Children's Literature Review

Guide to Gale Literary Criticism Series

For criticism on	Consult these Gale series
Authors now living or who died after December 31, 1959	*CONTEMPORARY LITERARY CRITICISM (CLC)*
Authors who died between 1900 and 1959	*TWENTIETH-CENTURY LITERARY CRITICISM (TCLC)*
Authors who died between 1800 and 1899	*NINETEENTH-CENTURY LITERATURE CRITICISM (NCLC)*
Authors who died between 1400 and 1799	*LITERATURE CRITICISM FROM 1400 TO 1800 (LC)* *SHAKESPEAREAN CRITICISM (SC)*
Authors who died before 1400	*CLASSICAL AND MEDIEVAL LITERATURE CRITICISM (CMLC)*
Black writers of the past two hundred years	*BLACK LITERATURE CRITICISM (BLC) AND BLACK LITERATURE CRITICISM SUPPLEMENT (BLCS)*
Authors of books for children and young adults	*CHILDREN'S LITERATURE REVIEW (CLR)*
Dramatists	*DRAMA CRITICISM (DC)*
Hispanic writers of the late nineteenth and twentieth centuries	*HISPANIC LITERATURE CRITICISM (HLC)*
Native North American writers and orators of the eighteenth, nineteenth, and twentieth centuries	*NATIVE NORTH AMERICAN LITERATURE (NNAL)*
Poets	*POETRY CRITICISM (PC)*
Short story writers	*SHORT STORY CRITICISM (SSC)*
Major authors from the Renaissance to the present	*WORLD LITERATURE CRITICISM, 1500 TO THE PRESENT (WLC)*
Major authors and works from the Bible to the present	*WORLD LITERATURE CRITICISM SUPPLEMENT (WLCS)*

87938
VC -Sub

volume 59

Children's Literature Review

Excerpts from Reviews,
Criticism, and Commentary
on Books for Children
and Young People

Deborah J. Morad
Editor

GALE GROUP

Detroit
San Francisco
London
Boston
Woodbridge, CT

87938

STAFF

Deborah J. Morad, *Editor*

Arlene M. Johnson, *Associate Editor*

Sara Constantakis, Motoko Fujishiro Huthwaite, Tom Schoenberg, Erin E. White, *Contributing Editors*

Tim White, *Technical Training Specialist*

Joyce Nakamura, *Managing Editor*

Maria Franklin, *Permissions Manager*
Sarah Tomasek, Edna Hedblad, *Permissions Associates*

Victoria B. Cariappa, *Research Manager*
Corrine A. Boland, *Project Coordinator*
Andrew Guy Malonis, Gary J. Oudersluys, Cheryl D. Warnock, *Research Specialists*
Tamara C. Nott, Tracie A. Richardson, *Research Associates*
Phyllis J. Blackman, Tim Lehnerer, Patricia L. Love, *Research Assistants*

Mary Beth Trimper, *Production Director*
Stacy Melson, *Production Assistant*

Gary Leach, *Graphic Artist*
Randy Bassett, *Image Database Supervisor*
Robert Duncan, Michael Logusz, *Imaging Specialists*
Pamela A. Reed, *Imaging Coordinator*

Since this page cannot legibly accommodate all copyright notices, the acknowledgments constitute an extension of the copyright notice.

While every effort has been made to ensure the reliability of the information presented in this publication, The Gale Group neither guarantees the accuracy of the data contained herein nor assumes any responsibility for errors, omissions, or discrepancies. Gale accepts no payment for listing, and inclusion in the publication of any organization, agency, institution, publication, service, or individual does not imply endorsement of the editors or publisher. Errors brought to the attention of the publisher and verified to the satisfaction of the publisher will be corrected in future editions.

This publication is a creative work fully protected by all applicable copyright laws, as well as by misappropriation, trade secret, unfair competition, and other applicable laws. The authors and editors of this work have added value to the underlying factual material herein through one or more of the following: unique and original selection, coordination, expression, arrangement, and classification of the information.

All rights to this publication will be vigorously defended.

Copyright © 2000 Gale Group
27500 Drake Road
Farmington Hills, MI 48331-3535

Gale Group and Design is a tradmark used herein under license.
All rights reserved, including the right of reproduction in whole or in part in any form.

Library of Congress Catalog Card Number 76-643301
ISBN 0-7876-3224-4
ISSN 0362-4145
Printed in the United States of America

10 9 8 7 6 5 4 3 2 1

Contents

Preface   vii
Acknowledgments   xi

Preface

Literature for children and young adults has evolved into both a respected branch of creative writing and a successful industry. Currently, books for young readers are considered among the most popular segments of publishing. Criticism of juvenile literature is instrumental in recording the literary or artistic development of the creators of children's books as well as the trends and controversies that result from changing values or attitudes about young people and their literature. Designed to provide a permanent, accessible record of this ongoing scholarship, *Children's Literature Review (CLR)* presents parents, teachers, and librarians—those responsible for bringing children and books together—with the opportunity to make informed choices when selecting reading materials for the young. In addition, *CLR* provides researchers of children's literature with easy access to a wide variety of critical information from English-language sources in the field. Users will find balanced overviews of the careers of the authors and illustrators of the books that children and young adults are reading; these entries, which contain excerpts from published criticism in books and periodicals, assist users by sparking ideas for papers and assignments and suggesting supplementary and classroom reading. Ann L. Kalkhoff, president and editor of *Children's Book Review Service Inc.*, writes that "*CLR* has filled a gap in the field of children's books, and it is one series that will never lose its validity or importance."

Scope of the Series

Each volume of *CLR* profiles the careers of a selection of authors and illustrators of books for children and young adults from preschool through high school. Author lists in each volume reflect:

- an international scope.

- representation of authors of all eras.

- the variety of genres covered by children's and/or YA literature: picture books, fiction, nonfiction, poetry, folklore, and drama.

Although the focus of the series is on authors new to *CLR*, entries will be updated as the need arises.

Organization of This Book

An entry consists of the following elements: author heading, author portrait, author introduction, excerpts of criticism (each preceded by a bibliographical citation), and illustrations, when available.

- The **Author Heading** consists of the author's name followed by birth and death dates. The portion of the name outside the parentheses denotes the form under which the author is most frequently published. If the majority of the author's works for children were written under a pseudonym, the pseudonym will be listed in the author heading and the real name given on the first line of the author introduction. Also located at the beginning of the introduction are any other pseudonyms used by the author in writing for children and any name variations, including transliterated forms for authors whose languages use nonroman alphabets. Uncertainty as to a birth or death date is indicated by question marks.

- An **Author Portrait** is included when available.

- The **Author Introduction** contains information designed to introduce an author to *CLR* users by presenting an overview of the author's themes and styles, biographical facts that relate to the author's literary career or critical responses to the author's works, and information about major awards and prizes the author has received. The introduction begins by identifying the nationality of the author and by listing the genres in which s/he has written for children and young adults. Introductions also list a group of representative titles for which the author or illustrator being profiled is best known; this section, which begins with the words "major works include," follows the genre line of the introduction. For seminal figures, a listing of major works about the author follows when appropriate, highlighting important biographies about the author or illustrator that are not excerpted in the entry. The centered heading "Introduction" announces the body of the text.

- **Criticism** is located in three sections: **Author's Commentary** (when available), **General Commentary** (when available), and **Title Commentary** (commentary on specific titles).

  - The **Author's Commentary** presents background material written by the author or by an interviewer. This commentary may cover a specific work or several works. Author's commentary on more than one work appears after the author introduction, while commentary on an individual book follows the title entry heading.

  - The **General Commentary** consists of critical excerpts that consider more than one work by the author or illustrator being profiled. General commentary is preceded by the critic's name in boldface type or, in the case of unsigned criticism, by the title of the journal. *CLR* also features entries that emphasize general criticism on the oeuvre of an author or illustrator. When appropriate, a selection of reviews is included to supplement the general commentary.

  - The **Title Commentary** begins with the title entry headings, which precede the criticism on a title and cite publication information on the work being reviewed. Title headings list the title of the work as it appeared in its first English-language edition. The first English-language publication date of each work (unless otherwise noted) is listed in parentheses following the title. Differing U.S. and British titles follow the publication date within the parentheses. When a work is written by an individual other than the one being profiled, as is the case when illustrators are featured, the parenthetical material following the title cites the author of the work before listing its publication date.

    Entries in each title commentary section consist of critical excerpts on the author's individual works, arranged chronologically by publication date. The entries generally contain two to seven reviews per title, depending on the stature of the book and the amount of criticism it has generated. The editors select titles that reflect the entire scope of the author's literary contribution, covering each genre and subject. An effort is made to reprint criticism that represents the full range of each title's reception, from the year of its initial publication to current assessments. Thus, the reader is provided with a record of the author's critical history. Publication information (such as publisher names and book prices) and parenthetical numerical references (such as footnotes or page and line references to specific editions of works) have been deleted at the discretion of the editors to provide smoother reading of the text.

- Centered headings introduce each section, in which criticism is arranged chronologically; beginning with Volume 35, each excerpt is preceded by a boldface source heading for easier access by readers. Within the text, titles by authors being profiled are also highlighted in boldface type.

- Selected excerpts are preceded by **Explanatory Annotations,** which provide information on the critic or work of criticism to enhance the reader's understanding of the excerpt.

- A complete **Bibliographical Citation** designed to facilitate the location of the original book or article precedes each piece of criticism.

- Numerous **Illustrations** are featured in *CLR*. For entries on illustrators, an effort has been made to include illustrations that reflect the characteristics discussed in the criticism. Entries on authors who do not illustrate their own works may also include photographs and other illustrative material pertinent to their careers.

Special Features: Entries on Illustrators

Entries on authors who are also illustrators will occasionally feature commentary on selected works illustrated but not written by the author being profiled. These works are strongly associated with the illustrator and have received critical acclaim for their art. By including critical comment on works of this type, the editors wish to provide a more complete representation of the artist's career. Criticism on these works has been chosen to stress artistic, rather than literary, contributions. Title entry headings for works illustrated by the author being profiled are arranged chronologically within the entry by date of publication and include notes identifying the author of the illustrated work. In order to provide easier access for users, all titles illustrated by the subject of the entry are boldfaced.

CLR also includes entries on prominent illustrators who have contributed to the field of children's literature. These entries are designed to represent the development of the illustrator as an artist rather than as a literary stylist. The illustrator's section is organized like that of an author, with two exceptions: the introduction presents an overview of the illustrator's styles and techniques rather than outlining his or her literary background, and the commentary written by the illustrator on his or her works is called "illustrator's commentary" rather than "author's commentary." All titles of books containing illustrations by the artist being profiled are highlighted in boldface type.

Other Features: Acknowledgments, Indexes

■ The **Acknowledgments** section, which immediately follows the preface, lists the sources from which material has been reprinted in the volume. It does not, however, list every book or periodical consulted for the volume.

■ The **Cumulative Index to Authors** lists all of the authors who have appeared in *CLR* with cross-references to the biographical, autobiographical, and literary criticism series published by The Gale Group. A full listing of the series titles appears before the first page of the indexes of this volume.

■ The **Cumulative Index to Nationalities** lists authors alphabetically under their respective nationalities. Author names are followed by the volume number(s) in which they appear.

■ The **Cumulative Index to Titles** lists titles covered in *CLR* followed by the volume and page number where criticism begins.

A Note to the Reader

CLR is one of several critical references sources in the Literature Criticism Series published by The Gale Group. When writing papers, students who quote directly from any volume in the Literature Criticism Series may use the following general forms to footnote reprinted criticism. The first example pertains to material drawn from periodicals, the second to material reprinted from books.

[1]T. S. Eliot, "John Donne," *The Nation and the Athenaeum,* 33 (9 June 1923), 321-32; excerpted and reprinted in *Literature Criticism from 1400 to 1800,* Vol. 10, ed. James E. Person, Jr. (Detroit: Gale Research, 1989), pp. 28-9.

[1]Henry Brooke, *Leslie Brooke and Johnny Crow* (Frederick Warne, 1982); excerpted and reprinted in *Children's Literature Review,* Vol. 20, ed. Gerard J. Senick (Detroit: Gale Research, 1990), p. 47.

Suggestions Are Welcome

In response to various suggestions, several features have been added to *CLR* since the beginning of the series, including author entries on retellers of traditional literature as well as those who have been the first to record oral tales and other folklore; entries on prominent illustrators featuring commentary on their styles and techniques; entries on authors whose works are considered controversial; occasional entries devoted to criticism on a single work or a series of works; sections in author introductions that list major works by and about the author or illustrator being profiled; explanatory notes that provide information on the critic or work of criticism to enhance the usefulness of the excerpt; more extensive illustrative material, such as holographs of manuscript pages and photographs of people and places pertinent to the careers of the authors and artists; a cumulative nationality index for easy access to authors by nationality; and occasional guest essays written specifically for *CLR* by prominent critics on subjects of their choice.

Readers who wish to suggest authors to appear in future volumes, or who have other suggestions, are cordially invited to contact the editor. By mail: Editor, *Children's Literature Review,* The Gale Group, 27500 Drake Road, Farmington Hills, MI 48331-3535; by telephone: (800) 347-GALE, (248) 699-4253; by fax: (248) 699-8065.

Acknowledgments

The editors wish to thank the copyright holders of the excerpted criticism included in this volume and the permissions managers of many book and magazine publishing companies for assisting us in securing reproduction rights. We are also grateful to the staffs of the Detroit Public Library, the Library of Congress, the University of Detroit Mercy Library, Wayne State University Purdy/Kresge Library Complex, and the University of Michigan Libraries for making their resources available to us. Following is a list of the copyright holders who have granted us permission to reproduce material in this volume of **CLR**. Every effort has been made to trace copyright, but if omissions have been made, please let us know.

COPYRIGHTED EXCERPTS IN CLR, VOLUME 59, WERE REPRODUCED FROM THE FOLLOWING PERIODICALS:

AB Bookman's Weekly, v. 92, July 12, 1993. © 1993 by AB Bookman Publications, Inc. Reproduced by permission of the publisher.—*The ALAN Review,* v. 22, Fall, 1994; v. 22, Spring, 1995; v. 25, Spring, 1998. All reproduced by permission.—*Appraisal: Science Books for Young People,* v. 1, Fall, 1968. Copyright © 1968 by the Children's Science Book Review Committee. All reproduced by permission.—*Best Sellers,* v. 43, July, 1983; v. 43, January, 1984; v. 45, September, 1985. Copyright 1983, 1984, 1985 by the University of Scranton. All reproduced by permission.—*Booklist,* v. 62, October 1, 1965; v. 62, November 1, 1965; v. 63, March 1, 1967; v. 63, May 1, 1967; v. 64, October 15, 1967; v. 65, June 15, 1969; v. 66, October 15, 1969; v. 66, May 15, 1970; v. 67, September 1, 1970; v. 67, February 1, 1971; v. 68, June 15, 1972; v. 68, July 15, 1972; v. 69, September 1, 1972; v. 69, November 1, 1972; v. 72, December 1, 1975; v. 76, June 15, 1980; v. 78, December 1, 1981; v. 81, December 1, 1984; v. 83, August, 1987; v. 84, December 15, 1987; v. 84, February 1, 1988; v. 86, November 1, 1989; v. 86, December 15, 1989; v. 86, April 1, 1990; v. 87, November 15, 1990; v. 87, March 1, 1991; v. 87, April 15, 1991; v. 89, October 15, 1992; v. 89, January 1, 1993; v. 90, September 1, 1993; v. 90, November 15, 1993; v. 90, March 15, 1994; v. 91, September 15, 1994; v. 91, December 15, 1994; v. 91, February 1, 1995; v. 91, May 1, 1995; v. 92, September 15, 1995; v. 92, October 1, 1995; v. 92, April 1, 1996; v. 92, May 15, 1996; v. 92, August, 1996; v. 93, April 15, 1997; v. 93, May 1, 1997; v. 93, June 1 & 15, 1997; v. 94, September 15, 1997; v. 94, November 1, 1997; v. 94, March 1, 1998; v. 95, September 1, 1998. Copyright © 1965, 1967, 1969, 1970, 1971, 1972, 1975, 1980, 1981, 1984, 1987, 1989, 1990, 1991, 1992, 1993, 1994, 1995, 1996, 1997, 1998 by the American Library Association. All reproduced by permission.—*Books for Young People,* v. 2, April, 1988 for "Potpourri of pictures and words satisfies at different levels" by Bernie Goedhart./ v. 3, April, 1989 for "Birthday cake, pizza served up in new books" by Sarah Ellis. Both reproduced by permission of the authors.—*Books in Canada,* v. 17, December, 1988 for "Animal Crackers" by Linda Granfield./ v. 17, December, 1988 for "Of tropical jungles and runaway soap" by Linda Granfield./ v. 18, October, 1989 for "Dislocation" by Linda Granfield. All reproduced by permission of the author.—*Bulletin of the Center for Children's Books,* v. XV, October, 1961; v. XV, March, 1962; v. 20, March, 1967; v. 20, April, 1967; v. 20, July-August, 1967; v. 21, April, 1968; v. 22, September, 1968; v. 22, June, 1969; v. 23, September, 1969; v. 23, January, 1970; v. 24, March, 1971; v. 29, May, 1976; v. 33, June, 1980; v. 35, December, 1981; v. 41, October, 1987; v. 41, December, 1987; v. 43, June, 1990; v. 44, October, 1990. Copyright © 1961, 1962, 1967, 1968, 1969, 1970, 1971, 1976, 1980, 1981, 1987, 1990 by The University of Chicago./ v. 49, May, 1996; v. 50, April, 1997; v. 50, July, 1997; v. 51, October, 1997; v. 52, March, 1999. Copyright © 1996, 1997, 1999 by The Board of Trustees of the University of Illinois. All reproduced by permission.—*Canadian Children's Literature,* 1983, 1988, 1990, 1991, 1992, 1995. Copyright © 1983, 1988, 1990, 1991, 1992, 1995 Canadian Children's Press. All reproduced by permission.—*Chicago Tribune,* September 27, 1987. © 1987 Tribune Media Services, Inc. All rights reserved. Reproduced by permission.—*Chicago Tribune Books,* September 9, 1990. © 1990 Tribune Media Services, Inc. All rights reserved. Reproduced by permission.—*Children's Book Review Service,* v. 4, February, 1976. Copyright 1976 Children's Book Review Service Inc. Reproduced by permission.—*The Christian ScienceMonitor,* November 4, 1965; May 1, 1969. © 1965, 1969 The Christian Science Publishing Society. Both reproduced by permission from The Christian Science Monitor./ December 14, 1940; December 10, 1942; June 12, 1947; March 4, 1954; May 10, 1956; November 6, 1958. © 1940, renewed 1968; © 1942, renewed 1970; © 1947, renewed 1975; © 1954, renewed 1982; © 1956, renewed 1984; © 1958, renewed 1986 The Christian Science Publishing Society. All reproduced by permission from *The Christian Science Monitor.*—*CM: A Reviewing Journal of Canadian Materials for Young People,* v. 16, November, 1988; v. 17, September, 1989; v. 18, May, 1990; v. 19, May, 1991; v. 22, March-April, 1994; v. 22, October, 1994; v. 3, November 29, 1996; v. 4, January 16, 1998. Copyright 1988, 1989, 1990, 1991, 1994, 1996, 1998 The Canadian Library Association. All reproduced by permission of the Manitoba Library Association.—*The Commonweal,* v. 33, January 3, 1941. Copyright © 1941 Commonweal Publishing Co., Inc. Reproduced by permission of Commonweal Foundation.—*The Dalhousie Review,* v. 44, Summer, 1964 for "The Animal Story: A Challenge in Technique" by William H. Magee. Reproduced by permission of the publisher and the author.—*English Journal,* v. 72, December, 1983 for a review of "The Majipoor Chronicles" by Elizabeth A. Belden. Copyright © 1983 by the National Council of Teachers of English. Reproduced by permission of the publisher and the author./ v. 74, April, 1985. Copyright © 1995 by the National Council of Teachers of English. Reproduced by permission of the publisher.—*Fantasy & Science Fiction,* v. 58, May, 1980 for a review of "Lord Valentine's Castle" by Algis Budrys/ v. 79, November, 1990 for a review of "Nightfall" by Algis Budrys/ v. 82, January, 1992 for a review of "The Face of the Waters" by Algis Budrys. © 1980, 1990, 1992 by Mercury Press, Inc. All reproduced by permission of the author.—*The Five Owls,* v. 7, January-February, 1993. Reproduced by permission.—*Growing Point,* v. 9, July, 1970 for a review of "The World of the Ocean Depths" by Margery Fisher/ v. 11, May, 1972 for a review of "Mammoths, Mastodons" by Margery Fisher. Both reproduced by permission of the Literary Estate of Margery Fisher.—*The Horn Book Magazine,* v. XLI, February, 1965; v. XLI, December, 1965; v. XLIII, June, 1967; v. XLIV, February, 1968; v. XLV, June, 1969; v. LXIII, September-October, 1987; v. LXIV, January-February, 1988; v. LVIV, May, 1988; v. LXV, March-April, 1989; v. LXVI, September, 1990; v. LXVI, November-December, 1990; v. LXIX, March, 1993; v. LXX, January-February, 1994; v. LXX, May-June, 1994; v. LXXI, July-August, 1995; v. LXXII, March-April, 1996; v. LXXII, November-December, 1996; v. LXXIII, November-December, 1997; v. LXXIV, March-April, 1998; v. LXXIV, September-October, 1998; v. LXXV, March-April, 1999. Copyright, 1965, 1967, 1968, 1969, 1987, 1988, 1989, 1990, 1993, 1994, 1995, 1996, 1997, 1998, 1999 by The Horn Book, Inc., 11 Beacon St., Suite 1000, Boston, MA 02108. All rights reserved. All reproduced by permission./v. XVII, July, 1941; v. XXIII, May, 1947; v. XXVI, July, 1950; v. XXX, April, 1954; v. XXXI, August, 1955; v. XXXII, April, 1956; v. XXXII, December, 1956; v. XXXIV, October, 1958; v. XXXV, February, 1959; v. XXXV, June, 1959; v. XXXV, October, 1959; v. XXXVII, June, 1961. Copyright 1941, renewed, 1969; copyright 1947, renewed 1975; copyright 1950, renewed 1978; copyright 1954, renewed 1982; copyright 1955, renewed 1983; copyright, 1956, renewed 1984; copyright 1958, renewed 1986; copyright 1959, renewed 1987; copyright 1961, renewed 1981 by The Horn Book, Inc., 11 Beacon St., Suite 1000, Boston, MA 02108. All rights reserved. All reproduced by permission.—*Journal of Adolescent and Adult Literacy,* v. 41, September, 1997. Reproduced by permission.—*Journal of Canadian Fiction,* v. II, Summer, 1973. Reproduced by permission from *Journal of Canadian Fiction,* 2050 Mackay St., Montreal, Quebec H3G 2J1, Canada.—*The Junior Bookshelf,* v. 36, April, 1972; v. 36, June, 1972; v. 53, August, 1989. All reproduced by permission.—*Kirkus Reviews,* v. XXXVII, January 15, 1969; v. XXXVII, March 1, 1969; v. XXXVII, April 1, 1969; v. XXXVII, September 15, 1969; v. XL, August 1, 1972; v. XLIII, August 15, 1975; v. LII, November 1, 1984; v. LIV, July 15, 1986; v. LVI, March 15, 1988; v. LVII, December 15, 1989; v. LVIII, May 1, 1990; v. LVIII, August 15, 1990; v. LVIII, October 15, 1990; v. LIX, August 15, 1991; v. LXI, July 1, 1993. Copyright © 1969, 1972, 1975, 1984, 1986, 1988, 1989, 1990, 1991, 1993 The Kirkus Service, Inc. All rights reserved. All reproduced by permission of the publisher, Kirkus Reviews and Kirkus Associates, L.P.—*Kirkus Service,* v. XXXV, January 1, 1967; v. XXXV, March 1, 1967; v. XXXV, April 1, 1967; v. XXXV, May 1, 1967; v. XXXV, May 15, 1967; v. XXXVI, February 15, 1968; v. XXXVI, March 1, 1968; v. XXXVI, August 1, 1968. Copyright © 1967, 1968, The Kirkus Service, Inc. All rights reserved. All reproduced by permission of the publisher, Kirkus Service and Kirkus Associates, L.P.—*KLIATT Young Adult Paperback Book Guide,* v. XIII, January, 1979. Copyright © 1979 by *KLIATT Paperback Book Guide.* Reproduced by permission.—*The New Advocate,* v. 12, Spring, 1999. Reproduced by permission.—*New York Herald Tribune Book Review,* July 16, 1950; July 1, 1951; April 13, 1952; January 29, 1956; July 5, 1959. Copyright © 1950, renewed 1987; © 1951, renewed 1979; © 1952, renewed 1980; 1956, 1984; © 1959, renewed 1987 by The New York Times Company. All reproduced by permission.—*New York Herald Tribune Books,* December 20, 1925; August 13, 1961. Copyright © 1925, renewed 1953; © 1961, renewed 1989 by The New York Times Company. Both reproduced by permission.—*New York Herald Tribune: The Lively Arts and Book Review,* February 19, 1961. Copyright © 1961, 1989 by The New York Times Company. Reproduced by permission.—*New York Herald Tribune Weekly Book Review,* March 23, 1947; October 10, 1948; June 12, 1949. Copyright © 1947, renewed 1975; © 1948, renewed 1976; © 1949, renewed 1977 by The New York Times Company. All reproduced by permission.—*The New York Times,* November 11, 1984; December 15, 1991; March 14, 1993; November 14, 1993; March 13, 1994; June 30, 1996; November 16, 1997; October 4, 1998. Copyright © 1984, 1991, 1993, 1994, 1996, 1997, 1998 by The New York Times Company. All reproduced by permission.—*The New York Times Book Review,* November 1, 1964; May, 1967; July 7, 1968; November 3, 1968; March 5, 1972. Copyright © 1964, 1967, 1968, 1972 by *The New York Times.* All reproduced by permission./ June 24, 1951; June 22, 1952; December 27, 1953; March 28, 1954; November 13, 1955; October 18, 1959; April 10, 1960; February 12, 1961. Copyright © 1951, renewed 1979; © 1952, renewed 1980; © 1953, renewed 1981; © 1954, renewed 1982; © 1955, renewed 1983; © 1959, renewed 1987; © 1960, renewed 1988; © 1961, renewed 1989 by The New York Times Company. All reproduced by permission.—*Publishers Weekly,* v. 191, April 3, 1967; v. 194, August 12, 1968; v. 195, January 20, 1969; v. 195, February 3, 1969; v. 196, July 21, 1969; v. 197, May 18, 1970; v. 198, August 24, 1970; v. 199, June 21, 1971; v. 200, October 25, 1971; v. 201, January 31, 1972; v. 203, April 2, 1973; v. 203, April 16, 1973; v. 208, August 4, 1975; v. 220, September 18, 1981; v. 222, August 6, 1982; v. 224, September 30, 1983; v. 226, September 21, 1984. Copyright © 1967, 1968, 1969, 1970, 1971, 1972, 1973, 1975, 1981, 1982, 1983, 1984 by Xerox Corporation. All reproduced from *Publishers Weekly,* published by R. R. Bowker Company, a Xerox company, by permission./ v. 227, June 7, 1985; v. 230, August 1, 1986; v. 232, August 14, 1987; v. 237, February 9, 1990; v. 237, April 13, 1990; v. 237, August 31, 1990; v. 238, February 1, 1991; v. 239, September 21, 1992; v. 240, November 1, 1993; v. 240, December 20, 1993; v. 242, January 2, 1995; v. 242,

January 16, 1995; v. 242, April 24, 1995; v. 237, July 27, 1996; v. 244, June 23, 1997; v. 245, March 2,1998; v. 245, June 29, 1998; v. 245, September 21, 1998; v. 245, October 12, 1998. Copyright 1985, 1986, 1987, 1990, 1991, 1992, 1993, 1995, 1996, 1997, 1998 by Reed Publishing USA. All reproduced from *Publishers Weekly*, published by the Bowker Magazine Group of Cahners Publishing Co., a division of Reed Publishing USA., by permission.—*The Quarterly Journal of the Library of Congress,* v. 39, Spring, 1982. Reproduced by permission. —*Quill and Quire,* v. 46, June, 1980 for a review of "Lord Valentine's Castle" by Paul Stuewe/ v. 48, November, 1982 for a review of "World of a Thousand Colors" by Paul Stuewe/ v. 56, March, 1990 for a review of "Daniel's Dog" by Joanne Findon/ v. 57, March, 1991 for a review of "Sarah Saw a Blue Macaw" by Frieda Wishinsky/ v. 58, December, 1992 for a review of "Sarah Saw a Blue Macaw" by Fred Boer/ v. 59, October, 1993 for a review of "Mama's Bed" by Janet McNaughton/ v. 60, April, 1994 for a review of "Two Too Many" by Kenneth Oppel/ v. 60, September, 1994 for a review of "Gifts" by Linda Granfield/ v. 64, January, 1998 for a review of "Jeremiah Loves to Read" by Sheree Haughian. All reproduced by permission of the authors.—*Riverbank Review,* Spring, 1999. Copyright © 1999 by the Riverbank Review. All rights reserved. Reproduced by permission.—*Saturday Review of Literature,* v. XXIII, December 7, 1940. © 1940 *Saturday Review Magazine*, © 1979 General Media International, Inc. Reproduced by permission.—*Saturday Review,* v. 38, November 12, 1955; v. 39, April 21, 1956; v. 39, June 23, 1956; v. 41, October 25, 1958; v. 43, April 16, 1960. © 1955, 1956, 1958, 1960 *Saturday Review Magazine*, © 1979 General Media International, Inc. All reproduced by permission.—*The School Librarian,* v. 25, December, 1977. Reproduced by permission.—*School Library Journal,* v. 19, May, 1973; v. 21, May, 1975; v. 22, February, 1976; v. 23, February, 1977; v. 27, September, 1980; v. 28, May, 1982; v. 29, December 29, 1982; v. 31, May, 1985; v. 33, March, 1987; v. 34, January, 1988; v. 35, September, 1989; v. 36, March, 1990; v. 36, June, 1990; v. 36, July, 1990; v. 36, August, 1990; v. 36, November, 1990; v. 37, March, 1991; v. 37, December, 1991; v. 38, November, 1992; v. 39, December, 1993; v. 40, June, 1994; v. 41, February, 1995; v. 41, March, 1995; v. 41, June, 1995; v. 41, October, 1995; v. 42, March, 1996; v. 42, September, 1996; v. 42, November, 1996; v. 43, April, 1997; v. 43, September, 1997; v. 43, November, 1997; v. 44, May, 1998; v. 44, October, 1998. Copyright © 1973. 1975, 1976, 1977, 1980, 1982, 1985, 1987, 1988, 1989, 1990, 1991, 1992, 1993, 1994, 1995, 1996, 1997, 1998. All reproduced from *School Library Journal,* a Cahners/R. R. Bowker Publication, by permission.—*Science Books,* v. 3, September, 1967; v. 3, March, 1968; v. 6, March, 1971; v. 8, December, 1972. Copyright 1967, 1968, 1971, 1972 by AAAS. All reproduced by permission.—*Science Fiction and Fantasy Book Review,* November, 1983. Reproduced by permission.—*The Times Literary Supplement,* March 26, 1982; January 2, 1987. © The Times Supplements Limited 1982, 1987. Both reproduced from *The Times Literary Supplement* by permission.—*Virginia Kirkus' Bookshop Service,* v. XVIII, February 15, 1950; v. XX, February 15, 1952; v. XXI, October 15, 1953; v. XXII, February 1, 1954. Copyright © 1950, 1952, 1953, 1954 The Kirkus Service, Inc. All rights reserved. All reproduced by permission of the publisher, Virginia Kirkus' Bookshop Service and Kirkus Associates, L.P.—*Virginia Kirkus' Service,* v. XXIV, January 1, 1956; v. XXV, July 15, 1957; v. XXVII, August 1, 1958; v. XXVII, July 1, 1959; v. XXVII, July 15, 1960; v. XXXIII, January 1, 1965; v. XXXIII, March 15, 1965; v. XXXIII, April 1, 1965; v. XXXIII, May 15, 1965. Copyright © 1956, 1957, 1958, 1959, 1960, 1965 The Kirkus Service, Inc. All rights reserved. All reproduced by permission of the publisher, Virginia Kirkus' Service and Kirkus Associates, L.P.—*Voice of Youth Advocates,* v. 5, June, 1982; v. 7, June, 1984; v. 10, October, 1987; v. 11, June, 1988; v. 12, December, 1989; v. 13, June, 1990; v. 13,August, 1990; v. 13, October, 1990; v. 13, February, 1991; v. 14, August, 1991; v. 15, December, 1992; v. 16, April, 1993; v. 17, June, 1994; v. 13, August, 1995; v. 18, August, 1995; v. 19, August, 1996; v. 19, October, 1996; v. 19, February, 1997; v. 20, October, 1997; v. 21, April, 1998; v. 21, June, 1998; v. 21, February, 1999. Copyrighted 1982, 1984, 1987, 1988, 1989, 1990, 1991, 1992, 1993, 1994, 1995, 1996, 1997, 1998, 1999 by *Voice of Youth Advocates.* All reproduced by permission.—*Washington Post Book World,* September 9, 1990 for a review of "Two Little Savages" by Noel Perrin. © 1990, Washington Post Book World Service/Washington Post Writers Group. Reproduced by permission of the author.—*Wilson Library Bulletin,* v. 69, May, 1995 for a review of "The Well" by Linda Perkins. © 1995 by the H. W. Wilson Company. All rights reserved. Reproduced by permission of the author.—*Wilson Library Journal,* v. 65, May, 1991 for "Young Adult Perplex" by Cathi MacRae. © 1991 by the H. W. Wilson Company. All rights reserved. Reproduced by permission of the author.—*The Writer,* v. 98, June, 1985. Reproduced by permission.

COPYRIGHTED EXCERPTS IN *CLR,* VOLUME 59, WERE REPRODUCED FROM THE FOLLOWING BOOKS:

Hamburger, Susan. From *Dictionary of Literary Biography, Volume 188: American Book and Magazine Illustrators to 1920.* A Bruccoli Clark Layman Book. Edited by Steven E. Smith, Catherine A. Hastedt, and Donald H. Dyal. Gale Research, 1998. © 1999 The Gale Group. Reproduced by permission.—Kingman, Lee. From *Children's Books and Their Creators.* Edited by Anita Silvey. Houghton Mifflin Company, 1995. Copyright © 1995 by Houghton Mifflin Company. Reproduced by permission of the publisher.—Nudelman, Edward D. From *Jessie Willcox Smith: A Bibliography.* Pelican Publishing Company, 1989. Copyright © 1989 by Edward D. Nudelman. Reproduced by permission.—Nudelman, Edward D. From *Jessie Willcox Smith: American Illustrator.* Pelican Publishing Company, 1990. Copyright © 1990 by Edward D. Nudelman. Reproduced by permission.—Smith, Karen Patricia. From *African-*

American Voices in Young Adult Literature. Edited by Karen Patricia Smith. The Scarecrow Press, Inc., 1994. Copyright © 1994 by Karen Patricia Smith. Reproduced by permission.

PHOTOGRAPHS AND ILLUSTRATIONS APPEARING IN *CLR,* VOLUME 59, WERE REPRODUCED FROM THE FOLLOWING SOURCES:

Bogart, Jo Ellen, photograph. Reproduced by permission of Jo Ellen Bogart.—Hays, Wilma Pitchford, photograph. —Hobbs, Will, photograph by Jean Hobbs. Reproduced by permission.—Nye, Naomi Shihab, photograph. Reproduced by permission.—Seton, Ernest T., photograph. The Library of Congress.—Seton, Ernest Thompson, illustrator. From an illustration in *Wild Animals at Home* by Ernest Thompson Seton. Grosset & Dunlap, 1913. Copyright, 1913, by Ernest Thompson Seton.—Silverberg, Robert, 1993, photograph. Reproduced by permission.—Silverberg, Robert, with Algis Budrys and Charles Harris, at World Science Fiction Convention, 1956, photograph. Reproduced by permission.—Silverberg, Robert, with wife Karen, 1998, photograph by Alison V. Haber. Reproduced by permission of Robert Silverberg.—Smith, Jessie Willcox, illustrator. From an illustration in *A Child's Garden of Verses* by Robert Louis Stevenson. Charles Scribner's Sons, 1905.—Smith, Jessie Willcox, illustrator. "Meg, Jo, Beth and Amy," 1915. From *Little Women* by Louisa May Alcott.—Smith, Jessie Willcox, 1915, photograph by Haeseler. —Smith, Jessie Willcox, illustrator. From an illustration in *Heidi* by Johanna Spyri. McKay, 1922-.—Smith, Jessie Willcox, illustrator. From an illustration in *The Jessie Willcox Smith Mother Goose.* Foreword by Corey Nash. Derrydale Books, 1986. Copyright © 1986 by OBC, Inc.—Taylor, Mildred, photograph. The Toledo Blade. Reproduced by permission.—Whitney, Phyllis A., photograph by Malice Domestic. Reproduced by permission of the author.

Children's
Literature
Review

Jo Ellen Bogart

1945-

Canadian author of picture books.

Major works include *Malcolm's Runaway Soap* (1988), *Daniel's Dog* (1990), *Sarah Saw a Blue Macaw* (1991), *Mama's Bed* (1993), *Gifts* (1994).

INTRODUCTION

Bogart is well known in the sphere of Canadian children's literature for her eclectic collection of picture books designed to enlighten and entertain preschoolers and primary graders. Rarely plot-driven and often written in verse, Bogart's works exhibit a varied mix of themes ranging from pure fancy to fun with numbers to sensitive portrayals of childhood relationships. A distinguishing feature of much of Bogart's writing is its focus on imagery, words, and sounds rather than story line. *Dylan's Lullaby* (1988), for instance, is a dreamy, magical portrayal of the images in a little boy's bedtime song. In a similar vein, Janet McNaughton noted of Bogart's *Mama's Bed* that the absence of plot "proves what a powerful device simplicity can be in a picture book." Still, a few of Bogart's stories carry a single theme. Reviewers noted that the depiction of ten lovably individualistic guests in *10 for Dinner* (1989), for example, is as much about being different as it is about numbers. One of Bogart's later works, the award-winning *Gifts*, was also lauded by critics for its simultaneous celebration of travel, imagination, and the close relationship between a grandmother and granddaughter.

Throughout her writing career, Bogart has built several stories based on her own experiences, as well as thoughts and comments from children. The idea for the fanciful *Malcolm's Runaway Soap*, for instance, came to the author after her own confrontation with a squishy bar of soap at the bottom of her bathtub. Bogart's desire to share her love of pets and exotic animals also comes through in her work, as she casts a host of unusual creatures as significant characters, particularly in *Sarah Saw a Blue Macaw*. Paired with its vibrant illustrations, the text of *Sarah Saw a Blue Macaw* "imparts a sense of wonder and appreciation for an endangered environment," noted reviewer Jennifer Johnson.

Some of Bogart's most acclaimed stories are those which focus on the creative ways in which children use imagination to cope with stress, establish comfort, and create meaningful relationships with important people in their lives. *Daniel's Dog*, for example, was particularly well received for its sensitive treatment of a little boy's struggle to accept a new baby sister into his household. Bogart explained that the story was influenced by her own memories of accepting new siblings after five years as

an only child. "[T]he experience of having three siblings born in four years helped me understand how Daniel felt," Bogart noted in *Something about the Author* (*SATA*). Critic Anna DeWind described *Daniel's Dog* as a "fine book [that] gracefully covers topics ranging from the arrival of a new sibling to imaginary companions to the resolution of inner conflict."

Consistent throughout all of Bogart's books, particularly those written in verse, is a celebration of language and sounds. In addition to her ability to empathize with the fears and feelings children experience in day-to-day life, reviewers have lauded Bogart's simplicity and her facility with rhyme. Bogart's own hope in writing her books, which she expressed in *SATA*, is that her readers will learn to "appreciate their own creativity and increase their joy in the written and spoken word."

Biographical Information

Bogart was born in Houston, Texas, in 1945. In her original career choice, Bogart followed in the footsteps of her mother, an elementary-school teacher. After earning degrees in education and psychology from the University of Texas, Bogart spent the next several years working as a supply teacher in Austin. In 1967, she married Canadian zoologist James Bogart. Shortly afterward, she had the unique opportunity to accompany her husband on two scientific expeditions to South America. While James studied exotic amphibians and reptiles in the Peruvian rainforests, Jo Ellen spent her days in the local library learning about animals native to the Amazonian region. One such four-month period of study laid the early groundwork for *Sarah Saw A Blue Macaw.*

After moving to Guelph, Ontario with her husband in 1975, Bogart continued to work as a supply teacher, as well as a volunteer speech therapist. In addition to becoming a reporter, illustrator, photographer, and editor for the *Guelph Examiner,* a small weekly newspaper, she began contributing stories to *Owl* and *Chickadee* magazines. Since publishing her first book in 1988, Bogart has continued to blend her background in teaching with her passion for writing. The author commented in *SATA* that at the outset of her teaching career, she had no intention of writing children's books. Yet, after two decades in the field, which included one year teaching mentally challenged teens, Bogart realized that she could also educate children by creating fun stories that they "could enjoy and maybe even learn something from." Bogart currently lives with her family in Guelph. Having obtained Canadian citizenship in 1995, she is now a dual citizen of both Canada and the United States. She is an active member of the Society of Children's Book Writers and Illustrators, The Writers' Union of Canada, and the Canadian Society of Children's Authors, Illustrators, and Performers.

Major Works

Bogart's repertoire includes two works that could be used as counting books. *10 for Dinner,* a depiction of ten unique dinner guests, and *Two Too Many* (1994), about a child's confusion when there are too many of everything, are mathematical mind-twisters that teach children about numbers in an entertaining way. *Malcolm's Runaway Soap* is a whimsical story of a little boy's adventures chasing after the slippery bar of strawberry soap that has escaped from his bathtub and traveled all the way to the center of town. Swathed in his favorite blue towel, Malcolm chases his soap as it pops up in several unlikely locations throughout the neighborhood. Kathleen Corrigan noted that Bogart traces the path of the runaway bar "in nice descriptive detail." Malcolm finally catches up to the soap as it froths away in the city hall fountain.

Daniel's Dog tells of a little boy who, feeling sad and left out after the arrival of his new baby sister, finds companionship in a "ghost" dog named Lucy, which he claims has been sent to him by his deceased grandfather. While his mother is busy looking after the new baby, Daniel occupies himself by tending to the needs of his imaginary pet. As Daniel grows more comfortable with

his sister and his place in the family, his attention to Lucy diminishes. When his friend Norman is sad about his father going away on a long trip, Daniel helps out by producing another imaginary dog to help comfort Norman, too.

Sarah Saw a Blue Macaw, inspired by Bogart's impressions of the Amazonian fauna of South America, offers a fanciful glimpse of a typical day in the Peruvian rainforest. Sarah, a spider monkey, leads the way as readers are introduced to a cast of characters composed of a wide variety of indigenous species. Written in rhyme, with a question-and-answer format, the book invites readers to search for Sarah among the colorful denizens of each page. Frieda Wishinsky noted that the book "displays a fine use of verse," while a *Publishers Weekly* reviewer stated, "[T]his gentle book never hits readers over the head with its 'save the earth' message. Instead it allows them to experience the forest and its diverse inhabitants through words and art."

Mama's Bed again shows Bogart's attention and sensitivity to the day-to-day concerns of young children. The book places a cozy and familiar piece of furniture at the center of a little girl's need to establish a sense of security at home. Her mother's bed becomes a cherished locale in which to share closeness and fun with members of her family, whether playing, doing chores, or just relaxing. Janet McNaughton opined that "children age five and under will identify strongly with the small protagonist's feelings about the safety and comfort provided by her mother's bed."

Also told in verse and question-and-answer format, *Gifts* celebrates the exceptional relationship between a little girl and her world-traveling grandma. Rather than requesting typical souvenirs, the girl asks for special gifts, such as memories, pieces of sky, or strips of a rainbow, which will help her share her grandmother's unique and exciting experiences abroad. "When someone I know returns from a trip, what I most want is to hear stories about what happened," Bogart explained in *SATA*. "Stories take time and effort and make a wonderful gift." As the grandmother travels throughout Africa, the Arctic, Australia, England, India, and Mexico, she shows a distinctive understanding of her granddaughter's creativity and inventiveness, always managing to bring back just the right present. Linda Granfield commented that "the text of *Gifts* is full of zing and zest, redolent with images of a child's limitless imagination and the loving responses of a spunky grandparent." Accompanied by lively Plasticine illustrations, the book creates a positive portrayal of imaginary journeys as well as actual travel to faraway places.

Awards

Several of Bogart's books have been selected for the "Our Choice" list by the Canadian Children's Book Centre, including *Malcolm's Runaway Soap* in 1990, *Daniel's Dog* in 1991, *Sarah Saw a Blue Macaw* in

1992, *Mama's Bed* in 1994, *Two Too Many* in 1995, and *Gifts* in 1996. Bogart received particular recognition for *Daniel's Dog*, which was made a Choices List selection by the Cooperative Children's Book Center of the University of Wisconsin in 1990, and a Children's Choice selection by the International Reading Association/Children's Book Council (IRA/CBC) in 1991. The critically acclaimed *Gifts* was shortlisted for the Ruth Schwartz Award, the Mr. Christie's Book Award, and the International Board on Books for Young People (IBBY) Honour list.

GENERAL COMMENTARY

Linda Granfield

SOURCE: "Animal Crackers," in *Books in Canada,* Vol. 17, No. 9, December, 1988, p. 12.

Every season there are new names in the publisher's catalogues, the names of first-time authors and illustrators. People wonder who these newcomers are; cynics and critics wonder if they have what it takes to stay in the business. Jo Ellen Bogart, author of last spring's *Dylan's Lullaby* and this season's *Malcolm's Runaway Soap,* has four more children's titles awaiting publication. Obviously, someone likes what she's writing.

Born in Houston, Texas, Bogart has degrees in elementary education and psychology from the University of Texas, where she met her husband, Jim, a Canadian zoologist. Before their children were born, the Bogarts travelled through Central America to Peru to study exotic amphibian fauna. Bogart has taught school and is currently a supply teacher in Guelph, Ontario. In her earlier writing for *Owl* and *Chickadee* magazines the subject was usually animals, which Bogart confesses is her favourite topic. Her four forthcoming titles, all picture books, will present more animal characters.

Bogart is refining *Sarah Saw a Blue Macaw* for publication by Scholastic in 1989. "I'm including animals from a specific Amazonian area, and I have to be very careful that I have my information straight. Some animals are only active in the daytime, some in the night; I have to be sure they're doing the right things at the right time," says Bogart. "Sometimes an idea will jump on you while you're in the middle of another project. That's what happened in my *10 for Dinner.* The story of 10 baby opossums at dinner gives all sorts of mathematical permutations of what they will do or want."

Not an "everyday writer" is how Bogart describes herself. "I'll think about an idea for two or three months and maybe write the book in one day. Sometimes it will be two months before I rewrite; most of the time the text is close to the way it was when I first wrote it." Ideas for her many projects sometimes come from "some little comment from a child." At other times Bogart is inspired by some little problem of her own. *Malcolm's Runaway Soap* stemmed from her own squishy soap sticking to the bottom of the bathtub. The story of Sarah and her blue macaw began when Bogart did some volunteer work with children who had minor speech problems. "I worked with them on grammar and rhyming and ended up with Sarah." Life experiences have also given this newcomer to writing for children the subjects for the other two titles forthcoming from Groundwood and Scholastic. And there seems to be no end to Bogart's enthusiasm and ideas: "There may be a novel in my future, though not now. Eventually I'd like to write a book of poems—I like every genre of children's literature." With six children's titles in two years, and who knows how many ideas brewing, the permutations of Bogart's possible output are astounding.

TITLE COMMENTARY

📖 *DYLAN'S LULLABY* (1988)

Charlotte Waterson

SOURCE: A review of *Dylan's Lullaby,* in *Canadian Children's Literature,* No. 51, 1988, p. 99.

Where do we go when we fall asleep? Like Eugene Field in his poem *Wynken, Blynken and Nod,* Jo Ellen Bogart describes the voyage of the child through the night sky. The story's rhythm moves along more or less successfully with the events of the dream.

Dylan meets a flock of birds, runs down a silver road with a horse, comes across the "Face in the sky", and enters a sky pool for the fishes. Having a lullaby pull Dylan from one adventure to the next is an original idea, but a rather abstract one for a young child to grasp.

As Dylan's dream unwinds we discover inevitably that adults are rarely able to visit the sky. Presumably they have forgotten how to dream in the way children do. The book finishes on this note and leaves us with an unresolved, unsatisfying ending.

Although *Dylan's Lullaby* will stir the child's imagination, the dialogue has a superficial quality that detracts from our enjoyment of the story. Cheryl Lowrey's simple illustrations match the story line but lack in visual appeal. *Dylan's Lullaby* is suitable for early primary children.

Bernie Goedhart

SOURCE: "Pot-pourri of Pictures and Words Satisfies at Different Levels," in *Books for Young People,* Vol. 2, No. 2, April, 1988, pp. 14, 18.

Dylan's Lullaby, which I had mentally dismissed as cloyingly sentimental and visually cutesy, [my son] found appealing enough to insist on reading aloud himself. . . .

Dylan's Lullaby, however, is marred by the greeting-card art of illustrator Cheryl Lowrey: sweet and flowery images that bear no resemblance to the real world. Starry skies with ethereal, disembodied faces; a too-pretty horse with flowers entwined in its mane; a constantly smiling, apple-cheeked, sleeper-clad boy who floats out of his bed on a lullaby and meets "the Face in the Sky"—it's all a bit hard to swallow. But Jo Ellen Bogart's text is good for reading aloud at bedtime, and my son, for one, thought it had the stuff that dreams are made of.

Brenda Watson

SOURCE: A review of *Dylan's Lullaby,* in *CM: A Reviewing Journal of Canadian Materials for Young People,* Vol. 16, No. 6, November, 1988, pp. 227-28.

The Dylan in *Dylan's Lullaby* calls his own lullaby to wrap him in a satin ribbon and whisk him off to the Face in the Sky. The Face uses his magic to show Dylan birds, horses, a silver ball, fish and a magical tree laden with food. Dylan joins in the dance of the fish, eats a prickly fruit and then returns home.

The idea of a night journey is reminiscent of Sendak's *Where the Wild Things Are,* but, unfortunately, this story lacks the enchantment of the former. The story is too wordy and the Face in the Sky lacks the appeal of the Wild Things—being at times grotesque and at other times almost parental.

The format and illustrations are not outstanding. A page of text alternates with a water-colour picture of Dylan floating around in a starry blue sky. The print is round and slanted. Most disturbing is the unnaturalness of Dylan's appearance. He appears plastic rather than warm and his features are not drawn consistently from page to page.

There are many more imaginative and successful bedtime stories to choose from.

MALCOLM'S RUNAWAY SOAP (1988)

Linda Granfield

SOURCE: "Of Tropical Jungles and Runaway Soap," in *Books in Canada,* Vol. 17, No. 9, December, 1988, pp. 11-16.

The antics of a bar of strawberry soap, not animals, are the subject of Jo Ellen Bogart's *Malcolm's Runaway Soap.* "It all started with Malcolm's bath." A very dirty boy climbs into the bathtub one afternoon and a squishy bar of soap pops out of his hand. So begins a wild chase through town. Readers know this really couldn't happen, but Bogart manages to keep the soap believably wet and in motion. Malcolm, clothed in a blue terry towel (good thing it's summer!) is followed by a growing audience of "people in your neighbourhood." Linda Hendry's illustrations are vivid—and non-sexist: the letter-carrier and house-painter are women, and fathers mind babies. The tall tale's rascally soap is finally subdued in a public fountain and Malcolm, squeaky clean by now, is taken home in style. What an entertaining exaggeration!

Kathleen Corrigan

SOURCE: A review of *Malcolm's Runaway Soap,* in *Canadian Children's Literature,* No. 63, 1991, pp. 97-8.

The repetition in Jo Ellen Bogart's **Malcolm's Runaway Soap** is more in the plot than the telling, and thus less successful than [Allen] Morgan's usage [in *Sam and the Tigers*]. Malcolm's strawberry soap escapes from the bath and "pops" from one place to the next through town before finally settling on a toy sailboat in the city hall fountain. Bogart has the soap pop in a great variety of places, and she writes in nice descriptive detail about each one, but by the fifth or sixth escape of the soap a feeling of *déjà vu* creeps in. The ending is fine, however—one which will appeal to the child's love of public nudity.

And this is a great looking book. Linda Hendry's slightly whimsical illustrations are full of life and detail (almost as good as an Ahlberg picture, and that's high praise). She creates movement by including at the edge of several drawings a hint as to where the soap will land next, causing the reader's eye to move across the page and her hand to turn it. Text and illustrations balance in a pleasing symmetry, a sign that someone at Scholastic thought hard about the design of this book.

10 FOR DINNER (1989)

Sarah Ellis

SOURCE: "Birthday Cake, Pizza Served up in New Books," in *Books for Young People,* Vol. 3, No. 2, April, 1989, p. 12.

Another party book, Jo Ellen Bogart's **10 for Dinner,** uses a theme-and-variations structure. Margot invites 10 friends to a birthday party. Nine behave conventionally with respect to clothing, presents, food, and games, but the tenth is eccentric. Catalogues and number games can work well in a picture book, and the elements of a birthday party are certainly close to every pre-schooler's heart, but in this effort the events are simply not very interesting: "On the day of the party 5 guests came right on time at 5 o'clock, 2 came at 5:10, and 2 came at

5:15. But 1 guest arrived early—at a quarter to 4." The odd behaviour of guest number 10 starts to seem a bit pallid.

This kind of text could function as a springboard for the illustrator, but in the pictures of Carlos Friere one looks in vain for an extra dimension—for delineation of character, for interaction between the guests, for running jokes, or for a sense of story shape. Bogart set a high standard last year with her excellent *Malcolm's Runaway Soap*. *10 for Dinner* doesn't measure up.

Nancy Tully

SOURCE: A review of *10 for Dinner*, in *CM: A Reviewing Journal of Canadian Materials for Young People*, Vol. 17, No. 5, September, 1989, p. 216.

In Canadian author Jo Ellen Bogart's [third] book for children, Margo invites ten friends for dinner on her birthday. One guest stands out more than the others. He arrives early wearing his Halloween costume, asks for a peanut butter sandwich with olives and sauerkraut, makes a hat like the Loch Ness monster, sings a solo, wants to play "dirty-double no-hands blindfolded marbles," and brings the most interesting present. The best part was that he also stayed to help with the dishes when the party was over.

The colourful illustrations on each page by Carlos Freire invite children to examine them carefully as well as count and match the numbers with the items on each page. The bold, simple text is especially readable and the bright attractive cover makes the story inviting for younger readers.

An excellent addition to a library or classroom picture book collection, *10 for Dinner* is also a nice alternative for teachers looking for another number or counting book.

Linda Granfield

SOURCE: "Dislocation," in *Books in Canada*, Vol. 18, No. 7, October, 1989, p. 36.

One of the birthday guests in Jo Ellen Bogart's latest picture-book, *10 for Dinner,* surprises everyone with his creativity, guaranteeing he'll be invited back. Young Margo has invited 10 friends to her party. Bogart presents different combinations of guests: "3 guests wore T-shirts and shorts, 1 guest wore a pink lace dress" and so on. The number of guests, and the action, changes with each illustrated page, challenging a young reader to keep track of the numbers *and* solve the mystery of the enigmatic person in the Halloween devil costume. The illustrations by Carlos Freire are colourful and humorous and match the text precisely. Children can see their own reactions mirrored in the expressions of a wonderful cat, especially when the odd guest asks for "a peanut butter

sandwich with olives and sauerkraut." Here's a guest who dares to be different, yet doesn't alienate. And when the party is over, guess who stays to clean up? Bravo!

Allan Sheldon

SOURCE: A review of *10 for Dinner*, in *Canadian Children's Literature*, No. 61, 1991, pp. 97-8.

Carlos Freire, a Chilean lawyer turned Canadian artist, finds good grist for a picture book in Jo Ellen Bogart's *10 for Dinner*. This book is about numbers and about being different (awkward at times but not a bad thing). It is also nonsensical, very funny and economically written. Freire's sense of humour is irrepressible. His coloured drawings are bright and crisply executed in full and double-page spreads. The glee overflows the pages, and the spare text appears boldly and clearly right where it belongs. This is the kind of book that calls for accuracy, being after all a book about numbers. Ten birthday party guests are hilariously depicted.

DANIEL'S DOG (1990)

Joan McGrath

SOURCE: A review of *Daniel's Dog*, in *Canadian Children's Literature*, No. 59, 1990, pp. 81-2.

Daniel's problem is as old as family life, but just as unexpected and shattering every single time it happens. The little boy has a new baby sister. She's tiny and beautiful, and he really loves and welcomes her. BUT . . .

His mother, his very own mother, spends an enormous amount of time taking care of the baby, bathing her, changing her, holding and cuddling her. Lovely illustrations show a young mother smiling down at the infant who for the moment absorbs her entire attention, while in the background a small boy hovers between wistfulness and jealousy. Daniel's solitary games grow louder and angrier, while mother remains oblivious to his attention-getting ploys.

Children find different ways of working through the readjustment of family dynamics. Daniel's solution is the arrival on the scene of Lucy, his "ghost dog", a present, he says, from his dead grandfather, who "always has time for me, no matter what". *Somebody,* even if it has to be an imaginary somebody, is going to put Daniel *first*.

Rich, warm colours—indeed, fiery colours [used by Janet Wilson] to suggest Daniel's frustrations—brighten a lovely evocation of a handsome black family, and are generally extremely attractive, with the unfortunate exception of awkward cover art which somehow seems to misplace Daniel's foot.

Joanne Findon

SOURCE: A review of *Daniel's Dog,* in *Quill and Quire,* Vol. 56, No. 3, March, 1990, p. 20.

Daniel's Dog by Jo Ellen Bogart deals with the all-too-familiar problem of a child who suddenly has to share parental attention with a new sibling. Daniel turns to an age-old solution: he finds an invisible friend. But the author gives it a twist; she has Daniel befriending Lucy, a ghost dog. The book's cover notes explain that the story stems in part from "the tales of dog ghosts which are part of American Negro oral tradition [and which are] typically seen to represent a departed loved one who returns to play a comforting role."

When Daniel tells his mother that Lucy likes to be read to, she wisely asks if he'll read to baby Carrie. The illustration showing Daniel reading aloud while his mother nurses the baby is one of the most touching images in a book that owes much of its appeal to the beautiful artwork of Janet Wilson.

It should be noted, for the benefit of adults who seek picture books that better reflect society's diversity of race and colour, that the illustrations in this book depict a black family—a perfectly ordinary black family. And Daniel has a best friend who looks decidedly Oriental. That's all. No big deal. But a definite change from the homogeneous pink-cheeked people we encounter in far too many picture books.

Anna DeWind

SOURCE: A review of *Daniel's Dog,* in *School Library Journal,* Vol. 36, No. 3, March, 1990, p. 188.

Daniel's new sister can't throw a ball, play catch, or even talk; worse yet, she occupies much of his mother's attention. Feeling neglected, Daniel turns to the companionship of a friendly ghost dog sent from his grandfather in heaven. As he begins to realize that there is room in his mother's heart for both himself and his sister, his dependence on the dog lessens. The story reads well, and the vibrant illustrations of the young black protagonist are remarkably lifelike. Crayon-hued borders outline the text, which is well spaced and easy to read. The warm family atmosphere is nicely captured, particularly in a tableau of Daniel reading aloud while his mother nurses the baby. The book, however, is not without flaws. Although Bogart attributes her use of a ghost dog to African-American folklore, in which canine spirits representing departed loved ones play a comforting role, Daniel's explanation of the dog's arrival from heaven seems contrived. When he offers another imaginary dog to a sad friend, Daniel seems wise beyond his years. The final page, depicting Daniel still leaning on the ghost dog, is surprising, given his growing acceptance of the baby. Still, this fine book gracefully covers topics rang-

ing from the arrival of a new sibling to imaginary companions to the resolution of inner conflict.

Beth Herbert

SOURCE: A review of *Daniel's Dog,* in *Booklist,* Vol. 86, No. 15, April 1, 1990, pp. 1543-44.

Daniel's baby sister takes up so much time that the young black boy feels left out; to compensate, he invents Lucy, a ghost dog. Through Lucy's healing magic, Daniel is able to accept his sister and even shares his fanciful creation with his playmate, Norman, by creating an invisible dog for him as well. Wilson's realistic illustrations ingeniously capture Daniel's facial expressions as he plays with his imaginary pet and learns to take care of his tiny sibling. According to dust-jacket copy, this story was inspired by tales of dog ghosts, part of the Afro-American oral tradition. The story will also speak to children's penchant for inventing imaginary friends.

Publishers Weekly

SOURCE: A review of *Daniel's Dog,* in *Publishers Weekly,* Vol. 237, No. 15, April 13, 1990, p. 63.

Jealous, neglected and unloved: that's how Daniel feels since the arrival of his baby sister, Carrie. As his mother spends most of her time caring for the infant, Daniel feels threatened by her lack of attention and creates an imaginary companion—a ghost dog named Lucy, sent to him by his dead grandfather. Lucy represents a positive spirit, bringing Daniel comfort and understanding. As a result he becomes more receptive to the baby's needs, and is able to share his fantasy with his friend Norman, who is also experiencing a personal crisis. Inspired in part by the dog ghosts of American Negro oral tradition (which supposedly represented a deceased loved one returning in a comforting role), Bogart's story gives a fresh and unusual slant to this familiar theme. Wilson's homey, realistic illustrations—and Lucy, depicted in an appropriately "translucent" fashion—add a reassuring touch to a potentially unsettling situation.

Patricia Fry

SOURCE: A review of *Daniel's Dog,* in *CM: A Reviewing Journal of Canadian Materials for Young People,* Vol. 18, No. 3, May, 1990, p. 117.

This book deals effectively with that age-old problem, the displacement of the first-born when the second child arrives. With his mother so busy, Daniel has lots of time to play with his toys, but it's his imaginary dog that helps him cope so well with his loneliness.

One evening, as his mother is tucking him into bed, she apologizes for spending so little time with him and assures him that the situation will improve. Daniel just smiles and says he's fine since Lucy, his ghost dog, arrived to keep him company.

After meeting Lucy, Daniel's mother makes a greater effort to include Daniel in the baby's daily care. He is asked to check the baby, he gets a diaper for her, reads a story to her while she's being fed, and finally holds her. The book ends when Daniel's friend Norman wishes that he too had a special someone to keep him company and Daniel arranges for him to have Lucy's friend, a shaggy dog named Max.

The illustrations deserve special mention. They really bring the story alive with their bright colours and attention to detail. Particularly intriguing is the way the ghost dog is drawn. Lucy is so easy to see yet she blends right into the background! Janet Wilson is also very talented at depicting expressions—from wistful to angry to content—and that makes the characters even more appealing.

The book is set up with text on one page and a full-colour illustration on the facing page. It's an excellent choice for a read-aloud selection at the Primary level because most children can identify with Daniel's loneliness and because the illustrations are so eye catching. It's also worth nothing that Daniel and his family are black and that might be another reason for including this title in a collection.

📖 *SARAH SAW A BLUE MACAW* (1991)

Frieda Wishinsky

SOURCE: A review of *Sarah Saw a Blue Macaw,* in *Quill and Quire,* Vol. 57, No. 3, March, 1991, p. 20.

Sarah Saw a Blue Macaw also displays a fine use of verse, although the stress is more on mood and place than story. From the first page we are transported to the rain forest of Peru, where we meet a wide array of exotic animals. By gradually deepening and darkening the colours, illustrator [Sylvie] Daigneault conveys the passage of time, and with it the appearance of different animals. The back of the book provides a useful "Cast of Characters" that gives the reader the names of all the animals in the pictures.

Unlike the spate of pedantic environmental titles released recently, this gentle book never hits readers over the head with its "save the earth" message. Instead it allows them to experience the forest and its diverse inhabitants through words and art.

Jennifer Johnson

SOURCE: A review of *Sarah Saw a Blue Macaw,* in *CM: A Reviewing Journal of Canadian Materials for Young People,* Vol. 19, No. 3, May, 1991, p. 170.

The talents of Jo Ellen Bogart and Sylvie Daigneault combine beautifully in *Sarah Saw a Blue Macaw,* a gentle rhyming tale of animal life in the Peruvian rain forest.

Bogart begins each page with a question. To the first, "Where did Sarah swing?" she replies, "Sarah swung where branches hung." This pattern of question and answer is carried on throughout the book until at the last, "Sarah said, It's time for bed." Creatures of the rain forest are referred to in the text by personal names. Clues about the characters are provided in the illustrations. The text flows smoothly and uses alliteration and repetition to good effect in introducing the rain forest inhabitants.

The illustrations by Sylvie Daigneault provide an accurate and inviting setting for Bogart's characters. Daigneault has correctly portrayed the animals and vegetation of the rain forest environment. The pages are not cluttered but indicate a lush, multi-layered ecosystem. Her progression from daylight to an exotic, star-filled night is done gradually and illustrates the cycle of diurnal and nocturnal animal movement.

An added feature of the book and one which should appeal in families where older children pour over Waldo books is the hide-and-seek element. A "cast of characters" is available at the end of the book listing each animal by its personal and species name. Other animals on the same page are indicated so that the searcher can identify each one. Sarah, the spider monkey of the title, is also hidden on each page and can be searched out.

Bogart and Daigneault have created a lyrical and artistic book which imparts a sense of wonder and appreciation for an endangered environment.

Ted McGee

SOURCE: A review of *Sarah Saw a Blue Macaw,* in *Canadian Children's Literature,* No. 66, 1992, pp. 82-3.

Sarah Saw a Blue Macaw tracks Sarah, a little spider monkey, from day until dusk. What Sarah sees are the animals of the rainforest; the verse on each two-page illustration focuses attention on one of the animals, while others are identified in a "Cast of Characters" at the back of the book. To little children, the book offers the opportunity to find Sarah somewhere in each picture, a predictable question-and-answer structure in the verses, emphatic alliteration and rhyme (internal and end), and a story that culminates at bed-time when the promise for the next day is more play. But children will need an adult to identify some of the animals in the illustrations and to explore the words that are most delicious in themselves: "marsupial frog," "collared peccaries," "morpho butterfly," "blue-crowned motmot," and the like. Indeed adult readers may have to do some research, as I did to make sure which was the baby skink and which the Brazilian tapir.

It is difficult to exaggerate how beautifully designed a book *Sarah Saw a Blue Macaw* is: flora and fauna, accurately drawn and brilliantly coloured, are set on monochromatic backgrounds, some flat, some textured. The resulting tension between verisimilitude in the representation of the figures and obvious artificiality of the background captures the richly exotic quality of the rainforest. The strange beauty of Sylvie Daigneault's illustrations may well engender support for efforts to protect the rainforests. . . .

Because Jo Ellen Bogart's months in Peru also inform *Sarah,* the political insensitivity of the book is the more surprising. The problem is in the naming: instead of Juan or Domaso or Evita or Esmeralda, the animals are dubbed Maggie and Charlie, Morton and Horton, Sherman and Clyde—as if the Peruvian rainforest were an Anglo-Saxon habitat. In addition to appreciating the humour, subtlety, beauty, and perceptiveness of . . . *Sarah Saw a Blue Macaw,* resisting this kind of linguistic colonialism is a good reason why . . . [this book] ought to be read, and discussed, by adults and children together.

Fred Boer

SOURCE: A review of *Sarah Saw a Blue Macaw,* in *Quill and Quire,* Vol. 58, No. 12, December, 1992, p. 28.

This delightful new picture book will quickly become a favourite with young children. Sarah, a spider monkey, spends a busy day watching the activities of the many strange and wonderful animals who live in the South American rain forest. The rhyming text is printed in appropriately large type and follows a simple pattern that is easy to learn. Children will love looking at the rich, colourful illustrations. A helpful list of the animals is included at the back of the book.

📖 *MAMA'S BED* (1993)

Janet McNaughton

SOURCE: A review of *Mama's Bed,* in *Quill and Quire,* Vol. 59, No. 10, October, 1993, pp. 38-9.

This book has no plot at all. Instead, a little girl talks about why she loves her mother's bed—the comfort she finds there when she is sick or sad or frightened, and the happy moments she shares with her mother and siblings on and beneath the covers. Jo Ellen Bogart's text is as sparse as that of a first-grade reader; the most exciting moment in the book involves a little bouncing on the mattress. How will a book like this fare with children raised on Saturday-morning cartoons? Just fine. *Mama's Bed* proves what a powerful device simplicity can be in

a picture book. Children age 5 and under will identify strongly with the small protagonist's feelings about the safety and comfort provided by her mother's bed. Bogart's simple writing creates a sense of domestic content that all children long for and need. *Mama's Bed* is especially likable because this is obviously a single-parent family, but the presentation is not at all self-conscious. This is not one of those well-retain intentioned books designed to belabour the fact that children of single parents can be well adjusted. It is simply a pleasant story about an ordinary family that happens to have one parent.

Sylvie Daigneault's wonderful illustrations, drawn with coloured pencils on coloured paper, are another reason to admire *Mama's Bed.* Daigneault used the same technique in *Sarah Saw a Blue Macaw,* another collaboration with Bogart. In both books, the colour of the paper sets the tone for each illustration. Daigneault, yet another of the many exceptional illustrators from Quebec, achieves remarkably fine lines, shading, and detail in her work. This is one of those books parents will look forward to at bedtime for at least as long as their preschoolers do.

Patricia L. M. Butler

SOURCE: A review of *Mama's Bed,* in *CM: A Reviewing Journal of Canadian Materials for Young People,* Vol. 22, No. 2, March-April, 1994, p. 45.

Many of us have memories of the security found in mama's bed after a nightmare or during a thunderstorm.

The team that produced *Sarah Saw a Blue Macaw* has ventured into the comfort zone with a story that describes the security a little girl finds in her mama's bed when she's frightened or sick, and the fun to be had there during the day while bouncing or folding clean laundry. Mama's bed has all sorts of uses, including cutting out Halloween costumes—something we hope young readers will request permission for before wielding their scissors around the eiderdown.

Each two-page drawing has one or two lines of simple text superimposed, easily read by a second year reader. As in *Simon's Surprise,* Daigneault has provided meticulous drawings, but the large presentation and colours used sometimes undermine the quiet tone of the story.

📖 *TWO TOO MANY* (1994)

Kenneth Oppel

SOURCE: A review of *Two Too Many,* in *Quill and Quire,* Vol. 60, No. 4, April, 1994, pp. 36, 38.

"Maxwell Moose had two too many antlers on his head/ Bernadette had two too many bedposts on her bed." So begins Jo Ellen Bogart's playful new picture book, *Two Too Many.* Children will undoubtedly enjoy hearing (and reading aloud for themselves) Bogart's extravagant rhyming couplets, all, of course, illuminating the humorous consequences of having two too many of something: a ukulele with too many strings, a balaclava with too many holes. Yvonne Cathcart's vivid oil-pastel illustrations offer bold, imaginative interpretations of Bogart's text, and also capture and sometimes slyly augment its rambunctious sense of humour.

Bogart's rhymes lend themselves to lively illustrations, and she's obviously had fun choosing unusual names, too, like Arabella or Teresina. The repetition of the text is sure to delight and hold the attention of a young audience. This is a light, pleasant book. The ending seems a little artificial, though, as readers are encouraged to share out their own extra things. Cathcart's final illustrations skillfully show how some objects in the book can be shared out, but how do you share dragon's flames, or bedposts, or elephant knees? Children are not likely to let this minor quibble interfere, however, and will enjoy the high-spirited fun of this attractive book.

Catherine McInerney

SOURCE: A review of *Two Too Many,* in *CM: A Reviewing Journal of Canadian Materials for Young People,* Vol. 22, No. 5, October, 1994, pp. 183-84.

This is a very simple book. Kids of all ages will enjoy the nutty things that go on when there are simply two too many things. Also counting the objects and deciding which pair were the "last straw" will be a good game.

The illustrations, done in pastel, have a wonderful crayon-like quality kids will be able to identify with. The two-page spreads feature kids and animals tumbling in and out of the frame of the pages. All have brilliant borders that function like picture frames to stop the action and capture it on the page. The children's faces express surprise, fright, disappointment, and shock as we go from page to page.

The message of the text is that when you have extra of something, the best thing to do is share. How can anyone disagree with that? The text features many unusual words like "balsa," which kids may even feel the need to look up in a dictionary. However, there are not too many words to make the text too tough to decipher for even the most beginning reader.

Melody Collins Thomason

SOURCE: A review of *Two Too Many,* in *Canadian Children's Literature,* Vol. 78, No. 21:2, Summer, 1995, pp. 69-73.

Bogart is well-known for her previous books, and she has a deceptively simple but very distinctive style. Like Richard Stevenson, she is fond of alliteration and internal rhyme. Unlike him, she knows how to use them sparingly, forcefully, and to good effect.

Using the simple concept of "two too many," whether it be spouts on a teapot or wheels on a tricycle, Bogart manages a funny, verbally pleasing and challenging book which will easily bear many re-readings to young children. Yvonne Cathcart's riotous, wildly colourful illustrations, often escaping their own borders in their good-humoured abundance, complement the verse beautifully. "Lulu's ukelele had two too many strings," and "Cleo's balaclava had two too may holes," says Bogart. Each line is a small perfect structure of sound and image. The rhymes are unexpected and precise, and she has fun using long four-syllable names, like Desdemona and Arabella, which match exactly the metre and the mood. *Two Too Many* works as a book, with its seamless mixture of repetition and variety, married well to the laughing excess of the illustrations.

GIFTS (1994)

Linda Granfield

SOURCE: A review of *Gifts,* in *Quill and Quire,* Vol. 60, No. 9, September, 1994, p. 70.

We're off on a world tour with Grandma in Jo Ellen Bogart's *Gifts,* following her adventures as she goes "a-travelling." The story is told in verse by her grandchild, whose souvenir requests are a delightful mixture of the easily accessible (a bell) and the abstract (a rainbow to wear as a ring). Grandma never disappoints—she always delivers.

Just like Grandma, the text of *Gifts* is full of zing and zest, redolent with images of a child's limitless imagination and the loving responses of a spunky grandparent. Bogart's rhymes are never forced, although her word choice occasionally does break the rhythm of the poetry. The Australian visit, for example, brings requests for "Just a didgeridoo, / some billabong goo, / and a boomerang I can fling." "Didgeridoo" is a fabulous word, but it's not easy to read aloud the first (or even fifth) time through the text.

In her trademark Plasticine illustrations, Barbara Reid provides the details that are missing from the brief text. She determines the sex of the grandchild (female) and creates the vistas that represent Grandma's travels, capturing the flora and fauna of each country, with its animals, birds, and historic buildings. We also are taken to sites of interior travel—Reid also shows us the two characters' bedrooms, those private places most associated with dreamy landscapes of the mind. Ethnic clothing (Grandma is a sharp dresser) and the faces of India, China, and Australia provide a wealth of multicultural details that will prolong enjoyment of the book. See the Taj Mahal! Visit Mayan ruins!

Throughout the travels, Grandma's knapsack collects more

travel badges and her granddaughter grows up. Grandma's aging, too. She's in a wheelchair for her final trip, to England. In a wonderful piece of work, Grandma's feet in the chair become legs on a swing as the page turns, and the story is thus brought full circle—the granddaughter was in a swing when we first met her.

In the end, the granddaughter pushes her own child in a stroller, wearing a grown-up version of the shoes she wore on that swing long ago. They've been to the library; they're carrying travel books home in Grandma's knapsack. Grandma's legacy of get-go, vision, and love is obviously cherished and alive.

Rachele Oriente

SOURCE: A review of *Gifts,* in *Canadian Children's Literature,* Vol. 78, No. 21:2, Summer, 1995, pp. 77-8.

The success of *Gifts* may be measured by its versatility: it may be integrated into a lesson plan, and it will entertain an audience. The text is a series of apparently random and unconnected memories, narrated in short, descriptive sentences by a first-person voice. There is no conventional plot.

The artwork tells of the loving relationship between the aging grandmother who travels the world and the growing granddaughter who requests souvenirs or gifts from those travels. The joy and intimacy of shared moments that make a bond of love between them is conveyed not, for example, by the granddaughter's request for a gift of "the roar of a jungle king," but by the scene of the old and young kneeling face to face on the scrambled rug roaring at each other.

The illustrations do more than accompany the text. They open up the world of the characters created by the text; and, they give a non-linear text its shape. The plasticine illustrations have both painterly and sculptural qualities. Indeed, they are narrative and may be read. For instance, the text does not mention time, but the art portrays its passage. It is only when we see that the child has grown to a woman with a child of her own that *Gifts* has a resolution. The first person narration that seems to be present time is actually memory—a grown woman is telling a story of her own childhood to her child. The woman says she will teach her child what she has learned from her grandmother: that life is a journey of discovery, that there is adventure in the everyday world as well as the exotic, and that every experience may be translated into a poem.

Gifts will appeal to librarians and storytellers with its musical rhyme scheme and its arresting illustrations. Also, the text is didactic in the most appealing way. By speaking of the exotic in casual terms it arouses curiosity. What *is* a didgeridoo? Could *I* eat a baobab seed? The culture-specific vocabulary may be difficult but it may prompt children to share their home culture in the multicultural classroom or library.

Jody McCoy

SOURCE: A review of *Gifts,* in *School Library Journal,* Vol. 42, No. 3, March, 1996, p. 166.

Another glorious, globe-trotting grannie joins the ranks of elderly travelers. Unlike Jill Paton Walsh's *When Grandma Came,* Bogart's Grandma is a happy soul who offers to bring back "gifts." As she heads off to nine very different locales, she asks, "What would you have me bring?" Her granddaughter's exquisitely fanciful replies presented in rhyme celebrate the imagination: a piece of sky, a roar, billabong goo, a memory, a rainbow to wear as a ring, etc. Reid's wonderful plasticine illustrations, with touches of acrylic for shine, seem so three-dimensional that they beg to be touched. The wealth of texture, depth, and detail is sure to mesmerize even the most jaded eye. The colors are scrumptious. The loving relationship between grandma and granddaughter as each ages is tenderly captured in hugs, smiles, and subtle physical changes. Perhaps this traveler doesn't carpet a town with lupines like Barbara Cooney's *Miss Rumphius,* nor is she as rambunctiously silly as the character in Grahame Base's *My Grandma Lived in Gooligulch,* but *Gifts* is a treasure to read alone, aloud, to a group, or to give to anyone who loves the unique.

Wendy Zwaal

SOURCE: A review of *Gifts,* in *CM: Canadian Review of Materials,* Vol. III, No. 7, November 29, 1996.

Gifts is the story of an adventurous grandmother who asks her granddaughter what she would like from her travels. The granddaughter does not request the usual souvenirs, but asks for such things as a mountain, a rainbow, a sunrise, a roar, an iceberg and a memory. The grandmother complies and through the gifts, the granddaughter shares in the grandmother's experiences. In the course of the grandmother's travels, both the child and the grandmother grow older and by the end of the story the child has grown up to be a mother who promises to share her grandmother's gifts with her own child.

Gifts demonstrates a positive relationship between grandmother and grandchild—one that is full of love and sharing, where the true gifts that the grandmother gives are not material. *Gifts* also portrays a positive image of aging; the grandmother, although grey-haired, is full of life and vigour. Even as she ages and is in a wheelchair, she retains her energy and zest for life.

Gifts is an outstanding picture book. In 1995, it won the Amelia Frances Howard-Gibbon Medal for best illustrated Canadian children's picture book. Illustrator Barbara Reid, whose previous works include the award-winning *Two by Two, Have You Seen Birds?* and the Zoe board book series, continues her wonderful work here. The illustrations are detailed, colourful and magical. The grandmother appears vigourous and energetic; the child is joyful and adoring. Action and emotion are both wonderfully portrayed.

Author Jo Ellen Bogart has written several other children's books including *Sarah Saw a Blue Macaw, Daniel's Dog,* and *Two Too Many.* In *Gifts* she employs rhyme effectively to create a special relationship.

Gifts is a delightful book that children will enjoy.

JEREMIAH LEARNS TO READ (1997)

Sheree Haughian

SOURCE: A review of *Jeremiah Learns to Read,* in *Quill and Quire,* Vol. 64, No. 1, January, 1998, p. 37.

Jeremiah does not fit the down-and-out image of an illiterate old man. He's led a particularly successful life on the farm, where he builds split-rail fences, cooks buttermilk pancakes, and grows delicious vegetables. Although he can read the signs of the seasons and the code of the natural landscape, letters and words have somehow never been accessible to him. Supported by his family in his desire to learn to "be even better," Jeremiah heads off to the rural schoolhouse. As he learns the alphabet and phonics with the help of the children who are his classmates, Jeremiah also teaches the curriculum he has already mastered so well—bird sounds, applesauce making, and the whittling of wood. One day he takes a book of poetry home from school. That night his wife is so moved by his readings on nature that she, too, decides to learn to read, and he offers to be her teacher.

With his snowy beard and sensitive temperament, Jeremiah is a character of great personal dignity. Jo Ellen Bogart's story is tender and lyric; key phrases are repeated just often enough to give rhythmic flow to the narrative. The illustrations for the book, from oil paintings on canvas, are created by Laura Fernandez and Rick Jacobson, who also collaborated on *Tchaikovsky Discovers America.* Rich and mellow, these pictures enhance the heartwarming quality of the text. The sociological question of why such a capable couple have never learned to read remains unexplored. This is neither a flaw nor an oversight, but a tribute to the power of

Bogart's writing and the accompanying illustrations. Literacy is viewed, not as a commodity essential to productivity in the contemporary workplace, but as a kind of magical door that allows those who enter an opportunity to experience beauty and truth more fully. Reading this book is a testament to that perspective.

Gail Hamilton

SOURCE: A review of *Jeremiah Learns to Read,* in *CM: Canadian Review of Materials,* Vol. IV, No. 10, January 16, 1998.

> Jeremiah knew how to build a split-rail fence and he knew how to cook buttermilk pancakes, but he didn't know how to read.

In fact, Jeremiah, a wise old grandfather, can do almost anything—from making a table out of a tree to understanding animal tracks on the ground. Yet Jeremiah feels that a part of him is missing. He announces to his brother and to his wife, Juliana, that he desperately wants to learn to read. The next morning, he accompanies the children to the one-room schoolhouse and joins Mrs. Trumble's class. Jeremiah is welcomed by the students who help him learn to sounds of the letters; and he, in turn, shares his wisdom with them, teaching them how to make bird calls and whistles, how to whittle with a pocketknife and how to make applesauce. In the evenings he studies hard, practising his newly acquired reading skills and writing stories inspired by his personal experiences. When he feels confident enough to read to his wife, Jeremiah reads from a volume of poetry. Juliana decides that she, too, wants to learn to read. The next day, she joins her husband and the children as they walk to school.

Bogart has written a heartwarming story about sharing and learning from one another and about the joy and wonder of reading. The text is simple, soft and soothing. Full page illustrations [and several double-page spreads], rendered in oil on canvas, depict the beauty of the countryside with its changing seasons. Illustrators Rick Jacobson and Laura Fernandez, a husband and wife team, used real models for the book's characters, an approach which resulted in wonderful life-like portraits which make the characters come alive. Use this book to kick off "I Love to Read" Month in February. It's a sure-fire winner!

Additional coverage of Bogart's life and career is contained in the following source published by The Gale Group: *Something about the Author,* **Vol. 92**

Wilma Pitchford Hays

1909-

(Born Wilma Pitchford) American author of fiction.

Major works include *Pilgrim Thanksgiving* (1955), *Freedom* (1958), *The Fourth of July Raid* (1959), *Drummer Boy for Montcalm* (1959), *Siege! The Story of St. Augustine in 1702* (1976).

INTRODUCTION

The prolific author of over forty-five books for primary and middle graders, Hays is known for her historical fiction that brings America's past to life for young readers. Although Hays initially began writing for adults, she turned exclusively to a child audience after the publication of *Pilgrim Thanksgiving*, her first work for youngsters, which provides an authentic account of the Pilgrims' first Thanksgiving celebration. In an essay for *Something about the Author Autobiography Series* (*SAAS*), Hays commented, "Letters pouring in from children, teachers, and librarians after publication of my first book . . . influenced me to leave adult fiction and write for these appreciative young readers." Hays produced a series of works highlighting Pilgrim history. In addition, she has written fiction set during the American Revolution, holiday stories, regional tales that depict the lives of children in various parts of the United States, and accounts of her childhood in the Sioux Indian territories of Nebraska and South Dakota. In a similar vein, Hays's fiction espouses the family stories of her ancestors, who were among the early settlers in North America.

Throughout her many writings, Hays strives for historical accuracy in creating an authentic atmosphere. In *SAAS* she noted, "The books came from my own experiences with people, animals and places I had known, merged with research, to make the story come alive in readers' minds." Reviewers praise Hays's precise historical details, her simple storytelling, and her ability to give meaning to the histories she tells. She is further recognized for the unique narrative perspectives she brings to her texts, which are often told by children from typically unheard points of view. The events in *Drummer Boy for Montcalm*, for example, are not described from the victor's perspective. Instead, the tale is narrated by a young French boy who witnesses France's loss of Quebec to the British Army. In a similar vein, the events in *Siege! The Story of St. Augustine* are described by the Spanish occupants of Fort Castillo de San Marcos, rather than by the fort's English assailants. Recognizing Hays's uncommon bent on history, Ellen Lewis Buell opined in a review of *Easter Fires* (1960), "Wilma Pitchford Hays . . . has a knack of finding unusual items in our country's past."

Biographical Information

Hays was born on November 22, 1909, in Nance County, Nebraska, to Clarence and Grace (Lull) Pitchford. During her early childhood she lived on her family's homestead near the Rosebud Indian Reservation in South Dakota, where her father worked building houses for the government. She later described her childhood memories with the Sioux in her books *Little Yellow Fur: Homesteading in 1913* (1973) and *Yellow Fur and Little Hawk* (1980). Hays recounted one memory in *SAAS*: "[T]he Indian women, intrigued by their first contact with a little white child, took me from our yard to their village nearby. They returned with a papoose and offered her to Mama saying 'Trade, trade.'" Hays spent so much time near the reservation that, as a child, she was able to speak the Dakota Sioux language. When Hays came of school age, a drought struck near her home, so her family returned to Nebraska. There, Hays's grandmothers filled her with stories of her family's history, including tales of her ancestors who lived through the U.S. Civil War, as well as of her great-great-great-grandfather, who was a drummer boy during the 1759 Battle for Quebec between the French and the British. Hays relates his story in *Drummer Boy for Montcalm*. *Abe Lincoln's Birthday* (1961) and *The Scarlet Badge* (1963) are also based on true stories of her early ancestors. "[The] first sixteen years of my life influenced many of the stories I wrote later," she noted in *SAAS*. She added in *Third Book of Junior Authors*, "I grew up with a strong sense of being a part of history. When I began to research and to write books for children, historians provided accuracy. The *feeling* for the times, and the people who lived in them, was already a part of me."

When Hays was in second grade, her family moved to a farm in Nance County, Nebraska—memories of which she explored in *The Apricot Tree* (1968). Two years later her family bought a home in nearby Fullerton, where Hays spent most of her childhood. With her mother's failing health and, as the oldest of six children, Hays watched over her younger siblings. She commented in *SAAS*, "I cannot remember a time when I was not surrounded by children, at home and at school. I read to them, made up stories to tell them." She also spent many hours at the public library, reading fairy tales, biographies, history, mythology, Bible stories, and novels such as *The Secret Garden*, *The Jungle Book*, and *Tarzan*. After graduating from high school, seventeen-year-old Hays began teaching in a nearby one-room school. In 1928, she entered the University of Nebraska, where she studied English, history, drama, and education. That same year she married R. Vernon Hays, a high-school teacher who had worked in Fullerton. The couple settled in Ansley, Nebraska, where they lived for nine years, during which their daughter Grace Ann was born.

In the late 1930s, Vernon received a scholarship to attend Harvard University. The Hays family spent several years in New England, moving throughout Massachusetts and Connecticut as a result of Vernon's career as a high-school principal and school superintendent. During this time Hays occasionally wrote stories and articles for adults. Others began to take notice of her work after one of her short stories received a prize in a national short-story contest sponsored by the Literature and Poetry Division of the National Federation of Women's Clubs. Throughout the 1930s and 1940s Hays published more than one hundred stories and articles in such magazines as *Collier's* and *Today's Woman*. She eventually shifted gears when her husband prompted her to write a children's book about the first Thanksgiving. After researching the accounts of Pilgrim governors William Bradford and Edward Winslow, Hays wrote *Pilgrim Thanksgiving*. The book's warm acceptance from teachers and children encouraged her to write exclusively for youngsters. She followed *Pilgrim Thanksgiving* with four more books about the Pilgrims, finding them, as she once commented in *Something about the Author* (*SATA*), "very interesting and much more human than most stories about them suggest." Hays's enthusiasm for history, places, and people has led her to travel across the United States. Throughout her fiction, she has attempted to pass on this excitement to children. "In all my historical books," Hays continued in *SATA*, "I added the oral history to the research and study that I continued all my life, to give my readers a feeling of 'being there.'"

Major Works

Hays was personally familiar with many important parts of Pilgrim history, and attempted to give an authentic depiction of their lives in *Pilgrim Thanksgiving*. She recounted in *SAAS*: "I had visited the hill above Plymouth harbor where the Pilgrims had buried their dead in a common grave to prevent the Indians from knowing how few were left after that first winter of sickness and death. Standing here, looking out over the harbor, my mind and body responded to the *feel* of those times: the loneliness, uncertainty, and courage of those isolated Pilgrims. . . . I knew Indians, too, from my Rosebud reservation days. I wrote from the viewpoint of a little girl and her brother who were there on that [Thanksgiving] day and met the Indians." Unlike Thanksgiving books about events leading up to the first Thanksgiving, *Pilgrim Thanksgiving* celebrates the day itself, as seen through the eyes of two young Pilgrim children, Damaris and Giles Hopkins. The story focuses on food preparation, prayers of thanks, and special Indian dances. Mary Peacock Douglas praised Hays's book, saying, "The first Thanksgiving Day in America comes alive as we share it with Damaris and her brother Giles, both of whom experienced that memorable occasion. . . . Mrs. Hays has given real meaning to Thanksgiving in her story for youngest readers."

A compilation of twenty-six historical documents dated from 1776 to 1945, *Freedom* articulates the beliefs, values, and ideologies of American democracy. The work includes facsimiles of the Declaration of Independence, the Bill of Rights, the Nineteenth Amendment, and the United Nations Charter. Accompanying each document is an explanation of its historical context and significance. Ruth Hill Viguers dubbed *Freedom* "an inviting introduction for children to the documents having to do with America's freedom," while Frances Lander Spain commented that through the book "one glimpses highlights in the growth and development of the idea of freedom and the country's integrity."

Taking place during the American Revolution, *The Fourth of July Raid* recounts the British invasion of New Haven, Connecticut, on July 5, 1779. Young Tom Morris narrates his account of the invasion, describing how General Tyron and his troops raided and torched many of the homes in town. Virginia Haviland called the book "a vivid, if brief piece, convincing in its picture of patriot staunchness and courage and of a boy's quick-wittedness." Similar in theme and style is *Drummer Boy for Montcalm*, a story about the 1759 Battle for Quebec told from the perspective of twelve-year-old Peter Demo. Peter, having dreams of becoming a fur trapper in North America, stows away on a French ship bringing reinforcements to General Montcalm's troops in Quebec. Eager to support the defenders of Quebec, Peter enrolls in Montcalm's army as a drummer boy, and witnesses the siege and eventual defeat of Canadian city to the British, as well as the death of his general. A *Virginia Kirkus' Service* reviewer characterized *Drummer Boy for Montcalm* as "[a]n unusual depiction of defeat rather than victory for the teen-age hero and a poignant portrayal of a cause overthrown." The reviewer concluded, "mark this as a teen-age novel of distinction." A reviewer for *The Booklist and Subscription Books Bulletin* noted that "[a] feeling of authenticity pervades this exciting and poignant narrative of the siege and fall of Quebec." Similarly, *Siege! The Story of St. Augustine in 1702* recounts the British invasion of St. Augustine's Fort Castillo de San Marcos from the viewpoint of a young Spanish boy, Juan Olfosno, whose family is staying in the fort. Norma Feld noted that "through the thoughts of young Juan . . . the pride and strength of the Spanish people is portrayed," adding that the book is "a quiet, but absorbing story on a period not usually touched upon for this age."

On another note, *The Goose That Was a Watchdog* (1967) is a more peaceful story about a young boy and his pet goose. Tad's father, a sharecropper, is charged with taking care of the landowner's geese, which are used to weed the cotton fields. Young Tad grows fond of one particularly tame goose that watches over Tad's baby sister and performs the job of a faithful watchdog by stopping chicken thieves. The owner eventually gives Tad the goose as a pet. Zena Sutherland appreciated Hays's simple story line and gentle telling, stating, "the writing style is direct and easy, the events are believable, and the book gives a quiet picture of a [black] family's life in the rural south."

Awards

Three of Hays's books have been Junior Literary Guild selections: *Pilgrim Thanksgiving, Little Lone Coyote,* and *The Pup Who Became a Police Dog.* In 1958, Hays won the New Haven (Connecticut) Festival of Art Award for outstanding contribution to literature for *Freedom. The Hawaiian Way* won the first prize for juvenile manuscript from the Wagner College Writers Conference in 1960 and was named to a select list of World Friendship Books for Children in 1961. Hays was also the runner-up for the Mark Twain Award in 1974 for *For Ma and Pa.*

TITLE COMMENTARY

📖 *PILGRIM THANKSGIVING* (1955; reprinted
   in *A Lizard to Start With,* 1976)

Virginia Kirkus' Service

SOURCE: A review of *Pilgrim Thanksgiving,* in *Virginia Kirkus' Service,* Vol. XXIII, No. 17, September 1, 1955, p. 646.

Very similar in style and content to Alice Dalgliesh's *The Thanksgiving Story,* this changes the focus somewhat and relates something of the pilgrim's story through events on Thanksgiving Day itself. The central characters are Damaris and Giles Hopkins again and their feelings about the Indians and their own life, reflect the tension and the hope. As Damaris wakes in the morning and spends the day helping her mother with preparations for the feast, she wonders what would become of them should the Indians suddenly decide not to follow the friendly examples of Massasoit and Squanto. Giles is less apprehensive. When the Indians come and the feast is under way, Giles exchanges presents with an Indian boy. This and the festivities that follow serve to symbolize a new understanding. Thoughtful—a good supplement to Miss Dalgliesh's more extensive story. Soft brown drawings by Leonard Weisgard.

The Booklist

SOURCE: A review of *Pilgrim Thanksgiving,* in *The Booklist,* Vol. 52, No. 4, October 15, 1955, p. 82.

As simple in style, and as welcome, as *The Thanksgiving Story* by Dalgliesh, this story tells of the first Thanksgiving Day as experienced by apprehensive Damaris Hopkins who looked forward to the feast but wished the Indians had not been invited. It was only at the end of the day of feasting, prayers, Indian dances, and speeches, that Damaris realized it had been a wonderful day and that one of the things she had to be thankful for was learning to be friends with the Indians.

Mary Peacock Douglas

SOURCE: A review of *Pilgrim Thanksgiving,* in *Saturday Review,* Vol. 38, No. 46, November 12, 1955, p. 64.

The first Thanksgiving Day in America comes alive as we share it with Damaris and her brother Giles, both of whom experienced that memorable occasion. Damaris's fear of the Indians was quieted after the day of prayers, of good food, of speeches, and of strange and beautiful Indian dances. Her little dog, who had pressed close to her ankles, was more at ease also. Mrs. Hays has given real meaning to Thanksgiving in her story for youngest readers. Leonard Weisgard, well known as a Caldecott Medal winner, is the illustrator.

C. E. Van Norman

SOURCE: A review of *Pilgrim Thanksgiving,* in *The New York Times Book Review,* November 13, 1955, p. 45.

Damaris Hopkins was afraid. Today the Pilgrims were sharing their feast of thanksgiving with the Indians. But there were so few Pilgrims and so many Indians! Brother

Giles, however, felt no fear for he was certain they could all be friends. At the end of the day Damaris admitted Giles was right. The great feast, the prayers of the Pilgrim Fathers, the strangely beautiful Indian dances and the friendly speeches of Chief Massasoit and Governor Bradford had brought them together in mutual understanding.

The true meaning of Thanksgiving is here brought out in an authentic and personal narrative of a real Pilgrim family, and in the beautiful saffron, brown and black illustrations by the well-known artist, Leonard Weisgard. *Pilgrim Thanksgiving* is a worthy companion to Alice Dalgliesh's *The Thanksgiving Story*, which is also centered upon the Hopkins family, but which stresses the rigors of the Mayflower voyage and the first winter rather than the day itself. Both are examples of superior workmanship and fine feeling and are excellent additions to Pilgrim literature.

📖 THE STORY OF VALENTINE (1956)

Virginia Kirkus' Service

SOURCE: A review of *The Story of Valentine*, in *Virginia Kirkus' Service*, Vol. XXIV, No. 2, January 15, 1956, p. 46.

Timed for St. Valentine's Day, this story of one of the first Roman priests is dignified and sympathetic. Living during the reign of Claudius, Valentine kept hidden in his garden. He saw few people but among them was a group of boys who visited and grew to love him though they didn't understand his religion. When the decree that all Christians be taken puts Valentine in prison, he sends his pet pigeon to the boys with messages and Octavian, one of them, manages to send Valentine a scroll. In the prison, Julia, a blind girl, has also become a friend of Valentine's and when she and Octavian meet, their faith enlarges, a miracle takes place, and Julia regains her sight.

Louise S. Bechtel

SOURCE: A review of *The Story of Valentine*, in *New York Herald Tribune Book Review*, January 29, 1956, p. 8.

Here is a lovely valentine to send a child eight to eleven, a story about the real St. Valentine, who lived in Rome so long ago, and was not called a Saint until long after the days of this story. A footnote at the end tells how this "day" was named, and the story makes clear why St. Valentine is connected with loving messages. It is about a Roman boy, Octavian, who played in the garden of this brave Christian priest who owned a clever pet pigeon, Smoky. When Valentine was arrested, Smoky and young Octavian and the blind girl Julia played their part in the finale. It leaves the boy a believer in "the One God," but does not tell us what finally happened to Valentine, which is rather disappointing. Nevertheless, it

is a moving story. It will give younger children some idea (though a very gentle one) of the courage of early Christians, and a colorful, brief glimpse of Rome in its most civilized era.

Mr. Weisgard's beautiful two-color pictures will rank among his best illustrating. His characters are real, his portraits and action are clear for children, while of subtle decorative quality, and his Roman backgrounds are superb. With the excellent type and fine printing, it is a distinguished piece of bookmaking.

Jennie D. Lindquist

SOURCE: A review of *The Story of Valentine*, in *The Horn Book Magazine*, Vol. XXXII, No. 2, April, 1956, p. 108.

It was a happy idea to make a lovely St. Valentine's Day book from a story about the good Saint himself who lived in Rome and let the children play in his garden. Mrs. Hays tells how Valentine was thrown into prison because of his belief in one God; how he sent messages by carrier pigeon to his young friends; and of what happened when Octavian, a young Roman boy, and the prison guard's little blind daughter managed to get to Valentine the book he wanted so much to read. Both illustrations and bookmaking are exactly right for the story. . . . [I]t is a good book for any time of year, particularly in schools and libraries that have a continual call for easy-to-read stories of the saints.

Ruth Gagliardo

SOURCE: A review of *The Story of Valentine*, in *Saturday Review*, Vol. 39, No. 16, April 21, 1956, pp. 32-3.

Valentine, whose birthday is celebrated on February 14, becomes a very real person instead of just a day in Wilma Hays's distinguished story of Rome during the persecution of the Christians. The boy Octavian loves the wise, friendly Valentine, who permits Octavian and his friends to play in his garden. When Valentine, a believer in "the one true God," is taken prisoner his carrier pigeon, Smoky, delivers a message to Octavian and his friends. What follows makes exciting reading for boys and girls of eight to ten. Mrs. Hays's beautifully told tale is a real find for the storyteller. The illustrations by Leonard Weisgard, Caldecott medalist, give a remarkable picture of ancient Rome. This is a truly beautiful book.

📖 CHRISTMAS ON THE MAYFLOWER (1956)

Virginia Kirkus' Service

SOURCE: A review of *Christmas on the Mayflower*, in *Virginia Kirkus' Service*, Vol. XXIV, No. 16, August 15, 1956, p. 570.

Another quietly portrayed historical incident, by the author of *Pilgrim Thanksgiving* and *The Story of Valentine* gently accents the spiritual role of children in times of trial. With the *Mayflower* anchored in Plymouth harbour but the Pilgrims not yet ashore by Christmas, there is grumbling among the crew that they will not have enough food and water for their trip home. Young Giles Hopkins and his sister Damaris feel the growing hostility and Giles leaves with an anxious heart on Christmas day to help the men set up the first foundations of their Common House ashore. But during the day enough game is shot to bring a feast for everyone aboard ship and in the evening a sense of well being returns to Pilgrims and crew alike.

The Booklist and Subscription Books Bulletin

SOURCE: A review of *Christmas on the Mayflower,* in *The Booklist and Subscription Books Bulletin*, Vol. 53, No. 5, November 1, 1956, p. 125.

Although not outstanding this quiet, pleasingly illustrated story has obvious uses. On Christmas day Giles Hopkins, a Pilgrim on the *Mayflower,* goes ashore to help lay the foundations for the first shelter, promising his sister to bring back something to make Christmas. Returning with game, yule log, greens, and even birch to make stick horses for the children, the work party finds the crew mutinous because of their delayed return to England. On the captain's order Pilgrims and crew sit down to the Christmas meal together, Christmas traditions are shared, and the spirit of Christmas and a sense of well-being prevail.

Heloise P. Mailloux

SOURCE: A review of *Christmas on the Mayflower,* in *The Horn Book Magazine*, Vol. XXXII, No. 6, December, 1956, p. 453.

The Pilgrims' home, at the time of their first Christmas in America, was still aboard the Mayflower in Plymouth Harbor. The children Giles and Damaris wondered how they'd celebrate. They knew many of their elders believed traditional customs frivolous. They also knew that the sailors were impatient to sail for home and that only the captain's determination that the Pilgrims be given time to build shelters kept them from weighing anchor. Giles and Damaris appeared first in *Pilgrim Thanksgiving.* The format of the two books is similar and both are based on facts from William Bradford's diary.

📖 *FREEDOM* (1958)

Virginia Kirkus' Service

SOURCE: A review of *Freedom,* in *Virginia Kirkus' Service*, Vol. XXVI, No. 15, August 1, 1958, pp. 546-47.

A graphic view of American freedom and the documents which assert it is the subject of this interesting supplement to the study of our history. Twenty-six documents in photostat are reproduced here and accompanied by a summary of the events which led up to the issuing of the specific paper. These documents span the years between 1776 to 1945 and include such manuscripts as the original draft of the Declaration of Independence, the Star Spangled Banner, the Nineteenth Amendment (Civil rights for women), and the United Nations Charter. Each photostat can be placed in a projector or examined by the student with a magnifying glass. Wilma Hays, whose *Pilgrim Thanksgiving* was a Junior Literary Guild selection, offers an engrossing new technique for classroom and home study.

The Booklist and Subscription Books Bulletin

SOURCE: A review of *Freedom,* in *The Booklist and Subscription Books Bulletin, Vol. 55*, No. 1, September 1, 1958, p. 29.

Twenty-six documents significant in America's history from the Declaration of Independence to the United Nations Charter are reproduced here in full or in part, with a facing page of text giving a brief historical background for each. Among the documents included are the Monroe Doctrine, the Treaty of Paris, the Bill of Rights, Nineteenth Amendment, the Agreement for invasion of Western Europe in 1943, and the Instrument of Surrender in the Pacific, 1945. Because many of the documents are reproduced in manuscript form, the use of a magnifying glass or an opaque projector is suggested. Interesting and valuable.

Ruth Hill Viguers

SOURCE: A review of *Freedom,* in *The Horn Book Magazine,* Vol. XXXIV, No. 5, October, 1958, p. 390.

This is an inviting introduction for children to the documents having to do with America's freedom which have become increasingly familiar to American young people in recent years. It should be noted, however, that these facsimiles can be found among the thirty-five in the official book of the Freedom Train, *Heritage of Freedom,* which also gives the history of each of more than one hundred and twenty documents exhibited on the tour of the Freedom Train through the United States.

Frances Lander Spain

SOURCE: A review of *Freedom,* in *Saturday Review,* Vol. 41, No. 43, October 25, 1958, p. 33.

This book contains facsimile reproductions of twenty-six documents important in the history of the United States. From the first one, Jefferson's rough draft of the Declaration of Independence, to the last, the Charter of the

United Nations, one glimpses highlights in the growth and development of the idea of freedom and the country's integrity through letters and public documents. Each document is accompanied by a note giving its historical setting and something of its significance. Though of wide general interest, this will be especially valuable in history classes.

THE LITTLE HORSE THAT RACED A TRAIN (1959; included in "Reading for Meaning" series, 1963)

Virginia Kirkus' Service

SOURCE: A review of *The Little Horse That Raced a Train*, in *Virginia Kirkus' Service*, Vol. XXVII, No. 2, January 15, 1959, p. 37.

Based on actual fact, this story by the author of *The Fourth of July Raid, Pilgrim Thanksgiving,* and other books, tells the story of a runaway horse and the winter he spends, trapped by snow, on a Colorado mountain top. Young Elmer Horne's concern for the animal is contagious, and before long, anxious adults enlist the aid of television and a helicopter to keep the horse alive. When the snows thaw, various ranchers claim the horse, but it is to Elmer he is ultimately awarded. Illustrated in black and white by Wesley Dennis, an easy vocabulary is the vehicle for this valid little adventure.

The Booklist and Subscription Books Bulletin

SOURCE: A review of *The Little Horse That Raced a Train*, in *The Booklist and Subscription Books Bulletin*, Vol. 55, No. 17, May 1, 1959, p. 487.

An easy-to-read story about a lonely boy who lived in a construction camp in the Rocky Mountains and rode the construction train to school and a little black horse that ran wild in a high canyon and raced Elmer's train each morning. When the snow came and Lightning was trapped on a mountaintop the anxious boy sought help through the newspaper to rescue the horse which he had come to regard as a friend. A satisfying story based on an actual happening.

THE FOURTH OF JULY RAID (1959)

Virginia Haviland

SOURCE: A review of *The Fourth of July Raid*, in *The Horn Book Magazine*, Vol. XXXVII, No. 3, June, 1959, p. 215.

This account of a day and a night of fighting in the American Revolution around Old New Haven Harbor seems like a chapter from a longer historical story. A family's preparations for a Fourth of July feast are suddenly interrupted by the arrival of British vessels. Valuables are removed from the home, and mother and the younger children flee, but Tom, just too young to fight, lingers to play a brave and helpful role in more than one direction. A vivid if brief piece, convincing in its picture of patriot staunchness and courage and of a boy's quick-wittedness. Its brevity, plus large print on a generous page, will recommend it to lower elementary grades. Strong blue-and-black [by Peter Burchard] illustrations suit the atmosphere of the story.

Margaret Sherwood Libby

SOURCE: A review of *The Fourth of July Raid*, in *New York Herald Tribune Book Review*, July 5, 1959, p. 9.

The author of the two gently charming holiday stories for eight-year-olds, **Christmas on the Mayflower** and **Pilgrim Thanksgiving,** has written another very simple tale with a seasonal interest, **The Fourth of July Raid,** based on an incident in our early history. It is more of an account than a story for it tells in detail the experiences of Tom Morris on July 5, 1779, when General Tyron and the British troops invaded New Haven, burning his home and many others. Much is made of the bravery of the Tuttles, neighbors of Tom, who refused to accept their freedom at the price of forsaking the American cause. The story is short, printed in fairly large type and made most attractive by Peter Burchard's dusky pictures which are dramatically high-lighted with brilliant blue-green. This book has an advantage the previous ones did not have. It can appeal to the older slow readers who will be interested in hearing of the exciting experiences of Tom (who appears to be a big boy well over twelve) on that fateful day. Although these books do not have as much literary charm as the similar group by Alice Dalgliesh, *Columbus Story, The First Thanksgiving* and *The Courage of Sarah Noble,* they offer authentic bits of Americana to the eight-and nine-year-olds.

DRUMMER BOY FOR MONTCALM (1959; selections included in *Beckoning Trails*, 1962)

Virginia Kirkus' Service

SOURCE: A review of *Drummer Boy for Montcalm*, in *Virginia Kirkus' Service*, Vol. XXVII, No. 13, July 1, 1959, p. 452.

The summer siege of Quebec by the English in 1759 forms a colorful background for this historical novel of a young French boy's adventures as a drummer. Peter, instilled with ardor for the French cause, vigorously supports General Montcalm in his heroic defense of Quebec. But ruthless profiteering cuts off supplies from the French; betrayal at the hands of French compatriots, and insurmountable military advantages held by the British turn Peter's dream of French victory into a nightmare of defeat—General Montcalm dies and the French, once and for all, lose their hold on the new continent.

An unusual depiction of defeat rather than victory for the teen-age hero and a poignant portrayal of a cause overthrown, mark this as a teen-age novel of distinction.

Margaret MacBean

SOURCE: A review of *Drummer Boy for Montcalm,* in *The New York Times Book Review,* October 18, 1959, p. 46.

As a switch from the usual accounts of how the British won Quebec, Wilma Pitchford Hays's **Drummer Boy for Montcalm** tells how, despite their valiant efforts, the French lost it—as witnessed by young Peter Demo. Arriving from France with dreams of becoming a trapper in the New World, Peter is hardly down the gangplank before he finds himself counterspying against the French traitors who are undermining General Montcalm's plans for strengthening Quebec's defenses against imminent British attack. His first bold assignment completed, Peter, now fired by the loyalty to Montcalm that inspires his colonial friends, postpones his trapping plans and enrolls in the General's army as a drummer boy.

Inevitably, Peter's view of the ensuing desperate months of battle and siege is a limited one, with the result that the reader occasionally has trouble keeping track of the campaign, despite the battle plan and calendar thoughtfully provided by the author. However, Mrs. Hays's enthusiasm for this colorful slice of North American history is infectious. Her fine feeling for the spirit of those days is understandable, since Peter Demo was her own great-great-great-grandfather.

The Booklist and Subscription Books Bulletin

SOURCE: A review of *Drummer Boy for Montcalm,* in *The Booklist and Subscription Books Bulletin,* Vol. 56, No. 12, February 15, 1960, p. 358.

To seek his fortune in the New World Peter Demo, a French orphan, stows away on a ship bringing recruits to Quebec—and the news that the walled fortress is soon to be attacked by a large British fleet. Too young to bear arms Peter serves the cause of New France as drummer boy for General Montcalm during the siege of Quebec. A feeling of authenticity pervades this exciting and poignant narrative of the siege and fall of Quebec; based on historical fact and on family stories of the author's great-great-great-grandfather who, as a boy, was present at the battle of the Plains of Abraham.

Ingis F. Bell

SOURCE: "Mountains with Legends," in *Canadian Literature,* No. 4, Spring, 1960, pp. 74-6.

[*Drummer Boy for Montcalm*] is quite unlike other [historical fiction] since the struggle is seen from the viewpoint of the harassed and ultimately defeated defenders in the 1759 battle for Quebec and through the eyes of the drummer boy Peter Demo. Peter, at the opening of the story a twelve-year old stowaway on a ship bringing recruits to Montcalm's forces at Quebec, was in real life the great-great-great-grandfather of the author and actually served under Montcalm during the siege and battle. Miss Hays spent several years in research and in the writing of the book, and she does, as she states on the dust cover, follow closely the true incidents of the battle.

And here is what is becoming a consistent mark of Canadian historical fiction for young people. The storytellers do not rewrite history *à la* "swamp-fox" as do many children's writers in the United States. Nor do their historical characters bear any resemblance to the unbelievably inflated and distorted Disney-like creations—the Davy Crocketts, Kit Carsons and Buffalo Bill Codys—so familiar across the border. . . .

Perhaps this is just as well. Since we live in a land so recently wrested from the Indians perhaps our heroes, like their gods, should be invested with defects as well as virtues.

Miss Hays's historical characters are in this tradition. Montcalm bears his full share of the blame for the loss of Quebec as do Bougainville and Vaudreuil and, of course, Bigot and Cadet. Wolfe if anything escapes too easily, but Miss Hays's book was no doubt completed before C. P. Stacey's recent *Quebec 1759: The Siege and the Battle* removed some of the gilding from this romantic figure.

Indeed, the characters in **Drummer Boy for Montcalm** are, in the main, ably portrayed. Peter Demo is a well-realized boy of twelve, and his friends Philippe and Bomazeen are presented convincingly. The book's only major shortcoming, for younger children at least, is the diminishing of excitement as the siege draws towards its conclusion. Events overshadow the hero, and he becomes primarily a narrator. However, even if at that point the younger reader's interest may flag somewhat, I do not think he will wish to put the book aside.

EASTER FIRES (1960; published as *Easter Treasures,* 1989)

Virginia Kirkus' Service

SOURCE: A review of *Easter Fires,* in *Virginia Kirkus' Service,* Vol. XXVIII, No. 2, January 15, 1960, p. 47.

Based on a custom which has been observed for over one hundred years in Fredericksburg, Texas, this is the story of the revelation of Easter to the Indians. When the tribe is oppressed by a drought, it is decided to sacrifice a beautiful young girl to the gods. Little Bow, unreconcilable to this, seeks out the aid of the medicine man who has learned the story of Easter. This story he reveals to his tribe and as the rains fall and the girl is saved, the Indians recognize that God wishes love not death from his worshipers. An engrossing Easter story which in simple vocabulary combines a religious and a regional theme.

Ellen Lewis Buell

SOURCE: A review of *Easter Fires*, in *The New York Times Book Review*, April 10, 1960, p. 38.

Next Saturday night bonfires will blaze on the hilltops about Fredericksburg, Tex., just as they have burned there for more than a hundred Easter Eves. They are lighted to commemorate the treaty of peace between the white settlers from Germany and the Tonkawas Indians, but long before that time the Tonkawas had lit fires in memory of the tribe's first knowledge of the Easter festival.

Wilma Pitchford Hays, who has a knack of finding unusual items in our country's past, tells here a story based on that custom. It begins with a drought which threatened the very life of the tribe and with the medicine man's decision that a maiden must be sacrificed to bring rain. Only the chosen girl's little brother, Little Bow, rebelled. Secretly he went in search of Silver Arrow, the brave who loved Little Bow's sister. It is Silver Arrow, guide to the Spanish priest, who brings back to the tribe the story of the first Easter and the understanding that the Great Spirit does not require human sacrifice. Quietly, with a sure touch for the drama and the terrible urgency of the boy's quest, Mrs. Hays brings her story to a moving climax.

The Booklist and Subscription Books Bulletin

SOURCE: A review of *Easter Fires*, in *The Booklist and Subscription Books Bulletin*, Vol. 56, No. 16, April 15, 1960, pp. 518-19.

To save his sister from being sacrificed to bring rain to the drought-stricken village Little Bow seeks the help of the brave, Silver Arrow, who is on the mountain with the missionary padres. Arriving just as the final prayer song is being sung the young brave tells the people the Easter story which he has learned from the missionaries; as he reveals the true meaning of Easter, the rain comes and White Fawn is saved. Based on fact the book is likely to be enjoyed more as an Indian tale than as an Easter story. Easy to read and effectively illustrated [by Peter Burchard].

Eve Merriam

SOURCE: A review of *Easter Fires*, in *Saturday Review*, Vol. 43, No. 16, April 16, 1960, p. 49.

Suffering from drought, an Indian tribe plans to sacrifice the hero's sister to the rain god. This is the story of

Little Bow's long journey for help, and the eventual conversion of his tribe to Christianity. The thesis that the new religion is more appropriate for the Indians than their ancient one, and the implication that a sudden rainstorm is less fortuitous after than before conversion, may not be acceptable to all children or their parents. But the dignity of the writing, and the evocative pictures of boy and horse against wide landscapes and spacious skies, make this book compelling.

ABE LINCOLN'S BIRTHDAY (1961)

George A. Woods

SOURCE: A review of *Abe Lincoln's Birthday*, in *The New York Times Book Review*, February 12, 1961, p. 38.

On Feb. 12th, as Abe Lincoln awoke in the dark cabin loft at Pigeon Creek, he wondered if anyone in the family would remember it was his twelfth birthday. The day, however, was much like all days in young Abe's life—one of hard work, frontier style, and an evening of reading by the fireplace. But his birthday was remembered.

Wilma Pitchford Hays's account of this one day is a somewhat moody fictionalized narrative, foreshadowing the greatness to come. The backbone of her story is formed by accurate historical and factual material plus her own ancestors' reports on pioneer life in Indiana. Mrs. Hays neatly compresses a great deal of information on Lincoln's boyhood into her single-day episode for an unvarnished, realistic portrait of the man whose birthday we celebrate today. Peter Burchard's soft, textured illustrations are pleasing and appropriate.

Margaret Sherwood Libby

SOURCE: A review of *Abe Lincoln's Birthday*, in *New York Herald Tribune: The Lively Arts and Book Review*, February 19, 1961, p. 36.

As each February rolls around new stories of Washington and Lincoln appear, with few authors resisting the temptation to moralize since that first cherry tree bit was added to Washington's story. Wilma Pitchford Hays, who has written a series of holiday tales for the young (of which our favorite is *Easter Fires*), is not one to eschew this favorite sport of educators. Her whole report of Lincoln's twelfth birthday works up to the final sentence in which she quotes him as saying that, although he does not know what he wants to be, he would study and prepare himself, and maybe his chance would come. For the rest the emphasis is on the common places of pioneering experiences—fear of a wildcat jumping for the meat hung outside the cabin, felling the trees and grinding corn—which Mrs. Hays adapted from reminiscences of her own family. The little book is very pleasing to look at with Peter Burchard's sketches in greenish blue and black, but it really has little to add to the more substantial and vivid books we already have.

Zena Sutherland

SOURCE: A review of *Abe Lincoln's Birthday,* in *Bulletin of the Center for Children's Books,* Vol. XV, No. 7, March, 1962, p. 111.

A fictionalized description of the way in which Abraham Lincoln spent the day on his twelfth birthday. The tempo of the writing is quiet and uneventful, but the author gives a very clear impression of Lincoln's personality and of the family activities. Some of the family's past history is incorporated into the story; the illustrations—like the text—give both the pioneer background and a good picturing of the boy himself: tall, gangling, kind, and courageous.

📖 LITTLE LONE COYOTE (1961)

Virginia Haviland

SOURCE: A review of *Little Lone Coyote,* in *The Horn Book Magazine,* Vol. XXXVII, No. 3, June, 1961, p. 261.

A second "regional" easy-to-read book by Mrs. Hays, this one set in Nebraska hills tells most appealingly of a third-grade boy's delight in having a baby coyote for a pet and his later heartbreak but eventual satisfaction in having Little Lone find freedom on the prairie. The incidents of mischievous animal behavior and the theme of recognizing what is right for a wild creature are nicely handled.

Margaret Sherwood Libby

SOURCE: A review of *Little Lone Coyote,* in *New York Herald Tribune Books,* August 13, 1961, p. 13.

Slighter and less dramatic than the first of Wilma Pitchford Hays's regional stories, this brief tale for beginning readers will nevertheless provide sufficient interest to hold the attention of seven- and eight-year-olds. First of all it will intrigue them that a boy should go to school in a place wild enough for a coyote to be seen lurking around the building. Then they will want to read on to find out if the lonely wild creatures can be kept safe and protected at the boys' ranch and not pine for the wilds. It is a familiar problem in stories for children, but capably handled here and most attractively presented. . . .

📖 THE GOOSE THAT WAS A WATCHDOG (1967)

Zena Sutherland

SOURCE: A review of *The Goose That Was a Watchdog,* in *Bulletin of the Center for Children's Books,* Vol. 21, No. 8, April, 1968, p. 127.

Since machines had been used to pick cotton, more and more of the sharecroppers had lost their jobs. Now the owner was buying geese to do the weeding, and Tad's father felt he'd be fired, too. But the geese needed some care, and Tad's father was hired to tend them; one goose became very tame and Tad made a pet of her. She watched his baby sister and raised an alarm that made it possible for the men on the farm to catch some chicken thieves. Appreciatively, the owner gave Tad the watchdog goose for his own. The storyline is not unusual, but the writing style is direct and easy, the events are believable, and the book gives a quiet picture of a Negro family's life in the rural south.

📖 THE OPEN GATE: NEW YEAR'S 1815 (1970)

The Booklist

SOURCE: A review of *The Open Gate: New Year's 1815,* in *The Booklist,* Vol. 67, No. 11, February 1, 1971, p. 450.

Because Lucie's Maman has not forgiven the U.S. for purchasing Louisiana from the French, she locks the courtyard gate of their New Orleans home when a family of Americans moves next door. After the Battle of New Orleans, Maman, along with other Creoles, experiences a change of heart toward the Americans. She invites the American boy to a delayed New Year's celebration and allows Lucie to unlock the gate between the two homes. A slight story, but useful for easy-to-read supplementary material on the War of 1812 and for the descriptions of the Creole festivities on New Year's Day.

Zena Sutherland

SOURCE: A review of *The Open Gate: New Year's 1815,* in *Bulletin of the Center for Children's Books,* Vol. 24, No. 7, March, 1971, p. 107.

When Louisiana was purchased by the United States, many of the Creole families refused to recognize their separation from France. Lucie's mother was one of many who closed the gate between her home and the one next door when Americans moved in. But the French and American men were fighting together against the British, and their victory brought rapport. So, during the holidays of this episode of the 1812 war, Lucie's mother agreed to open the gate, and Lucie's American friend Stephen went home in the traditional way of New Orleans neighborliness. The historical background is one seldom used in books for the middle age group, and the style is capable but fairly staid, the fiction rather overburdened by the history.

📖 FOODS THE INDIANS GAVE US (with husband R. Vernon Hays, 1973)

Publishers Weekly

SOURCE: A review of *Foods the Indians Gave Us,* in *Publishers Weekly,* Vol. 203, No. 14, April 2, 1973, p. 66.

"Eighty percent of our present food plants were unknown to Europeans before 1492. Early Spanish explorers invaded the New World in search of silver and gold . . . they also carried home a treasure of far greater value—native American plants, seeds, and roots." In what they state is a long overdue thank-you to the American Indian for introducing us to corn, potatoes, beans, squash, cocoa, tapioca and other foods, the authors present an appealing and informative text and the bonus of some delicious recipes. The book is a valuable addition to the home library, and one that good cooks of whatever age should appreciate.

SIEGE! THE STORY OF ST. AUGUSTINE IN 1702 (1976)

Norma Feld

SOURCE: A review of *Siege! The Story of St. Augustine in 1702,* in *School Library Journal,* Vol. 23, No. 6, February, 1977, p. 65.

In 1702 the English attacked St. Augustine and besieged the Fort Castillo de San Marcos for 50 days. In this brief story the author recreates the events of the siege through the lives of the fictitious Olfonso family. While Captain Olfonso seeks help from Cuba, his wife and two children remain at the Fort. It is through their eyes—and especially through the thoughts of young Juan—that the pride and strength of the Spanish people is portrayed. The black-and-white charcoal illustrations [by Peter Cox] are occasionally melodramatic but underscore the courage of a people defending their home. A quiet, but absorbing story on a period not usually touched upon for this age.

YELLOW FUR AND LITTLE HAWK (1980)

Zena Sutherland

SOURCE: A review of *Yellow Fur and Little Hawk,* in *Bulletin of the Center for Children's Books,* Vol. 33, No. 10, June, 1980, p. 191.

The Sioux Indians on the South Dakota reservation near which Susanna lives call her "Yellow Fur" because of her blond hair, and in this story set in 1915, Susanna is disturbed because the Sioux won't move into the houses her father is building. He's been told to build the houses by a government agent, and the Sioux have been ordered to abandon their tepees and move into the houses. They refuse, and Susanna's friend Little Hawk explains why his grandfather prefers to live in the old way. Not until there is a hailstorm does dignified old White Bull move into a house, and then he moves the tepee into the house and sits therein. The Sioux, he has explained to Susanna, make round tepees because the sun is round, that all nature is a circle. The book gives some facts about the Sioux and conveys the affection and respect Susanna feels, but the question of forcing a people to live in a certain way seems blandly accepted, and the story is weakened by the flat writing style and by the fact that a sizable portion of the story has to do with the disappearance of Susanna's dog during the drought that precedes the hailstorm, an element that gives no impetus to the story line.

Denise M. Wilms

SOURCE: A review of *Yellow Fur and Little Hawk,* in *Booklist,* Vol. 76, No. 20, June 15, 1980, p. 1532.

This simple story of friendship between a young white girl and a Sioux boy accomplishes a great deal within its elementary confines. The differing circumstances of the two children show both cultural disparities and the effects of nineteenth-century government policies aimed at subduing native American peoples. They also show the hardships both groups faced in the dry, hot terrain. In the story, Susanna, called Yellow Fur by the Sioux, worries that Indian reluctance to move into the wooden housing built for them will bring trouble. However, her efforts to find out Indian objections to leaving tepees takes a back seat to both groups' immediate need for water. The conclusion features compromise: a respected holy man moves his tepee into one of the frame houses, thereby satisfying government orders while still holding to the Sioux tradition of living within a circle. [Anthony] Rao's drawings are sparely washed in orange and yellow; his lines are loose yet articulate and project a light-hearted quality. They're a nice complement to a story that is a good deal more substantive than most at this level.

Additional coverage of Hays's life and career is contained in the following sources published by The Gale Group: *Contemporary Authors New Revision Series,* Vol. 45; *Major Authors and Illustrators for Children and Young Adults; Something about the Author Autobiography Series,* Vol. 3; and *Something about the Author,* Vols. 1, 28.

Will Hobbs

1947-

(Full name William Carl Hobbs) American author of fiction.

Major works include *Changes in Latitudes* (1988), *Bearstone* (1989), *Downriver* (1991), *The Big Wander* (1992), *Beardance* (1993).

INTRODUCTION

Hobbs is known for his exciting wilderness adventures featuring troubled teenagers who learn about themselves and their places in the world when their resources are challenged. Set in such evocative landscapes as the upper Pine River country of the Weminuche wilderness, Hobbs's fiction incorporates his personal outdoor experiences in the mountains, rivers, and canyons of the Southwest. These settings are as much characters as any of the human beings in Hobbs's stories. Shaped and influenced by their encounters with nature's wild beauty, his characters emerge significantly changed and victorious. Often based on the students he taught during his career as a teacher, Hobbs's adolescent protagonists discover their inner strength and understand the power they have over themselves as they battle the odds and learn to survive alone. In an article for *Horn Book,* Hobbs wrote, "I've been exploring survival themes in all of my novels, and as I look back at them, I see survival issues 'micro and macro,' *micro* concerning the survival of the individual and *macro* concerning the survival of a world worth living in." Ultimately, however, his protagonists are able to achieve personal goals by establishing a strong relationship with someone else. Hobbs's work has been praised for its careful research, realistic backgrounds, strong characters, and well-developed plots. His themes include not only endurance, perseverance, coming of age, and environmental consciousness, but the spiritual beliefs and culture of Native American tribes and the lives of cowboys as well. His books are especially appreciated by teachers who find that the suspenseful plots and dynamic characters draw even reluctant readers into Hobbs's narratives. Hobbs once told *Something about the Author* (*SATA*), "As I write about the crucial choices facing people today, their struggle for identity, their relations with others, I hope to be increasing their awareness of their relationship with the natural world. I'd like my readers to be appreciative and to care more about what's happening with wild creatures, wild places, and the diversity of life."

Biographical Information

Born in 1947 in Pittsburgh, Pennsylvania, Hobbs was raised with a love of the outdoors. His family moved to

Panama when he was six months old, and as a youth, Hobbs often explored nature with his family and with the Boy Scouts. He spent a few summers during high school and college as a guide and camp director at Philmont Scout Ranch. He credits his parents for encouraging his adventurous spirit—his father introduced him to the rivers of Alaska and his mother lived life to its fullest. He said of his father, "He joined me for three trips up the Pine River, where *Bearstone* takes place. It's my idea of heaven on earth, and I'll always be able to find him up there." Of his mother, he once commented, "She contributed the gusto to my makeup. She feels that life is best lived as an adventure. At the age of seventy-three she rafted the Grand Canyon."

Hobbs received a bachelor of arts degree in 1969 and a master of arts degree in 1973, both from Stanford University. In 1972 he married Jean Loftus, a fellow teacher, and the following year the newlyweds moved to Colorado, where Hobbs taught junior high and high school English and reading for almost seventeen years, primarily in Durango. In 1979 Hobbs and his wife decided to build a home near Durango, and a year later, at the age of thirty-three, Hobbs began writing his first book, *Bear-*

stone. The work took six manuscripts and eight years to be published; the house of his dreams took ten years.

In 1990 Hobbs quit teaching to write full-time. He motivates himself with a windup dinosaur that he sets to walk across his desk in the morning. By the time it reaches the other side of his desk, he begins to write. The dinosaur has helped him to produce an impressive number of books, well received not only by the critics, but, more importantly, by young readers, even reluctant ones, who find them spellbinding. "I'll always be a reader," noted Hobbs, "because it's endlessly fascinating to look at life from someone else's perspective, someone very different from you. . . . For me and for almost all writers, it's reading that primes the pump for writing. Your reading is the rain and snow that's absorbed into your language water table. Writing is sinking a well."

Major Works

Changes in Latitudes is a story about a family falling apart told from the perspective of the older boy, Travis. When the mother takes her three children to Mexico, Teddy, the youngest, becomes fascinated by some endangered sea turtles, and spends his vacation studying and watching them and protecting their nests. Travis is annoyed and self absorbed, but he does help Teddy rescue the turtle eggs and hatchlings. When Teddy accidentally drowns, Travis blames himself because he was off looking for girls instead of spending time with his brother. As a narrator, Travis is cynical and self-righteous, but also critical of himself. Called a "tender story" by Claudia Moore, *Changes in Latitudes* was appreciated for convincing dialogue as well as its "sometimes amusing, sometimes dramatic, and occasionally lyrical and poignant" narrative, according to Deborah Bennet.

Hobbs's best known book, *Bearstone* features a lonely teenage Ute boy named Cloyd whose mother is dead and whose father is hospitalized and cannot take care of him. Cloyd wants to stay with his grandmother in the hills of Colorado, but instead is sent to a school for remediation, and during the summer, to a ranch to work for an elderly old farmer named Walter. One day Cloyd discovers an ancient burial site, and resenting the white domination of his native land, he decides to keep it a secret. At the site he discovers a turquoise bear, which he takes as his spirit guide according to Ute tradition, naming himself Lone Bear and vowing to protect the bears in the mountains. Angered by bear hunters who come to the ranch, Cloyd destroys all the work he has done for Walter. In a gesture of loving understanding, Walter forgives the impulsive youth, imparting some of his wisdom as well. Cloyd later returns his affection for Walter when he saves the old man from a mining accident and ultimately saves himself. Critics praised Hobbs's well-developed and believable characters, as well as his blending of poetry and Colorado landscape, myth, and reality. George Gleason noted, "Extremely well-drawn characters and vivid incidents around the mountains of the continental divide, and powerful yet sensitive moments between the boy and the old man put this far above other coming-of-age stories."

The idea for *Downriver*—which is set in the Grand Canyon—came from Hobbs's desire to have readers experience one of the great American adventures. Having rowed his raft through the rapids of the Grand Canyon several times himself, Hobbs knows intimately the dangers and the beauty of the journey. Narrated by Jessie, a fifteen-year-old girl who has been sent away from home, this adventure story takes seven teens on a white water rafting excursion where they are tested over and over again. At the instigation of the charismatic Troy, the group ditches their guide and embarks on its own over the dangerous rapids. Troy is romantically interested in Jessie, although she does not return his interest, and this leads to conflict. Without an adult guide, the teens learn their own hard lessons about responsibility, facing consequences, and working together. It is the journey down the river that helps Jessie find a new life and her way back home as well. Mary Ojibway noted Hobbs's beautiful descriptions of scenery and the believable characters, stating, "I wanted these kids to have a great time on their venture, to experience success, gain self-confidence, and come out of the adventure relatively unscathed, but strong, wider, smarter, and better individuals."

The Big Wander is the story of fourteen-year-old Clay Lancaster, left on his own in the Southwest wilderness to survive as best as he can and find his way home. He knows he has an uncle in the area who is a cowboy, so he sets out to find him, acquiring a burro, a horse, and a dog along the way. He also falls in love. Describing his second draft of the story, the author said in *The ALAN Review*, "I'd be dreaming about the story as I slept, and wake up reaching for a scratch-pad. I'd find myself writing intuitively, racing, just trying to keep up with my fingers. . . . When I wrote that last chapter, I was Clay Lancaster, and I was galloping down the Escalante on that spotted pony." Kathleen Beck commented, "Hobbs gets better with each novel. His characters are real, the setting is vivid, and the adventure/survival story is exciting and engrossing."

In *Beardance*, the sequel to *Bearstone*, Cloyd and Walter return to the mountains to search for a lost Spanish gold mine. In the wilderness Cloyd meets an old Tinglit woman, Ursa, who is looking for the last of the grizzly bears. The Beardance is Cloyd's spirit dream and, having taken the bear as his spirit guide, Cloyd is drawn to Ursa and her quest. He becomes her assistant, and they find a mother and three cubs, possibly the last grizzlies on the mountain. When the mother and one of the cubs is killed in an accident, Cloyd protects the surviving cubs. He puts on the mother's skin to fool the cubs into believing that he is their mother and to prevent them from becoming attached to humans. To ensure their survival though the winter, he dens with them, slipping in and out of a dreamlike state as he faces starvation. At times his soul drifts above the scene, shifting between images of boy and bear as Cloyd connects to his ancient heritage and the lore of the Utes. At last the cubs sleep, and Cloyd returns to civilization, changed forever by his weeks of endurance, and anxious to see Walter again. To honor him and his commitment, Ursa names him Fights-for-Bears. *Beardance* was praised for its absorbing action and memorable characters, as well as for its descriptions of the mountains and the Native American legends that arose from them.

Awards

Hobbs received many acknowledgments for *Bearstone*. In 1989 the work was named a Notable book by the Children's Book Council and received the Best Book for Young Adults Award from the American Library Association; in 1990 it received the Teachers' Choice Award from the International Reading Association and the Regional Book Award from the Mountain and Plains Booksellers Association. *Changes in Latitudes* was runner-up for the 1990 Earthworm Children's Book Award and won the Colorado Blue Spruce Young Adult Book Award in 1992. *Downriver* was voted Best Book for Young Adults and Best Book for Reluctant Young Adult Readers from the American Library Association in 1992, and received a Pick of the List Citation from the American Booksellers Association. *The Big Wander* was recognized as a Best Book for Young Adults from the American Library Association, as was *Beardance*, both in 1993. In that same year, *Beardance* was named Pick of the List by the American Booksellers Association. Hobbs also has been nominated for state awards in California, Colorado, Florida, Indiana, Kansas, Kentucky, Maryland, Nebraska, Oklahoma, South Carolina, Texas, Utah, Vermont, Virginia, and Washington.

AUTHOR'S COMMENTARY

Cathi MacRae with Will Hobbs

SOURCE: "Young Adult Perplex," in *Wilson Library Bulletin,* Vol. 65, No. 9, May, 1991, pp. 126-27.

Golden aspen leaf "coins" rustled in the breeze at a lodge near Rocky Mountain National Park last fall as I addressed a group of Colorado librarians. A lanky man with a shy smile slipped into the back row, exuding a quiet presence. Afterwards he approached me, saying, "Hi, I'm Will Hobbs. I really enjoyed hearing about all those great YA books."

Later he spoke to a packed house in his slow western drawl, showing slides of the settings of his books. No wonder he wrote of sea turtles with such authority in *Changes in Latitudes* (1988); there he was pictured sharing their Mexican beach. He knew how it felt to the Ute boy Cloyd in *Bearstone* (1989) to stand amid "pouring air" in the Window rock formation on the Continental Divide. Hobbs hiked up there himself, capturing its

sheer joy in a spectacular photograph. His newest book, *Downriver* (1991), grew from splashy scenes of white-water rafting through the Grand Canyon.

Will Hobbs spoke of his seventeen years teaching high school English, of his longing to reach young people through reading, and of helping them express themselves in writing. When he finished speaking, I scheduled this interview, for "Perplex" readers must know this major new YA talent. Hobbs's first novel, *Changes in Latitudes,* was a runner-up for Britain's environmental Earthworm award. *Bearstone* was a Best Book for Young Adults. *Downriver* is already winning YA readers who crave its exciting treatment of their favorite theme of rebellion, as seven teenagers ditch their instructor to raft 240 miles of white water on their own.

At forty-three, Hobbs has left teaching to write full-time. He lives in the country near Durango, Colorado with his wife, Jean, in a house that they built themselves. He is fresh, enthusiastic, wise, and committed—essential qualities for a young adult author.

Cathi MacRae: Where did you get the idea of using an outdoor education setting for *Downriver?*

Will Hobbs: I had personal experience with a program at Aztec High School in the late seventies, just across the river in New Mexico. They identified likely dropout kids and put them in an outdoored class. I had been teaching a course based on the Foxfire idea called "Living in the Southwest." The curriculum was based on interviewing people over eighty years old who had pioneered in the area, and going out in the canyon country, rappeling off cliffs. I met some really neat kids there. Through all the years I've been teaching, a lot of kids I really bond with are out of it academically, but they're really deserving, worthy kids. They can be real bright and yet not do well in school.

CM: Like Cloyd in *Bearstone.*

WH: Yes, Cloyd is based on a native American boy who had been out of school for four years and hadn't learned to read. He'd been sent away from home, and he was really lonely. I thought, that's something I can build a character on. I have worked with kids like Freddy in *Downriver* who have come from rural places. If you live forty-five miles from town like the kids on Navajo reservations, you have wide open spaces in your head. It's a really different point of view. In my program there was a kid rappeling off cliffs who took these amazing leaps, going thirty feet at a shot before he put on the brake. He had no fear—he was actually burning the rope with the friction. That's enough to get started on a character—somebody who has that wildness and joy in him.

CM: In *Downriver,* you make it seem so appealing to have survival skills. Freddy, who has grown up herding sheep in isolated mountains, is so good at everything from relocating Adam's shoulder to scouting the wilds. You mention that some skills help you depend on yourself, and some are based on cooperation with others. In your books are you advocating a return to simplicity and coexistence with nature?

WH: Any teaching you're doing in a novel can't be didactic. That's the wonderful thing about my second career as a fiction writer. I can still find opportunities to teach, but in another mode. Fiction touches you in the heart. In *Changes in Latitudes* I can make readers care about endangered species. They learn to respect their existence, to share the earth with them. That's the kind of ethic that is always a bass note in my books.

When I'm writing best, the teaching is integrated; every detail must either reveal character or advance the plot. I wanted to pass along the theory that sea turtles might be navigating by the stars. They travel way out in the ocean, coming back to the same beach where they were hatched to lay their eggs. How do they get there? In *Changes,* the little brother Teddy, who empathizes so strongly with turtles, tells his older brother that he dreamed he was a sea turtle. "I was out at sea and I felt my flippers." I want the reader to feel like their arms are flippers, that they're like turtles. Teddy told Travis that the funny thing was that *he* was navigating by the stars.

CM: What about the survival skills I mentioned?

WH: I lean more toward cooperation than the strongly individualistic. I don't think the survivalist stance has that much to offer because we're such an interdependent society. But how can we live on the earth among all these other life forms and achieve more of a balance?

CM: All your books embody your deep love of nature. Armchair travelers will never forget *Downriver*'s palpable experience of facing the Crystal rapid, "waiting in its lair and growling like all the monsters of mythology combined into one." You make us feel "giddy, sick, high, panicky, and courageous all at the same time. But most of all, you're tuned in, you're right there." Tell about nature's "thereness," and why you communicate it so strongly.

WH: You have to write about what's in you. I discovered early the way I felt when I worked really hard to climb a mountain pass with a heavy backpack, which I started doing through the Scouts when I was about eleven. We'd go out for as long as thirteen days along the crest of the Sierra Nevada in California. I was inspired for life. I'll be doing that for as long as I can walk.

In *Changes,* Teddy felt so strongly about turtles because I had held a box turtle in my hand when I was five or six and I just imprinted. I thought they were the most admirable creatures. If your characters care about turtles or the canyon wren, then the reader, who cares about the characters, will care too. That transference is what I shoot for.

CM: There is always a point in Hobbs novels where one

chokes up through some spiritual insight: Travis's agonizing loss in *Changes,* Cloyd's sacrifice of the bear to save Walter in *Bearstone,* Freddy's visit to the Hopi sacred place in *Downriver.* Would you expand on your view of spirituality, especially native American?

WH: I have people of different cultures in my stories, whether Hispanic or native American—those I know the best living in southwestern Colorado—because there isn't one worldview that has all the answers. I'm hoping to pass on that open-mindedness. I want that to lie in my work, that just as no one culture has the truth, also no one species does. There's a spiritual dimension to all life forms. We're so dominant that we're rapidly extinguishing a lot of the others. That's what I admire about native American spirituality. They know that they are sharing the earth with other species and are essentially houseguests here. It's not theirs to plunder. When people incorporate that as a spiritual value, they make the hard choices so we won't abuse the earth as much as we're doing now. I see a real strong environmental consciousness in young people. They know that Americans use fifty to a hundred times more of the earth's resources per capita than people do in Third World countries.

CM: Your river is such a powerful symbol. Jessie describes being on the river and "thinking less and less of everything I'd left behind. Maybe it's because you're literally moving downstream, with no chance of going back."

At the end, she remembers "how, not so long ago, I'd thought of my future as a black tunnel. Now it was all light, with the promise of living in this kind of light." Does Jessie's experience of the river come from yours?

WH: The river is a powerful symbol and a powerful reality in my life, because my wife, Jean, and I spend about twenty nights a year on the river. It's one of the strongest and most beautiful forces in nature. It's a powerful theme in literature too—look at Huck Finn. A trip down the river has that feeling of cutting your bonds. There's only one way and it's forward. It's symbol of freedom.

The theme of moving forward in time was good for this novel, because Jessie is realizing that she must break from the past. Her situation is changing; she wants to live in the past.

CM: When kids have that first big experience of change, they resist it mightily.

WH: Yes, she's fighting it tooth and claw. She thinks it's the end of the world when her dad plans to remarry and leave their home. At first she thinks of leaving the past behind in a dark way. Going downriver is cutting her bonds to her father and the life she has known. There's a lot of fear there. Farther downriver, she has learned enough about her strengths to know it's a journey into light instead of that black tunnel. With each new mile, there's a possibility of joy and discovery. That image of the black tunnel, by the way, came from one of my students, who wrote that she saw her future as a black tunnel. I thought, how scary, how sad. With Jessie I wanted to take a girl who saw a black tunnel, and show that by believing in yourself and getting help from relationships, you can discover light and growth and joy.

CM: You did that so well. What's next?

WH: Every time I write I try to do something different. My new novel will seem realistic, yet whimsical. It starts with the image of a boy leading a burro out in the canyon country. Burros are about as fascinating as turtles. Somebody's going to say, give me some other book! So, it has to be about character. I can work in burros and their beautiful long ears and what great characters they are and how they have a sense of humor.

This boy is longing for true love in his life. He's a movie buff, and he dreams about saving a girl who's like Marilyn Monroe in *A River of No Return,* a girl who's totally helpless. But it's not going to turn out like he thought. He's going to be up to his neck in quicksand and he's going to get saved by the girl! I want it to have a lighthearted tone.

As I'm writing, I'm visualizing a couple of kids who I taught when they were seventh graders. Would they like this to happen or that to happen? They're now in late high school, but I have them frozen in time as seventh graders, and I'm writing to them.

CM: Are they aware of this?

WH: I saw one of their parents in the grocery store and told him I'm writing to Mike back when he was a seventh grader. I hope Mike still likes it because I think within each of us, we're still seventh graders. That's why adults can enjoy these books, too, especially if they have a playful side. I bet a lot of young adult writers are in touch with that earlier self, and they can bring it back.

Will Hobbs

SOURCE: "Survival Micro and Macro," in *The Horn Book Magazine,* Vol. LXXII, No. 2, March-April, 1996, pp. 174-77.

If I were to say that adolescents are known for being highly social, for spending a lot of their time hanging out with their friends, probably most of you would agree. Ah, but what a paradox teenagers are, as parents and teachers know so well. I've been reading about adolescents growing up in a small community on an island in the Arctic Ocean. While these teenagers spend a great deal of time hanging out with other kids, they also spend a significant amount of their time alone. In a culture in which families share only a few rooms, these kids want their own bedrooms, their own space. Does this sound familiar?

The article went on to say that these teenagers are becoming more and more like their counterparts in southern Canada and the United States, who spend about thirteen percent of their waking hours in their bedrooms, alone. I think I've come up with a term to explain this phenomenon: *cocooning.* Parents want to know what's going on in there. The teenager only wishes he or she knew.

I remember how my older brother went into his room in 1961, closing the door behind him, seemingly for good. I remember routing him out once with a stink bomb under the door. When my time came, I realized what this was all about: survival, a struggle for raw survival. Privacy is a basic need when you're undergoing a metamorphosis.

Almost all of young-adult literature is in a sense survival literature. Young-adult novels almost always are about kids surviving on their own—thinking for themselves, making decisions, trying to build wings without a manual, taking off, crashing, taking off again. The story often called the first novel, the *Odyssey,* was largely a survival story, and so was *Robinson Crusoe,* sometimes referred to as the first modern novel. When we think of survival stories as a genre, we think of the combination of adventure and nature; adversity, challenges, ingenuity, struggle, courage, growth, triumph—often focused on one isolated or stranded character. Hence their perennial appeal for young people, who often feel very much alone and up against the world.

I've been exploring survival themes in all of my novels, and as I look back at them, I see survival issues "micro and macro": *micro* concerning the survival of the individual and *macro* concerning the survival of a world worth living in. As I write a book, its theme evolves embedded in the fabric of the story, rather than as something I impose upon the story. It develops subconsciously. I almost feel as though trying to pin it down or name it would cause it to flee. But after the fact, I can talk about it. As I look at two of my books, *Bearstone* and its sequel *Beardance,* I see them illustrating a progression from the micro level, the survival of the individual, to the macro, the survival of that world worth living in.

Bearstone begins with a Ute boy very much in a cocoon: all Cloyd enjoys is being alone out in remote canyons, herding his grandmother's goats. When he's sent to a group home in southwestern Colorado, he's miserable, antisocial, more alone than ever. When he's placed for the summer with an old rancher named Walter, his first act is to run away. He finds an ancient turquoise fetish of a bear that reminds him of the powerful connection between his Ute people and bears, and he names himself "Lone Bear."

Bearstone includes the sort of physical tests that readers are looking for in a survival story, when Cloyd is up alone on the Continental Divide; but mostly it's about Cloyd's moral survival, as many coming-of-age stories are. His moral survival will depend on his forging a relationship with the old rancher, caring about more than himself, trying to be worthy of the faith that Walter has placed in him. When he's out on his own, he can draw on the strength of that relationship, a fresh triumph in his life. He fails in his attempt to save the last grizzly in the mountains, but he succeeds in saving the old man.

Both *Bearstone* and *Beardance* got their start in my imagination from real-life events involving the "last grizzlies in Colorado." I began writing *Bearstone* shortly after a grizzly was killed in the San Juans in 1979. This was news around the country—Colorado's previous "last grizzly" had been killed in 1952. I never saw the possibility of a sequel to *Bearstone* until a rancher sighted a mother grizzly and three cubs in our area in the summer of 1990. That's when I began to think about Cloyd's returning to the mountains to meet the mate and the cubs of the bear in *Bearstone.*

From the very start, I thought that the sequel would be much more about the bears than *Bearstone* was, and about Cloyd's relationship to the bears. In my reading I plunged into the natural history of grizzlies and the traditions of native peoples all across the continent in regard to bears. I learned that in the old days, at the end of the Ute Bear Dance, several dancers would appear in the skins of bears. The image of Cloyd wearing the skin of the mother grizzly, offering fish to her starving cubs, came to mind.

Something I had read suggested that the story could live on a mythic level as well as a realistic level. It goes like this: "In the old times, there was magic that went back and forth between people and bears. People could look at bears and see people, and bears could look at people and see bears." I began to think of inviting the reader to look at animals from a pre-Columbian viewpoint, when the land itself was alive and numinous. When Cloyd took the bearskin off, those cubs would regard him as a bear. They wouldn't become habituated to human beings; in fact, Cloyd would go to great lengths to make sure that they wouldn't. The stage would be set for a humdinger of a survival story.

Significantly, in *Beardance,* Cloyd's secret name is no longer "Lone Bear." A Tlingit Indian woman who has dedicated her life to grizzlies renames him "Fights for Bears." And indeed he does fight for bears. Starving, with the winter coming on at 11,800 feet, he won't leave them, not until they den. He's decided to risk his own life for the survival of these two grizzly cubs.

I do hope that readers are moved by this story to believe that we would be diminished by living in a world without these remarkable creatures, and to insist that we preserve sufficient habitat for our ultimate symbol of wildness.

I know from being a reader, and having been a reading teacher as well, that well-written stories engage hearts and minds and sometimes change them. Contemporary survival literature includes an increasing number of stories that move from the survival of the individual to the survival of the natural world itself, and I'm happy to be part of it as a writer. I hope that by taking readers outdoors in their imaginations, I can bring to life for them the beauty and the wonder as well as the excitement and the dangers of the natural world. I hope to celebrate what diversity of flora and fauna remains to us, as well as the remaining diversity of the family of man. I'd like to think of our young readers surviving their metamorphosis, drawn to beautiful places, with adventures awaiting and important battles to be fought.

Joel Shoemaker with Will Hobbs

SOURCE: "An Interview with Will Hobbs," in *Voice of Youth Advocates,* Vol. 21, No. 2, June, 1998, pp. 99-102.

From an altitude near 8,000 feet in the San Juan Mountains of southwestern Colorado, Will Hobbs and Jean, his wife of twenty-five years, live and work in the gambrel-roofed house they designed and built near Durango. Will's upstairs office window overlooks a hillside of Ponderosa pine as he writes surrounded by mementos including photos of Virginia Falls, the Grand Canyon, family, and friends. Maps of favorite places cover the walls. Bookshelves containing reference materials Will has used to research various books are within close reach of the corner desk where he writes on his Macintosh computer. Since the publication of *Changes in Latitudes* in 1988, he has written nine novels, numerous articles, and a picture book.

Will taught reading and English in southwestern Colorado for seventeen years, both at the junior high level and in high school. He has been writing full-time now since 1990. He stays in touch with his readers by spending about thirty days each year visiting schools across the country. Jean, also a former teacher, now works with Will full-time as his agent. She handles Will's travel calendar, helps with arrangements for conferences and school visits, and works directly with his publishers on the business aspects of Will's writing career.

Having read and admired Will's novels for many years, I first met Will and Jean at the YALSA pre-conference "What Young Adults Really Read—And Why" during the 1997 American Library Association conference in San Francisco. Traveling through the Southwest a month later, my wife, Becky, and I were glad to be able to arrange a visit to their home where this interview began.

Shoe: *Will, your first five award-winning novels*—**Changes in Latitudes, Bearstone** *and its sequel,* **Beardance, Downriver,** *and* **The Big Wander**—*established that you write exciting, contemporary, realistic coming-of-age novels set primarily in the wilderness of the southwestern United States. Your newer books build on the environmental and survival themes in those books while also breaking some new ground.*

In **Kokopelli's Flute,** *for example, your protagonist, Tepary Jones, turns into a pack rat. Many readers (both* *adult and YA) I've talked with as they begin this book are skeptical about this metamorphic premise. Yet, as the novel develops, the excitement, magic, and mystery win them over. How did this story come about?*

Hobbs: Like the rest, it began with personal experience—not turning into a packrat myself, although Jean would probably tell you I am one, but from hiking into remote canyons in the Southwest over a period of decades. I've always been fascinated with the rock art depicting Kokopelli, the humpbacked flute player and seedbearer of the ancient Americas. My "What If" for this story was the image of the magic flute player coming into the life of a modern kid. Given that one of my characters would be thousands of years old, I knew from the outset I was thinking in terms of fantasy. This was an exciting prospect since I'd always loved reading fantasy. I saw the opportunity to write one with indigenous American roots rather than the much more common European sources. In addition to Kokopelli, my cast of characters could include Coyote and Raven.

This was one of my books that involved a tremendous amount of research, primarily in archeology, ethnobotany, and paleobotany. Jean and I visited a seed farm in New Mexico that was growing out rare strains of native food crops in order to perpetuate them. I realized that Tep, my main character, could be growing up on such a farm, and that Kokopelli could have been secretly sending them seed. I owe the idea for the packrat metamorphosis to the bushy-tailed woodrats who serendipitously built a nest in the motor of my truck as I was wondering what was going to happen to Tep when he put the flute to his lips. I recalled that this same animal lives in the cliff ruins, and that paleontologists are currently analyzing packrat middens for clues to the ancient people who once lived there.

Shoe: *The overall mood of the story has great depth of feeling. I was surprised by how familiar and comfortable the family became to me. Are they based on anyone in particular?*

Hobbs: There's a whole lot of me in Tepary Jones. The exploring he did on his own comes from my own memories of roaming the hills almost every day after school, in northern California. At that same time I was doing a lot of gardening with my father—that's where all the feeling about watching seeds sprout comes from. The scene where Tep and his dad are raking side-by-side was very emotional for me to write. Tep's parents, Art and Lynn, are patterned after friends of ours, archeologists who worked for years on the dig in southwestern Colorado mentioned in the story. I'm pleased that you sensed the emotional reality in the characters. . . .

Shoe: **Kokopelli's Flute,** *as fantasy, is really only a little more fantastic than Cloyd's inner vision of becoming a grizzly bear in* **Beardance.** *What do the mythological/spiritual elements of your books say about what Will Hobbs believes? What do they say about what you think teen readers ought to believe?*

Hobbs: In **Beardance** I developed that mythic component quite fully, but it's there in many of my novels, weaving in and out with the natural science and history. My seed idea for **Beardance** was a mythic image—a boy denning with bears. The challenge was to make that happen within the context of a realistic contemporary novel. While on a mythic journey of connectedness to bears and nature, the reader is going to learn a whole lot about the natural history of grizzly bears. As you can tell, myth and natural science are major interests of mine. I see them as complementary rather than contradictory. Myth takes our longing to know where science can't, getting at deep meaning through story. By nature, we're all story-lovers.

Tep's mother *(Kokopelli's Flute)* and I have a lot in common. She has a mostly rational, scientific nature, yet she has her "mystical" side as her husband calls it. "There's more on heaven and earth," she tells Tep, "than is dreamt of in our philosophy." I've always appreciated this sentiment of Hamlet's and a similar one of Albert Einstein's: "The most beautiful experience we can have is the mysterious. It is the fundamental emotion which stands at the cradle of true art and true science."

Given my outlook, I'm ill-equipped to give young people a laundry list of "what to believe." It's the last thing I'd want to do anyway, and readers don't appreciate being hit with 2x4s. A novelist's outlook and beliefs as they filter through the events and the characters do comprise a basic element of what we call "style," but our work, thank goodness, has more to do with illuminating than prescribing.

I think that young readers have a big leg-up over non-readers when it comes to their own life choices. They've imagined being countless people they'll never be, which tends to make them more open-minded, I believe. They've seen all these characters making crucial choices, both good ones and bad ones. There's no question that readers are learning from that. That's why I try to embrace so much that's positive: individual responsibility, self-reliance, courage, friendship, empathy, kindness, compassion . . . wait a second, this sounds like a laundry list. I do try to convey a sense of wonder, of discovery, exploration, hope, and possibility. Being young is difficult enough; kids need to glimpse promise and potential, optimism and idealism. I've discovered that taking kids into the untrammeled natural world—in real life and through fiction—can provide much of the inspiration and challenge that adolescents are innately looking for.

Shoe: *Speaking of inspiration and challenge, you've rafted the Colorado River through the Grand Canyon ten times in the last fifteen years. It's a setting that's very familiar to you, and you've incorporated that knowledge into two books,* **Downriver,** *and the exciting new sequel,* **River Thunder.** *Tell us especially about the new one.*

Hobbs: *River Thunder* is once again narrated by Jessie, and it's much more about her coming into her own. She's going to row a raft at flood stage all the way through the Grand Canyon. It's based on my own experiences on our first Grand Canyon trip during the high-water emergency of 1983.

The story begins as Jessie and the others are tricked by Troy into a reunion river trip. Jessie's furious when she discovers it's Troy, but here's her chance to row the Grand Canyon. At the last second she jumps in the raft and takes the oars. She'll have to deal with a powerfully manipulative and needy ex-boyfriend as well as huge rapids, standing waves, suckholes—the Colorado river in flood. Aside from all the excitement, though, I kind of like thinking of this novel as a love story—the story of a girl falling in love with the river, with rowing a white-water raft, with living in what she comes to see as "the real world."

Although it's a sequel, I worked hard at making sure **River Thunder** can be read as a "stand-alone" story, for readers who may not have read **Downriver**. I had set out to achieve that same effect with **Beardance**, and I believe it's worked in both cases. As you probably noticed, **River Thunder** is described on the cover as a *companion* to **Downriver** rather than a *sequel*.

Shoe: **Far North** *is a survival adventure story set in the remote Northwest Territories of Canada. What kind of research did you do to write that book?*

Hobbs: A lot of my books have originated with falling in love with a place and then wanting to set a story there. This was the case again with **Far North**. After hearing about the South Nahanni River up in Canada, Jean and I went up there in the summer of 1993 and had a bush pilot fly us in with our raft. When we were portaging Virginia Falls (twice as high as Niagara), a park ranger told us about a floatplane that had stalled after landing upstream and then came very close to being swept over the falls. On the spot, I thought: What if a plane did go over the falls after stranding a couple of characters on the shore?

Evenings in camp, I was reading a book written by an adventurer who'd built a cabin on the Nahanni in 1927 and wintered there. I started thinking in terms of a winter survival story. All sorts of memories from my early years growing up in Alaska came flooding back, including the winter darkness and the northern lights. Before I started writing, a year later, I had read a couple dozen books on the region written by bush pilots, anthropologists, adventurers, and the native people of the area, the Dene. Learning about the young Dene, caught as they are between two worlds, gave me the insight that the novel could be not only about physical survival but about the survival of a way of life as well.

Shoe: *I really enjoyed reading* **Far North.** *Its nonstop action makes it a fast read, and yet there are deeper issues about individual responsibility, cultures in transition, and spiritual beliefs. Like most of your books, it features male protagonists and a plot that may appeal to more males than females. Did you write this book thinking mostly about male readers?*

Hobbs: From my years as a reading teacher, I know how readily girls will read books featuring boys as main characters, if they're interested in the content of the story itself. There are so many girls today involved with outdoor sports and adventure—backpacking, mountain climbing, skiing, river running, mountain biking—that I felt confident my readers would be girls as well as boys. It's my first novel without female characters (Gabe's mother is often in his thoughts, but she's deceased), yet I'm getting very enthusiastic responses from the girls.

Shoe: **Ghost Canoe,** *set in the Pacific Northwest, is quite a hike from Colorado. Again, the protagonist is a determined, curious, and capable male teen. The author's note says the story was inspired by the canoes themselves. How did you happen to see them? Have you ridden in one or paddled one?*

Hobbs: We've been exploring the Northwest quite a bit in recent years. There's been a lot of press coverage in that area lately about native people once again carving the great canoes from cedar trees and making journeys on the inside waters of the Pacific. When you visit native cultural centers, you are often invited to watch the carvers work. The canoes are an amazing sight to see, true works of art. I've seen them in the water, but haven't had a chance to paddle in one myself—maybe one day! With their high, tapering wolfhead prows and graceful hull lines, they almost seem like animate beings. I wanted to learn how they were made. That was the beginning. It led to a ton of book research.

At the same time I fell in love with the lighthouse on Tatoosh Island, just off the tip of the Olympic Peninsula in Washington. What an astonishingly dramatic setting! I read the history of the lighthouse, built in 1857. The era of the 1870s especially caught my interest, a fascinating crossroads of history. Sailing ships, steamships, and native canoes were plying the Strait of Juan de Fuca simultaneously. The Makahs were still hunting the great whales from their canoes. Since lighthouses have always suggested mystery to me, I started thinking about writing my first mystery. It would be a great way to hook readers before they realized they were reading an historical novel.

The main character is Nathan MacAllister, the son of the lighthouse keeper. The mystery begins with the wreck of a sailing ship, the discovery that its captain has been murdered, and the possibility that the murderer has survived and is hiding in a sea cave. I gave Nathan the mobility that he would need to try to solve the mystery by making him the paddling partner of the Makah fisherman who delivers the mail to the lighthouse.

I had a wonderful time writing this story. Among other things it's a treasure story about Spanish gold. In my dreams I think of it as my *Treasure Island*. I hope readers will come away entertained and in awe of the amazing seafaring Makahs.

Shoe: *You provide such great detail in explaining native fishing techniques—how did you do this?*

Hobbs: There's a marvelous book on precisely that subject by Hilary Stewart. You should have seen all the detail I wrote in my first draft that didn't end up in the book! A page and a half just on making a halibut hook! Don't get me started!

Shoe: *Librarians and booksellers lament the speed with which many books go out of print. Remarkably, all of your novels are still in print, in both hardcover and paperback editions. What accounts for this?*

Hobbs: To begin with, it's teachers, librarians, and booksellers. My books would never get into kids' hands without them. After that, it's up to the books themselves. I think voice is a huge part of it. More than anything, it's voice that keeps kids turning pages. Sense of audience is really important. Mine comes from all those years of doing book reports as one-to-one conversations with kids. I developed a sense for why they'll put one book down and keep reading another. It's the *way* the story is written that's the key. Kids are very impatient with writing that's confusing or lacks narrative authority. As I'm writing I'm listening for that sigh I would often hear when a kid put a book down.

As a writer, I want to snag them all, from the reluctant readers to the most advanced. And I believe that's attainable. There can be lots of content, lots of deep undercurrents to challenge even the brightest readers, yet as long as I write with clarity, I won't lose anyone. I hear from a lot of teachers that my books are working for *all* the kids. That's extremely gratifying, especially to realize that kids who didn't like to read are now reading a number of my titles and increasing their reading fluency along the way.

Shoe: **Bearstone, Beardance, Changes in Latitudes, Kokopelli's Flute, Downriver,** *and* **The Big Wander** *are now also available on audio tape cassettes from Recorded Books, Inc., to be followed by the others. What do you think of those productions?*

Hobbs: I'm blown away by them, they're so good. The actors they have reading these stories do such a great job, I find myself wondering if I could possibly have written them. Teachers and librarians appreciate that the tapes are unabridged, and so do I. I've always thought that hearing stories read aloud is enormously beneficial for kids of all ages. It helps readers to improve their inward ear as they return to their silent, individual reading. They start "hearing" all that expression in the text. For a teacher who lacks the cast-iron vocal cords to read a chapter dramatically five or six times a day, recorded books are an amazing tool.

Shoe: *Tell me about the new book you're working on now,* **The Maze.**

Hobbs: It takes place in the Maze, a natural puzzle of sandstone thirty square miles in size that sits to the west of the confluence of the Green and the Colorado rivers in Canyonlands National Park, in Utah. It's about a boy whose life has been one dead end after another—a maze in itself. He's always had dreams about flying. The book has a lot to do with flying: with the reintroduction to the wild of the nearly-extinct California condor, and with hang gliding.

Shoe: *Do I sense a mythic component?*

Hobbs: You bet. The kid, Rick Walker, is fascinated by the Icarus story. He identifies with Icarus trying to escape the labyrinth.

Shoe: *Your first picture book,* **Beardream,** *has come out recently, and another is in the works. Tell me about them.*

Hobbs: **Beardream** dramatizes the essence of the various Ute stories that tell the origin of the Bear Dance: that the people learned the dance from the bears. I wrote it primarily for young children but knew it would tie in to **Bearstone** and **Beardance** and would be of interest to older readers as well. Jill Kastner, the artist, came to Colorado to research her illustrations. We hiked together above timberline and she took hundreds of photos. The authenticity really shows in her gorgeous oil paintings.

Jill and I are collaborating right now on a second picture book called **Howling Hill** that takes place in the same setting as **Far North**—Canada's Nahanni River. It's about a wolf pup getting separated from her family, and all of her adventures getting back home. No humans in this one, but there is one great big bear. I've just seen the art and I'm delighted. **Howling Hill** will come out at the same time as **The Maze,** in the fall of 1998. . . .

Shoe: *What's the best thing, to you, about being in the mountains?*

Hobbs: It's the indescribable beauty of all those natural forms. I tried to describe it as Cloyd is approaching the Window in **Bearstone,** and as he reaches the top of the Rio Grande Pyramid. That's me, that's my heart. The beauty makes me feel that being alive, being a conscious part of life, is really pretty wonderful.

Shoe: *And it's that heart, that love of life and wonder that come through so clearly to your readers.*

TITLE COMMENTARY

CHANGES IN LATITUDES (1988)

Nancy Vasilakis

SOURCE: A review of *Changes in Latitudes,* in *The Horn Book Magazine,* Vol. LXIV, No. 3, May, 1988, p. 358.

Will Hobbs offers an affecting portrayal of the breakup of a family and the havoc this dispersal wreaks on young people already gripped by the turbulence of their own adolescence. The story focuses on Travis, the eldest of three children. When his mother takes them on a vacation to Mexico without their father, it is clear to Travis, if not to his younger siblings, that she is about to make a fateful decision concerning her troubled marriage. To avoid getting hurt in the crossfire, Travis adopts a cool, smart-alecky persona that succeeds only in alienating him from everyone in his family except nine-year-old Teddy who openly adores his older brother. Initially against his will, Travis is caught up in Teddy's worries over the endangered Pacific ridley sea turtles that lay their eggs on the beaches of the resort village where the three are vacationing. Even less to his liking, he discovers that his mother is involved in a romantic liaison. The author neatly balances the perilous situation of these ancient lumbering sea creatures against the breakdown of his family. Teddy's death, which occurs when he tries to rescue some captured turtles, finally brings matters out into the open. Travis must confront the discomforting truth that his approach—to run away from his problems— · has been the same as his mother's. This tendency of teenagers to adopt a public show of cockiness in order to cover up their sense of powerlessness is skillfully depicted by Will Hobbs, who, along with his sensitive ear for the language of the young, creates in his first novel an all too recognizable contemporary family in jeopardy.

Deborah Bennet

SOURCE: A review of *Changes in Latitudes,* in *Voice of Youth Advocates,* Vol. 11, No. 2, June, 1988, pp. 86-7.

Travis has fantasies about meeting erotic, beautiful women on a vacation with his family to the beach resort of Punta Blanca, Mexico. Teddy, Travis's nine year old brother, is thrilled to be going to Punta Blanca because he is intrigued by animals, especially reptiles. Punta Blanca is where the Pacific ridley turtle nests, and turtles are Teddy's favorite reptile. Travis's father has stayed home, ostensibly to work, but it is soon evident to Travis and his 14 year old sister Jennifer that their mother has planned this week as a time to think about a divorce.

Teddy, unaware of the family's problems, becomes a crusader on behalf of the turtles who are endangered because greedy people are selling the turtle eggs as aphrodisiacs and slaughtering the turtles to make lotions that supposedly rejuvenate skin. Soon Travis (who is not having much success finding sexy women who are interested in him) is sharing Teddy's interest and enthusiasm about the turtles. They meet Casey, a marine biologist, who not only gives them lots of information about the ridleys, but takes them on a memorable snorkeling excursion where they swim among the turtles going to the beach to nest.

Travis as narrator gives the reader insight into his thoughts and emotions. He carries on interior monologues and occasionally makes comments directly to the reader. His various feelings are reflected in the narrative which is sometimes amusing, sometimes dramatic, and occasionally lyrical and poignant. Travis is very critical of himself and states, "Cynicism and self-righteousness have always coursed through my veins like addictive drugs." But the reader observes Travis helping Teddy rescue turtle eggs and hatchlings, and confronting the men who are killing the turtles. He offers comfort to Jennifer when they talk about their parents, and she turns to Travis when she is confused or panic-stricken. Everyone but Travis can recognize that he is a loving person, and not as self-centered as he claims to be. In this "coming of age" novel, it is only a more mature Travis who is surprised at the depth of his loyalty and loving.

Hobbs has believably portrayed teenage emotions and dialogue in this novel. The focus of the story on the endangered sea turtles will appeal to readers interested in wildlife and conservation. The novel would have wider reader appeal, but the scientific information is occasionally so lengthy that it slows the action and detracts from the characters. Despite this shortcoming, this is an excellent novel and has moments when it comes touchingly close to being as well written as *Bridge to Terabithia.*

Claudia Moore

SOURCE: A review of *Changes in Latitudes,* in *School Library Journal,* Vol. 43, No. 11, November, 1997, p. 70.

Will Hobbs's sensitive, sad story about Travis, a typical American teenager, portrays the rapid coming-of-age during a family vacation on the coast of Mexico. The trip ends tragically when Travis's younger brother dies helping to save endangered sea turtles. Travis believes he could have prevented his brother's death if he had not been off in search of girls, and must cope with feelings of guilt. Told in the first person, Johnny Heller's versatile voice is excellent for the dialogue between the siblings. He easily copes with the quick changes from frustration and humor to caring and love, and is comfortable with teen jargon. His speech is much slower during the dramatic climax and conclusion. A tender story for mature teens.

BEARSTONE (1989)

George Gleason

SOURCE: A review of *Bearstone,* in *School Library Journal,* Vol. 35, No. 13, September, 1989, p. 272.

At 14, Cloyd, a Ute Indian lad, is dominated by the white authority figures who have kept him in school when he'd rather be with his grandmother and hiding out in the inaccessible canyons of the southern Utah/Colorado high country. Cloyd is almost an orphan: his mother is dead; his father is a hospitalized vegetable on a life-support system; and now he must spend the summer with an old, recently widowed farmer who is near the end of his life's tether. Exploring the hills above the ranch, Cloyd discovers an ancient burial site, finds a small turquoise bear, and in the Ute tradition, gives himself a new name, "Lone Bear." Cloyd works hard, but when angered by some bear hunters, undoes everything by chainsawing the fence posts he'd set and sawing down Walter's beloved peach trees that his wife had brought from Missouri. Walter's understanding lets Cloyd redeem himself—even to the point of saving the old man's life. Drawing on his legacy of the Indian "old ways," Cloyd struggles with the injustices he sees everyday and ultimately succeeds in learning "how to live in a good way." Extremely well-drawn characters, vivid incidents in and around the mountains of the Continental Divide, and powerful yet sensitive moments between the boy and the old man put this far above other coming-of-age stories.

Nancy Cleckner

SOURCE: A review of *Bearstone,* in *Booklist,* Vol. 86, No. 5, November 1, 1989, p. 540.

When 14-year-old Cloyd Atcitty is taken to a Colorado ranch to live with Walter Landis, a lonesome old miner, the boy is overwhelmingly resentful—the only emotion, besides loneliness, he has ever experienced. Having been abandoned by his parents, raised by his Ute Indian grandmother, and finally (because of supposed incorrigibility) placed in a government home for Indian children, Cloyd greets this new development in his life with cool, calculating silence. Exploring the high mountain cliffs surrounding the ranch, Cloyd finds a small carved turquoise bear in an Indian burial cave. While educating him in the old ways, his grandmother had portrayed the bear as the Utes' most important animal—friend, relative, and bringer of strength and luck. Secretly Cloyd becomes Lone Bear and vows he will strike out on his own as soon as possible. However, his plans are curtailed when he discovers that Walter, unlike other adults, is honest, genuine, and trustworthy and that the surrounding mountains, the land of his people, strengthen and beckon him to see his life anew. When Walter is injured in a mining accident, Cloyd's love for the old man transcends his resentment, and he desperately works to save him. Hobbs effectively combines heartwarming adventure and a traditional rite of passage.

Mary E. Ojibway

SOURCE: A review of *Bearstone,* in *Voice of Youth Advocates,* Vol. 12, No. 5, December, 1989, p. 276.

Cloyd is an American Indian boy, lonesome, without parents, a failure in school, and a resident in a group home his tribe sent him to. All he really wants is to go back to tending his grandmother's goats in the remote canyons of Utah. Instead he is to spend his summer with an old man, Walter Landis, on a ranch outside of Durango, Colorado. Although Cloyd is sure he won't like Walter, or the ranch, and runs away before even meeting his summer guardian, he reluctantly returns to the ranch and begins a summer that changes him forever.

Walter is as lonesome as Cloyd, and has a desire not unlike Cloyd's desire to return to his Utah home. Walter's desire is to mine, again, the Pride of the West. Together the old and the young survive, learn to understand one another, *and* learn to love and be loved—a first for Cloyd, and a return to giving and receiving love for Walter.

The growth and maturity that Cloyd acquires as the summer progresses is juxtaposed poetically against the majestic Colorado landscape. Hobbs has creatively blended myth and reality as Cloyd forges a new identity for himself, learns what caring is all about, and accepts responsibility for his actions and learns to care deeply about another human being. At the same time, Hobbs has created an elderly role model who has the ability to understand Cloyd's anger, anxiety, and longing, with patience and without being judgmental.

Bearstone is . . . definitely a best books candidate! A must purchase. The expression of the faces and in the eyes of Cloyd, Walter and the bear, on the jacket are sure to entice even the reluctant reader. This story has something for everyone—regardless of age!

DOWNRIVER (1991)

Publishers Weekly

SOURCE: A review of *Downriver,* in *Publishers Weekly,* Vol. 238, No. 6, February 1, 1991, pp. 80-1.

Against her wishes, rebellious Jessie is sent on an Outward Bound-style camping program in Colorado. The trip takes an unexpected turn when charismatic Troy persuades the group to abandon their leader in order to take an unguided white-water rafting trip through the Grand Canyon. Ironically, the group's mutiny brings about just the sort of character-forming insights that were the original goals of the trip—and shows at least some of the members the difference between healthy nonconformity and reckless irresponsibility. Similar to Julian Thompson's *The Grounding of Group Six,* Hobbs's narrative lacks that novel's consistently anti-authoritarian stance and quirky, memorable characters. With personalities that do not progress beyond their easily identified traits established at the story's beginning, Jessie and her friends lack depth and substance. Still, the abundance of rugged action and the faithful depiction of the wilderness program milieu should appeal to fans of the great outdoors.

George Gleason

SOURCE: A review of *Downriver,* in *School Library Journal,* Vol. 37, No. 3, March, 1991, p. 212.

Eight problem kids (four boys, four girls, high school age) have been sent to a camp called Discovery Unlimited where they are to meet problems, make responsible decisions, and develop as adults. "Hoods in the Woods" the kids call themselves. Action occurs in the outback of southwestern Colorado and northern Arizona as Al, their adult leader, programs the group first to climb Storm King Peak (which nearly results in fatalities) and then to raft the white water of the San Juan River. The Hoods decide rafting the Colorado River will be wilder; so they steal Al's van and equipment, drive to the put-in at Lee's Ferry, sneak past the park rangers, inflate their rafts, and seven embark—one deserts. Rafting the wild Colorado is heady but difficult and dangerous. Misadventures develop the kids, but also breed disasters. So when the rangers capture the group near Havasu Creek, not all resent the rescue. The book is exquisitely plotted, with nail-biting suspense and excitement. Jean Craighead George's *River Rats* is similar but lacks such intricate development of characters and interpersonal relationships.

Candace Smith

SOURCE: A review of *Downriver,* in *Booklist,* Vol. 87, No. 13, March 1, 1991, p. 1377.

Jessie, 15, is one of eight problem teens, participating in a nine-week outdoor survival education program known fondly as "Hoods in the Woods." Jessie's problems are hanging around with the wrong crowd and lots of friction with her widowed father over his new girlfriend. The idea of the program is to help kids "find themselves" and "come of age" by putting them in life-threatening situations that they work as a group to resolve. The first part of the program, mountain climbing, almost ends in disaster when Jessie panics and has to be talked down. But the real challenges start when the group, led by charismatic Troy Larsen, decides to ditch the counselor and head for the Grand Canyon to do some unsupervised whitewater rafting. Although the characters are stock (Adam is the clown, Star plans her life with Tarot cards, Freddy is silent but resourceful) and the adults aren't very visible or trustworthy, there are some interesting group dynamics, and the kids learn to face consequences. The rafting sequences are exciting, although it's hard to believe the teens would be so successful without experience or maps. (Troy doesn't believe in planning.) There's not the depth the plot promises, and the ending is too tidy to be believable, but there's enough action to keep kids reading.

Mary Ojibway

SOURCE: A review of *Downriver,* in *Voice of Youth Advocates,* Vol. 14, No. 3, August, 1991, pp. 171-72.

Jesse is a sophomore in high school, has had two car accidents and doesn't even have a driver's license, skips school constantly, drinks, hates her father's new woman friend, Madeline, and is being packed off to what her school counselor, father, and therapist have decided is the solution—a nine week program called Discovery Unlimited that involves hiking in the mountains and various other outdoor activities. At camp Jesse meets seven other young adults trying to find themselves, all with some kind of problem in their life that has made them a participant in Discovery Unlimited, or as the YAs call it "Hoods in the Woods." But, the story does not revolve around the problems, rather it revolves around these eight young adults "ditching" their adult leader and completing the "Wil-der-ness Ther-a-py" on their own.

Al, the leader, and the young adults climb Storm King Mountain together and then set out for Utah to do some river rafting. They want to do white water but Al has them scheduled to run the San Juan River. While Al is getting permits for the San Juan, the kids decide to abscond and do the white water, so they take off at dusk, drive all night, and eventually get to the Grand Canyon area. They begin their trek down the river and learn about each other's strengths and weaknesses in order to survive. One of the girls leaves and returns to the safety of Discovery Unlimited and "rats" on the others. They are survivors and throughout *Downriver,* they find themselves, learn to be independent, to trust, to make decisions for and about themselves and what's best for the rest of the group, and best of all to be survivors.

The scenery description is beautiful and the kids are believable, even Heather who "rats." I wanted these kids to have a great time on their venture, to experience success, gain self-confidence, and come out of the adventure relatively unscathed, but strong, wiser, smarter, and better individuals. Yes, the story has a happy ending but it is not contrived. Not everyone is better for the experience but most are. In fact, one of the real rebels, Adam, is going to start working for Discovery Unlimited: as he says—"kind of a junior counselor, too, the idea being that if this fool can get something out of the program, anybody can."

THE BIG WANDER (1992)

Will Hobbs

SOURCE: "On the Beautiful Trail We Go: The Story behind *The Big Wander,*" in *The Alan Review,* Vol. 22, No. 1, Fall, 1994, pp. 5-9.

With each of my novels, I've begun from a single image. Long before I start scratching around for a story, there's that image so full of promise and so laden with emotion. With *The Big Wander,* the image was of a boy, a burro, and a dog adventuring into Utah's matchless redrock country. It came from reading the letters of the young artist Everett Ruess, that "vagabond for beauty," who disappeared in the canyons of the Escalante in 1934 after four years of wandering.

The emotion I brought to the image was stirred by those evocative lines from Aldo Leopold's *A Sand County*

Almanac. "I am glad I shall never be young without wild country to be young in. Of what avail are forty freedoms without a blank spot on the map?"

I wanted to write a novel worthy of those words. I posted them on my bulletin board at the outset of my search for this story.

In Gary Snyder's *Axe Handles,* there's a marvelous poem entitled "On Top" that seems to be about composting. The "new stuff" goes on top; then there's turning, waiting, watering, sifting. . . . His last line, "A mind like compost," makes us realize he's been describing the creative process. The writing of my novels, too, I realize, has been a whole lot like composting.

With a novel, there's a compost pile building long before you recognize it as such. Everett Ruess and Aldo Leopold were part of the "old stuff" for **The Big Wander,** so too was Oliver La Farge's *Laughing Boy,* Frank Waters's *Masked Gods,* and countless other titles, along with my own life experience in the Southwest. My teenage summers working as a guide at Philmont Scout Ranch in northern New Mexico sparked my sense of place here, and since 1973 Jean and I have been living in southwestern Colorado, hiking in the San Juan Mountains and exploring the nearby Utah canyon country every chance we get.

I'd written a novel set in the San Juans *(Bearstone),* and one in the Grand Canyon *(Downriver);* now it was time for what I'd come to regard as the most beautiful "blank spot" on the map of North America, the canyon country surrounding the confluence of the San Juan and the Colorado Rivers. Intrigued by the canyons in which Everett Ruess had disappeared, Jean and I hiked down Coyote Gulch to the Escalante River and were stunned by the beauty. Even before I had a story, I knew I wanted it to end here.

On our way home, we swung by one of our favorite places, Monument Valley. I began thinking about a character traveling between Monument Valley and Escalante in Everett's mode: on foot, accompanied by a burro and a tiny dog. Hiking through the northern edge of the reservation, my character would inevitably meet Navajo people, as Everett had, and he would meet the Mormon people of the Escalante country, again as Everett had. In his last letter, Everett Ruess had written, "I stopped a few days in a little Mormon town and indulged myself in family life, church-going, and dances. If I had stayed any longer I would have fallen in love with a Mormon girl. . . ." Maybe my protagonist *would* fall in love with a girl of the Escalante country . . . These were my first inklings of plot as I plunged into my reading.

Before I start writing, I always go on a reading binge. Partly it's procrastination, but it's pleasure too, and I always learn a little here and a little there, sparks of ideas for the novel. I reread Everett's letters in W. L. Rusho's *A Vagabond for Beauty,* and I read *Land of Living Rock* and *Standing Up Country* by C. Gregory

Crampton, as well as his *Ghosts of Glen Canyon,* with its photographs of historic sites in Glen Canyon before it and its hundred side-canyons were flooded by Lake Powell in 1963. I realized that 1962 was the last summer that the Colorado was free-flowing through Glen Canyon, "The Place No One Knew." I began to think about setting the novel in that summer; it seemed especially right since that was the summer I was the age of the character I'd be writing about. On this trek of my hero's, he could discover Glen Canyon in its last summer.

I read John Wesley Powell's descriptions of Glen Canyon and Dellenbaugh's descriptions in his account of the second Powell expedition, and I read Russell Martin's *The Story That Stands Like a Dam,* about the building of Glen Canyon Dam and the nascent environmental movement's efforts to preserve Glen Canyon. At that time I thought my novel would be about the building of the dam and the flooding of Glen Canyon, but of course **The Big Wander** didn't turn out to be about that at all. In fact, there's only a brief scene in the novel set in Glen Canyon.

There are always going to be tangents, especially in a first draft as you pick one horse and not another. In my reading I had learned that John Wayne was in Page, Arizona, in the summer of 1962, filming *The Greatest Story Ever Told.* In my first draft, I had Clay meeting John Wayne at the Empire House Café in Page. Clay had long been drawn to the Southwest by the John Wayne/ John Ford westerns filmed in Monument Valley, and so of course assumed that his hero was filming a western there. Searching for his burro the morning after he'd met John Wayne, Clay encountered several camels grazing in Wahweap Wash, then a throng of people in togas on the banks of the Colorado, who were intently watching one long-haired man douse another in the river. As Clay wandered into the scene, the director was yelling "Cut! Cut!" which is exactly what readers of this first-draft episode advised me to do.

You never know, though. Some of my favorite images in the final form of **The Big Wander** did come from the research. For example, my reading included two books on burros. It had been twenty-five years since I'd worked with burros, and I wanted to brush up. I read an American book entitled *The Burro* and a British one entitled *Donkey Care.* In *The Burro,* there was a photograph of an oldtimer in a 4th of July parade in Flagstaff in 1967. He was marching down the street with a backpack on his back, and sticking out of that backpack, just above his shoulder, were the improbably large head and ears of a baby burro. I knew right then I had to get a baby burro into my story, and somehow I had to get him into a backpack as well.

In the British book I learned a lot about burro psychology, in chapters entitled "The Obstinate Donkey" and "The Mind of the Donkey." Among the photographs was one of a burro inside a house. I thought of my baby burro and what fun it would be to have him rampaging around inside a house. I didn't know he'd be all dressed up for the county fair.

I scanned the *Life* magazines from 1962 and found a photo-essay on an old man who lived along the highway in the Mojave Desert and made his living recycling junk he picked up along the road. He called himself "Hubcap Willie." I began to think of a character based on him and decided to keep the name as a tribute. My Hubcap Willie would be leading a burro rather than pushing a cart, and that burro would somehow become Clay's companion. . . .

While I was doing all the reading, I was scratching down plot outlines; I must have ten altogether in my compost-file on *The Big Wander.* For a few days I'd get all excited about the new plot, but then my balloon would burst as I perceived some major flaw. A novel has to have a worthy problem to solve, and it took me some time to decide that Clay would come out to the Southwest searching for someone, namely his Uncle Clay, who would have disappeared several years before the story starts. His uncle would be a former rodeo star; in Clay's mind that would qualify him as a hero akin to his big-screen heroes from the westerns.

In the evenings Jean and I would watch old westerns ourselves, especially the ones filmed around Monument Valley. But it was a 1962 contemporary anti-western that I happened to bring home, *The Misfits,* that got me started thinking about how wild horses might figure into the novel. *The Misfits* had a lot to do with wild horses being rounded up for slaughter. I went to the library and found Hope Ryden's *Mustangs: A Return to the Wild.* In 1962 the mustangs were indeed on the verge of being wiped out, for chicken and dog food and for fertilizer. I began to imagine that Clay's missing uncle had gotten involved trying to save wild horses in the Escalante country and had gotten into some hot water. . . .

I realized that Sarah, the girl Clay would meet in the Escalante country, would also know and love the local wild horses. She would be eager to try to save them and would enlist Clay's help. Having grown up on a ranch, Sarah would be even more capable than Clay in this world he was discovering. What a team they would make.

I didn't know during the research phase that the novel would turn out to be a song of innocence, with such a whimsical tone and so many comic incidents. The tone was set by the conversation on the first page, as Clay and his big brother Mike are backfiring their way in an old pickup truck from Seattle into the desert Southwest along Route 66. Now that I think about it, that tone of the novel, from the first page, flowed from my choice of audience for this story. I had two reluctant readers in mind from my days as a reading teacher; I had "hooked" them with books that were high adventure and also made you laugh. I wanted to snag them as well as all my other readers, right up through the most advanced.

When Clay sets out from Monument Valley, with only the burro and then a tiny dog for companions, he heads into the canyons east of Navajo Mountain, where his uncle was last seen. This may well be the most rugged section of the Navajo Reservation, so remote that even today people don't winter there. Clay will meet a Navajo family at their sheep camp; they know of his uncle and will help him on his way. I wanted Clay to acquire something of their sense of place, their ethic of "walking in beauty," of living in harmony with their surroundings. I walked that stretch only in my imagination, but I felt I could faithfully write about it. I had Everett's descriptions in his letters and Gregory Crampton's photo of the mouth of Paiute Creek. I also had taken photographs of the big three-dimensional relief map at the museum at Glen Canyon Dam, showing the route that Clay would take—every mesa and canyon he would cross.

It's the Yazzie family who make Clay a gift of a former mustang his uncle had brought out of the Escalante country. When I think of *The Big Wander,* I think of Clay newly-mounted on that spotted pony. He wears that string of red coral around his neck, the big silver-and-turquoise bracelet on his wrist, and the black Stetson, ringed by those hammered buffalo nickels. "Bik'e Hozhoni," he says to himself. He's on the Trail of Beauty. It's just where I hope my readers will be as they read this story, feeling this sense of place, of connectedness.

The Navajo Office of Historic Preservation in Window Rock was a great help. I had a lot of reading as well as my years visiting on the reservation behind me, but I wanted to make sure I got things right. For example, I wanted to verify that I was using Navajo terms correctly. "Old Age River" was the translation of a Navajo term I'd run into in two different books, in one referring to the San Juan and in the other to the Colorado. I figured one of the writers had made a mistake. When I asked the man in the office in Window Rock, he chuckled and said, "Oh, the people who live up by the San Juan, they call it 'Old Age River,' and the people over by the Colorado, they call it 'Old Age River.'" The Yazzie family in my story lived close to the San Juan River, so I had my answer.

The Yazzies accompany Clay as far as the fording of the Colorado at the mouth of the Escalante in Glen Canyon. Their parting, at that place, was one of my peak moments in the writing of the story. Here the story line converged with my earliest aspiration of the story, as readers and I got a glimpse of one of the lost wonders of the world. Clay learns that these "hundred tall canyons" will be going underwater the following spring. I left it to the reader to ponder the enormity of the loss. A novel dies when it preaches.

Clay rides on into Escalante and discovers that his uncle is in jail. Although Clay doesn't realize it, the writer has destined him to become the hero of his own western. Painfully shy, he's not only going to meet a girl but he's going to end up living with her family, and together Sarah and he are going to carry on the rescue of the wild horses his uncle has begun. A few traces of my reading on local Mormon history wound up in the novel. There are several references to the "Hole in the Rock Expedition," which traversed some of the most rugged country on earth—Escalante to Bluff, Utah—in the winter of 1879-80, without losing a man, woman, or child.

Like each of the novels I've written, *The Big Wander* was a journey of discovery, a Big Wander of its own. At first it was all egg shells and coffee grounds and a hundred other bits and pieces. But at some point, in the dark of my subconscious I suppose, it all started to cook. I'd be dreaming about the story as I slept and I'd wake up reaching for a scratch-pad. I'd find myself writing intuitively, racing, just trying to keep up with my fingers, and grateful that the compost had somehow reached the point of spontaneous combustion. When I wrote that last chapter, I was Clay Lancaster, and I was galloping down the Escalante on that spotted pony. At my neck, the red coral; on my wrist, the silver-and-turquoise bracelet; on my head, the black Stetson ringed with hammered buffalo nickels. At my side, my Uncle Clay, almost safe. Past the mouth of Davis Canyon we rode, and I remembered a cloudburst and a burro being born. All the while, I was scanning the rims a thousand feet above, looking for a girl waving where I guessed she'd be.

Between the sheer red walls we rode, between the waving willows at the Escalante's edge. No cloudburst coming today. The sky was as blue as the walls were red and the willows were green. *"Bik'e Hozhoni,"* I said aloud.

"Yes sir," my uncle agreed. "On the beautiful trail we go."

Charlene Strickland

SOURCE: A review of *The Big Wander,* in *School Library Journal,* Vol. 38, No. 11, November, 1992, p. 92.

Clay Lancaster, 14, has dreamed of adventures on what he calls the Big Wander (his name for a journey without planned destinations), and finds them aplenty in this coming-of-age saga. He ends up on his own in the Southwest of 1962, without parent or older brother to rule him. Clay searches for his cowboy uncle (located in a Utah jail); befriends Navajos; and acquires a mustang, a dog, and a burro. Hobbs skillfully blends action scenes (flash flood, quicksand, and wild chases) with moments of humor and insight. Clay copes admirably with a series of incidents, although coincidence and friends' actions resolve some of his problems. He shows his stuff in tracking his way through the desert and rescuing a band of wild horses; while starry-eyed about the Wild West of John Wayne, he experiences real life pleasures and relationships, including an episode of unrequited love. Hobbs makes Clay a believable character, and creates a memorable supporting cast—even a villain with a heart of gold. Frequent references to classic Westerns, J.F.K., the Bomb, and Navajo traditions could lead readers to further investigations of these topics.

Kathleen Beck

SOURCE: A review of *The Big Wander,* in *Voice of Youth Advocates,* Vol. 15, No. 5, December, 1992, p. 279.

Bumping along Route 66 in his brother Mike's very used pickup, 14 year old Clay Lancaster envisions a summer of adventure on their long-planned "big wander." They'll roam the Southwest searching for their missing uncle, whose last letter came from New Mexico. But Mike's thoughts are on his girlfriend back in Seattle and his preparations for college in the fall. When Mike decides to turn back, Clay talks his brother into letting him stay and work for the summer at an isolated trading post on the Navajo reservation in Arizona. A chance encounter with Navajo sheepherders who knew his uncle leads Clay to set out into the remote reaches of the reservation, accompanied only by a stubborn burro and a little dog he collects along the way. There Clay finds adventure, friendship, and even a first romance amidst the dramatic landscape he comes to love. When he finally meets up with his missing relative, the circumstances plunge Clay into an escapade worthy of his favorite Western movies.

Hobbs gets better with each novel. Here his characters are well-drawn, the setting is vivid and the adventure/survival story is exciting and engrossing. Readers will identify with Clay's longing for independence, his insecurity around girls, his earnest attempts to fit into this new way of life. The 1960s setting provides enough distance that the reader can smile at Clay's naiveté and at the same time appreciate the simplicity of an isolated lifestyle which even then was fast disappearing. And if the Navajo sheepherders and Mormon ranchers of the region are somewhat idealized, who cares? It's a rousing adventure with an appealing hero and it won't sit on your shelves.

Mary Lou Burket

SOURCE: A review of *The Big Wander,* in *Five Owls,* Vol. 7, No. 3, January-February, 1993, p. 65.

At first this seems to be a book about two brothers on a road trip into Utah, searching for the uncle someone describes as "One of the Men Who Don't Fit In." But after awhile the older brother, whose heart was never in the project to begin with, calls it quits, while the younger brother leaves the "road" entirely for the pack trails and isolated canyons.

He is fourteen-year-old Clay, and the story is his. Clay is a city kid from Seattle, fond of westerns and shy with girls. Although he's looked forward to spending the summer with his brother, he really grows when they're apart.

The year is 1962, and there are still wild mustangs in the canyons. Popular tunes like "Only Love Can Break a Heart" play on the air. As Clay sets out, he makes the most of every adventure. Despite his awareness of the threat of a nuclear war, he's taking big, hopeful leaps with his life—learning to ride through rugged country by himself, to dance the slow dance, and to kiss his first kiss.

Author Will Hobbs lives in Durango, Colorado, and he warms his story of Clay's trip with his love for this beautiful region and its people. The strongest chapters are about the time Clay spends with a Navajo family, who summer in one of the canyons and befriend him, giving him precious information about his uncle. When he sees what the woman is weaving on a loom, Clay reflects: "How could she make that design, and make it right out of her head?" Compared to her, "What had he ever done?"

Hobbs has an easy sense of humor, which is useful for revealing Clay's feelings. The character of Sarah, an accomplished rider Clay's age whose competence and daring are appealing, is another big plus. It's unfortunate that none of these pleasing elements are suggested by the jacket, which shows the handsome Clay with his able burro Pal and dog Curly. (I liked them, too.) To be fair, there's such a lot going on in this book that it would be hard to imagine a single defining image. Although I might have preferred a more direct beginning and a tighter focus throughout *The Big Wander,* it grew on me and I enjoyed its positive spirit. Readers who love a happy ending and stay the trail will be glad they did.

BEARDANCE (1993)

Janice Del Negro

SOURCE: A review of *Beardance,* in *Booklist,* Vol. 90, No. 6, November 15, 1993, p. 614.

While prospecting for gold, Cloyd Atcity meets the woman Ursa, who is searching for the last grizzlies in Colorado. With Cloyd's help, she finds them—a mother bear and three cubs. When the mother and one cub are killed in an accident, Cloyd remains behind to ensure the survival of the remaining two cubs through the winter. A member of the Ute Indian nation, he has always felt an affinity to the bear, especially since experiencing the traditional bear dance the year before. Cloyd's decision to stay in the isolated mountain area is a dangerous one, and he and the cubs face natural disasters as well as those engineered by humans. This combination of spiritual quest and adventure story has a likable main character and, after the discovery of the cubs, an escalating plot that should make it an easy booktalk. It is also a book that will appeal across gender lines.

Todd Morning

SOURCE: A review of *Beardance,* in *School Library Journal,* Vol. 39, No. 12, December, 1993, p. 134.

In the sequel to Hobb's *Bearstone,* Cloyd Atcitty returns to the high country with his rancher friend Walter. But whereas the elderly man is searching for a lost cache of Spanish gold, Cloyd is hoping to find a family of grizzly bears that has been sighted. The previous novel ended with Cloyd believing that he had failed to save what could have been the last of the Colorado grizzlies, and he clings to the belief that its mate and cubs may be alive. Eventually, his search for the bears and his commitment to their survival becomes a journey of self-discovery. This novel works as an effective adventure story, an exploration of the Ute Indian culture, and a natural-history lesson rolled into one, all set in the rarefied atmosphere of the Continental Divide. As compelling as the first book, *Beardance* should prove to be equally popular.

Elizabeth S. Watson

SOURCE: A review of *Beardance,* in *The Horn Book Magazine,* Vol. LXX, No. 1, January-February, 1994, p. 70.

In this intriguing sequel to *Bearstone,* Cloyd Atcitty is once again in the high-mountain meadows with his friend and mentor, Walter Landis. While Walter searches for a lost gold mine, Cloyd searches for a mother grizzly and three cubs reported to be the last grizzlies in Colorado. Cloyd's compulsive fascination with the bears is, he is sure, connected to his Ute heritage. He is given the name "Fights for Bears" by Ursa, a Tlingit woman who is a wildlife biologist specializing in grizzly research. The two find the mother and cubs, but a flash flood kills one cub and the female grizzly; the book details how the other two survive with Cloyd's help. There's plenty of action and memorable characters, and the descriptions of Ute rituals and legends, the setting, and Cloyd's first experiences with spirit dreams are particularly well done and well integrated into the text.

KOKOPELLI'S FLUTE (1995)

Darcy Schild

SOURCE: A review of *Kokopelli's Flute,* in *School Library Journal,* Vol. 41, No. 10, October, 1995, p. 134.

This unique and compelling fantasy/adventure is set in northern New Mexico. The mood is created immediately as Tepary Jones, 13, sets out to view a total eclipse of the full moon from the ruins of a cliff dwelling near his family's farm, but the quiet mystery of the Ancient Ones is shattered by illegal pothunters. Tep finds an eagle-bone flute they leave behind, and his adventures become complicated by a magic older than the ruins. He finds himself changing into a bushy-tailed woodrat each night, which both hinders and helps him to find the pothunters; develop drought-resistant seeds with his father; and save his mother from the hantavirus, a disease thought to be contracted from rodent droppings. Both parents are scientists and have encouraged their son to enjoy and respect nature, and to help preserve the variety of life on earth as well as the beauties of the past. They are both fully developed individuals who capture and hold readers' interest. Even Dusty, the dog, has a rare personality. Hobbs vividly evokes the Four Corners region and blends fantasy with fact so smoothly that the resulting mix can be consumed without question. Subplots flow together naturally, and ancient stories and sensibilities become one with modern lives. Outstanding characters, plot, mood, and setting combine in this satisfying and memorable book.

Frances Bradburn

SOURCE: A review of *Kokopelli's Flute,* in *Booklist,* Vol. 92, No. 3, October 1, 1995, p. 304.

When 13-year-old Tepary Jones and his dog Dusty are camping out at the Picture House, an ancient Anasazi cliff dwelling not far from his father's Seed Farm, they encounter some grave robbers. After scaring them away, Tepary cannot resist taking the small bone flute the thieves left behind. Playing the ancient flute marks the beginning of a strange yet fascinating story, for Tepary triggers his gift as a changeling, and each night after dark, he becomes a pack rat. Ludicrous as this may sound, the novel works because of Hobbs's easy style and his ability to make readers suspend disbelief. Additionally, the information that young people will learn about ancient farming and seed-gathering practices and the habits of desert animals, especially pack rats—all part of Hobbs's obvious but unobtrusive environmental message—make the story not only an entertaining fantasy, but also an interesting ecological education resource.

FAR NORTH (1996)

Joel Shoemaker

SOURCE: A review of *Far North,* in *School Library Journal,* Vol. 42, No. 9, September, 1996, p. 227.

From the compelling cover illustration to the terrifying and plausible details, this survival adventure clearly demonstrates the author's love for and familiarity with the northern wilderness. Gabe, 15, formerly of San Antonio, enrolls in a boarding school in Canada's Northwest Territories to be closer to his father, an oil field worker. Gabe's likable but depressed roommate, Raymond, is an Athapascan Indian. A map helps readers follow along as circumstances involving a plane crash leave the teens and Johnny Raven, an elder from Raymond's village, stranded with minimal supplies as winter hardens. The plotting is fast paced and action filled as the teens' cultures clash, and as they struggle against the cold, blizzards, isolation, starvation, injury, a wolverine, grizzly bear, and Johnny's death before finally reaching safety. The weakest elements of the book may be the sermonlike "testament" the boys find in Johnny's pocket after his death, and the thread of mythic raven lore that

is mentioned, then given up before becoming a major element again. Quibbles aside . . . this satisfying tale will engage YAs' hearts and minds.

Mary M. Burns

SOURCE: A review of *Far North,* in *The Horn Book Magazine,* Vol. LXXII, No. 6, November-December, 1996, pp. 745-46.

Motherless, fifteen-year-old Gabe Rogers comes to Canada's Northwest Territories to a boarding school in Yellowknife to be near his father, who is working on a geological dig. Events succeed one another in an inevitable progression when a routine sightseeing flight ends in disaster near the dangerous Nahanni River, stranding Gabe, his roommate Raymond Providence (a Dene from a remote village), and the latter's ailing great-uncle, Johnny Raven, the only one of the trio with any real survival skills. What follows is a thrill-a-minute account of their struggle, against seemingly impossible odds, to satisfy the basic needs for shelter, food, security—and ultimately, for rescue. This is not just another page-turner; there are deeper issues which are addressed, including the contrast between Gabe's culture and Raymond's, and between Raymond's and his uncle's. And there is tragedy as well, for the old man does not live to see how well his pupils learn the lessons he so painfully taught them. Comparisons with [Gary] Paulsen's *Hatchet* are inevitable, but while many elements are similar—a downed plane, delayed rescue, reformation of character under trying circumstances—tone, style, and intent are quite different. *Hatchet* is an introspective homage to Hemingway; *Far North* is in the more expansive tradition of the suspense-filled adventure tale, with character changes being suggested rather than emphasized. Neither will disappoint the armchair thrill-seeker. A map and an author's note describing Hobbs's research add verisimilitude.

Diane Tuccillo

SOURCE: A review of *Far North,* in *Voice of Youth Advocates,* Vol. 19, No. 6, February, 1997, p. 328.

Fifteen-year-old Texan Gabe Rogers decides to attend boarding school in Yellowknife, Northwest Territories so that he can be near his father, who is working at a diamond drilling project. When his roommate, Raymond Providence, a native from a remote Dene village, chooses to leave the boarding school and return home, Gabe is invited by his pilot buddy, Clint, to fly along. With them is Raymond's great-uncle, Johnny Raven, who has just been released from the hospital in Yellowknife and is also returning home to the village. Clint decides to take a detour up the Nahanni river to show his passengers the spectacular Virginia Falls, even though his radio is not functioning well enough to allow him to report his change in flight plans. When the engine dies after the plane lands on the river, everyone is nearly swept away by the strong current. The boys and Johnny Raven manage to get some supplies and themselves to the river bank, but Clint is not so lucky. He and the plane are dragged over the falls. So begins a battle of survival for the wise elder and two resourceful teens, with the intense Arctic winter descending upon them.

This classic Hobbs adventure takes readers to a rugged, amazing wilderness few know. Characters are well-drawn, and excitement and energy penetrate their entire trek from above Virginia Falls through the looming canyon of the almost-frozen Nahanni below. Smart and faulty choices are made the whole journey until the boys realize they must follow Johnny Raven's guidance if they are to make it back home. When Johnny Raven dies, the boys have learned so much from him they are able to continue their journey. Raymond is even able to recognize the spirit of the raven as their guide. . . . Readers clamoring for more superior adventure . . . will find their wish satisfied here.

📖 GHOST CANOE (1997)

Elizabeth Bush

SOURCE: A review of *Ghost Canoe*, in *Bulletin of the Center for Children's Books*, Vol. 50, No. 8, April, 1997, p. 285.

Nathan MacAllister is finding life on Cape Flattery, Washington, a stretch more exciting than he had anticipated when his father, a retired clipper-ship captain, took on the job of Tatoosh lighthouse keeper. Bodies have washed ashore from the wreckage of a ship bound for Canada; footprints indicate there was a survivor, and a robbery at the trading post, charcoal residue in a secluded cave, and the corpse of a murdered sea captain lead Nathan to suspect that the survivor is still in the area pursuing his own nefarious agenda. Hobbs freshens up a tried and true adventure plot with intriguing details of nineteenth-century Makah Indian life—seal and whale hunting, canoe building, burial customs, and potlatches—and a cast of equally intriguing characters, from Nathan's Makah friend and mentor Lighthouse George, to the crazed Makah outcast Dolla Bill and his villainous employer, Mr. Kane. Although the mystery itself isn't much of a puzzler, there's plenty of action between the dark-and-stormy-night opener and the murderer's inevitable demise (plunging off a cliff, weighed down by his ill-gotten gains) to keep the pages flipping.

Gerry Larson

SOURCE: A review of *Ghost Canoe*, in *School Library Journal*, Vol. 43, No. 4, April, 1997, pp. 137-38.

With characteristic skill, Hobbs blends together a number of elements to create an exciting adventure set in 1874 on Washington's rugged Olympic peninsula. Nathan, 14, tries to unravel the mystery of a shipwreck and the captain's murder. With Lighthouse George, a Makah fisherman, the boy paddles canoes on delivery runs to the damp, inhospitable island of Tatoosh, where his father is the lighthouse keeper, and on hunting expeditions for whales and seals. Curious about footprints found on a desolate beach near the shipwreck where all were supposedly lost, the boy explores the peninsula and encounters a shadowy figure brandishing a knife in a dark cave, a nervous local trader burying a small metal box, and a burial "ghost" canoe mounted high among tree branches facing the sea. When the boy's father receives a letter referring to a lost treasure map and the likelihood of foul play in the shipwreck, Nathan begins to piece together the truth. In a climactic scene, he is threatened by the murderer, and Lighthouse George and an eccentric village outcast come to Nathan's rescue. A gallery of good, evil, eccentric, and misunderstood characters teaches him the meaning of friendship and enriches his appreciation of another culture. Dramatic, vivid descriptions of the Pacific landscape and Makah lifestyle and customs create a rich backdrop for Nathan's adventures and discoveries. A winning tale that artfully combines history, nature, and suspense.

Chris Sherman

SOURCE: A review of *Ghost Canoe*, in *Booklist*, Vol. 93, No. 17, May 1, 1997, p. 1489.

Hobbs really knows how to please his readers. This time he's created an exciting historical adventure touched with a real mystery and set in a remote, exotic locale. To that, he's added Spanish treasure, a nasty villain and his quirky companion, and lots of action. What a read! Fourteen-year-old Nathan MacAllister helps his father tend a lighthouse off the northwest coast of Washington State. When his mother's health fails, he moves with her to the Makah village on the mainland, hoping the slightly drier climate will speed her recovery. From the moment he arrives, it's clear that something strange is going on: the captain of a wrecked ship has been murdered, someone is hiding in the caves around the coast, money and supplies have been stolen, and there's a mysterious stranger around. As Nathan unravels the puzzling goings-on, he discovers that he has endangered himself. As always, Hobbs delivers well-developed characters and a plot that never falters. Here, he also provides a respectful view of Indian life through Nathan's eyes.

📖 BEARDREAM (1997)

Leda Schubert

SOURCE: A review of Beardream, in *School Library Journal*, Vol. 43, No. 4, April, 1997, p. 104.

Hobbs explores the relationship between a young boy and a bear in his first picture book, a theme he has pursued in his novels for older children. In early spring, Short Tail, a young Ute, is concerned because no one has seen the Great Bear. He is worried that the animal will starve and goes to find him. But the boy tires and sleeps; in a dream he finds the Great Bear and wakes him. The creature appreciates Short Tail's respect and shares with him the annual bear dance, which celebrates the end of winter. The child in turn teaches the dance to his people. This layered tale, which is based on a Ute story, is respectfully told, but it may be confusing for readers, and the art doesn't clarify matters. [Jill] Kastner's oils are often impressive; dark, soft-edged, with large figures set against mountain landscapes. In several of the dream spreads, images of the dreamer (bear or human) are incorporated into the landscape, but they are not set far enough apart. In some scenes it's not obvious which character is Short Tail. The primary focus of the story is also not clear: Is it the survival of the Great Bear, Short Tail's relationship with it, the end of winter, Short Tail's bravery, or the teaching of the dance—or all of the above.

Karen Morgan

SOURCE: A review of *Beardream,* in *Booklist,* Vol. 93, No. 16, April 15, 1997, p. 1436.

As spring comes to the mountains, a great bear remains sleeping. His absence is noted, and village people worry that the grandfather bear has not survived the winter. So great is the concern that one young boy from the village climbs high into the mountains to look for the bear. Exhausted by the climb, the boy dreams of finding and waking the bear. Together boy and bear join other bears dancing "to the rhythm of thunder." It is this dance that the boy later teaches his people. Hobbs's fictionalized version of the traditional Ute bear dance story is enhanced by the large picture-book format featuring Kastner's double-spread oil paintings, in which the illustrator cues the dream sequences, subtly exposing the bear and the boy as part of the landscape. Kastner's evocative dance scenes add a fine note of drama to the story.

Journal of Adolescent and Adult Literacy

SOURCE: A review of *Beardream,* in *Journal of Adolescent and Adult Literacy,* Vol. 41, No. 1, September, 1997, p. 83.

Short Tail and the others in his village are concerned that winter will have no end this year. Spring cannot begin until Great Bear awakens. On his search for Great Bear, Short Tail falls asleep and dreams that he finds Great Bear, wakes him from his winter nap, and is taught the secret of the beardance in exchange for his respect.

Hobbs, author of **Bearstone** and **Beardance**, bases this picture book upon a Ute story and tradition. The illustrations by Kastner are beautifully rendered oil paintings that mirror the ancient spirituality of the text. The sleeping bear is carefully painted into mountains and creek beds, showing the close relationship between humans

and nature. Use this book as an introduction to the novels of Will Hobbs, as part of a study of Native American culture, or simply read it aloud so that students might experience the beautiful use of language that is a hallmark of Hobbs's work.

RIVER THUNDER (1997)

Deborah Stevenson

SOURCE: A review of *River Thunder,* in *Bulletin of the Center for Children's Books,* Vol. 50, No. 10, July, 1997, pp. 397-98.

In **Downriver**, Jessie and her fellow rebellious adolescents took off from the main group and rafted the Colorado on their own; here they're a year older and a few experiences wiser, but when a chance to finish the run comes up, they return. Though they were lured there under false pretenses (the troublemaking Troy sent letters in the name of their old guide) they're game for the experience, even when record rainfalls and runoff make the trip through the canyon uniquely demanding and dangerous. The plot runs aground on the interpersonal matters, which are mostly residual from the first book and deal with Troy's possible maturation and his relationship with Jessie. All readers will really want is for the group to get back on the river, where Hobbs's terrific and involving descriptions of high-pressure adventure, river lore, and Jessie's developing skill at this monumental task will keep pulses racing. Without being flashy, the book's knowledge permeates the story and keeps the narration credible, allowing audience members who don't know a canyon from a culvert to understand the situation and its challenges, and many of them will be pleased to see a girl as the capable real-life action hero. An author's note explains his rafting experience and the record-breaking year on the Colorado that provided the details for his group's fictional trip.

Joel Shoemaker

SOURCE: A review of *River Thunder,* in *School Library Journal,* Vol. 43, No. 9, September, 1997, p. 217.

The premise is that the cast from **Downriver** has been asked to work as interns by "Discovery Unlimited" owner Al, rejoining him for a raft trip down the Colorado River through the Grand Canyon. Their joyful reunion at the launch site is stressed almost to the breaking point when they find out that Troy, the manipulative, buffed, bad boy who nearly sank their earlier escapade, has bankrolled this trip, and that Al is not involved at all. Setting aside misgivings about Troy's duplicity, they row off, settling into a realistic rhythm of river work, problem solving, play, and stress management. The characters are interesting individuals who have changed in mostly positive ways since their first trip together. Jessie gains confidence and knowledge with each challenge. Troy's problems escalate with the rising level of the water, and it's gradually revealed that he has stalked Jessie throughout the previous summer, obsessed with making his fantasy of a relationship with her take shape. The climactic resolution with Troy comes just before they plummet through Lava Falls, which, if predictably plotted, is thrillingly told. The culture of the commercial canyon runners is aptly described. From the raft-eating big drop on the cover to the author's informative note at the end, the vivid descriptions deliver high-volume excitement sure to entice many readers into booking a ride on any subsequent sequels.

Cindy Lombardo

SOURCE: A review of *River Thunder*, in *Voice of Youth Advocates*, Vol. 20, No. 4, October, 1997, p. 244.

Thanks to some secretive wheeling and dealing, the self-proclaimed Hoods in the Woods group from *Downriver* is back for a second attempt at conquering the mighty Colorado River—this time without the aid of a professional counselor or guide. Fans of Hobbs's earlier whitewater adventure tale will be disappointed in this uninspired sequel. None of the characters are more fully developed than they were the first time we met them, and the interaction among them seems forced and trite. Young adults who appreciate veracity in their fiction may find themselves questioning how realistic it is, from a safety standpoint, that the group is allowed to continue its journey through the Grand Canyon despite unusually dangerous and turbulent weather conditions. The detailed blow by blow descriptions of how the group tackles various rapids combine with a host of technical terms to make this a must-read for only a small group of YAs, those with a strong interest in whitewater rafting. Even Troy's attempt to rekindle a romance with Jessie fails to raise any genuine interest in what happens to either of them.

📖 *HOWLING HILL* (1998)

Ilene Corsaro

SOURCE: A review of *Howling Hill*, in *Booklist*, Vol. 95, No. 1, September 1, 1998, p. 126.

Hobbs, master of the YA survival story, turns his attention to picture books with this riveting fictionalized account of a lost wolf cub. Although disappointed when she is unable to howl like the rest of the pack, Hanni is soon laughing with her brothers and sisters along the river bank. But before she realizes what is happening, she is floating down the river on a log, alone for the first time in her life. Hanni's survival depends on learning how to swim, convincing an enormous, sleepy bear (whom she eventually saves) to lead her home, and finding that elusive howl of hers. Although it's hard initially to discern Hanni from the rest of the pack, the oversize format is used to good advantage by [Jill] Kastner, whose thickly brushed oil paintings display a mastery of both color and texture. This should have enormous appeal to Hanni's human counterparts as they venture into the larger worlds of school and neighborhood.

Virginia Golodetz

SOURCE: A review of *Howling Hill*, in *School Library Journal*, Vol. 44, No. 10, October, 1998, p. 102.

This fresh adventure story introduces some new elements to the ever-popular theme of losing and finding home. Here, a wolf cub and a sleepy brown bear play out the drama in Canada's vast Northwest Territories. Little Hanni (named for the Nahanni River) is frightened when she is separated from her pack during an outing. She is, however, a survivor, and on her journey home she learns some valuable lessons. She finds out that she can swim when she is forced to jump into the river just before the log she is riding goes over the falls. Next, she meets a large bear that brings her close to home and teaches her to use her sense of smell to guide her the rest of the way. When she finally reaches Howling Hill and is reunited with her family, she discovers that her wish has come true—she has grown up enough to howl and can join the pack in song. In the text, the water of Howling Hill is described as "hot" and "stinky;" unfortunately, no explanation is given for this and children will wonder why. The full-color oil paintings laid out in double-paged spreads give some idea of the grandeur of the area and its wildness. The details of the wolves' activities invite close inspection. The last illustration dramatically shows the animals howling into a blood-red dawn.

Publishers Weekly

SOURCE: A review of *Howling Hill*, in *Publishers Weekly*, Vol. 245, No. 41, October 12, 1998, p. 77.

Hobbs delivered a wintertime survival tale in his YA novel *Far North*; here he brings that same type of suspenseful adventure to picture book format. His protagonist this time, however, is no adolescent but a wolf pup. Somewhat anthropomorphizing his characters, Hobbs sets up a problem for Hanni straightaway: a la Eric Cane's *The Very Quiet Cricket*, she can't howl ("Don't worry," her mother tells her. "It's inside of you, somewhere deep inside."). Then mishap overtakes her. While playing on a log in the river, Hanni is separated from her family and swept fast away. She plunges bravely into the water (and discovers she can swim) just before reaching a deadly waterfall. A bear drifting in and out of hibernation helps her most of the way home; returning to the apparently deserted *Howling Hill*, Hanni finally finds her voice and howls for the first time and thus summons the pack. The coming-of-age theme overloads the story a bit, but the tension stays strong. Kastner, previously paired with Hobbs for *Beardream*, contributes exciting, motion-filled oils. Rendered in broad, blurry strokes, her wolves and bears are realistic, with only some subtle posing to give Hanni the occasional childlike attitude.

📖 *THE MAZE* (1998)

Mary M. Burns

SOURCE: A review of *The Maze,* in *The Horn Book Magazine,* Vol. LXXIV, No. 5, September-October, 1998, p. 609.

Rick Walker, product of too many foster homes, is sentenced to serve six months in Blue Canyon Youth Detention Center near Las Vegas. His crime—throwing rocks at a stop sign—hardly seems to warrant such severe punishment. Aware that Rick is not a hardened criminal and concerned for the environment in which he will serve time, his social worker pleads unsuccessfully with the judge. The facility is worse than imagined. Except for the librarian, Rick has little support in a corrupt organization. When he learns that he is in danger from the other inmates, he escapes, eventually finding refuge with a bird biologist in the canyons of southwestern Colorado. As he learns to work with the giant condors that Lon, the biologist, is attempting to introduce into that area, he learns much about himself—his capacity for growth, endurance, and commitment. Ultimately, he must return to society, face the judge who had sentenced him, and resolve his future—but not before he has helped Lon to bring two dealers in illegal weapons to justice and negotiated the Maze, a harshly beautiful landscape of deep canyons and awesome pinnacles. This time, his social worker is not alone in attesting to his character, for Rick bids fair to extricate himself from the maze in which life has placed him. As in *Far North,* Hobbs spins an engrossing yarn, blending adventure with a strong theme, advocating the need for developing personal values. Again, as in the earlier book, there is a character who serves as mentor and explicator of those values— but the author's sure sense of story prevents him from overwhelming his narrative with philosophical commentary.

Todd Morning

SOURCE: A review of *The Maze,* in *School Library Journal,* Vol. 44, No. 10, October, 1998, p. 136.

Fourteen-year-old Rick Walker feels that his life is a maze. He's been bounced around from one foster family to another and is sent to a detention center for hard-core juvenile offenders after committing a petty offense. After he reports corruption at the facility, the boy is forced to flee for his life and ends up in an isolated part of Utah's canyon country, near an area called the Maze. Here he forms a friendship with Lon, a biologist who is trying to reintroduce condors into the wild. The two work together, observing and assisting the birds, and Lon teaches Rick to hang glide. When they run afoul of a pair of nasty anti-government types who are hiding a cache of weapons in the area, their lives are placed in danger. Certain elements of the plot are pretty conventional, appearing in countless young adult novels (troubled teen runs away and finds redemption with wise friend in a remote area). What sets this book apart is the inclusion of fascinating details about the condors and hang gliding, especially the action-packed description of Rick's first solo flight above the canyons in the face of an approaching thunderstorm. Many young readers will find this an adventure story that they can't put down.

Sarah K. Herz

SOURCE: A review of *The Maze,* in *Voice of Youth Advocates,* Vol. 21, No. 6, February, 1999, p. 434.

Fourteen-year-old Rick Walker runs away from Blue Canyon Youth Detention Center near Las Vegas, hides out in the rear of a camper truck, and finds himself "at the end of the world"—Canyonlands National Park in Utah. The truck delivers supplies to an isolated campsite, where bird biologist Lon Peregrino is feeding and observing fledgling condors recently released in the area. Rick is afraid that Lon will notify the authorities, but Lon proves to be the best person Rick could hope to meet. Rick has been in a series of foster homes, and does not trust adults—they have let him down too often. Lon does not pry into Rick's past; he accepts Rick's help in tracking and feeding the condors, and teaches Rick hang-gliding. Gradually Rick trusts and respects Lon, and tells Lon about his past. When Rick risks his life to save Lon, he learns what it means to care about another human being. Through his relationship with Lon, Rick is ready to become responsible for his actions and prepare for his future.

Hobbs has written an exciting adventure story about a teenager who changes his negative attitude about rules, adults, and authority. Rick is a richly-textured character who reveals his curiosity about the condors, his appreciation of the Canyonlands, his theory about the Icarus myth, and his realization that his anger and self-pity will not help him mature.

Additional coverage of Hobbs's life and career is contained in the following sources published by The Gale Group: *Authors and Artists for Young Adults,* **Vol. 14 and** *Something about the Author,* **Vol. 72.**

Naomi Shihab Nye

1952-

Palestinian-American author of poetry, fiction, and nonfiction; editor and anthologist.

Major works include *This Same Sky: A Collection of Poems from around the World* (compiler and editor, 1992), *Sitti's Secrets* (1994), *Benito's Dream Bottle* (1995), *Habibi* (1997), *The Space Between Our Footsteps: Poems and Paintings from the Middle East* (compiler and editor, 1998).

INTRODUCTION

Nye is celebrated for her poetry, fiction, essays and, above all, for her anthologies of poems from around the world, particularly from the Middle East. As an Arab American growing up in two distinct cultures, Nye strives in her own life to define the ways in which her experiences merge two unique ways of doing things and two different perspectives of the world. In her writings and her anthologies, she explores humanity's connections with each other, with family histories, with people from foreign cultures, and with other times and peoples. Although Nye originally wrote poetry for adults, after the birth of her son, she began compiling and writing works for children of all ages, including *Benito's Dream Bottle,* a picture book for very young children, and *Habibi,* a novel for young adults. Much of her work has been as a compiler and editor of the poetry and paintings of artists worldwide, especially from Arab countries. Encountering prejudice against Arabs in America, typically arising from misguided understanding, Nye once told *Something about the Author (SATA),* "It was during the Gulf War . . . I found some poems by Iraqi poets and had the kids read them and let them see that these people were no different than we were. They had the same daily needs, the same inner lives." The desire to establish a connection between children of various ethnic backgrounds inspired Nye to gather multicultural poems for her first anthology for children, *This Same Sky: A Collection of Poems from around the World.* Likewise, Nye's experiences with her own grandmother are played out in *Sitti's Secrets;* yet Sitti retains characteristics that many children will recognize in their own grandmothers, regardless of nationality. Reviewers praise Nye's ability to create texts to which children of all backgrounds can relate. It is this commonality that is the thread of all of Nye's work, both her collections of other artists' works, as well as her own original compositions. Nye has a unique ability to show how, despite our differences, all people are united through our common humanity, needs, and feelings, and that there is more about us to bring us together than there is to separate us. Marcus Crouch described *Sitti's Secrets* as a "book that builds bridges," an observation that applies to the rest of Nye's work as well.

Biographical Information

Born in 1952 in St. Louis, Missouri, to a Palestinian father and American mother, Nye spent much of her childhood listening to the stories her father told of his homeland and of his family who lived there. Young Nye was a voracious reader; at five she read Carl Sandburg's stories and grew fascinated by the power of words. She credits a second grade teacher, who had the class memorize poems, for engendering her love of poetry. During Nye's high school years, her family moved to Jerusalem and Nye met her father's Palestinian family for the first time, establishing deep connections. Her father, a journalist, was editing the *Jerusalem Times*, an English language paper, and asked Nye to write a teen column. The Six Day War forced the family to return to the United States, and they came back to San Antonio, Texas, where Nye finished high school and continues to live today. She studied English and world religions at Trinity University in San Antonio, and throughout her college years she wrote and published poetry. She graduated with a bachelor of arts degree in 1974, and shortly after, accepted a position with the Texas Writers in the Schools Project, through which writers worked directly with school children on writing projects. Nye stayed with the project for about twelve years, working in different schools all over the state and, at the same time, firmly establishing herself as a published poet. In 1978, she married photographer and lawyer Michael Nye. When their son, Madison, was born in 1986, she wanted to find a new working situation that allowed her to stay at home with her child. Familiar with poets from all over the world, Nye wrote letters soliciting work for her anthology, *This Same Sky*, and received many enthusiastic responses. The anthology launched Nye's career as an anthologist/writer for children. She told *SATA*, "I always tell young writers how important the link is between reading and writing. You just cannot be a good writer without reading, reading. It's a way of sharing."

Major Works

To compile *This Same Sky: A Collection of Poems from Around the World,* Nye solicited and collected poems celebrating the natural environment and its human and animal inhabitants. The poems are of everyday life and show how each person—no matter what his or her culture, background, or religion—harbors similar needs, hopes, and dreams. The anthology features the works of 129 poets from 68 countries. Mary M. Burns noted that the collection "should prove invaluable for intercultural education as well as for pure pleasure," while Jim Morgan opined, "The most striking aspect of this collection, and the book's greatest potential appeal to adolescents, is the sense of real human life behind the words; these poets are people in distant lands and cultures who have experienced real human emotions."

Nye explored her own cultural background in *Sitti's Secrets*. "Sitti" is the Arabic word for grandmother. In this book, an Arab-American girl named Mona visits her grandmother in Palestine, and although they do not speak the same language, they find wonderful ways to communicate as Mona watches her Sitti go through her daily chores. When she comes back to the United States, Mona writes a letter to the President asking him to find a way to make peace between all people. *Sitti's Secrets* "serves as a thoughtful, loving affirmation of the bonds that transcend language barriers, time zones, and national borders," commented Luann Toth. Maeve Visser Knoth concluded, "The emotional story is rich in images of life in the Middle East but is most importantly about the love of a family separated by space but united in spirit." Inspired by Nye's son, the picture book, *Benito's Dream Bottle,* is also about the relationship between a child and his grandmother. Benito's grandmother says that she never dreams. Benito feels so sorry for her that he asks everyone he knows where dreams come from, concluding that dreams come from a bottle inside you and that his grandmother's dream bottle is empty. He tries to help his grandmother think about images for her dreams until her dream bottle finally is filled and she can dream again. When she does, she dreams of Benito taking her outside to cook leaves inside a broken toaster oven. "The child's close relationship with his family, especially his warm

concern for his grandmother, irradiates the story," noted Judy Constantinides. "The text has a lyrical quality that serves its subject well and underlines the importance of dreams and imagination."

Habibi, an Arabic nickname meaning "darling," is a novel for young adults that explores the experience of growing up in an Arab family. Liyana, a fourteen-year-old girl, moves with her family from St. Louis to Palestine where they are welcomed by their relatives. Liyana encounters situations and traditions very different from those she is used to, and becomes homesick for St. Louis. When she falls in love with Omer, a Jewish boy, her homesickness begins to fade, but the Palestinian conflict in the background intrudes into her family's lives, and can never quite be forgotten. Reviewers observed the story as a sweet and leisurely tale of growth against a background of conflict. "*Habibi* succeeds in making the hope for peace compellingly personal and concrete," Kate McClelland remarked.

The Space between Our Footsteps: Poems and Paintings from the Middle East is a collection of poetry and paintings by 127 contemporary Arab poets from 19 countries in the Middle East. The poems and illustrations speak of such universal themes as childhood, family roles, and relationships, as well as depict scenes of village, country, and homeland. Angela J. Reynolds wrote, "Good poetry evokes emotion and brings feelings and images to light; this collection exquisitely touches the senses through well-crafted language." Reynolds continued, "Nye's respect and admiration for Middle-Eastern culture, and for poetry, come through in the expertly chosen, artistically arranged entries."

Awards

This Same Sky won the Jane Addams Children's Book Award and was designated an Honorary Book for Christians and Jews from the National Association for Christians and Jews in 1992. In 1994 *Sitti's Secrets* received a Best Book Citation from *School Library Journal* and a Pick of the List Citation from the American Booksellers Association. In 1995 it received a Notable Children's Trade Book in the Field of Social Studies Citation from the National Council for the Social Studies and Children's Book Council and the Jane Addams Children's Book Award for picture book.

AUTHOR'S COMMENTARY

Naomi Shihab Nye

SOURCE: "Lights in the Windows," in *The ALAN Review,* Vol. 22, No. 3, Spring, 1995, pp. 5-6.

Years ago a girl handed me a note as I was leaving her

proud town of Albany, Texas, a tiny, lovely place far in the west of our big state. "I'm glad to know there is another poemist in the world," the note said. "I always knew we would find one another someday and our lights would cross."

Our lights would cross. That girl had not stood out to me, I realized, among the other upturned, interested faces in the classroom. How many other lights had I missed? I carried her smudged note for thousands of miles.

I was fascinated with the earliest poems I read and heard that gave insight into all the secret territories of the human spirit, our relationships with one another. Somehow those glimpses felt comforting, like looking through the lit windows of other people's homes at dusk, before they closed the curtains. How did other people live their lives? Just a *sense* of so many other worlds out there, beginning with the next house on my own street, gave me a great energy. How could anyone ever feel lonely? One of the first books I loved in my life was a thick, gray anthology edited by Helen Ferris, called *Favorite Poems Old and New*. I still have my early edition, though it is coming a little loose at the spine. Rich, intelligent voices spoke to me each time I opened its covers. I found Rabindranath Tagore, Carl Sandburg, Emily Dickinson, living side-by-side. I imagined I was part of a much larger family.

To me the world of poetry is a house with thousands of glittering windows. Our words and images, land to land, era to era, shed light on one another. Our words dissolve the shadows we imagine fall between. "One night I dreamt of spring," writes Syrian poet Muhammad al-Maghut, "and when I awoke/flowers covered my pillow." Isn't this where empathy begins? Other countries stop seeming quite so "foreign," or inanimate, or strange, when we listen to the intimate voices of their citizens. I can never understand it when teachers claim they are "uncomfortable" with poetry—as if poetry demands they be anything other than responsive, curious human beings. If poetry comes out of the deepest places in the human soul and experience, shouldn't it be as important to learn about one another's poetry, country to country, as one another's weather or gross national products? It seems critical to me. It's another way to study geography!

For this reason I was always carrying poems I found from other countries into classrooms where I worked as a visiting writer. If American students are provincial about the literary histories of other places, imagining themselves to be the primary readers and writers on the planet, it is up to us to help enlighten them. When I first traveled to India and Bangladesh as a visiting writer for the Arts America program of the U.S. Information Agency, friends commented helpfully upon our departure, "Why do you suppose people over there will care about poetry? They can barely get enough to eat!" Stereotyping ran rampant among even my educated community. In India, poems were shared with us which were 7,000 years old. In Bangladesh, an impromptu poetry reading was called one evening and 2,000 enthusiastic listeners

showed up. Could either of those things happen in the United States?

Anyone who feels poetry is an alien or ominous form should consider the style in which human beings think. "How do *you* think?" I ask my students. "Do you think in complete, elaborate sentences? In fully developed paragraphs with careful footnotes? Or in flashes and bursts of images, snatches of lines leaping one to the next, descriptive fragments, sensory details?" We *think* in poetry. But some people pretend poetry is far away.

Probably some of us were taught so long and hard that poetry was a thing to *analyze* that we lost our ability to find it delicious, to appreciate its taste, sometimes even when we couldn't completely apprehend its *meaning*. I love to offer students a poem now and then that I don't really understand. It presents them with the immediate opportunity of being smarter than I am. Believe me, they always take it. They always find an interesting way to look through its window. It presents us all with a renewed appetite for interpretation, one of the most vibrant and energetic parts of the poetry experience.

I'm reminded of a dear teacher I had in high school who refused to go on to the next poem in our antiquated textbook until we had all agreed on the same interpretive vision of each poem—*her* vision. Wearily we raised our hands. Yes, yes, that poet was just about to jump off a cliff. Onward! If we can offer each other a cognizance of *mystery* through the poems we share, isn't that a greater gift? Won't a sense of inevitable mystery underpinning our intricate lives serve us better than the notion that we will each be given a neat set of blanks to fill in—always?

Poems offer that mystery. Poems respect our ability to interpret and translate images and signs. Poems link seemingly disparate parts of experience—this seems particularly critical at the frenzied end of the 20th century. I have yet to meet one person in all my travels who doesn't say they are too busy, they wish they had a little more time. If most of us have lost, as some poets suggest, our meaningful, deep relationships with the world of nature, poems help us to see and feel that world again, beyond our cities and double-locked doors. I have learned as much about nature from the poems of Mary Oliver as I have ever learned walking in the woods.

And since we now live in a world where activities in one person's woods have a direct relationship on countries far away—the disappearing rain forests in southern Mexico and Hawaii and the changing weather everywhere, for example—we need to know one another. It is an imperative, not a luxury. What will we recognize? As the daughter of a Palestinian immigrant, steeped since early childhood in Palestinian folktales, I found it critical the older I grew to read Israeli Jewish writers too. I had to know how many links we had. When Yehuda Amichai of Israel writes, ". . . the field needs it: *wild peace . . . ,*" he is talking about the same fields my ancestors wept over for years. I have no doubt these cousins of the human race could learn to work in them together.

During the Gulf War, I carried poems from writers in Iraq into classrooms I was visiting. It seemed important to remember that there were real people in Iraq, real fears and hopes, real chimneys and children and shoes and bread. A friend warned me, "You won't get away with it," but the exact opposite response occurred. Teachers said, "Where can we get more of these?" Did it matter that a third grader said, "I wonder what those little children in Iraq are thinking about today. I wonder if they slept at all last night." It mattered to me. Did it matter that high school girls ended up discussing the coldness of media euphemisms—"collateral damage" for innocent people dead, for example—how the television made everything seem somehow cold and distant, but the poems written in a personal human voice made that so-called enemy feel very close? That was the *job* of poems, we decided. To give us a sense of others' lives close up. Poems could be a zoom lens in a world of wide-angle sweeps. And the teachers at Hockaday School in Dallas said, "Do a book for us, okay? Give us a lot of voices from everywhere—we'll be waiting."

I love that the word *anthology* comes from the Greek for *flower gathering.* We walk through the garden—one plant stands out to one person, one vine to another. There are possibilities of choice. So I got to work on *This Same Sky: A Collection of Poems From Around the World* (1992). I wrote letters to all the poets and translators I knew in many countries. "Send me poems appropriate for younger readers, but also appealing to adults"—I wanted a book that didn't condescend. I have a very slim appetite for the limericks and cutesy ditties some people toss out when you say "younger readers." Ever since second grade, when our ambitious, poetry-loving 75-year-old teacher had her entire class memorize William Blake's *Song of Innocence,* I knew children were capable of more. She used to say, "If you don't understand something, just turn it over and over in your head like a lozenge or a lemon drop." We did that, and it worked. We were left with lovely phrases in our memories, to savor as we grew older. We were left with a sense that words had something to *give us.*

And the poems came flying in, some stitched together at the top, some on thick, old-country paper, some fully illustrated with 20-page autobiographies accompanying. One fellow from a remote island asked if I could please nominate him for the Nobel Prize. A poet in American Samoa thought she was supposed to pay the permissions fee to *me.* Some of the poems, of course, I'd already had and loved for years. Then I just had to track down their authors or translators for permissions. No slim feat. The only day in my life I ever drank a glass of wine at 10 in the morning was one of those permission days.

Finally my trusty mailman Mario pounded on my door with a handful of exotically stamped letters. "I can't stand it anymore," he said. "What are you *doing* in there?" I love how Four Winds Press/Macmillan includ-

ed some of the fabulous stamps as a detail in the front and back of the book. And I feel deeply lucky that my generous, wonderful editor Virginia Duncan and her excellent staff felt as enthusiastic about the book as I did. They even gave it a blue marking ribbon. Some teachers have said, "I thought you had to be the Bible to get a ribbon."

As will happen with collections, the poems ended up gathering themselves into sections that felt almost organic—related to family, or words and silences, or losses, or human mysteries. The sky seemed to occur surprisingly often as a universal reference point, which gave us the title. I loved receiving the autobiographical notes almost as much as the poems. An example from Amanda Aizpuriete: "I'm raising 4 children and translating Emily Dickinson into Latvian in my spare time." Or a note on Shuntaro Tanikawa by one of his translators, Harold Wright: "He entered a poetry contest because he didn't want to study for his college entrance exams and went on to become one of Japan's best-known contemporary poets." When Al Mahmud of Bangladesh describes his early life with poetry—"Poetry was . . . carefully collected bird's eggs/fragrant grass, the runaway calf of a sad-looking young farm wife,/neat letters on secret writing pads in blue envelopes."—he gives us a world we can touch and smell and share. When Benilda Santos of the Philippines describes the elaborate, loving way her little son said goodbye to her when he was in kindergarten and she left him at school, and the way he says goodbye to her now, years later—"his standard reply's/ a tight smile/an eyebrow's twitch' or sometimes/the slightest of nods./Nothing remains of the old goodbyes . . ." —I cry every time because I am a mother now, and because I was also a daughter saying goodbye in both ways, and because human beings need to be reminded of themselves simply to see who we all are and how we fit together.

I am happy to say that the collection *This Same Sky* was picked by the American Library Association as a Notable Book, received numerous "Editor's Choice" awards, the Jane Addams Award for Social Justice, and was called one of the Best Books of the Year for teenagers by the New York Public Libraries. It went into a third printing within one year of publication. And I am still getting letters from students and teachers in small towns and big cities, saying "Thanks for making my family larger." This all makes me happy because it suggests a real appetite for poetry still thriving in our rushed, modern souls. It suggests the windows of the house are still open. One by one, in quiet corners, we will turn on a small light, read a poem, and feel our own soft wings spreading out into the dark. They will carry us. We have so many places to go.

Naomi Shihab Nye

SOURCE: "Singing the Long Song: Arab Culture in Books for Young Readers," in *The New Advocate,* Vol. 12, No. 2, Spring, 1999, pp. 119-26.

What is our responsibility to our ethnic and cultural communities? "Everybody's Ethnic" is the title of a wonderful multicultural alphabet series for classroom and library walls. Certainly, that's true. We celebrate one another's variations by learning more, tasting more, listening to each other's music. We widen our worlds. How many ways can reading and writing help us on this journey?

I was born Arab-American in the geographical center of the United States, my father a Palestinian immigrant from Jerusalem. His family became refugees during the 1948 creation of the state of Israel. When he came to this country in 1951 to continue his university studies, he met my mother, who had grown up in St. Louis. About three months later they were married. I was born before their first-year anniversary. People have asked if I felt like an Arab-American as a child, and I say, "No, I just felt like a *kid.*" It is true I was very aware of my father's interesting accent, his intriguing recipes, his mysterious family far away . . . and I was very proud of him, too. Living first in St. Louis, then back in Jerusalem, we moved to Texas as a family in the late sixties. I now live in a center-city neighborhood in San Antonio with Mexican-American neighbors on both sides. The mining of heritage has turned out to be an essential element of much of my writing—something I could never have predicted early on. I mean, I was in college before I realized it might be possible to write about my own cousins!

Recently I received a letter from the Arab Arts Council inviting me to send work to *Jusoor,* the Arab American Journal of Cultural Exchange. "You will agree with me," wrote poet Khaled Mattawa, founder and executive director of the Council, and guest editor of an upcoming issue, "that we, as minority writers from a demonized community, have of necessity tended to address communal concerns more than individual ones. . . . What adjustments are we making, in our self-image and our understanding of our Americanness, now that our Arabness has a more visible presence?"

I thought of his words for days, particularly the haunting term "demonized." Having long been described as "the exaggerator of my family," there are, nevertheless, painful things I prefer to minimize. I might have said, "We are an ethnic community that is not exactly top-of-the-pops among those who don't know it." Many people are quite aware that Arabs are frequently portrayed negatively in the U.S. media and in movies. . . . Still, there is often a linguistic inequity in media stories about the Middle East. I have written numerous letters to editors to remind them that, if an Arab who engages in a violent act is a "terrorist," so is a Jew, or any other person. Yet many times that word seems to be reserved strictly for Arabs.

Jews frequently claim that Arabs are anti-Semites. I laughed out loud when a review in a Jewish paper called my book *Sitti's Secrets* anti-Semitic, simply because it respected the details of Arab life. Jews were not mentioned once in the book. Such reviewers would do well to remember that Arabs are Semites, too. . . .

I receive letters from people I never met, asking, "Was it harder to get your work published because you are Arab-American?" I don't think so. "Are you offended to be called a Palestinian-American?" Not at all. I now call myself that. I *am* that. Sensitive since childhood to certain word choices—"black," for example, being used to indicate negatives, as in black mood, black heart, Black Monday, etc.—I have thought often about the relationship of language to, essentially, everything and the ways that "labels" may both identify and connect us.

For me, the word "different" always felt like a compliment, not an insult. Within the savory atmosphere of San Antonio, ethnicity these days feels more like a calling-card than a burden. I realize it was not always this way. Anglos are a minority population here. It is easy to enjoy being what I call a "minority minority" as well. Yet a sorrow abides about misperception of anyone else's cultures, a disgust over ethnic or racial stereotyping of any kind, anywhere, and a wish to help balance, in any way one can, the images that are conveyed.

The ongoing stance of victimization is simply not very appealing for very long, since complaint is such a thin drone. We must move beyond it, keeping our radars keenly tuned, not only to the victimization of our own groups, but to attitudes that marginalize any kind of "other." Ethnocentricity, also, will not get us very far. How may we *live* in a way which will counteract injustices and inequities that continue to exist? How may we help extend one another's perceptions?

Writing for children is certainly one important way. Theirs are the opinions not only of tomorrow, but of today: crucial sensibilities, vigorously alert. I continue to wish politicians, in the Middle East especially, but these days, just about everywhere, would turn to children more often for wisdom. I cannot believe children are prejudiced in any instinctive ways when they are born. They learn or don't learn prejudice from their models. It is doubtful that children who grow up with a sense of general compassion for others—other ethnicities, traditions, socio-economic backgrounds, and religions—will suddenly close in or shrink up to become narrow-minded adults. Hopefully their hearts will keep widening.

We noted, as our son began kindergarten in Hawaii as one of only two non-Asians in his class, that never once did he refer to anyone's ethnicity, except, perhaps, as related to food. "Teddy brought some great Japanese candy for the party." More often classmates were described simply as "Billy, who loves to draw buses." To this day I have never yet heard the same son, now twelve, refer to anyone by race or ethnic background, even in a neutral way. He dislikes such designations, leaving that categorizing technique to grown-ups, who, try as they might to avoid it, often lapse into easy identifiers: the black woman, the Latino guy. Why not expand children's hearts, as we continue to work on our own, when they are most supple for the learning?

"I had no idea how large my family was," a poet wrote

me, after her poem was included in my first international anthology, *This Same Sky.* This can be one of the deepest ongoing hopes of books—to bring us into closer, more caring contact with one another. How better may we discover empathy beyond our own backyards and blocks? A good way to engage students with international poetry is through the universality of theme ("Who likes to run? Here's a poem about running!" only mentioning afterwards that it was written in Poland vs. a geographically-good-for-you approach: *It would be good if we read something by someone in Poland.*) Intriguing poems and books do this automatically. Very happily, the numbers of books that help us to engage with our "larger family" have been blossoming in recent years—a fact to be celebrated together. Every time I go to the library I am struck by the abundance available to us now—biographies of Arafat and Sadat, Ghandi and Ralph Nader and Sacajawea—holding their own amongst the best ten slam dunkers in basketball history and the tales about Thomas Edison and Henry Ford.

Two books by other people I would particularly like to mention are the very wonderful *Sitti and the Cats, A Tale of Friendship,* written by Sally Bahous, and illustrated by Nancy Malick (1993) and *Children of Israel, Children of Palestine: Our Own True Stories,* edited by Laurel Holliday (1998). This second book, a collection of remarkably moving, well-written essays about childhood, is part of the "Children of Conflict" series, one of those books I would like to give to every library I walk into, if they don't already have it.

Oddly, I met Sally Bahous, born in Tabgha, Palestine, in Dahlonega, Georgia, the town where the infamous and tragic "Trail of Tears" began. The intricate sorrow of *other* displaced people still lingered in that fragrant mountain air, reminding us how long the echoes of oppression and occupation can be. Visiting with Sally, talking about her childhood and life journey, and telling my father's similar story of loss and exile, was a touchingly congruous counterpoint for my visit to the museum of Native American history there.

At that time, my book *Sitti's Secrets* (1994) and Sally's *Sitti and the Cats: A Tale of Friendship* were both forthcoming. We cheered the arrival of two Sittis, "grandmother," in Arabic, in close succession on children's bookshelves in the USA. My son fell in love with Sally's book the minute it entered our house. We have read it together again and again over the years till now, never tiring of the talking cat in the lavender dress or the wonderful ageless story of generosity, fussiness, and cheer. Based on a folk story of Palestine, my father remembers being told a less delicious version of the tale almost seventy years ago.

One of Sally's gifts to us in this book is her use of interesting little "boxes of information" as inserts that describe even more about the culture and life of old Palestine. In *Sitti's Secrets,* I included daily details about domestic activities in a village setting, favorite Arabic foods, and so on. . . . I was gratified to receive letters from children who were obviously of other cultures—Chinese-American from California, for example—saying, "My grandmother is just like yours." Even children in Texas who had grandmothers in New Hampshire said they related to the theme of "distances between loved ones" as well as getting together to learn "how that person does all their little things they do." Despite different clothes, different languages, different daily habits, the girl in my book and her grandmother feel an intimate bond. Never once did a child write to me, "Sorry, my grandma doesn't look anything like yours," even when the letters were obviously class assignments. . . .

Children of Israel, Children of Palestine: Our Own True Stories draws its indelible power from the simple fact that these are real voices of real people, born (in the cases of the Palestinians) or raised (as many of the emigrating Israelis were) in the hotly disputed Palestine/Israel lands. Even the biographical author notes at the top of each section are eerily gripping, giving their own insight—how many of the Palestinian voices have been forced *out* of their homes as the Israeli voices were moving *in.*

The book is far more interesting than the ongoing tedious debate about land percentages: it travels behind stark headlines, sharing intimate family stories, fears, hopes, animated conversations. There's no way young readers who explore this book will be able to forget that the Arab/Israeli anguish is doublesided. They will have a deeper picture. It will be harder for them to jump to conclusions and easier to comprehend the attachments of both peoples to this stony, holy terrain, as well as the long desperation of the conflict. They will feel the story-behind-the-story that leads to so many of the tragic news accounts reported in newspapers. They will never be able to say, as the stunningly deluded Golda Meir, past prime minister of Israel, announced, "There *are* no Palestinians." Also, they could never say what a teacher once proclaimed at-large in an American teacher's lounge, after pitching a newspaper down onto a couch. "Oh, well—Arabs never had any brains anyway." Sitting at a nearby table reading students' poems, I felt as though I had been unexpectedly electrocuted.

The poet Morton Marcus in California wrote me a marvelous letter recently in which he said, "I've just returned from Croatia, that devastated country where the Serbs really did it to the poor Croatian farmers, my truly wonderful in-laws. But every moment I was there I was aware that the Croats had done it to the Serbs, gypsies, and Jews several decades before, and the Jews did it to the Palestinians afterwards, and the gypsies are doing it now to everyone, and everyone is doing it to everyone else. . . . What we [writers] do [is] sing the songs of our ancestors, the dispossessed, or, rather, they sing through us, and we let them, even though we know all the while that they'll do it to others when they get the chance. It will be then that the songs will be ours as much as they ever will be, and we'll keep singing them, knowing that they're now reminders to everyone that they were once the sufferers and should remember and should open their fists and extend their palms."

These books are palms extended.

A need to hear one another's voices and see one another's visions encouraged me to edit *The Space Between Our Footsteps: Poems and Paintings from the Middle East* (1998). Also, I was urged on by Houston librarians who said their high school libraries contained almost zero "cultural" material relating to the Middle East, and they had many Arab-American students attending their schools.

In my anthology, the works of more than a hundred poets and artists from the Middle East sit side-by-side on elegant pages, thanks to editors who assured the pages would be generous and uncrowded. Reviews of this book have commented on its engaging appearance, as well as engaging content. I quote from my introduction: "If you are going to the Middle East, people around you often raise their eyebrows. It is quite possible that the Middle East is one of the most negatively stereotyped places on earth. How did this happen to a place which has been the center of so much dramatic cultural and religious history? Unless American adults and teenagers have lived or traveled in the region themselves, many know only what they hear in the news or see in flamboyant movies . . . Of course, the violent or unhappy news stories are usually the ones that get transmitted. But what a terrible fragment they are of the fuller story, which is as rich and interesting as life anywhere else. . . . "

The book includes poems about childhood, families, breakfast tables, rivers, trees, exile, homelands, journeys, romance, and memory, among other topics. No reader should feel "foreign" to these subjects. Reviews from teachers, students, and journals have been warm and enthusiastic, frequently mentioning "getting to know and appreciate a world which many of us only know through troubled news reports."

Only a couple of reviewers have telephoned to inquire about my inclusion of Israeli authors and artists among the majority of Arabs from many countries—this was, of course, a deliberate inclusion. Troubled as I am by enormous inequities still ongoing in Palestine/Israel, the last thing I want to do in my life is perpetuate separations between peoples. Anyone who still imagines we can pretend the "others," whoever they might be to us, don't exist, is living in a lonesome fantasy.

I also hoped to offer more of the story-behind-the-story when I wrote the novel for young readers, *Habibi* (1997). An Arab-American girl, Liyana, moves from St. Louis to Jerusalem with her Palestinian father, American mother, and brother, Rafik. An observant, sensitive girl, she keeps a journal; each chapter begins with a line from her own notebook. Moving is hard, initiation into her father's culture is clumsy, being 14-turning-15 has its own rough edges. Then she finds a friend, a Jewish boy whom she thinks is an Arab at first. Again, one of my major concerns in this book was conveying that stories do, must, and always will have even MORE than two sides, in a way that was pleasurable and occasionally funny to experience, as opposed to merely didactic.

Readers' responses to *Habibi* have been kinder than I ever could have hoped. Young readers demanding a sequel! They want to know "what happens next?" What does this say to me? People are interested. Many people *want* to enter "other worlds." Borders are not barriers, but simple geographical distinctions. Many of us *desire* to cross them. It is a human instinct to *go there and know*. Writers have the opportunity to invite wary travelers across, and to whet the appetites of younger readers, assuring them that *more worlds may be yours than just the one you were born into*.

Surely, among adults, it is often a challenge for the voices of "regular people" to be heard above the blare of those in the spotlights. The Israeli poet Yehuda Amichai once said to me, "If only the moderates could speak more loudly!" He is right. If children are reminded there are moms and kids and books and bread and schoolrooms and bicycles and hopes and grandma's hands behind every tyrannical ruler in every distant locale, they will be less inclined to imagine "Enemies!" when they think of that place. To counteract negative images conveyed by blazing headlines, writers must steadily transmit simple stories closer to heart and more common to everyday life. Then we will be doing our job.

TITLE COMMENTARY

📖 ***THIS SAME SKY: A COLLECTION OF POEMS FROM AROUND THE WORLD*** **(edited and compiled by Nye, 1992)**

Hazel Rochman

SOURCE: A review of *This Same Sky: A Collection of Poems from around the World,* in *Booklist,* Vol. 89, No. 4, October 15, 1992, p. 425.

This is an extraordinary anthology, not only in its global range—129 contemporary poets from 68 countries, their work translated from many languages—but also in the quality of the selections and the immediacy of their appeal. From Palestine, Argentina, Latvia, Israel, and Lebanon to India, New Zealand, and El Salvador, diverse voices connect us all. Many poets, especially those from eastern Europe and the Middle East, have barely appeared in YA books before. Editor Nye, a fine writer herself who visits schools across the country to talk about poetry, shows us what we've missed. Most of the poems are upbeat (Who says comedy doesn't travel?) and loosely organized into sections that include families, animals, and the natural world; there are also poems about suffering, several about prison. Browsers will dip into this, and teachers will find the index by country useful for curriculum units. No illustrations distract from the verbal imagery; there's just a bright wraparound cover and endpapers made up of the signatures and stamps of the poets who wrote to Nye and mailed her their work. The brief notes on each contributor include some terse personal comments and stories that are nearly as stirring as the poetry. Nye includes a suggested list of anthologies, like those by Janeczco, that focus on the U.S. The translations are casual, even colloquial, getting away from the idea of poetry as something special and exotic. As the Estonian poet Kaplinski says, "Everything that is is very ordinary / or, rather, neither ordinary nor strange." Yes, says Nye, something must be lost in translation— but look at what's gained.

Lauralyn Persson

SOURCE: A review of *This Same Sky: A Collection of Poems from around the World,* in *School Library Journal,* Vol. 38, No. 12, December, 1992, pp. 139-40.

In the preface, Nye says, " . . . what lovely, larger life becomes ours when we listen to one another?" This question states the purpose of this anthology that emphasizes selections from the Middle East, Asia, Africa, India, and South and Central America. They are indexed by country as well as by poet. This is a lengthy collection, close to 200 pages long, brimming with much lovely material. The poems are about many things: the nature of poetry (and language itself), the beauty of the natural world, how feelings about childhood are colored by memory, the love of parent for a child (and vice versa). Some are more political in subject matter. Determining the audience is problematic. The preface states that the poems have been especially chosen for young people, but many of them will be of marginal interest to them, and several require an adult perspective to be appreciated. The book may be useful, but it will have to be introduced by a sensitive adult (preferably a very talented teacher who can lead students to draw connections that may seem unlikely at first). For senior high and public libraries where multicultural material is a priority.

Mary M. Burns

SOURCE: A review of *This Same Sky: A Collection of Poems from around the World,* in *The Horn Book Magazine,* Vol. LXIX, No. 2, March, 1993, p. 215.

One hundred twenty-nine poets from sixty-eight countries are represented in this substantial anthology of transglobal visions. The anthologist, herself a poet, has provided a lyrical arrangement for these international treasures in six major groupings: "Words and Silences: 'Sawdust from under the Saw'"; "Dreams and Dreamers: 'Eyes the Color of Sky'"; "Families: 'The First Tying'"; "This Earth and Sky in Which We Live: 'Water That Used to Be a Cloud'"; "Losses: 'Kissed Trees'";

and "Human Mysteries: 'White Bracelets.'" The subheadings are drawn directly from a poem within each section which reflects the thematic threads woven into that unit. Thus, "sawdust coming from under the saw" is Estonian poet Jaan Kaplinski's metaphor for describing poetry as ordinary rather than exotic. This interpretation is reflected in Al Mahumud's comments on his childhood in Bangladesh, where "poetry was the memory of adolescence." It is re-echoed in Tunisian poet Muhammad al-Ghuzzi's observation that "the whole world is a sky-blue butterfly / And words are the nets to capture it." Each of the selections in this introductory section celebrates the power of language to effect change, to transform. As Greek poet Yannis Ritsos proclaims: "Every word is a doorway / to a meeting, one often canceled, / and that's when a word is true: / when it insists on the meeting." His words anticipate the remarkable experience afforded those who read this book, for it speaks with myriad voices of feelings and events which are universal yet distinctly individual. For each poem, the name of the translator is provided. That every effort has been made to reflect the cadence of the original may be assumed from the lilting yet poignant lines of Irish poet Máire Mhac an tSaoi's "The First Shoe," a haunting evocation of a mother's regret that her son must grow up: "[A] manbaby you are in your walk and your bearing, / the height of my knee, and so soon to leave me!" As Naomi Shihab Nye so succinctly observes in her introduction, "Whenever someone suggests 'how much is lost in translation!' I want to say, 'Perhaps—but how much is gained!'" And how right she is. This collection rightfully inhabits what Paul Hazard called "the world republic of childhood"—where the frontiers are open to all who would pass through. Notes on the contributors, a map, suggestions for further reading, an index to countries, and an index to poets are appended, adding additional luster to a book which should prove invaluable for intercultural education as well as for pure pleasure.

Jim Morgan

SOURCE: A review of *This Same Sky: A Collection of Poems from around the World,* in *Voice of Youth Advocates,* Vol. 16, No. 1, April, 1993, p. 59.

This is an excellent selection of poetry from sixty-eight countries, including something from nearly every corner of the globe (excluding the United States). The poems are loosely organized into six thematic units: "Words and Silences," "Dreams and Dreamers," "Families," "The Earth and Sky in Which We Live," "Losses" and "Human Mysteries." Authors are primarily of the twentieth century, with an occasional poem by an earlier writer as well as a few traditional folk poems to contribute to the diversity. Included are such great (but fairly unknown in the West) poets as Yannis Ritsos (Greece), celebrated author of more than 115 books of poetry and other writings; Nirendranath Chakravarti (India), author of more than 20 volumes of poetry; and Amanda Aizpuriete (Latvia), poet, mother, and translator of Emily Dickinson.

The quality of the poetry ranges from average to exemplary, with almost no didacticism and only occasional lapses into sentimentality. The most striking aspect of this collection, and the book's greatest potential appeal to adolescents, is the sense of real human life behind the words; these poets are people in distant lands and cultures who have experienced real human thoughts and emotions. The book as a whole reflects the universality of human concerns across cultures. References to historical events abound, such as the Vietnamese poet Lan Nguyen's *My Life Story,* which recalls the pain of the Vietnam war: "What shall I tell about my life?/a life of changes/a life of losing/remembering/eighteen years ago/ a little child was born/surrounded by the love of family/ so warm and tender/surrounded by mountains and rivers/ so free and beautiful/But life was not easy/the dearest father passed away/and left a big scar in the child's head/She grew up with something missing in her/She had seen the people born and dying/born from the war/dying from guns and bombs . . . The only thing she can do/ is keep hoping/one day her dream will come true/God cannot be mean to her forever." To Western adolescents, who know about other cultures almost exclusively through television, these poems offer a deeper and more meaningful perspective on the lives of people from around the globe.

Most adolescents should find the book reasonably accessible; words that are not easily translatable into English are explained in short notes below some of the poems. Included are helpful indices of poets and countries, the names of the translators and an excellent introduction which briefly discusses the richness and variety of world poetry. This would definitely be a strong multicultural contribution to any poetry collection.

📖 *SITTI'S SECRETS* (1994)

Hazel Rochman

SOURCE: A review of *Sitti's Secrets,* in *Booklist,* Vol. 90, No. 14, March 15, 1994, p. 1374.

Sitti means *grandmother* in Arabic, and in this lyrical picture book an American child misses her grandmother who lives in a Palestinian village "on the other side of the earth." The child remembers when she visited Sitti. They didn't speak the same language: at first they talked through her father, who spoke both English and Arabic, and then they invented their own language with signs and hums and claps. She remembers the house and the countryside, the culture and the clothes, and the intimacy of brushing Sitti's hair. She also remembers the painful leave-taking ("Even my father kept blowing his nose and walking outside"), and back in the U.S., she writes a letter to the President: "If the people of the United States could meet Sitti, they'd like her, for sure." Carpenter's paintings show the physical bond between child and grandmother when they're close and their imaginary connection when they're far away from each other. Like the human embrace, the pictures [by Nancy Carpenter] flow

with soft curving lines of clothes and hills, birds and sky, all part of the circle of the rolling earth. There are too few books like this one about Arabs and Arab Americans as people. Nye edited the powerful global poetry collection for older readers, *This Same Sky* (1992); that title applies here, too, showing that "people are far apart, but connected." Every child who longs for a distant grandparent will recognize the feeling.

Maeve Visser Knoth

SOURCE: A review of *Sitti's Secrets,* in *The Horn Book Magazine,* Vol. LXX, No. 3, May-June, 1994, pp. 317-18.

Mona lives halfway around the world from her grandmother, her *sitti.* "Between us are many miles of land and water. Between us are fish and cities and buses and fields," recounts Mona as she remembers her trip to the Palestinian village where her grandmother lives. Her story takes the reader back with Mona to witness a relationship unfold between a grandmother and grandchild who do not speak the same language. At first, they speak through Mona's father, but soon they begin to understand each other and invent their own language. Sitti takes Mona to a field where they watch men pick lentils and shows Mona how to bake the flat bread that she eats for breakfast with yogurt and cucumbers. Mona comes to love her grandmother as she learns about the daily life of one elderly Palestinian Arab woman. When she returns home, Mona writes a letter to the president of the United States asking that he understand that the people he speaks about on the news are human beings, like her Sitti, with secrets, dreams, and the need for peace. The author writes a compassionate story in poetic, rich language. The simple sentences are dotted with imagery that is often picked up in the illustrations. Mona tells us that her grandmother's voice "danced as high as the whistles of birds"—and the Arabic letters hovering near Sitti's mouth turn gradually to birds as they glide across the page, while birds adorn Sitti's dress and a bird tattoo can be glimpsed on Sitti's hand. The emotional story is rich in images of life in the Middle East but is most importantly about the love of a family separated by space but united in spirit.

Luann Toth

SOURCE: A review of *Sitti's Secrets* in *School Library Journal,* Vol. 40, No. 6, June, 1994, p. 112.

When Mona travels from her home in the U. S. to visit her grandmother's small Palestinian village on the West Bank, she must rely on her father to translate at first, but soon she and Sitti are communicating perfectly. With verve and a childlike sense of wonder, Mona relates some of the sights, sounds, and tastes she is introduced to as well as "the secrets" she learns from spending time in the wise, elderly woman's company. Upon her return home, Mona writes to the president describing the woman and expressing her concerns about the situation in her homeland. "I vote for peace. My grandmother votes with me," says Mona. The simple, poetic text is accompanied by exquisitely rendered mixed-medium paintings. They are suffused with the light and colors of the desert, and incorporate subtle and evocative collage touches. A story about connections that serves as a thoughtful, loving affirmation of the bonds that transcend language barriers, time zones, and national borders.

Marcus Crouch

SOURCE: A review of *Sitti's Secrets,* in *The Junior Bookshelf,* Vol. 59, No. 2, April, 1995, pp. 65-6.

Sitti's Secrets is . . . for, or about, ethnic minorities. . . . Mona, in her American home, thinks about her visit to her grandmother 'Sitti' in the Middle East, the unfamiliar activities, especially the love that she gave and was given. Sensitively and quietly written, and with illustrations by Nancy Carpenter which reveal landscape and character with equal success, the book might well have slipped into sentimentality. It does not. This is a book that builds bridges.

 BENITO'S DREAM BOTTLE (1995)

Publishers Weekly

SOURCE: A review of *Benito's Dream Bottle,* in *Publishers Weekly,* Vol. 242, No. 17, April 24, 1995, p. 71.

When his grandmother confides that she hasn't dreamed in a long time, a concerned Benito proceeds to ask "everyone he knew" where dreams come from. The responses are varied and fanciful, but Benito has his own solution: "dreams really came from the Dream Bottle," which is located between the chest and the stomach and pours dreams into the head when a person lies down. Determined to fill up his grandmother's bottle, Benito helps her think hard about "stoplights blinking and trees shivering in the wind and telephone answering machines full of voices. . . ." Nye then presents a tiresome mishmash of dialogue and snippets from Benito's own dreams and those of family members, including—eventually—his grandmother, who "dreamed she had a little grandson who took her by the hand and led her outside. He showed her how to cook leaves inside a broken toaster oven. . . ." More noteworthy are newcomer Yu Cha Pak's strategically patterned, vividly hued watercolors, which creatively interpret the story's plot as well as the dream sequences.

Hazel Rochman

SOURCE: A review of *Benito's Dream Bottle,* in *Booklist,* Vol. 91, No. 17, May 1, 1995, p. 1580.

What are dreams, and where do they come from? A small boy asks everyone in his family and community as he tries to help his grandmother recapture her dreams. Nye is a fine poet, and the words here have a nice rhythm and a joy in the domestic and the imaginary. The bright, dancing folk-style illustrations express the leap from the ordinary to the surreal. But however much kids will enjoy the idea of everyday things becoming magical, the lists of images never develop. Nye's moving picture book *Sitti's Secrets* (1994) is also about a child and her grandmother, but this time there's no story and most kids will tire of the reverie.

Judy Constantinides

SOURCE: A review of *Benito's Dream Bottle,* in *School Library Journal,* Vol. 41, No. 6, June, 1995, p. 94.

When Benito discovers that his grandmother no longer dreams, he sets out to fill her "dream bottle" again. Believing that all people have a bottle located between their stomachs and chests that pours dreams out when they lie down, he helps his grandmother gather sights and sounds and experiences to add to hers, and she finally "gets full again." This is an inventive book, both in text and illustrations. Soft, watercolor pictures create a lovely feeling of weightlessness as people, fairies, flora, and fauna float dreamily through the air. The child's close relationship with his family, especially his warm concern for his grandmother, irradiate the story. The text has a lyrical quality that serves its subject well and underlines the importance of dreams and imagination. A fine choice.

 THE TREE IS OLDER THAN YOU ARE: POEMS AND STORIES FROM MEXICO (edited and compiled by Nye, 1995)

Hazel Rochman

SOURCE: A review of *The Tree is Older Than You Are: Poems and Stories from Mexico,* in *Booklist,* Vol. 92, No. 2, September 15, 1995, p. 151.

Nye, who edited the fine YA world anthology *This Same Sky* (1992), has once again gathered literature in translation from a host of voices seldom heard in English. These Mexican poems and traditional stories in the original Spanish appear side by side with excellent English translations. The spacious, large-size volume includes magnificent, richly colored paintings by contemporary Mexican artists. The art is never a literal interpretation of the words; it expresses the magic realism of many of the verbal images. There's an elusive quality to the writing, whether it's by the famous (such as Octavio Paz) or by the relatively unknown. The focus is on the universals of nature and rural life rather than on urban or popular culture. This is dreamy, lyrical writing with sudden leaps from the real to the magical. Some of the poetry isn't easy, but browsers in this lovely volume will find pieces to startle them out of the mundane, as when

Erika Ramirez Diez writes: "I will never be able to know the sea / Every time it arrives / it leaves." Nye includes notes on the poets, painters, and translators and on the folklore.

📖 *I FEEL A LITTLE JUMPY AROUND YOU: A BOOK OF HER POEMS AND HIS POEMS COLLECTED IN PAIRS* **(edited by Nye, with Paul B. Janeczko, 1996)**

Hazel Rochman

SOURCE: A review of *I Feel a Little Jumpy around You: A Book of Her Poems and His Poems Collected in Pairs,* in *Booklist,* Vol. 92, No. 15, April 1, 1996, p. 1351.

An anthology needs a unifying theme, and this collection focuses on the experience of gender—how men and women see things differently and the same. Two fine YA anthologists have collaborated in gathering nearly 200 rich, subtle poems about "the multitudes of hes and shes" among children, parents, siblings, friends, lovers, spouses, outsiders. The politics is great fun as a framework. Janeczko and Nye each contribute a lively introduction in which they open up issues of gender and of anthology making. The brief excerpts from their faxes to each other are argumentative, irritable, profound, and teasing ("Is this a boy thing?" Nye asks him). Notes at the back by the contributing poets are earnest, comic, sometimes lyrical; one famous poet is furious at being asked to think about gender in relation to his poetry. The pairing arrangement seems a bit tight: always a poem by a man and a poem by a woman set off together. Instead of enjoying each poem for itself, you feel pushed to read the companion piece and work out why they're together. (Is my problem a "girl" thing?) Best of all, of course, are the individual poems; you dip into this great collection anywhere and discover something astonishing to read, one poem at a time.

Deborah Stevenson

SOURCE: A review of *I Feel a Little Jumpy around You: A Book of Her Poems and His Poems Collected in Pairs,* in *Bulletin of the Center for Children's Books,* Vol. 49, No. 9, May, 1996, pp. 311-12.

Nye and Janeczko have each independently produced worthy poetry anthologies; here they join forces for a collection with a twist. The poems come in pairs, the male-authored entry always leading and the female-authored one always getting the last word. The coupled poems sometimes share a subject, sometimes a setting, sometimes a theme or an image (Agha Shahid Ali's "Snowman" and Robin Boody Galguera's "Alloy" both address questions of culture, E. Ethelbert Miller's "Dressed Up" and Naomi Stroud Simmons' "With Reservation" offer quirky takes on fancy dress) that directs readers to a specific way into each poem. The poems

themselves, almost all contemporary free verse and from poets ranging from famous (Rita Dove, W. S. Merwin) to less known, are of a high standard. Though the gender counterpoint really plays little part in the juxtaposition, the pairings are piquant and provide a manageable way to start talking about a very large collection of poetry. An engaging marginal dialogue, taken from Nye's and Janeczko's collaborative fax correspondence, appears alongside the appendix and permits a revealing peek behind the scenes. Highly readable notes from contributors are included, as is an index of poems and a gender-segregated index of poets.

Anthony Manna

SOURCE: A review of *I Feel a Little Jumpy around You: A Book of Her Poems and His Poems Collected in Pairs,* in *Voice of Youth Advocates,* Vol. 19, No. 3, August, 1996, p. 178.

The 194 poems in this fascinating anthology go a long way in revealing the extraordinary range of perspectives and sensibilities that females and males bring to bear on whatever piece of human experience they happen to be pondering at the moment. By arranging these mostly free verse poems into 97 provocative he/she pairs wherein a male and female fathom the same or a thematically related phenomenon, Nye and Janeczko reveal the role gender plays in the ways this culturally diverse community of contemporary poets makes sense of the world. Included among the phenomena these poets reach into with characteristically spare, sharp-edged wonder are the forces that shape one's identity, the power of memory, family ties, friendship, estrangement, loss, death, and, of course, the complex ways in which men and women perceive each other. What ultimately makes this gathering so intriguing, thanks to the careful lay out, is the degree to which the voices blend and gender boundaries give way to quests, quirks, and needs which signal the ties that bind us. Augmenting the all-of-a-piece feel of the entire volume are amusing, often emotionally charged excerpts from the compilers' correspondence about the anthology, which illuminate both the selection process and their own sense of equity, and the contributors' responses to Nye's and Janeczko's query about gender. What an eye- and heart-opening experience!

Nancy Vasilakis

SOURCE: A review of *I Feel a Little Jumpy around You: A Book of Her Poems and His Poems Collected in Pairs,* in *The Horn Book Magazine,* Vol. LXXII, No. 6, November-December, 1996, p. 755.

This timely anthology provides visceral proof of how men and women perceive the world differently and what dreams and memories we hold in common. Nye and Janeczko have assembled almost one hundred pairs of poems that examine a variety of subjects from a male and a female perspective. The individual poems, of course, but the pairings as well, are frequently provocative. Sometimes the juxtapositions are obvious, but not always, and part of the fun of the book is delving into the poems deeply enough to discover some faint or unexpected clue to the male-female conundrum. These tenuous lines of communication are embodied in Harryette Mullen's "Jump City": "I feel a little jumpy around you, / Like when I think a house has / roaches, and I watch everything / out the corner of my eye to see / if it crawls away." It would be difficult to read this book alone; it needs sharing, discussion, and, no doubt, argument. Each editor has written an introduction, and the book includes their frequently humorous faxes, which give the rationale behind many of their selections. Also included are notes in which the contributors explain how gender plays a part in their poetry.

📖 *NEVER IN A HURRY: ESSAYS ON PEOPLE AND PLACES* (1996)

Hazel Rochman

SOURCE: A review of *Never in a Hurry: Essays on People and Places,* in *Booklist,* Vol. 92, No. 22, August, 1996, p. 1875.

Nye is a Palestinian American poet whose world anthologies, such as **This Same Sky** (1992), have brought a host of new voices to American readers. Her picture book **Sitti's Secrets** (1994), about an American child's visit to her grandmother on the West Bank, is clearly autobiographical, and several of the lyrical essays and memoirs in this stirring collection draw on her experience across borders. The power of her writing is in the personal particulars, loving and rueful, whether she's talking about cleaning house in San Antonio, where she lives with her husband and son, or about the fun of gossip, or about the anguish in her six long years of infertility. It's the absence of rhetoric that makes unforgettable the scene where she returns with her father (the refugee) to his childhood home in Jerusalem and finds a friendly, innocent New Yorker (the settler) moving in. They like each other.

Dottie Kraft

SOURCE: A review of *Never in a Hurry: Essays on People and Places,* in *School Library Journal,* Vol. 42, No. 11, November, 1996, p. 142.

This collection of essays is an excellent addition to any library. Nye is a Palestinian American, married to a Swedish American, and has lived much of her life in San Antonio, TX. The essays are autobiographical reflections of people and places she has encountered throughout her life. She and her parents lived in Jerusalem for a year until the Six-Day War caused them to flee back to the United States; Nye and her husband have returned to her ancestral country on several occasions. The essays are short, quiet reflections on a variety of subjects. The

author has the ability to perceive and describe her surroundings so skillfully that readers are drawn into these experiences and are enriched in the process. Such essays as "Favorite Cleaners, San Antonio" help readers step back, slow down, and contemplate the everyday role of the all too familiar in one's life. This collection is guaranteed to make YAs laugh, cry, reflect, or think about life from another point of view. Literature by and about the Arab experience in America is rare; to discover a well-written collection suitable for young adults is a joy.

📖 *LULLABY RAFT* (1997)

Publishers Weekly

SOURCE: A review of *Lullaby Raft,* in *Publishers Weekly,* Vol. 244, No. 25, June 23, 1997, p. 90.

This uneven picture book, essentially a bedtime poem, begins in a child's cozy room at night and ends with a child's dream journey on a moon rowboat. The text is based on a lullaby Nye sings in schools (the music appears on the book's final page). Although filled with lovely phrases ("My lizard licks the darkness clean/In the leaves outside my room"), the text often ends abruptly on the page, perhaps to accommodate the musical line of the song. Words and art unite most effectively when focusing on the details, as in: "My mama sings me a lullaby all my own/And I dream of her hands/And the years I'll live alone." [Vivienne] Flesher accompanies these lines with a close-up of the child's face held gently in her mother's hands, set against a deep velvet-red curtain of color rendered in pastels. An ambitious sense of composition creates emotional depth. The artist's work exudes a sense of stillness and reverie, of gently ebbing consciousness. Things get a bit confusing, however, as the book makes a textual and visual transition from the concrete to the metaphysical. As the book moves toward its conclusion, Nye turns from the child's thoughts to an adult's point of view, and the child, who appears to be a toddler in the opening spread, now looks 10 years old. Even with its moments of verbal and pictorial harmony, this lullaby ultimately ends on a dissonant note.

Alicia Eames

SOURCE: A review of *Lullaby Raft,* in *School Library Journal,* Vol. 43, No. 9, September, 1997, p. 189.

In this original lullaby, Mama sings of animals who settle down for the night as her red-haired child helps them along. Chicken hums on the windowsill, bunny snuggles in a sock drawer, turtle withdraws into its shell, and lizard seeks comfort on the "sleepy ground." Each finds the perfect note to hold all night long. While the language and images are not always completely accessible to young listeners, this poem/song has a satisfying rhythm and soothing tone; it is best appreciated when read or sung aloud. Simple music is provided. Soft but vividly hued chalk pastels provide the perfect medium for the dreamy illustrations. One caveat—the child's face is portrayed with a distracting inconsistency. Is she a sleepy toddler, a porcelain doll, a boyish youngster, or a young adult? It's just not clear. Also, the brilliant colors used to close the song are surprisingly stimulating, not the typical finish for a bedtime story.

Deborah Stevenson

SOURCE: A review of *Lullaby Raft,* in *Bulletin of the Center for Children's Books,* Vol. 51, No. 2, October, 1997, pp. 64-5.

Noted poet Nye here translates into picture-book form the lyrics to a song she performs in schools. In seven verses, the young narrator describes how her mama sings her to sleep, how her chicken settles down, her turtle folds up, the moon floats away, the bunny curls up, the lizard quiets down, and the speaker plans a "lullaby raft" to get to the other side of night. There's some lovely imagery here, and the softening nighttime mood is evocatively conveyed. The concepts get awfully ethereal for the age group, however, and the text's gentle patterning isn't sufficient to support the winding narrative. The illustrations, glowing pastel on dark paper, have a dreamy flow reminiscent of Judy Pedersen, but the soft texturing and full-bleed color give them a distinctive mood. Young listeners fond of gentle fancy may enjoy floating along to sleep with the story. The final page includes musical notation (complete with chording) and lyrics for all verses.

Stephanie Zvirin

SOURCE: A review of *Lullaby Raft,* in *Booklist,* Vol. 94, No. 5, November 1, 1997, p. 483.

Cutout stars on the jacket, which let the soft velvety colors of the book underneath peek through, are but a few of the lovely touches that make this sleepy-time book special. Nye's soothing words, actually a song she wrote (musical arrangement appears on the last page), become a mother's cooing as she lulls her child into a sleepy fantasy world. Encircled by the warmth of the lullaby, the child and his animal pets settle for the night. Reminiscent of Chagall's work at times, Flesher's naive-style pictures are extremely appealing. Her luminous, saturated pastels play cleverly with scale and shape as they sweep little ones to a magical place, where the moon becomes a golden raft that floats the boy and the animals to a land of sweet, sweet dreams.

📖 *HABIBI* (1997)

Kate McClelland

SOURCE: A review of *Habibi,* in *School Library Journal,* Vol. 43, No. 9, September, 1997, pp. 223-24.

An important first novel from a distinguished anthologist and poet. When Liyana's doctor father, a native Palestinian, decides to move his contemporary Arab-American family back to Jerusalem from St. Louis, 14-year-old Liyana is unenthusiastic. Arriving in Jerusalem, the girl and her family are gathered in by their colorful, warm-hearted Palestinian relatives and immersed in a culture where only tourists wear shorts and there is a prohibition against boy/girl relationships. When Liyana falls in love with Omer, a Jewish boy, she challenges family, culture, and tradition, but her homesickness fades. Constantly lurking in the background of the novel is violence between Palestinian and Jew. It builds from minor bureaucratic annoyances and humiliations, to the surprisingly shocking destruction of grandmother's bathroom by Israeli soldiers, to a bomb set off in a Jewish marketplace by Palestinians. It exacts a reprisal in which Liyana's friend is shot and her father jailed. Nye introduces readers to unforgettable characters. The setting is both sensory and tangible: from the grandmother's village to a Bedouin camp. Above all, there is Jerusalem itself, where ancient tensions seep out of cracks and Liyana explores the streets practicing her Arabic vocabulary. Though the story begins at a leisurely pace, readers will be engaged by the characters, the romance, and the foreshadowed danger. Poetically imaged and leavened with humor, the story renders layered and complex history understandable through character and incident. *Habibi* succeeds in making the hope for peace compellingly personal and concrete . . . as long as individual citizens like Liyana's grandmother Sitti can say, "I never lost my peace inside."

Hazel Rochman

SOURCE: A review of *Habibi,* in *Booklist,* Vol. 94, No. 2, September 15, 1997, p. 224.

What is it like to be young in Palestine today? That is the focus of this stirring docunovel, which breaks new ground in YA fiction. Liyana Abboud, 14, moves with her family from St. Louis to Jerusalem. For her physician father, it is going home to where he was born and educated. To Liyana, her younger brother, and her American mother, it is a huge upheaval. At first Liyana misses the U.S., can't speak the languages, and feels uncertain at school, "tipped between" the cultures. She is awkward with her bossy grandmother ("Sitti") and overwhelmed by her huge extended family when she visits their village on the West Bank. The military occupation is always there and the simmering conflict between Jew and Arab. In one horrifying scene, Israeli soldiers tear into Sitti's house and smash her bathroom. In a climactic episode, after a Palestinian bomb has injured civilians, the Israelis shoot an innocent boy in the leg, and Liyana's father is held in prison overnight. Yet it doesn't have to be that way. Liyana meets and loves a Jewish boy, and together they join the Jews and Arabs trying to make peace.

Nye is an Arab American author and anthologist, and, as

in her fine essay collection, *Never in a Hurry* (1996), she writes from a unique perspective, as the American newcomer/observer and as the displaced Palestinian in occupied territory. The story is steeped in detail about the place and cultures: food, geography, history, shopping, schools, languages, religions, etc. Just when you think it is obtrusive to have essays and journal entries thrust into the story, you get caught up in the ideas and the direct simplicity with which Nye speaks. She does try to cover too much—no book can tell the whole story of the Middle East—but this is a story that makes us "look both ways."

Jennifer M. Brabander

SOURCE: A review of *Habibi*, in *The Horn Book Magazine*, Vol. LXXIII, No. 6, November-December, 1997, pp. 683-84.

When Liyana Abboud is fourteen, her father decides that the time is right to move the family from St. Louis to his native Jerusalem; before she knows it, Liyana is studying Arabic in school and baking bread in a giant outdoor oven with Sitti, her Arab grandmother. Inevitably, Arab-Israeli tensions enter into the story: Israeli soldiers ransack and destroy much of Sitti's house one day, and later, Liyana's doctor father is briefly arrested for trying to protect a young Palestinian boy shot by soldiers. Liyana's attraction to and eventual friendship with a boy whom she is shocked to discover is Jewish, not Arab, is believably rendered, as is the unexpectedly warm welcome he ultimately receives from Sitti. The message isn't preachy and remains almost secondary to the story of Liyana's search for her identity as she goes from feeling homesick to feeling very much at home. *Habibi*, or *darling*, is what Liyana's father calls her and her younger brother; it is a soothing, loving word, and Liyana gradually finds herself comfortable "living in the land of *Habibi*," where she is showered with love by her huge extended family. The leisurely progression of the narrative matches the slow and stately pace of daily life in this ancient land, and the text's poetic turns of phrase accurately reflect Liyana's passion for words and language.

Karen Leggett

SOURCE: "Where Rage Lives," in *The New York Times Book Review,* November 16, 1997, p. 50.

Adolescence magnifies the joys and anxieties of growing up even as it radically simplifies the complexities of the adult world. The poet and anthologist Naomi Shihab Nye is meticulously sensitive to this rainbow of emotion in her autobiographical novel, *Habibi.* Nye weaves threads of her own life into the story of Liyana Abboud, the daughter of a Palestinian father and an American mother. Raised in St. Louis, Liyana moves with her family to Jerusalem in the 1970s to live in her father's homeland. Fourteen years old and ready to start high school, she is troubled and fascinated by the notion of moving to

a place "where no one but your own family had any memory of you." Suddenly she is the immigrant, not her father.

The Abbouds move into a white stone house between Jerusalem, where her father, a physician, will practice, and Ramallah, where his relatives live. Liyana sees, as the epigram to one chapter notes, that Jerusalem "was a cake made of layers of time." An apolitical youngster, she learns from confounding experience how the city is continually fragmented by contemporary politics. Israeli soldiers, for instance, appear at her grandmother's house, looking for a grandson who has been living in Jordan. Not finding him, they arbitrarily destroy the old woman's bathroom. "That poor little bathroom," says Liyana's mother. "But why?" "There is no why," Liyana replies, surprising herself by quoting her father. When Liyana's father talks about living harmoniously, it all seems so straightforward—until he has to put his beliefs into practice. Incidents escalate around them. Her father is jailed and released. Meanwhile, of course, Liyana has made friends with a boy—a nice boy, a Jew who has never visited an Arab village—and wants to invite him to dinner.

"Didn't you say before you went in jail that it would be great if people never described each other as 'the Jew' or 'the Arab,'" Liyana asks her father indignantly, "didn't you just SAY?" Yes, but as she herself observes, "in Jerusalem, so much old anger floated around. . . . The air felt stacked with weeping and raging and praying to God by all the different names."

Nye is an award-winning poet, and the novel is filled with poetic images. The word *Habibi* means *darling.* The children, she says, "had 'Habibi, be careful, Habibi, I love you,' trailing them like a long silken scarf." Elsewhere, an "afternoon puffed up lightly, joyously, a delicate pastry, a sweetened shell of hours."

From kisses to politics, Liyana shares her secrets with her journal, including stories about her father as a boy in old Jerusalem, when Palestinians, Jews and Greeks all lived on the same street. In those days the children traded desserts after dinner, because everybody liked everyone else's dessert better than his own. She writes: "My father used to wish the politicians making big decisions would trade desserts. It might have helped." *Habibi* gives a reader all the sweet richness of a Mediterranean dessert, while leaving some of the historic complexities open to interpretation.

THE SPACE BETWEEN OUR FOOTSTEPS: POEMS AND PAINTINGS FROM THE MIDDLE EAST (edited by Nye, 1998)

Hazel Rochman

SOURCE: A review of *The Space between Our Footsteps: Poems and Paintings from the Middle East,* in *Booklist,* Vol. 94, No. 13, March 1, 1998, p. 1131.

As in her stirring global anthology *This Same Sky* (1993), Palestinian-American writer Nye brings us a wealth of new voices, many in translation. This time Nye's focus is on the Middle East, with more than 100 poets and artists from 19 countries. With the poetry, she includes full-page gloriously colored paintings that range in style from narrative folk art and intricate Arabic calligraphy to surrealism and contemporary graphics. The design of the large square volume is open and beautiful, with lots of white space and thick, quality paper. The biographical notes at the back reveal how many of the contributors have lived in several places, including the U.S., so it is not surprising that displacement is a dominant theme ("I was a kid, in a house they called a shanty / in a neighborhood called a transit camp"). The lyrical verse about family, friendship, nature, and daily life includes Majaj's intimate tribute "I Remember My Father's Hands" and Cohen-Assif's "Class Pictures." Several poets are Palestinian (most of them writing in English), but there are also eloquent pieces from Israel, Turkey, Iraq, Egypt, and elsewhere. Some are famous—including Yehuda Amichai (Israel), Naguib Mahfouz (Egypt), and Hanan Ashrawi (Palestine)—but most will be new to YA readers. Adults as much as teens will appreciate the poetry of place and the longing for home.

Publishers Weekly

SOURCE: A review of *The Space between Our Footsteps: Poems and Paintings from the Middle East,* in *Publishers Weekly,* Vol. 245, No. 9, March 2, 1998, p. 69.

Vibrant images and emotions fill this impressive anthology as Nye invites readers to experience the Middle East as portrayed by 127 contemporary poets and artists from 19 countries. Many of the themes are universal: images of childhood; family roles and relationships; scenic villages and countryside; and fleeting encounters with strangers and animals. Here, culture, history and politics shape these experiences. One powerful prose poem, "Unveiled" by Gladys Alam Saroyan, describes a woman's anger at having been devalued as a girl: "'Cover her face:' my grandmother told my parents on the way to the beach. 'She is already too dark.'/ 'Where did you get such black hair?' she said, with obvious concern./ 'From you, grandmother.'" Facing this poem, Reza De Rakshani's arresting oil painting shows a woman in a yellow veil, her black, kohl-lined eyes staring out at the viewer, her hand holding two blue eyes on stems like flowers. Many of the poems deal with longing for a lost homeland and the hope of return, as in Joseph Abi Daher's "Memoirs in Exile:" "Tomorrow looms in sight./ The homeland will return./ We will throw our wanderings and our suitcases/ into the sea." The illustrations throughout have particular strength and diversity, ranging in style from realistic to abstract to folk art. Buttressed by biographies of the poets and authors and a map of the region, the collection amply achieves Nye's goal of acting as a type of *hors d'oeuvre* to stimulate further interest.

Susan P. Bloom

SOURCE: A review of *The Space between Our Footsteps: Poems and Paintings from the Middle East,* in *The Horn Book Magazine,* Vol. LXXIV, No. 2, March-April, 1998, pp. 229-30.

In a volume whose aesthetic pleasure rivals Nye's 1992 *This Same Sky,* a collection of poems from around the world, Nye sets herself a smaller geographic landscape but as daunting a task—to capture in art and poetry the "secrets [which] live in the spaces between our footsteps" in the multifarious cultures of the Middle East. The book's square white pages generously and elegantly set off the poetry and luxuriously accent the full-color art of the more than one hundred contributors from nineteen Middle Eastern countries. Nye's poignant and intelligent introduction invites us to alter our image of this most complicated region and get behind the stereotypes to see the human connections in (poetic and artistic) themes as diverse and universal as reverence for the child and childhood, love of family, passion for one's homeland, and sadness and anger about exile from one's land. The anthology is divided into four sections ("A Galaxy of Seeds," "The World Is a Glass You Drink From," "Pick a Sky and Name It," "There Was in Our House a River"), each of which take their name from a line of poetry. Although many of the poems and art present ponderous issues, this collection is everywhere lightened with joyous language and fanciful art. . . . Like Turkish poet Yusuf Eradam, we are encouraged to "play hide-and-seek" in and with these poems. In her thoughtful notes on the contributors, Nye intersperses canceled postage stamps of birds, of peace signs, of vegetables and trains, even one charming Israeli stamp of *The Little Prince.* With the final poem "Quintrain," Lebanese Said Aql speaks of a mother bird "eloquently telling / its child: / Fly away, / soar high." Perhaps it needs only a few bread crumbs to exist, "but the sky / you need . . . / the whole sky." Nye once more reminds the world's children about "this same sky" and the imperative to know it in its fullness and complexity. Indexes of names, poems, and illustrations are appended, as is a generalized map of the region (which optimistically labels both Israel and Palestine).

Angela J. Reynolds

SOURCE: A review of *The Space between Our Footsteps: Poems and Paintings from the Middle East,* in *School Library Journal,* Vol. 44, No. 5, May, 1998, p. 159.

Over 100 poets and artists from 19 countries are gathered in this feast of poetry and paintings. The anthology is a potluck of Middle Eastern tastes, and every dish is full of flavorful surprises. Thirty-nine paintings, done in a rich assortment of styles and mediums, from figurative to folk art, abstract to collage, are scattered throughout. The artwork enhances, but in no way outshines the poetry contained within these pages. Good poetry evokes emotion and brings feelings and images to light; this collection exquisitely touches the senses through well-crafted language in glimpses of bright sun, watermelons, a rose on an uncle's lapel, a grandfather's footsteps, and heartbreaking images of children maimed by revolution. Nye's respect and admiration for Middle Eastern culture, and for poetry, come through in the expertly chosen, artistically arranged entries. Many of the selections have been translated into English for this compilation, and the poets' lyrical voices have been retained. The universality of topics—childhood, nature, love, homeland, war, family, school—gives insight into a culture and proves that differences are only skin deep. Students of the region and of poetry will be pleasurably served by this volume that includes a comprehensive introduction, a map, and short biographies of the contributors.

WHAT HAVE YOU LOST? (edited and compiled by Nye, 1999)

Betsy Hearne

SOURCE: A review of *What Have You Lost?*, in *Bulletin of the Center for Children's Books,* Vol. 52, No. 7, March, 1999, p. 251.

Young adult readers in the throes of realizing the infinite possibilities of loss are bound to connect with these 140 dynamic poems ranging so widely in tone and style. "You become what you lose," says Diana Der-Hovanessian in "Secrets of Life"—and there are many things to lose. The protagonist of Carla Hartsfield's "Shrink-wrapped" fears "losing something to do." The narrator in John Brandi's "Wilderness Poem" considers "the universe a fragile empire/ dissolved on the tongue." But there are things to find, as well. Reza Shirazi in "Learning Persian" recovers "a hibernating language/ lying in the dark corners of my mind." And there is the search, in every language, to name what has come and gone: " . . . this is the difficulty—/ *lo que se pierde* what gets lost/ *no es lo que se pierde en traducion sino/* is not what gets lost in translation but more/ what gets lost in language itself." This mixture of Spanish and English in Alastair Reid's "What Gets Lost/ *Lo Que Se Pierde*" is indicative of the many cultures represented here. Michael Nye's photographic portraits are intensely engaging, though sometimes not as interlinked with the poems as their placement implies. Rich in quantity, quality, and variety, the poetic selection is based on a broadly interpreted theme of important losses expressed by poets who are for the most part not commonly anthologized. May they find through this an audience as fresh as their own voices. Notes on the contributors are included.

Jennifer M. Brabander

SOURCE: A review of *What Have You Lost?*, in *The Horn Book Magazine,* Vol. LXXV, No. 2, March-April, 1999, p. 218.

In her thought-provoking introduction, the anthologist-poet considers loss—its certainty, scope, and effect, and its ability to give rise to art. The topic is thoroughly explored by the one hundred and forty poets whose work is collected here in twenty-two unlabeled, thematically arranged sections. The poems focus on specific losses, including those we experience as we grow up, leave home or homeland, fall in love, grow old; what we suffer when someone dies suddenly—or slowly; what we're deprived of by acts of violence and anger; and losses accrued through travel and distance. The poets are all contemporary, with a dozen or so hailing from outside the United States. That the great majority are previously unpublished or at least relatively unknown (contributors include a software engineer, a sportswriter, and a priest) should intrigue and encourage reader-writers: established poets obviously don't have a monopoly on publishable, memorable poems. Young adults, finding their way and wanting so much, will appreciate this collection about losing—and regaining—oneself through the experience of loss. Accompanying the poems are mostly affectless black-and-white portraits whose inclusion is puzzling. Notes on contributors include their thoughts on the question "What have you lost and found?"; indexes handily include an "index of losses."

Jessica Roeder

SOURCE: A review of *What Have You Lost?*, in *Riverbank Review,* Spring, 1999, pp. 42-3.

One day, when all of the poems ever published are indexed and cross-referenced on a single computer database, we will be able to determine with a few keystrokes what percentage of poems concerns loss. For now, we can only guess that the number is considerable. Which of Shakespeare's sonnets were not written against loss? How many of Emily Dickinson's poems aren't tinged by losing? Naomi Nye's latest anthology takes a fresh look at this perennial theme.

Nye does not reprint old favorites or the overanthologized. All of the poets represented here are contemporary. Most write in free verse. Some have not published before. Even the luminaries, such as Lucille Clifton, are less celebrated than they deserve to be. And Nye includes as a matter of course translations of poems from Japan, Nicaragua, Mexico, Chile, and Italy.

In the hands of a different anthologist, this would be a thinly disguised self-help tract for the treatment of adolescent angst. We'd have poems on lost boyfriends and girlfriends, lost football games, *gained* weight, perhaps lost grandparents. Nye takes a different tack. Most of the poems do not concern adolescence. Nye trusts her readers to care about points of view that are not their own. A father loses his son to kindergarten; a child frees a rescued wren; an old poet wins fame long after losing his desire for it. The book becomes an exercise in expanding compassion. Losses extend beyond the personal or individual—whole towns, lands, languages, and cultures are lost—and responses include bewilderment, grief, anger, bemusement, and joy.

The photographs, black-and-white portraits taken before a generic school-photo backdrop, come to resonate with the poems. The people in the photos take on the role of witnesses. Gestures that at first glance seem forced or hermetic become sympathetic, if not quite interpretable. They are expressions of loss and assertions of survival. It would be a lonelier project to read all these poems without the very real presences in the photographs.

Readers will want to spend time with this anthology, stopping to think, to reread—and to write. The quiet "conversations" that emerge from groups of poems about similar losses are well worth joining. From the introduction (which ends, "Maybe you are writing one now") to the expansive contributors' notes (which give a sense of where these poems came from), *What Have You Lost?* encourages readers to pick up a pen themselves.

Additional coverage of Nye's life and career is contained in the following sources published by The Gale Group: *Contemporary Authors New Revision Series*, **Vol. 70;** *Authors and Artists for Young Adults*, **Vol. 27;** *Dictionary of Literary Biography*, **Vol. 120; and** *Something about the Author*, **Vol. 86.**

Ernest Thompson Seton

1860-1946

(Born Ernest Evan Seton Thompson; also wrote as Ernest Seton-Thompson) English-born Canadian author and illustrator of fiction and nonfiction.

Major works include *Wild Animals I Have Known* (1898; Canadian edition, 1900; British edition, 1902), *Two Little Savages* (1903), *Animal Heroes* (1905; British edition, 1906), *Rolf in the Woods* (1911; Canadian edition, 1917), *Wild Animal Ways* (1916).

INTRODUCTION

Renowned as one of the founders of the Boys Scouts of America, Seton was a writer, artist, and naturalist who is best remembered for his fiction and nonfiction that portrays the lives, habits, and individual characteristics of animals, and appeals to audiences of all ages—from elementary graders to young adults and adults. Influenced by the writings of Charles Darwin, Seton viewed animals as the forebears of humankind and therefore deserving of more respect than they were generally accorded. He deplored mistreatment of animals and in his fiction, often written from an animal's point of view, he exposed the needless suffering inflicted upon wild creatures by human beings. His tales illustrate his beliefs concerning the kinship of man and beast and humanity's moral responsibility toward the animal kingdom. Similarly, Seton published his nonfiction works, which are thorough and painstaking records of his own observations, in the hope that wider knowledge of animals' lives would lead to increased respect for their rights.

Drawing his fiction from his experiences in the Canadian wilderness, Seton sought to provide a corrective to the concept of wildlife expressed in nineteenth-century anthropomorphic tales, in which animals spoke, wore clothing, and generally behaved like human beings. Finding the reality of animal existence more compelling and dramatic than any fictional treatment could be, he attempted to describe simply and accurately the phenomena he had observed during his years as a naturalist. As a result, Seton favored a genre he called the animal biography, which recounted the life of an animal from birth to death, thus enabling the author to include comprehensive information about the behavior, development, and social interactions of a given species. His stories, accompanied by his own beautifully rendered wildlife drawings and paintings, emphasize the animals' heroism and uniqueness, and his characters have their own stories to tell. Leonard R. Mendelsohn wrote in *Twentieth Century Children's Writers*, "Seton's animal characters, posed against a natural landscape and confronting circumstances conforming to the environs, retain a lively caricature quite surpassing the dull personifications which

dominate and denude animal denizens of many a children's book." Thematically, Seton's tales attempt to emphasize the "real personality of the individual and his view of life," rather than the ways of the species, as Seton expressed in his preface to *Wild Animals I Have Known*. Most of his fiction ends tragically, which, as Seton once observed, is realistic, and the way of the wilderness.

Although Seton has described his animal biographies as life histories and factual accounts, they are in fact compilations of his observations in nature and his imagined interpretations of the feelings and motives of animals. His combination of fiction and nonfiction details have made his works difficult for readers and reviewers to categorize. Despite this, however, Seton's works have been celebrated for their promotion of the beauty and strength of the natural world, as well as for their appeal to the reader's interest and emotions. Fred Bodsworth argued that in light of the traditional animal story as practiced before Seton, his work was "a monumental step toward realistic animal portrayal," and further contended that "the anthropomorphic flaws are more than offset by the sound scientific realism that characterizes most of Seton's work." His stories, though not as widely read today as they were during his lifetime, continue to entertain and are particularly popular with children. Mendelsohn also concurred, "Even though [Seton's] works abound in precise detail and acute observation derived from unrelenting study . . . his controlled ebullience and knowing naivety demonstrate that Seton is legitimately within the ranks of writers for children."

Biographical Information

Born Ernest Evan Seton Thompson in South Shields, Durham, England, in 1860, Seton was the eighth of ten sons. At the age of six, his family emigrated to Canada, first to a farm near Lindsay, Ontario, and four years later to Toronto. During the 1860s and 1870s, Lindsay was pioneer territory, and Toronto was a small city whose ravines and lakeside marshes afforded Seton a rich variety of bird and animal life. Seton's encounter with the Canadian wilderness during this period inspired the fascination with nature that shaped the rest of his life. From his early youth, he was touched by the courage and feelings of animals. In his autobiography, *Trail of an Artist-Naturalist* (1940), he recalls hearing the older children "reading from Franklin's *Polar Sea*." The story of a polar bear and her two cubs being shot impressed him greatly and brought "a choking sorrow in [his] throat over the fate of the noble old mother bear." Seton's first response to nature was an attempt to capture its beauty in drawings; possessed of much innate talent, he rapidly advanced as an adept wildlife artist. His interest in becoming a naturalist emerged when he returned to the Lindsay farm to recuperate from an illness. Faced with his father's objections, however, the sixteen-year-old Seton began working as an artist's apprentice and shortly thereafter enrolled in night classes at the Ontario School of Art. In 1879, Seton won a seven-year scholarship to attend the Royal Academy School of Painting and Sculpture in London. Ill health and financial burdens drove him back to Canada in 1881 to his brother's homestead in Manitoba.

Manitoba in the 1880s was the scene of Seton's golden period as an observer and illustrator of wildlife. There began the fat notebooks crammed with sketches and measurements of Canadian birds and animals, which Seton later declared to be the first necessity for an artist-naturalist. It was there also, along with his Lindsay and Toronto years, that much of the material for Seton's first and most famous collection of realistic animal stories, *Wild Animals I Have Known*, was gathered. In 1883 Seton moved to New York City, where he secured a job illustrating animals for the second edition of *The Century Dictionary*. In 1887, he began to write stories based on his experiences with wild animals, and also completed his art training at the Julian Academy in Paris between 1890 and 1896. In Paris he met and married an American girl, and the couple settled in Greenwich, Connecticut. By the late 1890s, Seton was so confident of the success of his first collection of animal stories that he contracted with Scribners for no royalties on the first

two thousand copies, with twenty percent on every copy thereafter. The immediate popularity of these stories resulted in frequent speaking invitations, and Seton soon became know as an expert on North-American wildlife. He received letters of congratulations from his friends, Rudyard Kipling and Charles G. D. Roberts, who both acknowledged his influence on their own writing. The financial success of his lecturing, writing, and illustrating endeavors thereafter enabled him to spend much of his time in the wilderness

Seton's career as a naturalist was not, however, unmarred by controversy. In 1898 he collected several of his most popular animal stories in the volume *Wild Animals I Have Known*, a book that was denounced as a "nature-fakery" by another leading naturalist, John Burroughs. Burroughs doubted whether Seton had witnessed the events depicted, noting that in his own vast experience of nature he had never seen or heard of such events and denouncing what he considered Seton's misrepresentations. This set off quite a discussion among naturalists and literary critics. In his autobiography, Seton describes the attack as bitter, unfair, and reeking with jealousy. In a later article, however, Burroughs praised Seton as an artist and raconteur, but warned his readers against Seton's "romantic tendencies." In any case, questions of accuracy did not diminish the wide popularity of Seton's fiction, and he continued to publish animal stories throughout his lifetime.

Closely tied to Seton's respect for nature was his reverence for North American Indians, and he gradually came to believe that children growing up in an industrial society would benefit greatly from exposure to the healthful and highly moral Indian way of life. As a result, he invited a group of boys to his estate to practice woodcraft, learn Indian ways and culture, and participate in outdoor activities. Seton expounded on his methods and theories in a series of articles for the *Ladies' Home Journal* in 1902. Later that year he founded the Woodcraft League for boys, which grew rapidly and spawned other chapters throughout the country. A few years later, Seton's groups were supplanted by the Boy Scouts of America, whose founder, Robert Baden-Powell, had in fact appropriated Seton's ideas from his *Birch-Bark Roll of the Outdoor Life* (1908). Seton, however, served as Chief Scout from 1910 to 1915 and wrote the first American scout manual. His idealization of the Native Americans and dislike of the movement's militarism led to an open rupture with the Boy Scout board and Seton's eviction from the organization he had helped to found. He continued to lead the Woodcraft League, which had over eighty thousand members by 1934.

In 1930 Seton and his second wife moved to a 2,300-acre ranch near Santa Fe, New Mexico, where they established a home, library, museum, camp, and school for youth leaders. Seton's creative gifts continued to flower until his death on October 23, 1946, at the age of eighty-six. In his essay "Black Wolf," printed in the *Smithsonian*, Bill Gilbert stated, "No one did more than Ernest Thompson Seton to promote the message that nature is a very good thing in itself and contemplation of it an uplifting tonic for the human psyche."

Major Works

Wild Animals I Have Known is described by the author as the "personal histories" of eight animals, including Lobo the wolf, Silverspot the crow, Ruggylug the cottontail rabbit, Bingo the dog, the Springfield fox, and others. To a high degree, the tales demonstrate Seton's vision of the human-like thoughts and emotions of animals. The volume is enhanced by the author's paintings and thumbnail sketches of wildlife. Reviewers emphasized the drama and excitement of Seton's biographies. Fred J. Pierce, in an article for *AB Bookman's Weekly*, observed, "Instead of dreary pages of prose for adolescent readers to wade through, the animals and birds fairly leaped from the print and were clearly fixed in the minds of those following the adventures. . . ." Bodsworth hailed the book, stating that it "started a whole generation looking with new understanding at the world of nature," while a reviewer in *The Nation* (New York) opined, "Mr. Thompson [Seton] holds our unflagging interest in his stories. He knows his animals as individual characters, and sets forth their lives vividly, making us feel for and with them, through all their vicissitudes to the appointed death by violence."

A thinly veiled autobiography, *Two Little Savages* is a nostalgic story for boys based on Seton's own childhood experiences. Eleven-year-old Yan, feeling estranged from his family, secretly dreams of being an Indian. He takes odd jobs to earn money to purchase a nature book, by which he hopes to familiarize himself with Indian ways and customs. When Yan is fourteen, however, he contracts tuberculosis and is sent to a farm to recover. There he meets Sam, a young boy who shares Yan's passion for nature. The two boys live like Indians over the summer—learning to make arrows, track animals, build a tepee, make a fire by rubbing sticks together, and trap a lynx. In a 1962 essay for *Canadian Literature*, S. E. Read wrote that *Two Little Savages* was the "best and most evenly written of [Seton's] works, evidencing not only his superb knowledge of animal life, but also his ability to tell a good story, to handle dialogue and to catch the sounds and accents of dialects, to write clear expositions, to preach unobtrusively a good sermon, and to create convincing characters. . . . [Seton] knew of what he wrote and was able to convey that knowledge with enthusiasm to the millions who were to read the work." Nearly twenty years later, Noel Perrin commented, "*Two Little Savages* has some four or five separate charms. The greatest, of course, is the wonderful if vicarious sense of accomplishment the reader gets watching Yan and Sam acquire skill after skill."

Animal Heroes contains eight stories about heroic animals with unusual gifts, and features a cat, a dog, a jackrabbit, a pigeon, a lynx, a reindeer, and two wolves. Unlike *Wild Animals I Have Known*, however, not all of the animals meet tragic outcomes. A reviewer in *The Nation*

(New York) celebrated Seton's ability to invoke human emotion in his stories, noting, "He does touch the heart and the imagination, his methods are not sensational, his literary art is excellent, his knowledge is wide."

Dedicated to the Boy Scouts of America, *Rolf in the Woods* is the story of fifteen-year-old orphan Rolf Kittering, who runs away from his cruel uncle to live in the woods with Quonab, a solitary Indian trapper. A historical tale, the adventures occur during the War of 1812 along the U.S./Canadian border and Rolf takes on the role of a scout and dispatcher to the American General. In *Canadian Literature*, Read stated, "The inherent didacticism in the work is not repulsively obvious, for both preaching and teaching are well blended with the exciting events of the narrative itself. . . . It all makes for good reading, and inasmuch as there is something of a plot with considerable suspense, it is a good yarn, too. Seton wrote nothing else quite like it." A reviewer for *The Spectator* wrote, "The story has all the qualities which a boys' book should have and many which are often lacking."

Similar in style to *Wild Animals I Have Known* and containing over two hundred drawings by the author/artist, *Wild Animal Ways* is a collection of seven stories about a razor-back (or wild boar), a raccoon, a bat, a dog, a monkey, a wild horse, and some wild geese. A reviewer for *The Times Literary Supplement* noted that "the stories are in substance good, the narrator thoroughly knows his heroes and heroines and villains. . . . And they make good drama; their doings are interesting, full of movement."

Awards

Seton won the Camp Fire Gold Medal in 1909 for *Life Histories of Northern Animals*. He later enlarged *Life Histories* and published them in four volumes between 1925 and 1928 as *Lives of Game Animals*, for which he won the John Burroughs Memorial Society's Bronze Medal in 1926 and the Daniel Girard Elliot Gold Medal in 1928.

GENERAL COMMENTARY

Fred Bodsworth

SOURCE: "The Backwoods Genius with the Magic Pen," in *Maclean's Magazine*, Vol. 72, No. 12, June 6, 1959, pp. 22, 32, 34, 38-40.

In *Wild Animals I Have Known*, Seton originated a strikingly new literary form known now as the "realistic" animal story. In all previous fiction of this type the animals talked and thought like humans, but Seton tried to show animal lives and personalities as they are in nature. Many biologists today, viewing Seton in the sharper light of modern biological knowledge, claim he fell short of depicting animals as they actually are; but sixty years ago *Wild Animals I Have Known* was a new and monumental step toward realistic animal portrayal. It revealed to millions of readers that animals have loves and tragedies not unlike our own. It started a whole generation looking with new understanding at the world of nature. It was the real beginning of the movement which grew into today's vigorous conservation crusade.

Probably a majority of today's naturalists and biologists had their interest sparked first by Seton's stories, for he turned thousands of boys to the outdoors. I remember vividly the impact of Seton on my own generation—the classroom in tears as the teacher read **"Raggylug"** or **"Lobo, King of the Currumpaw"**; the library waiting list for *Two Little Savages,* which most boys reread religiously each year; the hours in the woods trailing animals, building Indian tepees, with a Seton woodcraft book as our Bible and constant guide. Seton is still in demand, I hear, holding his own despite the Lone Ranger and Wyatt Earp. It was a moving and reassuring thing recently to lift a tattered copy of *Two Little Savages* from a library shelf and find a bundle of dried pine needles in its pages—evidence that Seton is still going into the woods with boys. I hope that, like Tennyson's brook, he goes on forever, and he shows good signs of doing so. Recent paperback editions have pushed Seton book sales to three million. The Seton message—"We and the beasts are kin"—lives on.

But Seton has a special significance to Canada other than the fact that he has kept three generations of us animal-conscious. Our homegrown belittlers of Canadian art and culture, who bemoan that Canada has originated nothing of artistic merit, overlook that Seton's wildlife fiction was an original Canadian literary form that was quickly imitated by Kipling and other literary greats throughout the world. Though he was born in England and lived most of his life a U.S. citizen, Ernest Thompson Seton wrote his first stories in Canada, and most of his wildlife characters were animals he studied here. Because of this, and because another Canadian, Charles G. D. Roberts, followed quickly along the literary trail that Seton blazed, the realistic animal story is now recognized as a Canadian contribution to world literature.

Seton had three careers—art, science and writing—and he won recognition in all of them. But his fiction writing, the career that interested him least, was the one that brought him wealth and fame. He had begun it merely as a hobby, as an expression of his love for nature, and even after it had thrust him into world prominence he still wished to be known first as a scientist. The recognition he gained in scientific circles as a competent, self-taught biologist he prized more than all the fame and wealth he won as a teller of animal tales. Of his forty-two books, he was proudest of his huge four-volume *Lives of Game Animals,* a scientific work to which he devoted ten years of his life. He obtained a wry satisfac-

tion from the fact that his *Lives,* though it established him as a scientist, sold only twenty-six hundred copies while his animal fiction sold millions and made him a millionaire. Today, almost fifty years later, Seton's *Lives* is still a must for every mammalogist's library and second-hand copies are in demand at five times the original price.

But despite his reputation as a scientist, there are glaring scientific flaws in his popular fiction. Some of Seton's stories show a fallacy common for his time—the error of anthropomorphism, or unduly humanizing of animals. Modern biologists contend that Seton's animal heroes are too liberally endowed with human emotions like love, grief and hate. Some possess too much reasoning power to be acceptable as animals today. There is the small bear in *The Biography of a Grizzly,* for example, which rolls a log up to a tree and stands on it so that it can reach up and leave a higher claw mark in the bark, hoping to make other grizzlies believe there is a monstrous bear inhabiting the region. Modern authorities on animal behavior say this and other episodes imply a degree of intelligence that animals just don't possess. But the anthropomorphic flaws are more than offset by sound scientific realism that characterizes most of Seton's work.

S. E. Read

SOURCE: "Flight to the Primitive: Ernest Thompson Seton," in *Canadian Literature,* No. 13, Summer, 1962, pp. 45-57.

Slowly I closed the book, and, after an envious look at the last illustration—a magnificent sketch of Yan in the full regalia of an Indian chief—placed it back on its shelf, along with *Rolf in the Woods, Lives of the Hunted,* a few Hentys, some Horatio Algers, a simplified Homer, a *Gulliver,* a *Swiss Family Robinson,* some recent numbers of *St. Nicholas,* a collection of annuals (chiefly *Boys' Own* and *Chums*), the *Books of Knowledge,* a Bunyan, and a Bible. As I did so, I knew that I would never completely forget Yan, who proudly bore the name of Little Beaver, or Sam, the Great Woodpecker, or Sappy Guy Brown, or Caleb, the kindly old trapper, or even the aged Sanger Witch, Granny de Neuville.

Fifty years later—give or take a year or two—I saw the book again—not *my* book, but one fresh from the presses. The old illustrations were still there—the footprints, the flowers, the birds, the designs for tepees and bows and arrows, the glowering lynx, repulsive Sappy Sam, with and without war-paint, and noble Yan, erect as ever in full regalia on the last page of the text. Ernest Seton Thompson and his *Two Little Savages* had survived not only the bite of time, but also the world's violent entrance into an age of atomic hazards and ever-expanding horizons.

Part of the reason for this extraordinary survival is to be found in the man himself, part in the central theme that repeats itself with modest variations in all he wrote, and part in the skills he employed. Let me start with the man.

He was born in South Shields on the east coast of England on the fourteenth of August, 1860, and was duly named Ernest Evan Seton Thompson. Largely, I gather, because of the violent antipathy with which he regarded his father, he was not happy with his name and early in his career started signing his sketches and writings Ernest Thompson Seton, a name he legalized in 1898. For a brief period, he succumbed to maternal pressure and changed to Ernest Seton-Thompson—this time with a hyphen; he regarded this as a pseudonym and after his mother's death reverted to Ernest Thompson Seton, dying as such in Santa Fé, New Mexico, on the twenty-third of October, 1946. His little name game has confused at least two generations of readers, librarians, and bibliographers.

In 1866 the family migrated from South Shields to Lindsay, Ontario, at that time a frontier village not far from the eastern edge of Lake Simcoe. Here the father, a financially broken ship-owner, intended, with more romantic imagination than hard-headed realism, to start life anew as a "gentleman farmer." It was a mass migration, for Mrs. Thompson, a true Victorian, had been fruitful; she had given birth to fourteen children, ten of whom, all boys, had survived. Ernest Evan was the eighth. He was dominated by his older brothers and had little in common with them. He despised his father, whom he describes as a financial failure, an indolent individual, an overbearing husband, and a tyrannical, brutal parent. Even toward his mother his feelings were ambivalent. A deeply religious woman, she was much given to prayers and long Biblical quotations, to hopes of salvation and threats of damnation. Her unthinking orthodoxy repelled him. At times, too, she neglected him, burdened and confused as she was by the complexities of her responsibilities. But in moments of crisis, especially those arising from the lad's recurring illnesses, she lavished tenderness and affection upon him. The confused, harried, and sensitive boy rebelled against the accepted conventions of religion and against his family. For refuge he fled to the world of the outdoors—first in the still wild, open country around Lindsay; later amidst the fields, streams, and the marshes that were yet within walking distance of the growing town of Toronto; still later in the vast, mysterious spaces of an opening Manitoba; and finally in the great wastelands and mountains of the American West. Nature became his sanctuary. In it he found clarity, order, and comfort rather than darkness, confusion, and anguish; and through his detailed observations of the world he had chosen he developed his skills as artist and writer.

Of the genius of the man and the complexities of his life little of value has been written. The available encyclopædic articles give some facts about his life and work but nothing else. . . .

In short, I am reasonably convinced that the best source of information on Seton is still Seton himself, primarily his erratic and sketchy autobiography, *Trail of an Artist-Naturalist,* and *The Arctic Prairies,* an unevenly written but sporadically interesting account of a canoe trip down the Athabasca to the plains country near the Arctic Circle, made by the author and a friend in 1907. Of only slightly less value as sources of self-revelation are his other major works, for rarely could he keep himself out of the picture. *Two Little Savages* is thinly disguised autobiography; *Lives of the Hunted* and *Wild Animals I Have Known* are well larded with personal anecdotes; and *Rolf in the Woods* and *The Gospel of the Red Man* reveal his basic religious beliefs and ethical principles.

The foremost impression I get from a reading of his works is that of a deeply sensitive and introspective man, somewhat egocentric and opinionated, who concentrated all his powers on the observation and minute study of nature and, especially in his later life, on the spreading of his "gospel". With the move to Lindsay, the boy was brought into an intimate, exciting contact with primitive, unkempt nature.

He quickly learned the simpler lessons of woodcraft and eagerly listened to tales of great hunts and Indian warfare told by men who had lived out their lives on the edges of civilization. He read tales of adventure and survival, such as *Robinson Crusoe* and *Swiss Family Robinson,* and later, in Toronto, the works of the naturalists, starting with A. M. Ross's *Birds of Canada* and eventually moving into the formidable works of Alexander Wilson, the great Scottish-American ornithologist of the late eighteenth and early nineteenth centuries, and of James Audubon, the most famous of all naturalists of the frontier world. Under the influence of such men, the young boy soon began to keep his daily journals, and began, too, to sketch much that he saw—animal tracks, animals, birds, leaves, flowers.

By his early teens he had begun to retreat from his family and from his schoolmates, in order to develop his own peculiar, off-beat interests. He was an intellectual eccentric, an anti-social, juvenile hermit, an explorer in search of an earthly paradise. Eventually he found it in a quiet, cool, isolated glen near the River Don. With a typical egocentric gesture he named his Eden "Glenyan", for Yan was the name he had given his hermit-self. It was in Glenyan that, with crude tools, he fashioned his first crude shanty. Here he methodically studied the flora and fauna around him, and began to develop his conviction that in the world of nature man can find comfort and consolation, an ever-renewing strength, and all the essential rules for ethical and moral behaviour. Here, too, he first assumed in full the role of the romanticized Red Man.

In some ways Seton undoubtedly regarded himself as a mystic. His "voice" and his visions directed him in his activities, his way of life, and his beliefs. Though he eagerly sought for fame—and fortune—he preached the doctrine of the simple life close to nature, and in the spiritual shrine that he erected he placed in his holy of holies an idealized symbolical figure—the American Indian, the Red Man. From his childhood on he was deeply moved by anything even remotely associated with the Indian way of life. As he matured he not only came under the influence of the writings of [James] Fenimore Cooper, but he also met many Indians in his wanderings through Manitoba and during his long canoe trip down the Athabasca. Generally he admired them, but he was not blindly consistent. He found many of the Indians in the far north indolent, dirty, superstitious, and savage. But these, he would have argued, had been corrupted by the corrosive influences of a white civilization. Actually his ideal was the Indian of the past, untainted by external forces.

This ideal is partially developed in the character of Quonab, "the last of the Myanos Sinawa", the profoundly religious, highly moral, and friendly Indian, who teaches Rolf Kittering, an abandoned white orphan, the true way of life; it is deeply imbedded in *Two Little Savages,* when Yan and Sam are brought to maturity and wisdom through studying and practising Indian manners and customs; and it reaches full bloom in *The Gospel of the Red Man; An Indian Bible,* a work compiled by Seton and his second wife towards the end of Seton's life. This is an anthology of sorts in which are gathered "the inspiring teachings of the Red man," prayers, ethical codes, laws of behaviour. Its most revealing section is the preface, in which Seton takes a last, lingering look at his own age. In it he finds little that is good. The white man's way has failed. His culture is materialistic and poisonous; his religion arid, punitive, fruitless. Slowly but all too surely he is destroying himself. But salvation can yet be found through following the new *Gospel.* For this work, Seton expressly hoped, was to have a universal religious appeal; it would bring unity and peace into a world fraught by dissension and torn by fears; it would satisfy Christian and Buddhist, Catholic and Protestant, Presbyterian and Methodist—all alike. If man would only retrace the tracks of the noble Indian, he could once again find his way back to nature—and survive.

To the sceptic and the scientist, Seton's beliefs doubtless appear naïve—the products of a simple mind. But to Seton himself they were fundamental. They provided the main thrust that led to his establishment of the Woodcraft Movement and to his early support of the Boy Scouts in America, and they run as a central strand in all that he wrote. His sincerity is obvious; and it is this sincerity that is one of the great factors in his success as a writer.

From his earliest days in Lindsay and Toronto Seton studied the world of nature around him. Animals, birds, flowers, trees, the signs of changing weather, the medicinal folk lore of herbs—all came under his scrutiny. By curious games and devices to sharpen the memory he increased his powers of observation. Though he finally submitted to his father's commands that he should be an artist rather than a naturalist, he satisfied his own longings by becoming an artist who sketched and painted animals and birds to the almost total exclusion of all

else. In 1879 he was gold medalist at the Ontario College of Art in Toronto, and in the following year, according to his own account, he won a seven-year scholarship at the Royal Academy School of Painting in London, only to abandon it after twelve months or so to return to Canada because of ill health. Later, in the 1890's, he went twice to Paris to study and paint. At a time when he might have come under the influence of the French Impressionists—Cézanne, Monet, Renoir, Van Gogh—he preferred to carry the bodies of dead dogs to his attic rooms to perfect his knowledge of the anatomy of the wolf. The anatomy studied, he then painted—and exhibited—wolves, large and small, and realistic. He prepared one massive canvas, four-and-a-half feet by seven, entitled "The Wolves' Triumph," for entry in a Paris exhibition. It was rejected. The subject, said the critics, was revolting. They had some reason on their side: a picture of a wolf pack finishing off the skeletal remains of a human body is a gruesome sight even though the winter setting is done with skill and feeling. The picture was eventually exhibited at the Chicago World's Fair of 1893, much against the wishes of some members of the Toronto selection committee who were inclined to believe that it might leave an unfavourable impression of the Canadian way of life.

In brief, Seton never became a great painter. He remained basically a skilful illustrator doing what he loved to do—portray animals and birds, sketch the tracks to be seen in wilderness sand and mud; illustrate, with patient detail, the best ways to make tepees and bows and arrows, or to start a camp fire, in the Indian way, by rubbing-sticks. And his specialization paid off. Not only did he do a thousand drawings of animals and birds for Merriam's *Century Dictionary;* he also used his skill to illustrate all that he wrote.

But what of Seton, the author? First he was prolific, especially in the period from the 1890s to the 1920s. He started in a modest way with articles and short stories, but eventually he wrote more than thirty volumes, ranging from scientific and semi-scientific works to the vast bulk of his writing, which is specifically directed towards the younger reader. In all his works, however, Seton centres his interest on one focal point—the world of nature.

From the moment he bought Ross's *Birds of Canada* (he was then thirteen), he was well on his way to becoming a self-taught naturalist. Early in his career he published scientific articles on birds and animals, and in 1909 he produced his *Life-Histories of Northern Animals: An Account of the Mammals of Manitoba.* Not until some nineteen years later, however, when he was approaching seventy, did Seton complete his most ambitious work, his *Lives of Game Animals.* This vast work, originally published in four volumes, immediately brought him recognition as an outstanding naturalist. Professor McTaggart Cowan, himself a wild life specialist of international reputation, tells me that the *Lives* still stands as an invaluable reference work in its field, in spite of errors and unscientific observations and of its anecdotal passages and personal reminiscences. For Seton, even in his scientific garb, could never get far away from the technique of the tale, nor from the personal approach he exhibited with such skill in his more popular writings.

In some ways Seton was actually in revolt against the scientific method. To him the type of natural history then current was too general, too vague, to be effective. Scientists, he said, placed their emphasis on the species. For him a true understanding of animals and birds came through a study of the individual. To him each animal was different, possessing its own particular characteristics, its own special profile of behaviour. Moreover the line of demarcation setting man apart from animal was a slight one. He even endowed his heroes and heroines with human virtues—dignity, sagacity, mother-love, love of liberty, obedience, fidelity—and encouraged man to look closely at the beasts of the fields and the birds of the air so that he, man, might learn from them ways to a better life.

At times, especially in his early stories, he so humanized his figures as to strain the credulity of his more critical readers and to antagonize the scientifically minded. At first, he even made his animals talk, not as the animals of Aesop talked, but as human beings talk when caught in situations that arouse such emotions as terror, love, or pity. He translates the single "thump" of a rabbit into "look out" or "freeze" and the triple "thump, thump, thump" into "run for dear life." In his later stories, however, he declared this conversational technique to be "archaic", but he never ceased to endow his heroes with human characteristics far beyond the accepted reaches of instinct. In **"The Springfield Fox,"** for example, his heroine, Vix, leads the pursuing hounds across a railway trestle just in time to have an engine overtake and destroy them. And Wahb, the aging and heroic figure in *The Biography of a Grizzly,* is given a truly Roman end when, worn out and burdened by a sense of defeat, he courageously enters a cave filled with fumes he knows to be lethal.

It was, I believe, because of this same stress on the importance of the individual, with its consequent narrowing of the gap between animal and man, linked of course with his ability to tell a good tale, that Seton as a wild life biographer was from the first successful. He started in a modest way with such tales as **"The Story of a Little Gray Rabbit,"** which appeared in that grand old magazine for children, *St. Nicholas,* in October, 1890, and he was soon in full flight as a writer of animal fiction. With the great success of *Wild Animals I Have Known* (it was published in 1898 and ran through four editions in two months) his fame was firmly established.

It would be a mistake to suppose that Seton's path to fame was completely smooth. Naturalists especially regarded his works with scepticism. Foremost among them was the famous and formidable John Burroughs, who turned his sharp pen against Seton in "Real and Sham Natural History", in the *Atlantic Monthly* for March, 1903. The attack opened obliquely and ended frontally.

Early in the article Burroughs warmly praises Roberts's most recent work, *Kindred of the Wild,* a volume in which "one finds much to admire and commend, and but little to take exception to . . . in many ways the most brilliant collection of animal stories that has appeared." This was a bitter dose for Seton to swallow, but more bitter was the one given a page later. "Mr. Thompson Seton says in capital letters that his stories are true, and it is this emphatic assertion that makes the judicious grieve. True as romance, true in their artistic effects, true in their power to entertain the young reader, they certainly are; but true as natural history they are not."

Seton was deeply hurt. He was, if one can judge by his writings, a self-centred man—opinionated and sincerely convinced of the validity of his techniques. He was also sensitive, especially to this unfavourable criticism from a man he had long admired. . . .

Standing quite aside from all of Seton's other works are two books that demand special comment—*Rolf in the Woods* and *Two Little Savages.* The first is nominally an historical novel for the young; the second a rich brew in which are mixed nearly all the ingredients found in varying degrees elsewhere in his writings. It is the quintessence of Seton.

I first read *Rolf* shortly after it appeared in 1911. In the half-century that had slipped away since then the details of the yarn had disappeared beyond recall, but the general impact of the book still lingered. When I re-read it recently I could easily see why. Set in the era of the border war of 1812-14, the story revolves around its two central figures—Rolf Kittering, a desolate, insecure white orphan, and Quonab, a noble Indian, with whom Rolf seeks refuge and through whom he learns the ways of life in the woods, and the values of a simple and primitive religious faith. The inherent didacticism in the work is not repulsively obvious, for both preaching and teaching are well blended with the exciting events of the narrative itself, including Rolf's escape from the combined tyranny of a besotted uncle and a rigid New England society, the struggle for survival in the deep woods of the Green Mountains, and the dangers of acting as scout and guide for American forces along the Canadian border.

The actual war, with its causes, events, and attendant horrors, is carefully kept in the background, for Seton hated war and the military mind. Only towards the conclusion of *Rolf* does he allow the excitement of armed combat to creep in at all; he prefers—and in this he is consistent—to concentrate on the more peaceful thrills of camping, canoeing, hunting, trapping, and learning the Red Man's way of living. It all makes for good reading, and inasmuch as there is something of a plot with considerable suspense it is a good yarn, too. Seton wrote nothing else quite like it.

But another work also stands by itself—the classic in the Seton canon—*Two Little Savages.* It contains the essence of all of the beliefs that Seton held so dear. It is also the best and most evenly written of his works, evidencing not only his superb knowledge of animal life, but also his ability to tell a good story, to handle dialogue and to catch the sounds and accents of dialects, to write clear expositions, to preach unobtrusively, a good sermon, and to create convincing characters. It has been, I would guess, the most widely read of his books, and it is the book, I believe, that will last the longest.

Basically the ingredients are autobiographical. In the summer of 1875 the fifteen-year-old Thompson was seriously ill, and, under the doctor's orders, he was sent to Lindsay to live with the Blackwell family, who had moved into the large house formerly owned by Mr. Thompson when he was attempting, without success, to be a "gentleman farmer." William Blackwell, the head of the household, was a practical, hard-working, hard-bargaining man. Superficially he was tough and severe, but under the surface he was kindly and understanding. To Ernest he was a better man by far than his own father. As for Mrs. Blackwell, she was a fountain of motherly sympathy. Quickly the lonely, sickly boy became a member of the family group. In *Two Little Savages* the Blackwells become the Raftens, and one of the Blackwell boys is transformed into the second little savage—Sam. As for Ernest himself, he is given the name of Yan—his favourite nickname from his Toronto days. Even the minor characters are drawn from the folk of the village and its neighbouring farms—dirty, snivelling Guy; old Caleb, wise in woodcraft and Indian lore; and the Sanger (Lindsay) Witch, the ageless Granny de Neuville, who, though a repulsive crone, proves an unending source of folklore and herbal knowledge, which she transmits to Yan in a thick Irish accent. Around these characters the plot is formed, and thin though it is, it is sufficient to hold most readers to the end. The vicious three-fingered tramp is duly caught and subdued, and the evidence extracted from him is enough to terminate the bitter quarrel between Raften and old Caleb, and to restore that poor but dignified ancient to his rightful place in the community.

The obvious plot, however, is really a subsidiary affair. The real purpose of the work is to show how Yan, the insecure, sensitive, unhealthy boy, achieves status among his fellows. This he does through his unremitting study of nature, through practical camping, through learning *and* using Indian woodcraft lore, and through his willingness to venture into the dark and mysterious recesses of the forest and to face danger.

To Sam and Yan achievement brought excitement. It was exciting to make a tepee—not any old tepee but a real Indian tepee. It was exciting, too, to make a fire with rubbing-sticks, to cook, Indian fashion, to listen to the strange night noises, to track animals (even the family cat), to trap, to hunt, to kill—not a coon but a spitting, vicious lynx. It was exciting for these two little savages to do all these things for the very reason that in such things Seton himself found his own particular, exciting way of life. He knew of what he wrote and was able to convey that knowledge with enthusiasm to the millions who were to read the work.

Thus far I have said nothing about his ability as a writer in the more limited sense of that word. To avoid some comment on him as a literary person would be a continuation of the silence with which he has been generally treated by literary historians and critics. But to separate his skill as a stylist from the other ingredients that he poured into his moulds is not an easy task. Perhaps he did not even regard himself as a literary figure. His writings indicate little interest in the great works of literature and he seldom refers to other writers. Yet he did formulate for himself a simple theory of composition from which he seldom wavered. It is found in an interesting passage in *Rolf*, and, reduced to its fundamentals, is this: follow the practice of Wordsworth and write of what you know and of the times in which you live. To do otherwise is folly. In following this theory Seton placed severe limits on himself, but it may be said that it was partly through his limitations he achieved success. He knew of what he wrote; he knew for whom he wrote; and what he said was generally stated with apparent simplicity, and effective lucidity.

I at one time thought that Seton was not really interested in writing as an art. But I am now convinced that he was a conscious stylist, quite willing to alter and to prune in order to produce the effects he desired. As a writer of expository passages he was a master; he could handle dialogue with an easy naturalness (this is especially evident in the *Two Little Savages*); and in his best descriptive passages he writes with sensitivity and poetic feeling. Take, for example, this description of a marten, from *Rolf in the Woods:*

> Into a thicket of willow it disappeared and out again like an eel going through the mud, then up a tall stub where woodpecker holes were to be seen. Into the largest so quickly Rolf could scarcely see how it entered, and out in a few seconds bearing a flying squirrel whose skull it had crushed. Dropping the squirrel it leaped after it, and pounced again on the quivering form with a fearsome growl; then shook it savagely, tore it apart, cast it aside. Over the ground it now undulated, its shining yellow breast like a target of gold. Again it stopped. . . . Then the snaky neck swung the cobra head in the breeze and the brown one sniffed, and sniffed, advanced a few steps, tried the wind and the ground. Still farther and the concentrated interest showed in its outstretched neck and quivering tail.

This, which is not atypical, illustrates Seton's competence as a writer. The structural quality of the sentences is such as to produce impressions of rapid motion and of tension. The language, basically simple, is precise and concrete, and appeals to the multiple senses of the reader. And the well controlled occasional metaphor or simile adds a touch of poetic magic to the overall effects.

But Seton nods much more frequently than Homer. His punctuation can be not only erratic but erroneous; his grammar is by no means always precise; and when sentimentality or moralizing overpowers his judgment he produces bathos of the worst order. This will serve to make the last point. It comes from the story of Tito, the wily coyote. She is quietly approaching a prairie-dog, just before the kill:

> She soon cut the fifty yards down to ten, and the ten to five, and still was undiscovered. Then, when again the Prairie-dog dropped down to seek more fodder, she made a quick dash, and bore him off kicking and squealing. Thus does the angel of the pruning-knife lop off those that are heedless and foolishly indifferent to the advantages of society.

It should be evident from the quotations above that no valid claim can be made for Seton as a great writer; but it can be argued that, within his limitations and for his particular purposes, he was usually competent, and at times good. But—and again it must be said—he cannot be finally judged solely as a writer. His success came from his extraordinary ability to fuse into a unified and an artistic whole his manifold gifts—his wide and deep knowledge as a naturalist, his skill as an artist, and his competence as a writer, especially for the young.

Today the success that he first achieved some seventy years ago has been reaffirmed by the myriads of people who have read, and loved, and remembered his works. His brilliant successors, such as Williamson, Gerald Durrell, and Haig-Brown, all of whom write with deep insight of the animal world, have not driven the ancient Nimrod off the stage, nor have the radical changes that have occurred in our own civilization; a brief bibliographical excursion reveals that at least twelve of his volumes are in print and that a limited number of his works are being translated abroad.

Some day, perhaps, old Seton Thompson—or Thompson Seton—will be forced into the limbo where dwell forgotten authors. But for the moment he sits securely on his small throne in the hierarchy of the living. And I believe that he will continue to hold his place so long as the young pitch tents (even backyard, drugstore tents), or gather around camp fires with the gloom of the forests as a backdrop, or look with inquiring eyes into the world of nature.

Patricia Morley

SOURCE: "Seton's Animals," in *Journal of Canadian Fiction,* Vol. II, No. 3, Summer, 1973, pp. 195-98.

"How many of us have ever got to know a wild animal?" Not in a cage, Seton continues in the opening paragraph of the story of Silverspot, but in its natural state and over a continued period of time? We know the answer only too well. Very few. Very few indeed. If we choose to make their acquaintance via the art of Seton, Roberts, Fraser and Saunders, we may end up with an unexpected bonus—namely, knowledge of ourselves. The realistic animal story is a peculiarly Canadian genre and serves to hold a mirror up to certain aspects of the national psyche.

Conservationist John Livingston believes [as he wrote in "Man in the Perspective of Infinite Time"] that Western society is, and traditionally has been, indifferent to the rights of non-human nature: "Perhaps this is because we cannot conceive of having any ethical responsibility to that which is not capable of reciprocating. Ethics, morals, fitness and propriety of behavior—these are human attitudes." Western society is a big subject, and it's not mine, here. But the point is of interest because, while this exploiting attitude towards the natural world may be typical of Western technology, it is emphatically not the attitude of many Canadian writers of both the last century and the present one.

In the preface to *Wild Animals I Have Known,* Seton writes that his stories emphasize "a moral as old as Scripture—we and the beasts are kin." Animals, he insists, are creatures with wants and feelings differing from our own only in degree, and hence they have *rights;* Moses knew this, as did the Buddhist of two thousand years ago. As Redruff, the Don Valley partridge, hangs in the air in a snare, "slowly dying; his very strength a curse," Seton asks: "Have the wild things no moral or legal rights? What right has man to inflict such long and fearful agony on a fellow-creature, simply because that creature does not speak his language?"

Seton's interest in animals as in men lay not in the species but in the individual, the individual hero. It is a romantic bias, and Seton was a romantic by temperament and by choice. He was in search of the picturesque, and he regretted that he had not lived in the wilderness or on the frontier during an earlier epoch, before the natural glories of lakes and woods were forced to give way before "progress" and "the higher beauties of civilization and art." He believed that man's great work is to develop and know himself, and that in order to know himself he must study all things to which he is related: "Each animal is in itself an inexhaustible volume of facts that man must have in order to solve the great problem of knowing himself."

Animal Heroes (1905), the title of one of Seton's books, is the constant theme of his stories about individual animals. In the prefatory note to this collection of eight tales, Seton writes: "A Hero is an individual of unusual gifts and achievements. Whether it be man or animal, this definition applies; and it is the histories of such that appeal to the imagination and to the hearts of those who hear them." The sub-title of *Wild Animals I Have Known* declares the book to be the Personal Histories of Lobo, Silverspot, Ruggylug, Bingo, the Springfield Fox, the Pacing Mustang, Wully, and Redruff. The prefatory note to this first book of Seton's refers to the high degree of heroism and personality in these animals, and the author emphasizes that his theme is "the real personality of the individual, and his view of life" rather than the ways of the species.

Most animals of one species all look alike to human beings, as Seton acknowledges at the beginning of his story of Silverspot the crow: "But once in awhile there arises an animal who is stronger or wiser than his fellow, who becomes a great leader, who is, as we would say, a genius, and if he is bigger, or has some mark by which men can know him, he soon becomes famous in his country, and shows us that the life of a wild animal may be far more interesting and exciting than that of many human beings."

Julia Seton's biography of her husband includes the text of an early poem by Seton called "**The Kingbird**" (1876). He greatly admired this little bird for its ability to defy and repel birds many times its own size. The concluding lines of his poem describe the kingbird as a sparrow in size, an eagle in spirit. Mrs. Seton acknowledges that "**The Kingbird**" is not great poetry, and we can only agree. But she tells us that Seton himself considered it to be the beginning and foundation of all his work as a writer of wild animal stories. The poem celebrates the courage and individuality of the tiny hero-bird.

The first two parts of *By a Thousand Fires* [by Julie M. Seten] paint a horrifying picture of Seton's father and their relationship. Joseph Logan Thompson was a tyrant, a despot, an ego-maniac who was willing, rather reluctantly, to play second fiddle to God and only to God. After many beatings and confrontations, Seton came to hate his father with a warm and lasting passion. (His other life-long hatred was for General Custer.) I have long been suspicious of psychological criticism, but I must confess that Seton's admiration for the little kingbird and other such animal heroes strikes me as not entirely unconnected with his personal experience as a sickly, sensitive but courageous little boy standing up to his tyrannical father.

From his mother, a martyr to his father's selfishness and fits of rage, the child learned that kindliness was "the only thing worthwhile." This faith Seton retained, along with an Emersonian belief in a divine Oversoul. The following quotations are taken from a burial service performed by Seton in Seton Village, New Mexico: ". . . we are adherents of the oldest church of all, the Church of the All-Father, the Great Spirit, the Maker and Ruler of the Universe . . . the Oversoul . . . We feel that all ground is consecrated if we approach it with reverent attitude, realizing that the whole world is the Holy Ground of the Great Spirit . . . We are ever in the consciousness of the Great All-Father . . . a God of love and kindness . . ."

Seton's attitude towards his writings, and towards his vocation as an artist-naturalist, reflects his basic religious orientation. He shows the Victorian preference for truth over art or beauty, and his primary intention is to write what is true, edifying, and moral. His Note to the Reader in *Wild Animals I Have Known* begins, "These stories are true." Seton admits to often leaving "the strict line of historical truth" and to having "pieced together" some of the characters, while noting that in some

of the stories there is "almost no deviation from the truth." The preface to *Animal Heroes* reveals the same preoccupations. While the stories are admitted to be "more or less composite," they are founded on "the actual life of a veritable animal hero." Seton duly records which tales are the most and which the least 'composite,' preferring this strangely technical or scientific word to any reference to imagination or art.

Critics have taken Seton at his word and seen his animal stories as the simple case-histories of a naturalist. In his 1958 Introduction to the New Canadian Library edition of Charles G. D. Roberts' *The Last Barrier and Other Stories,* Alec Lucas states: "Roberts wrote as a creative artist and Seton as a naturalist, and one dependent on his imagination and the other on his powers of observation to give his natural-history meaning, or, more briefly, for Roberts it was art first; for Seton it was science." Seton, had his opinion been asked, might well have agreed. But should we? Certainly I have no quarrel with the view that Roberts is a creative artist, and never more so than in the best of his animal stories. Seton's tales, however, have a unique strength and beauty. The animal protagonists are living personalities who hold the reader's attention throughout. Our interest in their fate is reinforced by the fine sense of detail, the delightful humour, the simple yet vivid language and, occasionally, the perceptions of a mystic. In these 'composite' portraits, the artist in Seton worked better than he knew.

Julia Seton notes [in *By a Thousand Fires*] that a previously unpublished Seton manuscript reveals her husband's single-minded intention to record the truth. Seton's article refers to the fairy tale and its near kinsman, the romantic animal story. A few of these tales retain a permanent hold on old and young alike: "Their strength lies in this: THEY ARE TRUE. They may be mixed with error, they may be disguised by the fanciful . . . But still, in the main they are true . . . As with all lasting work, they are *the truth from the heart through the head* of a man of genius."

Aesop's Fables, Seton writes, humanize the animals in order to exemplify a moral truth, thereby "creating a false picture on the whole." St. Francis of Assisi struck a new note in the twelfth century with the gospel that the animals were meant to share with man in the benefits of Christian charity. In the middle of the nineteenth century, the evolutionists preached that animals are not simply our spiritual breathren but our blood kin. These are the literary and philosophic antecedents which Seton sees for the new type of animal story which begins to appear in the late nineteenth century. It differed from the fable chiefly in the degree of sympathy evoked for the animal hero. In crediting the evolutionists with the view that the animals are our kin, Seton ignores for the moment the fact that he had ascribed this knowledge, in his 1898 preface, to Moses and the ancient Buddhists.

The truth, then, was Seton's touchstone. While remaining faithful to what he saw as the truth, Seton felt free to choose unusual individuals (animal *heroes*), to ascribe to them the adventures and attributes of several of their race (his 'composite' method), and to allow them to do things which although never observed were completely possible and even probable. To the anticipated criticism that he has added a human atmosphere, a sensibility foreign to his animal subjects, Seton replies: "No man can write of another personality without adding a suggestion of his own. The personal touch may be the poison of science, but may also be the making of literature, and is *absolutely inevitable.*" All fiction, Seton implies, is a kind of autobiography.

Seton's autobiography is entitled, significantly, *Trail of an Artist-Naturalist* (1940). While Seton may not have thought of himself as an artist in words, he was also the illustrator of his own books. He studied art in Toronto (winning a gold medal at the Ontario College of Art in 1879) and in Paris. Seton was a man of diverse talents: practical architect, sculptor, portrait painter, graphic artist. He worked in many mediums, including pencil, charcoal, ink, wash and water colour. Julia Seton writes that her husband "never thought of his work as art presentation—although he knew it was good. Each delineation was to him merely a documentary record of what he had seen, but each an authoritative portrait of an experience in his life." Merely? This may be Julia Seton's view and now Seton's; or perhaps Seton undervalued the artistic element in his visual art as in his written tales, in his effort to honour the 'truth.'

However that may be, Seton's sketches and paintings speak for themselves. I came to them first at the age of twelve, and both drawings and stories remained vividly in my mind. The stories in *Wild Animals I Have Known* each begin with an illustrated capital letter, as in medieval manuscripts. These depict, often with whimsical humour, the hero of the tale or some aspect of his story. Miniature sketches of plants and animals enliven the margins of many pages. Four foxcubs polishing off a too-curious squirrel are tagged "And the little ones picked his Bones e-oh!" Along with these numerous small drawings are thirty full-page illustrations: "There she had lain, and mourned;" "Frank retreated each time the world turned;" "No chance to turn now;" "The hound came sniffing along the log." Seton's ability to depict animal movement is remarkable, his sense of composition authoritative, and he includes the telling detail while suggesting vast space.

His drawing, like his writing, testifies to his imagination and humour. Seton illustrated his *Life Histories of Northern Animals* (1925-28) with 1500 illustrations. These included not only scientifically accurate drawings but others that Seton called his synoptic drawings. These sketches caught the life and character of the animal, its very essence. The publisher was horrified to find humorous and imaginative sketches in "an otherwise erudite book" and attempted to persuade the author to remove them, but Seton held firm and won out.

His illustrations are also comments on his philosophical and religious concepts. A small two-inch square drawing on the title page of *Wild Animals I Have Known* depicts the Peaceable Kingdom. A man, seated at the foot of a giant tree, is surrounded by birds and animals: a horse, two foxes, a rabbit, dog, wolf, partridge, crow—a Canadian version of the lion lying down with the lamb. The final sketch in this volume shows a naked man flanked by a large bird and a dog or wolf. A flaming sun encircles the trinity of creatures, and this mandala is placed at the centre of a double-spiraling 'eye.'

Seton's love for his animal heroes is one of the most striking features of his tales. In his outline of the historical development of the animal story, he characterized the late nineteenth-century animal story by the sympathy it evokes for the animal hero. This sympathy takes two forms: firstly, an interest in the doings of creatures whose lives, as Seton claims, are often more dramatic and exciting than those of many human beings; and secondly, pity for their fate. In the Note to *Wild Animals*, Seton writes: "The fact that these stories are true is the reason why all are tragic. The life of a wild animal *always has a tragic end.*" In the story of Silverspot. Seton observes that there are no hospitals for sick crows.

When Lobo, the "grand old outlaw" and King of the Currumpaw range, has finally been trapped through his love for his mate, Seton eulogizes the fallen king in a passage of great tenderness: "Poor old hero, he had never ceased to search for his darling, and when he found the trail her body had made he followed it recklessly, and so fell into the snare prepared for him." Lobo is staked out with a collar and chain. He refuses food and water, and dies of a broken heart; "A lion shorn of his strength, an eagle robbed of his freedom, or a dove bereft of his mate, all die, it is said, of a broken heart; and who will aver that this grim bandit could bear the three-fold brunt, heart-whole? . . . his spirit was gone—the old King-wolf was dead."

Seton admires courage, and also common sense, which he describes as a thousand times better than the reckless courage of the bulldog. The Springfield foxes know better than to try to dig for a woodchuck: "hard work was not their way of life; wits they believed worth more than elbow-grease."

Seton describes in detail the social organization of the band of crows who made their headquarters near Castle Frank in Toronto's Don Valley. He says the crow organization is admitted by the bird kingdom to be the best that there is, and that crows, "though a little people, are of great wit, a race of birds with a language and a social system that is wonderfully human in many of its chief points, and in some is better carried out than our own." Since it is essentially a benevolent monarchy where the leader and his lieutenants are the oldest, wisest and bravest, and since this form of government obviously evokes the author's admiration at the time he wrote *Wild Animals I Have Known* (1898), it is surprising to discover that in later years Seton declared himself to be "deeply in sympathy with the American ideal of government."

Margaret Atwood and James Polk have recently made the point that Canadian animal stories present animals as victims, and that this may indicate a willingness or even a need on the part of Canadians to see themselves in the role of victim. Atwood sees in this tendency violence repressed, violence turned in upon itself in a kind of death wish. This is the way in which Hugh MacLennan views the form of puritanism he sees in North America today. Polk speaks of the "tight-lipped Presbyterian endurance" of the suffering Canadian animal, and speculates about the influence of Roberts' and Seton's books, as popular reading for children, on the collective Canadian psyche.

American animal stories are usually hunting stories, where sympathy is directed towards the hunter; or psychological dramas such as *Moby Dick,* where the animal symbolizes something in man's own nature which is to be appropriated or subdued. A recent American adaptation of Seton's ***Wild Animals I Have Known*** provides a striking illustration of the American preference for the hunting story and the tendency to identify sympathetically with the human hunter. On the cover, valiant old Lobo, whom Seton describes as king and hero, is transformed into a demonic red-eyed, red-tongued beast who is just about to be lassoed by the big brave hunter. Lobo becomes "the wicked king of the Corrumpa (sic)" and "another killer wolf," appellations completely foreign to both the language and spirit of the original. The closing pages of Lobo's story in the adaptation make none of the effect of heroism, steadfastness or nobility that is found in the original, and Lobo's reunion with Blanca in death is cut out, as is the passage I quoted earlier which begins "A lion shorn of his strength . . ."

In the story of Redruff, the Don Valley partridge, the adaptation omits Seton's impassioned protest against man's inhumanity to the animal kingdom and his rhetorical question about animal rights. In "Silverspot," it omits the numerous references to crow government and social organization. Seton's "the old chieftain," "the strict teacher," are changed to "the leader;" and the communal emphasis in Seton's eulogy to Silverspot ("His long life of usefulness to his tribe was over") is lost in the adaptation's "His long life was ended."

In comparing this adaptation with the original, I found that all the passages I had marked in the latter as being of particular beauty and interest, and/or indicative of Seton's attitudes, were passages that had been not merely reworded but dropped entirely from the American version. The adaptation claims to be "adapted by language-arts experts to the needs of today's children." It claims, further, to retain the flavour of the original and to provide mature content. My reaction is, God help the children who are fed this pap.

Marshall Saunders (1861-1947), a Maritimer, was born one year earlier and died one year later than Seton. She offered the manuscript of *Beautiful Joe: An Autobiography* (1894) in a competition sponsored by the Humane Society, and dedicated it to the President of the American Humane Education Society and the Massachusetts Society for the Prevention of Cruelty to Animals. Her frank purpose was heart-education: to awaken in the reader a sympathy for animals which might improve his behaviour towards them.

Like Seton and his martyred mother, Saunders's watchword is kindness. Cruelty towards animals filled her with horror. In her fictional autobiography of the dog whose ears and tail have been cut by his first master, another animal tells Beautiful Joe: "We animals kill mercifully. It is only human beings who butcher their prey, and seem, some of them, to rejoice in their agony." Hezekiah Butterworth's enthusiastic Introduction finds kindness to animals to be a basic principle in the growth of true philanthropy, and Saunders's sympathetic insight, "ethically the strong feature of the book." Butterworth refers to Moses' recognition of this principle. One of the novel's characters instructs a visitor that children may be taught to be thoughtful and unselfish by giving them animals to care for. "The Lord made us all one family," says Mrs. Morris, moving easily from neglected animals to neglected humans. Children should learn that just as alcohol will destroy their bodies, so "cruelty to any of God's living creatures will blight and destroy their innocent young souls." And Saunders makes it quite clear, through Joe and other animal protagonists, that animals have *rights*.

Saunders has her own version of the Peaceable Kingdom. Miss Laura succeeds in teaching Malta the cat not to hurt birds. Saunders's mood, unlike Seton's, is predominantly sentimental, and Miss Laura's tears fall thick and fast at the sight of any animal in distress. She is depicted as attempting to control this tendency in herself, in order to channel all her energies into opposing cruelty.

Saunders resembles Seton in being concerned with truth rather than art. Her preface notes that the human characters are drawn from life, that "the smallest detail is truthfully depicted," and that nearly all the incidents are founded on fact. Sentimentality is not in fashion today. And there are unintentionally comic scenes such as the one where Joe acts with social consciousness ("I got up and stood in front of her, for a well-bred dog should not lie down when a lady speaks to him") or accuses himself of being selfish. Despite such flaws, the technique of first person narration is well done (the dog relates his own story) and many of the scenes are memorable. I loved it as a child, and find it still has the power to hold my attention. But for a twentieth-century audience, *Beautiful Joe* is a children's book, while Seton's stories could appeal to any age.

How many of us have ever had the chance to know a wild animal? But we can know Seton's. Conrad, in his Preface to *The Nigger of the 'Narcissus',* says that the task of the artist is, before all, to make us *see*. And that is exactly what Seton does. His vision is leavened with humour, as in the picture of Slum Cat, held against her will in an antiseptic house and a garden *polluted* with roses: "The very Horses and Dogs had the wrong smells; the whole country round was a repellent desert of lifeless, disgusting gardens and hayfields, without a single tenement or smoke-stack in sight . . . altogether it was the most unlovely, unattractive, unsmellable spot she had ever known."

He moves easily between homely comparisons (it is as impossible for the crows to protect their spoil from kingbirds as it is for the fat apple-woman to catch the small boys who have raided her basket) and poetic descriptions such as that of the barren uplands where battles of sun and frost have split the grey-green rocks and exposed "their inner fleshy tints." From time to time an incident will suggest a parallel between animal and human experience: "The life game is a hard game, for we may win ten thousand times, and if we fail but once our gain is gone." The Bible supplies some of his metaphors: the mourning Vixen watches over her dead cubs "like Rizpah" (Saul's concubine); and the little mare used to snare the Pacing Mustang is tagged Delilah.

Seton, whose long life-time spanned two eras, was one of our first conservationists. Was it necessary to agriculture that the wonderful things of the wilderness be exterminated? Certainly not, he told the Canadian Club in 1924: "We have desolated our heritage, absolutely devastated these wonderful wilds. We have robbed our children. We have robbed our country."

The naturalist and the artist were wonderfully complementary in this man. One thinks of Frederick Philip Grove, whose *Over Prairie Trails* exhibits this same combination of scientific detail and artistic vision; or Henry Jackson, Ottawa mycologist and watercolourist, whose technically accurate paintings of mushrooms are at the same time works of beauty. Woodcraft is the oldest of all sciences. Art's lineage is equally ancient. In Seton's work, they make a great team.

TITLE COMMENTARY

📖 *WILD ANIMALS I HAVE KNOWN* (1898; Canadian edition, 1900; British edition, 1902)

The Nation (New York)

SOURCE: A review of *Wild Animals I Have Known,* in *The Nation* (New York), Vol. LXVII, No. 1746, December 15, 1898, pp. 454-55.

The motive of this charming book reminds us of the more formal treatise on the personality of animals by Prof. Shaler, reviewed at length in these columns not long ago, though the method is entirely different. Both books bear upon the kinship of man with other animals;

bespeak kindly, sympathetic feelings towards our fellow-creatures of a lower order than ourselves; and dwell upon the marked individuality or personal peculiarities which every beast will be found to possess when studied closely enough. Prof. Shaler gave us the more scientific aspect of the theme which Mr. Thompson now presents from a more artistic point of view. The latter strikes his keynote in these passages of his preface:

> The fact that these stories are true is the reason why all are tragic. The life of a wild animal *always has a tragic end.*
>
> We and the beasts are kin. Man has nothing that the animals have not at least a vestige of, the animals have nothing that man does not in some degree share. Since, then, the animals are creatures with wants and feelings differing in degree only from our own, surely they have their rights.

By way of pointing out an extreme case of human possibility in the brutes, let us ask, who would imagine a Jekyl and Hyde dog? But there are such. Mr. Thompson tells us the story of Wully, the mongrel sheep-dog, and elsewhere speaks of another case—

> a similar yaller dog who long lived the double life— a faithful sheep-dog by day, and a bloodthirsty, treacherous monster by night. Such things are less rare than is supposed, and since writing these stories I have heard of another double-lived sheepdog that added to its night amusements the crowning barbarity of murdering the smaller dogs of the neighborhood. He had killed twenty and hidden them in a sandpit, when discovered by his master. He died just as Wully did.

One can never be indifferent to tragedy, and Mr. Thompson holds our unflagging interest in his stories. He knows his animals as individual characters, and sets forth their lives vividly, making us feel for and with them, through all their vicissitudes to the appointed death by violence. Not that these lives are all sad—on the contrary, there is plenty of fun, and keen enjoyment of living, and development of all sorts of traits; it is the inevitableness of fate that lends a sombre undertone to the whole recital. The treatment of these themes is not less artistic with the pen than with the pencil, in both of which modes of expression Mr. Thompson shows himself easily master of his subject.

The eight stories are of Lobo the wolf, "King of Currumpaw"; Silverspot the crow; Ruggylug the cottontail rabbit; Bingo the dog; the Springfield fox; the pacing mustang; Wully the "yaller" dog above mentioned; and Redruff the partridge. Each is illustrated with one or more full-page plates, which merit more than a mere word of praise. Mr. Thompson is now drawing the best mammals of any American artist; from a strictly technical or zoological standpoint they surpass his birds, in fact, and in the present case he has been able to give his fancy free play in depicting the sentiments and passions of animals, and the shifting scenes in their personal lives,

From Rolf in the Woods, *written and illustrated by Ernest Thompson Seton.*

as true to nature as their mere forms. It is not easy to pick out one of the stories in point of our remarks, they are all so good; but the Springfield fox particularly arrested our attention and excited our sympathy. Compare the plates . . . the cruel complacency and exultation of the first, the cunning and expectancy of the next, the utter woe of the third, where Vixen watches "like Rizpah" by her dead cubs, stretched stiff-legged in the snow—we can even see that their noses are cold!

This is artistic fidelity to nature in high degree—a kind of realism that the technical naturalist requires, to which is added that lifelikeness which satisfies the most ardent imagination. Besides these striking plates, the broad margins of the pages are utilized with more than 150 very telling thumbnail sketches, as a sort of running commentary on the text. Nothing of equal simplicity could be more effective than these little oddities and whimsies. The book is thoroughly good, both in purpose and execution; it should find a wide circle of interested readers, to whose sympathies it appeals so strongly and so humanly.

William H. Magee

SOURCE: "The Animal Story: A Challenge in Technique," in *The Dalhousie Review,* Vol. 44, No. 2, Summer, 1964, pp. 156-64.

[Sir Charles G. D.] Roberts in *Earth's Enigmas* stimulated several kinds of animal stories, but neither the naturalists nor the romancers succeeded in discovering any other distinctive patterns in plots. Naturalists and wild-animal lovers like Ernest Thompson Seton and Grey Owl tried using animal stories to make natural history memorable, but they also made it bizarre. Explaining the choice in the prefatory "Note to the Reader" in *Wild Animals I Have Known,* the first of more than a dozen volumes, Seton applies hero worship to the animal world as the most memorable device for informing the reader about a species. In the stories themselves, however, he stresses individual rather than representative aspects of heroism. Lobo the wolf organizes a pack in deliberate opposition to man, and Lobo proves his superiority to man in incident after incident (**"Lobo, the King of Currumpaw"**). Vixen the fox eludes a watch at both the hen house and the kennel, to bring freshly killed chickens to his captured cub night after night (**"The Springfield Fox"**). At best these stories create a dramatic tension comparable with Roberts', and Seton can deepen them with a similarly tragic vision: "No wild animal dies of old age. Its life has soon or late a tragic end. It is only a question of how long it can hold out against its foes." (**"Raggylug, the Story of a Cottontail Rabbit"**). Thus Vixen the fox counters every human attempt to thwart her feeding her cub, but when she concludes that she can never free the cub she kills it, in a particularly moving climax. Most of Seton's stories, however, are too episodic to build up such drama. Without a representative unifying drive like the constant search for food in Roberts' stories (in these stories the animals seldom eat), Seton's animals usually drift from crisis to unrelated crisis. Silverspot the crow learns many separate things in his recounted life (**"Silverspot, the Story of a Crow"**), and Redruff the partridge sees his young die one by one (**"Redruff, the Story of the Don Valley Partridge"**), and then each is by chance eaten by an owl. Even less promising are the stories in which Seton turned desperately to conventions of human fiction, which are not only trite but gratuitous in the animal world. Lobo the wonder wolf abandons its fight against man and lets itself be trapped when its mate is caught. Seton was unable to expand the genre of the animal story with any new patterns of plot or characterization.

Clarence Petersen

SOURCE: A review of *Wild Animals I Have Known,* in *Chicago Tribune,* September 27, 1987, p. 4.

Your grandparents, and indeed your great-grandparents, may well have read this book as children, and for good reason. Published in 1894, when it inspired Kipling to write his *Jungle Books,* it become a popular classic of natural history. From track and wing marks in the snow, Seton could reconstruct the struggle between a snowshoe rabbit and a horned owl. He wrote with a raconteur's verve, knew his stuff—at least most of the time—and this book made him rich. But because Seton believed animals could think and could be motivated by emotion, it also made him controversial. In 1903, John Burroughs, one of the great natural scientists, denounced Seton in print for insisting his stories were true and listing the "lies" Burroughs had found in this book. But no matter. What Seton saw and the actions he recorded were not in dispute, only the implicit suggestion that he could read the animals' thoughts.

📖 *THE TRAIL OF THE SANDHILL STAG* (1899)

The Canadian Magazine

SOURCE: A review of *The Trail of the Sandhill Stag,* in *The Canadian Magazine,* Vol. XIV, No. 4, February, 1900, pp. 393-97.

The big game of Canada are the equal of the big game of any other country in the world. Yet it is surprising the number of people who know not the differences between the goat and the big horn, or the moose and the musk-ox, or the elk and the black-tail. It is also noteworthy that the romance of the lives of our big game is so little sought after, although it is one of the most wonderful of all natural romances.

Among those who have been impressed by the wonders of the animal-life to be seen in this country, is Ernest Thompson Seton, a Canadian artist, whose pictures of wolves first brought him into prominence. Seven or eight years ago, when a large canvas of his was on exhibition in Canada, the Canadian critics, with their usual unenthusiastic conservatism, said that he could paint wolves, but he couldn't do anything else. Since then he has written: *Wild Animals I Have Known, Art Anatomy of Animals, Mammals of Manitoba, Birds of Manitoba, The Trail of the Sandhill Stag.* It is this latest work which claims especial mention here. It is a handsome volume containing some sixty drawings and ninety pages of well-printed text. The story describes how for years Yan the hunter followed the great hoof-marks in the Sandhill wilderness about Carberry, Manitoba. Other hunters had caught glimpses of this noted stag, but it was a long quest before Yan even saw him.

> Then gray among the gray brush, he made out a great log, and from one end of it rose two gnarled oaken boughs. Again the flash—the move of a restless ear, then the oak boughs moved and Yan trembled, for he knew that the log in the brush was the form of the Sandhill Stag. So grand, so charged with *life*. He seemed a precious, sacred thing—a king, fur-robed and duly crowned.

But Yan didn't shoot him then, the stag escaped and Yan followed.

The feelings and thoughts of the hunter, the ruses and deceptions of the hunted, the denouement of the great game the two were playing, are well described. The whole picture is artistically drawn, with the high-mindedness of the author to preserve it from being the representation of a ruthless slaughter.

The Spectator

SOURCE: A review of *The Trail of the Sandhill Stag,* in *The Spectator,* No. 4487, June 27, 1914, pp. 1062-64.

The second volume from the pen of this fertile writer is *The Trail of the Sandhill Stag,* "dedicated to the old-timers of the Big Plain of Manitoba." It is a slender tale, with many pretty illustrations, of a lad who has the hunting fever strong on him, but cannot bring himself to pull the trigger when he has at last made a successful stalk. An atmosphere of snow, lakes, pines, wolves, and Indians surrounds the subject. There is nothing on the title-page to inform the guileless English reader that this is not a new book; but the story was copyrighted in the United States as long ago as 1899.

Robert Wegner

SOURCE: A review of *The Trail of the Sandhill Stag,* in *AB Bookman's Weekly,* Vol. 92, No. 2, July 12, 1993, pp. 100-01.

In 1899, Ernest Thompson Seton, that brilliant naturalist who waxed so eloquently on deer and deer hunting, put the final touches to the blue-chip deer books of the 19th century by adding to the list *The Trail of the Sandhill Stag,* one of the most thought-provoking, sensitive, moving tales ever written on the long, endless pursuit of a black-tailed stag. I highly recommend it for boys of 20 and for boys of 60 and over. In this deer hunting tale, Seton challenges and examines the basic philosophy of the chase.

Although the original edition of this book is out of print—only 250 copies were published—it went through numerous editions, and copies of these later editions can be readily found in used bookstores and at a reasonable price. This little volume of less than 100 pages will arouse the spirit of any deer hunter. It is a fascinating record of long searches that usually end in an unsuccessful manner; it captures the spell of the woods and the joy of the hunter. A story to read and reread! In the fall of 1899, *The New York Times* instantly recognized it as a classic. "It is in every way thoroughly pleasing, both through the beauty of the story—one which once read, we think, can never be forgotten—and in its illustrations and general make-up, all the details of which are worthy of the charm of Mr. Seton's style."

📖 *THE BIOGRAPHY OF A GRIZZLY* (1900)

The Canadian Magazine

SOURCE: A review of *The Biography of a Grizzly,* in *The Canadian Magazine,* Vol. XV, No. 1, May, 1900, pp. 91-2.

Not being a popular novelist Ernest Seton-Thompson's reputation grows slowly, but it is growing. The foundations have been laid broad and deep, and the structure may be as lasting as a Rhine castle or the Appian Way. His latest book *The Biography of a Grizzly* with its seventy-five drawings, is a work of art, of art in its two-fold sense. It is an artistic story, this biography of Wahb, the huge grizzly bear that was once a little yellow ball rolling over and over on the grass with three other little yellow balls, and a great mother grizzly looking on contentedly. What Wahb learned about traps, smells, roots, ants, and the pleasure and pain of life is admirably set down by this sage interpreter of the animal kingdom. The book is artistic in another sense, for the drawings by Mr. Thompson and his accomplished wife have been reproduced so as to reveal and interpret what the story tells. The volume is most dainty, a pearl among the many gems now being produced to satisfy the rising taste of an appreciative public. And Mr. and Mrs. Thompson are Canadians.

The Dial

SOURCE: A review of *The Biography of a Grizzly,* in *The Dial,* Vol. XXVIII, No. 334, May 16, 1900, p. 408.

One of the most charming books that have recently issued from the press is that in which the Century Co. have reproduced Mr. Ernest Seton-Thompson's *The Biography of a Grizzly."* It is not quite safe to call any writing a classic that is only a year old, but we feel reasonably confident that this piece of sympathetic delineation of animal life will have a longer life than most books. The illustrations by the author, and the decorative designs by his talented wife, present many unusual and even startling effects, but they are unfailingly artistic in their feeling, and no less important than the text in accounting for the attractiveness of the book.

LIVES OF THE HUNTED: A TRUE ACCOUNT OF THE DOINGS OF FIVE QUADRUPEDS AND THREE BIRDS (1901; British edition, 1902)

Charles Atwood Kofoid

SOURCE: A review of *Lives of the Hunted: A True Account of the Doings of Five Quadrupeds and Three Birds,* in *The Dial,* Vol. XXXI, No. 371, December 1, 1901, pp. 439-40.

The hunting instinct is by no means eradicated from the human breast, though it plays but little part, directly, in the economy of the civilized life of to-day. The old habit still lurks in our veins, and most of us follow a good animal story with something of the zest of the chase. Authors—and publishers too—have found this out; and, following in the wake of *The Jungle Books* and *Wild Animals I Have Known,* come new claimants for our interest.

Some naturalists and more scientists are half inclined to

quarrel with this newly-fledged method of depicting animal life, and some would even relegate the whole anthropomorphic menagerie to the forests of Wonderland. Mr. Seton-Thompson seems to have heard of these criticisms, for in the preface of his latest collection of stories, *Lives of the Hunted,* he takes particular pains to state that "The material of these accounts is true. The chief liberty taken is in ascribing to one animal the adventures of several." Nevertheless, we note that a particularly interesting adventure of "Johnny," the dyspeptic bear cub of Yellowstone Park, is told by Mr. Seton-Thompson—and it loses nothing in the telling—on the authority "of three bronzed mountaineers." It is obviously unfair to ask for an extension of the list of authorities. It is equally unfair to fail to recognize the fund of animal lore from which the material of these tales is drawn. They should not, however, be judged as scientific reports upon the habits and instincts of animals where unvarnished fact and cold logic admit of no embellishment for the reader's delectation. They are essentially and primarily stories with an underlying basis of fact and observation. In any case, the court of final appeal is open, and we can all take to the woods and plains and obtain a first-hand acquaintance with their furred and feathered denizens. The stories in Mr. Seton-Thompson's present collection include his recent as well as some of his earlier contributions to periodical literature. Krag, Biddy and Randy, Johnny Bear, Tito, Chink, and the Kangaroo Rat, are most of them old friends; and whether old or new are sure of a welcome from hosts of readers among the children of all ages. In the humor and the human element which this author finds in his animal friends, lies one of the secrets of his well-deserved popularity.

TWO LITTLE SAVAGES (1903)

The Dial

SOURCE: A review of *Two Little Savages,* in *The Dial,* Vol. XXXV, No. 419, December 1, 1903, pp. 429-30.

Intended for those of fewer years and more imaginative qualities, Mr. Ernest Thompson Seton has limited himself more than usually to facts in *Two Little Savages,* wherein a party of youngsters have good times playing at being Indians. This book, with its numerous illustrations and enticing make-up, should add many new recruits to Mr. Seton's, large juvenile following.

The Canadian Magazine

SOURCE: A review of *Two Little Savages,* in *The Canadian Magazine,* Vol. XXII, No. 3, January, 1904, pp. 304-05.

The index at the back of Thompson Seton's new volume, *Two Little Savages* tells a tale. The book is intended to be more than a story for boys who love animals and the experiences of the bush; it is a handbook of flower, bird and animal lore. . . .

It is much the same style of book as Sandys' *Trapper Jim,* but is more artistic in style and illustration. It is doubtful, however, if either book would be classed as literature. Both are books which will interest boys and divert their minds into wholesome channels of exploration and research. On the other hand, White's *The Magic Forest* is real literature, a genuinely artistic story. Mr. Seton's book is beautifully illustrated, printed and bound.

Joan McGrath

SOURCE: "The Red and the White: Canadian Books for Children," in *School Library Journal,* Vol. 27, No. 1, September, 1980, p. 41.

One interesting departure from [Seton's] usual animal-hero format was the somewhat autobiographical *Two Little Savages,* a story of two young farm lads who are permitted a rare holiday, living in a tepee and attempting to master the Indian survival crafts of which they have read. Even now, so many years later, every spirited youngster dreams of such a Robinson Crusoe existence, free of everyday concerns and full of challenge. Seton provided all the instruction one could require for attempting a similar adventure, in both the text and his own marginal sketches.

Noel Perrin

SOURCE: A review of *Two Little Savages,* in *Washington Post Book World,* September 9, 1990, p. 11.

For the last 130 years or so, small boys in America have played the game called cowboys and Indians. Even now, in the age of Nintendo games and Native Americans, they continue to.

The curious thing is that nearly all the small boys want to be Indians. When I was little myself, I used to pretend I *was* part Indian. . . .

There is one book above all other books that will appeal to boys (and girls) who have had such fantasies. And it is quite capable of creating the fantasy in those who haven't. This is Ernest Thompson Seton's *Two Little Savages.*

The book takes place in Canada, but not in one of the wild parts. It's set in tame farm country, where deer are extinct and Indians have long been gone. The nearest thing to wilderness is a big swamp 10 miles away, where no one lives because no one has gotten around to draining the water yet. The time must be around 1880.

The main character is a boy named Yan. Yan is no farm kid; he has grown up in a small provincial city, one of the many children in a shabby-genteel family.

Yan is the family misfit. What he cares about is pure nature. He dreams—what else?—about being an Indian, and in his secret fantasies he tries to talk and act like one. What his parents and most of his siblings care about is respectability, plus a particularly deadening kind of religion. When Yan is trying to get a dollar together to buy his first nature book—he is about 11—he starts doing odd jobs for neighbors, to earn a nickel here, a dime there. His father finds out, and instantly forbids him to continue. Stacking firewood is not work fit for a gentleman's son, the father thunders. But this same father gives him no allowance at all, not even a nickel a week. Says he can't afford to.

When Yan is 14, he gets tuberculosis, and is sent off to live on a farm for a year and regain his health. He will earn every penny of his room and board doing farm chores, so this the father can afford.

William Raften, the Irish-born farmer who takes Yan in, has a son the same age, a boy names Sam. Sam shares Yan's passion for the woods—and quickly gets infected with his equal passion to live like an Indian. Before Yan has been a week on the farm, the two boys have started to build a tepee in the patch of weeds down by the creek that runs through Raften's farm. The farmer is perfectly willing to let them, provided they get all their chores done first.

They hit a problem almost immediately. They are trying to fasten the tepee poles together with willow withes, which keep slipping. The farmer comes down to see how his son and the city boy are doing—and offers them some baling wire from the barn. Yan answers, "We ain't allowed to use anything but what the Indians had or could get in the woods."

"An' who don't allow yez?"

"The rules."

Raften is amused by this, and promptly shows them how to find and use the tough branches of a shrub called leatherwood.

Yan and Sam soon have their tepee and their camp. They now constitute themselves the Sanger Indians. Sam has metamorphosed into the Great Chief Woodpecker, and Yan is the almost as great chief Little Beaver. And the book is fully launched.

A long series of adventures follows. Woodpecker and Little Beaver learn to paint themselves with war paint. They learn to make arrows, to hunt, to track, to read the forest floor like a book. They encounter an imaginary banshee and a horribly real three-fingered tramp. With help from Mrs. Raften, they get permission to spend three weeks entirely in the woods, extra chores to be done when they get back. They admit a third boy to the tribe. They get a technical adviser in the person of a lonely old man named Caleb Clark, who many years ago had lived with real Indians. There's a grand climax, involving a trip to the big swamp, a new and rival "Indian" tribe, and the three-fingered tramp.

Two Little Savages has some four or five separate charms. The greatest, of course, is the wonderful if vicarious sense of accomplishment the reader gets watching Yan and Sam acquire skill after skill. It isn't entirely vicarious, either. Seton is unobtrusive about his instruction—but relying only on *Two Little Savages,* a reader could fletch his or her own arrows, make a very beautiful wood and leather drum, build an excellent small dam. All this using only what the Indians had or could get in the woods.

But the book offers other pleasures almost as great. The character studies of Yan and Sam, for example—and of many other people as well, such as Guy Burns, the irrepressibly boastful third member of the tribe. There are the marginal illustrations, by my count numbering well over 200. My two favorites are a study of 12-year-old Guy Burns with and without war paint (the difference is amazing), and a tiny set of a dozen tepees as decorated by different tribes. Seton, a master artist, drew all these himself.

Then there's Seton's ability to keep two or three plots going at once, all of them exciting. There are the formal full-page illustrations (22 of them); there is Sam's lively wit, and so on.

I can think of only two flaws. Seton does have a certain taste for melodrama when dealing with grown-up characters. And in true Victorian style he is impossibly sentimental about little girls. But there is only one of these in the book—Sam's kid sister Minnie—and only one scene where you actually cringe.

I can never be First Stabber (and now that as a grown-up I know what the name means, I wouldn't want to be). But maybe I can be that milder thing, First Recommender. I'll recommend. *Two Little Savages* would make a stunning present for almost any kid who loves the woods.

📖 MONARCH, THE BIG BEAR OF TALLAC (1904; British edition, 1905)

The Canadian Magazine

SOURCE: A review of *Monarch, the Big Bear of Tallac,* in *The Canadian Magazine,* Vol. XXIV, No. 2, December, 1904, p. 189.

Ernest Thompson Seton gives us of his genius in small parcels. His latest book contains about 30,000 words as compared with 70,000 in Roberts's *Watchers of the Trail.* Mr. Seton's book has one hundred drawings, where as Mr. [Charles G. D.] Roberts's volume has but sixty; yet of the one hundred, only eight are full-page, while of the sixty, forty-seven are given the limit of space. Thus economically Mr. Seton's book is worth about one-third the price of Mr. Roberts's. Mr. Seton's book is a high price because the author believes in introducing his productions in good clothing, giving in quality what they lack in quantity. *Monarch, the Big Bear,* is a splendidly

dramatic story and is well worth reading. Still, with all its beautiful type, nice paper and artistic ink blotches, one cannot but feel that the public seeking a good book investment will pass it over. As a Christmas present for a dainty maiden with artistic bent, it will be quite suitable; but if similar presents are required for strong, healthy boys, I should recommend *The Watchers of the Trail* and *The Kindred of the Wild,* which are uniformly bound. Every Christmas present of books should be suited to the recipient.

The Dial

SOURCE: A review of *Monarch, the Big Bear of Tallac,* in *The Dial,* Vol. XXXVII, No. 443, December 1, 1904, p. 374.

The story of *Monarch, the Big Bear of Tallac* is Mr. Ernest Thompson Seton's contribution to the year's holiday literature. As he takes pains to state distinctly in the foreword that his story is not intended to be pure science, but is rather an historical novel of Bear life, its aim being to convey the truth, but the truth about an unusual and composite animal, we do not see how it can result in any prolongation of the recent controversy about the genuineness of Mr. Seton's writings. The story of *Monarch* is longer than most of his narratives, so that it fills out an attractive little volume, which has of course been illustrated and decorated by its author. The marginal drawings are not so clever as some of his earlier work, but the full-page pictures of the cub 'Jack' are irresistibly humorous, and the story of his evolution from an affectionate and mischievous little household pet into the mysterious and ruthless sheepkiller of Tallac is as thrilling and pathetic as anything Mr. Seton has given us.

📖 WOODMYTH AND FABLE (1905)

The Bookman

SOURCE: A review of *Woodmyth and Fable,* in *The Bookman,* Vol. XXIX, No. 170, November, 1905, p. 93.

There is a good deal of shrewd common-sense and worldly wisdom in many of these quaint little prose and verse fables of Mr. Seton's, and others mask nothing at all but an odd and delightful spirit of tricksy humour; mingled with them are amusingly grotesque or poetically imaginative myths and legends of the Chaska-water Indians, and the book is illustrated throughout by the author, whose grotesque or eerie sketches are admirably in harmony with the text. If you want to know "How the Giraffe Became," here you may learn all about it, and draw a moral from his dissatisfied desires; or you can turn to the "Fable of the Yankee Crab," and read how the young may know better than their elders, which is not a sound, orthodox moral, of course, but is, nevertheless, in this case, as true as it is amusing. Here is one of the fables in verse, which we quote not because it is absolutely the best, but because it is the prettiest, and happens to be short:

> The Meddy she was sorry
>   For her sister sky, ye see,
> Coz, though her robe of blue wuz bright,
>   'Twas plain as it could be.
>
> An' so she sent a skylark up
>   To trim the Sky robe right,
> Wi' daisies from the Meddy
>   (Ye kin see them best at night).
>
> An' every scrap of blue cut out
>   To make them daisies set,
> Come tum'ling down upon the grass
>   An' growed a violet.

The book is very daintily got up, with a cover design and title and page decorations by Miss Grace Gallatin Seton, and . . . would be appreciated by older as well as by younger readers.

ANIMAL HEROES (1905; British edition, 1906)

May Estelle Cook

SOURCE: A review of *Animal Heroes,* in *The Dial,* Vol. XXXIX, No. 467, December 1, 1905, pp. 372-73.

No Christmas-tree is fully equipped which has not a flowering of animal story-books somewhere among or beneath its branches, and no child counts his gifts complete without some new tale of outdoor life. This year there is satisfaction for all who love such stories—and in this count we all enroll ourselves as children; . . .

Among these books none will be more justly popular than Mr. Thompson Seton's *Animal Heroes.* "A hero is an individual of unusual gifts and achievements. Whether it be man or animal this definition applies." And Carlyle himself would scarcely deny a deed of hero-worship to the eight "individuals" whom the book celebrates. The fact that most of them belong to the common tribes rather enhances the appreciation of their qualities. Even the Slum Cat, it seems, is worthy to enter the class of animals Mr. Seton has known, and though her heroism may not have exactly the same fibre as that of the Sandhill Stag, it is nevertheless genuine and admirable. The author's power has increased as his style has become more simple and his allegiance to plain facts more indisputable. He has never told a story more dramatically than that of Little War-horse, the Jack Rabbit, or more touchingly than that of Arnaux, the Homing Pigeon. As if to prove, too, that his greater command of the commonplace has not lessened the wealth of his imagination, he closes his volume with the **"Legend of the White Reindeer,"** a haunting story in which plain fact runs off confessedly and most alluringly into pure

fancy. With regard to the illustrations, one might suggest that here and there they are too sketchy and uncertain to add either the humor or the illumination that the author intends. But this suggestion is only a marginal note.

The Nation (New York)

SOURCE: A review of *Animal Heroes,* in *The Nation* (New York), Vol. 82, No. 2116, January 18, 1906, pp. 53-4.

Animal Heroes, by Ernest Thompson Seton, gives the histories of a cat, a dog, a pigeon, a lynx, a rabbit, two wolves, and a reindeer. The stories are more or less composite, the author says, but are each founded on the life of a veritable animal hero. "A hero is an individual of unusual gifts and achievements. Whether it be man or animal, this definition applies; and it is the histories of such that appeal to the imagination and to the hearts of those who hear them." Mr. Seton thus defines his subject and his literary aim. Probably few readers will unsettle their enjoyment of his stories over the question whether it is he or Mr. Burroughs that is right about the existence of animal heroes, or whether they see his animals in the light of his fancy or that of common day. He does touch the heart and the imagination, his methods are not sensational, his literary art is excellent, his knowledge is wide. Of all the modern nature students in whom the human interest in wild creatures dominates the merely scientific interest, he is, in Mr. Burroughs's opinion, the best, though with "romantic tendencies" that must be remembered when one reads his works as natural history.

Punch, or The London Charivari

SOURCE: A review of *Animal Heroes,* in *Punch, or The London Charivari,* Vol. CXXXI, July 18, 1906, p. 54.

In the old days a hero was a man, and a heroine a woman, and that was the end of it. But we know better now, and find heroes and heroines elsewhere, on four legs as well as two. Mr. Thompson Seton, who is Naturalist to the Government of Manitoba, as well as a lecturer and author, has written a book about several of his acquaintances, called *Animal Heroes,* wherein you may read of the great merits of a certain slum cat, and a certain bull-terrier, and a pigeon, and a lynx, and a reindeer, and two wolves, all of whom touched nobility. The result is a book that no child should be without. I give it as my opinion that as a writer about animals

> Thompson Seton.
> Can't be beaten.

The Bookman

SOURCE: A review of *Animal Heroes,* in *The Bookman,* Vol. XXX, No. 179, August, 1906, p. 189.

On the subject of wolves and bears and deer Mr. Seton has held our warm regard for many a long day. Occasionally his very enthusiasm for animals leads him to touch up their portraits into something a little too human for our taste, leaving for a while in the eye of our mind a deficient man rather than an efficient animal; but in spite of this the strongest impression left is that this historian of wild creatures really does know them intimately and affectionately and comprehendingly. In this new volume, however, we have the excitement of new animals, at least, of some animals new to us in Mr. Seton's hands, and perhaps it is a certain taste for novelty which makes the stories of the cat, the pigeon and the dog our three favourite chapters out of a good eight. Never again shall we look at a slum cat with quite the same eyes, for we now know the past of a "Royal Analostan," her rise, her vicissitudes, her courage, and her placid age; and who knows but that the lank animal, stealing over the garden wall any day, may not be such another, and have the courage and endurance of a hero, and a record any athlete might envy? Perhaps the most beautiful story of all is that of "Arnaux," the Homing Pigeon. This chapter is a lesson in bird culture and in humanity. The brave little messenger, with his work and his triumphs, his dangers and his domestic trials, is as enthralling a hero as any of the monsters of the woods. We pardon the touch too much of sentiment at the end for the sake of the little Arnaux we have watched eagerly from his first journey to his last. Two hundred illustrations in Mr. Seton's admirable style add two hundred additional charms to an already attractive book.

The Spectator

SOURCE: A review of *Animal Heroes,* in *The Spectator,* No. 4075, August 4, 1906, pp. 158-59.

"A Hero," Mr. Ernest Thompson Seton writes in his new book, **Animal Heroes** "is an individual of unusual gifts and achievements. Whether it be man or animal, this definition applies; and it is the histories of such that appeal to the imagination and to the hearts of those who hear them." And so he has taken the lives of a number of wild and captive or pet animals, and out of the typical incidents and accidents of their careers has evolved half-a-dozen heroes,—creatures who do and suffer rather more than their fellows. The lives of the heroes, thus, are "composite," but are founded mainly on one particular life, and the result, as is usual with Mr. Seton's stories, is wonderfully interesting. How far the stories can be regarded as scientific natural history is, of course, another matter.

There can be no doubt as to the success of the "appeal to the imagination." Few writers excel Mr. Seton, in the modern school which began with Mr. Kipling's *The Jungle Books*, in enlisting the sympathy of the reader on the side of individual animals in the struggle to live; and the fascination of the personalities of Little Jack Warhorse, the Slum Cat, Snap, the bulldog terrier, and Arnaux, the

homing pigeon, is as strong as that of any of Mr. Seton's animals, even though it is in some ways less convincing than the fascination of Bagheera or Baloo. Occasionally, it would appear, Mr. Seton is rewriting history. Little Jack Warhorse, for instance, is the name of a rabbit who actually existed; he was a jack-rabbit caught up in a big rabbit-drive in the West, and kept for coursing. The course was from the starting-pen on one side of a large park, across the open ground in front of the grand stand, to the Haven, or home-pen, on the other; and the Warhorse was faster than any greyhound that was ever slipped after him. He was promised his liberty if he covered the course thirteen times without giving his pursuers a turn,—that is, if he could run straight from the starting-pen to the Haven; and his last run, Mr. Seton tells us, is still talked about by Kaskadoans, besides having already been made immortal in the daily papers. The story of Arnaux, the homing pigeon, again, is largely a matter of fact. Arnaux was a pigeon who was sent up from a steamer in distress, and who actually flew two hundred and ten miles home, in a fog, in four hours and forty minutes, and so, perhaps, saved the lives of the passengers and crew of the drifting steamer. He had a brother, Arnolf, also a pigeon with three fine records, and nothing is more moving in the book than the reproach of Arnolf's owner to a brute who had shot his pigeon flying home. "There were tears in the wrath of the pigeon-man: 'My bird, my beautiful Arnolf, twenty times has he brought vital messages, three times has he made records, twice has he saved human lives, and you'd shoot him for a pot-pie. I could punish you under the law, but I have no heart for such a poor revenge. I only ask you this, if ever again you have a sick neighbour who wants a pigeon-pie, come, we'll freely supply him with pie-breed squabs; but if you have a trace of manhood about you, you will never, never again shoot, or allow others to shoot, our noble and priceless messengers.'" That is sound enough work, even for those who refuse to be so sentimental as to allow that animals possess a consciousness in any degree similar to man's; but Mr. Seton is hardly on such safe ground in his description of the death of Arnaux himself, shot at on his last homeward journey by another brutal gunner, and so falling a victim to a pair of peregrine hawks. "A dark stain appeared on his bosom, but Arnaux kept on, homeward bound . . . under the pirates' castle where the great grim peregrines sat; peering like black-masked highwaymen, they marked the on-coming pigeon. Arnaux knew them of old. Many a message was lying undelivered in that nest, many a record-bearing plume had fluttered away from its fastness. But Arnaux had faced them before, and now he came as before,—on, onward, swift, but not as he had been; the deadly gun had sapped his force, had lowered his speed. On, on; and the peregrines, biding their time, went forth like two bow-bolts; strong and lightning-swift they went against one weak and wearied. Why tell of the race that followed? Why paint the despair of a brave little heart in sight of the home he had craved in vain? In a minute all was over. The peregrines screeched in their triumph." Now, that is surely not a transcript, but a translation. It is the transference into the mind of a pigeon of the emotions which would be felt by a human being who, having been exiled from his home for years, realised that he was about to be struck down by a violent death. To assert that a pigeon is capable of suffering such intense agony of thought as such a situation would produce in the mind of a human being, is to imbue the whole scheme of Nature with a cruelty that is unthinkable.

It must be admitted that Mr. Seton seldom allows himself such latitude of emotion. Nothing, for instance, could be more restrained or more successful than the narrative of the Slum Cat. The contrast between the dignity, the grace, and the comfortable habits of a well-fed cat, and the shifts to which hunger drives the guttersnipes of catdom, would be unhappy enough, if treated on certain lines, to conjure into maiden ladies' wills any number of codicils endowing cats' homes. But the hero-cat in this book is regarded more wisely. She of the Slums is not happy when, full-fed and fat, she wins the gold medal at the cat-show, and, purchased with a falsely royal pedigree, is asked to live on cream and lie on velvet. She prefers an unfettered life among the chimney-tops and the chance of finding an occasional fish-head in a rubbish-heap. The story is one of the most successful in the collection because of the absence of a maudlin insistence, into which the author might so easily have fallen, on the miseries afflicting cats which cannot depend on regular meals and lined baskets to sleep in.

Yet the author of **Animal Heroes** does somehow contrive to strike a main note of unhappiness, not the less impressive because cold reasoning about the possibilities of pain in the scheme of Nature is not always readily listened to, however logical may be the syllogisms. Now and then, of course, the existence of avoidable suffering on the part of animals is unquestionable, and a book may be written with unhappiness as the keynote, and be perfectly in accordance with ascertained facts. Take, for instance, such a book as *Black Beauty,* which is perhaps still read in some nurseries. The avowed object of the writer of the book is to bring to the knowledge of the reader the cruelties which may result from the improper use of the bearing-rein. But the misery which she describes is due to the conditions of an artificial existence. The pain inflicted is inflicted by man, and the insistence upon the necessity for its removal is not only legitimate, but right. But when the pain described is inflicted by animals upon animals, under perfectly natural conditions of existence, it is surely logical to argue that unhappiness does not enter into the scheme of things at all. The scheme must be wise, or it would not be the Scheme; and it would not be wise if animals felt the unhappiness in contemplating the violent endings of lives all round them which human beings would feel if they were similarly tortured and preyed upon and destroyed. So far, then, as the author of any collection of animal-stories contrives to convey the impression that his animal heroes are consciously unhappy in the same sense and to the same degree as men and women can be consciously unhappy, he is translating, not transcribing. He is writing, in reality, not about animals, but about men. But, of course, that line of argument brings you

to the equally sound contention that if animals cannot be unhappy as men are unhappy, neither can they be happy as men understand happiness. That is incontestable; but where, then, it may be asked, is there any opportunity for an animal to become a "hero"? The deliberate acceptance of danger or pain in obedience to the dictates of what is known to be right is of the essence of heroism: how can that, for animals, be a possibility?

It is, of course, impossible. But Mr. Seton would be justified in urging that he has already defined and limited the word "hero." An animal hero is "an individual of unusual gifts and achievements." That may, perhaps, be put in another way, which would be that an animal hero is the animal who survives. He is perpetually proving himself fitter than the others. Little Jack Warhorse gets the opportunity of becoming a "hero" because he happens to run faster than the others in the rabbit-drive, and so gets caught up in the traps towards which the rabbits are driven before the others, who are slower and weaker, arrive. Yet it must be owned that in certain senses the definition of an animal hero as merely an animal who proves his fitness to survive is not wholly satisfying. That is particularly the case when the "heroic" action is performed in relation to man,—in pursuance, for instance, of such a duty as guarding a child from harm. There is room, no doubt, in the contemplation of such actions for a good deal of confusion of thought. We seem to discern, perhaps very dimly, something akin in the uplifting of the being of an animal into a plane near our own. But that may lead to dangerous argument. One point, at least, stands out clearly enough. It is man who makes the animal the hero. He does not know that he is a hero himself. No other animal admires him as heroic, nor, most certainly, would understand how it could be possible for so commonplace a creature as Dash, the collie, or Peter, the tom-cat, to provide material for books over which wonderful and powerful human beings can laugh, or weep, or philosophise.

📖 ***THE BIOGRAPHY OF A SILVER FOX; OR, DOMINO REYNARD OF GOLDUR TOWN (1909)***

The New York Times Book Review

SOURCE: A review of *The Biography of a Silver Fox; Or, Domino Reynard of Goldur Town,* in *The New York Times Book Review,* April 10, 1909, p. 209.

Lovers of the gentle art upon which an eminent faunal naturalist, now upon his travels, has fixed the short and ugly name of "Nature Faking" cannot have forgotten Mr. Charles G. D. Roberts's ingenious and diverting story of *Red Fox.* **The Biography of a Silver Fox** represents a parallel performance in the same gentle art by Mr. Ernest Thompson Seton.

Mr. Seton—the world cannot quite get out of the habit of thinking of him as Mr. Thompson—declares that the resemblances between his fox-epic and Mr. Roberts's fox-epic arise from the circumstance that both have narrowly observed the fox race. The two books were being written at the same time, he says.

As a matter of fact, Mr. Roberts's chief advantage over Mr. Seton, aside from priority of publication, is that his is the better, more vivid, and more dramatic story. Mr. Seton, however, is the bolder idealist. He asserts that his purpose is not merely "to show the man-world how the fox-world lives," but "above all to advertise and emphasize the beautiful monogamy of the better class fox."

The volume is illustrated by the author in his familiar manner and decorated somewhat elaborately by his wife, Grace Gallatin Seton.

The Spectator

SOURCE: A review of *The Biography of a Silver Fox; Or, Domino Reynard of Goldur Town,* in *The Spectator,* No. 4221, May 22, 1909, p. 824.

Mr. Seton tells one of his stories of woodland life with all his accustomed skill and sympathy. We are introduced at the beginning of the book to a litter of fox cubs at play—a very pretty sight, but not often seen—and we follow the career of the sprightliest cub, a dark little chap with a black band across his eyes. These biographies commonly end in tragedy. We come into contact with these creatures of the wild only when we kill them. Mr. Seton contrives to avoid this catastrophe. The story of the last run, when a great fox hunt had been started to avenge misdeeds of which our hero had not been guilty, is quite admirable. Usually our sympathies are found to be with man and man's servant, the dog, but in this case we cannot help feeling glad that 'Domino'—this is the silver fox's name—is left in possession.

May Estelle Cook

SOURCE: A review of *The Biography of a Silver Fox; Or, Domino Reynard of Goldur Town,* and *The Biography of a Grizzly,* in *The Dial,* Vol. XLVI, No. 551, June 1, 1909, pp. 363-64.

Mr. Thompson Seton has written *The Biography of a Silver Fox* as a companion volume to *The Biography of a Grizzly.* The author calls attention to the fact that the story contains incidents similar to those in Mr. Roberts's story of Red Fox; but those who know both writers will know that this was mere accident. The story is well told, and is as interesting as any of those that have come from this author's pen—which is as high praise as a critic could well give. Compared with the quite unpretentious and simple stories in such a book as Mr. [Enos] Mills's, it perhaps raises the question whether the points are not a little strained—a little melodramatic—to represent truly the life of our brothers of the field, who after all have a great deal of the commonplace in

their lives, just as humans have. The book is artistically bound in blue and silver, beautifully decorated and illustrated, and will be a most acceptable giftbook for children.

The Canadian Magazine

SOURCE: A review of *The Biography of a Silver Fox; Or, Domino Reynard of Goldur Town,* in *The Canadian Magazine,* Vol. XXXIII, No. 4, August, 1909, p. 376-78.

According to Ernest Thompson Seton's latest story of animal life, *The Biography of a Silver Fox,* the silver fox is a freak of nature and not the offspring of parents similarly endowed. The author says:

> The silver fox is not of different kind, but a glorified freak of the red race. His parents may have been the commonest of red foxes, yet nature, in extravagant mood, may have showered all her gifts on this favoured one of the offspring, and not only clad him in a marvellous coat, but gifted him with speed and wind, and brains above his kind, to guard his perilous wealth.

The story is fascinating, and is delightful reading for children.

BOY SCOUTS OF AMERICA: A HANDBOOK (1910)

The New York Times Book Review

SOURCE: A review of *Boy Scouts of America: A Handbook,* in *The New York Times Book Review,* September 24, 1910, p. 520.

Brimful of lore of woods and field, alluring with hints of the life out of doors, and containing the suggestive link between woodcraft and "life-craft," this handbook of woodcraft, scouting, and life-craft, by Ernest Thompson Seton and Lieut. Gen. Sir Robert S. S. Baden-Powell, K. C. B., appeared at an opportune moment. In the Summer season thousands of boys in large cities, and even in small towns and in the country, are thrown on their own resources for amusement and recreation. Keen observers have noticed the degenerating influence of undirected boyhood activities and particularly the rapidly growing numbers of spectators and lookers-on, rather than participators, in the sports and activities of our older boys and young men. We seem to be slowly evolving into a race of anaemics; the self-reliance, resourcefulness, and adaptability of our fathers are wanting. A remedy is sorely needed. "Something to do, something to think about, something to enjoy in the woods, with a view always to character building—for manhood, not scholarship—is the aim of education," best expresses the basis of the Boy Scout idea.

Under the direction of the Young Men's Christian Association and other influential societies and individuals, the

Boy Scouts of America have been formed into a National organization, with Mr. Seton at its head, as "Chief Scout," Boys everywhere—in city and country—are collected into groups, competent volunteer instructors being appointed to guide their sports and recreations, and the secrets and rules of "life-craft" being taught through the interesting media of woodcraft, scouting, and real-boy games.

As a first step, *Boy Scouts of America* has been issued in convenient and easily procurable form as the manual of organization of the movement. It contains all necessary information for instructors, as well as for the boy scouts themselves, and, in addition, a wealth of material on camping. Practical directions for the selection of camp outfits, instruction in wig-wag signaling, tracking, rope-knotting, first aid to the injured, and, in fact, everything one can imagine as necessary for the camper, we find in well-arranged, simple form, well adapted to the class of readers the book will reach. And even of greater value are the many pages of well-selected outdoor games, many of them new to the boys of America, that will go far toward holding the interest of those obliged to remain at home, as well as the more fortunate campers.

A.L.A. Booklist

SOURCE: A review of *Boy Scouts of America: A Handbook,* in *A.L.A. Booklist,* Vol. 7, No. 3, November, 1910, p. 132.

The "book of organization" of the Boy Scouts, including Mr. Seton's articles reprinted from many periodicals, and all of General Baden-Powell's *Scouting for Boys* that is applicable in this country. Primarily a book for leaders of this popular and worthy movement, containing compact information, from many sources on games, sports, camping, signs and signalling, tracking and trailing, etc., and suggestions for carrying on the various phases of the work. Some libraries will prefer placing it in the adult collection. Much of the contents, however, will be useful in the children's room.

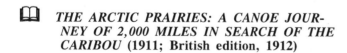 THE ARCTIC PRAIRIES: A CANOE JOURNEY OF 2,000 MILES IN SEARCH OF THE CARIBOU (1911; British edition, 1912)

Robert H. MacDonald

SOURCE: A review of *The Arctic Prairies: A Canoe Journey of 2,000 Miles in Search of the Caribou,* in *Canadian Children's Literature,* No. 30, 1983, pp. 64-7.

In the spring of 1907 Ernest Seton Thompson set off north from Edmonton in a livery rig, to begin a journey of over 2,000 miles that was to take him six months to complete, by canoe down the Athabaska River system, through Great Slave Lake and onward to Aylmer Lake, till he reached the treeless country of the Arctic plains.

From Wild Animals at Home, *written and illustrated by Ernest Thompson Seton.*

His declared intention was to find the summer range of the great caribou herds, to document the wildlife seen along the way, and to explore the largely unknown waters of Aylmer Lake. His, he thought, was only the fourth white expedition to penetrate so far north, and for the last third of the journey he would be travelling beyond the knowledge of the native guides. In spite of various adventures and one near disaster he did what he set out to do, though at considerable cost. His romantic dreams, both of the Indian life that he had promoted with such devotion in New York City, and of the paradise of the north lands, came up against the reality of the native Chipewyans and the harsh climate, and suffered grievously. This is one theme of the book: the diary of a sensitive and scrupulously fair man, forced to come to terms with his own illusions. . . .

Ernest Seton Thompson is remembered as the writer of nature stories—*Wild Animals I Have Known, Animal Heroes, The Biography of a Grizzly, Lives of the Hunted* and many more. He wrote about animals from the animal's point of view, he wrote with sympathy and most of all with knowledge, he wrote clearly and simply, and he illustrated his stories with his own instantly recognizable drawings. From the 1890s on these books went into edition after edition, and some are still in print. They were written with children in mind, and they have been popular with children (perhaps as much as anything because Seton never wrote down to his audience, nor did he prettify animal life).

After about 1901, however, Seton abandoned the nature story, and turned his energies to his other great interest, the imitation of the life of the Indian. He re-imagined his childhood and youth—spent in the Don Valley and the prairie of Manitoba—through the mind of an Indian boy, and the autobiographical *Two Little Savages* (1903) was the result, a hymn to the outdoor life and the wisdom of the Indian. His *Birch-Bark Roll* further advanced the principles of woodcraft, and led to the formation of his band of Woodcraft Indians, a scouting organization for boys. For Seton, Woodcraft was "the first of all the sciences. It was Woodcraft that made man out of brutish material, and Woodcraft in its highest form that may save him from decay." The living symbol of the healthy outdoors was the Indian, who lived in Harmony with Nature, respecting and reverencing all wild creatures. Seton became a tireless advocate of living with Nature rather than exploiting Nature, of preserving the wilderness and its inhabitants, and of defending the Indian against all criticism. These were truths that had to be taught to children; the Woodcraft Indians, and later, the Boy Scouts, were the means for the new teaching.

In his promotion of his ideals through youth organizations Seton was not always successful, perhaps being too nice a man, not ruthless enough in his dealings with others. The lore, the rituals and the games of the Woodcraft Indians were cannibalized by Baden-Powell in *Scouting for Boys* (1908), and Seton found himself fighting a rearguard action to save the integrity of his own principles. He agreed to serve as Chief Scout of the Boy Scouts of America, but again, he found his expertise used while his aims were ignored. He became alarmed by the increasing militarism of the Scouts; he was out-manoeuvred, and finally deposed from office on the grounds that he was not an American citizen. Seton's Indian as the model of American manhood lost out to Daniel Beard's idealization of the pioneer.

There is one other fact of Seton's life that bears on *The Arctic Prairies.* Seton began his career as an artist, and his first successes as an illustrator of wildlife, together with his own interest in and knowledge of animals, led him to make claims as a naturalist. Here he overreached himself. His attempts at scientific studies were savaged and he was deeply wounded by the criticism. Subsequently, with painstaking industry, he tried to gain professional recognition, and with the publication of *Life-histories of Northern Animals: An Account of the Mammals of Manitoba,* he largely succeeded. His expedition to the Barren Lands in 1907, at the age of forty-seven and in imperfect health, was surely spurred by his desire to be taken seriously as a scientist.

In *The Arctic Prairies* these three dominant interests—wild life, the image of the Indian, and scientific observation—meet and sometimes conflict dramatically. The book is essentially a diary, telling in short chapters and straightforward narrative the incidents of the expedition,

but we are always aware of Seton's own personality, and of the tensions when ideals meet reality. The Seton party set out from Athabaska Landing as soon as the river was clear of ice, and for the first stretch accompanied the scows taking supplies to the Hudson's Bay posts downstream. Here Seton experienced his first disappointment, finding the sixty Indians and Metis that made up the scows' crew a noisy, savage and ungrateful crowd, liable to loose off their rifles at anything that moved on the banks. Seton's only success was as Medicine Man, dispensing rhubarb pills for all complaints. In the country east of the Great Slave River he tried to find guides that would take him to the range of the wood buffalo; the Indians were unhelpful and evasive. For the voyage across Great Slave Lake he had to hire a boat and a crew; his problems increased. He had trouble getting the Indians to rise in the morning, he found it impossible to satisfy their frequent complaints, he grew impatient and then desperate at their habit of stopping every two hours to eat—at his expense. As the voyage continued he lectured them on the sanctity of life but could do little to stop their wanton killing. When it came to the parting he was heartily glad to be rid of them. Taking with them only one docile old man, Seton and his companion Edward Preble—an American naturalist—and their servant Billy, journeyed on in their own canoe to the Barren Lands.

This then is the strongest undercurrent in the book: the degeneracy of man. Seton tried his hardest to set an example, for he carried no whiskey, he put out his campfires, and he taught reverence for all Nature. He tried to make every allowance for the Chipewyans, and he did find one or two to admire, but there is a poignancy in his evident disappointment with his model of manliness.

There were devils, too, among the wild-life. The paradise of the north country was close to being impenetrable, for the mosquitoes were "a terror to man and beast." Seton tried to preserve a scientific attitude, and devised a mosquito gauge to count them—his bare hand held up for 5 seconds one day and "125 long-billed mosquitoes boring away." He discovered that frogs were immune, and he tried rubbing frog slime over his skin as a repellent. Finally, the best he could do was confine the mosquitoes to one chapter of *The Arctic Prairies,* and treat them afterwards as the great unmentionables.

On the whole, and in spite of the disappointments and the hardships, the note that Seton strikes most often is one of cheerful interest in everything, whether it is the tales of the Hudson Bay traders, the magnificent scenery, or the abundant wildlife. He did see the caribou that he travelled so far to meet, he saw buffalo herds, and muskox, he saw lynx, white wolf and silver fox, he saw pelicans, he ate the prized whitefish, he recorded and collected the plant life. (His lists of both fauna and flora are given in the appendices.) "Have I not found for myself a kingdom and become a part of it?" he asks in a last lyrical outburst.

This is not a book that was written for children, nor is

it a book that makes much concession to the reader who is not already interested in nature and the north. The lists of the contents of lynxes' stomachs might seem tedious, and the discussion of the fluctuations of the northern rabbit population might seem dry. Yet Seton had a story to tell, and his own very real involvement with the things he observed—whether human, animal or vegetable—is good reading. Our present concern with ecology makes Seton's idealism fresh and modern.

This is a useful reprint to add to the literature of exploration and the north, and with some introduction . . . it could be recommended to an intelligent student who already had some interest in the subject. One word of caution: the maps, which are small and blurry, and were no better in the first edition, are worse than useless. Seton's photographs are a loss, but a small one, for he was operating in the days before the telephoto lens, and we have become habituated to seeing rather more dramatic shots.

📖 *ROLF IN THE WOODS* (1911; Canadian edition, 1917)

A.L.A. Booklist

SOURCE: A review of *Rolf in the Woods,* in *A.L.A. Booklist,* Vol. 8, No. 2, October, 1911, p. 79.

Details the adventures of fifteen-year-old Rolf, who ran away from a cruel uncle to live with Quonab, the Indian, in the woods, and learned much forest-lore during several years' living in Connecticut and New York woods—knowledge which made him valuable later as a scout in the War of 1812. A good boys' story, though very long, and a *vade mecum* for Boy Scouts, to whom it is dedicated. Two hundred characteristic drawings by the author.

The Athenaeum

SOURCE: A review of *Rolf in the Woods,* in *The Athenaeum,* Vol. II, No. 4383, October 28, 1911, p. 525.

If the boy who takes up **Rolf in the Woods: The Adventures of a Boy Scout with Indian Quonab and Little Dog Skookum,** written and illustrated by Ernest Thompson Seton, does not read the Preface, it will come as a disappointment to him, when he nears the end, to learn that it all relates to conditions of a hundred years and more ago. Rolf is a boy who had no relatives, and took to the woods with an Indian. The narrative is that of their innumerable adventures, and is dedicated to the Boy Scouts of America.

The story is written from the point of view of an American boy, who is represented as taking some (American) part in the war of 1812. We had always claimed Mr.

Seton as British and Canadian. However, that is of no significance. Even British boys will forgive Rolf and his author for the sake of the woods and the adventures. There are over four hundred pages about them, and here you may learn how to hunt woodchucks, and coon, and deer, and even snapping turtle, to say nothing of fiercer quarry. There is a most exciting (and crude) account of a tussle with the "demon of the deep."

On every page Mr. Seton displays his remarkable familiarity with wild nature. He does not wield his pen with the cunning of Mr. Charles Roberts, also a Canadian, but his knowledge is probably much more intimate. Indeed, this is an ideal boys' book—one which (despite the unnecessary close) all adults would have welcomed in their "salad days." The wash drawings by the author are effective, but we do not care for his practice of scattering sketches in the margin.

The Bookman

SOURCE: A review of *Rolf in the Woods,* in *The Bookman,* Vol. LXI, December, 1911, p. 46.

Mr. Ernest Thompson Seton's new book once more displays its author's extraordinary knowledge of wild animals and their habits, but it is, in addition, something of a departure from this author's general methods. The volume is dedicated to the Boy Scouts of America, and it is an account of the adventures of a boy scout of a past age. Rolf is a young American citizen of a hundred years ago, and he with his *fidus Achates,* Quonab, a Red Indian, and his no less valuable dumb companion, the little dog Skookum, take a leading part in the campaign round Lake Champion. The author has made good use of his historical knowledge, but the volume will perhaps be more useful and more interesting to a juvenile public for its "tips" on scouting.

The Spectator

SOURCE: A review of *Rolf in the Woods,* in *The Spectator,* No. 4353, December 2, 1911, p. 937.

Mr. Ernest Thompson Seton has written an extremely good boys' story. It deals with the adventures of Rolf Kittering, a Yankee lad of fifteen, who, to escape a cruel uncle, joins a solitary Indian trapper in his wigwam. The scene is chiefly laid in the Adirondacks a century ago. Mr. Seton's knowledge of wildlife, wild animals, and wild Indian ways stands him in good stead, and though there is no crowding of adventures the short chapters are never for a moment dull. The fur traders prosper. Then comes a journey to Albany, and Rolf and Quonab are engaged as guides to young Van Cortlandt, the Governor's son, who is to pass three months in the woods for his health. Then comes the War of 1812 between England and the United States, when Rolf acts as scout and despatch-carrier to the American General. Fighting and narrow shaves succeed each other till the

Peace of Ghent. The tale ends when Rolf is twenty-one and married to Annette, the daughter of a Dutch farmer. The story has all the qualities which a boys' book should have and many which are often lacking. It is profusely illustrated with the author's familiar and clever sketches. We have described the book as one for boys. Let us add that *one* old boy at least has enjoyed it, and with this we recommend it to our readers.

📖 THE BOOK OF WOODCRAFT (1912; revised and enlarged from *The Birch-Bark Roll of the Outdoor Life,* 1908)

The New York Times Book Review

SOURCE: A review of *The Book of Woodcraft,* in *The New York Times Book Review,* December 29, 1912, p. 797.

Ernest Thompson Seton, so long known as an enthusiastic exponent of the principles of woodcraft and of the necessity to civilized man of more or less life in the open, has brought together in one sturdy volume a comprehensive collection of the activities, customs, laws and amusements that have been developed in his own camps. He calls it *The Book of Woodcraft.* He long ago took the American Indian as his model for life in the open, and he devotes considerable space in this book to a defense of the Red Man against the accusations the whites have been making ever since they began taking his possessions. But the greater part of it is concerned with the principles of scouting, the laws and purposes of the "Woodcraft Indians," the songs, dances, ceremonies of the "Woodcraft" camps, the honors and degrees to be won therein, campcraft, first aid, wildwood remedies and simple lessons upon natural history and forestry. A great number of illustrations, drawings and diagrams add to the value and interest of the work.

The Nation (New York)

SOURCE: A review of *The Book of Woodcraft,* in *The Nation* (New York), Vol. 96, No. 2481, January 16, 1913, p. 63.

The Book of Woodcraft and Indian Lore, by Ernest Thompson Seton, is a revised and enlarged edition of the author's *Birch-Bark Roll.* It forms a bulky volume, in which the American youth who is "tormented with an insatiable instinct for the woods" may find an inexhaustible store of information and incentive, from forest ceremonies to "wildwood remedies" and camp-fire stories. And the adult amateur camper, as well as the boy scout, will learn much from these heavily-loaded pages. The illustrations, half a thousand pen sketches, are as neat and accurate as Mr. Thompson Seton's usually are. From its predecessors the new edition differs mainly in the inclusion of a deliberate attempt to rehabilitate the Indian ideal, in which attempt the author seems to us zealous rather than wary.

A.L.A. Booklist

SOURCE: A review of *The Book of Woodcraft,* in *A.L.A. Booklist,* Vol. 9, No. 10, June, 1913, p. 465.

The first comprehensive collection of the customs, laws, amusements and activities that have developed in the camps established by Mr Seton, revised and greatly enlarged from his annual **Birch-Bark Roll.** A mine of information on scouting, camping, forestry, wildwood remedies, natural history and the customs and ceremonies of the Indians, including typical Indian stories and legends. Useful to the adult amateur camper as well as to the boy scout.

📖 WILD ANIMALS AT HOME (1913)

The Bookman

SOURCE: A review of *Wild Animals at Home,* in *The Bookman,* Vol. XXXVIII, No. 4, December, 1913, pp. 443-44.

Outstanding among the season's books about animals is Ernest Thompson Seton's **Wild Animals at Home.** Just a glance at it revives the thrill of several years ago, when Mr. Seton was writing enchanting biographies of grizzly bears and other tales with memorable titles like **The Trail of the Sandhill Stag.** In his preface the author says that in all his thirty years of trailing through the Rocky Mountain regions he has found no place more rewarding than Yellowstone Park. Owing to its protective laws the wild things there, unlike any place else at present in the northwest, "have resumed their traditional Garden-of-Eden attitude toward man," making the place a paradise for the naturalist. His new book offers the most intimate and unforgettable sketches of coyotes, prairie-dogs, fox, martens, beavers, otters, deer, buffalo, antelope, the "well-meaning skunk," badgers, squirrels, rabbits, bears, the "misunderstood" Canada lynx, and "the shyest thing in the woods"—the mountain lion. Mrs. Seton has had a big share in the work, having accompanied her husband on nearly all the expeditions and contributed many of the illustrations. There is an amazing assortment of photographs, a valuable appendix, and woodcraft information "by the peck." This ought to be one of the most delightful books a young person could imagine as a Christmas gift.

The Dial

SOURCE: A review of *Wild Animals at Home,* in *The Dial,* Vol. LV, No. 659, December 1, 1913, p. 484.

Mr. Ernest Thompson Seton has long ago proved that he can see with his eyes and draw with his hand and reason with his brain. In his **Wild Animals at Home** there is much sketching and photographing of untamed creatures in their native haunts, and admirable discourse concerning them. In the Yellowstone Park and elsewhere in the great West the author has carried on the nature-studies now reduced to writing and presented in twelve enjoyable chapters with a wealth of illustrations. The coyote, the prairie-dog, the famous fur-bearers, the swift runners, the squirrel and the rabbit, and other wild animals, are intimately interviewed by this skilled reporter of the forest and the field; and what he has to say, combined with his manner of saying it, is not likely to disappoint. Humor of a choice kind speaks in both the printed page and in the accompanying marginal sketches, while the half-tone plates have the soberer excellences of such products of the illustrator's art. Human nature is not neglected in the author's studies; animals were not the sole living beings he encountered. Mrs. Seton furnishes an original and appropriate cover design, and has otherwise assisted in the preparation of the book.

The Athenaeum

SOURCE: A review of *Wild Animals at Home,* in *The Athenaeum,* Vol. II, No. 4496, December 27, 1913, p. 758.

It is given to few people to know the Yellowstone Park and its inhabitants in Mr. Thompson Seton's intimate way, and this "great mountain haven of wild life," as he calls it, is an attractive region to explore under his guidance. The establishment of the Park forty-one years ago has made an astonishing difference in the attitude of its animal inhabitants towards man, and their lack of fear, together with their insatiable curiosity, makes the place ideal for the naturalist and the hunter who travels without weapons. In this account of the author's adventures among coyotes, moose, bears, and other animals we find both new and old acquaintances, and it is of the everyday aspects of their lives that ostensibly we are to learn. But Mr. Thompson Seton knows his friends so intimately that he cannot help introducing most of their private affairs, their joys and tragedies, and the skeletons in their small cupboards. If the reader does not shut the book with increased sympathy, for example, for two popularly "misunderstood" animals, the "well-meaning" skunk and the Canada lynx, the fault will be on his side. Popular prejudice has no place in the author's attitude towards animals.

It is, perhaps, inevitable in an account of a community of living beings that we should meet with tragedy, and the story of the kindly badger who petted and fed for days a little lost boy, only to be cruelly shot by an acquaintance of his father's, is one of the saddest in the author's collection. But the book as a whole deals with a comparatively even level of experiences, and the author speaks modestly of the few "thrillers" he can offer to his readers. They may, however, learn much of the ordinary events of camp life with him in the Park, whether it be of the cold feet of the deer-mouse running over their faces as they sleep, or of the inquisitive sniffing of mountain lions round their beds.

The Nation (New York)

SOURCE: A review of *Wild Animals at Home,* in *The Nation* (New York), Vol. 98, No. 2536, February 5, 1914, p. 140.

At the back of **Wild Animals at Home,** by Ernest Thompson Seton, is an appendix containing a list of the mammals living in the Yellowstone Park, most of which were observed by the author in 1912. The book deals with bits of the lives of these animals. Their actual habits as observed in the Park are supplemented by tales of earlier days and incidents of other trips, the chapters affording easy and light reading, with about the range of treatment of a popular lecture. A few headings selected at random are The Cute Coyote, The Well-Meaning Skunk, and Sneak-Cats, Big and Small. We could wish that, even in so evidently popular a book, the author had put something of comparative comment, the leaven of a philosophic touch here and there. Even a single page of discussion of the strange instinct which drew the bull back to the bloody milk, time after time and finally to its death, would have been much more worth while than the mere narration of the episode. We are glad to read the five "nots" of the beaver, that it neither uses its tail as a trowel nor uses big logs for its dam; neither drives stakes nor throws trees any given way, and does not finish its lodge outside with mud. But we fear the author is gullible in believing the story of the crippled buffalo bird which wintered with a bull, searching for seeds during the day and roosting at night for warmth deep buried in the woolly fur between the horns of the great animal. Is not the cowbird the buffalo-bird of olden times, and not the normal nesting blackbird? The comical thumbnail sketches are good, the photographs fair. It is an ideal book for the Pullman car en route for the West. The most important thing which can be said about a book of this type is that the light and frivolous pattern of its diction is woven on a framework of real scientific truth.

The Spectator

SOURCE: A review of *Wild Animals at Home,* in *The Spectator,* No. 4487, June 27, 1914, pp. 1062-63.

With all the knowledge that he has of the wild fauna of North America, he tells us that he has found no place more rewarding than the Yellowstone Park, "the great mountain haven of wild life." **Wild Animals at Home,** illustrated with many photographs and hundreds of characteristic little marginal sketches, gives a wonderful account of this paradise of the naturalist and camera hunter. It is an account, sometimes a little disjointed by journalistic cross-headings, into which some anecdotes of other places are introduced. But the great national reserve, which was established in 1872, is Mr. Seton's main theme. Here, as everyone knows, animals have lost their fear of man. Black bears and grizzlies visit the backyards and garbage-heaps of hotels. Wapiti, mule-deer, and white-tail pose for the photographer. Moose have increased from fifty in 1897 to five hundred and fifty in 1912. Bighorn are now common along the western boundary. The wild herd of bison numbers about fifty, and there are, besides, about a hundred and fifty more in fenced corrals. The pronghorn is almost the only steadily diminishing species. The interesting appendix, with a catalogue of the mammals, which Mr. Seton prints, informs us that the carnivora include about a hundred pumas, which never show themselves, besides lynxes, bobcats, foxes, otters, mink, wolverine, and badgers. The timber wolf is very rare, but coyotes are abundant. With such abundant material at his disposal, Mr. Seton makes a pleasant series of chapters. None is more entertaining than that on the skunk, an animal which, for reasons that do not commend themselves to all Americans, he maintains should be the proper national emblem of America instead of the eagle.

📖 WILD ANIMAL WAYS (1916)

The Nation (New York)

SOURCE: A review of *Wild Animal Ways*, in *The Nation* (New York), Vol. 103, No. 2668, August 17, 1916, p. 159.

Ernest Thompson Seton is always interesting, always replete with first-hand information as to nature in the wild, and in his wild animal fictions, like the traditional riding horse on the mountain trails, apparently always delights to walk with at least one foot over the precipice of improbability. *Wild Animal Ways* is a collection of seven animal stories in the author's well-known style, enlivened by some two hundred whimsical marginal drawings. Some of the protagonists in these stories have been among his personal animal friends, he tells us, while others are composites, intended merely to present facts of natural history in story form. The most exciting episode in the collection, the killing of an especially vicious bear by "Foam" and "Grizel," a pair of Virginia "razor-back" hogs, is based on a story told to the author by a Michigan lumberman, whose name he has forgotten. This recalls the fact that the writer of this note heard from the lips of a Michigan lumberman, name forgotten, a story of a train which came down the Duluth road from Trout Lake to St. Ignace so fast that it was on the ferryboat and well out into the straits before its shadow arrived at the St. Ignace docks. But the restriction of Ernest Thompson Seton to the limits and methods of rigid scientific investigation would mean a loss to "nature" literature which even a characteristically scientific age would be reluctant to tolerate.

The Times Literary Supplement

SOURCE: A review of *Wild Animal Ways*, in *The Times Literary Supplement*, No. 763, August 31, 1916, p. 411.

If you like animal stories told in this form, then you will like these stories. That is not the mere truism that it may

sound. The stories are in substance good, the narrator thoroughly knows his heroes and heroines and villains—the razor-back, or wild boar, the wild geese, Way-Atcha, the racoon, and the rest of them. And they make good drama; their doings are interesting, full of movement; but is this the most satisfactory way of telling us about them? The way may be described very shortly; it is this: to make the animals think very human thoughts, and to tell the tale of their doings as if they were ordered by very human motives. In our opinion this is a mode which gets the whole psychology of the animals wrong, and so sets all in an unreal atmosphere. A tinted, artificial light is thrown on it, quite unlike the open-air sunshine or natural gloom of cloud. The writer, Mr. Ernest Thompson Seton, is American. It is of American wild creatures that he writes. There can be no doubt of that as you read, even before the species of the persons of the story is named. "Foam moved toward the place, with Grizel, hip near, following. The way was down the hill toward a black muck swale." That is not a description of any locality in a British woodland, neither is it a British way of description. It is not suggested that on that account it is not as good a way, or as good a locality; only, that it is distinctively American.

Here and there we meet some very charming passages. It is something of a triumph to make a reader's eyes grow a little misty over the death of a young porker. Mr. Seton achieves it.

> And Runtie [Runtie was a little wild pigling, slain by the wild cat—a death gloriously avenged by Foam, his father], he was lying deep in the brush on the other side of the stump. His mother came and nosed him over, and nudged him gently, and came again to nudge. But the brothers were lively and thirsty; she must go on with them. She raged against the fierce brute that had killed her little one. She lingered about, then led the others to the brook. Then they all came back. The little ones were once more merry and riotous. The mother came to nudge and coax the limp and bloody form, but its eyes had glazed. The father tossed the furry trash aside, and then all passed on.

Delightful and very deft, too, are the thumbnail sketches, full of humour, drawn by the author himself in the margins of the pages. There are some full-page plates, too, but these are less interesting and more ordinary. There is so much that is pleasant and true in this, as in the other books of Mr. Seton's, that it seems niggardly to deal it out such grudging praise as the above. They may indeed be taken as a type. Of their own sort they are very good. But is it the right sort? Is it the best way of telling animal stories? That is the question, and it is largely a question of taste. The present writer has to confess it not entirely to his taste. Tales of the talking animals—folklore and the *Jungle Book*—are one thing. Frankly, we are in the atmosphere of fiction, of poetry, or whatever you please to call it. It is an atmosphere that has its own truth to nature for all that. But here, where are we? In an atmosphere in neither sense real, scarcely quite honest, neither frankly fictitious and poetic nor severely true to fact. It is just a little too theatrical for the one and not quite candidly enough imaginative for the other. But there are many whom it pleases, and to those who like the form the substance here given us may be commended unreservedly.

The Spectator

SOURCE: A review of *Wild Animal Ways,* in *The Spectator,* No. 4604, September 23, 1916, pp. 345-46.

Mr. Seton's books range all but the most perverse of human beings on the side of the animals. The interest of boys in wild animals—except birds possibly—characteristically expresses itself in the desire to pursue, trap, or kill. Even the common domestic cat, if a stranger, is fair game. But it is difficult to imagine that such thoughtlessness (for it is generally nothing more) would survive the reading of a book by Mr. Seton. Each of his books might have as a sub-title, "The Animal's Point of View." For our part, we have never been able to read Mr. Seton without a poignant sense of what the human world has lost by its probably inevitable estrangement from wild animals. The reader, if he shares our feeling, will also experience some degree of humiliation. . . .

The first narrative in Mr. Seton's [*Wild Animal Ways*] is about a horse which was a renegade from the beginning, defied man and all his schooling, and escaped in the end to enjoy perfect freedom as a wild horse of the prairie. The normal horse-lover does not love a vicious horse, particularly when the horse shams lame and is capable of every kind of low cunning. Even Whyte-Melville's sympathy would have broken down at that. It is a triumph of Mr. Seton's skill that he does create in us something like satisfaction when Coaly-Bay escapes from the hunters, who are going to use his carcase as bear-bait, and storms like a whirlwind along the track to ultimate freedom. . . .

In his biography of Foam, a razor-backed hog, Mr. Seton extorts sympathy and admiration once again in difficult circumstances. . . .

The other animals introduced to us in this book are a coon-raccoon; a bear-hunting dog, who, having been considered the "dunce of the family" from puppyhood, distinguishes himself by tackling a bear magnificently in a terrific emergency; a bat; wild geese, whose instinct to migrate is in humorous conflict with the fact that they are pinioned; and a dangerous monkey, who was dangerous only because she had been ill-treated. The experiments with the captive bat prove, if it needed any proof to-day, that the miraculously deft steering of the bat among obstacles in the dark is due to the intense nervous sensitiveness of the wings. The experiments were conducted by carefully covering the bat's eyes—a method which Spallanzani might well have used in his notorious experiments many years ago, instead of blinding the wretched creature. The character of the keeper who tamed

the dangerous monkey is, we imagine, Mr. Seton's ideal of what such a character should be. It is a fine combination of strength and tenderness.

THE PREACHER OF CEDAR MOUNTAIN: A TALE OF THE OPEN COUNTRY (1917)

Clarence Rowe

SOURCE: A review of *The Preacher of Cedar Mountain: A Tale of the Open Country,* in *The New York Times Book Review,* Vol. 22, May 6, 1917, p. 177.

It is nineteen years since **Wild Animals I Have Known** was published, and in those years Mr. Thompson Seton has given us twenty-five books—animal books, woodcraft books, boys' books. Now he has written a novel. And a most interesting novel it is. *The Preacher of Cedar Mountain* is a tale of the upbuilding of a part of the "wild West," and of the days when the West was very wild indeed. Its general theme is conventional enough—the familiar presentation of a young mission pastor at work in the rough-and-tumble life of the "new country" in the early "booming" days. Yet the idea, often as it has been used, is one which admits of wide variations of interest, both in character and incident. And there is nothing conventional in Mr. Thompson Seton's treatment of it. *The Preacher of Cedar Mountain* is a vivid story of men, of horses, of the "open country." And the actual conflict of the young preacher's missionary work takes place, not in the effort to change the lives of those about him, but to control and arrange his own. The "horse preacher" is a vitally interesting human figure, moving in the midst of exciting events. And next to the interest of the story as it traces the development of Jim Hartigan's life and the varied experiences in which he plays a part, the book is to be recommended for its vigorous presentation of historic scenes and figures in the West of the later nineteenth century.

Jim Hartigan, the "horse preacher," is a young Irishman of much physical strength of high honor and courage, the child of an interesting heredity, who is undisciplined, intolerant, and freakishly "wild" until chance leads to his "conversion" at the age of twenty-three. It is characteristic of Jim that the determination to reform his own life should not be enough—he must give his whole future existence to the helping of other men and the preaching of the Gospel. So, in the settlement of Cedar Mountain, near Deadwood, he sets manfully to work, and finds that the struggle with intemperance and gambling which he must assist in other men are as nothing beside the fight that he must wage with them himself.

The Preacher of Cedar Mountain is the story of how Jim met varied events, vastly differing problems, unexpected temptations, and how, falling often, he at last grew out of his weakness and immaturity and became a strong man. As a story of this character development it is very interesting. And it is also unusual. For there is no sentimentality in the tale of Jim's evolution, and the things that happen to him are full of concrete interest themselves. The whole story of his struggles with his native gambling instinct, for example, resolves itself into a really thrilling tale of men and horses, of Jim's deep love for all horses, and for his own horse most of all, and of the great Fort Ryan races, which, as the author points out, many a man now living remembers with excitement still. This picture of the great races, the "boom in betting," the Indian participation, the thrilling dénouement that took victory away for the white man, is intensely interesting reading. And Mr. Thompson Seton has very cleverly woven it into the vital matters in the life history of the "horse preacher" himself. The love story, too, is full of interest, and the heroine is presented with no little charm.

As the author points out, most of the characters in the story are "taken from life," and some of the events, such as the horse races at Fort Ryan, are historical. The background of the Dakotas is sketched with complete sympathy, and the pictures of community life are always illuminating. Of plot, in the sense of one developed situation, the book has little; it is rather a series of happenings, each with its place in the building up of Pastor Jim's life. But the interest of character and of event is well balanced, and always cleverly combined. Mr. Thompson Seton's first novel will be very thoroughly enjoyed.

The Nation (New York)

SOURCE: A review of *The Preacher of Cedar Mountain: A Tale of the Open Country,* in *The Nation* (New York), Vol. 105, No. 2716, July 19, 1917, p. 72.

Mr. Thompson Seton loses his distinction when he begins to write about human beings. His books about animals opened a comparatively new trail; there were no conventions to follow, and Mr. Seton established conventions for other people. But in his first novel, **The Preacher of Cedar Mountain,** he follows pretty closely the conventions of what may be called the Y. M. C. A. type of Western story. The hero is a big, athletic, half-educated young preacher, with a weakness for whiskey and a grand passion for horses and horse-racing; he has a strong "haroldbellrighteous" flavor. In the new Dakota

From Trail of an Artist-Naturalist, *written and illustrated by Ernest Thompson Seton.*

town to which he is sent, he makes a great success, but his weakness for whiskey gets him into serious trouble, and his love of horse-racing threatens to prove his ruin. He is saved, of course, by a girl of the wise, strong, and serene type, who, however, has to marry him rather hastily to prevent his becoming entangled with another girl of very different character. Almost anybody might have written such a yarn; and it is perhaps to Mr. Seton's credit that he seems more interested in the horses than in the men and women of the story. The best parts of the book are the spirited descriptions of the historic races at Fort Ryan, in which soldiers and Indians wagered all their possessions on their respective favorites. The trick by which the Indians won the great race is worthy of the best traditions of Indian subtlety. But the author's friends must hope that he will go back to his wolves and grizzlies.

The Catholic World

SOURCE: A review of *The Preacher of Cedar Mountain: A Tale of the Open Country,* in *The Catholic World,* Vol. CV, No. 629, August, 1917, p. 685.

Mr. Seton's contribution differs in character from the writings we are accustomed to receive from him. It is a picture of life in the Western country some fifty years ago; not life in mining camps, but in the open. It tells the story of James Hartigan's struggle to fulfill the wish of his dying mother, that he should enter the Methodist Church and become a preacher, a calling for which he possesses one qualification, the gift of oratory; of how he is handicapped by two powerful factors for evil, an inheritance from his father in the shape of a craving for strong drink, and a love of horses and horse-racing that nearly causes his undoing; of how he is helped to conquer by the woman who as sweetheart and as wife holds him to high standards and restores his courage when he falls. He is an attractive hero, handsome and brawny, giving more than one practical demonstration of the muscular quality of his Christianity.

The book is vaguely reminiscent of others along similar lines; it is readable, however, and, as might be expected, it breathes a spirit of love of nature, and contains many beautiful word-pictures of landscapes.

The Times Literary Supplement

SOURCE: A review of *The Preacher of Cedar Mountain: A Tale of the Open Country,* in *The Times Literary Supplement,* No. 822, October 18, 1917, p. 507.

Well-known on both sides of the Atlantic as is Mr. Seton for his books about animals and the Wild West, he has not so far been known as a novelist. In this tale of the Canadian backwoods he turns his knowledge to excellent account. His picture of the life of the country in the 'eighties glows with the enthusiasm of one who was intimate with it all; and not the least telling of all his

descriptions is that of Fort Ryan horse races, though he tells us he did not actually witness them himself. But the whole centres round the story of Jim Hartigan, and the moulding, through many influences, of his character from a reckless dare-devil youth into a preacher of strength and power, a fine type of muscular clergyman. He and his devoted wife, who for a time take up work in Chicago, but return to Cedar Mountain, grip the reader throughout; and one is not surprised to learn that a story of so much breadth and reality is for the most part historical, and many of its characters, including its hero, drawn from life.

BANNERTAIL: THE STORY OF A GRAY SQUIRREL (1922)

Mabel H. B. Mussey

SOURCE: A review of *Bannertail: The Story of a Gray Squirrel,* in *The Nation* (New York), Vol. 115, No. 2996, December 6, 1922, p. 619.

Bannertail is an aristocrat among animals. This story of a gray squirrel is told in Thompson Seton's familiar way, with his inimitable pen-drawings flashing humor on the wide margins. After years of paper famine the spaciousness of this beautiful volume seems to spread as luxuriantly as the squirrel's plumy tail. Surely of all our wildwood folk the gray-squirrel is the closest friend to childhood, and his story should be widely read. But Bannertail is no portly and pauperized park bencher—he is the silver streak that flashes through the forest. The lessons he acquires in youth, his courtship of Silvergrey, his part in and out of the family life, and his encounters with weasel and snake, sickness, famine, and plenty, fill out the measure of his days. Dignity in the telling and fun in the picturing make an excellent combination. Better one such book than scores of the to-bed-going variety of near-animal stories.

Punch, or The London Charivari

SOURCE: A review of *Bannertail: The Story of a Gray Squirrel,* in *Punch, or The London Charivari,* Vol. CLXV, October 10, 1923, p. 360.

I have read several of Mr. Ernest Thompson Seton's books, and I hope that he will give me opportunities to read many more of them; for to anyone with a taste for natural history they are real treasures. *Bannertail* is the story, delightfully told, of a grey squirrel. We are given the history of him from his infancy until he is the father of a grown-up family and in considerable awe of his extremely competent wife. *Silvergray* loved and appreciated her husband, but saw to it that he did not become too domineering. With this tale of domesticity we are also told how squirrels contrive to live, and how they manage, if they are careful, to outwit their enemies. Mr. Seton's admirable illustrations add much to the charm of a fascinating volume.

GREAT HISTORIC ANIMALS: MAINLY ABOUT WOLVES (British edition as *Mainly about Wolves*, 1937)

E. Frank Allen

SOURCE: A review of *Great Historic Animals: Mainly about Wolves,* in *New York Times Book Report,* August 29, 1937, p. 4.

A wolf, says Mr. Thompson Seton, is "simply a big, wild, but very doggy dog, getting his living by his wits and the strength of his jaws"; and as in all highly specialized creatures, there is a vast difference between individuals. It is these differences in individuality among wolves which form the basis of most of the stories told in this latest book by the author of **Wild Animals I Have Known.** Good wolves, bad wolves, with a few other animals (a wild bull, a squirrel, some dogs, a rat, a leopard and a bear), wander back and forth through these pages, showing qualities and talents which are not only "doggy," but human as well. Some of the happenings are culled from the author's own wide experience. Some are stories other students of the wild have told him. A few are old historic tales.

The red-headed Cody wolf, for example, was certainly a good wolf in his own way. He had lived in captivity for a while, on the Cody ranch—hence his name—but he distinguished himself, and at last heroically sacrificed himself, in freedom. The story of the dog that found a wolf companion is another unusual tale. The story of the wolf on a motor car's running board is a merry little joke on the author himself, told in high good humor. The story of the Breton wolves and the child who lived with them is a grim tale until it reaches its happy ending. And here in this book, too, are the "last two wolves of northern Ireland," strangely caught in the seventeenth century; and Courtaud, the "king wolf" of fifteenth-century France; and the gaunt and dreadful beast of Gevaudan.

Along with the stories which fill the greater part of the book, Mr. Thompson Seton traces a number of "wild ways of tame beasts," like the wagging of a dog's tail, and even some of the inborn habits and feelings of the "tall naked two-legged animals" that are ourselves.

TRAIL OF AN ARTIST-NATURALIST (1940; British edition, 1951)

Alan Devoe

SOURCE: A review of *Trail of an Artist-Naturalist,* in *Saturday Review of Literature,* Vol. XXIII, No. 7, December 7, 1940, p. 18.

Ernest Thompson Seton, twelfth of the fourteen children of a shipowner, was born in South Shields, England, but he was only six years old when in 1866 the whole considerable family came to Canada to take up a life of backwoods farming. It was a pioneering life . . . a life of sheep-shearing and cattle-driving, woodcutting and log-cabin-chinking, learning to deal with snow and cold and stock-diseases and the encroachment of the wilderness. To young Ernest Seton, as he grew into older boyhood, it was a life of enchanted happiness. He loved the making of things with his hands, the fashioning of bull-toggles out of hickory and silver-brooms out of blue beech; he loved the company of trees and sky and earth and changing elements; particularly he loved the wild birds and animals which were everywhere around him in the unspoiled forest. There was something in the wilderness to which Ernest Thompson Seton's boyish heart deeply responded, and was soon inalienably dedicated. He was able to decide while still a lad that he wanted to grow up to be a naturalist. He was able to be sure that he wanted to give his life to a career of studying the outdoors and its creatures and its spirit, and to arousing public enthusiasm for these things.

Save for the art-study periods and one or two other brief interludes, young Ernest Thompson Seton's life was almost wholly spent in the wilder places of the American outdoors. He travelled the Great Plains, hunting and camping and growing Indian-wise; trapped wolves in New Mexico; voyaged deep in the wilderness of Manitoba. Always he was sketching the things he saw, studying minutely at first-hand the behavior of wolf or deer or beaver, shooting and skinning and dissecting in order to learn those nature facts which he had no textbooks to tell him. His life was that of an absorbed field-naturalist and frontiersman, fascinated by the dramatic elements in animal life, interested less in pallid scientific book-learning than in what he could observe with his own eyes in his own beloved wilderness.

Seton's **Wild Animals I Have Known** appeared in 1898. It was an instantaneous success, and was followed by other nature-books as fast as he could write and illustrate them. The Canadian backwoodsman became before long famous as the most popular naturalist in America, a constant lecturer at large fees, a founder of the Woodcraft movement, a high-priced animal illustrator for *Century,* and an idol to all boys who were early interested in nature lore (including this reviewer). With the passing of the years Ernest Thompson Seton achieved in full measure success in the role that as a boy he had dreamed of playing: the role of "Prophet of Outdoors."

Such is the life-story told in the fat and handsome autobiography called **Trail of an Artist-Naturalist.** It is an uncommonly interesting story, the more so because Seton speaks only briefly of the last thirty or forty years of his long life and instead devotes most of his account to a minutely detailed and vividly told chronicle of his earlier years as backwoods farm boy, wilderness hunter, and roving camper-naturalist. It is hard to imagine that anyone who loves the outdoors will fail to find it fascinating reading, or indeed that any reader at all will fail to find a good deal of entertainment in its recital of picturesque adventures. The book has its share, of course, of that kind of imaginatively presented animal lore which in 1904 infuriated the sober-minded Burroughs into publicly (and I think unwarrantably) attacking Seton as a sham naturalist, and it has, too, occasional outcroppings of a curious sort of naive vanity and egotism. But the "nature-faker" issue has been dead these many years now, and Seton's occasional romantics need not trouble anyone too much; and a little complacent self-congratulation is perhaps permissible to an old man who has fought many battles and fought them stoutly. As the record of a colorful, incident-crowded life, and particularly as the record of an American wild scene that is now gone forever with the passenger pigeon and the thundering wild bison, *Trail of an Artist-Naturalist* is excellent reading.

The Christian Science Monitor

SOURCE: A review of *Trail of an Artist-Naturalist,* in *The Christian Science Monitor,* December 14, 1940, p. 16.

The story of his life and labors written by Ernest Thompson Seton in *Trail of an Artist-Naturalist* would fit very well into the Horatio Alger series of stories about conservative, ambitious, poor boys who struggled to make their mark in the world, went to the big city and after hardship and adventure, achieved fame and fortune.

Born in the north of England of Scottish lineage, he was taken by his family to Canada and homesteading when he was almost six. There began the pioneer lessons that determined first his interest in wild life and second his love for art. But father Seton wasn't a very successful homesteader and after four years the family moved to Toronto, where in near-by swamps and woods (long since relinquished to the march of progress and the city real estate operator) the artist-naturalist-to-be puzzled over mysteries encountered on the north shore of Lake Ontario.

When it came time to study art Ernest went to London. After paying his passage over, he had so little left of the allowance his father advanced him that he had to find an immediate market for such sketches and drawings as he made under tutelage of the British Museum School. He supposed that he would go from London to wherever British art should lead him, but a "vision" told him his future would be in Canada for a time and finally New York.

The wild lands of western Canada and the United States were really wild then, and the greatest difficulties experienced were not so much in seeing new species and varieties of wild life as in identifying them. There were no really good books available yet on the subject. Artist-Naturalist Seton was to play a big part in making these available by illustrating for such authors as Frank Chapman and C. Hart Merriam as well as himself. His own *Life-Histories of Northern Animals* and *Lives of Game Animals,* ten volumes in all, are classics in the library today of any serious student of nature.

But Ernest Thompson Seton is perhaps best known for popular stories like *Lobo (the Wolf) and Other Stories,* and *Old Silver Grizzle. Two Little Savages,* and *Trail of the Sandhill Stag.* A condensed story of Lobo and parts of many other famous yarns are repeated in his latest work for the benefit of those who are not familiar with his writings; but of course they lose a great deal of their charm and chuckle appeal through condensation.

In general this autobiography is a gem of sparkling anecdotes, loaded with practical advice gleaned from years of living on the western plains and hills.

E. P. Richardson

SOURCE: A review of *Trail of an Artist-Naturalist,* in *The Commonweal,* Vol. XXXIII, No. 11, January 3, 1941, p. 284.

Whether by accident or design, Ernest Thompson Seton has chosen to write down his memories, not of his successful life as an author and naturalist, but of the experiences in his youth which formed and nourished his later life. That is perhaps as it should be, for the important part of an author's life is in his books; whereas the unwritten story of his youth is that of the formation of his talent. The result is a book which is written from fresh and happy memories, memories of the forest frontier in Ontario in the 1860s and 70s, which are the bases of Seton's masterpiece of writing for boys, *Two Little Savages,* which I was interested to find is autobiographical; memories of the splendid, untouched spectacle of bird and animal life on the plains of Manitoba, before it vanished at the coming of the homesteader; memories of an art student's life in London and Paris; of the Southwest in the great days of the cattle industry. It is a life in which impressions of nature mean more than impressions of people, except for a story about the author's father that is certainly one of the most extraordinary tales ever told of any parent. But the chief actors in this autobiography are the prairies and the forest, the marshes of Toronto Bay, the Winnipeg wolf, Lobo the desert wolf, the bird which for years he knew only as the Voice in the Tamaracks and their like. Many of them are characters familiar to the reader of Seton's books.

Of the importance of Seton's serious scientific work I cannot speak, for I have not read his *Life-Histories of Northern Animals* or *Lives of Game Animals.* But of the imaginative stimulus he gave to a whole generation of boys who grew up before the war of 1914, I feel as well able to speak as anyone, for no one, I feel certain, poured over *Two Little Savages, Rolf in the Woods* and *Wild Animals I Have Known* with more delight. It is no small achievement to color the imagination of a generation. Seton was, it is true, not alone in this work; for we can see, as we look back, that a great part of the best thought in America was devoted in the later nineteenth century to discovering the importance that nature had for our civilization, an effort which resulted in a rich literature and some of our best painting, as well as the conservation movement and its attendant professions, much important work in natural history, and the foundation of the great boys' and girls' organizations of today. But Seton was a great popularizer, perhaps the greatest popularizer, of animal and forest life. The self-revelation of such a man has its importance. What was the secret of his achievement? He gives a vivid record of his struggle against poverty and lack of advantages. But others have worked as hard and shown equal will and intelligence with other results. Seton himself gives the clue to his special achievement in a passage written as he looked over his old notebooks, in search of a bird which had meant much to him in his unknown years of self-training on the western plains: "As I look over the ancient record written by the campfire at night, I am conscious of this: that the detail of birds and beasts, with set and science names, as given in my paper record, is not she real thing. This was the new light—the spiritual joy, the lasting memories of life—life—beautiful life on every side." This seems to me the key to Seton's importance. He was sound naturalist enough to come unscathed through the "nature-faking" controversy of the early years of the century. But he had also esthetic gifts and a love of life which enabled him to transcend the limits of specialized knowledge and to captivate the imagination of a generation. His ability to go beyond the narrow professionalism of modern knowledge is more important to our civilization, I think, than the world has recently been inclined to admit. We are accustomed to popularization which means vulgarization. Seton showed that it can be an independent, imaginative achievement that makes abstract knowledge a living part of general culture. In boys' magazines today pseudo-science and aviation head the list of interests, while nature, together with historical stories, hangs on by sufferance at the bottom of the list. Is this because the world has changed and values are now different, or is it the lack of a first-rate talent of the rare sort that Ernest Thompson Seton possessed?

The Booklist

SOURCE: A review of *Trail of an Artist-Naturalist,* in *The Booklist,* Vol. 37, January 15, 1941, p. 215.

Though uneven in interest, Mr. Seton's account of his long career as a naturalist, writer, artist, and lecturer will appeal especially to readers who grew up with his nature stories. Born in the 1860s, he spent his childhood in Scotland and in frontier Canada, with subsequent intervals in London, Paris, New York, the Northwest and Southwest. Emphasis is on the first half of his life.

ERNEST THOMPSON SETON'S AMERICA: SELECTIONS FROM THE WRITINGS OF THE ARTIST-NATURALIST (1954)

Mary N. Barton

SOURCE: A review of *Ernest Thompson Seton's America: Selections from the Writings of the Artist-Naturalist,* in *Library Journal,* Vol. 79, No. 2, January 15, 1954, p. 142.

Miss Wiley, of the American Museum of Natural History, has selected and edited this representative collection of Seton's best writings taken from scattered and sometimes inaccessible sources. The naturalist-artists' passionate interest in wild animal and bird life is the unifying thread in this varied assortment which includes: excerpts from his autobiography; methods of tracking and trailing; woodcraft; the art anatomy of animals; observations on the life and habits of many of his wild life friends, birds and mammals; and a few of his famous stories, including such old favorites as the wolf story **"Lobo."** Although Seton is no stylist and one wishes at times that his writing were less slipshod, it is always readable, and the suspense and adventure in his animal stories make them enthralling to amateur naturalists of all ages, though the greatest appeal is to young people.

The Booklist

SOURCE: A review of *Ernest Thompson Seton's America: Selections from the Writings of the Artist-Naturalist,* in *The Booklist,* Vol. 50, No. 12, February 15, 1954, p. 234.

The biographical sketch and interpretations of the English-born artist-naturalist of American wildlife by both Mrs. Seton and the editor, Farida Wiley, make more meaningful for the present generation the 21 skillfully arranged chapters from Seton's 40 books and articles. Youthful years in Canada, true stories and life histories of animals, ideas on zoos and wildlife preserves, a successful experiment in overcoming vandalism of boys, legends, ethical teachings of Indians, and well reproduced examples of his drawings unfold a wide range of interests and talents. It is regrettable that there is no list of illustrations in an otherwise finely made book.

T. Morris Longstreth

SOURCE: A review of *Ernest Thompson Seton's America: Selections from the Writings of the Artist-Naturalist,* in *The Christian Science Monitor,* March 4, 1954, p. 10.

Once more the Buffalo Wind is blowing through the bookstores. Lobo, the King of the Currumpaw, is back, and Krag, the Kootenay Ram. Grandfathers may read "Hank and Jeff" to the children they feared had become television addicts and find that they respond to one of the most remarkable dog stories ever told. Grandmothers who once were moved to tears by "Molly Cottontail" will be glad to know that Kipling wrote to Seton that it was this story which got him started on his Jungle Tales.

This is a book of a generation's memories, as well as a reminder to our times that a great man lived among us. It is a joy to report that time has stolen nothing that matters from the author of *Wild Animals I Have Known.*

The book is a collection of samples indicating Seton's versatility, depths, heights, and usefulness to North America. Julia Seton gives "Impressions" of her husband, and Farida Wiley a brief biography. Then come excerpts from one of the most simple and entrancing autobiographies in English. *Trail of an Artist-Naturalist,* followed by short selections from the stories, natural history, and travels.

Seton's Woodcraft League of 1900 was a forerunner of our country's youth programs, and the story of its birth is told here from a privately printed pamphlet. Read it and laugh, and get a new insight into the real man. The Annual Report of the Smithsonian Institution for 1901 reveals one of Seton's finest investigations into animal nature.

Dip into this book anywhere and you will want to turn back to the living, if neglected, sources. And everywhere you will find integrity, searching, persistence, imagination, humor, all borne on a tide of natural joy in his boundless lifework. "Greatness," says Thoreau, "is well proportioned, unstrained, and stands on the soles of his feet," and he might have been describing Ernest Thompson Seton. The man's contribution to the soundness of our country's life over half a century is literally incalculable.

Alan Devoe

SOURCE: A review of *Ernest Thompson Seton's America: Selections from the Writings of the Artist-Naturalist,* in *The Saturday Review,* Vol. 36, No. 10, March 6, 1954, p. 20.

Two or three years ago Miss Farida Wiley, staff member of the American Museum of Natural History and lecturer in nature education to many groups, edited an admirable volume, *John Burroughs' America.* This selection did much to acquaint a new generation with the best work of the Sage of Slabsides, rescuing it from the threatened dusty oblivion of his *Collected Works.* In *Ernest Thompson Seton's America,* second volume in a projected American Naturalists Series, Miss Wiley has now performed the same service for Ernest Thompson Seton. Seton had not been moldering away in any set of collected works; his forty-some books were mostly out of print, and the atomic space-rocket generation was in danger of missing altogether the picturesque tales of grizzly bears, moose, wolves, and pacing mustangs with which Seton had spellbound several generations. (The "several generations" is no casual phrase. Seton was born in 1860, was a best seller by 1898, and lived until 1946.)

Miss Wiley has selected and edited well, with sound taste and scholarship. In under 400 pages, taken from Seton's enormous output, she has caught him at his most authentically magical and has preserved a remarkably

large part of what is best worth preserving. The selection of Seton's drawings—he made thousands and thousands of them; his surviving second wife, Julia Seton, possesses something like 7,000—is as sound as the selection of prose. There are several drawings here published for the first time. Altogether, the one-volume Seton has been excellently composed, from the touching memoir by Julia Seton to the condensed bibliography and efficient index. For any old friend of Seton's, however, or for any informed student of the American nature-writing scene early in this century, there is about this volume a fascinating aspect of the Unsaid. It requires a little comment.

A reader meeting Seton for the first time in this book would take him to have been an almost stuffily "respected" figure (as was Burroughs) in his nature-writing heyday. After all, he comes presented by a conservative and scholarly editor, of Museum standing, who speaks reverently of his "research," his "authoritativeness," his "great understanding of the world of natural science," and so on. One would think, from her introduction, that there had never been any question of Seton's standing.

It was just over fifty years ago (in the *Atlantic* for March 1903) that good gray Burroughs, sage and dean of American nature-writing then, let loose his comments on Seton's *Wild Animals I Have Known.* The article was one of the nastiest in the history of responsible critical journalism. Seton's book, said Burroughs, ought to have been called *Wild Animals I Alone Have Known.* Its author, he went on, was a deliberately unreliable sensation-monger. Seton's stories might be "true as romance, true in their artistic effects, true in their power to entertain the young reader; . . . but true as natural history they certainly are not." And so on. It was a massacre, or an attempted one. It touched off the whole bloody shindig that raged for years as the controversy about "nature-faking," a controversy notable, among other cruel things, for the war-whoops of President Theodore Roosevelt.

Ernest Thompson Seton did have "great understanding of natural science"; he did do a prodigious lot of field-research, and the rest. But also he was primarily an artist; he loved to present his nature-lore in bright, fantastic colors; he was a gorgeous yarn-spinner. This extravagant temperament endeared him and his work to the public, and it let him write and draw with memorable vividness. But also it caused a great many of the less imaginative naturalists and prosiness-at-any-price scientists to—speaking simply—hate him. It gives an eerie feeling, reading *Ernest Thompson Seton's America* and nothing the grave homage of its tone, to reflect that some readers, scanning it, may never know what a hardy and valiant-spirited man Seton had to be to win to such estate.

Additional coverage of Seton's life and career is contained in the following sources published by The Gale Group: *Contemporary Authors,* Vol. 109; *Dictionary of Literary Biography,* Vol. 92; *Junior DISCovering Authors; Something about the Author,* Vol. 18; and *Twentieth-Century Literary Criticism,* Vol. 31.

Robert Silverberg

1935-

(Also wrote as Walker Chapman, Don Elliott, Franklin Hamilton, Walter Drummond, et al) American author of fiction and nonfiction.

Major works include *Lost Cities and Vanished Civilizations* (1962), *Mound Builders of Ancient America: The Archeology of a Myth* (1968; abridged version as *The Mound Builders*, 1970), *Lord Valentine's Castle* (1980), *Project Pendulum* (1987), *Letters from Atlantis* (1990).

INTRODUCTION

A prolific writer and one of the most influential in his field, Silverberg is credited with helping to turn science fiction from a pulp form to legitimate literature. Although he himself wrote pulp in the beginning, in mid-career he began to fulfill his vision of science fiction as a form of art. Silverberg's primary themes were how alienation can be confronted and overcome; how individuals can discover and develop a new concept of beingness; how individuals with special abilities, usually psychic, learn to embrace those abilities and forge new relationships with other individuals; and how individuals adapt to different physical and social environments. This was a tremendous innovation at the time, and although critics found his work to be exciting, refreshing, and the manifestation of his early promise, it did not win as large a popular audience as his earlier and lesser work. Another claim to Silverberg's reputation is the sheer quantity of material he has written. At the beginning of his career, Silverberg produced so many writings that he had to use pseudonyms to keep his name from appearing too often. His first science fiction book, *Revolt on Alpha C* (1955), written for young adults, has been in print for over forty years. Later, when he switched for a time from writing fiction to writing popular nonfiction science books for both juveniles and adults, he was just as prolific. Some of his nonfiction, such as *Lost Cities and Vanished Civilizations*, *The Auk, the Dodo, and the Orynx: Vanished and Vanishing Creatures* (1967), and *Mound Builders of Ancient America: The Archeology of a Myth,* have become classic reference books. Commenting on the diversity of Silverberg's works in the *Washington Post Book World*, George R. R. Martin observed that "few writers, past or present, have had careers quite as varied, dramatic, and contradictory as that of Robert Silverberg."

Biographical Information

Born in Brooklyn, New York, in 1935, Silverberg discovered science fiction in the eighth grade. As a child he was fascinated by the past as understood from dinosaur and other fossils, and would speculate about the future,

intrigued by any time not *this* time. A lonely child, he prodigiously read literary classics and science texts, but when introduced to science fiction magazines and anthologies, he became addicted to them. An early writer as well, Silverberg wrote for the school newspaper, and churned out story after story, hoping one day to be published in one of the science fiction magazines. He thought for a time about a career as a scientist, but realized he lacked the ability that some of his classmates had to "[grasp] fundamental principles and [draw] new conclusions from them." While a student at Columbia University, he continued writing and submitting science fiction stories. His collaboration with already established science fiction writer Randall Garrett led to the publication of Silverberg's stories in small magazines, and in 1954, he sold his first novel, *Revolt on Alpha C,* to Thomas Y. Crowell. When he graduated from Columbia in 1956 with a Bachelor of Arts degree, he was a professional. In the late summer of that same year, Silverberg got married and received his first Hugo for Best New Science Fiction Writer of the Year. During the 1950s he wrote hundreds of stories under such pseudonyms as Walter Chapman, Dan Eliot, Don Elliott, and others, which he considered mere potboilers.

By the end of the decade, when the market for science fiction began to shrink, he tried to find a new niche by proposing a book about Pompeii to one of his editors. After some consideration, the editor suggested he do a book about several ancient sites, rather than just one. *Lost Cities and Vanished Civilizations* was published in 1962 and launched Silverberg on a new phase of his writing career. Throughout the 1960s he wrote an enormous number of popular science books for both adults and juveniles, usually picking his subject according to his own scientific interests, ranging from archeology to biographies, to a book on American Indians and a history of medicine. When his friend Frederik Pohl, the well-known science fiction writer, became editor of the science fiction magazine, *Galaxy,* Pohl sought out Silverberg and offered to publish his short stories, giving him complete creative freedom. The resulting story, "To See the Invisible Man," was a mature and complex piece, the kind Silverberg had been wanting to write for a long time. As he wrote and submitted more stories to Pohl, Silverberg found himself drawn back into the world of science fiction.

In 1966, after a serious illness, Silverberg began to write serious literary works with complex plots and developed social situations, some with dark, unsatisfying endings, such as *Thorns* (1967), which he considered to be crucial to his oeuvre and one of his best works. To much of his science fiction audience, *Thorns* was a radical departure from the formulized work they had come to expect from him, and while some were pleased that he had begun to show his potential, others were appalled at this proof of his dark and disturbing side. The book was nominated for both the Hugo and the Nebula. After a devastating house fire in 1968 and a long recovery period, Silverberg returned to write serious adult science fiction. Although the critics were favorably impressed, the troubling psychology, highly emotional content, and sometimes brutal images made his work less appealing to the general audience. Nevertheless, his *A Time of Changes* (1971), considered the first serious work in the genre of science fiction, won the Nebula Award from the Science Fiction Writers of America, and helped to change the face of science fiction. Silverberg moved to California in 1971, but dissatisfied with his work, unhappy with the public response to his serious endeavors, and caught in a failing marriage, he announced his retirement. Four years later, in order to raise money for an expensive divorce, Silverberg decided to write one last book. The result was *Lord Valentine's Castle*, the first of his works set in the complex alien world, Majipoor, and certainly his most popular work and a tremendous success. In recent years he remarried happily, collaborated on three novels with Isaac Asimov before Asimov's death, produced anthologies, wrote more books for a young adult audience, and has continued to add to his books about Majipoor.

Major Works

Lost Cities and Vanished Civilizations, the first of Silverberg's nonfiction science books, received several awards and launched him on a secondary writing career. In it he explores six ancient civilizations recovered by explorers and archeologists in the last two centuries. These civilizations include Pompeii, Troy, Mycenae, Babylon, Chíchen Itza, and Angkor. The book addresses archeological findings for each civilization, as well as legends arising from them. A source of archeological science and lore, *Lost Cities* was researched and written to spark an interest in archeology, and was favorably received by critics. Even more praised was *Mound Builders of Ancient America: The Archeology of a Myth*. When it was published, many reviewers, even those writing for archeological journals, assumed Silverberg was himself an archeologist, and he was embarrassed by invitations to lecture, teach, and review articles on archeological findings. Silverberg's comprehensive and scholarly study of the ancient Indian mounds in the Mississippi Valley explores the history of the exploration of the mounds, as well as the results of research, among which led to the founding of the Smithsonian Museum. *Mound Builders* examines modern surveys of Indian culture and discredits vague theories regarding the meanings of these mounds. A classic text, the work is still considered to be one of the best scholarly writings on the subject.

In *Across a Billion Years* (1969), written for young adults, Silverberg united his aptitude for archeology and science fiction. A young archeological apprentice goes on an expedition to the planet Dinamon IX, where an outpost of an ancient race known as the High Ones has been recently discovered. In their search for artifacts, the excavation team uncovers evidence that the High Ones, who lived a billion years ago, may still be alive. Guided across the galaxy to the home planet of the High Ones, the excavators find that they have arrived a billion years too late. Critics thought the book was humorous, inventive, and provocative, and included many interesting and lively characters and important points about prejudice. *Lord Valentine's Castle*, Silverberg's most well-known book, brought him out of his self-imposed retirement with a resounding popular success. Using many elements of fantasy, the story tells of a young man who wanders around his planet acquiring new companions and eventually discovers that he is the true prince of the kingdom, whose body has been switched with an interloper. Silverberg creates a unique alien world called Majipoor, which has been settled by explorers from Earth for several centuries and is also populated by many unusual and entertaining aliens and a mysterious and hostile subjugated aboriginal race. *Lord Valentine's Castle* was praised for its quirky characters and inventive world, and the evocative and absorbing writing. Silverberg continued the tales of Majipoor with *The Majipoor Chronicles* (1982), *Valentine Pontifex* (1983), *The Mountains of Majipoor* (1995), *Sorcerers of Majipoor* (1997), and the possibility of more in the future.

Along with his science fiction for adults, Silverberg wrote many books for juveniles and young adults. Among these is *Project Pendulum*, about twins Eric and Sean who are chosen as the first subjects of a new time travel experiment. They are shunted back and forth over time on a pendulum, with each time period becoming more distant. Each era they pass through is unique. They see in succession their younger selves, robots, cavemen, aliens, and dinosaurs. *A reviewer for Publishers Weekly* noted, "This imaginative story, suggesting much more than is stated in its brief length, is a deft evocation of Silverberg's theme of dislocation." Also for young adults, *Letters from Atlantis* is about time travel and dislocation. Young researchers studying thought patterns go back in time to inhabit the minds of people from the past. One researcher, Roy, travels to Atlantis and inhabits the mind of Prince Ram. Roy causes the prince to write letters about Atlantis and send them to Roy's fellow researcher and lover. When Ram discovers Roy in his mind, Roy goes against the scientific code and reveals himself to Ram. Roy finds out that not only is Ram an alien, but he also can see the future in which Atlantis is doomed by the gods. Reviewed as inventive and entertaining, *Letters from Atlantis* presents an original setting in which Silverberg cleverly combines detailed descriptions and finely tuned nuances with traditional legends.

Awards

Silverberg has won a host of awards and has been nominated for many others. Of the two major science fictions awards, he has won four Hugo Awards, given by the fans of science fiction at the World Science Fiction Convention, and five Nebula Awards, given by the Science Fiction Writers of America. These include best new author in 1956, the novella *Nightwings* in 1969, the novella *Gilgamesh in the Outback* in 1987, and the novelette *Enter a Soldier, Later: Enter Another* in 1990. He has received the Nebula for the short story "Passengers" in 1970, the short story "Good News from the Vatican" in 1971, the book *A Time of Changes* in 1972, the novella *Born with the Dead* in 1975, and the novella *Sailing to Byzantium* in 1986. In 1970 Silverberg was the guest of honor at the World Science Fiction Convention. Some of his awards for young adult works include the Spring Book Festival Award from the *New York Herald Tribune* in 1962 for *Lost Cities and Vanished Civilizations* and in 1967 for *The Auk, the Dodo, and the Orynx*; an award from the National Association of Independent Schools in 1966 for *The Old Ones*, the Locus Award for *Lord Valentine's Castle* in 1982, and the Woodward Park Award for *Letters from Atlantis* in 1991.

TITLE COMMENTARY

📖 *LOST RACE OF MARS* (1960)

H. H. Holmes

SOURCE: A review of *Lost Race of Mars,* in *New York Herald Tribune Book Review,* May 8, 1960, p. 32.

S. F. for pre-teen readers is infrequent and usually incompetent; so Robert Silverberg's agreeable *Lost Race of Mars* should be welcomed by the eight to twelve group. This simple story of how two children make contact with the Old Martians when their elders have failed has enough warmth and charm to it to make one overlook a few scientific slips and the fact that Leonard Kessler's illustrations seem overcute and out of tone with the text.

Pamela Marsh

SOURCE: A review of *Lost Race of Mars,* in *The Christian Science Monitor,* May 12, 1960, p. 3B.

Sally and Jim, good companions for the 9-12s, go to Mars for a year with their father who is searching for the original Martians. Life in 2017 doesn't seem to have changed much. Children are still misunderstood by other children but are still triumphant in the end, and cats (a Mitten, or Mars kitten in this story) are still Terribly Important Creatures. A danger that immature readers may not notice is that the Mars colony is so rigidly organized that imagination, children's writers and books as delightful as this one may be ruled out.

📖 *LOST CITIES AND VANISHED CIVILIZATIONS* (1962)

Virginia Kirkus' Service

SOURCE: A review of *Lost Cities and Vanished Civilizations,* in *Virginia Kirkus' Service,* Vol. XXX, No. 3, February 1, 1962, p. 150.

From the excavated ruins to the digging now going on in the Mayan Indian country of Mexico, this book tells the story of six ancient civilizations which disappeared centuries ago, then were rediscovered by archeologists and explorers in the last two centuries. In a series of vinettes—supported by archeologist's discoveries today—the life of Pompeii is recreated just as nearby Mount Vesuvius erupted. Following this is the story of the famed explorer-archeologist Heinrich Schliemann and his diggings in ancient Troy and Mycenae. Babylon is examined too in all its complexity, as well as the Chíchen Itza of the Mayas, and the huge city of Angkor lost for centuries in the Cambodian jungle. Not only does this book recreate the life of those civilizations, but it explains the fascinating lore of archeology and stimulates interest in the science. Written for the layman.

📖 *THE MASK OF AKHNATEN* (1965)

Viriginia Kirkus' Service

SOURCE: A review of *The Mask of Akhnaten,* in *Virginia Kirkus' Service,* Vol. XXXIII, No. 1, January 1, 1965, p. 8.

One of this author's favorite subjects has been the archaeological excavations made in Egypt, and earlier this year he wrote an adult book about Akhnaten (*Akhnaten: The Rebel Pharaoh*). This ancient leader, who abandoned polytheism for the worship of Aten, is really the hero of this story about Tom Lloyd, who had been invited by his journalist uncle on an expedition to Nubia. The two joined up with a group of archaeologists just in time to participate in the resurrection of Akhnaten's tomb—quite a find, since it has always been thought to have been destroyed by the Pharaoh's numerous enemies. The subsequent incidents involve the theft of Akhnaten's golden mask, and its recovery by Lloyd and his young Arabic friend following a chase in a subterranean maze. It's a weak adventure story, shored up with details about Egyptology which are solid and plentiful.

MEN WHO MASTERED THE ATOM (1965)

Virginia Kirkus' Service

SOURCE: A review of *Men Who Mastered the Atom,* in *Virginia Kirkus' Service,* Vol. XXXIII, No. 6, March 15, 1965, p. 330.

As science knowledge grows more complex and research grows in terms of investigators, it becomes more difficult to pinpoint who invented what. In the case of nuclear physics, principles were built upon principles and Mr. Silverberg attempts to show the historic background of atomic energy from the Greeks speculating on the nature of matter, to post-Einsteinian projects. The discussion is easy to follow at first, combining as it does biographical information with the analysis of theories through logic rather than chemical or physical test. With the 18th, 19th and 20th century mathematicians and physicists contributing their mites to the final atomic breakthrough, the experiment and the chemical or mechanical proofs become of primary importance, so that the book predicates a thorough basic knowledge of procedures and first laws that only the more advanced students will be able to bring to it. Such readers as these will find it a handy single source of historic information economically arranged.

NIELS BOHR: THE MAN WHO MAPPED THE ATOM (1965)

Virginia Kirkus' Service

SOURCE: A review of *Niels Bohr: The Man Who Mapped the Atom,* in *Virginia Kirkus' Service,* Vol. XXXIII, No. 6, April 1, 1965, p. 389.

This is the story of the work done by Niels Bohr and by the other great nuclear physicists with whom he associated, rather than of his personal life. In many ways it is an expansion of the material offered in the later chapters of the author's recent **Men Who Mastered the Atom** (1965). Roughly the first half of this book describes Bohr's great discoveries about the nature of the atom.

The explanations are technical and require some background in physical principles. The remainder deals with the steps that went into the formulation of the atomic bomb. Here the text offers some interesting insights into the way historical events helped to shape the development of nuclear physics. In this respect the book is an intriguing blend of science and recent history.

THE OLD ONES: INDIANS OF THE AMERICAN SOUTHWEST (1965)

Virginia Kirkus' Service

SOURCE: A review of *The Old Ones: Indians of the American Southwest,* in *Virginia Kirkus' Service,* Vol. XXXIII, No. 6, April 1, 1965, pp. 389-90.

Only the finest piece of writing about the American Indian can quell the temptation to say "Here is another." This is a fine book. A comprehensive history of the Pueblos, the story (for it is, in the best sense, a story) begins with the first Spanish stories into the American Southwest: Cabeza de Vaca, the lost wanderer, and later, the resplendent Coronado, in vain search of more splendor. The author then flashes back more than 5000 years to the beginnings of the Anasazi, the Old Ones, and tells their story to the present. The author has drawn from archaeological discoveries, the writings of explorers and pioneers, and the record of today's Pueblo culture. Mr. Silverberg has written widely on archaeology and Indians. He writes with authority, with feeling for the great expanse of time and the desert, and with appreciation for a peace-loving, industrious, and tragic people. The almost text-bookish amount of detail is nevertheless readable because of a simple narrative organization and frequent summarizing paragraphs. Two directories append the text, listing the Pueblo ruins and the contemporary Pueblo reservations, and how and when the visitor may see them best. A bibliography of 46 related books and articles, grouped under four headings, extends a final irresistible invitation—symbols indicate those titles of technical interest and those with special appeal to young people.

The Booklist and Subscription Books Bulletin

SOURCE: A review of *The Old Ones: Indians of the American Southwest,* in *The Booklist and Subscription Books Bulletin,* Vol. 62, No. 5, November 1, 1965, p. 269.

Using archaeological studies and the writings of explorers Silverberg chronicles the history of the Pueblo Indians from their arrival in the Southwest through their conquest by the Spaniards. A final chapter examines the Pueblos of today and their attempts to preserve their ancient culture. A directory of historic sites and living pueblos and an extensive bibliography are appended. Photographs, maps, and drawings complement the extremely readable text. Will be useful as a guidebook or as supplementary social studies material as well as enjoyable for recreational reading.

📖 *THE GREAT WALL OF CHINA* (1965;
published as *The Long Rampart: The Story
of the Great Wall of China,* 1966)

Virginia Kirkus' Service

SOURCE: A review of *The Great Wall of China,* in *Virginia
Kirkus' Service,* Vol. XXXIII, No. 10, May 15, 1965, p. 516.

The Great Wall makes a convenient political paradigm in
this otherwise diffuse history of China. This is not only
an account of the Wall, but a general reference work as
well. For some, it may be unrewarding to read straight
through, since those unfamiliar with the government
turmoil of China's dynasties may be overwhelmed and
confused. The Wall itself helps to retain the outlines of
China's past. China here is constructed as southern China,
that part lying below the 3,900-mile wall. Above the
wall were the nomadic barbarians. The first Great
Wall, a mere 1,850 miles, was built in seven years about
2200 years ago. It was not built mainly as an article of
defense, but rather to consolidate the outlines of empire,
keep culture in and pure, and to burn up restless energy.
Little of that wall is left, for future empires rebuilt,
modified and extended this massive piece of engineering.
Today, it begins in a sea and ends on a precipice.
Some of the book's high points include the activities
of southern China's first great emperor; the effects of
Confucianism; the influx of Buddhism; the Mongol
invasion and the great khans. China's history boils at
a dead level and never really exploded until just recently.

📖 *THE WORLD OF CORAL* (1965)

Virginia Kirkus' Service

SOURCE: A review of *The World of Coral,* in *Virginia Kirkus'
Service,* Vol. XXXIII, No. 15, August 1, 1965, pp. 764-65.

A very thorough treatment of coral reefs and their ecological communities, ably researched and clearly written, but extremely detailed for casual reading. Dramatically, the first chapter is a fanciful snorkel swim through
a coral "sea garden" but the remaining sections lack
sustaining vitality, and do not inspire the eager attention
of Cousteau's writing, quoted here several times, with
his imaginative prose and authority. The bibliography,
entitled *For Further Reading,* is in three sections to satisfy
popular and technical interests, and includes a selection
of periodical articles, notably from *National Geographic,* dating from 1927 into the 1960s.

📖 *SOCRATES* (1965)

The Booklist and Subscription Books Bulletin

SOURCE: A review of *Socrates,* in *The Booklist and
Subscription Books Bulletin,* Vol. 62, No. 13, October
1, 1965, p. 147.

Socrates' life is ably sketched against a well-depicted
background of conditions in Greece, especially Athens,
during his time. Using the writings of Plato the author
presents in narrative style simplified yet real examples
of Socrates' method of searching for truth through questions and answers. May be useful as supplementary history material.

📖 *TO THE ROCK OF DARIUS: THE STORY
OF HENRY RAWLINSON* (1966)

Zena Sutherland

SOURCE: A review of *To the Rock of Darius: The Story
of Henry Rawlinson,* in *Bulletin of the Center for Children's Books,* Vol. 20, No. 7, March, 1967, pp. 115-16.

A rather ponderous biography of a romantic figure in the
history of archeological scholarship. Rawlinson's brilliant deciphering of the cuneiform inscriptions at Behistun are still impressive, still dramatic; the whole aura of
the British sahib in the mysterious East pervades this
account of the young soldier who became an Assyriolo-
gist, a Fellow of the Royal Society, an Ambassador to
Persia, and an M.P. The material is fascinating; the
writing style rather heavy.

The Booklist and Subscription Books Bulletin

SOURCE: A review of *To the Rock of Darius: The Story
of Henry Rawlinson,* in *The Booklist and Subscription
Books Bulletin,* Vol. 63, No. 13, March 1, 1967, p. 736.

A stimulating biography chronicles the life and multiple
careers of the English soldier-diplomat who achieved
lasting fame for his brilliant work in deciphering
Babylonian-Assyrian, Elamitic, and Persian cuneiform
texts and offers interesting sidelights on archaeological
research and British diplomacy in the Near East in the
nineteenth century. There is a detailed analysis of cuneiform writing and Rawlinson's methods of decipherment.
A map, two sections of photographs, and a partially
annotated bibliography are included.

Science Books

SOURCE: A review of *To the Rock of Darius: The Story
of Henry Rawlinson,* in *Science Books,* Vol. 3, No. 2,
September, 1967, p. 129.

The major theme is young Henry Rawlinson's decipherment of cuneiform writing during his term of service as
an officer of the East India Company in Persia and
Mesopotamia. A minor theme running through the book
is the role of the British East India Company in the
Orient—its policies, wars, and methods of dealing with
Asiatic peoples. There are good descriptions of 19th-
century oriental culture and of the ancient cultures of the
Assyrians, Babylonians and Sumerians. The author has

presented the intricate problem of cuneiform decipherment most skillfully and plainly for young readers. A better map and a diagram of the positions of Class I (Persian), Class II (Elamite or Susian), and Class III (Babylonian) on the Behistun Rock would have been helpful for those not familiar with the background. The illustrations otherwise are excellent. There is a good bibliography.

FORGOTTEN BY TIME: A BOOK OF LIVING FOSSILS (1966)

Marion H. Perkins and Fred Geis

SOURCE: A review of *Forgotten by Time: A Book of Living Fossils,* in *Appraisal: Science Books for Young People,* Vol. 1, No. 2, Spring, 1968, pp. 14-15.

LIBRARIAN [Marion H. Perkins]: This book develops the concept of gradual change in nature at varying rates as illustrated by pre-historic fossils. Interesting and seemingly factually scientific bringing together of the evolution of life with dramatic word pictures by the author, and striking illustrations by Leonard Everett Fisher of such familiar oddities as the kiwi, okapi, Galapagos tortoise, koalas, opossums, armadillos, etc., their discovery and place in history; a fascinating presentation for the junior high youngster.

SCIENTIST [Fred Geis]: In some respects the views put forth in this book are naive and/or mistaken, e. g., the representation of "Living Fossils" as "the débris left behind as time flows on," and it is unfortunate that an editor who understands the dynamics of evolution was not consulted. With this reservation I would recommend its purchase as a reference and source of stimulation for the browser. The vignettes of various forms of animal life are interesting, informative, and written in a personable manner.

THE DAWN OF MEDICINE (1967)

Kirkus Service

SOURCE: A review of *The Dawn of Medicine,* in *Kirkus Service,* Vol. XXV, No. 5, March 1, 1967, p. 286.

You may wonder if there is enough substantiated information about pre-Hippocratic medicine to make a book of general interest. *There isn't.* You may even wonder if there was enough scientific medicine to justify the title. *There wasn't, false dawn* would be more apt. The author has strung together suppositions about prehistoric man, circumstantial evidence and a few texts from the Egyptians, Mesopotamians, Chinese and Indians—and the conclusions can be summarized in a few sentences: the Egyptians separated examination, diagnosis and treatment, knew much about the body's workings, little about its care; the Mesopotamians had a code of medical practice (Hammurabi, of course) which wasn't enforced; the

Chinese studied diseases and recorded symptoms, discovered many valuable drugs and innoculation against smallpox—their tradition still has adherents as a counterpart to Western medicine; the Indians practiced plastic surgery and vaccination, put forth the notion of bodily hygiene and may have influenced the West. The recurrent theme, however, is the prevalence of magic, mixed in the Far East with philosophical concepts. Only in the fifth century in Greece does science begin to predominate, and then we have Hippocrates—and the end of the book. All this marshaling of minutiae to illumine pre-scientific practices in ancient cultures might be of interest to a student of those cultures; for youngsters, it's a great deal of repetitious deduction to support a few generalizations.

Harry C. Stubbs

SOURCE: A review of *The Dawn of Medicine, Horn Book Magazine,* Vol. XLIV, No. 1, February, 1968, pp. 81-3.

Robert Silverberg's **The Dawn of Medicine** follows a single theme—from distant past, since it goes back to the Cro-Magnon caves. Much of the material is necessarily based on legend, and much on educated guesswork. Historical figures such as Hippocrates and Galen accompany nameless magicians and medicine men across backgrounds of prehistoric and early historic Europe, Africa, and Asia. Here again emerges the historical point of view that magic slowly—very slowly—yields to an appreciation of material evidence. Even the scientist comes to feel some sympathy for magic-rooted "logic."

Science Books

SOURCE: A review of *The Dawn of Medicine,* in *Science Books,* Vol. 3, No. 4, March, 1968, p. 327.

The copious and rich melange of pre-Hippocratic medical history is too often merely "nodded to" in works dealing with the history of medicine. Mr. Silverberg presents a clear and most readable treatment of the mixture of science, magic, religion, and serendipitous discovery which characterizes the dawn of medicine. Beginning with the primitive medicine men of prehistoric times in Gothic hemispheres, he uses both archeologic data and contemporary anthropology in an attempt to reconstruct the status of the healer. He moves easily from this into a description of Egyptian medicine, drawing heavily from the seven medical papyri which were discovered in the latter half of the 19th century, particularly the Smith Papyrus and the Eber Papyrus (c. 1500 B.C.). Two chapters are devoted to Mesopotamian medicine, from which we have the oldest known medical document in the world, the Tablet of Zuppus, 4,000 years old. There is a fascinating chapter on the early history of Chinese medicine which is particularly relevant in view of the current political regime and China's resurrection of acupuncture as a contemporary mode of treatment. The brilliance of early Indian medicine is also portrayed and traced as it joins the Greek school of Cos and even, over a thousand years later, the Bagdad School (800 A.D.). The book is vivid and is particularly noteworthy in its integrating functions. Not only are patterns of medical history thoughtfully interwoven, but also an attempt is made to keep the reader's focus on the nature of science itself. The only significant erratum was the attribution of the staff with two serpents in Asklepeos; it is that of Hermes in his function as God of Commerce. The staff of Asklepeos bore one serpent only.

THE AUK, THE DODO, AND THE ORYNX: VANISHED AND VANISHING CREATURES (1967)

Kirkus Service

SOURCE: A review of *The Auk, the Dodo and the Oryx: Vanished and Vanishing Creatures,* in *Kirkus Service,* Vol. XXXV, No. 7, April 1, 1967, p. 432.

Following a repetitious plea for conservation is a literate examination of "vanished and vanishing creatures"—the dodo, auroche, bison, Steller's sea cow, auk, quagga, moa, rukh, giant ground sloth, passenger pigeon, and heath hen—each treated in a complete essay. Some species brought "back from oblivion" and some which are "on their way out" are surveyed in the last two chapters, and the conclusion examines steps already taken to prevent extinction of existing wildlife. A general and a topical bibliography, an index, and excellent wood-engravings of each animal enhance the utility of the book; the fine balance of historical fact, apropos quotation and natural science makes it as fine to read as to study.

Diane Wagner

SOURCE: A review of *The Auk, the Dodo, and the Oryx: Vanished and Vanishing Creatures,* in *The New York Times Book Review,* May, 1967, p. 34.

Walk into the American Museum of Natural History and you will see the bones of the ungainly dinosaur. In life-like dioramas behind glass cases, the heath hen guards her newly-hatched chicks and the zebra-like quagga gazes over the African veld. This is our only opportunity for observing extinct animals. Some species have perished through the process of natural selection—reaching an apex and then, unable to adapt to changing conditions, dying out. Others have been hunted down by man to the point of no return. We are all the poorer for never having seen them.

Selecting historical accounts by such naturalists as Georg Steller, who studied the now-extinct sea-cow on Bearing Island, and John James Audubon, who devoted his life to painting American birds and mammals and described the wanton slaughter of the passenger pigeon, Robert Silverberg has written a taut and moving narrative. Dedicated conservationists have managed to save many species. But we cannot be told too often that only by preserving our natural heritage, and continuing to set aside protected

areas, can we postpone the day when man no longer shares the earth with the colorful whooping crane, the shaggy bison and the bellowing trumpeter swan.

Zena Sutherland

SOURCE: A review of *The Auk, the Dodo, and the Oryx: Vanished and Vanishing Creatures,* in *Bulletin of the Center for Children's Books,* Vol. 20, No. 11, July-August, 1967, p. 176.

A most interesting book, the information about animals and species that are extinct—or that are threatened with extinction—being prefaced by a lucid discussion of the evolutionary process and by a plea for conservation of wild life. Mr. Silverberg describes the processes of slow, natural extinction and of the extermination caused by man's rapacity; the description is given with dramatic impact because actual cases are followed, such as the hunting of the moa and the last recorded sight of a live passenger pigeon. Some of the attempts to save a species came too late, some are viewed with optimism at present, and some are still in doubt. The book's illustrations are helpful; an index and a very good divided bibliography are appended.

TO OPEN THE SKY (1967)

Publishers Weekly

SOURCE: A review of *To Open the Sky,* in *Publishers Weekly,* Vol. 191, No. 14, April 3, 1967, p. 59.

Superior science fiction, but not of the tightly-plotted variety. Rather, each chapter is almost a short story in itself, connecting loosely with the others to form a narrative of the future, of Earth in the 21st and 22nd centuries. The population explosion has caused earth to become one vast slum, filled with mile-high skyscrapers. A religious group, the Vorsters, thrives by providing the masses with psychedelic experiences, hypnotic blue lights that symbolize the power of the atom. Technology has become a religion. There is an opposing heretical group, the Harmonists, who believe that man, using ESP powers, can become one with nature. The stories run in time from 2077 to 2164, and in place from Earth to Mars to Venus, telling of the conflict between the sects, a conflict resolved when the groups combine their technological and supernatural powers "to open the sky."

THE WORLD OF THE RAIN FOREST (1967)

Kirkus Service

SOURCE: A review of *The World of the Rain Forest,* in *Kirkus Service,* Vol. XXXV, No. 9, May 1, 1967, p. 572.

A systematic study of that standard assignment, the rain forest—climate, characteristics, trees, plants, insects, animals, early explorers, agricultural potential—is heightened by a few well-chosen quotations from the original explorers. With enthusiasm and competence, Mr. Silverberg describes the flora and fauna, selecting for special attention some of more than average interest, like the driver ant and the strangler fig. An interesting safari that should inspire a young naturalist to look for more of the same . . . the extensive bibliography points the way.

Althea L. Phillips and Douglas B. Sands

SOURCE: A review of *The World of the Rain Forest,* in *Appraisal: Science Books for Young People,* Vol. 1, No. 3, Fall, 1968, pp. 23-4.

LIBRARIAN [Althea L. Phillips]: This beautifully written, fascinating account of the rain forest includes descriptions of some of the forest's numerous plants and animals, among them the strangler fig, driver ants of Africa, army ants of South America, and sloths. Brief excerpts from scientific journals are included. An index and list of books for further reading add to the usefulness of the book.

SCIENTIST [Douglas B. Sands]: Entertaining and extensive in its coverage, *The World of the Rain Forest* is a book to interest the youth of today who crave adventure in the manner of the pioneer naturalists of a century or more ago. The final success of a book of this sort is determined by its effect on our young men. Will it stimulate them to strike out for themselves? Silverberg's accounts of the early explorers are good reading. When he attempts to catalog the jungle trees, he does less well. The illustrations are not equal to their task.

📖 *THE GATE OF WORLDS* (1967)

Kirkus Service

SOURCE: A review of *The Gate of Worlds,* in *Kirkus Service,* Vol. XXXV, No. 10, May 15, 1967, pp. 609-10.

The Gate is "the gate beyond which all futures lie. And for each possible future, there is a possible world beyond the gate." In this world the black plague so devastated Europe that it wasn't able to repel the Turkish invasion. After years of domination it finally drove them out but Europe never really recovered. Now it's 1963 and the Aztecs are among the big powers. This 1963 still sees sailing ships, not airplanes, and this is the saga of Dan Beauchamp, Esq., an 18-year-old from an "impoverished and unimportant island" named England who sails to the New World named the Upper and Lower Hesperides in search of fame and fortune. He hopes to attach himself to an Aztec Prince as a mercenary. What a great, painless, adventurous way of observing ancient cultures—and this whole projection of "what if?" is marvelously alive in action aplenty on both sides of the border. What about a "what if?" book on Napoleon beating his Waterloo? The Gate is there thanks to the author.

The Booklist and Subscription Books Bulletin

SOURCE: A review of *The Gate of Worlds,* in *The Booklist and Subscription Books Bulletin,* Vol. 64, No. 3, October 15, 1967, p. 250.

An interesting interpretation of a world that might have been if the Black Death of 1348 had killed three fourths of Europe's population instead of one fourth and Europe had then been conquered by the Turks. Set in 1963 the story centers on the adventures of eighteen-year-old Dan Beauchamp of New Istanbul (London) who migrates to the New World to make his fortune in the land ruled by the mighty Aztecs. After attaching himself to an ill-fated expedition led by an Aztec noble Don travels throughout the northern part of the continent in a fast-paced action tale with appeal for younger boys.

M. Hobbs

SOURCE: A review of *The Gate of Worlds,* in *The Junior Bookshelf,* Vol. 42, No. 6, December, 1978, p. 323.

This lively and most moral adventure from the pen of a popular science-fiction writer carries the reader along with cliffhangers and dire hints of what is to come. The plot is ingeniously different. We find the narrator, though English and living in 1963, belongs to a race subject to the Turks. The Russians and the South American Indian races, Incas and Aztecs, are also world leaders. Dan leaves home to escape the hated conquerors and their language and seek his fortune in the New World. He saves the life of Quequex, King Montezuma's fat sorcerer, who befriends him until Dan prefers to join the King's nephew in various rash ventures to found a kingdom. Quequex teaches Dan about the Gate of Worlds, the point at which all possible paths of time are visible—even one where only a quarter of Europe's population dies in the Black Death instead of three-quarters, Vienna is not captured by the Turks who then over-run Europe, and Shakespeare, the greatest Turkish dramatist, writes in his native English. We leave Dan, who has fallen in love with a Red Indian girl and been separated after adventures with cannibals and others, on his way to a reunion in Africa, the rising country for young people. It is all very neatly worked out: national characteristics break through even in the new circumstances—the British are good at football and the Germans at scientific invention, though the cars they export to the Aztecs are primitive and coal-fired.

📖 *FOUR MEN WHO CHANGED THE UNIVERSE* (1968)

Kirkus Service

SOURCE: A review of *Four Men Who Changed the Universe,* in *Kirkus Service,* Vol. XXXVI, No. 4, February 15, 1968, p. 195.

Actually a history of cosmology from ancient times up to the Newtonian synthesis, this book takes its special character from the lives of the four brilliant men who immediately preceded Newton and made his work possible. To this extent the choice of Copernicus, Brahe, Kepler and Galileo is remarkably apt and at the same time unique. Rarely is the intimate and invaluable contribution of such forerunners emphasized so dramatically as to stop short at Newton, leaving the four lives richer in comparison. . . . [T]he treatment of Galileo, Kepler and Copernicus here is . . . thorough and useful. The style is similar to the author's **Men Who Mastered the Atom** in that once again the personal details of biography gained from letters, diaries and the like are used to portray a scientific era.

Harry C. Stubbs

SOURCE: A review of *Four Men Who Changed the Universe,* in *The Horn Book Magazine,* Vol. XLV, No. 3, June, 1969, pp. 323-25.

In Robert Silverberg's **Four Men Who Changed the Universe,** the change is in our concept of the earth's *place* in the universe; the four men are—one almost says "of course"—Copernicus, Galileo, Tycho Brahe, and Kepler. It must have been hard to leave Newton out of the title; it was impossible to leave him out of the last chapter.

A very good biographical background is supplied for each of the four; and the line of reasoning from observed motions in the sky to Newton's generalizations about moving bodies—the real central theme of the book—is followed about as meticulously as can be done in words. Clear contrast is shown between the groping of pre-Tychonic scientists in the fog of inaccurate measurements which surrounded them, and the "sudden" clearing of the view when Tycho had accumulated a few decades worth of *regular* celestial measurements in keeping with his own far more exacting standard. The importance of personalities is shown; the rather arrogant natures of Tycho and Galileo not only contrast with the more retiring ones of Copernicus and Kepler but influenced the flow of information and ideas among these men and their contemporaries. Mr. Silverberg makes all this clear and interesting, without losing sight of the main theme.

 MOUND BUILDERS OF ANCIENT AMERICA: THE ARCHAEOLOGY OF A MYTH (1968; abridged version as *The Mound Builders,* 1970)

Kirkus Service

SOURCE: A review of *Mound Builders of Ancient America: The Archaeology of a Myth,* in *Kirkus Service,* Vol. XXXVI, No. 5, March 1, 1968, p. 282.

The incredibly active Mr. Silverberg again illuminates some stunningly comprehensive research with his own vigorous style and considerable joy in the telling. Although now sometimes hemmed in by city streets, sometimes almost leveled by erosion, the ancient piles of earth which appear in the Mississippi Valley and southeastern United States at one time provided a basis for myths that sparked the imagination and fancies of Americans to such an extent that a book purporting to tell the truth about the mysterious "Builders of the Mounds" sold 22,000 copies in thirty months. Amateur archaeologists, including two Presidents (Jefferson and Harrison) began poking around the earthworks; conservative and radical branches centering on the identity of the Mound Builders researched, lectured, wrote and researched again. With scraps of contemporary writings from the violent invasions of Spanish explorers, the author begins a study of a developing body of scientific observations and romantic fancy which persisted through the nineteenth century. Unsung heroes of an infant American archaeology; the founding and growth of the Smithsonian Institute; modern surveys of the nature of Indian cultures that produces the Mounds; a few of the fuzzier theories—are given their just due.

Science Books

SOURCE: A review of *Mound Builders of Ancient America: The Archaeology of a Myth,* in *Science Books,* Vol. 6, No. 4, March, 1971, p. 284.

This is an abridged version of **Mound Builders of Ancient America: The Archaeology of a Myth,** published in 1968; yet it is still rich in detail, some of it from little-known 18th- and 19th-century sources, some from current archeological publications. The first half of the book describes the many misconceptions that developed as settlers moved into the midwest, which ascribed Indian mounds to a lost race, to the Vikings, to the Israelites, and to many others. Serious investigations, by the Smithsonian Institution and others, from the 1840s onward, substituted increasingly reasonable explanations, many of which have been displaced in turn by current research. The second half of the book summarizes (a little less readably) present-day archeological information on the groups that built the many kinds of mounds (burial, effigy, geometric, platform, etc.), their chronology, origins, and demise. This is a skillful and serious presentation of numerous details not easily available elsewhere, synthesized in a way that will be useful to student, scholar, or archeologically minded nonspecialist.

 THE WORLD OF THE OCEAN DEPTHS (1968)

Edward B. Garside

SOURCE: A review of *The World of the Ocean Depths,* in *The New York Times Book Review,* July 7, 1968, p. 16.

Mr. Silverberg's **The World of the Ocean Depths** sketches

out key information gained to date about the watery world and the creatures dwelling in it. Expertly organized and executed, it is a superior book in all respects. The enormous dimensions of the ocean depths are sweepingly suggested. Our mind's eye is made to see trenches far deeper than the Grand Canyon, world-circling mountain ranges with peaks higher than the Himalayas, vast plains of sediment resting on pure basalt, all lost in impenetrable darkness.

In Mr. Silverberg's hands Thomson and Schmidt's early exploration of the deeps and the great breakthroughs made possible by Beebe and Barton's bathysphere, Piccard's bathyscaphe and deep-diving minisubs such as the Alvin are relived in all their original excitement. Exciting, too, is the author's evocation of living things seven miles down, of the fantastic oceanic "chain of life," of the sea's mineral and food potential. The semi-legendary themes of sea-serpent and kraken are presented in a new light, and even the prosaic subject of fish protein concentrate takes on dramatic significance.

Zena Sutherland

SOURCE: A review of *The World of the Ocean Depths,* in *Bulletin of the Center for Children's Books,* Vol. 22, No. 1, September, 1968, pp. 17-18.

An excellent survey of one of the great areas of scientific research today focuses (although it also discusses theories of formation and physical attributes of the oceans) on the discoveries that have been—and are being—made about marine life. The book is well-written and is illustrated with interesting photographs and drawings; it gives information both about the men and machines used in exploration of the ocean depths and about the strange and wonderful creatures that have been found there.

Margery Fisher

SOURCE: A review of *The World of the Ocean Depths,* in *Growing Point,* Vol. 9, No. 2, July, 1970, pp. 1562-63.

This long discursive study for middle secondary readers covers the geology of the ocean bed briefly, discusses early exploration of the ocean's surface and depth from the biological point of view and gives some idea of the kinds of animals to be found under the sea. Legends of sea serpents and other monsters are examined and various explanations for them are suggested; by contrast, modern methods of fish farming find a natural place in the book too. I hope the rather flat prose style and the

Robert Silverberg with his wife Karen in their garden, 1998.

absence of coloured illustrations will not prevent children from discovering the interesting facts in this book.

STORMY VOYAGER: THE STORY OF CHARLES WILKES (1968)

Kirkus Service

SOURCE: A review of *Stormy Voyager: The Story of Charles Wilkes,* in *Kirkus Service,* Vol. XXXVI, No. 15, August 1, 1968, p. 829.

Biography only in courtesy, this is a pithy, sober and absorbing account of a remarkable expedition around the world—almost four years spent mainly in Antarctic waters highlighted by the first sighting of that continent. Although the other seventy-one years of Wilkes' life (including the memorable Mason and Slidell detention during the Civil War) are crammed into a few pages before and after the main narrative, there is a real sense of the man. Seizing leadership and thriftily securing his resources, he met challenges other men declined: faulty equipment, rotting ships, stormy seas, cannibals and a mutinous crew. There is a need for better mapping (with sequence and more detail) and more frequent identification of years with his day-by-days, but these are minor weaknesses. Descriptions to cool the hottest afternoon; aptly chosen anecdotes; pertinent quotes from the journals of Wilkes and his colleagues—all provide for a passage-by-proxy.

GHOST TOWNS OF THE AMERICAN WEST (1968)

Publishers Weekly

SOURCE: A review of *Ghost Towns of the American West,* in *Publishers Weekly,* Vol. 194, No. 7, August 12, 1968, p. 56.

With the cry of "Gold! Gold!" men stampeded to the Sierra Nevada in the late 1840's in search of wealth. Goldfield, Arizona, Deadwood, South Dakota, Bodie, California and Bullfrog, Nevada, were some of the towns that sprouted up over night, some of them to become metropolises with hotel, operas and shops, only to fall to quick death after the ground had been scourged. Some of these towns have been preserved as a heritage of American history, some are still thriving with new industries, but many are just stumps of rubble that only hint of the wild and exciting days gone by. The excellent illustrations of Lorence Bjorklund . . . bring alive an exciting era.

Dan Cushman

SOURCE: A review of *Ghost Towns of the American West,* in *The New York Times Book Review,* November 3, 1968, pp. 28.

This book is really a history of the prospector's West rather than another tome on the ghost towns. The author starts in the days of forty-nine, and moves from California's historic diggings to the silver camps of Nevada, to Colorado, Utah, Idaho, Montana, South Dakota and the Southwest, concluding at Goldfield and Rhyolite, Nev., in the early years of the present century. Choosing representative mining camps, and telling their individual stories (discovery, boom and, generally, bust), he has skipped most of the gunfighters, gamblers, vigilantes and lurid gals who have overpopulated such books since Bret Harte. He lapses when he reaches Virginia City and Bannack, Mont., where he finds Henry Plummer, Slade and company too much to resist. We'll forgive this, in view of his otherwise good record. We'll also overlook a couple of geological expositions that would make J. E. Spurr, the late master of mining geology, roll right over in his grave.

THE CHALLENGE OF CLIMATE: MAN AND HIS ENVIRONMENT (1969)

Kirkus Reviews

SOURCE: A review of *The Challenge of Climate: Man and His Environment,* in *Kirkus Reviews,* Vol. XXXVII, No. 2, January 15, 1969, p. 88.

"We are still playthings of the storm gods," Silverberg says early on in this compendious volume. "We know a great deal but not nearly enough." The book testifies to these truths on nearly every page with its impressive documentation of what is and is not known of climate, culture and man through geological and historical time. The book is too densely written to satisfy the uninitiated, and at times the trotting out of theory after theory of causes of climactic change will bewilder rather than comfort the reader. The lesson is too obvious that while man has risen to the top of the mammalian heap by his "conquest of climate," he has abused and despoiled nature, plowing fields, stripping forests, diverting streams and sowing the seeds of self-destruction whether in the midwest's Dust Bowl or the Indus Valley. In early chapters, Silverberg deals with megayear categories of the geological past and the technology of tracing climactic change (shell spiralings, oxygen take-up). Then comes a discussion of the causes of weather, including startling statements about how much turbulence has increased. In the second half of the book, man emerges. Surprisingly, Silverberg manages to relate climate and culture for nearly all the settlements and civilizations of the world, ending with a discussion of the origin of maize in America and the civilization of the Pueblo Indians. The short last chapter deals with rain-making, past and future.

Publishers Weekly

SOURCE: A review of *The Challenge of Climate: Man and His Environment,* in *Publishers Weekly,* Vol. 195, No. 5, February 3, 1969, p. 61.

Robert Silverberg plunges into his subject with an impressive show of learning. His book progresses from a comprehensive discussion of climatic changes over the aeons (Ice Ages and so on) and an analysis of the *causes* of weather from the modern meteorologist's book-of-knowledge, to the crucial problems of man's continuing "conquest of climate." Readers who have ever thought seriously about the decisive influence of climate on entire civilizations and races—and inevitably their cultures—will find Silverberg's broad survey of this aspect of weather the most instructive and absorbing part of his book. He writes of the Pueblo Indians, maize growing and sundry earthbound subjects, and closes with an interesting survey of old and new techniques in rain-making. Some readers will find themselves fogbound in Silverberg's more technical sections; but the book is essentially comprehensive and a reassuring response to Mark Twain: *now* somebody's trying to do something about the weather, even if we are still "playthings of the storm gods."

C. Martin

SOURCE: A review of *The Challenge of Climate: Man and His Environment,* in *The Junior Bookshelf,* Vol. 36, No. 2, April, 1972, p. 122.

Because this is an American book, not only the spelling but also the theories quoted and discussed tend to be U.S.-orientated; nevertheless it is a thoughtful account of man's reliance on climate, showing how civilisations rise and fall under long-term fluctuations such as the Ice Ages or shorter ones as seen in the deserted cities which can be found in our modern deserts (though the author realises that decay of irrigation works may be equally or even more responsible). While there is nothing new nor very profound in this book, grammar school students could find plenty of interesting information conveyed in very readable language calculated to provoke youthful discussion on matters such as the future of weather control which might well be vital to coming generations. Unfortunately, however, the book is far from attractive in appearance, consisting of three hundred pages of closely printed text, unbroken by map, diagram or illustration. The bibliography is rather overweighted in favour of the author.

THE MAN IN THE MAZE (1969)

Publishers Weekly

SOURCE: A review of *The Man in the Maze,* in *Publishers Weekly,* Vol. 195, No. 3, January 20, 1969, p. 272.

On a diplomatic mission to a distant planet, Dick Muller is captured and his neural system is short-circuited. Back on Earth, he finds that his brain emanations make him anathema to all other humans; so he exiles himself to the planet Lemnos and to the Maze, an ancient corkscrew city reminiscent of Dante's rings of hell. Muller manages to reach the safe core of the Maze and hopes to live his life there in solitude. But a mission from Earth arrives to tell him that his damaged brain is vitally needed as a defense against creatures threatening the whole galaxy. The efforts of the Earth team to penetrate the Maze and convince Muller to come home are the heart of the story, and a very well-told and suspenseful one it is, with a new diabolical obstacle popping up on every other page.

ACROSS A BILLION YEARS (1969)

Kirkus Reviews

SOURCE: A review of *Across a Billion Years,* in *Kirkus Reviews,* Vol. XXXVII, No. 7, April 1, 1969, pp. 385-86.

Tom, a twenty-one-year-old archaeological apprentice, is off to the dig of the century on Dinamon IX where an outpost of an ancient master race called "The High Ones" has been discovered. The expedition is a lively assortment: there's Kelly Watchman, a seductive android; Leroy Chang, a frustrated sex maniac; Jan Mortenson, attractive even if not quite human; Pilazinool, who can take himself apart and put himself back together again; Steen, a his/her combination; Mirrik, rhinoceros-sized (he gets drunk on flowers); three top Professors suffering from severe attacks of professional jealousy and others. . . . But it's Tom who makes *the* find, a movie that shows another outpost and a robot that can lead them to the "High Ones'" home planet. Then it's a chase across the galaxy with an assortment of near-misses and kooky misdemeanors (Mirrik can't stay off the flower power for instance) until the "High Ones" are discovered . . . a billion years too late. Mr. Silverberg is being almost altogether too cute in this one and a little flip for a juvenile audience.

Zena Sutherland

SOURCE: A review of *Across a Billion Years,* in *Bulletin of the Center for Children's Books,* Vol. 23, No. 1, September, 1969, p. 17.

The story of an archeological expedition in the year 2375. The story is told by Tom Rice in message-cubes dictated to a twin sister back on Earth. Searching for artifacts, the expedition (mixed life-forms, an android, and some humans) stumbles upon evidence that the High Ones, who lived a billion years before, may still be alive. One of their robots leads the group to a hidden world in which the High Ones are slowly, finally dying while their robot servants maintain the civilization. The story is rather heavily laden with fanciful creatures, names, inventions, and slang, but it is both inventive and provocative, with an occasional diatribe against prejudice and a mild love interest included.

Norman Culpan

SOURCE: A review of *Across a Billion Years,* in *School Librarian,* Vol. 25, No. 4, December, 1977, p. 362.

Four hundred years hence an archaeological expedition searches the Galaxy for remains of the High Ones who lived a thousand million (the American billion) years ago. What they find is amazing. Its credibility is eased, for those whose suspension of disbelief is not too willing, by the mode of narration. A junior member of the expedition, Tom Rice, dictates letters, in fact a diary narrative of events, to his twin sister back on earth, and these are the sole content of the novel. The style is colloquial and the mood affectionate. In the earlier part of the story Tom's relationships with his ten fellow-archaeologists—of various planetary origins, and variously he, she and it—are of more importance than the remains they find. Tom's account is at once completely frank and quite unexceptional. Skilfully written, though not really outstanding in imaginative quality, this novel will go down well, I think, with middle teenagers.

📖 *VANISHING GIANTS: THE STORY OF THE SEQUOIAS* (1969)

Kirkus Reviews

SOURCE: A review of *Vanishing Giants: The Story of the Sequoias,* in *Kirkus Reviews,* Vol. XXXVII, No. 7, April 1, 1969, p. 391.

Despite the conservationist efforts of the Sierra Club, the Save-the-Redwoods League, and many others, there is great probability that by 1980 only 4% of the original redwood population will remain. The redwoods are in greater danger than the sequoias for the latter are less likely to be logged but both kinds have been mishandled in the past. Some of this "history" is digressive: e.g. a discussion of the development of Linnaean nomenclature which precedes introduction of the naming controversy, or the elaboration of Archbishop Ussher's dating of creation (4004 B.C.) to put a tree in its 19th century perspective. For the most part, however, it concentrates on essentials—the sport of measuring trunks, counting rings and computing heights; attempts to cultivate seedlings outside of California; the aftereffects of loggers and tourists and fires and fire prevention. Preferable as a reference and more mature in orientation than the other monographs available, fuller than the other roundups.

📖 *THE CALIBRATED ALLIGATOR AND OTHER SCIENCE FICTION STORIES* (1969)

Zena Sutherland

SOURCE: A review of *The Calibrated Alligator and Other Science Fiction Stories*, in *Bulletin of the Center for Children's Books,* Vol. 22, No. 10, June, 1969, p. 164.

Nine science fiction stories are included in an original and varied collection, one of the best of which is the title story. In **"The Calibrated Alligator"** a prankster on a lunar base becomes involved in a biological experiment that succeeds in a totally unexpected way. One tale takes a poke at the fads in popularity of artifacts; another is the amusing account of a helpless man who gets shuttled from time belt to time belt when he calls the Friendly Finance Corporation to ask for an extension on his loan. Several are serious, but it is the humorous short story at which the author excels.

The Booklist and Subscription Books Bulletin

SOURCE: A review of *The Calibrated Alligator and Other Science Fiction Stories,* in *The Booklist and Subscription Books Bulletin*, Vol. 65, No. 20, June 15, 1969, p. 1172.

Combining humor, suspense, and adventure these nine stories will appeal to readers who enjoy science-fiction short stories. The title story features a 10-inch pet alligator that becomes part of a phenomenally successful growth-acceleration project. In another tale contemporary artifacts have no market value so a whole planet of aliens is busily turning out and planting antiquities for archaeologists from earth to find. A third story in the varied collection deals with the age-old question of why man goes out to explore. These stories first appeared in various science-fiction magazines.

📖 *TO LIVE AGAIN* (1969)

Publishers Weekly

SOURCE: A review of *To Live Again,* in *Publishers Weekly,* Vol. 196, No. 3, July 21, 1969, p. 55.

With the science of medical transplants becoming more sophisticated, it will be only a matter of time, according to Mr. Silverberg, until the mind itself can be transferred and reborn. In the 21st century this will be a luxury only the very rich can afford, their affluence measured by their number of transplants. Not only will you be able to enhance your personality, but by making recordings of your own mind twice yearly, you can assure yourself of a rebirth if death arrives. When a great financial wizard dies, a battle between his nephew and a new financier develops, with the great man's mind at stake. A readable, good science fiction novel with an exciting new twist.

📖 *BRUCE OF THE BLUE NILE* (1969)

Kirkus Reviews

SOURCE: A review of *Bruce of the Blue Nile,* in *Kirkus Reviews,* Vol. XXXII, No. 18, September 15, 1969, p. 1018.

A sage, almost magical mystery travelogue with James Bruce of Kinnaird, Scotland, who explored the no man's lands of eighteenth-century Africa and returned to tell the story . . . which few people then believed. It's since been proved that indeed the self-styled Don Quixote did spend twelve years battling the sea and the desert and disease, awing Abyssinian rulers and helping them fight a civil war, ministering to sick natives and addressing all in their own tongues, producing five volumes of notes, charts, and drawings, and drinking finally from the very source of the Nile. Silverberg is sensitive to Bruce's late discovery that "the pleasure lay in the quest itself, and not in the fulfillment"; it is with this kind of awareness that he documents the internal search that accompanied the fantastic journey. The "dark continent" takes a giant step out of the shadows in this insightful anthropography of Blue Nile cultures, thanks to both Messrs. Bruce and Silverberg.

The Booklist

SOURCE: A review of *Bruce of the Blue Nile*, in *The Booklist*, Vol. 66, No. 18, May 15, 1970, p. 1157.

The life and African travels of James Bruce, eighteenth-century Scottish gentleman-explorer, are related in an exciting narrative which incorporates excerpts from Bruce's own account of his explorations. Portraying Bruce as a brash, courageous, and stubborn man with great faults as well as virtues, the author follows his adventurous journey into Ethiopia, his locating the source of the Blue Nile, crossing of the Nubian desert to Cairo, and return to Europe, where his reports on his Ethiopian experiences, regarded as tall tales during his lifetime, were eventually accepted. Like Silverberg's ***To the Rock of Darius: The Story of Henry Rawlinson*** this is a thoroughly researched biography of a little-known but remarkable figure. A bibliography is appended.

WONDERS OF ANCIENT CHINESE SCIENCE (1969)

The Booklist

SOURCE: A review of *Wonders of Ancient Chinese Science*, in *The Booklist*, Vol. 66, No. 4, October 15, 1969, p. 298.

A prolific writer of science and history books for young people combines a succinct survey of Chinese history with an examination of some of the major scientific achievements and inventions developed by the Chinese from around the fourth century B.C. to the thirteenth century A.D. The enlightening account underscores the imaginativeness and resourcefulness exhibited by these early Chinese scientists and engineers and the stultifying effects of isolationist policies initiated by the Ming dynasty which led to a decline in China's scientific advancement. The delicate black-and-white drawings are both decorative and informative.

Zena Sutherland

SOURCE: A review of *Wonders of Ancient Chinese Science*, in *Bulletin of the Center for Children's Books*, Vol. 23, No. 5, January, 1970, p. 88.

Following a brief background history of China from 1994 B.C. this most informative book surveys the achievements of Chinese scientists, some of them familiar and many of them neglected for the hundreds of years in which the accomplishments were forgotten and the disciplines abandoned. Separate chapters describe the impressive astronomical observations, such scientific instruments as the magnetic compass and the seismograph, and such useful inventions as paper and printing, gunpowder and rockets, kites, wheelbarrows, umbrellas, and the fishing rod reel. A table of dynasties precedes the text.

TOWER OF GLASS (1970)

Publishers Weekly

SOURCE: A review of *Tower of Glass*, in *Publishers Weekly*, Vol. 198, No. 8, August 24, 1970, p. 46.

Simeon Krug, wealthy tycoon of the year 2218, had made his fortune manufacturing almost-human androids that make efficient slaves, but they are beginning to outnumber humans. Krug is now squandering his wealth building a giant tower in the Arctic tundra so he can answer radio signals coming from an intelligent source 100 light years away. The religious feelings programmed into his androids—Krug is their god—have kept them manageable, but now a radical faction is fighting for equality with humans and representation in Congress. Krug struggles against odds to get his tower to reach 1500 meters before the android revolution wipes out earth humans. This 23rd century world is neatly and imaginatively constructed and, with biology, astrophysics and religion smoothly blended into the tight plot, the novel is top-shelf Silverberg.

MAMMOTHS, MASTODONS AND MAN (1970; British edition, 1972)

The Booklist

SOURCE: A review of *Mammoths, Mastodons and Man*, in *The Booklist*, Vol. 67, No. 1, September 1, 1970, p. 54.

In a lively account Silverberg discusses the discovery and study of mammoth and mastodon remains from the first known finds during the Middle Ages to the present-day scientific study of prehistoric animals. He describes important and interesting discoveries and quests for information around the world and traces the ongoing controversy surrounding the huge bones, including the early giant theory and the turmoil created in religious circles.

Margery Fisher

SOURCE: A review of *Mammoths, Mastodons and Man,* in *Growing Point,* Vol. 11, No. 1, May, 1972, p. 1951.

The most impressive book in this batch is undoubtedly *Mammoths, Mastodons and Man,* an importation from America. The present fashion among the young for studying (or perhaps collecting is a more accurate term) the dinosaurs of the world may well be shaken, among older readers, by the scope and interest of Robert Silverberg's survey of a later evolutionary stage. Among his many virtues is the rare one of accepting doubt. He makes no generalisation without evidence, offers only with reservations the theory, held by many, that there may be still mammoths alive in the Siberian taiga, ends his book with the salutary principle "We know now that all things change except change itself." The book is admirable, too, in that it cuts through subject frontiers. Geology, history, biology, sociology—these and other disciplines contribute to compilation. The author traces the study of fossil remains in Old World and New, with a firm idea of the philosophy underlying each period. He explains that the Royal Society was unable to accept Peter Collinson's suggestion that the animal whose tusks were found in Ohio might be extinct, because in the eighteenth century religion still discouraged the idea that God, having created a species, would ever let it vanish. He discusses the "mammoth fever" in the United States in the last century and the competition between museums for fossil remains and reconstructions. He lays out the family tree of the elephant and explains the confusion of nomenclature that still exists. This is a work of scholarship written in a most lively and persuasive manner.

C. Martin

SOURCE: A review of *Mammoths, Mastodons and Man,* in *Junior Bookshelf,* Vol. 36, No. 3, June, 1972, pp. 190-91.

This is not a book for the child who wants bright pictures and an easy text on prehistoric animals but for the more serious reader interested in the story of how, where and when the remains of the first two mammals of the title were discovered and eventually classified after many mythological and unscientific misconceptions. Further, the book relates the dating of the bones of early man and his artefacts to the fossil remains of the mammoths and mastodons with which they were found. A lot of facts are given and some suppositions and the story is at times both enthralling and astonishing; for instance the past existence of the hairy mammoth may be common knowledge to every eight-year-old today but until very recent times the picture was far from clear and for this confusion the fundamentalists of the last century must take a good deal of responsibility. The number of black-and-white drawings is not over-generous considering the price of the book, and chapter 7 on the species of elephants would have been made clearer by a chart, while the bibliography is rather a list of sources than something of practical use to the British schoolchild.

A TIME OF CHANGES (1971)

Publishers Weekly

SOURCE: A review of *A Time of Changes,* in *Publishers Weekly,* Vol. 199, No. 25, June 21, 1971, p. 72.

The planet is Borthan (visited once and abandoned by Earthmen); the narrator is long-winded Kinnall Darival, second son of the Septarch of Salla. When his royal father dies, Kinnall leaves before his brother can assassinate him. He wanders through desert, wilderness and cities, lamenting the fact that Borthans are such hostile, suspicious and noncommunicative people, who consider the word "I" an obscenity. When he discovers a white powder that provides instant telepathic communications and tries to share his discovery, he finds only rebuffs and exile to the Burnt Lowlands. The milieu of this story is mixed up—with a model-T technology in a medieval society—the narrator not very sympathetic, and the plot loose and rambling.

SON OF MAN (1971)

Theodore Sturgeon

SOURCE: A review of *Son of Man,* in *The New York Times Book Review,* March 5, 1972, pp. 36-7.

Son of Man might be judged, by its title and last few pages, a messiah story. It might be a fable, or an allegory (the protagonist's name is Clay) but it is other things too. It's a hell of a good story—that you can be sure of. It's also a journey story, a narrative in which we travel strange landscapes and never know what is just over the hill. It is profligate, spendthrift, wildly generous with image and sensation. And with sexuality. It is explicit, surprisingly always meaningful.

Unlike so many of today's authors, who are aware of new freedoms but don't quite know how to handle them, Silverberg is aware of what sex he belongs to, is not afraid of it, doesn't care if Mommy reads his story; he finds sex joyful. His approach is that of a celebrant. To him sex is clearly much more than a sensual explosive, it is communication, linkage, the gate on the frontiers of very other places. Perhaps it is enough to say that it is revered. This is not a perfect book, but in light of what the man was and what he is, we can anticipate with fascination what he will become.

THE REALM OF PRESTER JOHN (1972)

Publishers Weekly

SOURCE: A review of *The Realm of Prester John,* in *Publishers Weekly,* Vol. 200, No. 17, October 25, 1971, p. 46.

Silverberg, author of much science fiction, has written

several books reflecting his special interest in myth and history. Here he revives the legend of Prester John, a mysterious personification of Marco Polo-cum-Errol Flynn who was believed to have brought Christianity to a huge area from interior Asia to Africa in the 12th century. So viable was the Prester John legend up until the time it was proved a myth (in the 18th century), that European explorers, obsessed with travelers' tales about him and his kingdom, were driven to go into both Africa and Asia to seek out the truth. Silverberg's examination of the Prester John story and its tenacious hold on the imagination of men of the Middle Ages should fascinate armchair historians and sleuths who are also El dorado or Atlantis buffs—for, after all, the legend was a projection of the dream of Utopia, and John himself "the ever enduring prince of the impossible."

The Booklist

SOURCE: A review of *The Realm of Prester John,* in *The Booklist,* Vol. 68, No. 20, June 15, 1972, p. 885.

Drawing on findings from historical sources and interpretations of the legendary medieval Prester John, allegedly a mighty Christian potentate in the East variously thought to be India, Central Asia, or Ethiopia, Silverberg presents a well-written, plausible, but not documented blend of history and legend. The prologue comprises the letter supposedly written by Prester John which circulated throughout Europe during the twelfth century, describing his realm as a kind of earthly paradise. Silverberg deftly interweaves speculations of other researchers as he relates that an Italian scholar Olschki in 1931 labeled the documentary letter a political allegory envisioning the perfect society. Silverberg himself interprets Prester John as a symbol of the hunger to know the unknown. A map of the legendary kingdom is included.

THE BOOK OF SKULLS (1972)

Publishers Weekly

SOURCE: A review of *The Book of Skulls,* in *Publishers Weekly,* Vol. 201, No. 5, January 31, 1972, p. 245.

Told in the words of Tim, one of the four college students embarked on a strange mission, the prose is a combination of mystical meditation and modern idiom. One of the boys had come upon the mysterious Book of Skulls and translated its promise that four must undertake the quest for life eternal, but two of them must die. When the four reach a place known as the Skullhouse in the Arizona desert, they begin the rituals of the Ninth Mystery. Who will live and who will die? What secrets—secrets the ritual of the Book of Skulls insists must be revealed—lie hidden in their pasts? Silverberg, who usually writes straight science fiction, deftly creates tension, probing the mind and the spirit of each of the

four, building to a climax that is as surprising to the four as it will be to the reader.

JOHN MUIR: PROPHET AMONG THE GLACIERS (1972)

The Booklist

SOURCE: A review of *John Muir: Prophet among the Glaciers,* in *The Booklist,* Vol. 68, No. 22, July 15, 1972, p. 1005.

Quoting frequently from Muir's writings, an author of many books for young readers has produced a sympathetic biography depicting the naturalist as a man of many talents who dedicated himself to preserving the wilderness from exploitation by ignorant or greedy men. After describing Muir's early life on the farm, his months at the University of Wisconsin, his successful experience in industry, and finally his decision to spend his life wandering in the wilderness, Silverberg devotes the greater portion of the book to Muir's adventures and discoveries in California and Alaska, his writing, and work as a conservationist.

Science Books

SOURCE: A review of *John Muir: Prophet among the Glaciers,* in *Science Books,* Vol. 8, No. 3, December, 1972, p. 204.

This well-written, authoritative biography of a man devoted to the conservation of America's natural areas is very timely. The sections on Muir's childhood and early manhood are slow-moving and dull, but once the chronology moves on to his adult activities the narrative is considerably more gripping. Muir was a crusader for conservation from 1875 until his death in 1914, and he is here portrayed vividly as a heroic figure who was, nevertheless, a misfit in his own time. Even so, he was both a national and international conservation activist. Silverberg points out Muir's brilliant leadership capacity yet makes it clear that he also had weaknesses. This book provides a good introduction to the turn-of-the-century conservation movement, a movement which greatly strengthened the national park system and led to the creation of the Sierra Club. A good index and bibliography are provided, making the book additionally useful as a reference.

THE WORLD WITHIN THE OCEAN WAVE AND THE WORLD WITHIN THE TIDE POOL (1972)

Kirkus Reviews

SOURCE: A review of *The World within the Ocean Wave* and *The World within the Tide Pool,* in *Kirkus Reviews,* Vol. XL, No. 15, August 1, 1972, p. 867.

Of these two handsome volumes, the **Ocean Wave** deserves special attention for pointing out the factors such as temperature, nutrient content, vegetation and marine life, which makes the superficially uniform seas a diverse web of interrelated environments. Within this context, Silverberg examines the constituents of plankton—concentrating on the most peculiar and widely known forms (sargasso weed, red tide, etc.), and includes an amusing chapter on the reactions of Heyerdahl's crew, oceanographer Alister Hardy and others who have attempted to survive on a plankton diet. The tour of the **Tide Pool** is more purely descriptive, but includes a good explanation of tidal phenomena and introduces many varieties of animals and the most common forms of vegetation. Both books end with strongly worded warnings on the dangers of pollution, though unfortunately relying on some of the same examples—the *Torrey Canyon* disaster and Heyerdahl's observations of solidified chunks of oil in mid-ocean. Silverberg teaches ecology instead of preaching it (his skeptical examination of the promise of unlimited food from the sea is particularly welcome), and Bob Hines' graceful and accurate black and white drawings are an accomplishment in themselves.

The Booklist

SOURCE: A review of *The World within the Ocean Wave* and *The World within the Tide Pool*, in *The Booklist*, Vol. 69, No. 5, November 1, 1972, p. 241.

Emphasizing the vastness of the ocean and the abundance of its living matter, the author discusses clearly and simply [in **The World within the Ocean Wave**] such factors as temperature, chemical content, and pressure which govern marine environment. He examines in detail several varieties of phytoplankton and zooplankton describing their maneuvers and distribution. In considering the desirability of obtaining food from the sea for the world's rapidly increasing population, he tells of numerous experiments using plankton for human consumption and points out how expensive it is at present to catch and prepare plankton in quantity. Finally he reports on pollution and the damage done to oceanic life and indirectly to man. Generously illustrated with attractive pencil sketches. Books for further reading appended.

After discussing the three littoral zones the author explains [in **The World within the Tide Pool**] how fluctuations in temperature, salt, and oxygen content influence life in the tide pools and how the sun and moon affect the tides. He describes such animals as barnacles, mussels, sponges, snails, starfish, octopi, sea cucumbers, and hydroids, reporting on their physical makeup, food, method of locomotion, if any, and protective features and concentrating very briefly on algae among the forms of plant life. Silverberg concludes with a chapter on pollution in which he uses examples, only some of which are mentioned in the companion volume above. Suggestions for further reading are appended. A fascinating examination illustrated with attractive pencil sketches.

THE LONGEST VOYAGE: CIRCUMNAVIGATORS IN THE AGE OF DISCOVERY (1972)

The Booklist

SOURCE: A review of *The Longest Voyage: Circumnavigators in the Age of Discovery,* in *The Booklist,* Vol. 69, No. 1, September 1, 1972, p. 26.

Often using quotations from original sources, an author of many historical books writes in detail of the men who first sailed around the world: Magellan, Drake, Cavendish, Noort, Spilbergen, Le Maire, and Schouten. He contrasts and compares the purposes and accomplishments of their voyages and describes their difficulties with weather, mutinous crews, conspiracies, natives, disease, and starvation, including the cruelties and barbarities practised by some of them. Silverberg has been able to make many parts of his book exciting and dramatic but the great detail will limit the book to confirmed Silverberg fans and to history buffs. A bibliography is appended.

THE STOCHASTIC MAN (1975)

Publishers Weekly

SOURCE: A review of *The Stochastic Man,* in *Publishers Weekly,* Vol. 208, No. 5, August 4, 1975, p. 52.

In New York in 1997 Lew Nichols calls the work of his stochastic consulting firm "the projection business," and he is making a good living providing businessmen with statistics-based predictions of future events. When he is introduced to fast-rising politico Paul Quinn, he is impressed with the man's magnetism and joins his team in a winning campaign for the New York mayoralty. The next Quinn goal is the Presidency in 2004, and Nichols is eager to help his man to the White House. Then he meets a mysterious millionaire who has the power to really *see* the future, and like a futuristic Faust, Nichols grabs at the chance to share that power. The gift has strings attached, though, and the uncomputerized predictions that the future-seeing Nichols supplies the Quinn machine bring disaster to the city and the party. An imaginative, easy-reading speculation on metropolitan life a few decades hence.

Dan Miller

SOURCE: A review of *The Stochastic Man,* in *The Booklist,* Vol. 72, No. 7, December 1, 1975, pp. 501-02.

The Stochastic Man qualifies as a brilliant finale to a brilliant career. Lew Nichols is a professional in stochastics, the science of skilled conjecture guided by the laws of probability, as distinguished from mere extrapolation. Nichols works for the mayor of New York in the year 2000, recommending policies based on his high-powered guesswork, until he is able to foresee the future in all its alluring and frightening inevitability. As usual, Silverberg is in full control of the plot, leading the reader through a fast narrative populated by characters with layer upon layer of complexity. Quintessential Silverberg.

Marcia Schneider

SOURCE: A review of *The Stochastic Man,* in *School Library Journal,* Vol. 22, No. 6, February, 1976, p. 58.

From available current data, Lew Nichols is able to guess future trends with a high degree of accuracy. This ability makes him a powerful ally to Paul Quinn, an up-and-coming mayoral candidate in the city of New York in the year 1998. Given the opportunity to actually see the future (under the tutelage of Martin Carvajal), Nichols jumps at the chance to increase both Quinn's power and his own. This ability to foresee, however, does not enable him to change or influence events. An interesting set-up carried through to a dramatic conclusion.

LORD VALENTINE'S CASTLE (1980)

Algis Budrys

SOURCE: A review of *Lord Valentine's Castle,* in *Fantasy & Science Fiction,* Vol. 58, No. 5, May, 1980, pp. 22-8.

Lord Valentine's Castle is or should be quite familiar to you, as a recent four-part serial in this magazine. It's a significant book, as the first new Robert Silverberg novel in years and as the first genuine Silverberg epic, and is undoubtedly selling like hotcakes. Its literary merits for me center on the fact that I had a hard time putting it down long enough to get some sleep or get to any work of my own.

It is that magical thing, the page-turner . . . a story which, even when less than felicitously told on any given page, keeps you going because you know that on the next page you will be shown something fascinating.

It has going for it one of SF's most effective variants on the age-old effectiveness of the Little Tailor plot; an amnesiac hero who comes to realize that he was once a king, and might be king again. But what legitimizes it as a creation in itself is the world in which this story takes place—huge Majipoor, planet of vast distances, vast populations, and, most important, plenty of room for a wandering protagonist to encounter richly imagined outré situation after exotic situation.

I have never seen Silverberg deploy so much of his imagination in one place—which is not too surprising, considering the size of both of the place and of the text, but it is surprisingly well sustained, which couldn't have been all that easy over such a compass. There are places where he helps himself along with little in-group jokes; among the great lists of cities he mentions are Thagobar, Larnimisculus and Verf, a little bow to the days of Robert Randall. And there are places where I rather suspect he is borrowing incidents from mythologies obscure to western audiences rather than creating them whole. But the world of Majipoor is real; its people jostle and crowd in real streets, and real rain falls.

And there is of course the introduction of juggling, that very nice gracenote which humanizes the wandering Valentine, and does a great many other kinds of work in the narrative.

What comes through as a result of all this is a sense of Silverberg's wittiness as well as of his intelligence: the book has charm, outweighing all other considerations. It operates on an intellectual plane of more than ordinary elevation, at the same time that it entertains, entertains, entertains.

Paul Stuewe

SOURCE: A review of *Lord Valentine's Castle,* in *Quill and Quire,* Vol. 46, No. 6, June, 1980, p. 39.

Silverberg is an established pro who moves with ease between the science fiction and fantasy genres, here working mostly within the latter as he fashions a fascinating alternate world of Tolkien-like dimensions. This is basically a picaresque romance of colourful incidents and exotic situations structured around the protagonist's search for his true identity, and it's capably if rather predictably narrated in a style that will appeal to aficionados of the fantastic-adventure novel. Whether or not they will feel compelled to purchase the hardcover edition is a more problematic question, but in any event this is a worthy contender in a field where we've seen some spectacular recent successes.

Claudia J. Morner

SOURCE: A review of *Lord Valentine's Castle,* in *School Library Journal,* Vol. 27, No. 1, September, 1980, p. 93.

Majipoor is an enormous planet inhabited by intelligent beings and ruled by a benevolent lord. In this peaceful, industrious, bustling world people of many races live in relative harmony and are controlled from committing crimes by the knowledge that they will be caught and by the unpleasantness of the punishment: bad dreams for the rest of their life. The story begins as Valentine, a young amnesiac, wanders into the city of Pidruid in time for a festival celebrating a once-in-a-lifetime visit of another Valentine, Lord Valentine, the supreme ruler of the planet. Early in the book readers know what Valentine is slow to understand: he is the real Lord Valentine and the one in power is an impostor. On a coming-of-age journey to Lord Valentine's Castle, gathering friends, supporters, and ultimately troops en route, Valentine discovers his true identity and gains a better understanding of the people and place he is destined to rule. A good story, inventively told, which abounds with adventure and curious characters, four-armed jugglers, shape changers, a dwarf with psychic powers, dream speakers, and an amazon-like woman who becomes Valentine's bodyguard.

📖 *MAJIPOOR CHRONICLES* (1982)

Claudia Morner

SOURCE: A review of *Majipoor Chronicles,* in *School Library Journal,* Vol. 28, No. 9, May, 1982, pp. 90-1.

Although the setting here is the same as that of **Lord Valentine's Castle,** this is not a sequel but another look at the large, fascinating world of Majipoor. Silverberg uses a clever device to permit glimpses into the past of this planet, unifying what would otherwise be only a series of unrelated short stories with the same setting. He binds the stories together through the adventures of Hissune, a bored teenage clerk in the House of Records who risks his job and more by delving into forbidden records of the Registry of Souls. This Registry holds every minute, every experience of billions of inhabitants of Majipoor since it was colonized thousands of years ago. By calling up a record, he is given the opportunity to live episodes from the lives of famous and ordinary people of both sexes. These experiences, both terrifying and exhilarating, are at the core of this exciting and well-written book, which belongs in every YA science fiction collection.

Elizabeth A. Belden

SOURCE: A review of *Majipoor Chronicles,* in *English Journal,* Vol. 72, No. 8, December, 1983, p. 69.

In this sequel to the popular **Lord Valentine's Castle,** sci-fi/fantasy fans continue their journey through the magically futuristic world of Majipoor. The guide is a young clerk named Hissune who finds his job in the House of Record tedious at best. To liven up his dull existence he sneaks into the forbidden Register of Souls where exist the experiences of all the millions of creatures who lived on Majipoor. When Hissune plugs in one of the memory capsules he can relive an event that took place eons before. Through Hissune we meet a dream-speaker, a soul painter, shape-shifters, Ghayrogs, and many more marvelous citizens of the wonderful world of Majipoor. Our readers were impressed by Silverberg's vivid characterizations and descriptions. "This is first class reading."

📖 *WORLD OF A THOUSAND COLORS* (1982)

Publishers Weekly

SOURCE: A review of *World of a Thousand Colors,* in *Publishers Weekly,* Vol. 222, No. 6, August 6, 1982, p. 60.

In 1956 Robert Silverberg was awarded a Hugo as most promising new author. In those days the magazines were still the main market for SF and Silverberg worked under a number of names with prodigious imagination and energy to help fill their pages. Most of the 19 stories in this collection date from the late '50s. Their efficient, effective development of the different single idea around which each of them is built epitomizes the period and demonstrates how he won his early popularity. They are workmanlike writing in the best sense, and still entertain. In the late '60s and the '70s, Silverberg underwent a metamorphosis, his output declined greatly and the human writing machine turned into a genuine artist. Five stories here dating from 1968 to 1971 show us that transformation under way. The sensitivity and depth that were only hinted at in the '50s are now present in full measure. It's good to have the best early short work of one of the field's major figures conveniently brought together and preserved, it's even better to contemplate those later stories and realize how well the promise recognized by that Hugo was fulfilled.

Paul Stuewe

SOURCE: A review of *World of a Thousand Colors,* in *Quill & Quire,* Vol. 48, No. 11, November, 1982, p. 29.

These science-fiction short stories from a prolific and often very good fantasist were originally published between 1957 and 1971, a period of consolidation rather than innovation in the sci-fi field. They are appropriately competent and workmanlike, if occasionally rather predictable. Although their hardcover publication is presumably intended to appeal to those who made Silverberg's novel **Lord Valentine's Castle** a steady seller, most fans of the genre will be satisfied with the inevitable paperback.

📖 *THE SCIENCE FICTIONAL DINOSAUR* (editor, with Charles G. Waugh and Martin H. Greenberg, 1982)

Ann G. Brouse

SOURCE: A review of *The Science Fictional Dinosaur,* in *School Library Journal,* Vol. 29, No. 4, December, 1982, p. 74.

All but one of the nine stories in this collection have been published previously in science-fiction magazines or anthologies. Their distinguished authors include Brian

Aldiss, Isaac Asimov and Harry Harrison. Four of the selections were written in the 1950s, while the remainder are more recent. The tone of these tales ranges from the humorous **"A Statue for Father,"** a tribute to the man who discovered "dinachicken," to the gruesome **"Poor Little Warrior,"** the last adventure of a disappointed big-game hunter. Outdated theories mentioned in the stories are updated and corrected in the introduction to each piece. Readers with piqued imaginations won't have to search for a factual text on dinosaurs after reading these fantasies about dinosaur life. Instead, they'll discover a wealth of information in the forms of a "Geologic Time Scale" chart, an 8-page glossary of "Selected Mesozoic Fauna" annotated in detail, a classification chart for 53 "Mesozoic Reptiles" and a list of supplemental reading—2 novels and 12 more short stories about dinosaurs.

LORD OF DARKNESS (1983)

Publishers Weekly

SOURCE: A review of *Lord of Darkness,* in *Publishers Weekly,* Vol. 223, No. 9, March 4, 1983, p. 91.

Essentially a historical fantasy though based on fact, this long and slightly ponderous first-person story recounts the 20-year experience in darkest Africa of an Elizabethan seaman-adventurer, Andrew Battell. Having been captured by the Portuguese in Brazil, Battell is shipped off to Angola, where he is forced to participate in the Portuguese slave trade as a pilot. After his attempt to escape and return to his beloved England has been foiled by his mistress, a beautiful half-breed, he is sent deep into the interior, again as a pilot, only to be captured by the cannibalistic Jaqqa tribe whose ferocious giant of a chief elevates him to blood-brotherhood at the price of his participation in unspeakable rites, both cannibalistic and erotic. The tale is colorfully told and has an exciting, gory climax; yet Silverberg invests it with little of the sinister power of Conrad's "Heart of Darkness," and Battell's lurid adventures grow a little monotonous for lack of variety.

Paul Granahan

SOURCE: A review of *Lord of Darkness,* in *Best Sellers,* Vol. 43, No. 4, July, 1983, p. 129.

Robert Silverberg has long been one of SF's most inspired luminaries, reminding us time and again that fine prose and skilled characterization are as important to that genre as to any other. Author of such triumphs as *Dying Inside* and *The Book of Skulls* (as well as shorter gems such as the Nebula winning **"Born with the Dead"**), his unwelcome decision to retire in 1975 was fortunately reversed with 1979's *Lord Valentine's Castle,* and he is once more producing both novels and short stories.

Lord of Darkness, however, is not science fiction—though

sharing some of its elements—but an historical novel set primarily in Portuguese Angola of the late sixteenth and early seventeenth centuries. It is the fact-based story of Andrew Battell, an English seaman stranded in western Africa for over twenty years. Questing for treasure as a privateer, Battell is marooned by his cowardly captain and captured by the Portuguese, who ship him to their colony in Angola. After a lengthy imprisonment in an old-fashioned dungeon, Battell is pressed into service as a pilot upon a Portuguese pinnance, the first of many compromises he makes to ensure continued survival. Following many adventures (not a few of them erotic in nature) and betrayals at the hands of his deceitful enemies, including an abortive escape attempt, Battel flees to the fearsome Jaqqas, wraithlike cannibals who inhabit the shadowy recesses of the inner jungle. Accepted readily due to his unfamiliar golden hair and the destructive power of his musket, Battell is transformed into "Andubatil," warlord of the nomadic Jaqqa nation, and made a brother of their monstrous leader the Imbe-Jaqqa Calandola, the title's "Lord of Darkness" whose dream it is to purge the earth of all civilization. Finally in a night of horror and conflagration, Battell's hellish stay with the cannibals ends and eventually he returns to his beloved England and pens these memoirs.

Silverberg's novel is something like a *Shogun* in Africa with a dash of Conrad's *Heart of Darkness* (which also influenced his *Downward to the Earth*). Essentially enjoyable, it doesn't noticeably drag despite its considerable length. The affable character of Battell is somewhat problematic in that he is perhaps too chameleon-like in his ability to adapt. Although Silverberg allows him to survive, the ease with which he does is rather questionable with too little consideration of the moral dilemma. I recommend the novel to those not overly squeamish about somewhat graphic sex and violent situations.

Steve Carper

SOURCE: A review of *Lord of Darkness,* in *Science Fiction and Fantasy Book Review,* No. 19, November, 1983, p. 42.

The exploration of imagined alien cultures has long been a favored theme in science fiction. Its overuse sometimes makes us forget the large sections of this planet which are alien to the western mind. In this straight historical novel, Silverberg explores, through the eyes of a late 16th century Englishman, the infinite wonders and oddities of the Africa just at the beginning of its colonization.

Andrew Battell truly existed. Captured by the Portuguese while sailing as a pirate, he was taken prisoner and long held in captivity in Africa before finally returning home to a newly strange England. Silverberg has taken the sketchy highlights laid out in Battell's memoirs and fleshed them out with a myriad of well-researched details until Africa comes to breathing, steaming life. The habits, peoples, and attitudes of early colonial outposts, Christianized and pagan African tribes, and professional mercenaries and adventurers seem perfectly real, even right.

Would that the novel itself come to such life. We know in advance that Battell is doomed to twenty years in Africa, his hopes for passage home always postponed by one or another twist of fate, his thoughts of the woman he left behind growing ever fainter. (Silverberg thoughtfully labels the last section "Ulysses" to make the parallel explicit.) What suspense there is comes from trying to guess whose betrayal will thwart Battell next. Worse, the book is plotted something like a cross between a traveler's tale and a Dickens novel, so that pages of close description ("coccodrillos," we learn, leave a musky taste to the water they infest) are followed by the improbable reappearance of a character left hundreds of pages and hundreds of miles behind.

The Battell of the novel is likable, mostly because his attitudes are determinedly rational modern. He sees the blacks as people, women as equals, oppressive slavery economically if not morally wrong, and all religions as different manifestations of worship of the same god. Silverberg claims that the real Battell "might find [much] scandalous or even libelous if he were to read this book," which is no doubt true, even without mentioning the varied and ribald (though hardly overgraphic) sex allowed him.

Lord of Darkness is a long, intricately detailed work of imaginative history, neither SF nor fantasy, an interesting associational item for those fascinated by the many facets of Silverberg's career. In the end, though, it remains an easier book to admire than to like.

📖 *VALENTINE PONTIFEX* (1983)

Publishers Weekly

SOURCE: A review of *Valentine Pontifex,* in *Publishers Weekly,* Vol. 224, No. 14, September 30, 1983, p. 112.

Silverberg emerged from self-imposed retirement in 1980 to give us *Lord Valentine's Castle,* followed last year by *Majipoor Chronicles.* Bringing the gigantic saga to a close with this expertly balanced novel, Silverberg demonstrates that a trilogy *can* get better as it grows—to the point where the third book raises the stature of the first retroactively. Having achieved the fairy-tale fate of rising from pauper to king, Valentine is now engaged in the "happily ever after" portion of his life and worrying about the timing of his promotion from visible, active Coronal to shadowy Pontifex. Likewise, Hissune, Valentine's young protegé, must deal with a rapid ascent from commoner to noble on the way to becoming Valentine's successor. Confronting them is a planetary crisis. The Metamorphs, shape-shifting natives of Majipoor displaced by its polycultural civilization, are sabotaging the crops the gigantic world's billions depend upon. There's an

almost symphonic grandeur to the thoughtful way Silverberg weaves the strands of the story together, effortlessly juggling the various motifs, while enhancing the central characters' solidity. Taken as a single work, the trilogy must now be judged the best of its type since Zelazny's classic, Hugo-winning *Lord of Light.*

Paul Granahan

SOURCE: A review of *Valentine Pontifex,* in *Best Sellers,* Vol. 43, No. 10, January, 1984, p. 364.

After a brief but entertaining respite with an historical novel, **Lord of Darkness,** Robert Silverberg returns in **Valentine Pontifex** to the field of science fiction, which his talent has so greatly enhanced for many years. A multiple award-winner, Silverberg completes with the present work the quasitrilogy begun in his 1980 novel **Lord Valentine's Castle** and continued in 1981's collection entitled **Majipoor Chronicles.** Valentine, capable but gentle Coronal of the immense and wondrous world of Majipoor, has regained the throne temporarily usurped (along with his original body) by the madman Barjazid, himself deceived by the chameleonic Metamorphs. Those hints of an organized Shapeshifter conspiracy are now bearing terrifying fruit. These native Majipoorans have legitimate grievances against the human colonizers who herded them into reservations millennia before. Now a renegade faction of these aborigines, led by the hate-consumed Faraataa, has initiated a many-pronged and subtle attack calculated to drive all of the "Unchanging Ones" from the face of the planet, despite their vast numbers. Mysterious blights cripple the food supply of Majipoor—an unprecedented situation on an always prosperous world—while grotesque and perilous creatures, products of genetic manipulation, appear further to threaten the subjects of Lord Valentine. Indeed it seems as if the favor of the Divine has been withdrawn from those owing allegiance to the Four Powers. It is Valentine's responsibility, as the most active of those Powers, to deal with the disasters threatening to tear the world asunder. Valentine's personal conflict as to whether the ancient Pontifex Tyeveras, cruelly being artificially kept alive, should be granted final rest gradually becomes the focus of the planetary crisis. For Valentine would be obliged to replace him in the tomb-like, underground Labyrinth—a fate dreaded by the Coronal beyond all else—and yet Valentine's pontificate along with the ascendancy of his successor as Coronal may well prove to be the salvation of both his people and the Metamorphs as well.

Although I was not overly impressed by **Lord Valentine's Castle** (despite its significance as Silverberg's return to SF following a several year hiatus), the richness and depth the author lent to his setting in **Majipoor Chronicles** altered my opinion. **Valentine Pontifex** makes good use of the colorful and fascinating cities, races, and characters of Majipoor. This multi-threaded tale stands as another testament to Silverberg's unique skill, and I found it wholly enjoyable.

John O. Christensen

SOURCE: A review of *Valentine Pontifex,* in *Voice of Youth Advocates,* Vol. 7, No. 2, June, 1984, p. 102.

In this third volume about the planet Majipoor and its gentle leader Lord Valentine, a new threat to Valentine's rule surfaces. Valentine must defeat a Metamorph radical who is waging a biological war of extermination to return Majipoor to Metamorph control after thousands of years of alien occupation. Valentine must also face the inevitable step of becoming Valentine Pontiflex, the figurehead emperor, and relinquishing Castle Mount to a new Coronal Lord Hissune.

Majipoor is rich with the color of many races, life forms, and wonders. Lord Valentine and his cast of thousands enrich the landscape. Silverberg has truly done an excellent job of writing. It would be helpful to read the previous two, **Lord Valentine's Castle** and **Majipoor Chronicles,** before reading this one but **Valentine Pontifex** does stand by itself as a masterpiece.

GILGAMESH THE KING (1984)

Publishers Weekly

SOURCE: A review of *Gilgamesh the King,* in *Publishers Weekly,* Vol. 226, No. 12, September 21, 1984, p. 91.

Though it is little read today, the ancient Sumerian legend of Gilgamesh has achieved a wide audience at second hand. Elements of this work dating from c. 1700 B.C. were echoed in the Old Testament (Noah and the flood), the *Odyssey,* the *Aeneid* and other works. Silverberg's novelistic retelling draws on two areas of expertise: his excellent, visionary SF and his fine, lesser-known nonfiction on archeology and prehistoric cultures. In fact, the pairing of author and tale seems inevitable in retrospect, for Gilgamesh might be the original of Silverberg's own tormented protagonists. Atypical of epic heroes, Gilgamesh is obsessed with death. He vigorously pursues and rejects the palliatives of religion, sex, love and friendship. Finally, bereft, he goes in quest of Ziusudra, survivor of the flood and, it is said, immortal. What he finds is a bitter disappointment but in the process he is reconciled to a life whose years are numbered. Until this knowledge makes him whole, Gilgamesh has been a stranger to himself. That condition of alienation, key to Silverberg's work, also helps to create a prose style appropriate to this fascinating, oddly modern epic. The first-person story of a demigod, earthy, boastful, yet deeply pessimistic, this is one of Silverberg's best—and most personal—books.

William L. Moran

SOURCE: A review of *Gilgamesh the King,* in *The New York Times Book Review,* November 11, 1984, p. 13.

The memory of Gilgamesh is fresh again, his story told once more and now in many ways. This Sumerian king, who reigned in his city, Uruk, around 2650 B.C., achieved fame and honor unique in Mesopotamian history, and for more than 2,000 years he was celebrated in cult and legend, only to disappear under the sands of Iraq and the ruins of Mesopotamian civilization. But then he reappeared a little more than a century ago—"Out of dark night where lay / The crowns of Nineveh," in Yeats's phrase—and tablet by tablet, fragment by fragment, his story began to be put together and told again. Today it takes its place next to the *Iliad* and the *Odyssey,* and it is known to students of literature everywhere. . . . Now here it is again, in a translation by a distinguished novelist [John Gardner] and in an imaginative elaboration by a well-known writer of science fiction.

The earliest legends we have about Gilgamesh are found in Sumerian lays of the late third millennium B.C. By a process of sifting out, adaptation and radical transformation, probably in the early second millennium B.C., these legends were reworked into a single epic. This epic was composed, however, not in Sumerian but in Semitic Babylonian; this is the Old Babylonian version. Though the text is quite fragmentary, the story line can be seen: Gilgamesh the King becoming restless; the creation of the savage Enkidu by the mother goddess; his seduction by a harlot and his becoming Gilgamesh's companion; the journey of Gilgamesh and Enkidu to the Cedar Forest and Enkidu's slaying of the guardian monster; the death of Enkidu and the terrible grief of Gilgamesh, which becomes an obsessive fear of death and drives him to the end of the world to find the one man who has escaped death, Ut-napishtim, the Babylonian Noah and survivor of the Flood. . . .

In *Gilgamesh the King,* Robert Silverberg has turned his considerable imaginative and narrative power from the world of pure fantasy to a civilization in many ways more alien and remote than the planet Majipoor of his own creation. He draws on the archeological record, written sources such as the Sumerian King List, various Sumerian myths and the Gilgamesh legends as well as the Babylonian epic, and he presents us with the memoirs of Gilgamesh. They begin as Gilgamesh recalls the day when, as a mere boy of 6, he was fetched from play to attend the funeral of his father, Lugalbanda. There he had his first experience of death. The memoirs end years after his return from his visit to Ut-napishtim, the survivor of the Flood. He tells us he is sitting in his palace, inscribing the last of his tablets, feeling his tale is told, for though many years may still remain to him, the real story is over. The hatred and fear of death with which it began and which stalked him through life are gone. He feels, he tells us, a certain peace. No more is he the restless king—and all is well.

Between the frightened child of 6 and the mature man completing his memoirs is a story Mr. Silverberg tells very well. Of the Dumuzi that follows Lugalbanda in the Sumerian King List he makes a pliant and ineffective creature of temple and palace politics who eventually becomes a threat to the life of Gilgamesh. Gilgamesh flees to Kish to enter the service of its king, Agga. Thus does Mr. Silverberg give us the background of the legend of Gilgamesh's relations and his eventual struggle with his northern neighbor. After Agga is defeated, the story line of the Babylonian epic takes over; the walls of Uruk are built, but still Gilgamesh is restless. Early in the story, at Dumuzi's coronation, Gilgamesh meets a young devotee of the goddess Inanna who, as the high priestess of the goddess whose name she shares, is to become a central force in his life, even more important in some ways than Enkidu. Her love and then her hatred shape his days. This is Mr. Silverberg's transformation of the spurned goddess of the sixth tablet of the epic.

The most ingenious part of Mr. Silverberg's story is the visit to Ut-napishtim. He demythologizes the Flood, but since I do not wish to spoil the story, I will not reveal how. The message Gilgamesh receives and the profound change it causes in him in *Gilgamesh the King* are, in my opinion, right on target. I like very much the ending and the man at peace with himself. What Mr. Silverberg seems to have come to by sensitivity and intuition is actually in the opening lines of the epic: "He made a long journey, then was weary but at peace." As Mr. Silverberg implies, this is what the epic is all about.

Rebecca Blevins Kaery

SOURCE: A review of *Gilgamesh the King,* in *English Journal,* Vol. 74, No. 4, April, 1985, p. 86.

The story of Gilgamesh is probably the oldest story known to humankind. It exists, at least in fragments, in Babylonian, Assyrian, and Hittite versions—some more than a thousand years older than *The Iliad* or *The Odyssey.* It tells of the legendary exploits of the king of Uruk—his disputes with the immortals, his encounter with the wild man Enkidu, his rival and friend, their clashes with wicked demons and monsters, his ceremonial marriage to the temple prostitute, and finally his mourning the death of Enkidu and his desperate quest to learn the secret of death and rescue his friend from the underworld.

Unfortunately, there are few retellings of the story appropriate for young adult readers. . . .

Now Robert Silverberg, an old hand with fantasy and science fiction, has undertaken a retelling of the story. He writes, "I have attempted to interpret the fanciful and fantastic events of these poems in a realistic way, that is, to tell the story of Gilgamesh as though he were writing his own memoirs. . . ." Though he expands freely on details, his central narrative line generally follows the originals. His storytelling is robust, artful, and engaging. We regret that he did not choose a subtler version of Gilgamesh's encounter with the underworld for the ending, but young readers will find this an immensely appealing tale—a good introduction to the heroic Gilgamesh.

TOM O'BEDLAM (1985)

Publishers Weekly

SOURCE: A review of *Tom O'Bedlam,* in *Publishers Weekly,* Vol. 227, No. 23, June 7, 1985, p. 78.

One of the most impressive careers in SF now boasts another fine novel, as Silverberg again explores the messianic themes characteristic of his work. His characters—in this book they range from a psychotherapist and a conman to a lapsed priest and a San Diego cab driver—are typically eager for transfiguration, but their detachment and disaffection are not so easily shed. Their lives are all profoundly changed by contact with one man, Tom O'Bedlam, who seems to first to be just another crazy, ragged wanderer, begging his way through a post-holocaust California. But Tom has been subject since childhood to ecstatic visions of other worlds; as more and more people begin having these same "space dreams," an apocalyptic religion springs up around them. Tom offers to help his friends shed their bodies and make the crossing to the transcendent planes glimpsed in those visions. Although Silverberg's narrative manipulation of his characters is sometimes facile, his mastery comes through in a characteristic examination of the tug-of-war between Dionysian fervor and the surrounding world of Augustan rationality.

Paul Granahan

SOURCE: A review of *Tom O'Bedlam,* in *Best Sellers,* Vol. 45, No. 6, September, 1985, p. 203.

Lest anyone doubt that Robert Silverberg is once again firmly ensconced in the genre for which he's labored so mightily, along comes *Tom O'Bedlam* to allay lingering skepticism. After the excellent Majipoor trilogy, which at least bordered on science fantasy, and two historical novels which were quite good, with the present novel (and the shorter work he's finally resumed with a vengeance), set in the relatively near future, he solidly returns to the mainstream of science fiction.

If you're unaware of how significant this reunion of Silverberg and SF is, let me attempt briefly to apprize you of his status in the field and perhaps entice you into savoring some outstanding fiction. Silverberg's incredibly prolific career began in the fifties, when he published some more-than-competent adventure SF. It wasn't until the late '60s that the author took a step back and honed his craft, becoming a true stylist whose works plumbed the depths of the human soul. During this fertile period he produced such classics as *Thorns, The Man in the Maze, Downward to the Earth, The Book of Skulls,* and perhaps his most brilliant novel, *Dying Inside* (along with shorter gems like "The Feast of St. Dionysus" and "Born with the Dead"). In the mid-seventies, Silverberg retired somewhat disillusioned, but this proved to be merely a short-lived hiatus with the publication several years later of *Lord Valentine's Cas-*

tle. Returning to the current novel, **Tom O'Bedlam** takes place in 2103, in an America the mid-section of which has been wiped out by a different kind of nuclear attack—clouds of radioactive dust which ravaged entire cities. Yet this is not a typical "after the holocaust" story, since Silverberg purposely reveals little about his setting, for the thrust of the novel is "somewhere else." Tom, the wandering focus of the book, is a supposed madman who has received visions of other planets with wondrous inhabitants all his life. Now, however, everyone seems to be sharing these dreams and Tom appears to be the point of interface between actual alien worlds and the people of Earth. Various well-drawn characters, including "poor Tom" and his nomadic "scratcher" companions, thousands of members of a voodoo-like cult based upon the visions, an anthropologist studying the movement who becomes a believer, and the staff and patients of a futuristic mental health institution all come together for "the Crossing"—when humans are to pass over to these beautiful new worlds.

Tom O'Bedlam is a novel both joyous and disturbing for Silverberg deliberately leaves us wondering whether this "crossing over" is the ultimate culmination of human destiny or a cowardly release from our own mistakes. This is a thoughtful work, not Silverberg's best effort (that would be a mean feat indeed), but an enjoyable one nonetheless.

John Clute

SOURCE: "Unto this Dust," in *The Times Literary Supplement,* No. 4370, January 2, 1987, p. 21.

A sickness unto death reigns in the California of 2100 as Robert Silverberg's smoothly elegant new novel begins its slow course to apocalypse. **Tom O'Bedlam** is about the end of things, even though the sustained note of ambivalence in its last pages does manage to suggest the possibility of transcendence.

Some time in the twenty-first century, a Dust War has occurred, seemingly between the two superpowers. Since that point, everything has been running down. It is not hard to see why.

> For a hundred years everyone worries about the horrors of atomic war . . . and then the atomic war comes, not with bombs but very quietly, with its lethal radioactive dust . . . great chunks of land made permanently unlivable overnight while life goes on in an ostensibly normal way outside the dusted places. Nations fall apart when bands of hot dust are spread through their midsections.

For the characters in the novel, even though complex relics of the hi-tech world continue to ease their days, it is too late. The best lack all intensity; it is the twilight of the species.

Tom O'Bedlam, whose mother was impregnated in a Dust storm, comes to California, bearing waking dreams of great urgency. Though distant space is barred to humanity because of the limiting factor of the speed of light, these dreams take the shape of messages of clarity and hope, clemently and meltingly ironic, from innumerable species that throng the universe. For Tom, who may be insane, the message is clear: having fouled its nest, humanity must now leave the planet Earth, must make the Crossing. This will involve dropping the body, for the corruptible must put on incorruption.

In northern California, at the Nepenthe Center where psychotherapists mind-pick criminal patients until they are cured by forgetting whatever has twisted them, Elszabet finds her staff and inmates increasingly dominated by shared dreams of the Nine Planets, and of hieratic beckoning figures. To the south, in San Diego, a cult with origins in Brazilian spiritism begins to espouse Chungira-He-Will-Come and Maguali-ga, hieratic beckoning figures who signal the end of humanity's time on Earth.

Wherever Tom, a ragged mendicant, happens to be, such dreams proliferate. Either he creates them, or merely augments them. Either they are manifestations of a race's despair, or the tortured species may indeed have new life, as it says in Revelations, which is quoted throughout, along with the seventeenth-century poems that give Tom his name. When the cultists and Tom finally converge on the Nepenthe Center, the Crossing begins. With the aid of some extraordinary narrative effects, Silverberg makes it manifest that it simply cannot be said whether or not the Crossing is death or transcendence. Of human culture on this planet, however, one way or another, it is the end.

One of the American academic firms whose interest in science fiction has done much to legitimate the form for scholars has published a two-volume bibliography of Robert Silverberg. It is far from complete. Like Georges Simenon, Silverberg wrote many pseudonymous "apprentice" novels in his early years, and it is unlikely that anyone knows just how many books have preceded **Tom O'Bedlam.** This latest novel shows the benefits of Silverberg's intense professionalism. Such competence seems capable of doing its job without heightened emotion. Only in the closing pages does one feel the author genuinely stretching himself in acts of technical bravura, keeping the reader on tenterhooks and giving intense delight.

STAR OF GYPSIES (1986)

Kirkus Reviews

SOURCE: A review of *Star of Gypsies,* in *Kirkus Reviews,* Vol. LIV, No. 14, July 15, 1986, p. 1074.

A big, bustling, but curiously uninvolving space-fantasy that depends on the quite unbelievable premise that the wandering Rom (Gypsy) peoples of Earth are human/

alien refugees from space who built Atlantis before migrating to India and thence dispersing across the globe. In the fourth millennium, the Rom have multiplied and prospered; and, thanks to psi-powered Rom spaceship pilots, humans have spread through the galaxy. The King of the Rom, Yakoub, has retired from the pressures of the office to a remote ice-world where he meditates on his (intermittently interesting) past and goes astro-travelling—"ghosting"—through history (these matters constitute the bulk of the yarn). While in exile he is visited by various emissaries of galactic civilization: the Rom are threatening to choose a new King; the Gaje (non-Rom) are about to choose a new Emperor, but all three candidates are mutually hostile. Eventually, Yakoub is forced to return when news arrives that his evil, embittered son Shandor has usurped the kingship; too, the old Emperor has died and the three potential successors have declared war on one another. Through patience and guile Yakoub comes out on top, finally becoming both Rom King and Gaje Emperor. Plenty of embroidery, then, but not much of a plot—and Yakoub simply doesn't have enough personality or drive to carry readers through the long boggy stretches. Even the Silverberg inventiveness falters, often blurring into meaningless lists of names or descriptives. Overall: a hardworking but frequently tedious, decidedly patchy saga—and a major disappointment.

Publishers Weekly

SOURCE: A review of *Star of Gypsies,* in *Publishers Weekly,* Vol. 230, No. 5, August 1, 1986, p. 72.

In the 32nd century, Gypsies are no longer horse traders and fortune tellers but planet brokers and starship pilots. As a key power bloc in the far-flung Imperium whose 15th Emperor is now in failing health, their sovereign nation is courted by contenders to the throne—all in vain, for Yakoub Nirano, king of Romany, has abdicated and gone into self-exile. Yakoub's journey back to his royal duties and the conflict with his usurping son becomes a struggle with himself and a journey back through his own 172 years of life and the millennia of his people's past. His vigorous, lusty, sometimes painful recollections—of being a slave and space explorer, prince and prisoner, merchant and manure harvester—are rich, inventive and surprising. Once more Silverberg returns to a favorite theme, asking provocative questions about the meaning of being chosen—as gypsy, king, near-immortal and demigod. Sadly, the political story and the somewhat schematic narrative structure are less successful, which leads to a final letdown in an otherwise excellent novel.

Dorcas Hand

SOURCE: A review of *Star of Gypsies,* in *School Library Journal,* Vol. 33, No. 7, March, 1987, p. 178.

Silverberg strikes again. Starting with bits of commonly known gypsy lore, he has built a fascinating extrapola-

Silverberg (center) with writer Algis Budrys (left) and Charles Harris (right) at the World Science Fiction Convention, New York City, 1956.

tion into a future as well as a mythological past for the Rom people. Romany Star is their planet of origin, one made unlivable by eruptions on its sun. The exiles are forced into millennia of wandering—Atlantis, Earth until it too becomes uninhabitable, and on into space. Yakoub, the Gypsy king, tells his—and his people's—story through narrative and flashback. The tale is spellbinding, the characters carefully drawn, the future fantasy quite believable—although the conclusion loses some of this strength in its speed and predictability.

PROJECT PENDULUM (1987)

Publishers Weekly

SOURCE: A review of *Project Pendulum,* in *Publishers Weekly,* Vol. 232, No. 7, August 14, 1987, p. 106.

This title in the Millennium series of illustrated SF is a striking time-travel story by much-honored Silverberg. Twins Eric and Sean Gabrielson, a paleontologist and a physicist, are chosen as the first human subjects of a secret Cal Tech experiment in 2016 that will transport them into the past and the future. As if on a pendulum, they are automatically shunted back and forth, at increasing distances—a few minutes, hours, years, centuries. . . . Their brief stays in other times produce vivid, dreamlike vignettes: encounters with their younger selves, with robots, Neanderthals, aliens and dinosaurs, each era with its own smell and taste. This imaginative story, suggesting much more than is stated in its brief length, is a deft evocation of Silverberg's theme of dislocation.

Zena Sutherland

SOURCE: A review of *Project Pendulum,* in *Bulletin of the Center for Children's Books,* Vol. 41, No. 2, October, 1987, p. 37.

Silverberg's concept is intriguing: identical twins Eric and Sean have been chosen from other volunteer-twins to participate in a project that will take them, separately, in wider and wider arcs of time, into the past and the future. Thus, Project Pendulum. It's an appealing concept and the writing has pace and vigor; there are moments of high drama and flashes of wit. What makes this less than Silverberg's best is the format, as the short accounts of the pendulum-swing visits proliferate to the extent of losing impact.

Susan Rice

SOURCE: A review of *Project Pendulum,* in *Voice of Youth Advocates,* Vol. 10, No. 4, October, 1987, p. 180.

Sean and Eric Gabrielson are twins involved in Project Pendulum. It is the year 2016 at Cal Tech in California and Project Pendulum is the first experiment in time travel. The pendulum takes Eric and Sean alternately between the past and future, then 50 minutes into the past, then 500 minutes into the future, and so on until the pendulum swings back to where the experiment started. Sean and Eric start on opposite sides of the pendulum, but do reach each shunt, only alternately. The mission the twins have taken up is to experience time travel, but also to try and not interfere with anything happening. Twins are used because of their identical body mass, allowing scientists the opportunity to study their reactions. Eric, the physicist, wants to see the future, and Sean, the palaeontologist, wants the chance to see dinosaurs.

Silverberg helps the reader out by giving a note with each chapter as to which twin is experiencing which shunt. . . . This aspect helps with the sometimes confusing topic of time travel and where you are at in time. The twins don't spend enough time at each location to do any real harm. . . . What you do experience with each of the twins is their thoughts, emotions, and sense of wonder and hope as they experience the future and past. This novel is an excellent introduction to a major author, and illustrations by Moebius add to the overall quality of the novel.

My complaints are that I'd have liked to see more of each location the twins visit, and what happens after they finally connect back with each other. Did they see the same things, or as sometimes happens, witnesses have seen the same thing but tell very different stories? Sean and Eric are adults, but the appeal of the storyline and writing style seems to be for a younger audience. Recommended for science fiction collections.

Marcus Crouch

SOURCE: A review of *Project Pendulum,* in *The Junior Bookshelf,* Vol. 53, No. 4, August, 1989, p. 194.

The mathematics of ***Project Pendulum*** is beyond me, but

Robert Silverberg is as much philosopher and poet as scientist and his magnificent novel is accessible to all, not merely the committed SF addict.

The basic idea is clear enough. Some time in the 21st century identical twins, Sean and Eric, volunteer to take part in a scientific experiment. They occupy opposite sides of a pendulum which will swing them forward into the future, back into the past, by short stages at first, then by geometrical progression deeper and deeper into the unknown. The story is seen alternatively through the eyes of the two young men. Some of their experiences are slightly comic, some romantic, at least one (California suffering from the Greenhouse effect) horrifying. There is a lovely moment when Sean, having survived the spear of a Stone Age man and the attack of a giant ape, finds himself deep in the future in a forest of singing flowers. In a final chapter, before the pendulum swing is reversed, Sean sees a world in which the dinosaur is lord, 'snorting and mooing and grunting' in a leafy kingdom.

There is much here to think about and to wonder at. Mr. Silverberg has a command of words to match his imagination, and much of his story is told with real beauty of style. By its nature the story does not allow any development of character, and Sean and Eric, despite their wisecracking and their wondering acceptance of experiences, are not much more than stock figures. It could hardly be otherwise. In its command of detail and its consistent vision Robert Silverberg's book is in the true succession from Wells.

AT WINTER'S END (1988)

Roland Green

SOURCE: A review of *At Winter's End,* in *Booklist,* Vol. 84, No. 11, February 1, 1988, p. 889.

In the far future, the Earth suffers a massive meteoritic bombardment. Those humans who survive emerge into a world shrouded by dust clouds, only to have to fight both the other evolved Terran sapient races and an invading race of insects for humanity's birthright. This vast, sprawling novel—of the sort Silverberg seems to prefer these days, e.g., ***Star of Gypsies*** and ***Tom O'Bedlam***—makes minimal demands on narrative technique and seldom achieves coherence. However, Silverberg does offer a gallery of frequently fascinating characters, and his prose remains of a high order. Not a great book, but recognizably the work of a superior talent and a powerful imagination, and certainly likely to find readers in most sf collections.

Kirkus Reviews

SOURCE: A review of *At Winter's End,* in *Kirkus Reviews,* Vol. LVI, No. 6, March 15, 1988, p. 417.

Writer/editor Silverberg has finally done it: produced a long, absorbing, far-future saga with substantial characters *and* a plot that adds up.

For 700,000 years, "death-stars" from space have rained upon the Earth, destroying the ancient civilizations and creating a glacial climate. Now, as the bombardment ends and the land warms, various tribes of humans emerge from their protective "cocoons" to reclaim the world. One such tribe—led by stern, wise Koshmar, and stirred by the young, inquisitive Hresh—is determined to find the fabled ancient city of Vengiboneeza where, according to tradition, they will discover the means to rebuild civilization. Finally, after braving many dangers, they reach the city. Hresh, who has the most highly developed psi-powers of all the tribe, uncovers usable ancient machines, and rediscovers the city's ancient history—but to his shock and consternation, he learns that his people are not humans, but evolved monkeys. Still in the future for Hresh's folk: tragedy and a parting of the ways for the tribe; a challenge from a rival tribe, the advanced, knowledgeable, snobbish Beng; and an invasion by the teeming, insect-like hjjk, who have laid their own plans to dominate old Earth.

Tingling, fascinating work, richly detailed and satisfying: Silverberg's best full-length outing for many a long year.

Diane G. Yates

SOURCE: A review of *At Winter's End,* in *Voice of Youth Advocates,* Vol. 11, No. 2, June, 1988, p. 97.

Koshmar's little tribe of 60 has lived in its cocoon underground, safe from the ravages of the death stars that destroyed the Earth's surface and caused the 700,000 year Long Winter. But now it is the Time of Coming Forth, the long-awaited springtime, and Koshmar as chieftain leads her people to the fabled city of the lost sapphire-eyes folk where the Chronicles have foretold that humans will find machines to help them rule the Great World once again. Once outside, others in the tribe are seeking to establish their own identities, and the once-solid group finds itself torn apart and beset by enemies.

The Chronicler for the tribe is Hresh full-of-questions, newly appointed to the post and consumed with a passion for learning all that he can about the past in order to build a new and glorious future. But knowledge can be devastating; he learns that his people were not human, but only very clever, intelligent animals. Over the millennia they have acquired many traits of the humans, however. They have a language, they read and write, they think. Gradually he comes to realize that to become fully human is to plan and build, to grow and expand knowledge, to create and change the world, to do and not merely to be.

Scientists, theologians, and SF writers all have evolution theories, all of which must deal with the vastness of time and the seemingly inexplicable rise and fall of civilizations. Silverberg offers an intriguing theory of the way a species becomes human. . . .

Silverberg never disappoints; although not as compelling as his Majipoor trilogy, his new work entertains us while forcing us to think about the meaning of life and the nature of humanity. It could be the basis for stimulating discussions in sociology classes, as well as around the table at the local pizza parlor.

THE NEW SPRINGTIME (1990)

Diane G. Yates

SOURCE: A review of *The New Springtime,* in *Voice of Youth Advocates,* Vol. 13, No. 4, October, 1990, pp. 232-33.

Its been 40 years since the People, led by Hresh, emerged from their 700,000 year sojourn under the earth. They have expanded across the land, building great cities and developing all of the trappings of civilization, including a ruling caste and poorer workers.

The only threat to the People's continued peaceful existence comes from the hjjks, the last of the six great races that lived on Earth before the Long Winter. The hjjks are gaunt, towering insect creatures who live in great nests under the earth in complete harmony with each other and with the universe. Theirs is a very static, conservative society, with each member having its appointed task. They are ruled by a Queen whose love and power is all-encompassing.

The People loathe and fear the hjjks, and a peace overture from the Queen is met with much wrangling over how to best answer it. Different factions suggest different approaches: all-out war, negotiate in order to gain time, agree to the Queen's conditions. Each of the approaches has it proponents, and the different plot threads follow each group as they carry out actions designed to bring about their desired ends.

This sequel to **At Winter's End** is a very unsatisfying book. I suspect that Silverberg's intentions were good. He wanted to make several points: 1) Change is inevitable and the only constant in the world and those who don't adapt to change are doomed to disappear, and 2) Sometimes there can be no clear winner and both sides would do well to work out an accommodation so that all can live in harmony. These two admirable points of view are mired in a boring, repetitive narrative. Several of the People discover for themselves what makes the hjjks tick and we must suffer through ramblings about Nest-love, Nest-breath, Nest-truth, Nest-bond, Nest-plenty, Queen-love, Queen-peace, and Egg-plan until you want to crack a few eggs yourself. There is too little motivation for certain actions by characters, and several switch allegiances without enough preparation for it in the plot lines. Considering that all is resolved with a whimper not a bang, there is too much discussion about conflicting philosophies and too little action.

Silverberg has written many wonderful books, with the Valentine trilogy a notable example of his best work. Re-read them and forget this one. It is unclear from the inconclusive ending whether or not a third book is being planned.

NIGHTFALL (with Isaac Asimov, 1990)

Publishers Weekly

SOURCE: A review of *Nightfall,* in *Publishers Weekly,* Vol. 237, No. 35, August 31, 1990, p. 52.

This collaboration by two masters of the genre expands on Asimov's classic short story first published in 1941. Kalgash is a planet with six suns, a world where darkness is unnatural. Scientists realize that an eclipse—an event that occurs only every 2049 years—is imminent, and that a society completely unfamiliar with darkness will be plunged into madness and chaos. The novel traces events leading to this discovery, and the fates of the main characters immediately following the apocalypse. While the premise is convincing in the context of a short story, this longer version brings up too many unresolved questions. The original tale was tightly written, succinct and stunning, but the novelization seems flabby and drawn-out—the reader recognizes the significance and consequences of the impending events long before the characters do. An abrupt and simplistic ending further mars a hallowed SF tale.

Algis Budrys

SOURCE: A review of *Nightfall, in Fantasy & Science Fiction,* Vol. 79, No. 5, November, 1990, p. 51-5.

We all read it when we are at a relatively young age— I was 16—and were impressed by it. I speak, of course, of Isaac Asimov's *Nightfall,* the novelette, which, if you haven't read it, I feel sorry for you. And for you I will give a précis:

On a planet in another system, where the people are pretty much like you and me except that they have built up a civilization even faster than we have, it never gets dark because there are six suns, at least one of which is always in the sky. Unbeknownst to most inhabitants, once every 2000 years there is a total eclipse, which makes the stars appear, which causes just about everyone to go mad and burn everything, in an effort to stave off darkness and/or shut out the awful starlight, thus collapsing civilization, thus causing the planet to go through endless 2000 year cycles. The story concerns itself with the futile efforts of the knowledgeable inhabitants to save civilization; futile because even though they reason out that the eclipse must occur, and postulate even the appearance of a few stars, the actual reality is too great for their minds to encompass.

Almost as soon as you have read it, and been mightily impressed by it, certain logical if noncrucial objections occur. One by one, they get explained away, except for one: Is it the darkness, or is it the stars? But it's so good, you supress that.

I don't know exactly how many times I've re-read the story over the years—it's been a while since I was 16—but it retains its power, and Asimov—who has written better, but has not struck that peculiar blend of power and memorability very often again—is stuck with being the author of *Nightfall.* He wrote it so long ago, you see; toward the very beginning of his career, bent over a manual typewriter, in physical circumstances that must seem very straitened to him as he looks out his penthouse windows at Central Park now. Such a long time ago, and all the stories that have come since *Nightfall,* and still people remember him first for it.

I can think of worse fates than to be Isaac Asimov. And to be the author of a story like *Nightfall,* which is a landmark in a field that does not get many, and to have struck the peculiar blend of power and memorability which it is not given to most writers to strike at all; if out of, what is it, 500 books? he is known first as the author of *Nightfall* is a fact that occasionally galls, Christ, it's considerably better than being poked in the eye with a sharp stick.

Still, one can see how he would feel a certain bittersweetness. And now it has perhaps started all over again, with the publication of *Nightfall,* the novel.

Nightfall, the novel, is written in collaboration with Robert Silverberg, and I deliberately did not call up either Bob or Isaac to find out who did what, because you couldn't. What you can do is read the book to find out where the seams are—where the one hand took up and the other left off. And what you will find is that you can't tell. The thing is a whole, legitimately and seamlessly a novel, with the novelette rewritten and incorporated as the middle third, not the last third. *Nightfall* the novel stands by itself, just as *Nightfall* the novelette did.

It is not, in fact, a book that ends with the eclipse and the fires; it is, essentially, an after the disaster novel, although it has many other features.

But we'll get to that in a minute; I want to talk about Bob Silverberg first. Viz.: I don't know what's gotten into Bob, specifically, but this makes the second of these in a few months (the first being his novelette written as a companion piece to C. L. Moore's "Vintage Season," as published by Tor), and, once again, he's done a superb job. Once again, I don't see how he's going to make as much money out of this as he would devoting the same amount of time to doing his own work. So, once again, I have to assume it's because he couldn't resist. Granted, he's not exactly hurting for money, and he can probably afford it. But it makes me think about him in a way I'm not sure I've ever fully felt before; one is coincidence, but twice is something else again, and to not only do it but do it well. . . . Well, it's something; something nice.

Back to our story:

The novel begins with three principal characters: Sheerin, the psychologist; Siffera, the archeologist, and Beenay, the astrophysicist, who, all unbeknownst to each other, are grappling with different aspects of the same mystery.

Sheerin has been called in as a consultant to a theme park. After 2000 years, someone has for the first time gotten the idea of a tunnel of darkness ride, fifteen minutes in duration. Unfortunately, although the ride, newly opened, is a smash success, no one who undergoes it is not shaken, a few go permanently crazy, and a smaller but nonetheless real number just plain die. Sheerin spends some time interviewing survivors, in an insane asylum, and then takes the ride himself. Though he emerges essentially unscathed, he feels no doubt that the ride must be closed down permanently; people are not prepared to cope with darkness.

Siffera is in the midst of investigating Beklimot, the oldest known archeological dig on the planet, when she is caught in a horrendous sandstorm. When it passes, the nearby Hill of Thombo has been accidentally sliced open by the sand, and in it are at least seven city remains, each on top of the other, each separated from the others by a layer of charcoal, each layer of charcoal 2000 years less aged than the one below it.

Meanwhile, young Beenay is meticulously verifying, again and again, that there is something seriously wrong with the Theory of Universal Gravitation, which theory was recently announced to tumultuous applause by Athor, an eminent figure in science; in fact, the leading physicist of the day.

When Beenay tells his discovery to Theremon, the newsman, things start to unravel—or, rather, ravel. For Theremon has by coincidence arranged an interview with the Apostles of The Flame, a far-out religious cult which believes the planet is doomed to a 2000 year cycle in which it grows dark, the stars come out—whatever *they* are—and rain down fire to destroy the cities of Man. Which is due to happen in fourteen months. And although Theremon does not at first put things together, soon enough he is the thread that gathers in Beenay, Siffera, Sheerin, and Athor, who points out that Beenay's figures do not invalidate the Theory of Universal Gravitation; they point to the existence of a hitherto unknown astronomical body which will eclipse the one sun that will shine on a day fourteen months hence.

With this much information in their possession, and fourteen months to go until the big day, you would expect that something could be done. But, step by inevitable step, nothing is done, or what is done is pitifully inadequate. And the stars come out, in a scene in which they do not rain down fire, but the civilization destroys itself trying to build enough fires to drive away the darkness.

And then the survivors—the really few who have not gone hopelessly psychotic—must try to salvage . . . something. Which, in a way, they do; the book ends on a note of not exactly triumph, but at least human attainable hope.

But certain questions remain left over from *Nightfall.*

Sheerin, for instance, through his story demonstrates that the people of the planet really can't stand darkness; darkness pitch black, darkness everywhere they look. There are certain logical objections to this, but they can be patched over, for instance, everyone, every time, has been sleeping with a "godlight," so that even though they draw the curtain in their bed chambers, it still isn't dark. And if you go into a mine, as these people must if they are going to support a technological society, or cave, of course you carry a light. Less easy to gloss over is the fact that mines, aplenty, must exist from previous epochs and be known to archeologists, but somehow that doesn't bother me. I am left, really, only with the central puzzle; is it the darkness *or* is it the stars? Because it can't be both.

I am already troubled that in this story the stars all pop out at the same time, whereas in a real eclipse you get the first magnitude stars coming out almost as soon as the eclipse is fairly begun, then the second magnitude, then the third, and so forth, until the full majesty of the night sky is revealed if it doesn't happen to be raining. And, mind you, that's in *our* sky; this planet on which this story is set is apparently in a cluster such that our own sky pales—well, no—in comparison.

Now, then. Do you mean to say these stars shed no light? Obviously, you can't say *that*. But how much light do they shed? Could it possibly be as much as is shed on Earth by a full Moon? *More?*

Do you, for that matter, mean to say that no one, in 2000 years, has looked up at the sky from a deep well and reported that the sky is not what it seems? And gotten considerable attention paid to him, if not the first time, and the first reporter, but the hundredth? And what about this sixth sun? It appears to be, really, a rather feeble vessel, if people's fingers and toes start to go numb because by itself it sheds so little warmth. And yet *none* of the stars, in this starry, starry sky, are strong enough to be visible even at that relatively low level of illumination?

No. No. No, despite the strong efforts of the collaborators to paper over the central logical fallacy, it remains. Now—does it matter? No.

This is a very good book. True, it is another in a long series of books that demonstrates the strongest ingredient in science fiction is not the science, but we already know that. The point that counts is whether you believe it while it is happening, and you do. And, most important, what might have been an exercise just in milking *Nightfall* for another round, is anything but. It's a pleasure.

LETTERS FROM ATLANTIS ("Dragonflight" series, 1990)

Kirkus Reviews

SOURCE: A review of *Letters from Atlantis,* in *Kirkus Reviews,* Vol. LVIII, No. 20, October 15, 1990, p. 1460.

The *real* story of Atlantis: In the 21st century, scientists can send thought patterns of researchers back in time. Thus, Roy is cast back 180 centuries—into the mind of Ramifon Sigiliterimor Septagimot Stolifax Blayl (Ram), heir to the throne of Atlantis. There he finds a race of advanced architects and craftsmen who use electricity and call other humans "dirt people." Roy causes Prince Ram to write letters relating this fantastic information to his fellow researcher and lover Lora, half a continent away, who has been sent back to the same era. When the Prince discovers that he has an uninvited tenant, Roy is forced to break the first law of time travel by revealing himself to his host; he then finds that Ram is not strictly human but rather one of the survivors of a galactic catastrophe. Moreover, Ram can read the future and knows that Atlantis will be destroyed—but will take no action: it is the will of the gods.

In this first in the new "Dragonflight" series, Silverberg is as smooth and provocative as ever. Although neither the Atlantis theory nor the invented technology is original and the letter-writing ploy is a little far-fetched, the net effect is entertaining and affecting. Superior sf/fantasy.

Ilene Cooper

SOURCE: A review of *Letters from Atlantis,* in *Booklist,* Vol. 87, No. 6, November 15, 1990, p. 660.

Atlantis. The name evokes past glories and tragic ends. In a remarkable blend of legend and science fiction, award-winning writer Silverberg weaves every strand of the Atlantis legend into an intricate tale that is nevertheless so simply written it is accessible to a spectrum of readers.

The book takes the form of letters from Roy. Information is dispensed slowly, enticingly, until readers understand that Roy is a time traveler from the twenty-first century. His body lies comatose in the Home Era, but his essence has invaded the mind of Ram, the Crown Prince of Atlantis. Roy, along with his girlfriend, Lora—to whom the letters are written—is on a mission to learn the secrets of the fabled continent. And what secrets they are! Roy discovers the incredible origin of Atlantis and

must deal with the inevitability of its end—though against all his training, he tries to interfere with history.

Since Roy and Ram are the only real characters (to say nothing of their parasitic relationship), the story might have seemed claustrophobic, but Silverberg cleverly makes Atlantis itself one of the characters through detailed descriptions and finely tuned nuance. He also does an excellent job of juxtaposing modern, often witty prose against the stuff of legend. From the first sentence: "The prince is sleeping now" right through to the arresting conclusion, this is brilliant, in both senses of the word.

Sr. Mary Veronica

SOURCE: A review of *Letters from Atlantis,* in *Voice of Youth Advocates,* Vol. 13, No. 6, February, 1991, p. 367.

Have you ever wondered what it might be like to be both yourself and another person? What would it be like to really know what that person thinks and to be able, perhaps, to control that person's actions?

Roy Coulton, a time traveler from the 20th century, writes of his experiences as a spirit inhabiting the mind of Prince Ram, heir to the throne of Atlantis. Roy's letters to a fellow time traveler, give an exciting glimpse of a golden time in the legendary past. For a tantalizing moment, Roy seems to be in a position to alter the course of history.

Silverberg has crafted a story that will intrigue his science fiction fans. He works with several questions: Did Atlantis really exist? Where did its people come from? What happened to it? Where did its inhabitants go after Atlantis was destroyed?

This is another potential science fiction winner by an author who has won three Hugo Awards and Five Nebula Awards for his work. Young people will be drawn to this book because it is by Silverberg, and they will want more. While [Robert] Gould's artwork planned for inside the book was not seen, the book jacket is colorful, true to the story inside, and certain to draw readers.

Susan M. Harding

SOURCE: A review of *Letters from Atlantis,* in *School Library Journal,* Vol. 37, No. 3, March, 1991, p. 218.

In the future, scientists have developed a type of time travel in which the traveler's consciousness is transferred into the mind of someone actually living in the past—a useful way to observe history first hand. Roy has been sent into the mind of the Prince of Atlantis; Lora has been sent into the mind of a provincial governor existing at the same time. The title refers to Ray's letters to Lora, written after putting the Prince's mind to sleep and using his body. When Roy begins to feel lonely and depressed, he grows careless, and the Prince soon becomes aware of Roy's presence in his mind. Roy, revealing himself fully, breaks all rules of nonintervention and possibly sullies history. The premise is intriguing, and Silverberg's portrayal of Roy is convincing, especially his isolation and need for contact with another human. But Silverberg's vision of Atlantis is nothing new. He falls back on the old "mankind-wasn't-advanced-enough-at-that-time-so-such-a-high-civilization-must-have-been-a-colony-of-aliens-from-another-planet" cliché. He introduces, and then uses this excuse to explain away, without really exploring, topics such as why Atlantis was so technologically advanced, why racial hatred existed between the Atlantans and native earthlings, and why the earthlings kept no remembrance of Atlantis after its destruction. The triteness of these revelations betrays the freshness of the set-up. Readers will be ultimately disappointed because this could have been so much better than it is.

THE FACE OF THE WATERS (1991)

Kirkus Reviews

SOURCE: A review of *The Face of the Waters,* in *Kirkus Reviews,* Vol. LIX, No. 16, August 15, 1991, p. 1051.

After the sun goes nova and destroys the Earth, humans survive only in small groups on far-flung planets like Hydros, a world with no land masses at all; here, humans are permitted to share the floating islands built by the Gillies, one of several intelligent native species. But when ambitious capitalist Nid Delagard of Sorve Island accidentally kills some intelligent "divers" in the course of his operations, the Gillies somehow know—and order the humans off Sorve. Led by doctor Valben Lawler, in ships provided by Delagard, they sail off in pursuit of a distant uninhabited island. On the voyage, storms, tides, and deadly sea creatures take their toll of ships and people; then Lawler discovers that Delagard really intends to seek out the Face of the Waters, a fabulous, mysterious island avoided by the Gillies. At last, a handful of survivors reach the island, only to learn that the Face of the Waters is the focus of a planetary consciousness embracing all Hydran life—and they, isolated, orphaned humans, are being invited to join.

This far-from-original idea raises other questions, not least the problem of a food chain whose components share a consciousness, that Silverberg declines even to acknowledge, let alone confront. So: a mediocre ocean-world odyssey . . . from the veteran writer/editor, professionally turned but disappointingly superficial.

Gerald Jonas

SOURCE: A review of *The Face of the Waters,* in *The New York Times Book Review,* December 15, 1991, p. 21.

The title of Robert Silverberg's new novel, *The Face of the Waters,* comes from Genesis: "And the earth was without form, and void; and darkness was upon the face of the deep. And the spirit of God moved upon the face of the waters." In Mr. Silverberg's conceit, the waters are a world-encompassing ocean on a planet named Hydros that was once used as a human penal colony. The descendants of the original prisoners survive on small floating islands that obey the ocean currents. The humans share these islands with the intelligent Gillies, natives of Hydros who barely tolerate their presence. The waters themselves teem with ravenous forms of life that resemble the sea monsters found on old maps of Earth, the barely remembered home planet long since destroyed by a blast of "hard radiation" from its own sun.

When some of the humans learn that the Gillies fear and venerate an unusual island known in their language as "the face of the waters," they set sail in a fleet of ships to find out why. As Mr. Silverberg tells it, this quest is unabashedly mythic: there is a priest searching for God, a self-medicating doctor looking for love, a man of action looking for something to conquer, a woman searching for the truth and so on. But the people themselves are more than allegorical devices; their obsessions are believable, their pain all too real. The opening chapters set the scene with great economy and authority; the ending is both daring and persuasive. The problem comes in the middle, the quest-journey itself, which goes on and on and on, enlivened mainly by attacks from one terrifying monster after another.

Mr. Silverberg exercises considerable ingenuity in devising these creatures, but the exercise grows tedious and begins to look suspiciously like padding. Back in the 1940s and 50s, in the heyday of the science fiction magazine, editors welcomed stories of any length; if a story was too long to be called short and too short to be called a novel, it was published as a novelette or novella.

"Novelette" always sounded to me like something on sale at Woolworth's, but "novella" (which my dictionary defines as "a story with a compact and pointed plot") has been good English since the Renaissance. Many of science fiction's classic stories are novellas. Without its bloated middle, *The Face of the Waters* would have made a perfect novella; readers who don't mind skimming through the middle hundred pages or so may enjoy it as such.

Algis Budrys

SOURCE: A review of *The Face of the Waters,* in *Fantasy & Science Fiction,* Vol. 82, No. 1 January, 1992, pp. 45-50.

Robert Silverberg has written twenty or forty books I wish I had written. True, I would have written them differently, but that, too, is the point, which I will not explain further. If you are a writer, you will know what I mean.

The book we have to consider in the present context is *The Face of the Waters*. . . . Something has gone wrong with this Bob Silverberg book in particular; it is instructive to see what that is.

It is not the scope of the book, nor the idea for it. The idea is that, some generations before the story opens, the Sun went nova, and most of the human race, and the planet, Earth, perished. Only here and there are there outposts of humanity among the stars, and whether some of them are considerable or not, on the planet Hydros people are barely tolerated. A few hundred live on Hydros, a world apparently 100 percent covered by an ocean, dotted here and there with artificial floating islands built by the Gillies, a sort of humanoid race which pretty much represents the top of the evolutionary ladder on Hydros. It's a little hard to tell, because they don't communicate well with humans.

At any rate, there are lots of sentient beings on Hydros, large and small, living in the ocean, and some are casually deadly to humans. The rest pretty much are actively hostile.

There is no way off Hydros. It is the end of the line, and the humans who live there, in precarious balance with the environment, live on various islands, which float around in a complex pattern. The island we are particularly concerned with is Sorve Island, on which a band of about seventy humans have lived for several generations. They live pretty primitively. Everybody does. The Gillie culture is difficult to understand; they have been building an electrical generation system for some time, but are largely stone age in other ways.

The viewpoint character is Valben Lawler, the human doctor, fortyish, and a bachelor now that his wife, whom he has not stopped loving, one day shipped out for another island and has never been heard from again. Lawler moons over her. And he wishes he knew more about the Gillies. He wishes he knew as much as his dead father, who was the doctor before him and actually helped the Gillies crack a nasty plague. But what he mostly does is drink numbweed, which enables him to get from one day to the next. Days are pretty much the same.

Until Nid Delagard, among other things the owner of a small fleet that traffiks from island to island, offends the Gillies. Then nothing will fix the problem; all humans must be off the island in a month.

All attempts at suasion fail; the sentence is irrevocable. In the end, a fleet of ships, small in number, small in individual size, sets off with all the sixty-odd humans on board. Where are they going?

Where. Nid—on whose flagship Lawler embarks—has his radio man call various islands in an effort to find one that will take all the refugees from Sorve. But none will.

Some will take a few, but this option is unacceptable; broken up, the Sorve humans will lose their identity, and a chapter in human history will, it seems to them, be lost. Finally, Delagard declares that the most distant island, Graveyard, will take them all, and they set course.

But it turns out, after an interval in which various fascinating adventures befall Lawler and the others, that Graveyard did *not* offer to take them. Where they are sailing for instead is the Face of the Waters—a forbidden island continent (?), on the other side of the planet, of which only the most sketchy tales have ever been told, and on which Delagard hopes to find a place to live.

O.K. So far, so good. The tale Silverberg is spinning out is replete with menace and a kind of beauty; the ships plough through many exotic life forms, some of which drag crew members overboard, some of which spray them with various deadly poisons, and some of which are good to eat. One has a sense of Silverberg bringing the story ever closer to a grand denouement, and meanwhile inventing, inventing, and never flagging.

But things start to go subtly wrong. For one thing, all the other ships disappear, all but one of them presumably in a passing cataclysm. But we do not see this. The one ship did the same a few pages back. And we did not see that either. And the first suspicion grows; can it be that Silverberg is jettisoning all those crews because he does not know what to do with them. There is, for instance, the ship crewed by the Sisters, apparently a community of women with nun-like characteristics, who abhor men. This is an idea that seems to have, finally, proven unfruitful to Silverberg, because we never hear of them again. But I think most readers would have liked to.

Then, crewmen die on Nid's ship, and there is neither any particular reason for which ones are to die nor any particular *un*reason. There is, in other words, no sense that Silverberg planned these deaths one page before he got to them. And there is the affair with Sundira, who says she loves Lawler and falls in his arms—but not his arms exclusively—and this would seem to require an explanation which we never get.

Finally, after many perils, many of them fatal, they arrive at the Face of the Waters, the peculiarly named continent (?), which turns out to be very little like what we were led to expect either from old traveller's tales or Sundira's sometime researches among the Gillies. It could not support a castaway for years—In which case where did Lawler's boyhood confidant come from?—nor does it seem to contain the sort of deadliness against which Sundira was warned.

In the end, all the surviving crewfolk fall under the island's (?) spell, and go ashore, there presumably to live happily ever after, maybe. The island is somehow God; all creatures on Hydros are linked, and everything the crew had experienced was designed to lead them hither . . . a proposition which I, for one, doubt very strongly. What it reads like to me, much more, is as if Silverberg had to finally come up with an explanation to justify the evocative incidents that he had been writing more or less *ad libitum*. The explanation given in the text simply does not hold water—too many of the said incidents contradict it. I may be wrong. The whole structure of this book may in fact be tightly organized toward an end, had I but the wit to see it. But there is the other explanation—that this began as a half idea in Silverberg's head, evocative and compelling, and that he began to write it, thinking that somehow it would resolve itself satisfactorily. And as good as the first nine-tenths of the book are is a measure of how disappointing the last tenth is. Maybe. I said maybe.

THE UGLY LITTLE BOY (with Isaac Asimov, 1992)

Publishers Weekly

SOURCE: A review of *The Ugly Little Boy,* in *Publishers Weekly,* Vol. 239, No. 42, September 21, 1992, p. 80.

This expanded version of the late Asimov's classic 1958 tale is a collaborative effort that surpasses the original. There are no plot surprises; the authors have retained the basic story of an alien four-year-old child who is kidnapped from his time zone and brought into a future world. Yet this is a fresh and satisfying version, primarily because the characters have been made richer, the depiction of 21st-century society rounded out and the history of the Neanderthal tribe from which the eponymous boy was abducted more fully given. When the woebegone waif, now named Timmie, was snatched from his epoch, he was brought into a pool of no-time, which exists coincident with the present. Since Timmie is condemned to living within that pool forever, his presence raises moral questions: Is it abusive to leave him alone in this limbo for eternity? Would it be equally cruel to send him back to the Ice Age? Asimov and Silverberg explore these issues in an intriguing story supported by seamless writing.

KINGDOMS OF THE WALL (1993)

Roland Green

SOURCE: A review of *Kingdoms of the Wall,* in *Booklist,* Vol. 89, No. 9, January 1, 1993, p. 795.

Silverberg's latest is superficially the most basic sort of quest tale. Poilar Crookleg is called on to lead 40 pilgrims from his village in an attempt to scale the Wall that looms just beyond the village and in search of the wisdom of the gods, although he knows he will likely return a madman, if he returns at all. The novel's real protagonist is the Wall itself, with the humans that hurl themselves against it almost minor characters in compar-

ison. Although not absolutely at Silverberg's highest technical level, this book is vivid and compelling most of the way through. It also indicates that Silverberg's skill and ingenuity are not diminishing, for all that he is at or past his fortieth year as a published writer.

Gerald Jonas

SOURCE: A review of *Kingdoms of the Wall,* in *The New York Times Book Review,* March 14, 1993, p. 14.

It is becoming difficult these days to find a science fiction story that does not in some way confront the question of godhood. Robert Silverberg's **Kingdoms of the Wall** is a parable about the danger of seeking more intimate contact with the powers that control the universe. On a distant planet a race of people who superficially resemble humans lives at the foot of a mountain so steep and so tall that it is known as the Wall. Their myths tell of a Prometheus-like First Climber who ascended the Wall and brought back useful knowledge from the gods who live at the summit. In honor of this First Climber, the people periodically choose 40 of their best and brightest as Pilgrims, who try to climb the Wall and parley with the gods. Most fail to return; those who do are invariably mad, and their reports of what they have seen at the summit make little sense.

The band of Pilgrims to whom Mr. Silverberg directs our attention has better luck. The Wall turns out to be an entire range of mountains offering trial after trial as horrific as any observed by Dante in the Inferno. Many former Pilgrims have ended up in the clutches of monsters capable of stealing one's body, mind and will. The author makes some attempt to distinguish between these monsters, and there are hints that each Pilgrim's fate is determined by his or her character. But since the only Pilgrims we get to know well are those who escape the monsters, the fate of the less fortunate seems more arbitrary than ordained. Higher up the Wall, the obstacles become more subtle; some regions are so pleasant that the Pilgrims are tempted to settle down and forget their mission. What awaits those who persevere is a revelation that calls into question everything they believe (although it will hardly come as a surprise to the seasoned reader of science fiction).

The trouble with Mr. Silverberg's parable is that, for all its length, it ends too soon. I was more interested in learning how the believers deal with the blow to their faith than in following the rather repetitious challenges they must overcome on their way to the summit.

THE POSITRONIC MAN (with Isaac Asimov, 1993)

Publishers Weekly

SOURCE: A review of *The Positronic Man,* in *Publishers Weekly,* Vol. 240, No. 44, November 1, 1993, p. 70.

The third and final collaborative novel from Silverberg and the late Asimov follows Asimov's classic story, "The Bicentennial Man," step by step (whole sentences and paragraphs remain), adding extra scenes for length. The novel chronicles the quest of the robot Andrew Martin (dubbed NDR-113 at the factory) to achieve the rights, privileges, appearance and ultimately even the weaknesses of being fully human. When brought to the home of wealthy politician Gerald Martin, Andrew is little more than a standard household robot, but he quickly develops a remarkable, even artistic, skill in woodworking. He proceeds to stretch his increasingly human-like mind, seeking and winning his freedom and legal rights, grieving as human friends die and he lives on, replacing his robotic parts with organic prostheses of his own design. But he cannot replace his positronic brain, so he must finally appeal to the World Court to be declared human in all respects. Focused on the question of what it means to be human, Asimov's short story is a masterpiece in which the thinness of the background doesn't matter. The absence of a convincing future world or well-developed characters is glaring here. Readers interested in contemplating the human potential of robots would do better to reread the original.

Gerald Jonas

SOURCE: A review of *The Positronic Man,* in *The New York Times Book Review,* November 14, 1993, p. 74.

The Positronic Man, by Isaac Asimov and Robert Silverberg, is a novelization of an Asimov short story, "The Bicentennial Man," which won a Nebula Prize in 1976. Asimov, who died last year, and Mr. Silverberg, who continues to turn out provocative science fiction on his own, also collaborated a few years ago on a novelization of the classic Asimov story *Nightfall.* Like that book, *The Positronic Man* is no improvement on its source.

In the original story, Asimov took one theme of his well-known "Robot" series to a logical conclusion. The household robot NDR-113, known as Andrew to his owners, develops unusual capabilities and aspirations; not only can he create wood carvings of artistic merit, he conceives a longing for the personal freedom that human beings enjoy. Having achieved this freedom by legal means, he begins to replace the virtually indestructible parts of his mechanical body with more fragile but more lifelike substitutes, until only the immortality of his "positronic" brain separates him from what he imagines to be true humanity.

The sole justification that I can see for resurrecting and expanding this neatly contrived parable would be to delve more deeply into NDR-113's death wish. "The imperfections—the weaknesses—the imprecisions—they are the very things which define humans as human," the robot thinks. "And which drive them to transcend their own failings." Far from seizing the opportunity to investigate this premise, the authors take it as a conclusion. Andrew's march toward oblivion is without roadblocks:

"Pain was not an issue for him," we are told. As for second thoughts, Andrew assures himself, "You have achieved the thing you set out to accomplish and you must feel no regrets." And he doesn't, alas.

HOT SKY AT MIDNIGHT (1994)

Publishers Weekly

SOURCE: A review of *Hot Sky at Midnight,* in *Publishers Weekly,* Vol. 240, No. 51, December 20, 1993, pp. 54-5.

Silverberg's latest is his best novel in some time, returning from the extraterrestrial travelogues he offered in **The Face of the Waters** and **Kingdoms of the Wall** to Earth of the relatively near future, which has been polluted almost to uninhabitability. Even in the best areas, people wear breathing masks and inject a product called Screen, which darkens their skin as protection from the sun. Victor Farkas, operative of the megacorporation Kyocera-Merck Ltd., is blind but gifted with hypersensitive "blindsight." He comes to the massive orbital habitat Valparaiso Nuevo in search of a renegade geneticist of legendary skill. On Earth, Nick Rhodes wrestles with a midlife crisis and moral uncertainty as head of Samurai Industries, which is attempting to breed humans that can thrive in the horrendous conditions expected to prevail on Earth. Silverberg focuses on his characters and their ruined world, providing a convincing portrayal of life in a greenhouse effect-cursed future. In the background looms the efforts to save the human race, whether by emigration or transformation. The plot may tie up too neatly, but Silverberg delivers powerful images of a world blighted by ecological abuse, and a satisfying novel as well.

Gerald Jonas

SOURCE: A review of *Hot Sky at Midnight,* in *The New York Times Book Review*, March 13, 1994, p. 30.

It is hard to know what Robert Silverberg had in mind in his latest novel, **Hot Sky at Midnight**. His opening chapters skillfully introduce four promising characters: Juanito, a young hustler who lives on an artificial satellite noted for providing refuge, at a price, to fugitives from Earth; Victor Farkas, a man with no eyes who has been genetically engineered to function with a new sense called "blindsight"; Paul Carpenter, a restless "salary man" who works for a Japanese-run "megacorp," and Nick Rhodes, a restless research director with a drinking problem.

With his customary deftness, Mr. Silverberg sketches in the background. The time is the first half of the 24th century. The Earth is suffering from multiple ecological disasters: the seas are rising, there are crocodiles in San Francisco Bay, the Midwest is a desert and the air has become a "thick soup" of pollution that will be unbreathable in five or six generations. While keeping a steady eye on the bottom line, world-spanning megacorps secretly pursue competing technological solutions to the crisis—a faster-than-light starship drive for escaping the oxygen-depleted Earth and a drastic genetic makeover that will end "the human race's dependence on oxygen."

Having set all these intriguing elements in motion, Mr. Silverberg inexplicably shifts his focus to a group of far less interesting characters—a stereotypical Israeli spy and two women who might be charitably described as postmodern bimbos—and a murky subplot involving terrorists who want to hold Juanito's artificial satellite for ransom. In the end, nothing coheres, and some fine set pieces—Paul Carpenter's tour of duty on an iceberg trawler, Victor Farkas's confrontation with the "gene-splicer" who "worked me over in my mother's womb"—go to waste.

Diane G. Yates

SOURCE: A review of *Hot Sky at Midnight,* in *Voice of Youth Advocates,* Vol. 17, No. 2, June, 1994, p. 101.

Through man's mistreatment of the environment, Earth is gradually becoming too toxic for humans to survive there. The combination of holes in the ozone, the greenhouse effect, and global warming have played havoc with the climate. Two Japanese-run mega-corporations are working on solutions. One, the Samurai, is concentrating on genetic transformation, retrofitting humans to survive in a different environment. The other, Kyocera-Merck, is developing a starship with faster than light engines to allow humanity to escape to the stars.

The plot revolves around two men, friends since childhood. Nick Rhodes is a brilliant scientist who drinks too much, is emotionally involved with a woman who hates his work, and who is agonizing over his part in creating a new genetically different person. Will they still be human if their blood is green and they have gills? Paul Carpenter has slowly moved up the corporate ladder in a variety of different jobs until he makes a bad decision and finds himself cut off from the company and thus life as he has always known it.

Silverberg is an icon of the SF world, but this is far from his best work. In his zeal to remind us that we have little time to stop our headlong rush to destruction, he ignores the elements that make great fiction. Characters are one-dimensional stereotypes, events are too obviously controlled by the author's hand, and the frequent sex scenes seem thrown in to keep the male readers happy. Great cover art will sell it, but I'd rather re-read the wonderful *Lord Valentine* trilogy and pass on this one.

THE MOUNTAINS OF MAJIPOOR (1995)

Publishers Weekly

SOURCE: A review of *The Mountains of Majipoor,* in *Publishers Weekly,* Vol. 242, No. 3, January 16, 1995, p. 444.

Silverberg's fourth Majipoor book–his first in over 10 years—is, like the second novel in this popular fantasy series, *Majipoor Chronicles,* a bildungsroman. Set five centuries after the events in book three, *Valentine Pontifex,* it details the adventures of Prince Harpirias, a young bureaucrat exiled from Castle Mount when he commits an unintentional indiscretion during a hunting expedition. The prince is given a chance to redeem himself by rescuing a group of scientists who have been taken captive by a previously undiscovered, less technologically advanced people whom Harpirias considers "savages." Aided by a Shapeshifter and several others, Harpirias makes several discoveries that startle him much more than they will the reader. While there are moments here that recall the glorious descriptive passages displayed earlier in the series, these are infrequent, and sadder still is the author's apparent lack of interest in his characters. Hissune in *Majipoor Chronicles* and Valentine himself were living creations, but Harpirias and the Shapeshifter seem less full-fledged characters than elements tailored to further the plot. While fans may be grateful for any return to Majipoor, this shadow of a novel doesn't provide the journey they might have hoped for.

Roland Green

SOURCE: A review of *The Mountains of Majipoor,* in *Booklist,* Vol. 91, No. 11, February 1, 1995, p. 993.

Silverberg returns to what is now his best-known creation, the sprawling, complex, exotic world of Majipoor. It is now a thousand years after the time of Lord Valentine, hero of the earlier Majipoor books, and one of his descendants, young Harpirias, accidentally kills a rare and valuable animal belonging to another nobleman. By way of punishment, Harpirias is sent to the snow-covered mountains to ransom an archaeological expedition from the local inhabitants. He is accompanied by a shape-shifting interpreter whose kind is not the most exotic that we encounter in the course of the yarn. This is a modest story, but the marvelously well realized world of Majipoor and Silverberg's graceful prose carry it along in a fashion that most lovers of Majipoor will find highly satisfying.

STARBORNE (1996)

Carl Hays

SOURCE: A review of *Starborne,* in *Booklist,* Vol. 92, No. 18, May 15, 1996, p. 1573.

Like vintage wine, Silverberg's genius continues to improve with age and now yields a profound, masterfully rendered chronicle of humanity's first voyage to the stars. Earth is finally enjoying an era of peace and almost boring contentment when the first mission to colonize a new world is dispatched with a crew of 50 young scientists aboard the starship *Wotan.* As the ship moves faster than the speed of light through a featureless spatial wrinkle called "nospace," crew members maintain earthly contact through a blind telepath named Noelle and probe the worlds they pass for signs of promise. The first planetary landfall is disastrous, however, leaving one crew member dead and Noelle's telepathic link inexplicably fading, which leads to suspicions that something or some entity outside the ship is barring the way. While tapping the limits of sf's deepest philosophical possibilities, Silverberg offers rich and unforgettable characterizations in Noelle and the dour, commanding "year-captain" in another masterpiece that may be savored by sf fans and nonfans alike.

Gerald Jonas

SOURCE: A review of *Starborne,* in *The New York Times Book Review,* June 30, 1996, p. 28.

Starborne, by Robert Silverberg, represents another kind of maturity in science fiction. Mr. Silverberg belongs to the generation of writers who came to prominence just after Asimov and Heinlein. Prolific to a fault, he had to learn over the years to harness his energies to projects worthy of his talent. Despite his many awards and honors, he has never been unequivocally embraced by the science fiction community. This may have something to do with his predilection for downbeat subjects. Two of his best and most characteristic books, *Dying Inside* and *Born with the Dead,* deal respectively with a depressed telepath and the somber bliss of euthanasia.

The dominant mood of *Starborne* is world-weariness. Several centuries from now, humanity has solved all its problems, and so has grown bored with life itself. The healthy, wealthy, exceedingly comfortable people of Earth, in one last effort to revive their vitality, decide to dispatch a starship to look for habitable planets elsewhere in the universe. This is how Mr. Silverberg, who has clearly been there before, describes the mounting of the expedition: "The starship had to be designed and built and tested. Done and done and done. A crew of suitably fearless and adventuresome people had to be assembled. It was. The voyage had to be undertaken. And so it came to pass." Of course, the whole point of establishing a sense of ennui in the early chapters is to prepare us for some revelation, some epiphany, later on. Alas, Mr. Silverberg proves more adept at the setup than the payoff. When one crew member, the blind telepath Noelle, discovers the secret of the universe, Mr. Silverberg, who ought to know better, falls back on pages of stuff like this:

Oh.

She is dazzled by it.

Oh. Oh.

She hears it roaring, the way a furnace might roar. But what a deafening furnace-roar this is! Oh. Oh. Oh. Oh. She hears a crackling too, a hissing, a

sizzling: the sounds of inexorable power unremittingly unleashed.

Too much light! Too much power!

Christy Tyson

SOURCE: A review of *Starborne,* in *Voice of Youth Advocates,* Vol. 19, No. 4, October, 1996, p. 221.

Sit down. Get ready. From the first paragraph of this powerful adventure you know you're in the hands of a master. You are sixteen light years from Earth, traveling through the gray tube of nospace, searching for a possible new home for humanity. A bold quest, yes, but meanwhile the fifty passengers of the Wotan have plenty of time on their hands. Some keep busy with marathon games of "Go," others participate in the casual partnerings at the baths. However, for two of the crew their jobs are their whole lives. The year-captain, a former actor-turned-space-explorer-turned-mystic, is driven to find a place where human life can reignite that creative spark that old Earth's stability and comfort has extinguished. Noelle also stands apart from the rest of the crew. She is a blind telepath, linked with her twin sister on Earth and the ship's only means of "real time" communication with the home planet. But this is just the beginning. Ahead are worlds that promise much but turn out to be strange, unwelcoming, even lethal. Worse, Noelle's link with her sister becomes tenuous, then vanishes completely. The crew's monotony becomes concern, then desperation as they wonder if they will ever find a home at all. Maybe the Wotan will become some kind of nospace Flying Dutchman, endlessly seeking a compatible world that doesn't exist. Maybe they should just forget the whole thing and go home. But maybe Noelle's block is only temporary. Maybe she can re-establish contact after all. Maybe the interference has some external cause. Maybe there's something out there in nospace. Maybe another presence. Maybe angels. Maybe they should try to find out.

Silverberg has never been better than in this stunning combination of space adventure, psychological drama, and metaphysical speculation. Even though he has been writing prolifically since the 50s, he's managed to instill all the sense of wonder and mystery of a first-time discoverer of science fiction. His experience comes through in the deft characterizations, the carefully-paced plot and the sheer inventiveness of each new development. It doesn't get much better than this for fans of the genre or for first-time science fiction readers. This is the genre at its finest. Not to be missed!

📖 *SORCERERS OF MAJIPOOR* (1997)

Roland Green

SOURCE: A review of *Sorcerers of Majipoor,* in *Booklist,* Vol. 93, Nos. 19 & 20, June 1 & 15, 1997, p. 1620.

In his new novel, Silverberg returns to his most successful creation, the gigantic, metal-poor world of Majipoor. Nearly twice as long as *The Mountains of Majipoor* (1995), its immediate series predecessor, *Sorcerers* retreats to 1,000 years before the time of Lord Valentine—hence, a full 2,000 years before *Mountains*. In the Fifty Cities of Castle Mount, the aged Pontifex Prankipin, a renowned statesman, is dying. He will be a hard act to follow, but Coronal Lord Confalume, next in line to be pontifex, is less than happy over the fact that his successor as coronal is Prince Prestimion, who is better known as a hunter than as a courtier. There is, however, more to the prince than meets the eye, and indeed, an oracle has called him to follow in Prankipin's footsteps as a mover and shaker, and he rises splendidly to the prophecy. This novel has more sorcery and court intrigue than action, but it is not slow paced. Moreover, Silverberg uses the length of this yarn to develop both major and minor characters. As for the setting, Majipoor is already so well developed that Silverberg can drop almost any sort of story into it. The horde of readers who know and love it will swarm library shelves for this book.

Nancy K. Wallace

SOURCE: A review of *Sorcerers of Majipoor,* in *Voice of Youth Advocates,* Vol. 21, No. 1, April, 1998, pp. 60-1.

Pontifex Prankipin and Coronal Confalume rule Majipoor; but it is Majipoor's sorcerers and mages who predict its future, alter its past, and manipulate its present. Upon Prankipin's death, Confalume succeeds him. Against all ancient tradition, Confalume's son, Korsibar, urged on by his twin sister, Thismet, unlawfully seizes the crown and declares himself "Coronal." Prince Prestimion, the legitimate heir to the throne, is understandably upset and even though he tries hard to accept Korsibar's new reign, he is ultimately unable to bend his knee to the man who usurped his crown. Thrown into prison as a traitor, Prestimion's anger and frustration grow. Backed by loyal supporters, he is finally freed and wages a long and bloody war against his rival, which shakes peaceful Majipoor to its roots.

Initially a bit short on action, this novel's momentum inexorably increases toward a climactic finish. It follows two men's rise to power: one pushed inevitably toward greatness by an ambitious sister and his opportunistic mages; the other resisting magic's seductive lure until he is forced to use its power to win a war that is tearing his country apart. Underlying everything is the validity of Majipoor itself—Silverberg's creation takes on a life of its own, once again, and makes us a part of it.

THE ALIEN YEARS (1998)

Publishers Weekly

SOURCE: A review of *The Alien Years,* in *Publishers Weekly,* Vol. 245, No. 26, June 29, 1998, p. 40.

Silverberg returns to his 1986 short story "**The Pardoner's Tale**" as the inspiration for this sobering and frightening novel of extraterrestrial invasion. The narrative opens seven years hence, with the arrival of alien spaceships on Earth, an event that has a devastating effect on the Carmichael family. Pilot Michael Carmichael is killed trying to fight the huge fire storms in Los Angeles that erupt when the alien ships land; his wife, Cindy, leaps at the chance to go aboard one of the UFOs and become an interpreter for the "Entities"; and his brother, Colonel Anson Carmichael, is summoned by Washington to help cope with the situation. Before there is time to react, however, the aliens' intent becomes known as they disrupt all electricity and plunge civilization back into the Dark Ages. Silverberg's story is clear-eyed, credible and occasionally bleak. Faced with an omnipotent enemy, mankind's only alternative is to refuse to capitulate and to attempt to endure. Isolated and relatively safe in their mountain ranch, the extended Carmichael clan tries to go on with their lives while working on ways to resist their oppressors. Silverberg's technique of leap-frogging several years ahead between chapters furthers momentum, and while the enemy in his story is disturbingly inhuman, the focus of the tale is the humanity of his characters and their efforts to keep hope alive. The novel's ending seems arbitrary, but Silverberg's rich characters, his dead-on target vision of modern society, his mastery at building tension—all are in evidence in this notable outing from one of the very best.

Gerald Jonas

SOURCE: A review of *The Alien Years,* in *The New York Times Book Review,* October 4, 1998, p. 30.

In *The Alien Years*, Robert Silverberg wastes no time putting the unknown on a collision course with humanity. The aliens who invade Earth with devastating effect on the opening page manifest no recognizable pattern of behavior. They communicate with humans only through the universal language of pain. But their ultimate purpose, if they have one beyond mortifying human pride, remains as unguessable as their incentive for erecting a great wall around Los Angeles or rearranging the circle of monoliths at Stonehenge.

Arrayed against them, in the face of all odds, is the Carmichael clan, led by Col. Anson Carmichael 3d, a man unversed in the subtleties of human emotions but a genius at keeping alive his hatred without letting it subvert his judgment.

To stay sane, Colonel Carmichael and his descendants take the long view, and so does Silverberg. As one generation of Carmichaels gives way to the next with no great success against the aliens, resistance seems ever more futile; and a suspicion forms that the big question posed by the alien presence—what do they want from us?—may never be answered. A similar nonrevelation lay at the heart of Arkady and Boris Strugatsky's 1972 classic "Roadside Picnic" (which inspired the 1979 movie "Stalker"). But where the Strugatskys offered an outrageous metaphor to help readers grasp the ungraspable—comparing a mess of deadly but tantalizing alien artifacts to rubbish from an alien rest stop, the interstellar equivalent of a "roadside picnic"—Silverberg offers no help at all. In their stark, undifferentiated alienness, his aliens turn out to be not very interesting.

This shifts the spotlight to the Carmichael clan. Enough stresses and strains appear in the family saga to keep the principal characters from becoming stereotypes of dauntless resistance. Measured against the classic Robert A. Heinlein heroes of the 1940s and 50s, Silverberg's Carmichaels are paragons of self-reflection. But is this sufficient reason to track their generational shifts in attitude toward a stubbornly unknowable menace over 428 pages? Despite the considerable pleasures of Silverberg's lucid prose, this story might have been better told at half the length.

📖 *LEGENDS* (editor, 1998)

Publishers Weekly

SOURCE: A review of *Legends,* in *Publishers Weekly,* Vol. 245, No. 38, September 21, 1998, p. 78.

Microcosmic glimpses of broadly imagined worlds and their larger-than-life characters distinguish this hefty volume of heavyweight fantasy. Silverberg collects 11 previously unpublished short "novels" by genre celebrities, each a window on a sprawling saga that has shaped the way modern fantasy fiction is written and read. Stephen King weighs in with "The Little Sisters of Eluria," set early in the Dark Tower saga and deftly weaving threads of horror, quest fantasy and the western into a dangerous snare for his indefatigable gunslinger, Roland of Gilead. Ursula K. Le Guin contributes "Dragonfly," a tale about a young woman who would be a wizard that offers a savvy dissection of the sexual politics that govern Le Guin's Earthsea empire. Neo-Arthurian fantasy gets its due in George RR Martin's "The Hedge Knight," a prequel to the Song of Ice and Fire series. Only a sliver of fantasy insinuates Silverberg's own "**The Seventh Shrine,**" a Majipoor murder mystery that becomes a fascinating exploration of clashing cultures. Although most of the selections are sober sidebars to serious literary fantasy cycles, Terry Pratchett's "The Sea and Little Fishes" is a giddy Discworld romp that pits cantankerous witch Granny Weatherwax against her crone cronies, and Orson Scott Card's "Grinning Man" is corn-fed tall talk in which Alvin Maker outwits a crooked miller in the alternate America of Hatrick River. Some entries, among them Raymond E. Feist's Riftwar tale "The Wood Boy" and Anne McCaffrey's "Runner of Pern," shine only as light glosses on their authors' earlier achievements. Still, there's enough color, vitality and bravura displays of mythmaking in this rich sampler, which also includes tales by Terry Goodkind, Tad Williams and Robert Jordan, to sate faithful fans and nurture new readers on the stuff of legends still being created.

Additional coverage of Silverberg's life and career is contained in the following sources published by The Gale Group: *Authors and Artists for Young Adults,* **Vol. 24;** *Contemporary Authors New Revision Series,* **Vol. 36;** *Contemporary Literary Criticism,* **Vol 7;** *Dictionary of Literary Biography,* **Vol. 8;** *Major Authors and Illustrators for Children and Young Adults; Major Twentieth Century Children's Writers,* **Vol. 1; and** *Something about the Author,* **Vols. 13, 91, 104.**

Jessie Willcox Smith

1863-1935

American illustrator of fiction, poetry, and picture books.

Major works include *The Book of the Child* (written by Mabel Humphrey, with Elizabeth Shippen Green; 1903), *A Child's Garden of Verses* (written by Robert Louis Stevenson, 1905), *A Child's Book of Old Verses* (compiled by Smith, 1910), *The Jessie Willcox Smith Mother Goose: A Careful and Full Selection of the Rhymes* (1914), *The Water-Babies* (written by Charles Kingsley, 1916).

Major works about the author include *The Studios at Cogslea* (by Catherine Connell Stryker, 1976), *Jessie Willcox Smith,* (by S. Michael Schnessel, 1977), *The Subject Was Children: The Art of Jessie Willcox Smith* (by Gene Mitchell, 1979), *Jessie Willcox Smith: A Bibliography* (by Edward D. Nudelman, 1989), *Jessie Willcox Smith: American Illustrator* (by Edward D. Nudelman, 1990).

INTRODUCTION

Called "a multifaceted artist of immeasurable abilities" and "a woman who dearly and truly loved children" by Marilyn Nuhn in *Hobbies,* Smith is considered one of the only American women illustrators of her generation to have attained critical, popular, and financial success; in addition, she was a highly regarded portrait painter, commercial artist, and humanitarian. Smith illustrated approximately forty books for both adults and children, but is best known as an illustrator of classic stories and verse for a young audience. She provided the pictures for works by such authors as Henry Wadsworth Longfellow, Louisa May Alcott, Robert Louis Stevenson, Frances Hodgson Burnett, Clement Clarke Moore, George MacDonald, Johanna Spyri, and Charles Kingsley, and she illustrated such favorite books for children as *Little Women, Heidi, A Child's Garden of Verses,* and *The Water-Babies,* as well as the rhymes of Mother Goose. In addition, Smith edited an anthology of children's verse and created hundreds of magazine covers that depict popular child characters from literature such as Alice in Wonderland, Hans Brinker, and David Copperfield. In a career that spanned fifty years, she developed a reputation as an artist of versatility, charm, and technical skill, one who defined a view of childhood that came to typify the way that children were often perceived in the early twentieth century. Smith used a variety of media—most frequently watercolor, charcoal, and oil—to picture children in both real and imaginary settings, and she was acknowledged as both a naturalistic painter and a fantasist. Her illustrations capture the young as they played, studied, and dreamed, and she presents her subjects as innocent, winsome, and natural beings who are fascinated with the world around them. Smith became known for drawing and painting children who were always precious

even when they were being slightly naughty. Moreover, she often portrayed the tender interaction of mothers and children: her works are recognized for providing an idealized image of motherhood and childhood, one that acted as an homage to American motherhood while helping to define societal aspirations for idyllic, wholesome family life and sweet, happy children.

As an artist, Smith is credited with successfully evolving her style throughout her career. She worked in both color and black and white and created line drawings and color plates. Initially, Smith used dark borders to highlight bright colors, while later she muted her colors and softened her lines for a more ethereal effect. Working with artboard, canvas, and textured paper, she created works noted for their strong decorative elements. Smith's drawings and paintings are often called impressionistic, and she was influenced by the French Impressionists as well as by the French illustrator M. Boutet de Monvel, the American artist Mary Cassatt, the Pre-Raphaelite painters, and the flat, patterned look of Japanese woodcuts. In working with her child subjects, Smith encouraged natural movement. She often painted children at play outdoors, frequently in her own garden. She also told her subjects fairy stories to hold their attention and used a camera to record them for further study. Noted for the optimistic, pleasant quality of her work, Smith is often praised for bringing out the best in her subjects.

Biographical Information

It has been suggested that Smith's focus on idealized mothers and children was her way of recreating the kind of loving relationship that she desired as a child. Born in Philadelphia, Smith was the daughter of Charles Henry Smith, an investment broker, and Katherine Dewitt Willcox. The youngest in her family, which also included two sisters and two brothers, Smith did not demonstrate any particular artistic ability while growing up; however, she was always interested in children. Smith completed her elementary and high school education at private schools. At sixteen, she was sent to Cincinnati, where she studied to become a kindergarten teacher. When she was seventeen, an aunt asked Smith to act as a chaperone for her cousin, an advanced art student who was giving drawing lessons to a young teacher in a boys' school so that he could illustrate his lessons on the blackboard. Smith decided to attempt a drawing of a lamp. To her great surprise, her sketch was applauded by both her cousin and her mother, who was an illustrator. On the strength of that sketch, Smith was persuaded to drop teaching in order to study art. Smith stated in an essay for *Contemporary Illustrators of Children's Books,* "That lamp was the turning point in my life, and has shed its light before me ever since." Smith had a brief, but ultimately unsuccessful stint as a sculptor before determining her true talent lay in painting.

In 1885, Smith enrolled in Philadelphia's School of Design for Women. The next year, she transferred to the Pennsylvania Academy of Fine Arts, where she studied under the talented but demanding artist Thomas Eakins. Shortly thereafter, she sold her first picture, an advertisement for Ivory Soap; her first illustration was published in 1888 in the popular children's magazine *St. Nicholas.* She also took a job with *Ladies' Home Journal,* illustrating advertisements and borders for editorials. In 1892, Smith's first pictures appeared in book form: black-and-white illustrations for a work titled *Now and Then.* Two years later, Smith enrolled in an afternoon illustration class at the Drexel Institute of Art, Science, and Industry in Philadelphia. Her instructor was Howard Pyle, a highly respected artist and educator who was to become Smith's mentor. Pyle gave Smith an appreciation for color, as well as a commercial forum for her art. In addition, he taught Smith the importance of mentally projecting herself into a story in order to create illustrations for it. Pyle often arranged with publishers to have illustrations for new books done by his most outstanding students. In 1897, he invited Smith and Violet Oakley to illustrate an edition of Longfellow's poem *Evangeline;* each artist contributed five color plates to the volume, which was published the next year. After leaving Drexel, Smith was offered a teaching position, but turned it down because she was receiving so many commissions. In 1901, she

moved to an inn with fellow artists Oakley and Elizabeth Shippen Green. Two years later, Smith and Green published a calendar called *The Child;* its success led to the publication of *The Book of the Child,* which contained text by Mabel Humphrey. *The Book of the Child* gave national attention to both Smith and Green. In 1905, Smith moved with Green, Oakley, and another friend, Henrietta Cozen, to a farm in Chestnut Hill, Pennsylvania, which they christened Cogslea; the name was derived from the first initials of the farm's occupants. In the same year, Smith's illustrations for Robert Louis Stevenson's *A Child's Garden of Verses* were published to great acclaim. Her success allowed Smith to participate actively in the conceptualization of her works: she selected authors for whom to illustrate or to write texts for her drawings, and she also designed the formats for several of her works.

For the next twenty years, Smith continued to illustrate books, to provide artwork for periodicals and advertisements, and to create posters and postcards. As an illustrator for magazines, she contributed pictures to the *Century, Scribner's Magazine, Collier's Weekly, Woman's Home Companion,* and *Harper's,* among others. Smith worked for almost every women's magazine in the United States; however, perhaps her most successful association was with *Good Housekeeping,* for which she drew over two hundred covers in just fifteen years. As a commercial artist, Smith had a long affiliation with Proctor & Gamble, and she produced thousands of illustrations for advertisements for that company's Ivory Soap; she also did ads for such products as Kodak cameras, Cream of Wheat cereal, and Fleischman's yeast. In 1910, Smith compiled *A Child's Book of Old Verses,* a collection that included familiar traditional rhymes, as well as more contemporary selections by Lewis Carroll, Kate Greenaway, and Robert Louis Stevenson. In 1914, the artist and Henrietta Couzens moved to Cogshill, a large house and studio on a hill overlooking Cogslea. Smith published one of her most popular works, *The Jessie Willcox Smith Mother Goose,* in the same year. The next decade saw the publication of several of Smith's most well-received books for children: Louisa May Alcott's *Little Women* (1915), George MacDonald's *At the Back of the North Wind* (1919) and *The Princess and the Goblin* (1920), Johanna Spyri's *Heidi,* and Charles Kingsley's *The Water-Babies.* The latter is generally considered to contain her finest art; recognizing the quality of her work, Smith donated her originals from *The Water-Babies* to the Library of Congress.

In 1925, Smith decided to devote more time to portrait painting, an ambition that she had sustained since she was a young art student. Consequently, Smith stopped contributing illustrations to books; however, she continued her association with *Good Housekeeping* almost until her death. Smith also became known as a humanitarian, donating to various charities, especially those relating to children, and contributing posters for world relief and other organizations; for example, she designed posters for the Welfare Federation and the Liberty Loan drives. The most financially successful female illustrator of her day, friends called Smith "The Mint." She assumed fiscal responsibility for a brother, an elderly aunt, and for eleven children, including two of her sister's. Although Smith loved children, she never married. In 1933, Smith went on a trip to Europe; while overseas, she became ill and had to return home. In 1935, Smith died at Cogshill from arteriosclerosis and nephritis.

Critical Reception

Smith is considered an artist of great originality as well as an important interpreter of child life. Praised for the aesthetic merits of her works, she is also lauded for her draftsmanship and her knowledge of human anatomy; her drawings of hands are considered especially noteworthy. She is further recognized for her affinity with and insight into children and for portraying them with sensitivity, perception, and humor. In her day, Smith was extremely popular. Reproductions of her works decorated homes, nurseries and schoolrooms internationally, and she is credited with helping to bring fine art to the masses through her books, calendars, posters, and advertisements. Her works were acknowledged for their appeal to children, who saw themselves reflected in her art, and to adults, who felt the emotional resonance of her approach to childhood. In 1912, Algernon Tassin of the *Bookman* wrote of Smith, "More . . . than anyone else she can make you feel how serious to themselves are the little souls of children." Currently, Smith is regarded as an illustrator who created work that, although occasionally too sentimental, possesses strong vitality and narrative quality while capturing an important social viewpoint. In addition, Smith is acknowledged as being a groundbreaking female role model, a woman who achieved incredible success in a male-dominated field through talent and initiative. Marilyn Nuhn of *Hobbies* said, "Only a handful of women illustrators have ever attained artistic, commercial, and financial success in a field long dominated by men. . . . [U]nquestionably the greatest was Jessie Willcox Smith." Nuhn added, "[S]he caught the inquisitive, exploring enchantment of children. She painted them with love and affection, as if they were her own." In his biography *The Subject Was Children,* Gene Mitchell stated, "She had a remarkable insight into what set the children's world apart from that of adults, and she possessed a unique ability to place these images pleasingly before us. Her art began where that of her contemporaries left off." Mitchell concluded, "To have reached the peak of success, as Smith did, was an immense accomplishment, not only for herself but for other members of her sex as well."

Awards

Smith received a number of awards during her lifetime. While a student at the School of Design for Women, she received the George W. Childs Gold Medal for the best illustration of the year. In 1901, she won the Boston Chickering Hall Programme Prize as well as first prize from Proctor & Gamble for her drawing "Child Washing." Smith received the Bronze Medal at the Charleston Exposition in 1902. In 1903, she received the Mary Smith Prize at the Pennsylvania Academy of Fine Arts; the next year, she won the Silver Medal for illustration at the St. Louis International Exposition. In 1911, Smith received the Beck Prize from the Philadelphia Water Color Club. She won the Silver Medal for Watercolors at the San Francisco Panama-Pacific Exhibition in 1915. In 1925, an exhibition of Smith's illustrations and portraits was held at the Philadelphia Art Alliance. The 1968 edition of *Little Women* was bestowed the Lewis Carroll Shelf Award in 1969.

AUTHOR'S COMMENTARY

Jessie Willcox Smith

SOURCE: "Jessie Willcox Smith: An Autobiographical Sketch," in *The Subject Was Children: The Art of Jessie Willcox Smith,* by Gene Mitchell, Dutton, 1979, pp. 4-5.

[*The following article was originally printed in* Good Housekeeping, *October, 1917.*]

People probably care more about how I get that "particular look in children's faces" than where I was born; so I will begin this little autobiography backward, and tell where I was born last.

The way I do it is to tell fairy-stories—tell them with great animation! A child will always look directly at any one who is telling a story; so while I paint, I tell tales marvelous to hear. But to paint with half one's mind, and tell a thrilling, eye-opening tale with the other half is an art I have not fully conquered even yet. Alas, the resplendent Cinderella sometimes stops halfway down the stairs, slipper and all, while I am considering the subtle curve in the outline of the listener's charming, enthralled little face.

As for myself, when a child, I never showed any artistic ability whatever. The margins of my schoolbooks were perfectly clean and unsullied with any virgin attempts at drawing, and it was not until I was seventeen years old—and studying to be a kindergarten teacher—that I discovered, quite by accident, that I had entirely mistaken my vocation. Pictures had always had a wonderful fascination for me, but never as anything belonging to my world. I would spend hours at the galleries wondering and worshiping, but how they were made was a deep mystery. I never even expected to know, until one happy day I was asked by my cousin—a young girl like myself, but quite an advanced art student—if I would chaperon her while she was teaching a friend of hers to draw. The friend was a young professor in a boy's school who was anxious to learn enough drawing to illustrate on the blackboard his talks to the boys under his tutelage. So our class met in the evening.

From The Jessie Willcox Smith Mother Goose, *illustrated by Jessie Willcox Smith.*

Friday, I remember it was—not a propitious day on which to discover one's life work. We sat at a large center-table on which a student-lamp was burning, and possibly because that was the most obvious thing in the room, our teacher suggested that we draw the lamp. It would be difficult to give a harder problem to two persons absolutely ignorant of the first rudiments of drawing and perspective. However, it was a case of "Where ignorance is bliss," and we bravely went to work. After two nerve-racking, intense evenings, the young professor gave up in deep disgust—while I was told to stop teaching kindergarten—at which, I may as well confess, I was not making a brilliant success—and go to art school. This I did, with deep gratitude in my heart to that young professor who wanted to learn drawing. I began almost at once to draw little things for the children's magazines, and with what poignant memory do I recall my very first thrill—when *St. Nicholas* accepted a drawing I submitted.

After a few years of study and work, I joined a class that Howard Pyle was starting at the Drexel Institute. He seemed to wipe away all the cobwebs and confusions that so beset the path of the art-student, and with his inspiration and practical help, I was soon in the full tide

of book illustration. In order to give his students the stimulus of real work, he had an arrangement with some publishers by which they gave him books to be illustrated by his pupils, he, of course, to be responsible for the quality of the work. These books were given to the class for competition, and the student who submitted the best drawing was given the book to illustrate.

The first book that was allotted to me happened to be a thrilling story about Indians—a regular boy's book. I knew very little about Indians, and was not particularly interested in them, but with the aid of a friend who had a wonderful collection of Indian curios, and with very hard work on my part, I managed to turn out a fairly presentable set of drawings. At all events, they pleased the publishers, and I was much relieved. Later I was somewhat dismayed when a second book came, also about Indians, with the request that it be given me to illustrate. I was not by way of refusing a manuscript in those days, so I began another struggle with Indians, the result of which also met with the approval of the publishers. But when this was promptly followed by a third Indian book, I felt I must speak or forever after be condemned to paint Indians. So I wrote to the publishers that I did not know much about Indians and that if they had just an every-day book about children, I thought I could do it better. I was immediately rewarded with one of Louisa M. Alcott's stories, and a letter saying they were glad to know I did other things, as they had supposed Indians were my specialty!

So, after two narrow escapes from being forced into the wrong channel—first that of teacher, and second of becoming an Indian specialist—I came into my own, and ever since it has been one long joyous road along which troop delightful children—happy children, sad children, thoughtful children, and above all wondering, imaginative children, who give to their charmingly original thoughts a delicious quaintness of expression. I love to paint them all—all but noisy, rowdy, ill-mannered children—who are often like this, poor, little things, through no fault of their own.

I have lived in interesting old country places where children love to come. There were all sorts of fascinating nooks and corners for them to play in, and while they were playing and having a perfect time, I would watch and study them, and try to get them to take unconsciously the positions that I happened to be wanting for a picture. All the models I have ever had for my illustrations are just the adorable children of my kind friends, who would lend them to me for a little while. Such a thing as a paid and trained child model is an abomination and a travesty on childhood—a poor little crushed and scared unnatural atom, automatically taking the pose and keeping it in a spiritless, lifeless manner. The professional child model is usually a horribly self-conscious, overdressed child whose fond parents proudly insist that he or she is just what you want, and give a list of the people for whom he or she has posed.

Many of my portraits are painted out-of-doors. Out-of-doors seems the natural background for childhood. Given leaves, and flowers, and sunshine, which is theirs by right, their little faces glow in the full light as though illumined from within. Heavy draperies and dark shadows, with the strong, concentrated studio light, are not expressive of childhood to me. I want children under the blue sky, in the shining radiance and joy which is their birthright, and with the flowers of God's earth, of which they are only a higher bloom, at their feet.

Now I mustn't forget to tell where I was born. My parents were of New England, but I was born in Philadelphia, my childhood was spent here, I was educated here, and have done all my art-studying here. And here I have my home.

Jessie Willcox Smith

SOURCE: "As I Know Children from Painting Them," in *American Childhood*, Vol. 14, No. 4, December, 1927, pp. 5-6, 69, 71.

That artists prefer always to paint pretty children is an idea prevalent among many people. Parents, even, seldom think of having a portrait painted of any but a beautiful child. But beauty, mere beauty, in a child, is to my mind too apt to be doll-like. I much prefer individuality, some quaintness of manner, or a taking characteristic peculiar to the child. In painting a portrait, one's greatest difficulty is overcome if one can discover such qualities and fix them on canvas. You then find you have a soul behind the big child eyes that look at you so solemnly and seriously. People often ask me, "Why don't you make your children pretty?" And I always answer, "Because all children are not perfect in feature. I try to make them as I see them, and sweetness—even mischievousness—appeal to me more than beauty."

How do I manage to keep young children quiet long enough to paint them? Well, the fact is that I have never yet been able to get little children to "hold a pose," except on one occasion, when I hired a small girl of five years from a family that made "posing for artists" a business. They could supply all ages, from babies to grandmothers. A wonderful family, that. This little girl was to pose for one of the illustrations for *The Princess and the Goblin*. I first told her the story, as I always do, to create an interest. Then I put her in the pose desired. There she stood, not moving a muscle or winking an eyelid, but in a perfectly mechanical way, all interest, all spontaneity gone. She looked frightened, wan, and old. She had been trained to hold a pose, and she did it. I fear a severe punishment loomed in the background of her imagination if she moved. Such a lifeless, spiritless child was no use to me. I would rather have had her handling everything in the room, and asking a million questions as they usually do.

In despair, I finally opened my studio door on to the sunny outdoors, with its garden in the distance. "Go and play," I told her. "Forget that you have come to pose."

After that I borrowed my friends' children, and got them interested in pretending they were the different characters in the story I was illustrating. While they were having a beautiful time, acting out their creations, I was able to catch fleeting glimpses of what I wanted. It was natural. As soon as a child knows he is posing, he becomes stiff and self-conscious. And that is the end of everything. Of course, trying to draw children in full action has its difficulties. But with considerable knowledge of the anatomy of a child, and a trained memory for poses and actions, plus a sketchbook, I somehow am able to get what I want.

Posing a child for a portrait is quite another matter, and takes different handling. While an illustration for a story often calls for action in the pose, a portrait, in which the likeness is the essential characteristic, demands that the child be quiet. The only way to accomplish this and still have him look at you is to tell him stories.

In my younger days, I could tell thrilling fairy tales, and paint at the same time. But I find now that either the story or the painting stops without my knowing it, generally the story, and I am recalled from the absorbing question of color, values, and light, by a little voice saying, "And what happened then?" Children of five years will listen very well to stories read to them, but at three years the stories must be told and dramatized in a way to hold their attention. The fact that I am painting him does not interest a child under five years in the least. After that age he takes considerable notice, and often makes very intelligent remarks. By the time he is seven or eight years old, he is trying to help and wanting to look at the canvas every few moments.

I have often observed that a child of two or three years has no idea what he looks like. I will point to my painting, and ask him, "Who is it?" and he is utterly blank. But his brother can tell you at once whom I am painting. The shy child gives me no difficulty. He is quiet, and often very appealing. The restless child can be managed if you can attract his interest. Doing this is really the vital thing with all of them, holding their interest so that they forget to be either shy, or restless, boisterous, or wilful.

The stubborn child is perhaps the most difficult. When he persistently presents to me the back of his head, and nothing that I can do will make him turn around, I decide that I am too busy to discipline him; that this is his mother's prerogative. His portrait is not painted. Some children are just contrary. If they know I want them to look in a certain direction, that is the one spot they will avoid. Or if I ask them to keep the head still, while I am painting the eyes, the head immediately begins to turn and wag. Then I say, "Now, John, I am going to paint your shoes, so please keep your feet still," and as the feet begin to swing, I have a good chance to paint the head, which is now at rest.

Once a sitting had been arranged for a boy of four years, a high-strung, excitable child. He arrived at the appointed hour, accompanied by his mother, his aunt, a nurse, and his older brother. Bringing up the rear was the chauffeur, his arms full of new toys, shining and mechanical, that went top-speed all over the studio floor. I looked aghast at the cavalcade. The child to be painted was already down on the floor, flushed with excitement and starting off the toys. The other boy was shouting loudly as he commanded my model what to do. There was no question in my mind what to do! I looked at the young mother who had brought all these things and people to help in entertaining the boy. She seemed, in her little short skirt, like an older sister of the children.

"Please take all these toys away," I said. "I would like everyone to leave, except the child and his nurse." It took some time to get him over his disappointment, as he saw his toys going away. But his nurse was a wise and a sensible woman, and we soon had him sitting quietly, listening to a fairy tale.

On another occasion, I was asked to paint a little boy of about two or three years. His mother wanted him on his kiddy-car, to which he was devoted. She said he would sit on it by the hour. No trouble at all. She was perfectly right. But in order to keep him there, the kiddy-car had to be in motion. If it was still for half a minute, he got right off. So I cleared a big space in the studio, and settled myself with my easel in its center. I put a large chalk mark on the floor in a place where the light was good, and the background what I wanted. "Now," I said, "we will play a game. You ride all around me, and when you get to this spot," pointing to the chalk mark, "look at me and smile. Mother will count to see if you can do it ten times without once forgetting to look at me." The method proved highly successful, and the entire portrait was painted in this manner.

Most children can be interested in any quiet way, with a book, pictures or simple toys. But sometimes one finds a child who will not respond to any of them, and then it often takes some time to find what his interest is. If he is a boy, it is safe to say, "automobiles." For instance, there was a little fellow of three years posing for me. He was restless and fretful. Nothing held his attention until I asked him how he came to the studio. His face lighted up at once, and he said, "In the Marmon." Then he went on to tell me how much better he liked the Marmon than the Cadillac. From then on there was no more trouble. I was able to work for some time, while he talked about his enthusiasm for automobiles.

I began painting children because they interested me more than grown people or landscapes. I never drew a child in my student days, but always wanted to. Before I studied art, I spent a year teaching kindergarten. I knew I wanted to do something with children, but never thought of painting them until an artist friend saw a sketch I had made. She insisted that I stop teaching, and go to an art school. This I did, but for three years I never drew a child.

As soon as I had any time to myself, I naturally turned to children again, and made a few drawings which I sent to different magazines. And I have never had an idle moment since, although that was nearly thirty years ago. My first little drawings were published in *St. Nicholas;* then Scribner kept me busy for some years; and ever since, I have worked for all the various magazines, and have illustrated many children's books.

Of all the illustrations I have done, I think, perhaps, I like best those for Kingsley's *The Water-Babies,* or, to go even farther back, Stevenson's *Child's Garden of Verses,* and *At the Back of the North Wind,* a charming fairy tale by George MacDonald, and a series of *The Children of Dickens.* The subject-matter of the stories appealed tremendously to my imagination. I felt them very strongly, and that always makes for good work.

The present-day paintings of children that I like above all others are those done by Abbott Thayer. He is not modern—he is eternal—and his children have souls, minds, and noble beauty. Among the illustrators of children, it is not so easy to choose. The one, perhaps, who gives me the most joy, is Ernest Shepard, who made the drawings for *When We Were Very Young.* I have always loved the child paintings of Reynolds. His "Age of Innocence," and "Little Miss O'Brien" are sweet, natural, and unstudied. Alfred Stevens painted some children in about the 1850 period who have every characteristic we want to see in childhood.

The one quality that seems to me an essential in an attractive child is unself-consciousness, if this is accompanied by sweetness and good manners. I ask nothing more. I have no objection to beauty, but it is never essential.

Jessie Willcox Smith

SOURCE: In *Contemporary Illustrators of Children's Books,* compiled by Bertha E. Mahony and Elinor Whitney, The Bookshop for Boys and Girls, 1930, pp. 68-9.

It was quite by accident, when I was about seventeen years old, that I discovered I had any ability or talent for drawing. I was studying to be a kindergarten teacher. Children had always attracted and interested me and I naturally turned to them when selecting my life's work—but fate had other plans!

A young friend of my own age who was studying art had been asked by a friend of hers, a teacher in a boys' school, if she would give him some lessons in drawing. He wanted to be able to demonstrate talks to his boys on the blackboard. She spoke to her mother about it (which shows we were not living in this day and generation) and her mother consented, but suggested she make me join the class—"just for propriety's sake."

We had our first lesson that evening and were given to draw—of all things for beginners—a student lamp that stood on the table before us. I had literally never drawn an object from life before, but was perfectly unconcerned, as success or failure meant nothing, and I fully looked for failure. Much to my surprise and the young man's chagrin, my student lamp was a brilliant success—his might have passed for one in a modernistic exhibition of today, but certainly not back in the "gay nineties." That lamp was the turning point in my life, and has shed its light before me ever since. I feel profoundly grateful to it still.

Kindergarten was uphill work, but from the moment that I began studying in the Academy of Fine Arts in Philadelphia, which I did the following year, I have never had one moment that I should call "uphill." Difficult, exacting and constant? Yes. But always thrilling and absorbing, with something ahead that one was sure one could do better.

My interest and love of children and my close observation of them during my year in kindergarten stood me in good stead. When I had finished my early training, I began to make drawings for *St. Nicholas* and other children's magazines and then had the good fortune to be able to study under Howard Pyle. I owe a great debt to him. He made many things clear and through him I illustrated my first book and many others.

Busy years have passed since then, with book and magazine illustrations, and now, except for the covers of *Good Housekeeping,* my work is entirely portrait painting of children.

GENERAL COMMENTARY

Harrison S. Morris

SOURCE: "Jessie Willcox Smith," in *The Book Buyer,* Vol. XXIV, No. 3, April, 1902, pp. 201-02, 204-05.

There is so much in common between the members of that group of very clever young women who hang out modest shingles at 1523 Chestnut Street, Philadelphia, that when you have said praiseful things of one you have said them of all. The kind of work with pen and brush they do, the training they have had, the aims they express, are close allied; and they live out their daily artistic lives under one roof in the gentle camaraderie of some Old World "school," a band of independent partners in talent who have no time for rivalries and who would admit none if they had.

Perhaps the salient force of the group is, however, that, notwithstanding kindred impulses and common gifts, each shows a sturdy habit of being a person, which gives dignity and poise to her own productions much as they happen to be like the rest. In Jessie Willcox Smith this is marked. She may, like children of a clan, have the family nose, but her artistic features are distinctly her own. . . .

Jessie Willcox Smith's particularity is the decorative use of every-day subjects. She paints or draws in broad flat masses and is almost Japanesque in her use of the planes of her composition. Perhaps she has this trait from Mr. Pyle, who likes to force his design beyond the picture, thus to give width and openness, or she may take it legitimately from the decorative impulses now in the air. That her method is a quite individual one, like, but distinct, from that of her comrades, will be evident to every eye that sees more in illustration than simply a device to carry the text. Such, indeed, it used to be, but nowadays it is different. As a learned editor said to me not long ago, "You know I want enough text to carry the pictures." Illustration has outstripped its parent and makes the pace.

Dealing with subjects like "Rappacini's Daughter" and a "New England Village," by Nathaniel Hawthorne, Miss Smith has produced quite a new type of interpretation of the text. Of old this was a convention in which rather simpering figures appeared in a landscape or interior more or less unreal, as the composition or space at command required the sacrifice of truth. You were willing to accept the pictures in most books as a convenient resting-place, scarcely as a help in forming ideals of the characters, never as a needful adjunct to the story. Indeed, I have not got over feeling illustrations to a story a hindrance, simply because they used to be so often so. But in such work as this of Miss Smith and of her preceptors and her friends there are sympathy and reality which, apart even from the book, give pleasure, and, in conjunction with the text, are not only an embellishment, but a critical interpretation. Miss Smith's people are the people of the streets, the towns, the shops. Her houses are what charming typical houses ought to be. You would like to have her build you one and furnish its walls with her pictures. Her gardens smell of roses and old-fashioned blooms, and the children she draws so cunningly would pluck them as eagerly as you, were they not the foster-children of Silence, as Keats hath it.

Perhaps the delightful decorative impulse does slur the deeper possibilities in rendering a subtle text. But . . . I know of nothing more fresh and delightful than may be found in these new impulses.

Well, Jessie Willcox Smith is in the thick of these new impulses. She has had no long career and has had it exclusively in Philadelphia, of which maligned town an art editor in a neighboring borough said the other day: "When any of these new boys and girls hail from Philadelphia you've got to give them a hearing. The best things in the field come from there now."

Edith Emerson

SOURCE: "The Age of Innocence," in *The American Magazine of Art,* Vol. XVI, No. 7, July, 1925, p. 341-47.

An exhibition most appropriate to the Christmas season has just been opened at the Philadelphia Art Alliance, consisting of portraits, drawings, and illustrations by Jessie Willcox Smith. The visitor's first impression is that he has strayed into a children's party, and he gladly decides to stay and join in the fun. He must be hard-hearted indeed to resist the appeal of these winsome mites of humanity.

Miss Smith's well-known and widely circulated illustrations for books and magazines reach an enormous public both here and abroad, but her portraits will prove a revelation to those who have not hitherto had the opportunity of studying this phase of her art. Her inimitable set of illustrations for Kingsley's *The Water-Babies* is the feature of the West Gallery, simultaneously charming and disarming the spectator. Peals of sympathetic laughter greet the picture of Tom, paddling busily in a cool green stream as "he felt how comfortable it was to have nothing on him but himself." The artist's own eyes twinkle merrily when she contemplates her quaint creation.

The chief characteristics of Miss Smith's art are sympathetic insight and a tonic humor. This combination has irresistible power, and seldom does she fail to evoke a quick response. *The Water-Babies* should find a permanent place in the Children's Room of some great public library.

Immortal children of the imagination, courteous *Alice-in-Wonderland,* the appealing *Little Lame Prince,* gay *Hans Brinker, The Princess and the Goblin, Heidi,* and a host of others salute us from the walls. The pictures win the respect of those who recognize able draughtsmanship, felicitous composition, and gayly decorative color. Only a few know what they represent of steady devotion to work—continuous effort generously and unselfishly poured out that others may rejoice and be glad. Moral fibre is an even more essential part of a work of art than the warp and woof of the canvas, and back of these charming fantasies are many noble qualities, modesty, simplicity, honesty and candor. They attract and win without guile. . . .

The ideals of Jessie Willcox Smith have been woven into the fabric of contemporary thought, and her forms are impressed upon the consciousness of innumerable mothers, who hope that their children will look like the children she paints. With unerring directness she touches the heart of humanity and travels the only quiet road to fame.

Gene Mitchell

SOURCE: "Introduction," in *The Subject Was Children: The Art of Jessie Willcox Smith,* Dutton, 1979. pp. 1-4.

There can be no doubt that Jessie Willcox Smith was one of the most accomplished illustrators of children and fairy tales in America. Delightful as the work of her contemporaries was, it seldom attained the perfection and versatility that was reflected in Smith's pictures. She had a remarkable insight into what set the children's world apart from that of adults, and she possessed a unique ability to place these images pleasingly before us. Her art began where that of her contemporaries left off.

The work of such great children's artists as Maud Humphrey Bogart, Frances Brundage, and Ida Waugh usually arose from their pictures of individual, or groups of, children, portrayed as existing almost alone in a world devoid of anything else. On the other hand, Smith's pictures usually suggest something greater than the eye sees. There is a universal tone to her pictures, and she seems to be offering a new and romantic visualization of child life. It's as if she were appealing to all adults who have forgotten the joys of childhood. Along with Maxfield Parrish, she shared the ability to bring to mind a complete fairy tale with a single picture. This is evident in such pictures as *Snow White and the Seven Little Dwarfs* and *Jack and the Bean Stalk* (both 1911). Smith succeeded in a world dominated by men at a time when women were expected to stay at home and just raise children. Despite her love of and special affinity for children, she never married. Her lifelong goal was to be a successful artist and her favorite subject was children, as seen through a woman's eyes.

Her pictures reflect a feminine view of the joys of motherhood and childhood. Her love of children led her to fantasize through her art about how seemingly perfect mothers and children looked and acted. In short, she brought out the best in them. When one looks closely at her pictures of children, it is not difficult to find a suggestion of trust about them. When she shows a girl washing her younger brother's face, one recognizes the boy's acceptance of his sister's loving attentiveness. In her pictures children were always portrayed as being redeemable, even if she showed them acting mischievously, or while being punished. Optimism was her guide to a world limited to pleasant things.

In Smith's world only children and their mothers seemed to exist. And although she excluded adults from many of her pictures, adults were some of her most enthusiastic admirers. Her art was enjoyed by millions of people and the quite extraordinary level of her success is evidenced in the fact that she was the only woman artist to illustrate every cover of a major national magazine for more than fifteen consecutive years. That magazine was *Good Housekeeping.*

During that fifteen-year period Smith's work appeared on the covers of more than 180 issues of *Good Housekeeping.* She very likely earned about a quarter of a million dollars for this work. In addition, she retained the right to use these cover illustrations as plates for children's books. From 1916 to 1920 she illustrated three books that stand out as some of her finest work. These books were Charles Kingsley's *The Water-Babies;* and George MacDonald's *At the Back of the North Wind,* and *The Princess and the Goblin.* In the middle of the 1920s she began to devote less time to book and magazine illustrations, while doing more portraits of children for families in the Philadelphia area. In 1933 she ended her work for *Good Housekeeping* and traveled to Europe. It was during this trip that her health began to deteriorate. Her career was nearing its end. Upon returning to the United States she retired to her home near Philadelphia and on May 3, 1935, she died at the age of seventy-two.

There can be no doubt that Jessie Willcox Smith not only deserved her success, but had earned it through years of hard work. Being talented was an obvious advantage, but it wasn't always a guarantee of success. A certain amount of luck was necessary. Two of Howard Pyle's other students also had immense talent: Sara Stilwell and Ethel Franklin Betts. They had as much ability as Smith, but they never received the opportunities to develop their talents fully. The reason for this was simple: it was a man's world. One only has to look at such series of children's books as the Scribner Classics, Rand McNally's Windermere Series, and the Harper Illustrated Classics to discover that most of them were illustrated by

such eminent artists as N. C. Wyeth, Milo Winter, and Louis Rhead. When we add the names of Edmund Dulac, Arthur Rackham, Maxfield Parrish, and Kay Nielsen, we have most of the group that dominated the field of illustrated books during the first quarter of this century. The work that was available to women generally appeared in books that just couldn't compete with these very successful series.

Time and again the best and most prestigious illustration assignments were given to men. Thus when a woman decided to embark on a career as an illustrator, she faced an uncertain future at best. To have reached the peak of success, as Smith did, was an immense accomplishment, not only for herself but for other members of her sex as well. Smith, although certainly not an outspoken feminist, gave encouragement to many other women by proving that it was indeed possible to succeed in a man's world.

Helen Goodman

SOURCE: "Women Illustrators of the Golden Age of American Illustration," in *Women's Art Journal,* Vol. 8, No. 1, Spring-Summer, 1987, pp. 13-22.

Certainly one explanation for Smith's extraordinary success lies in the fact that her work fed the fantasies and aspirations of the middle-class society of her day by depicting idyllic, heartwarming images of wholesome family life and secure, happy children. As the editors of *Good Housekeeping* put it, her pictures "hold up to our readers . . . the highest ideals of the American home, the home . . . one associates with a sunny living-room and children."

She illustrated nearly 40 books, most notably *Little Women, A Child's Garden of Verses,* and Charles Kingsley's *The Water-Babies.* Other work included posters, and advertisements for such major companies as Ivory Soap, Quaker Oats, American Radiator, and Campbell Soup. An advertisement she did for the latter company in 1928 is an excellent example of her strongest work, in which the influence of the Japanese print and the turn-of-the-century poster is apparent. In it she divided her composition into a triptych-like arrangement. On the left stands a frock-coated hare and on the right, the mad hatter; each holds a bowl of soup and peers intently into the larger central image, where two beautiful children giggling infectiously sit facing one another from opposite ends of a table, their soup bowls before them. Smith compressed planes, cropped borders, and boldly outlined her forms so that the work had the simplicity and clarity of a stained-glass panel.

Smith's themes, almost exclusively those of idealized motherhood and childhood, were repeated so consistently that she may have been recreating through her art the sort of loving relationship she herself had longed for as a child. In an illustration for *Dream Blocks* by Aileen Higgins, published by Duffield & Co. in 1908, an adoring mother reverently caresses her daughter, who dreamily accepts as her due the comfort and love of her mother's embrace. The mother's posture, seated, with knees spread beneath a long gown, brings to mind the Madonna in Michelangelo's 1498 *Pietà* in St. Peter's. Smith's visual allusion to this sacred mother and her blessed child elevates the painting from a mundane image into a sort of hymn not only to mother-love in general, but to American motherhood in particular.

Edward D. Nudelman

SOURCE: "Introduction," in *Jessie Willcox Smith: A Bibliography,* Pelican Publishing Company, 1989, pp. 9-21.

[Howard] Pyle's influence as both a teacher and a model cannot be overemphasized. Smith, in comparing her work at *The Ladies' Home Journal* to this class stated, "When, however, I came under guidance of Howard Pyle, I began to think of illustration in a light different from that of a pot boiler." . . . Perhaps Pyle's greatest contribution to Smith during this period was a love and appreciation for color. He felt that painting more suitably captured the dramatic moment than drawing, and that drawing was prerequisite to illustrative reality: "Its [painting's] color and fluidity capture 'real things', real surroundings, real backgrounds. A tone for a background will not do." Apart from all this, Pyle also offered his students a forum for presenting their art. More than most teachers of the period, Pyle had a keen sense for the commercial feasibility of illustration, and he was always the supreme advocate for his pupils. In 1897, Pyle arranged with Houghton, Mifflin and Company to publish an edition of Longfellow's *Evangeline* containing chromolithograph illustrations by Jessie Willcox Smith and Violet Oakley. The book, with a preface by Pyle introducing his two students, was issued in both green and red gilt-stamped cloth, and contained five color plates by each artist, as well as head- and tail-pieces for chapter headings. As would be the case with many of Smith's future books, this book was also issued in England, with the same sheets and plates but with a cancel title page bearing the publishers Gay and Bird. The bold chromolithography in *Evangeline,* though failing somewhat in a technical sense, nevertheless offered the public for the first time a colorful representation of the ability of these two rising artists. Smith's style in these drawings was almost indistinguishable from that of Oakley's and the two styles reflected strongly the influence of Howard Pyle's tutelage.

The Head of a Hundred, by the popular Maud Wilder Goodwin, was issued in 1897 by Little, Brown and Co. and contained two black-and-white illustrations by Smith. These, along with the six illustrations for *The Young Puritans in Captivity* (1899, Little Brown and Co.), dealt with subject matter that was to Smith most unattractive: ". . . I wrote to the publisher that I did not know much about Indians and that if they had just an every-day book about children, I thought I could do it better. I was immediately rewarded with one of Louisa M. Alcott's stories, and a letter saying they were glad to know I did

other things as they had supposed Indians were my specialty."

Before this edition of Alcott's renowned *An Old Fashioned Girl* was to appear in 1902, Smith would illustrate four separate stories, contribute single illustrations to two Hawthorne classics, and produce a baby book with dozens of tinted illustrations. . . . The books illustrated by Smith during this time helped establish her name at last in the realm of publishers. However, all of the illustrations in this period were in black and white, and those such as appeared in the "Brenda Books" by Helen Leah Reed were unassuming and not comparable to her later work. In 1900, she illustrated a curious book entitled *Reminiscences of the Old Chest of Drawers* by Sarah Cauffman Sill. The slender book was very nicely produced by J. B. Lippincott and contained six full-page, black-and-white plates as well as line drawings by Smith. These illustrations are unique and not representative of her usual style. Executed in charcoal and watercolor, the drawings vary from pictures of a chest of drawers to sketches of a church and a house. In 1902, A. C. McClurg issued a story for young readers by Mary Imlay Taylor entitled *Little Mistress Goodhope.* Smith's illustrations for this work include a color frontispiece and headpieces throughout in tint. It is a nicely balanced work and it contains the first major color illustration used in the text (excluding the chromolithograph plates in *Evangeline* and minor color portrait in the 1900 reissue of *The Head of a Hundred*).

Though experiencing much commercial success, it was clear to Smith that for her to develop as a major illustrator, she would have to publish in color. The development of color in her art was influenced not only by Pyle's teaching, but also by her relationship with her close friends Violet Oakley and Elizabeth Shippen Green. In 1897, Smith rented a studio in Philadelphia with Oakley and Green, cementing friendships begun earlier in Pyle's initial class. During the next few years these three would rise to prominence in illustration in Philadelphia. . . . In the early development of their use of color, Green and Smith were more closely related. In fact, the two artists teamed on two different projects which were destined to bring them much acclaim and advancement in their respective careers. These were the Bryn Mawr Calendars in 1901 and 1902, and the publication of *The Book of the Child,* by the much admired Mabel Humphrey. . . . However, it was more the publication of *The Book of the Child,* and later in the same year the publication of a calendar with the book's illustrations, that marked the first major economic success for either artist. The enormous lapbook, measuring 38x35 cm, was issued by Frederick A. Stokes, a publisher that had already begun producing books illustrated by the renowned Mabel Humphrey. *The Book of the Child* was unique and, in many ways, an extraordinary production. The entire text is hand lettered, with each capital a bold letter, and the chapter headings are all printed in bright orange. Smith contributed four illustrations, including the cover illustration; Green added four more. The production costs for a book of this size and weight, with seven full-page color plates on coated paper, pictorial covers in color and even a printed dust wrapper, were enormous. Considering this, it is interesting that the book was bound with four heavy-duty staples and the signatures glued to a cloth spine. Because of this binding technique and the immensity of the book, very few copies remain. The drawings by Smith in this work are strikingly bold and colorful with large flat masses of color.

Both Smith's and Elizabeth Shippen Green's art in *The Book of the Child* reflect a number of influences including Japanese prints and the aquatints of Mary Cassatt. Smith was also a great admirer of the popular French illustrator Boutet deMonvel, who painted with a peculiar static quality. This aspect is readily visible in these drawings, where oftentimes the subject appears to be frozen in space, creating a visually pleasing effect. The illustrations are warm and inviting, full of the decorative element which would fill her canvases throughout the remainder of her professional career.

Also issued in 1903 was Betty Sage's enchanting *Rhymes of Real Children,* a children's lapbook in the truest sense

From A Child's Garden of Verses, *written by Robert Louis Stevenson. Illustrated by Jessie Willcox Smith.*

of the word. This was the first of Smith's books to be published by Duffield and Company of New York. The large, flat format was perfectly suited for the illustrations of Smith, and served as a prototype for the many future Duffield productions (including two more illustrated by Smith: *The Bed-Time Book* in 1907 and *When Christmas Comes Around* in 1915). The illustrations in *Rhymes of Real Children,* painted in water-color over charcoal, are among her most decorative and are full of sensitivity and warmth. The frontispiece, entitled "Mother" shows the back of a mother hugging her daughter, with more than half of the picture taken up by a huge patterned armchair. This theme would recur throughout Smith's art, that of the interaction and feeling between a mother and her child, and would come to be one of Smith's most memorable images.

In 1904, Smith teamed up with the famous Frances Hodgson Burnett in a handsome production of *In the Closed Room,* published by McClure, Phillips and Co. The book was issued in bright green cloth with bold gilt-stamped decorations on the front cover, on the decorated endpapers and throughout the text and was issued in a decorated dust wrapper. Smith contributed eight illustrations for the text, using pastel colors and different framing techniques. The work was reissued in the same year by Grosset & Dunlap, but with only four illustrations. About the same time Smith began work on these illustrations, she received a very important letter from the prestigious firm of Charles Scribner's Sons in New York. The well-known publishing company had seen brilliant success with their *Scribner's Illustrated Classics,* a series established by Joseph H. Chapin, art editor at Scribner's. It was Chapin's idea to showcase America's greatest illustrators by setting them to illustrate some of the most popular juvenile fiction. The first title in this series, *Poems of Childhood*, by Eugene Field, was issued in 1904 and contained brilliant illustrations by Maxfield Parrish. It was thus quite a compliment, if not an endorsement, for Smith to receive this commission. In a letter to Smith dated December 23, 1903, Chapin writes concerning the proposed contract: "It is understood that you are to illustrate (in colors) *A Child's Garden of Verses* for the lump sum of $3600, we to own the originals and have exclusive publication rights. . . . We will appreciate it greatly if you will make an early selection of the twelve (12) full-page subjects in order that *Collier's Weekly* may nominate from this list of twelve, the six (6) which they will reproduce. The six drawings which they will publish will, of course, have to be done first as we must begin to deliver these drawings to them for reproduction as early as October and November, 1904." This cooperative arrangement with a different periodical was somewhat unusual, as Scribner's could have also published these in their own journal. They must have felt that the larger format available in *Collier's* would more ably showcase the illustrations.

In 1904, Smith moved into a new home in Chestnut Hill with Oakley, Green and Henrietta Cozens, a gardener and close friend. The abode was called Cogslea, the first four letters standing for the first letter of each of the women's names. *A Child's Garden of Verses* was issued by Scribner's shortly after this move. A facsimile edition also appeared in England simultaneously, with the cancel title page bearing Longmans Green and Co. Among the illustrations for this work, "The Land of Counterpane" stands out as a compositional masterpiece. Smith uses foreshortened perspective to give the impression of a faraway city, all within the confines of the bedsheets. In these illustrations, the strong double contours of *The Book of the Child* are present, but are less distinct, and space is treated more naturally. More realistic color is also evident and there is greater attention to detail. Both the public and Scribner's were well pleased with the work. In a letter from Art Editor Joseph Chapin to Jessie Willcox Smith, this was expressed: "I have used up all the adjectives that I believe in using (there are certain ones which are ruled out) so I will simply say that the last two drawings which reached me today are delightful examples of the sort of thing of which you are master." A critic further echoed these sentiments: "Miss Smith has created for us more of a type of childhood. There is no mistaking a drawing or painting by this artist: that charm in children that appeals to all pervades her work, and although it is essentially illustrative in its rendering, a high order of craftsmanship is displayed. . . . "

Only one book appeared in 1906 with illustrations by Smith, a tiny volume by John Luther Long entitled *Billy-Boy*. The black-and-white illustrations are clever, but quite unassuming. On the other hand, there are some remarkably original and creative illustrations to be found in the *Collier's Weekly*. After seeing one of the covers from *Collier's Weekly,* the renowned author Bliss Carman wrote Smith: "I am sure you must be oversupplied with letters of admiration, and any words of mine would be superfluous. This is merely an exuberant note to vent my own delight. . . . "

The Bed-Time Book was published in 1907 and *Dream Blocks* in 1908, both issued by Duffield and Company with full-page color illustrations. These were also issued shortly thereafter by Chatto and Windus in London. Both works depict Smith's use of the decorative element in her illustration. Large, flat masses of color and dark contours typify these illustrations, with a poster-like quality to the composition. *Dream Blocks* contained fifteen color plates, color cover insert and a pictorial dust-wrapper. This was the largest number of color illustrations ever to appear in any of Smith's books. Due to the large number of inserted plates, printed on thick, glossy paper, the book is often found lacking one or more illustrations and is very scarcely found in fine condition.

In 1909, Moffat and Yard issued *The Seven Ages of Childhood,* a remarkably balanced and attractive work, with poems by the ever-popular Carolyn Wells. By now, Smith was established as a major illustrator to the point where she participated in the planning and the preparatory process of an idea. This was the case with the production of *The Seven Ages of Childhood.* It was Smith's hope to procure the talents of Edward S. Martin, who had written an exceptionally popular book entitled

The Luxury of Children, illustrated by Sarah Stillwell, and published by Harper's in 1904. But he declined, and Moffat urged Smith to try and persuade him to reconsider. Smith, however, wrote the publishers saying that this would not at all be appropriate. Moffat then wrote Smith: "We appreciate that there must be indeed many children's books with which you have no patience, and your advice and idea will be very valuable indeed from a business point of view as well as from the point of view of personal taste. . . . " In another letter to Smith, the editors elaborate on availability of an author. "Miss Wells is apt to be the higher priced of the two and it may be that we would not get her without a royalty because some of her books are such capital sellers. She would bring a very distinct public with her—a good deal more of a public, I can assure you, than Helen Hay Whitney." Smith was able to interpret Wells's simple verse with remarkable sensitivity and perception. One of the more universal of all her paintings is the one with the poem,

> The Sixth Shifts to lean and slender maidenhood.
> With thoughtful eyes and quiet mien.

It captures a young lady resting at the base of a willow tree, with book in hand, her gaze up from the book and into a realm we are not privileged to enter. . . .

In 1910 Smith produced for Duffield and Company a volume of illustrated verse entitled *A Child's Book of Old Verses.* The work represents Smith's first book of her own selected poems, and the illustrations and line drawing are very well suited for the text. For the frontispiece illustration, Smith won the coveted Beck Prize given by the Philadelphia Water Color Club in 1911. The illustration, entitled *A Child's Grace,* shows two young children, hands folded and at the table, with a loaf of bread in front of them. The first child's eyes are closed, but the second child's are open and staring at the bread.

In 1911, Smith illustrated three very successful books, all by different publishers: *The Five Senses, A Child's Book of Stories,* and *The Now-A-Days Fairy Book.* All three contained full-page color illustrations and all but *The Five Senses* were also issued in England. *The Now-A-Days Fairy Book* was a large, heavy book with tipped-in color plates mounted onto stock plates. These were the first of Smith's illustrations to appear in this manner. Though impressive, the production was not comparable to many of the limited, signed editions of Smith's English colleagues, and the color reproduction was not the highest quality. This was in contrast to the crystal clear reproduction of her ten, full-page color illustrations for *Dickens's Children,* published by Scribner's in 1912, and also issued simultaneously by Chatto and Windus in England. Printed on glossy card paper, the book was well-conceived and produced. The illustrations for this book were later added to a text by Samuel McChord Crothers in the 1925 production of *The Children of Dickens,* issued again by Scribner's. In this edition printed on cheaper paper, the plates do not show the same clarity and brilliance as the original 1912 issue.

Another work issued in 1912 was Clement Clarke Moore's *'Twas the Night Before Christmas*. The oblong book, with bright red pictorial covers, was illustrated by Smith with twelve full-page color pictures, vignettes, and line drawings. It was published by Houghton Mifflin, and originally issued in a pictorial dustwrapper. The illustrations are quite different from the style that Smith had shown in previous books, and the wispy, near-caricature figures are not found in any later illustrations. . . .

In [1914], Dodd, Mead and Company published the famous *Jessie Willcox Smith Mother Goose,* an immense book with twelve color and five black-and-white illustrations, and line drawings throughout. The oblong quarto, with plates on glossy, coated paper, was an instant success and brought Smith much fame. The book was originally issued in a pictorial box with a price of $2.50; the following year the price was changed to $5.00. The illustrations had appeared earlier in *Good Housekeeping Magazine* in consecutive issues from December 1912 to April 1914. However, these appeared in black and white, and were nothing compared to their combined presence in the book. One reason for the widespread popularity of these illustrations was Smith's portrayal of the nursery rhymes in a realistic, easily identifiable style. With the dark-lined borders almost entirely absent, and more subtle, muted coloring, Smith breathed life and vitality into these pictures. The shift of style toward realism is noteworthy and typical of the versatility of the artist. Unlike many of the English illustrators of her time, Smith was never locked into any one style, but adapted and evolved her style throughout her career.

In 1915 Smith's illustrations appeared in four books. *A Child's Stamp Book of Old Verses* was a unique book, reproducing the illustrations from *A Child's Book of Old Verses* in miniature stamps which came in an envelope inside the front of the book. A book by little-known Priscilla Underwood, entitled *When Christmas Comes Around,* was published by Duffield in 1915, and simultaneously in London by Chatto and Windus. The large, flat book had six full-page color illustrations by Smith. Though decorative and colorful, these illustrations appear rather hastily contrived and are not her best work. *The Everyday Fairy Book,* issued by Dodd, Mead and Co. in 1915 and reprinted several times in England, contained seven color plates, but was printed on cheaper wove paper, and the reproduction of the original *Collier's* illustrations were of poor quality. The other book published in 1915 was a superb production of Alcott's *Little Women,* published by Little, Brown and Company. Unlike the cheaper production of Alcott's *An Old-Fashioned Girl* (1902), this edition contained eight full-page color plates, a color insert on the cover and all edges gilt. These illustrations rank among the finest ever made for this story, and the book was very well received. . . .

During the four year period of 1916-1920, there appeared over ten books with illustrations by Smith, and all of them dealt with fantasy of fairy tale themes. The greatest of these were *The Water-Babies, The Way to Wonderland, At the Back of North Wind,* and *The Princess and the Goblin.* The latter two were classics by the universally admired George MacDonald. These works, published in 1919 and 1920 respectively, were issued by David McKay of Philadelphia, a publisher who had a reputation for books of quality and beauty. David McKay issued both of these in several different cloth states and the color reproduction of Smith's paintings is among the finest in all her books. Printed by the Beck Engraving Company, these illustrations, reproduced on coated, glossy paper, were in vivid and varied colors. Smith's art in these books is again decorative in style with an added ethereal quality. The subject matter made it necessary for Smith to blend colors and shapes as she never had done before. Unlike the hard line of Edmund Dulac or Arthur Rackham, Smith's fantasy world still belied a close relation to natural objects and shapes. Nowhere is this more evident than in the pictorial endpapers of *The Princess and the Goblin.* Here we see a legion of goblins marching in a line through a forest, all in the most natural of poses, carrying picks and lanterns on their backs.

In 1917, Dodd, Mead and Company continued their tradition of publishing Smith's illustrations with the production of a fantasy story by Mary Stewart entitled *The Way to Wonderland.* The book contained six, full-page color plates by Smith as well as a cover insert and pictorial endpapers. It was later issued in 1920 by Hodder and Stoughton in London with a lavish gilt pictorial cover. But Smith's greatest work of this period, and considered by many to be her greatest group of illustrations, was Kingsley's *The Water-Babies.* Issued in 1916 by Dodd, Mead, and Co., and reprinted many times in England in various formats, this work was the culmination of Smith's imaginative style and technical ability. The paintings were all executed on canvas using mixed media. The overlays of water color and oil over charcoal reveal a careful and methodical approach. The illustrations represent a return to decorative style with broad, flat patterning of shapes and colors. The publishers spared no expense in the production of this work. The original edition, issued in full-color pictorial box, was a heavy quarto with illustrations printed on glossy paper. Line drawings in green fill up the text as well as the endpapers. Smith considered these paintings to be her best work and bequeathed the entire set of twelve original oils to the Library of Congress. This is the only known group of paintings for any single book illustrated by Smith which has remained together as a group. The illustrations as compositions are very innovative and imaginative. One illustration shows a group of large fish approaching the tiny figure of a child hiding behind underwater foliage and gives both the feeling of either a friendly meeting or a foreboding adventure. The many illustrations involving underwater scenes would prove a challenge to any artist, but Smith executed them remarkably. It was said by one critic that Smith's paintings for *The Water-Babies* rank among the finest ever rendered for this classic.

In 1922, *Heidi,* the famous story by Johanna Spyri was

issued by David McKay. It contained ten full-page color plates, a color pictorial wrapper, a color insert on the cover, pictorial endpapers, and colored lined drawings. This was again a fine production, typical of David McKay's work. The book represents the last major children's story in which Smith specifically designed illustrations. Fourteen separate books followed until Smith's death in 1935, but all of these were either composites of illustrations previously published as *Good Housekeeping* covers, or they represented relatively minor contributions of only a few illustrations. This was not to minimize in any way her later work. In fact many of these books remain among the more popular and collected of all her work. A special group of these might be termed, "The Child's Book of . . . " Series. These were all published by Duffield, beginning with *A Child's Book of Modern Stories* (1920) and ending with *A Child's Book of Country Stories* (1925). In between, there were two additional titles: *A Little Child's Book of Stories* (1922) and *A Very Little Child's Book of Stories* (1923). All of these books had similar designs, with a color pictorial insert on the cover and various color plates. The basic quality of the production was average, but the overall effect was very endearing, and the books were very heartily bought and read with pleasure. In all, there were a total of thirty-one illustrations in these four books taken from covers of *Good Housekeeping* magazine. These four works, together with *A Child's Book of Old Verses,* were reissued by The Dial Press in 1935 with color pictorial wrappers and boxes. Smith also illustrated a book for the Cosmopolitan Book Corporation in 1923 with illustrations taken from *Good Housekeeping* covers. The book, entitled *The Boys and Girls of Bookland,* was issued in a pictorial wrapper, and although the quality of the paper for the text was average, the eleven full-page color plates were quite vivid and bright. The large quarto was later reissued by David McKay in a production inferior to those of his earlier publications.

Near the end of Smith's career, with the available time and energy for illustration declining, quite a few books appeared with only a frontispiece or a dustwrapper designed by Smith. This was the case with Annie W. Franchot's, *Bobs, King of the Fortunate Isle,* in 1928, where Smith contributed the frontispiece and the dustwrapper illustration. Smith had earlier done the same for this author's work, *Bugs and Wings and Other Things,* in 1918. Similarly, *The Lullaby Book* (1921) and *Rhymes and Reminiscences* (1929), had frontispiece illustrations by Smith.

Smith also contributed a few illustrations for various private publications. In 1924, Emily Eldredge Saville issued her story, *Memories and a Garden,* with a color frontispiece and wrapper design by Smith. *A Child's Prayer,* printed by David McKay, but privately produced for Cora Cassard Toogood in 1925, appeared with a full-color illustration on the cover by Smith, as well as numerous line drawings for the text printed in blue. The book was originally issued in cloth with a color pictorial wrapper. Another private production, by Kathryn Jarboe Bull entitled *Little Paul's Christ Child,* was published in

1929 and contained two black-and-white illustrations from *Harper's Weekly,* 1902. Smith's last illustration was for a cookbook for children entitled *Kitchen Fun,* published in 1932. This illustration first appeared as a cover of *Good Housekeeping* in 1931.

Smith's attention to portrait work became more pronounced about 1925, but she remained active in book and magazine illustration right up to her death in 1935. . . .

Upon the death of Jessie Willcox Smith in 1935 there followed a wave of commemoration and admiration, both in the art community and the general public as well. Never had an American female illustrator been so admired and recognized in her own lifetime. . . .

In the Philadelphia *Evening Public Ledger,* the article announcing her death and remembering her as an artist, bears the headline: "Death Takes Away Her Brush," a fitting eulogy, as it is sure that no other obstacle would ever have caused her to stop painting. Her energy and initiative was truly remarkable, but this was overshadowed by her keen sensitivity and awareness, not only for the composition of a painting, but also for the world around her. A tribute, offered by her close friend Edith Emerson, captures well the inspiration and personality of Jessie Willcox Smith, an artist whose painting was her life:

> Nothing morbid or bitter ever came from her brush. This is not because the difficulties of life left her untouched. She had more than her full share, but when they came she met and conquered them. She demanded nothing for herself but obeyed the simple injunction on the poster she designed for the Welfare Federation—GIVE. She helped those in need, the aged, the helpless, the unfortunate. She gave honest and constructive advice to students who came for criticisms. She rejoiced in the success of others and was modest about her own. Tall, handsome and straightforward, she carried herself well, with no trace of self-assertion. She always spoke directly and to the point. She lived quietly, and loved natural unaffected things and people. Altogether hers was a brave and generous mind, comprehending life with a large simplicity, free from all the pettiness, and unfailingly kind.

Edward D. Nudelman

SOURCE: In *Jessie Willcox Smith: American Illustrator,* Pelican Publishing Company, 1990, pp. 17-126.

Smith's illustrations for [*Evangeline*] were of a delicate nature, possessing a certain graphic quality. The medium was gouache, a method of watercolor painting using opaque colors. Pen and ink was used liberally as a high-light, and the end result yielded a softness which was quite unique and pleasing to the eye. Her illustrations for *Evangeline* captured a sort of dreamy element which was to be a characteristic quality in her art throughout her career. In the frontispiece illustration, captioned "Fair in sooth was the maiden," one can see this imaginative element in the posture and open gaze of a woman standing in a field. Pyle, commenting on the two artists' work in the preface, states: "I may hardly compare one with another, but I like the image of Evangeline standing in the hot radiance of the yellow fields gathered of their harvests. . . . "

One of Smith's most delightful series of illustrations, created for *The Book of the Child* published in 1903, was painted at the Red Rose Inn, and this production definitively marked the establishment of Smith as a leading American illustrator. . . .

Smith used colored charcoal and watercolor to portray a serene world of children, toys, and dolls. In one illustration, entitled *On the Hammock,* a young child is seen delicately balanced in a hammock, looking quietly down at the infant doll in her lap. The graphic element is strikingly evident in the composition, with the doll's dress forming a large portion of the picture and giving the entire illustration a posterlike quality. Also noteworthy is the use of the "double contour," where the figure is outlined with a dark, contrasting border. Smith used this technique to draw attention to a central figure or pattern, and it is one of the most recognizable features of her illustration. . . .

Both works [*The Bed-Time Book* and *Dream Blocks*] depict Smith's use of the decorative in her illustration. Large, flat masses of color and dark contours typify these paintings, with a definite posterlike quality in the composition. This is evident in an illustration for *The Bed-Time Book* entitled *Picture Papers,* which shows a young girl in bed, cutting out figures from a magazine. Our eyes are pleasantly drawn to a decorative vertical design of roses in the background, which is attractively set off by a huge white pillow. . . .

The cover illustration for [*The Jessie Willcox Smith Mother Goose*], showing two children nestled beneath the wings of Mother Goose, is one of Smith's most pleasing and warm images. The serenity portrayed in the posture and expression of the children, along with the maternal concern of Mother Goose, gives further evidence of the genius of Smith. This recurrent theme, the relationship between mother and child, is a dominant statement in much of Smith's art. One critic commented, "In her art the maternal note predominates. She is haunted by a vision of two faces, and the face of one is the face of a mother. . . . "

An excellent example of [Smith's close relation to natural objects and shapes] can be found in an illustration for *At the Back of the North Wind* entitled *On the Top of the Great Beech-tree.* Here we see "North Wind," a beautiful woman with long flowing hair, holding the tiny child Diamond in her arms, safely protected within the branches and leaves of a beech-tree. The child is purposely drawn out of proportion to the giant North Wind, giving an added dimension of fantasy. There are definite Pre-Raphaelite influences to be found in this painting, especially in the Rossetti-like face of North Wind and in

the mysterious, though otherwise natural elements of the painting.

A series of four paintings commissioned in 1916 by Swift's Soap Products strongly depicts Smith's expertise in portraying fantasy. The paintings were grouped together as a calendar and were printed in brilliant colors. The illustration for Cinderella is a marvelous blend of the natural and the supernatural, as we see an astonished Cinderella sitting at the foot of a wispy, ephemeral fairy godmother. . . .

Jessie Willcox Smith loved the classic boys' and girls' stories and painted illustrations for such notable characters as David Copperfield, Hans Brinker, and Alice in Wonderland, as well as fully illustrating *Little Women* (1915) and *Heidi* (1922). . . .

Smith's paintings for *Heidi* are quite unique in their use of coloration, with many shades of purple, green, and orange, giving an ethereal effect. One such illustration shows Heidi introducing various goats to her friend Clara and has a very Maxfield Parrish-like quality, especially seen in the bright orange and violet colored mountains in the background. . . .

One can find in [*Boys and Girls of Bookland*] delightful illustrations of Alice in Wonderland, Rebecca of Sunnybrook Farm, the Little Lame Prince, David Copperfield, Little Women, Tiny Tim, Jackanapes, and others. Many of these illustrations had appeared just months before this publication as covers for *Good Housekeeping,* and their appearance together for the first time in a picture book was very well received by the public. The illustration for *Little Women* is an excellently balanced composition with the four central figures being framed on each side by red curtains, and the heads of three of the figures are set off by the pale yellow drapes in the background. . . .

It remains clear that the legacy of Smith's art is in that certain feeling and recognition found in her compositions which can be identified with some experience in our past. Whether it is falling asleep on a hammock or reading a bedtime book, we are entreated to stop and appreciate the moment a little longer. Smith's art has left for us a large record of many experiences, most of them relating to our childhood, but not in any way thus limited. . . .

The children that Smith painted were reflective and a little sedate," wrote one contemporary critic, "and in her art the maternal note predominates." The image of a mother expressing her love and tender care for her child is probably the most recognizable feature in Smith's art. The sensitive compositions of mother and child which filled her canvasses were concerned with everyday emotions and situations: the reading of a storybook, comforting a fallen spirit, or simply cuddling in a quiet place.

But for Smith, the telling of a particular feeling or impression always involved more than simply the pictorial representation of the figures in any given illustration. She expertly made use of decorative elements, such as color and design, to evoke sentiment and warmth in her paintings. An example of this can be found in the frontispiece for *The Seven Ages of Childhood,* where we see a baby lying face down on its mother's lap. Much of the illustration is filled with the decorative design of the mother's dress, giving an impression of comfort and serenity.

Smith's draftmanship was exemplary, and contributed to the excellence of her compositions. Her knowledge of human anatomy was superb, and her skill in drawing hands is especially evident. In her paintings expressing maternal love, this ability to portray accurately the posture and movement of the hands dramatically added to the overall emotional impression of the viewer. In the cover design for *Dream Blocks* one can see this effect as the mother kisses her child's hand, palm in palm, while her other hand is gracefully supporting the child's body.

Although Smith never married, and chose a rigorous career for a woman of her time, she was nevertheless a champion for the role and responsibilities of motherhood. In a personal quote, Smith conveys this view: "A woman's sphere is as sharply defined as a man's. If she elects to be a housewife and mother—that is her sphere, and no other. Circumstance may, but volition should not, lead her from it." A few years before her death, Smith was asked the inevitable question, "Did she ever regret not marrying?" She responded, "No," but went on to say:

> To marry and have children is the ideal life for a woman. What career could ever be as fine? To give the world splendid men and women—isn't that the noblest thing a woman could possibly do?

What adult can forget the sheer delight of trying out new toys, warm summer days spent at the beach, or quiet hours perusing picture books? Smith has given us today a pictorial history of the preoccupations of the child in the early decades of the twentieth century. Through her paintings we see the styles of dress for the children of the period, the quaint toys and games, and we are led into a world less cluttered and noisy than our modern counterpart.

Smith was a master of observation, and her early art training taught her the necessity of patiently waiting for the right moment in which to capture the elements of a composition. Nowhere was this more evident than in her pictures of children at play. Often using a 4 x 5 inch viewfinder camera which gave sharp, detailed images of her subjects, Smith captured real children engaged in candid rather than posed play. She would welcome the active youngsters into her studio or courtyard, supply them with an abundance of toys, a hammock in which to lie, or maybe even sit with them for an afternoon tea.

Smith's great strength in relating to children was her sincere and natural affinity for the children themselves,

a prerequisite for the sensitivity that pervaded her art. Her first vocation, that of a kindergarten teacher, revealed her deep-rooted love for children, and this affection never waned throughout her artistic career.

In becoming the country's most popular children's illustrator of her period, Smith portrayed what one critic called "more a type of childhood than any one child." And although some of her illustrations revealed sorrowful moments, it is true that most of her art relating to childhood reflected an optimistic, triumphant view of children and the world around them. The acclaimed contemporary artist Henry Pitz pointed this out when he commented that Smith "espoused a consistently late-Victorian outlook—her children were charming, scrubbed, unrumpled, and always on the side of the angels."

In relating her technique for capturing the interest of her child models, Smith commented, "The way I do it is to tell fairy stories—tell them with great animation!" At the prime of her career, from 1916 to 1920, Smith was preoccupied with the illustration of fairy tales, producing over ten books dealing with fantasy themes.

From Heidi, *written by Johanna Spyri.*
Illustrated by Jessie Willcox Smith.

Prior to this period, however, Smith brought out a monumental illustrated book which was to become one of her most acclaimed and prodigious works. *The Jessie Willcox Smith Mother Goose,* issued in 1914, contained twelve wonderfully colored illustrations, as well as five black and white plates and dozens of pen and ink drawings. Smith's imaginative interpretations of the nursery rhymes contributed to her growing reputation as one of the leading illustrators of her day. In a triumph of composition, her illustration of "Peter, Peter, Pumpkin-Eater" shows a huge pumpkin with the tiny figure of a baby barely visible from inside, and the poised figure of a child is deftly positioned peering into the opening. It was this genius in interpreting the rhymes through a child's perspective that breathed new life into these well-known verses.

In painting fantasy, Smith often used mixed-media on artboard or canvas to obtain the required ethereal effects. Her illustrations for Charles Kingsley's *The Water-Babies* are generally considered to be the finest ever rendered for this enchanting tale. In order to give the impression of underwater scenes, Smith had to layer oil over varnished watercolor, and the resultant effect was a remarkable, wispy translucence.

Smith's illustrations for George MacDonald's *At the Back of the North Wind* (1919) and *The Princess and the Goblin* (1920) were extremely imaginative and full of vitality. One such example, pictured in *The Princess and the Goblin,* shows a host of goblins surrounding the young boy, Curdie, who is reciting a rhyme which is supposed to ward off the threatening foes. Smith uses the boy's own shadow to give a foreboding impression, adding a special tension and excitement to the composition.

From the beginning of her career, and extending to her latest illustrations, Smith was interested in illustrating the great classic boys' and girls' stories. As early as 1902, when she contributed twelve full-page black and white illustrations in a new edition of Louisa May Alcott's *An Old-Fashioned Girl,* Smith revealed her talent for creating pictures adapted around a preexisting story. A delightful illustration for this story shows a sophisticated use of perspective, in which we see a group of children sledding down a snow-covered hill. The gradually merging tree trunks in the distant background heighten the awareness of movement in the composition.

Smith's artistic training was a perfect foundation for her eventual illustration of storybooks. Specifically, Howard Pyle had relentlessly taught the necessity of mentally projecting oneself into the story and the characters. As a result, Smith's interpretations were very true to the intent of the author, and her illustrations supported the text, rather than distracting one's attention away from the story line.

This quality of mental projection was evident in Smith's creative illustration of Johanna Spyri's classic tale *Heidi.* The attractive color-plate book produced by David Mc-

Kay in 1922 was immensely popular and the ten full-page illustrations are brilliantly colorful and enchanting.

In her lengthy association with *Good Housekeeping,* Smith contributed many cover illustrations with themes taken from classic children's stories. Among those included were *Little Women, Hans Brinker,* and various scenes from Charles Dickens' famous stories.

A contemporary critic, in describing Smith's illustration, accurately captured some of the elements that have contributed to her greatness:

> In her work there is sympathy and reality which, apart even from the book, give pleasure, and, in conjunction with the text, are not only an embellishment, but a critical interpretation. Miss Smith's people are the people of the streets, the towns, the shops. Her houses are what charming typical houses ought to be. Her gardens smell of roses and old-fashioned blooms, and the children she draws so cunningly would pluck them as eagerly as you.

Lee Kingman

SOURCE: "Jessie Willcox Smith," in *Children's Books and Their Creators,* edited by Anita Silvey, Houghton Mifflin Company, 1995, p. 610.

During the early 1900s paintings by Jessie Willcox Smith illustrated handsome editions of children's classics, including *Little Women, The Water-Babies, At the Back of the North Wind, The Princess and the Goblin, Heidi, A Child's Garden of Verses,* and *'Twas the Night before Christmas.* Smith was a pupil of Howard Pyle, and, like many artists in the late 1880s, she began her career illustrating stories in magazines. This led to her doing cover illustrations for *Good Housekeeping,* and until Norman Rockwell came along in more recent times with his paintings for *The Saturday Evening Post,* she was the only artist whose work was used consistently on the cover of a national magazine—over 180 paintings in fifteen consecutive years. Her subjects were children, playing, dreaming, doing—often in family and school scenes—and were presented for the most part without sentimentality. Her compositions, while less painterly than those of Mary Cassatt, conveyed the same realistic look at the tenderness of mother and child together.

Smith brought a strong sense of storytelling to her illustrations, and in Robert Louis Stevenson's *Child's Garden of Verses,* the paintings of the little girl dressing by yellow candlelight, the small boy in bed with his toy soldiers strewn about the counterpane, and the child on the seaside rock contemplating his shadow are as evocative and memorable as the poems. Memorable, too, are her depictions of the frightening Mrs. Bedonebyasyoudid and the comforting Mrs. Doasyouwouldbedoneby in *The Water-Babies.* In that book her decorative line drawings and colorful paintings of naked, potbellied babies innocently preceded Maurice Sendak's later and more controversial nude babies. Smith presented illustrations with simplicity, making the story's actions and emotions clear, but her use of detail and texture enriched them just as it enhances fine paintings. In the frontispiece of *A Child's Book of Old Verses,* for example, the little boy and girl saying grace at the table are flanked by a fine still life of jug, bread, and plate, while the curtained window behind them recalls those in Dutch paintings.

Susan Hamburger

SOURCE: "Jessie Willcox Smith," in *Dictionary of Literary Biography, Volume 188: American Book and Magazine Illustrators to 1920,* edited by Steven E. Smith, Catherine A. Hastedt, and Donald H. Dyal, Gale Research, 1998, pp. 336-44.

Smith's illustrations initially appeared in black and white in the books and magazines up to 1900. The three calendars—two for Bryn Mawr in 1901 and 1902 using tinted colors and the self-published one that became *The Book of the Child* (1903), with its hand-lettered text, bold capitals, and bright-orange chapter headings—marked a publishing turning point for Smith. Her use of design and color shone through and defined the style for which she became known. Influenced by Japanese prints, Mary Cassatt aquatints, and the static art of French illustrator Louis-Maurice Boutet de Monvel, Smith and Green created decorative and visually appealing illustrations for *The Book of the Child.* As publishers sought Smith's work, they reproduced her illustrations in large formats best suited to her images. *Dream Blocks* (1908) included the largest number of color illustrations ever to appear in Smith's books; it included an illustrated dust jacket, color cover insert, and fifteen color plates.

One mark of Smith's renown is the commission she received from Joseph H. Chapin for a series for Charles Scribner's Sons, *Scribner's Illustrated Classics.* Chapin sought out America's greatest illustrators, including Maxfield Parrish, to illustrate popular juvenile fiction. He asked Smith in 1904 to illustrate *A Child's Garden of Verses* (1905) for $3,600. Her execution of the drawings for this volume drew rave reviews from critics, the public, and her editor. One illustration, *The Land of Counterpane,* is a compositional masterpiece in which Smith used foreshortened perspective, realistic color, and minute detail to give an impression of soldiers marching through the pass and over the mountain of rumpled blanket.

By 1909, her reputation established, Smith no longer waited for commissions and suggestions. She actively participated in planning and preparing ideas for books by seeking authors to write word pictures to accompany her drawings and at other times illustrating their words. These illustrations for series accompanied compilations of discrete poems or stories. Smith's work often stood alone without text or captions, just as Parrish's did.

Smith's artistic style gradually changed. In the beginning she used dark-lined borders to delineate brightly colored objects and people. In her later work she muted the colors and softened the lines until they nearly disappeared. Smith worked in mixed media—oil, pastels, charcoal—whatever would give her the desired effect. She often overlaid oils over charcoal on paper whose grain or texture added an important element to the work. This use of color lends an impressionistic tone to her work, an influence of the French impressionist painters. Smith adapted and evolved her style to suit the situation. She employed a sympathetic, sometimes humorous, approach in her imaginative compositions of brilliant colors. Her portraits include children in relaxed poses, painted with affection, not cloying sentiment. For *The Water-Babies* she painted the canvas with watercolor and oil overlaid on charcoal. Knowing these were her best work, Smith bequeathed the entire set of twelve originals to the Library of Congress. . . .

Despite critics' opinions that Smith's illustrations were too sentimental, her strongest appeal lay with the *ideal* of childhood: what an adult remembers of the best times, what a parent wishes to see in a child, and what a carefree childhood should be. That book and magazine publishers continued contracting with Smith and paying handsomely for her work attests to the attraction her work held for millions of readers. As an artist she reached more people through her magazine and book illustrations than any museum or gallery exhibitor could hope to attract. Gritty reality could be laid bare for the world by other artists; Smith concentrated on the pleasures of childhood—adulthood would come soon enough.

TITLE COMMENTARY

📖 *THE BED-TIME BOOK* (written by Helen Whitney, 1907)

The New York Times Book Review

SOURCE: A review of *The Bed-Time Book,* in *The New York Times Book Review,* November 2, 1907, p. 703.

One of the most charming books of the season is a baby book, one of those books for the little people which are equally interesting for adults. This is *The Bed-Time Book,* by Helen Hay Whitney, with pictures by Jessie Willcox Smith. It is a large, thin book with large, full-page colored pictures, and on every page, running around the text, little boys and girls in their nighties marching with their candles to bed. It is only necessary to mention the artist's name to prove the charm of the pictures.

The American Review of Reviews

SOURCE: A review of *The Bed-Time Book,* in *The American Review of Reviews,* Vol. XXXVI, No. 6, December, 1907, p. 766.

The engravers. The Beck Engraving Company, and the printers, S. H. Burbank & Co., deserve special mention for their clean and satisfactory work in connection with the illustrations of the *The Time Book,* by Helen Hay Whitney, illustrated by Jessie Willcox Smith, the most attractive picture book of the year. There is a strain of seriousness, we might almost say sadness, underlying the expression of Miss Smith's characters, that the young folks may not find attractive, though they may not penetrate deep enough into the philosophy of art to know the cause. But artistically these pictures would be hard to equal.

📖 *DREAM BLOCKS* (written by Aileen C. Higgins, 1908)

The New York Times Book Review

SOURCE: A review of *Dream Blocks,* in *The New York Times Book Review,* December 5, 1908, p. 744.

Miss Smith will be remembered as the realistic yet whimsical illustrator of Helen Hay Whitney's *The Bed-Time Book* and Betty Sage's *Rhymes of Real Children.* Her line, color, and atmosphere treatment is not unlike that of Maxfield Parrish, although evidently Miss Smith makes no use of the blowpipe or of superimposed photographs. The fourteen pictures, full quarto in size, which accompany Miss Higgins's verses, are of a high artistic merit. In color, pose, and movement they are sure to appeal to children, while the infantile pathos and humor, the prophetic element in form and feature of the figures, will cause adults to ponder over the philosophy of child play and its striking analogy to the beginnings of a race in all its simplicity, curiosity, and eager endeavor to solve elemental problems of necessity and happiness.

📖 *A CHILD'S BOOK OF OLD VERSES* (compiled by Smith, 1910)

The North American Review

SOURCE: A review of *A Child's Book of Old Verses,* in *The North American Review,* Vol. 192, No. DCLXI, December, 1910, p. 852.

The charm of Jessie Willcox Smith's children, if it does not quite match that of Kate Greenaway, falls at least not far short of it. The ten full-page drawings here of round, chubby children in a very solid and realistic child's world are as delightful as ever. Imagination or suggestion, of course, is not what these pictures have, but they have youth and truth. From the one hundred and ten children's poems chosen it is easily seen that Jessie Willcox Smith was properly brought up and trained on Whittier's "Child Life" and Christina Rossetti's "Sing-Song." All the poems included are permanently valuable; but since, by the inclusion of "She was a Treasure, She was a Sweet," the author proves her acquaintance with that

From Little Women, *written by Louisa May Alcott. Illustrated by Jessie Willcox Smith.*

most delightful writer upon child-life, William Canton, why should she have omitted his lovely "Prayer"?

> Dear Father whom I cannot see
> Look down from Heaven on little me,
> Let angels through the darkness spread
> Their holy wings about my bed.
>
> And keep me safe because I am
> The Heavenly Shepherd's little lamb.
> Teach me to do as I am told
> And help me be as good as gold.

Herrick's "Child's Grace before Meat," if somewhat quaint and odd in form, would yet be a good addition to a modern collection of children's verses. One also misses one or two of the best of William Motherwell's children's poems and quite indispensable poems by Kipling and Stevenson.

The Nation

SOURCE: A review of *A Child's Book of Old Verses,* in *The Nation,* Vol. 91, No. 2371, December 8, 1910, pp. 554-55.

Miss Smith has . . . turned anthologist in a sumptuous

volume, entitled *A Child's Book of Old Verses.* Not only are the illustrations quaint and poetically childlike, but the selections, largely old-fashioned, are chosen with discrimination—something which cannot be said of most recent compilations of this character.

William Elliot Griffis

SOURCE: A review of *A Child's Book of Old Verses,* in *The New York Times Book Review,* December 17, 1910, p. 711.

Both little boys and little girls ought to find much pleasure in *A Child's Book of Old Verses,* selected and illustrated by Jessie Willcox Smith. There are over a hundred of the selections, some of which have been read or quoted to the children many generations, while others are from pens as modern as those of Kate Greenaway, Lewis Carroll, and Robert Louis Stevenson. Here are the famous owl and pussy cat, and Father William, and grasshopper green, and that Meddlesome Mattie who opened her grandmother's snuffbox, concerning whom Col. Roosevelt lately provoked some inquiry among people who had forgotten their first readers. There are ten full-page plates in color, in which the illustrator has shown her usual understanding of child nature and her delightful art in its portrayal.

The American Review of Reviews

SOURCE: A review of *A Child's Book of Old Verses,* in *The American Review of Reviews,* Vol. XLII, No. 6, December, 1966, p. 766.

The most attractive picture book of the year is undoubtedly *A Child's Book of Old Verses,* selected and illustrated by Jessie Willcox Smith. The color printing, as has been usual in the last few years where Miss Smith's colored drawings have been reproduced, is really marvelous. One might do well to buy the book for the nursery, extract carefully the color prints, and frame them for wall decorations.

📖   *THE FIVE SENSES* (written by Angela M. Keyes, 1911)

The New York Times Book Review

SOURCE: A review of *The Five Senses,* in *The New York Times Book Review,* October 1, 1911, p. 585.

Five full-page colored illustrations by Jessie Willcox Smith give the final touch to excellence to an unusually attractive collection of short stories and poems for little children brought together under the title of *The Five Senses,* by Angela M. Keyes. Such writers as Kingsley, Longfellow, Stevenson, and Hans Christian Andersen have been drawn upon, with selections from various old tales and bits of folk lore, as well as contributions by the compil-

er, delightful little stories that the children like. The contents are brought together under the five heads—those of the senses—Tasting, Smelling, Touching, Hearing, and Seeing. It is a volume of 252 pages, the stories all fresh and unhackneyed. It is, as the foreword says, "An easy book of joyous literature for the children."

📖   *DICKENS'S CHILDREN: TEN DRAWINGS BY JESSIE WILLCOX SMITH* (1912)

Algernon Tassin

SOURCE: "Christmas Voyage and Picture Gallery," in *Bookman,* Vol. XXXVI, No. 4, December, 1912, pp. 391-403.

Jessie Willcox Smith in *Dickens's Children* succeeds very well in catching the spontaneous action which . . . photographs lack. Her drawing and colouring are delightful, and the pictures are pervaded with feminine sympathy for children in their appealing moods, and with her well-known expressive charm. More almost than any one else she can make you feel how serious to themselves are the little souls of children.

📖   *THE WATER-BABIES* (written by Charles Kingsley, 1916)

Mary M. Ison

SOURCE: "Things Nobody Ever Heard Of: Jessie Willcox Smith Draws the Water-Babies," in *The Quarterly Journal of the Library of Congress,* Vol. 39, No. 2, Spring, 1982, pp. 90-101.

Kingsley's tale lends itself wonderfully to illustration, with its make-believe creatures and interesting characters and vignettes, and through the years more than two dozen artists have illustrated it in various editions. Jessie Willcox Smith made thirteen color drawings in oil, charcoal, and pastel for a 1916 edition published by Dodd Mead & Company. Twelve of these original works were received by the Library of Congress in 1935 from the artist's estate. The thirteenth is in a private collection. . . .

Although of vastly different backgrounds, the team of Kingsley, the nineteenth-century man of religion, and Smith, the twentieth-century woman of art, brought about a book which is both charming and earnestly believable. Jessie Willcox Smith's illustrations invest the water-babies with such reality as to provide credence to Kingsley's story. Because she takes his tale seriously and portrays its subjects in ways which relate to human experience, she forces us to take the story and its message seriously too. At the same time, her delightful and charming drawings remind us of the final words of Kingsley's classic: "But remember always, as I told you at first, that this is all a fairy tale, and only fun and pretence: and, therefore, you are not to believe a word of it, even if it is true."

📖 THE LITTLE MOTHER GOOSE (1918)

The Nation

SOURCE: A review of *The Little Mother Goose,* in *The Nation,* Vol. 107, No. 2787, November 30, 1918, p. 657.

There are two editions of Mother Goose; one is a handy little volume which a child may enjoy without depending on stronger hands to manage the unwieldy bulk so often a hindrance in children's books. The colored pictures by Jessie Willcox Smith are captivating, especially Peter-Peter-Pumpkin-Eater, and Rain-Rain-go-away. The black-and-white drawings suffer, as do the color plates, by indifferent workmanship unfair to the artist.

📖 THE CHILDREN OF DICKENS (written by Samuel Crothers, 1925; illustrations reprinted from Smith's *Dickens's Children,* 1912)

Anne Carroll Moore

SOURCE: "Reading Dickens," in *New York Herald Tribune Books,* Vol. 2, No. 14, December 20, 1925, p. 8.

With the sure sense both of a critical child audience and of a true Dickens lover Dr. Crothers has searched for the children in all the Dickens books and presents his liberal and varied selection in their original form rather than in words of his own. Fortunately he seems to have been in no way limited by the ten color plates designed by Jessie Willcox Smith some years ago, which now appear as illustrations for this volume. They are pleasant pictures of children, but they give the book the appearance of another of the endless succession of child characters from Dickens in rewritten form rather than the distinction which belongs to it as a unique introduction to Dickens for both children and grown-ups who do not know how to think of the London of Dickens.

📖 AN OLD-FASHIONED ABC BOOK (written by Elizabeth Allen Ashton, 1990)

Publishers Weekly

SOURCE: A review of *An Old-Fashioned ABC Book,* in *Publishers Weekly,* Vol. 237, No. 6, February 9, 1990, pp. 58-9.

To parents with treasured early editions of *A Child's Garden of Verses* or *Heidi,* Smith's soft, period illustrations will be very familiar. An artist for *Good Housekeeping* during the 1920s and '30s, Smith depicted children involved in pastimes reminiscent of a simpler era: playing marbles, building sandcastles, learning to sew, lying in a hammock watching the clouds drift by. Ashton provides a sweet, melodic text that is perfectly synchronized with Smith's pictures: "L is for Luggage packed up for a trip. Laura is all set for her journey by ship." Youngsters may miss the pizzazz and punch of more contemporary-feeling alphabet books, but parents and grandparents will find this beautifully designed book a welcome change of pace.

Ann Stell

SOURCE: A review of *An Old-Fashioned ABC Book,* in *School Library Journal,* Vol. 36, No. 7, July, 1990, p. 55.

Selections from Jessie Willcox Smith's artwork depicting an idealized childhood circa 1920-1930 have been turned into an alphabet book with a verse for each letter. The full-color drawings are charming and sentimental and the verses—although far from great poetry—reflect the nostalgic mood of the pictures. ("A is for Apple, all shiny and red. Ann picked a whole basket with big brother Ted.") As a book to help children learn the letters of the alphabet, this has limitations. The initial letters are set in small squares with traditional vine and leaf designs that contribute to the harmonious layout of the pages, but are not clear enough for easy recognition. It's a book more likely to please the large audience of adults who view childhood as a time of innocence.

Additional coverage of Smith's life and career is contained in the following sources published by The Gale Group: *Dictionary of Literary Biography,* Vol. 188; *Major Authors and Illustrators for Children and Young Adults*; and *Something about the Author,* Vol 21.

Mildred D(elois) Taylor

1943-

African-American author of fiction.

Major works include *Roll of Thunder, Hear My Cry* (1976), *Let the Circle Be Unbroken* (1981), *The Friendship* (1987), *The Gold Cadillac* (1987), *The Road to Memphis* (1990).

For information on Taylor's career prior to 1981, see *CLR,* Vol. 9.

INTRODUCTION

Taylor is known for her writings that convey pride in her racial heritage and provide middle schoolers and young adults with well-researched historical fiction about African-American life and family relationships. As a child, Taylor enjoyed hearing stories of her ancestors—stories of people who were proud and dignified—but in school the history books told a different story. Believing that the textbooks diminished contributions of blacks and glossed over the injustices to which they had been subjected, Taylor vowed to write stories that offered a truer vision of black families and their racial struggles. In *Horn Book* she explained, "I wanted to show the endurance of the Black World, with strong fathers and concerned mothers; I wanted to show happy, loved children. . . . I wanted to show a Black family united in love and pride, of which the reader would like to be a part." Taylor does this in her chronicle of the Logans, a black family living in the South during the depression. She follows the family's activities and experiences during the mid-twentieth century, when their reaction to segregation and discrimination helped pave the way for the reforms of the Civil Rights movement. Critics have praised Taylor's ability to present emotional issues in an unsentimental, controlled style without losing the impact of her story. She has also been praised for the poetic quality of her prose, for her characterizations, and for the fact that her books are not social or political tracts disguised as fiction, but a successful interpretation of the universality of the black experience. Her ability to mix the events of everyday life with volatile issues and complex characters has gained the author both wide critical acclaim and popular appeal. "Mildred's words flow smoothly, effortlessly . . . and they abound in richness, harmony, and rhythm. . . . Her ability to bring her characters to life and to involve her readers is remarkable," commented Phyllis J. Fogelman. "This woman was born to write."

Biographical Information

Taylor was born in 1943 in Jackson, Mississippi, to

Wilbert Lee and Deletha Marie (Davis) Taylor. Three weeks after her birth, however, her father decided to move the family North because he did not want his daughters raised in the segregated, racist society of the South. They eventually settled in Toledo, Ohio, but made many trips back to the South to visit. "Each trip down reminded us that the South into which we had been born . . . still remained," recalled Taylor in *Something about the Author Autobiography Series* (*SAAS*). Yet the South also held pleasant memories as the home of her ancestors. When her extended family would get together, the adults would tell family stories, and Taylor would listen to the stories with interest.

Although Taylor's school was not segregated, she was often the only black student in the class. This caused discomfort for her for two reasons. One, she felt that her actions would be viewed as representative of her race. Secondly, she was aware of the discrepancies between her family stories of black Americans and the images presented in the history textbooks. By the time Taylor entered high school, the civil rights movement was underway. However, living in the North, Taylor felt somewhat removed, except for one incident. In 1957, when Taylor was a freshman in high school, a black senior was chosen as homecoming queen for her school. The student body reaction ranged from happiness (especially on the part of minority students) to anger which exploded into violence. Taylor remembers, "Though things returned to normal . . . those days . . . hammered home to all of us that racism was not only part of the South, but of the North as well."

As Taylor prepared for her future, she wrote stories, but found writing difficult and the style of her favorite authors, like Charles Dickens and Jane Austen, unnatural for her. After graduating from the University of Toledo with a bachelor's degree in education in 1965, Taylor joined the Peace Corps. During her service with the Corps, she taught English as a second language on a Navajo reservation in Arizona and taught at a small school in Ethiopia. After the Peace Corps, Taylor went back to school to study journalism. She received her master's degree from the University of Colorado in 1969.

Taylor's first success in the literary field came when she entered a contest sponsored by the Council on Interracial Books for Children. In a hurry to meet the deadline, she revised an old manuscript in just four days. To her surprise, *Song of the Trees* won in the African-American category, and various publishers expressed an interest in the story. Unable to let the Logan family go, she continued to write several more stories centered around them over the years.

Taylor has often mentioned the influence her father has had on her. Among other things, she described him as a great storyteller. In *SAAS* she noted, "He told me many of the stories upon which I have based the Logan books. The character of Stacey Logan is based upon him." Evidence of her father can also be found in the character of David Logan. Taylor's books are mostly based on the stories from her childhood, stories of her family, and of the black heroes she grew up learning about. They focus on family, self-reliance, determination, pride, and the land. Taylor noted, "It is my hope that to the children who read my books, the Logans will provide those heroes missing from the schoolbooks of my childhood, Black men, women, and children of whom they can be proud."

Major Works

Roll of Thunder, Hear My Cry is the most well known of the Logan books, focusing on how the family, and specifically the children, deal with racial discrimination over the course of a year. On a trip into Strawberry, Cassie gets her first real taste of the negative attitudes that pervade the South. Cassie and Stacey both go through a rite of passage and have to learn how to deal with the unfair world they are just now beginning to understand. The book explores the importance of land ownership, as well as the freedom and the hardships that it entails. Taylor also addresses the inaccurate portrayal of black history found in many textbooks. Through all the events, the parents offer wise and loving counsel to guide the

children on their emotional journeys. Stuart Hannabuss commented that the book is "full of episodes of emotional power." Noting the effect of such scenes, David Rees, in his work *The Marble on the Water: Essays on Contemporary Writers of Fiction for Children and Young Adults*, remarked that "it's impossible not to feel anger and a sense of burning in reading this book."

The next book in the Logan saga is *Let the Circle be Unbroken*. According to David A. Wright in *Dictionary of Literary Biography*, "Taylor's recurrent theme of family unity has its strongest appearance" in this book. Cassie once again narrates and tells the story of how her town and its people cope with the devastating effects of the Great Depression. The book examines how hard times can bring out both the best and worst in people. In the novel, white and black sharecroppers band together to give each other food and moral support, while an elderly black woman is criticized for memorizing the state constitution in order to vote, although ultimately she is refused this right. The novel also depicts the unfair trial of one of the Logan children's friends (a continuation from a situation started in *Roll of Thunder*). Christine McDonnell observed, "Though many of Cassie and Stacey's experiences happen because they are black, their growing pains and self-discovery are universal." She added, "The Logans' story will strengthen and satisfy all who read it."

The Friendship is based on a story that Taylor's father once told her and brings the issue of racial inequality to a dramatic climax. Tom Bee is an elderly black man who saved the life of John Wallace, a white storekeeper, when the two were younger. Grateful for Tom's assistance, John tells Tom that they will always be friends on a first-name basis. However, years later John retracts that promise when Tom refers to John by his first name in public—something that was considered insubordination in Southern society. Feeling pressured to respond to this public display, John follows Tom outside and shoots him in the leg. With quiet dignity, Tom pulls himself up and walks off, his leg dragging behind him, while repeating the name "John" over and over. Betsy Hearne claimed that the novel "elicits a naturally powerful response in depicting cruel injustice," with writing that is "concentrated to heighten that effect." Frances Bradburn stated, "This is a story that children will experience rather than simply read. . . . The humiliation, the injustice, but above all the quiet determination, courage, and pride of Mr. Tom Bee will speak to all children."

The Gold Cadillac is reminiscent of the trips Taylor took with her family as a child. Set in the 1950s, the story chronicles a black family's road trip to the South. Along the way, Wilma (the name of Taylor's sister), 'lois (an abbreviation of Taylor's middle name), and their parents are confronted with "whites only" signs and suffer harassment from white police officers who are both jealous and suspicious of the family's car and the prosperity it represents. Through these and other ugly encounters, the two sisters are better able to appreciate the greater freedom and opportunity they enjoy in their Ohio hometown. The Cadillac becomes an important symbol in the story. To their father it represents freedom and prosperity—the opportunities that are available to a black man in the North. To their mother it represents the frivolous spending of money that could be used to buy a house so that her daughters can live in a better neighborhood. For the girls it represents adventure. Unfortunately, it is also symbolic of the racial tensions and danger in the South. Helen E. Williams remarked, "Clear language and logical, dramatic sequencing of story events make this story bitter-sweet for adult readers but important for the social development of beginning readers."

The Road to Memphis is the most recent of the Logan books. Cassie is now a high school senior, attending school in Jackson, Mississippi, and dreaming of becoming a lawyer (partially the influence of a handsome young lawyer she meets). Cassie's brother Stacey and his friend Moe are also living in Jackson where they have found work in a factory. Away from home for the first time, the trio must deal with certain ugly realities on thier own. The outbreak of World War II, as well as several racial incidents, put a heavy strain on the young people; for instance, a friend dies because the hospital refuses to treat blacks. In addition, Moe is forced to flee the city because he defends himself against a white attack. Consequently, Cassie grapples with her decision to pursue a career in the white-controlled legal system. While allowing that Taylor loses a little narrative power in the novel, Susan Schuller concluded that *The Road to Memphis* "is a dramatic, painful book."

Awards

Taylor has received numerous awards and honors for her books, including the Newbery Medal in 1977 for *Roll of Thunder, Hear My Cry*. That book also was an American Library Association notable book in 1976 and a *Boston Globe-Horn Book* honor book in 1977. *Let the Circle Be Unbroken* received an outstanding book of the year citation from the *New York Times* in 1981 and the Coretta Scott King Award in 1982. *The Friendship* also received the Coretta Scott King Award, as well as the fiction award from *Boston Globe-Horn Book*, both in 1988. *The Gold Cadillac* was cited as a notable book by the *New York Times* in 1987 and was bestowed the Christopher Award in 1988. Finally, *The Road to Memphis* won the Coretta Scott King Award in 1990.

AUTHOR'S COMMENTARY

Mildred D. Taylor

SOURCE: "1998 Boston Globe-Horn Book Award Acceptance Speech," in *The Horn Book Magazine,* Vol. LXV, No. 2, March-April, 1989, pp. 179-82.

I am pleased and honored to accept the Boston Globe-Horn Book Award for *The Friendship.* It is an honor for me, and it is an honor to the memory of my father, for *The Friendship* is drawn from one of the many stories that he told me. Over the years he shared many stories about life in the South with me, and today in accepting this award I would like to share just a bit of that time in my life with you, that time in my life when my father and the other storytellers told the history.

For me the history began in the South, for I was born in Mississippi. When I was three months old, my parents took my sister and me to live in the North, yet over the years of my childhood I grew to know the South—to feel the South—through the yearly trips we took there and through the stories told. In those days of the late forties, in those days of the early fifties, in those days before the civil rights movement, I remember the South and how it was. I remember the racism, the segregation, and the fear. But I also remember the other South—the South of family and community, the South filled with warmth and love—and how it opened to me a sense of history and filled me with pride.

I remember during our trips South, speeding down winding red roads toward my grandparents' house, with rocks hitting the underbelly of the car. I remember my father pointing out landmarks of his own childhood or of incidents that had happened. I remember my grandparents' house, the house my great-grandfather had built at the turn of the century, and I remember the adults talking about the past. As they talked I began to visualize all the people who had once lived in that house, all the family who had once known the land, and I felt as if I knew them, too. I met them all through the stories told, stories told with such gusto and acting skills that people long since dead lived again through the voices and movements of the storytellers.

The history of the family and of the community was told through those stories acted out on moonlit porches or by brightly burning fires. Many of the stories told were humorous, some were tragic, but all told of the dignity and survival of a people living in a society that allowed them few rights as citizens and treated them as inferiors. Much history was in those stories, and I never tired of hearing them. There were stories about slavery and the days following slavery. There were stories about family and friends, and there was the story about a man—a black man—who befriended a white man and who later was shot by that same white man for refusing to address him as "mister," for refusing to show "the proper respect."

This story both enraged me as a child and made me proud. It enraged me because of the injustice of a society that expected blacks to bend to the will of whites. It enraged me that one man, because of the color of his skin, could consider himself superior to another. It made me proud because a black man chose not to see himself as inferior but to see himself equal to anyone. For me as a child hearing this story, this black man became my

John Wayne. He was a hero, and as a black child growing up in the forties and fifties, I needed black heroes. I needed them desperately and at no time more than the year I was ten years old; my family moved into a newly integrated neighborhood in Toledo, and I found myself the only black child in my class. During that year and the years that followed, classes devoted to the history of black people in the United States always caused me painful embarrassment. This was because history had not been presented truly, showing the accomplishments of blacks both in Africa and in this hemisphere. But, as it was, as the textbooks and the teachers presented the history, the indictment of slavery was also an indictment of the people who were enslaved—a people who, according to the texts, were docile and childlike, accepting their fate without once attempting to free themselves. To me this lackluster history of black people, totally devoid of any heroic or pride-building qualities, was as much a condemnation of myself as it was of my ancestors. I used to sit tensely waiting out those class hours trying to think of ways to repudiate what the textbooks said, for I recognized that there was a terrible contradiction between what was in them and what I learned at home.

Eventually there came a time when I tried to put some of the stories of heroism I had heard from my family over the years on paper. The story that later was to become *The Friendship* was one of the first I attempted to write. But in the beginning I didn't have the power to put the story on paper. For me the story had to be as powerful on paper as it had been when I had heard it told by the storytellers. I wanted the reader to feel what I had felt.

Over the years of my childhood the story of the man I call Mr. Tom Bee had been told by the finest of storytellers, and the finest of those was my father, for he was a master storyteller. The last most vivid memory I have of my father telling the story was shortly after my return from a two-year stay in Africa. I remember how special that time was. There was no large family gathering; there were no other storytellers present. In fact, it was just my father and me. Everyone else had gone to bed. It was late, after two o'clock in the morning. My father had to be up the next morning before six to go to work, and I had to be up early, too, for I was leaving for a job in Chicago. Yet my father talked on, telling the stories of his childhood, and I, as always, eagerly listened, not yet ready for sleep, not yet ready to have the stories end. Sitting by the living room fireplace, I heard each story anew. Then, as the night drifted on, and one story led to another, my father again told the story of the man I call Mr. Tom Bee.

I remember how my father's voice rang out as he told the story. I remember the sound he made in describing the awful explosion of the shotgun when the old black man was shot. But most of all, I remember the words of the old black man so long ago, the words as told by my father.

They were haunting.

My father has been dead twelve years now. I have not heard the story told since. Yet, the words ring out in my mind as if I had heard them spoken by my father only yesterday. Those words are now the last words spoken in *The Friendship.*

> The white men came out and sniggered. Mr. John Wallace, carrying the shotgun, came out onto the porch too. He stood there, his face solemn, and said, "You made me do that, Tom. I coulda killed ya, but I ain't wantin' to kill ya 'cause ya done saved my life an' I'm a Christian man so I ain't forgetting that. But this here disrespectin' me gotta stop and I means to stop it now. You gotta keep in mind you ain't nothin' but a nigger. You gonna learn to watch yo' mouth. You gonna learn to address me proper. You hear me, Tom?"
>
> Mr. Tom Bee sat in silence staring at the bloody leg.
>
> "Tom, ya hear me?"
>
> Now, slowly, Mr. Tom Bee raised his head and looked up at John Wallace. "Oh, yeah, I hears ya all right. I hears ya. But let me tell you somethin', John. Ya was John t' me when I saved your sorry life and you give me your word you was always gonna be John t' me as long as I lived. So's ya might's well go 'head and kill me cause that's what ya gon' be, John. Ya hear me, John? Till the judgment day. Till the earth opens itself up and the fires-a hell come takes yo' ungrateful soul! Ya hear me, John? Ya hear me? *John! John! John!* Till the judgment day! *John!*"

Mildred D. Taylor

SOURCE: "Acceptance Speech for the 1997 ALAN Award," in *The ALAN Review,* Vol. 25, No. 3, Spring, 1998, p. 3.

[The following is Mildred Taylor's acceptance speech for the 1997 ALAN Award, which she presented at the National Council of Teachers of English Convention].

Many years ago when I first started writing the stories told by my family about our family history and about neighbors and friends and the community in which my family lived, I envisioned presenting an aspect of American history which during my own childhood was not presented in the history books. I envisioned presenting a family united in love and self-respect, and parents, strong and sensitive, attempting to guide their children successfully without harming their spirits, through the hazardous maze of living in a discriminatory society. I wanted readers to know this family, based upon my own, and I wanted them to feel akin to them and to walk in their shoes. The presentation at the National Council of Teachers of English Convention of the 1997 ALAN Award signifies to me that perhaps I have achieved some of these goals I set so long also, and I sincerely thank you for this great recognition.

Writing the books based upon stories told by my family has been a long journey from my childhood to receiving the ALAN Award, but I have always tried to stay on course. From *Song of the Trees* to *The Well* I have attempted to present a true picture of life in America as older members of my family remember it, and as I remember it in the days before the civil rights movement. In all of the books I have recounted not only the joy of growing up in a large and supportive family, but my own feelings of being faced with segregation and bigotry. Writing these feelings was never easy, but when my first books were published, those feelings and the history I presented were understood. Yes, people would say. We remember how it was.

Today, however, younger generations have no experience of that time when signs over restroom doors, signs over water fountains, in restaurant windows and hotels said: WHITE ONLY, COLORED NOT ALLOWED. Today's generation of children, as well as many of their parents and teachers, have not had to endure such indignities or even worse aspects of racism that once pervaded America, and I am grateful for that. But, unfortunately, as we all know racism still exists and is growing.

In the writing of my books I have tried to present not only a history of my family, but the effects of racism, not only to the victims of racism but also to the racists themselves. I have recounted events that were painful to write and painful to be read, but I had hoped they brought more understanding. Now, however, there are those who think that perhaps my recounting are too painful, and there are those who seek to remove books such as mine from school reading lists. There are some who say the books should be removed because the "N" word is used. There are some who say such events as described in my books and books by others did not happen. There are those who do not want to remember the past or who do not want their children to know the past and who would white-wash history, and these sentiments are not only from whites.

In Texas recently a Hispanic father went to the school board and asked that *The Well* be removed from school reading lists because the "N" word was used. In Orange County, California a black mother objected to her son reading *Roll of Thunder, Hear My Cry* in a class where he was the only African-American, and the school's solution to her objection was to seat her son in the hall while the book was being read. In a Northern state, a black church questioned a book like *Roll of Thunder* being presented in the schools to its children.

I am hurt that any child would ever be hurt by my words. As a parent I understand not wanting a child to hear painful words, but as a parent I do not understand not wanting a child to learn about a history that is part of America, a history about a family representing millions of families that are strong and loving and who remain united and strong, despite the obstacles they face.

In the writing of my most recent work, titled *The Land,*

I have found myself hesitating about using words that would have been spoken in the late 1800s because of my concern about our "politically correct" society. But just as I have had to be honest with myself in the telling of all my stories, I realize I must be true to the feelings of the people about whom I write and true to the stories told. My stories might not be "politically correct," so there will be those who will be offended, but as we all know, racism is offensive.

It is not polite, and it is full of pain.

It is through you and through your great efforts that, if my books or books like mine are presented in the classroom, the children will be prepared for what they read. Before reading any of my books to my own eight-year-old, I talk to her about what life was like when I was a child and when her grandparents and great-grandparents were children; and we continue to talk as the story unfolds. I want only the best for my child in her learning of the past and of her heritage, just as we all want the best for all the children. I thank you for recognizing my books as a contribution to children. I shall always treasure your faith in my work, and shall always treasure the 1997 ALAN Award.

GENERAL COMMENTARY

Karen Patricia Smith

SOURCE: "A Chronicle of Family Honor: Balancing Rage and Triumph in the Novels of Mildred D. Taylor," in *African-American Voices in Young Adult Literature,* The Scarecrow Press, Inc., 1994, pp. 247-76.

Mildred D. Taylor is considered to be a major voice in African-American children's and young adult literature. Her books span both segments of youth genre, but given their depth and applicability to gaining an understanding of the historical role participated in by African-Americans, are particularly appropriate for the middle school (grade six through eight) young adult. Praised for the consistency of her writing style, her singular method of conveying the spirit, personality, and heartfelt convictions of a united African-American family, Tay-lor has been the recipient of numerous honors for her work. . . . Taylor's work is informed by historical verification, personal biographical, reflection and literary artistry. With the exception of *The Gold Cadillac* (written in 1987 and not part of the Logan family chronicle), winner of the Christopher Award, her work is set against the backdrop of Depression day Mississippi, a particularly perilous time for African-Americans.

One of the unique aspects of Taylor's work is her focus upon a strong, upwardly mobile family unit which consistently, and also realistically, manages to meet "head-on" the social challenges of racism and disfranchisement without projection of a self-conscious perspective. In the Mississippi of the 1930s and 1940s, African-American success was uneasily measured by African-Americans not only by one's general ability to survive economically but also more specifically, by ownership of land and one's capacity to retain that ownership. All manifestations of success had to be accomplished without attracting, to any great degree, the negative attention of discontented whites who, themselves struggling, directed their energies towards ensuring that the black standard of living not progress beyond a bare subsistence level. The most extreme forms of danger lay ahead for those blacks who were too "flamboyant" in their achievements.

The politics of family survival sustained by a strong spiritual and moral base serves as Taylor's most prominent theme, in what might be termed her "chronicle" of the Logan family. Taylor has stated that in great part, her Logan family stories are based upon personal experience:

> Through David Logan have come the words of my father, and through the Logan family the love of my own family. If people are touched by the warmth of the Logans, it is because I had the warmth of my own youthful years from which to draw. If the Logans seem real, it is because I had my own family upon which to base characterizations. And if people believe the book to be biographical, it is because I have tried to distill the essence of Black life, so familiar to most Black families, to make the Logans an embodiment of that spiritual heritage; for, contrary to what the media relate to us, all Black families are not fatherless or disintegrating. Certainly my family was not.

Such a factual basis for storytelling serves to underscore the reality stated above by Taylor, that many African-American families have in the past, despite the most oppressive of circumstances, succeeded in surmounting potentially overwhelming odds, and have done so *as a nuclear family*. Such a focus assists in illustrating to young people the positive and liberating possibilities, borne of that glorious combination of dreams and unabated hard work, that *can* await those who have the fortitude to prevail.

This does not mean that the hardships endured by a person of color should be submerged within a sea of optimism and certainly, Taylor does not do this. It also does not mean that one will not, or should not be entitled to experience a certain rage at injustices rendered. But what it does mean is that a youthful and also adult audience needs (and indeed *deserves*) to have the opportunity to see the good that can come of *not giving up and not giving in;* that there is the possibility of *triumph* at the end of adversity. . . .

Taylor reminds us that her family model flies in the face of stereotype. What is also evident upon further scrutiny, is the presence of *balance,* or as the Roman Horace referred to it, "the Golden Mean"; used here to indicate a mediating force which, when present within the most

adverse of circumstances, has the ability to offset a potentially destructive course of events. Balance, of a spiritual, social, economic, and political nature, . . . may be seen to be the key to the survival of the Logan family. These elements . . . are . . . the mechanisms through which Taylor works through the problem of balancing rage and triumph.

An analysis of Taylor's fictional family saga, one which we are reminded is informed by factual accounts, also serves to highlight through the literary vehicle, similar experiences of other African-American families of the era, and hopefully serves as a possible archetype for those contemporary African-American families for whom the dream still has not been realized. . . .

Noticeable in Taylor's work is the strong ability of the Logan family to incorporate spiritual belief and practice into daily living, without sacrificing a certain necessary awareness of the worldly environment. The Logan family embraces a non-charismatic form of Christianity, generally devoid of the more energetic physical manifestations of faith. Their spirituality is demonstrated through the quality of their actions in everyday life as well as through interactions with others, an approach totally consistent with that of the New Testament. The family avoids being totally subsumed within a religious framework which might prevent them from coming to terms with a generally irreligious world view. The Logans are totally at ease with their spirituality; it is neither overlooked during their progress through the outside world, or over-emphasized in a self-alienating fashion. Thus, in this regard, the Logans achieve equilibrium. . . .

Often, rationalization is called for; a circumstance which can be quite disorienting and even upsetting for those attempting to regulate their lives through Christian principles. In *Roll of Thunder, Hear My Cry,* Cassie tells her father of the confrontation she has had with the contemptuous Lillie Jean, daughter of a racist white storekeeper:

> When I had explained the whole . . . business to Papa, he said slowly, "You know the Bible says you're s'pose to forgive these things."
>
> "Yessir," I agreed, waiting.
>
> "S'pose to turn the other cheek."
>
> "Yessir."
>
> Papa rubbed his moustache and looked up at the trees standing like sentinels on the edge of the hollow, listening." But the way I see it, the Bible didn't mean for you to be no fool. Now one day, maybe I can forgive John Andersen for what he done to these trees, but I ain't gonna forget it. I figure forgiving is not letting something nag at you—rotting you out. Now if I hadn't done what I done, then I couldn't've forgiven myself, and that's the truth of it."

David Logan works out the problem in the presence of

his daughter, fully cognizant of her impressionable nature and the fact that anything he says or does will leave a lasting effect upon her psyche. He is a man of pride who is not pride-filled. He attempts to follow biblical principles in thought and action. He does not wish to leave a legacy of hatred behind him for his children and also his oppressors; on the other hand, he will not allow his children to be humiliated. Logan however, acknowledges his own humanity and also the reality that in order to survive and survive successfully, he must find a way to balance the situation without contradicting biblical practices—a constant struggle for all believers.

David Logan's decision making process does not go unwitnessed. The text tells us that the very trees seem to quietly await his response. They provide a divine setting for this moment. After a brief pause, Mr. Logan renders his decision of reconciliation rather than vengeful action, acknowledging that absolute forgiveness, while eminently desirable and required by Christian principle, is often in human terms, a goal to be honestly worked towards rather than one which can in every case be assumed and immediately attained. Forgiveness in effect, involves *process*, an active state of becoming or growth (in some instances a faster or slower process, as the case may be) culminating in an eventual product. Realistically, forgiveness is not always possible on demand, though it remains an expectation.

The concept of nature bearing witness to momentous events is established in the previous *Song of the Trees*, in which David Logan's forest is threatened by his avaricious neighbors. As the Logan children play unknowingly amongst the trees, Mr. Andersen and his men plot, and begin to carry out their plan to cut down the Logan trees and sell them for profit, taking advantage of the fact that David Logan is away from home, working in another city. For Taylor, land and spirituality are inextricably bound with one another. . . .

The image of a temple formed by the trees is a powerful one. The forest is to be revered, not for its own sake but for its presence as a representation of the work of the creative Deity. A legacy of time is established; time which has stood witness to many things. . . .

The inheritance of the Logan land is the major means through which the family is able to maintain its economic independence, thus curiously connecting spiritual matters with those of the world, in a way ironically similar to the statement "In God We Trust," which frames our coins. This appears to be a secularization of the most extreme form; and it is, if taken (pardon the expression), "at face value." How then can it be justified, or balanced? The answer I believe, for David Logan, lies in the fact that he believes that all things including the land which his family has been fortunate enough to own, come through the will of God, and as long as the origins of his ownership of this legacy are not forgotten, and the land is correctly worked, cared for, and utilized, the Logan family does not live in violation of their spiritual beliefs.

Living up to, or within ones beliefs, *totally*, is not always possible as we have pointed out. Sometimes belief codes are also violated through youthful ignorance or purposely put aside. Again, this is part of the human condition and representative of "balancing" of another type. In *Let the Circle Be Unbroken*, Cassie, Taylor's principal spokesperson in the Logan chronicles, covets Son-Boy's emerald-blue marble while in Sunday school, but feels no guilt about memorizing the Bible verse "Thou shalt not covet thy neighbor's house or anything that is thy neighbor's." She plots to get that marble with incredible calculation and adolescent mindlessness. This ironic act is both indicative of her "innocence" (in not sensing a dichotomy between the memorizing of the verse and covetous desire) and simultaneously, what many would deem typical adolescent self-centeredness. But Cassie's subconscious balancing of what she has been *taught* with what she *wants*, represents the covetous side of human nature, and as such is separate and apart from the type of compromise required for "safe" living in the Mississippi of the 1930s.

Overshadowing the same story however, is the aura of fear and anxiety brought on by the incident of T. J. Avery, a sad soul of a young man who takes up with the disreputable Simms brothers. They are the sons of Charlie Simms who is also father to the Christ-like Jeremy and to Cassie's nemesis, the unbearable Lillie Jean. T. J. has been enticed into participating in a scheme to steal a gun. The two Simms brothers accompany him, but are surprised by the owner and his wife. One of the Simms brothers (in a mask) hits and kills Mr. Barnett with the flat of an ax. The two boys later claim it was T. J. Avery who committed the assault.

A lynching is only averted when David Logan and his trusted hired hand Mr. Morrison, purposefully set fire to the Logan land to provide a distraction. The Logan family is outraged at the injustice of T. J.'s situation; everyone knows who is responsible for the killing. David Logan, through his actions has taken the initiative to do what he can for T.J.—at the expense of risking his own land. However, even he realizes that there is only so much one can do before ones own safety and the safety of ones family is jeopardized. Even burning his own land does not stop the wheels of injustice from grinding out their inevitable verdict on T. J. Avery. Mrs. Logan, David's mother and the children's wise grandmother, realizes this as well. Her utterance and response: "'Lord, Lord,' and [she] absently continued to stir the collards," is not indicative of an over preoccupation with cooking and a lack of interest in T. J.'s predicament. Rather, this response is an affirmation of the inevitability of T. J.'s situation, the belief that God does everything for a reason, and the acceptance of man's (and woman's) basic inability to understand His ways and also the villainy of human beings. . . .

A final powerful manifestation of "balancing" within the spiritual framework may be seen in the presentation of Taylor's most recent two books *The Road to Memphis* and *Mississippi Bridge*, both published in 1990. Here, the author takes the situation out of the hands of her characters and attempts to balance the scales in a larger, more overt fashion. Yet, the results are anything but "heavy-handed." The elements of vindication are skillfully interwoven in a starkly realistic manner. Though both books were published during the same year, according to the indications in the notes to *Mississippi Bridge. The Road to Memphis* was officially issued before *Mississippi Bridge* If *The Road to Memphis* is Taylor's angriest book to date, *Mississippi Bridge* is her most actively retaliatory. The plot line in the former novel is unrelenting in the magnitude of the injustices she lays bare for her readers. The resolution in *Mississippi Bridge* seems designed as a horrible (and yet frighteningly justified) commentary on mankind's inhumanity to man. A cycle is initiated in *The Road to Memphis,* where the Logan children anxiously await the return of their brother Stacey from Jackson where he works in a box factory. When Stacey does arrive it is in a marvelous new car, a self-bestowed present bought out of frustration. After all of the passengers in Jackson had boarded the bus, the only seats left were those in the front; seats reserved for whites only. Given the choice of either standing during the entire bus ride or getting off of the bus, Stacey leaves in anger and then decides to solve his situation by buying a used car, something he has wanted to do for a long time.

This incident initiates a shiver of foreboding in the sunny, late fall afternoon. The shiver soon turns to a terrifying chill when a young friend of the Logan children, Harris is chased and hunted by three young white brothers as a prank, attended by a reluctant but silently participating cousin, Jeremy Simms, the young man who has befriended the Logan family throughout the earlier books of the series. This terrible "prank" in which a hunter becomes the hunted, results not only in emotional trauma for Harris, but a permanent, debilitating injury from which we are led to believe, he will not recover.

Taylor continues to add injuries to insults, which accumulate at times with almost unbearable rapidity but yet, her writing avoids the pitfall of appearing contrived or clichéd. Another friend of the Logan children, Moe is forced into a no-win confrontation with the same three young white youths who persecuted Harris earlier. Driven beyond endurance when one of them knocks the cap off of his head, Moe strikes out with a tire iron, seriously injuring all three. This incident causes Moe to have to flee town, aided by Cassie and Stacey, and in a strange paradox, Jeremy Simms, who hides Moe under a tarpaulin in his wagon. En route to Memphis, Cassie is denied the use of a ladies room at a gas station, and in a crushing and demoralizing blow, kicked by the gas station owner. Later, at a hospital, the children's friend Clarence is denied crucial medical care at a white hospital—and subsequently dies.

In so establishing an escalating hierarchy of insult, injury, and injustice, Taylor leads the audience toward a conclusion that something devastating beyond the individual novel must take place to "balance" the scales.

That something involves divine intervention, the calling in of a power which has the ability to make a pronouncement and take action upon what has gone before, and what must come after. The pronouncement, and subsequent action comes in the form of the sequel *Mississippi Bridge.* Though Taylor chooses to set this novel approximately ten years earlier during the 1930s, at a time when the Logan children are in their youth, this chronological "interruption" complicates, but does not destroy the major premise. The reader is left with the feeling that spiritually, Taylor intended us to surmise that God seeks his own time and is present in every age as a mediating force. Time then, is not to be exclusively measured by chronological events, cause and effect, but rather by the overall condition of mankind. His imperfect nature was ordained before his imperfect actions were committed; therefore, divine responses are not necessarily "in tune" with individual acts.

On a day of a driving rainstorm, Jeremy Simms witnesses the humiliation of a black customer in the Wallace store, who is denied the right to try on a hat. He observes this incident and almost immediately after, the double standard treatment of a white woman, Miz Hattie, who comes into the store requesting the same, and is granted her request. . . .

Outside the store, a group of people wait for that bus. Cassie Logan's grandmother is among them. Cassie innocently tries to direct Big Ma to a seat in the front and is shocked when she is told that these seats are reserved for whites only. Later, in a final outrage, all blacks are ordered off the bus when a white family with many children arrive on the scene. One young black man, Josias who had been previously humiliated inside the store, is physically thrown off the bus with his belongings when he dares to beg the driver to allow him to ride the bus, because he knows he has a job waiting for him in the next town.

On the way over the bridge out of town, the bus careens off of the bridge, sending everyone on board to their death. *Mississippi Bridge* is Taylor's most explicit portrayal of the rendering of divine justice. This is Old Testament law at work; a unique commentary on an accumulation of evils displayed throughout the saga of this family, but most vividly expressed in *The Road to Memphis.*

Yet, despite the chilling finality of this bus ride, we are offered hope. Taylor does not wish to leave us with the unredeeming message of revenge as the only conclusion to injustice. She reminds us that there is more to the story. For it is Josias, the wronged young black man who was forcibly removed from the bus, who is the first to go down into the cold waters of the Rosa Lee and try and save the passengers, though to no avail. Josias is linked spiritually with the Josias mentioned in the King James Version of the Bible (in other versions, "Josiah"), a very young king who sought to correct the evils of his forefathers by reinstating correct Judaic practice in worship of the Lord.

It is Taylor's Josias who unknowingly forecasts the bus accident, when he jokingly refers to Noah and his building of the ark, an act which biblically preceded human destruction—destruction that is, with the exception of a select few.

> He [Josias] seen me [Jeremy] and he smiled that wide-toothed grin of his. "Wet 'nough for ya?" he asked, stepping onto the porch. I asserted it was and he laughed. "Keep it up 'round here and we gonna hafta start building ourselves an ark, just like ole Noah!"

When the devastating accident takes place, some in the reading audience will feel that Josias has every right to walk away from the bus passengers without attempting to aid them. After all, he has been wronged if not by each one of them personally, by the system collectively, which allows them to occupy the front seats on the bus or all of the seats on the bus. However, Taylor lets her audience know that there are other considerations of a higher order at work here. This is a story only in part about God's divine justice on those who have wronged others. The second level of the narration involves New Testament belief and man's ability, and indeed obligation to forgive, despite repressive and oppressive circumstances. Earlier, Josias has been forced to lie about going out of town to take a job because he is intimidated by Jeremy's father and friends who threateningly insist that no "nigger" could possibly have a job when white men are out of work. And yet, Josias does not hesitate to risk his own life to go into the cold waters on, as it turns out, a fruitless mission to rescue those who have presented themselves as so undeserving. This is a Josias who has a higher mission to fulfill, one that he does without hesitation because it is his duty to do so. When asked by the horror stricken Jeremy why he thinks this terrible thing has come to pass, Josias replies:

> "Ain't for me t' know. Can't go questionin' the ways of the Lord. Onliest thing I know is that the good book, it say the Lord He work in mighty mysterious ways."

Josias has fulfilled his unquestioning obligation to help those in need, thereby fulfilling his part of his personal covenant with God. In the end, he signifies not just the ordinary man who has been sorely served by white society, but all black men who suffer and yet, refuse to become victims of their suffering. . . .

Despite the fact that it is Jeremy who witnesses all events in this story, and that the narrative is told from his point of view, it is neither Jeremy, nor the Logan children who are the heroic figures. Josias emerges as a quiet, unsung hero, but one who, despite ill treatment and the potential if not inevitable loss of the job which he had waiting for him, can ironically be at peace with his actions.

Jeremy, on the other hand is in turmoil. His relatively passive role has cost him dearly. He is inert, unable to initiate, but rather merely to respond. This is in fact the state in which Jeremy Simms finds himself during most of the Taylor chronicle. . . .

Jeremy Simms' fate is to forever witness, internalize the wrongs committed against blacks, and be an outcast among his own people who accuse him of being "a nigger lover." He lacks the intellect to look beyond the situation and conceptualize the larger issue. Culpability by association eludes him; the punishing nature of collective guilt seems too harsh a judgment for him. Yet, the reader comes to know, as does indeed Josias, that the child Grace-Anne and her mother Miz Hattie are participants in a larger social system. Upon being removed from the water, Miz Hattie still wears the hat which she was able to try on and buy while others were previously denied the same right. Taylor suggests that the injustices in this Mississippi of the 1930s are so overwhelming that no white person there can ever claim total innocence. Perhaps the time shift between *The Road to Memphis* and *Mississippi Bridge* serves also to underscore the inevitability of oppression and response across the ages. The overall conception of Taylor's chronicle may be seen however, as part of an elaborate Biblical commentary on the nature of anger, human response and divine judgment. Through a series of incidents within all of the stories, and the tragedy of *Mississippi Bridge* in particular, Taylor attempts to balance rage and injustice with a deep sense of spirituality. While this may be seen to be the primary determinant in her stories, it is not only through spirituality that Taylor attempts to balance the scales. Imposed social/political and economic factors consistently challenge the participants in her "factions" but through Taylor's artistry and also her family's actual resilience, become mechanisms through which the Logan family both copes and triumphs. . . .

With a wary eye cast upon the present, but yet another turned towards the past, the Logan family adults in Taylor's series train their young people to live life as fully as possible, be a doormat for none, and to function and exist as the discerning protagonists of a cautionary tale: be prudent in what you say or do and never, never forget where you live. . . .

Surviving in the Mississippi of the 1930s, socially as well as politically, required delicate negotiations, mediations which are not always heeded by all of the participants in Taylor's chronicle. Those who fail to do so often meet harsh ends. Such circumstances come not as a result of didactic interference on the part of the author, but rather as the realistic, often tragic outcome of behaviors out of temperament with the times. Taylor's perception of the socio-political reasons for the condition of blacks during the 1930s is directly related to the racist viewpoint which she feels was held by most (though not all) white Mississippians of the time. This view was fueled by fear and, Taylor suggests, the underlying suspicion that given an opportunity, the black man might be able to best his white counterpart in the game of "one-upmanship." The white need to *accentuate* differences may well be based then, Taylor suggests, upon the frightening realization that there may be few differences among individuals at all beneath the surface of skin color. This is a revelation with which Jeremy Simms, in his supposed naiveté, was born. Jeremy undergoes no transformation of viewpoint in Taylor's stories; yet, he avoids the designation of a stereotyped character, a foil for his racist relatives, or even a true breath of fresh air for the Logan children. In fact, Jeremy is viewed by the Logan family with a careful eye, not because of what he individually represents, but because of what he has the power, in his innocence, to bring down upon the heads of any black child or adult whom he befriends. Jeremy's presence is a gadfly in the racist inheritance of his family; much of the time they seem angrily perplexed as to from where, Jeremy with his ability to accept people as people regardless of color, has come. After it is discovered that Jeremy has played a role in hiding Moe on his truck, "Mr. Simms emitted a horrendous scream and slammed his enormous first into Jeremy's jaw." Then later,

> Charlie Simms set a dead-eyed stare on his son. Then, in a voice as chill as well ice water and as low and quiet as a winter still night, he said, "Get outa my sight. Don't know where ya got it from, but you always was a nigger lover. Never thought I'd live to see the day I said that 'bout my own flesh, 'bout my own son, but it's so. I done tried to beat it outa you since you was knee-high, done tried to make ya see right, but you jus' had t' be 'round niggers. Well, ya might's well be one your ownself, 'cause you ain't white no more. Not after what you gone and done 'gainst your own kin. Your own blood, boy!"

The Logan children stand witness to this public disownment of a son, a chilling phenomenon. After such an experience, Taylor suggests, only death can resolve the situation for this young man. Indeed, he goes off to enlist in the army soon after and, we are told, never returns.

An explanation of basic racial hatred for the injustices which occur however, is too simplistic a reason for Taylor to offer her readers, given the perceptive nature of the author. As [F. Fitzhugh] Brundage suggests, there is more to the story. The onset of the Depression itself, fueled the situation faced by all of Taylor's characters. All must make a sometimes unconscious decision regarding whether or not to give in to despair, or struggle to cope and move on. Jeremy's family, and so many others like them, choose to given in, though ironically, they do not see it this way. They are, in effect, impotent in their abilities to move ahead both emotionally and physically. Paralyzed then, by their hatred, their static position in the social spectrum, and inner insecurities which reach deep into the recesses of their own souls as well as historically back to the subjugation of blacks whom whites fear might someday rise up in revolt, Taylor's white Mississippi populace, for the most part, are unable to balance their own rage. While they ironically see blacks as collectively representative of the uncivilized natural man incapable of learning, rationalizing, and projecting himself forward towards positive action, the Logans stand

before white society as an entire family living the reality that many whites cannot attain. Therefore, when in *Mississippi Bridge,* Josias walks proudly into John Wallace's store, a kind of theater for the absurd, and announces the fact that he has a job waiting for him in a nearby town, he inadvertently and quite naively, (some might think foolishly) places oil on ever smoldering flames. Put another way, such a pronouncement is the equivalent of screaming fire in a crowded movie theatre; it simply cannot be ignored.

Such is also the case when the elderly Tom Bee in *The Friendship* insists upon calling John Wallace by his first name, flaunting the deferential treatment historically given to whites. Again, the action is set in a store, in which are featured a crowd of witnesses, a situation which cannot be ignored by John Wallace. Tom Bee steadily insists upon the familiarity of calling John Wallace, "'John,' such a little thing . . . this thing about a name," Cassie Logan muses. But even at her young age, and in her innocence, Cassie *senses* though she does not understand, the ancient power of "naming." In European folklore, the one who knew your name was also the one who would consequently have power to bend you to his will. An imbalance in naming designation then, brought with it the potential of a power relationship; one that did not favor the black individual. . . . The whites in Taylor's Mississippi dreamed the nightmare of becoming invisible in a state in which they were outnumbered. . . . The power of "title" was one way that whites could psychologically maintain dominance over a numerically larger group of people; a group who, if they ever should decide to revolt—had a good chance of being successful. Cassie Logan views the issue of name designation as though it were one indicative of a childish sign of respect, one which she has been previously told, means nothing to her grandmother, who because of her advanced age, is referred to by white people as "auntie." These same individuals however, would never consider addressing the grandmother as "Mrs. Logan," the ultimate sign of respect. Yet, Cassie notes her older brother Stacey's words:

> Papa say white folks set an awful store 'bout names and such. He say they get awful riled 'bout them names too. Say they can do some terrible things when they get riled. Say anybody call a white man straight out by his name just lookin' for trouble.

Tom Bee agrees with Mr. Logan's assessment, but refuses to accede, dismissing the practice of calling white people "mister," as "foolishness." He feels this unjustified deference keenly since he has in years past, on two occasions, saved John Wallace's life. In return for these two incidents of embarrassing intimacy, John Wallace told Tom Bee that he considered him a friend and that consequently, Tom could always call him by his "Christian" name. But, for no explained reason other than perhaps perversity and old age, Tom has for years avoided the privilege of calling John Wallace "John." It is only recently, much to Wallace's anger that Bee now insists upon doing this.

The Logan children then, have two models before them. One, consisting of the words of an elderly man who now refuses to bow to none, and secondly, the advice of a loving father, whose discernment and strength are unifying forces for his family. The children sense that if they are being warned against such familiarity—even though they cannot immediately comprehend why, there must be a reason. The fate which befalls Tom Bee, shocking though it is, is perhaps one which comes as not so much of a surprise to the horrified children. It is also perhaps a fate which Tom Bee never expected or, on the other hand, perhaps it is. After Bee's repeated utterings of what John Wallace calls his "Christian name," Wallace shoots Tom Bee in the leg, giving a horribly ironic twist to the concept of "friendship." Tom Bee is ultimately a tragic-heroic figure, dragging himself away down the street still shrieking "John! John!," as the story closes. . . .

When sixty-four-year-old Mrs. Lee Annie announces to Big Ma and Cassie in *Let the Circle Be Unbroken,* "I thinks I wants to vote," she sets into action a chain of events which have resounding effects for the Logan family. Once over the shock of the announcement, the Logans make a decision to help Mrs. Annie study for the literacy test. This she does amidst warnings from her friends and relatives who tell her stories of dire happenings to other blacks who tried—and failed. Mrs. Annie is unmoved. Helping her prepare for the test becomes a family project, though each member is aware of the possible dangers ahead for Mrs. Annie and for anyone who is suspected of having assisted her. The Logans take a strong stand against injustice in making this decision. They choose to fight the system by coaching her in its rules. In the end, Mrs. Annie successfully learns all of the two hundred eighty-five sections of the Constitution and its fifteen amendments.

The Logan family goes a step further in showing their support for Mrs. Annie's project. David Logan allows his wife and Cassie to be with her during her appearance for the registration process. (He does not attend due to the fact that the male presence will be perceived as being more threatening.) Such a decision represents a major sacrifice and great potential personal risk. In making this choice, David Logan balances personal ideals and the opportunity to fight the system *through* the system in whatever small way he and his family can, against possible personal dangers. Nonetheless, his decision is not made irrespective of precautions for his family's safety; he realizes that were he to go to the courthouse, his presence alone might be enough to turn this encounter with "justice" into an immediate tragedy for all concerned. Therefore, David "bends" and refrains from being present during the event. The Logan children have grown through the experience of learning about the Constitution. They have gained first hand knowledge of the document that reflects the law of the state and the sections and articles designed to protect rights—and also the knowledge that in selective cases, those rights are not granted.

When in the end Mrs. Annie is denied the right to register, and tragically she and her relatives are thrown off the land which they tenant farm, the lesson becomes a harsh one indeed. But Mrs. Annie has successfully challenged the system, and the reader having the advantage of historical hindsight, acknowledges the fact that such brave acts laid the groundwork for successful voter registrations decades later. It is an acute historical irony that in devoting their attention to customizing racial hatred, and misusing the power vested in codified law, white Mississippians ultimately protected nothing and left themselves open to useless expenditures of energy, antagonism, and violence which might better have been used in uniting to re-build a shattered economy.

When Mrs. Logan accompanies Mrs. Annie to the courthouse, she is confronted by Harlan Granger, a plantation owner of some 6,000 acres, an unscrupulous man of considerable power and influence. Seeing her standing there, he attempts to intimidate her:

> " . . . Thought I'd stopped you from messing in what you got no business."

> "You stopped me from teaching at Great Faith."

> "Look like I ain't stopped nothing else."

Granger is referring to an incident in an earlier book, *Roll of Thunder, Hear My Cry* in which Mrs. Logan loses her job as a result of Granger's interference. Infuriated at Mrs. Logan's role in helping organize a boycott of the Wallace store which is located on Granger's property, he arranges to have her fired. The immediate reason given is that Mrs. Logan has "destroyed" school property, referring to some school books in which she pasted over the ownership record which listed the race of black students as "nigra." More importantly, Granger witnesses a lesson taught on the subject of slavery, a topic which does not appear in the assigned history book. These "infractions" remind him that Mrs. Logan is a person to be reckoned with, a clear threat. He attempts to eliminate that threat by taking her job, but as he discovers, the Logans are not to be so easily dispatched. Different from most families, they maintain their quiet strength, make their protests against the system in reserved, yet meaningful ways and force a certain respect from the white people around them. Large plantation owners like Granger, wielded tremendous power. Granger is on the school board, involved with voter registration and seemingly, just about every activity that involves money and power.

When one considers Granger's position on the one hand, and the Logans' on the other, it is clear that despite the fact that they are well thought of in the community, politically, there is no comparison to be made. The scale is tipped severely in Mr. Granger's favor. However, this is in terms of things which can be measured. What really infuriates Mr. Granger is the *weight of the intangible,* weight *not* tipped in his favor. He is aware of the dignity and the strength possessed by this family who, because they own the land they live on, are owned by no one.

The Logan elders possess an "elegance of approach," a self-confidence of which no white person has been able to rob them. Even when forced to accede to the formalities of "address," and to all of the elements attendant to racist policy and custom, somehow the Logans still maintain their dignity and their stature in the black community. Further, greatly against their individual wills, whites are forced to admire them as well, and in so doing, to some extent, they *fear* the Logan elders. Harlan Granger is aware of this and longs to bring them to their knees, but thus far, he has not been successful. He is aware that he has been successful in hurting the family peripherally in causing Mrs. Logan to lose her job, but he is also cognizant of the fact that he has not truly robbed the family of their total well being. He longs to see Mrs. Logan run down the street begging him to change his mind, as he has the sadistic pleasure of seeing Mrs. Ellis do after he has ordered her and her family off his land. . . .

> "Lordy, no, Mr. Granger!" Mrs. Ellis cried, running into the street to plead with him. "Mr. Granger, no!" Mr. Granger saw her coming, but disdainfully he gassed the Packard and sped away, leaving Mrs. Ellis desperately yelling after him. And I [Cassie] knew even as she stood there crying out for mercy, Harlan Granger would not change his mind. He had gotten what he wanted.

But he suspects that he will never have the "pleasure" of seeing Mrs. Logan do so. While the Logan family pays a high price for each challenge delivered, they manage to do so—and survive.

Mr. Wade Jamison, an attorney, offers the Logan family political support of a kind which is invaluable. Mr. Jamison stands alone as the only white adult who extends to the Logan family unconditional trust and assistance. Yet, ironically, he is not a friend. The barriers between true white and black friendship preclude such a relationship, Taylor lets us know. But, what Mr. Jamison has to offer is by far more valuable. His profession and position in the community make him a formidable adversary among whites. He also possesses tremendous common sense as well. Furthermore, since he is white, he has available to him the resources of the white community; he knows the people, how they think, how they will react. He can weigh the law on the one side, and human emotions and response on the other. He is a most valuable contact, *and* he is loyal.

> There was a mutual respect and, because the years had proven it justified, a mutual trust; but there was no socialization other than the amenities. Neither he nor we would have felt comfortable in such a situation, for the unwritten laws of the society frowned upon such fraternization, and the trust and respect were valued and needed more than the socializing.

It is Mr. Jamison who defends T. J. Avery against murder charges in *Let the Circle Be Unbroken,* though to no avail. It is also Mr. Jamison who in *Roll of Thunder,*

Hear My Cry, the earlier book, states his intention to David Logan to keep mention of the Logan children's assistance given to T. J. out of T. J.'s trial, and is later successful in doing so. And Mr. Jamison shares the deadly Logan secret, that in fact it was David Logan who purposely started the fire to distract the Night Riders and keep them from lynching T. J. for the assault on Jim Lee Barnett, the storekeeper. Through his actions, Mr. Jamison plays a not insignificant role in the lives of the Logans as an ally who can offer an equilibrium during times which are dangerously unbalanced.

At the heart of the Logan family's relative economic and social well being is their inheritance of land, 400 acres purchased by Big Ma's father between 1887 and 1918. This legacy allows the Logan adults to function as true breadwinners, rather than as tenants subject to the cruel turns and twists of fate so often delivered by plantation owners. Black ownership of land in the 1930s was an uncommon occurrence. . . . Tenant farming kept the black populace in servitude, forever at the mercy of the white landowner. The black individual who owned his land, had a leverage that was denied others. It is not surprising then, that such ownership could place a family at risk—if it were not managed correctly. Too much flaunting of ones good fortune, particularly during Depression times, could result in tragedy. The Logan family realizes the difficulties inherent in their situation. Their children are trained to be prudent and to exercise good judgement, to not shun risks but to take them on when the fight is worth fighting and when it is in the best interest of the family as a unit.

Having the land as an economic base allows the family to be relatively self-sufficient, even though David Logan is still forced to go north for a portion of each year to work so that he can bring in extra income. . . .

[However,] he successfully manages to keep his family together, avoiding the divisive effects that such actions had upon many families. In so doing, he is able to support his family, even though there is often very little left over for "extras." . . .

> Constrained by Jim Crow laws and racist attitudes, most black fathers found it extraordinarily difficult to support their families. In the South, the crop-lien system and the collapse of Reconstruction left black men economically marginalized and politically vulnerable, and these liabilities often dashed their hopes of supporting their families by farming.

Despite the fact that they, like many others, must struggle, owning land allows the Logans to consider the possibilities of upward mobility, something that others can only dream about. The Logan parents do not lecture their young excessively about the rewards of education, but when the children appear confused, angry, or victimized by the designs of white society around them, the Logan elders communicate to them the need for self-control, forbearance, and pride—and the future possibilities that education could afford them. In particular, Mrs.

Logan's interest in education, models for the children the benefits that may attend the educated. Big Ma further reinforces the necessity of schooling as a legitimate way of making ones mark on society. As she tells Little Man:

> One day you'll have a plenty of clothes and maybe even a car of yo' own to ride 'round in, so don't you pay no mind to them ignorant white folks. You jus' keep on studyin' and get yo'self a good education and you'll be all right.

Owning land also affords one the self confidence which allows one to take what may be perceived as necessary risks. The risks may be formidable. The Logans consider joining union efforts to organize tenant farmers and sharecroppers. As the organizers explain it, David Logan's endorsement will encourage others to join, since he is so highly thought of. Mr. Logan weighs his responsibility against the inherent dangers involved; he makes no commitment. Shortly thereafter, the agent who had approached him is found beaten up in his car. David Logan's decision to not become actively involved ultimately, turns out to be a good one. Later, another man involved in union business is found burned to death. In the final scene of *Let the Circle Be Unbroken,* union efforts are broken amidst gunfire and terror in the town center. David Logan's discernment in this matter saves his family from a possibly tragic involvement in this movement. This dilemma however, decided after a considered weighing of possible risks and probable outcomes, is one which could not have been seriously considered were it not for the reality of ownership of the land. . . .

In writing her chronicle of the Logan family, Mildred Taylor has indeed communicated a rare and special family relationship which has not lost its significance with time. Rather, she has offered her readers clear and compelling vignettes of a family whose spirituality, love, unity, and vision enable them to survive successfully despite overwhelming social, political and economic obstacles. Contemporary readers are offered the real possibilities of what *can be* despite the efforts of others to construct a negative and repressive reality. Taylor offers her audience the motivating gift of a message of positive action, one which while acknowledging history and memory, seeks to inspire a people with the ability to progress beyond a condition of oppression.

TITLE COMMENTARY

📖 *LET THE CIRCLE BE UNBROKEN* (1981)

Publishers Weekly

SOURCE: A review of *Let the Circle Be Unbroken,* in *Publishers Weekly,* Vol. 220, No. 12, September 18, 1981, p. 155.

The Newbery Medalist takes up the story of the black Logan family of Mississippi, begun in *Song of the Trees* and *Roll of Thunder, Hear My Cry,* in her new, profoundly affecting novel. The time is 1935, when the blacks in the South are oppressed by all but a few whites, as reported by Cassie Logan trying to understand the world with the ingenuousness of a 12-year-old. She describes the agony of her brother Stacey whose friend T. J. is hanged after a white jury decides, against the evidence, that he's guilty of murder; the riots when sharecroppers are attacked for trying to unionize; and other devastating happenings that are bitter reminders of what the fight for civil rights is for. This is a somber book, but lightened by Taylor's humor and by the indelible impression of a united, cherishing family.

Zena Sutherland

SOURCE: A review of *Let the Circle Be Unbroken,* in *Bulletin of the Center for Children's Books,* Vol. 35, No. 4, December, 1981, p. 79.

In a trenchant, dramatic sequel to *Roll of Thunder, Hear My Cry,* which won the 1977 Newbery Medal, Taylor continues the story of the Logan family. This is as well written but not as tightly constructed as the first book, covering a series of tangential events so that it is a family record, a picture of the depression years in rural Mississippi, and an indictment of black-white relations in the Deep South. A young friend is convicted of a murder of which he is innocent, a pretty cousin is insulted by some white boys and her father taunted because he had married a white woman, an elderly neighbor tries to vote, the government pays farmers to plow their crops under, etc. The story is told by Cassie, the only girl in a loving family, and is at its best when she is writing about her family and not about the period.

Denise M. Wilms

SOURCE: A review of *Let the Circle Be Unbroken,* in *Booklist,* Vol. 78, No. 7, December 1, 1981, p. 499.

Mildred Taylor's *Roll of Thunder, Hear My Cry* won the Newbery Award in 1976 and subsequently made its way to the television screen. Members of the book's wide audience will be interested to learn of the third installment in the Logan family's story, *Let the Circle Be Unbroken.*

Here the Logans are still struggling for enough income to keep up with costs, the most crucial of which is the tax on their 400-acre spread. Meanwhile the children are sobered by the sight of their neighbor and friend, T. J. Avery, who is wrongly sentenced to death for killing a local store owner. They watch, too, as furtive efforts at organizing a racially integrated farmer's union are firmly quashed, and their family unity is tested as 14-year-old Stacey, anxious to earn money for the family, leaves home in secret to work in the Louisiana sugar-cane fields.

These plot elements move the story along nicely and develop a vivid picture of the terrible physical and spiritual oppression of black by white. The impact is weakened, however, by the fact that after the televising of *Roots* and several strong juvenile novels on the subject, the material is now familiar territory.

What's less widely known and less frequently dealt with in popular media is the portrayal of the way race and class profoundly shape not only attitudes of whites toward blacks, but of blacks toward whites, and blacks toward each other. Taylor crafts a powerful sense of the whys and wherefores of that separateness. The Logans and their kith and kin avoid whites as much as possible; whites seem inevitably dangerous, either actively so or merely by accident. Even their white lawyer friend Mr. Jamison is kept at arms length: "He understood as well as we did that the friendship and goodwill we shared with him was different from that which we shared with our neighbors in the black community or that which we shared with his friends in the white community. There was a mutual respect and . . . a mutual trust; but there was no socialization other than the amenities."

This deeply felt separateness causes tension within the Logan family itself when Mama's Cousin Bud, who lives in New York, turns up to visit and reluctantly informs everyone that his second wife is white. They're having problems, and he's troubled that Suzella, their 15-year-old daughter, can and wants to pass for white. He asks Mama if the Logans will keep her for awhile. Suzella's presence in the local black community is telling too. Charming, attractive, and nearly white, she quickly gains the good graces of just about everyone.

While the story is absorbing and instructive in its exploration of southern black experience in the 1930s, there are some technical problems that interfere with the book's total effect. As narrator, 11-year-old Cassie sounds far too wise for her years. She is the one who elaborated, above, on Mr. Jamison; yet readers are supposed to believe that she's unaware of color distinctions in the washrooms and at the drinking fountain when she and her brothers travel to Strawberry for their friend T. J.'s trial. This just isn't convincing.

Another flaw is the overt way some information comes across. Background on Roosevelt's AAA, for example, is sometimes poorly woven into the unfolding story. But because characters are generally well developed, and because there is a good deal of drama in events, the story takes hold anyway. It's meaty, and a worthy continuation of *Roll of Thunder.* Readers will be eagerly awaiting further developments of the Logan saga.

Holly Eley

SOURCE: "Cotton Pickin' Blues," in *Times Literary Supplement,* No. 4121, March 26, 1982, p. 343.

Works of fiction with titles taken from blues or from popular song such as *A Good Man is Hard to Find* or *You Can't Keep a Good Woman Down* are often about hardship and intense relationships occurring below the Mason-Dixon Line. *Let the Circle Be Unbroken* is one of these, though it is written for children and large helpings of Black American history and race relations are hidden under the oiled sausage, grits and collard greens. By focusing on a rural community (during one year of the Depression) in which both black and white sharecroppers are equally, though separately, persecuted by landlords and government and by filtering the urge to instruct through accessible, descriptive prose Mildred D. Taylor achieves in fewer pages what Alex Haley attempted in *Roots.*

The first episode, an account of the trial and unfair condemnation of a black youth, seen through the eyes of eleven-year-old tomboy Cassie Logan, is obviously, and unfavourably, comparable to *To Kill a Mocking Bird;* but within this unpromising beginning Taylor establishes the credibility of the main characters (for blacks) and the romance of them (for whites). *Let the Circle Be Unbroken* is episodic but held together by the well-drawn Logan family; like many sagas it can seem soap operaish until one realizes how few concessions are made to the influence that television now has on children's reading. Imaginations are never required to leap gaps, although it is helpful to have read some of the classics of American children's literature such as the works of Twain, Alcott, the "What Katy Did" series, Gene Stratton Porter's *Michael O'Halloran* and in particular his *Girl of the Limberlost* which is not only a good fictional account of rural poverty during the Depression but also contains a marvelously accurate description of swamp flora in the deep South.

Seasons come and go; cotton is picked, ginned, sold at a low price, replanted and ploughed back into the land in compliance with Roosevelt's crop reduction plan. Uncle Hammer comes down from Chicago in his sunshine-yellow Packard and weak Cousin Bud, who has married a white New Yorker, leaves his daughter Suzella at Strawberry so that she can truly experience "blackness" before deciding (or not) to opt for a "white" future. Papa Logan, whose moral presence is needed at home, takes a summer job on the railway and in his absence Stacey (Cassie's teenage brother and idol) runs away to cut cane in Louisiana in order to pay family debts: before he is brought home he experiences the harshest of racial injustices. Throughout all this the writing is impressionistic but at the same time detailed. In avoiding short cuts Taylor paints an authentic picture of Southern segregation in the 1930s as well as giving solid dimensions to her black characters and delineating the predicament in which her white characters find themselves.

None of the many people in *Let the Circle Be Unbroken* are wholly good or bad; all are products of their time, place and circumstance. Through them, as well as through a series of rich narratives, Mildred D. Taylor gives us an historical perspective on racial issues which she insists can only be successfully resolved by recognizing the fundamental equality of all human beings; thereafter tolerating their differences. Among the many lessons which she gracefully imparts (lessons which include the meanings, workings and effects of organizations such as the Farm Workers' Union, the Works Progress Administration and the Civilian Conservation Corps) is an old one which says that a classic, even if supposedly written for a determined age group, will be enormously enjoyed by everyone.

Sharron Freeman

SOURCE: A review of *Let the Circle Be Unbroken,* in *Voice of Youth Advocates,* Vol. 5, No. 2, June, 1982, p. 36.

This sequel to *Roll of Thunder, Hear My Cry* is an absorbing continuation of Cassie Logan's story about growing up black in rural Mississippi in the depression year of 1935. Again, she and her family and friends are faced with racism, poverty, job deprivation and the daily struggle of maintaining their integrity and dignity in the face of constant harassment and prejudice by the surrounding white landowners. Cassie witnesses injustice in its many forms, from her brother's friend T. J.'s trial and subsequent imprisonment to the black community's struggles to raise cotton for landowners who try to cheat them out of the money they're due. She painfully watches while her brother breaks away from the family, while experiencing her own growing-up pains which surface when her cousin Suzella comes to stay.

The southern dialect and strong theme of pride and self-respect combine to make this a powerful, true-to-life story—one which will be remembered vividly by its readers. I can't think of a better novel to recommend, in the light of today's increasing tensions.

THE FRIENDSHIP (1987)

Betsy Hearne

SOURCE: A review of *The Friendship,* in *Bulletin of the Center for Children's Books,* Vol. 41, No. 4, December, 1987, p. 79.

A bitter short story about race relations in rural Mississippi during the Depression focuses on an incident between an old Black man, Mr. Tom Bee, and a white storekeeper, Mr. John Wallace. Indebted to Tom for saving his life as a young man, John had promised they would always be friends. But now, years later, John insists that Tom call him "Mister" and shoots the old man for defiantly—and publicly—calling him by his first name. Narrator Cassie Logan and her brothers, characters from Taylor's previous books, are verbally abused by Wallace's villainous sons before witnessing the encounter, along with a token non-hostile white child, Jeremy. The social drama elicits a naturally powerful response in depicting cruel injustice, and the writing is concentrated to heighten that effect.

Ilene Cooper

SOURCE: A review of *The Friendship,* in *Booklist,* Vol. 84, No. 8, December 15, 1987, p. 713.

Set during the Depression, this reintroduces Cassie Logan, the black heroine of *Roll of Thunder, Hear My Cry.* But this is not really Cassie's story. She and her three brothers are merely observers one fateful Mississippi afternoon when Mr. Tom Bee gets himself in trouble. Tom Bee has always called the white shopkeeper John Wallace by his first name. He was given that permission by Wallace himself, when Tom Bee took him in as a teenager. Now, however, Wallace's sons are displeased by what they conceive as disrespect, and even Wallace asks and then implores Tom Bee to call him Mister. Tom Bee will have none of it. He saved John Wallace's life and he is going to keep the man to his word. "He done promised me that. Promised me he wasn't never gonna forget what I done for him." Even the children know Wallace and Tom Bee are on a collision course, and as the afternoon grows hotter and tempers shorten, it happens—Tom Bee calls John by his first name once more and John Wallace takes out a gun and shoots him. Even the gun blast does not silence Tom Bee: "Ya hear me? John! John! John! John! Till the Judgement day! John!" He drags himself down the road crying out Wallace's first name all the way. A powerful story, there is no doubt. Readers will be haunted by its drama and emotion long after they have closed the book. Some will wonder about the uniformly despicable attitudes of the white people (except for one white child who makes a few overtures toward Cassie and her brothers), but considering the time and setting of the piece and the fact that Taylor has drawn on incidents her father related about his boyhood, this is probably a realistic representation. [Max] Ginsburg's pen-and-ink drawings are excellent, adding much to the intensity of the narrative.

Jeanette Lambert

SOURCE: A review of *The Friendship,* in *School Library Journal,* Vol. 34, No. 5, January, 1988, p. 70.

A hot, humid afternoon in Mississippi in 1933 is the setting for a tense drama and tragic confrontation between Mr. Tom Bee, an elderly black man, and a white store owner, John Wallace. The interaction between the two men portrays how severely the bonds of friendship can be tested against a backdrop of racism, peer pressure, and individual rights. This novella is narrated by Cassie Logan from *Roll of Thunder, Hear My Cry.* She and her brothers go to the country store for some medicine for a neighbor. At the store, they are hassled by Wallace's sons. They run into Mr. Bee, who addresses John Wallace by his first name. Blacks are forbidden to do so, but Mr. Bee had saved John's life on more than one occasion, and John had given him permission to call him by his first name. Under pressure and taunting by the men in his store, John reneges on his promise in an explosive and devastating outburst. The characterization is very strong in this brief drama, and the events of this fateful afternoon will be unforgettable. The black-and-white illustrations are noteworthy, and depict the story's mood and action well. This book lends itself well to discussions on various topics pertaining to human relations.

Ethel R. Twichell

SOURCE: A review of *The Friendship,* in *The Horn Book Magazine,* Vol. LXIV, No. 1, January-February, 1988, pp. 59-60.

Intended for a younger audience than readers of Mildred Taylor's *Roll of Thunder, Hear My Cry* and *Let the Circle Be Unbroken,* the brief but poignant story again features Cassie and her brothers but this time as spectators rather than as protagonists in the drama. When the children are sent to Wallace's store to pick up some "head medicine" for old Aunt Callie, they are uncertain about entering the unfriendly premises. Having been grudgingly served themselves, they watch apprehensively as elderly Tom Bee comes in and, as he asks to be served, addresses the white shop owner as "John." Given the era, the early thirties, the children know that no white person can be addressed without the proper "'missus'" or "'mistah.'" As the story unfolds, they also learn that old Tom Bee saved the life of the young John Wallace—in fact treated him much as a son—but with the passing years John has succumbed to the racist pressures of the community and his own sons. In a heart-wrenching climax Old Tom challenges the shop owner with his first name again. In answer John silently picks up his shotgun and with a violent, bloody display shoots his old benefactor in the leg. Horrified, the children watch Tom Bee drag himself along on his elbows away from the store shouting, "'John, John, John,'" in challenge and despair. Eloquent in both its brevity and understatement, the story underlines the author's skill in drawing from her family's experiences to enlarge her readers' understanding of a dark and still unresolved heritage. Numerous black-and-white illustrations are a sensitive addition to the drama of the text.

Beryl Banfield

SOURCE: A review of *The Friendship,* in *Interracial Books for Children Bulletin,* Vol. 19, Nos. 5 & 6, May, 1989, p. 11.

Mildred D. Taylor, winner of CIBC new writers award for *Song of the Trees,* has concentrated on producing works that will enable young readers to better understand the experiences of African Americans who lived in a rigidly segregated southern society prior to the Civil Rights movement. She continues the tradition in *The*

Friendship. Once again the impact of dealing with racism on a daily basis is revealed through the words of Cassie Logan who shares the experience with her brothers, Stacey, Christopher-John and Little Man. The story, based on a true incident related by Ms. Taylor's father, is a graphic and sensitive detailing of the strictly enforced codes that governed relationships between whites and blacks and the severe penalties inflicted for any violations of these codes. The central figure is an African American elder respectfully called Mr. Tom Bee by the black community. Mr. Tom Bee had once befriended a fifteen year old white youth by saving his life and then giving him food and shelter. Mr. Tom Bee cared for the young boy "like a daddy" until pressure from the white community forces the youth to leave. Now a grown man with two grown sons, Mr. Tom Bee's former ward, owns and operates a general store avoided by the black community because of the blatantly racist treatment of blacks. When Mr. Tom Bee acting on a presumption of friendship toward his former ward, violates a rigid social taboo, the result is a shocking violent response.

This is an important book for young readers. It effectively portrays the dehumanizing effects of racism on blacks and whites alike. Also, most importantly, it will evoke young readers to understand the courage of civil rights activists like Fannie Lou Hamer and Medgar Evers who lived in such a society and worked to change it.

THE GOLD CADILLAC (1987)

Denise M. Wilms

SOURCE: A review of *The Gold Cadillac,* in *Booklist,* Vol. 83, No. 22, August, 1987, p. 1753.

Daddy has bought a brand-new gold Cadillac, but Mother-Dear will have none of it. As far as she's concerned, the money should have gone toward a house instead of a new car. The family's Mercury, was, after all, only a year old. Mother-Dear's judgment is that if her husband bought the car alone, he can ride in it alone. Not until Daddy announces plans for a visit to the grandparents in Mississippi does Mother-Dear relent; the trip from Toledo taken in 1950, could be a matter of life and death for a black man driving a brand new Cadillac. For safety's sake, 'lois and other family members decide to go along; they pack lots of food and form a caravan south. In Memphis, however, 'lois' family gets separated from the group and ends up traveling on its own. Just over the Mississippi line the inevitable happens: 'lois' father is pulled over by the police and taken to jail. Not until three hours later is he allowed to go free. Instead of proceeding south, though, he heads back to Memphis to borrow a cousin's less conspicuous car. When the family is home once more, Mother-Dear tells Papa to keep the car, but he doesn't; another Mercury will take its place. "As fine as the Cadillac had been, he said, it had pulled us apart for awhile." Taylor's brief story is memorable for its economic portrayal of both complicated emotions and the social climate that so threatened blacks in the

South. The sense of family is strong and warm, and the skillful integration of drama and history is admirable.

Helen E. Williams

SOURCE: A review of *The Gold Cadillac*, in *School Library Journal*, Vol. 34, No. 1, September, 1987, pp. 171-72.

In this quiet story, 'lois explains a child's perspective of her fears when she, her sister Wilma, and their parents drive from Ohio to visit relatives in Mississippi in 1950. When 'lois' father buys a new gold Cadillac, his wife refuses to ride in it—until he declares his intentions to visit his parents in the South. Then the whole family goes, caravan style, for it's "a mighty dangerous thing, for a black man to drive an expensive car into the rural South." 'lois and Wilma are disquieted by the increasing appearance of "white only, colored not allowed" signs as they drive further south. After white policemen humiliate and arrest their father, they do visit their grandparents, but the trip results in their father giving up the car when they return home, realizing that it was pulling the family apart. Full-page sepia paintings effectively portray the characters, setting and mood of the story events as [Michael] Hays ably demonstrates his understanding of the social and emotional environment which existed for blacks during this period. 'lois' first-person narrative allows readers to understand the youthful perspective on the dehumanizing interactions of racism. Clear language and logical, dramatic sequencing of story events make this story bittersweet for adult readers but important for the social development of beginning readers.

Nancy Vasilakis

SOURCE: A review of *The Gold Cadillac*, in *The Horn Book Magazine*, Vol. LXIII, No. 5, September-October, 1987, p. 606.

The shiny gold Cadillac that Daddy brings home one summer evening marks a stepping stone in the lives of Wilma and 'lois, two black sisters growing up in Ohio during the fifties. At first neighbors and relatives shower them with attention. But when the family begins the long journey to the South to show off the car to their Mississippi relatives, the girls, for the first time, encounter the undisguised ugliness of racial prejudice. In subdued tones Taylor describes the awakening fear felt by her young heroines as they see the "WHITE ONLY" signs alongside restaurants, water fountains, and public rest rooms. The huge picnic lunch packed by their mother and aunts for the trip loses much of its appeal once the girls understand the reason for it. Further on, their father is stopped and frisked by police, who can't believe that a black man could have come by such a car honestly, and after a long, uncomfortable night spent by the side of the road, he turns back and leaves the car with a cousin,

fearing to drive the Cadillac any further into the South. Sure of herself, Taylor speaks softly but carries a big stick. She skillfully makes her point by contrasting the comfortable, carefree life the sisters have always known, surrounded by their large, extended family up North and later in Mississippi with the hostile no man's land between. Printed in warm sepia tones, with full-page illustrations that successfully complement the quiet strength of the story, *The Gold Cadillac* is a brief but important book, one that serves as a necessary reminder of how things used to be and how much remains to be done.

Claudia A. Logan

SOURCE: "Books in the Classroom," in *The Horn Book Magazine*, Vol. LXVI, No. 6, November-December, 1990, pp. 779-81.

The Gold Cadillac . . . recounts the story of two sisters and their parents who drive in their new car from Ohio to Mississippi. The 1950 Cadillac that had earned the family looks of admiration and envy up North becomes a source of angry suspicion once they enter the South. Both stories present the terrible pain and history of racial injustice but allow readers a chance to look at prejudice from a personal perspective. My sixth graders felt these books revealed history in a way that was more real than any lecture or movie could be. Their genuine feeling for these characters made them look at racial issues with a new slant and led them to certain insights into why people become prejudiced.

THE ROAD TO MEMPHIS (1990)

Publishers Weekly

SOURCE: A review of *The Road to Memphis*, in *Publishers Weekly*, Vol. 237, No. 15, April 13, 1990, pp. 67-8.

In the tradition of Maya Angelou and Alice Walker, Taylor uses powerful, vibrant prose to express the sentiments of a young black Southerner, as the Newbery Medalist continues the story of Cassie Logan. The year is 1941, and 17-year-old Cassie prepares for college by attending high school in Jackson, Miss., where her brother Stacey and friends Little Willie and Moe work in factories. No longer under the protective wing of her parents and Big Ma, Cassie confronts the hostility of the white community and faces new harsh realities including the betrayal of a childhood friend, the outbreak of World War II and an act of violence that forces Moe into hiding. Although Cassie experiences fear and humiliation, her determination to fight for justice remains undaunted. Offering the same captivating characters, honest dialogue and resonant imagery found in *Roll of Thunder, Hear My Cry* and *Let the Circle Be Unbroken*, this enlightening, moving novel will leave readers yearning for the next installment of the Logan saga.

Kirkus Reviews

SOURCE: A review of *The Road to Memphis,* in *Kirkus Reviews,* Vol. LVIII, No. 9, May 1, 1990, p. 656.

Continuing the saga of the Logan family—extraordinary as black landowners in pre-WW II Mississippi while also representative of the agonies of survival in a racist society—Cassie (age nine in Newbery-winner *Roll of Thunder, Hear My Cry*) recounts harrowing events during late 1941.

Now 17 and aiming for law school, Cassie goes to school in nearby Jackson, where older brother Stacey works and has earned his first car. At home, redneck bullying is as cruel as ever: as "coon" in a malicious "hunt," one friend is severely wounded; another, Moe, is attacked and goaded until he retaliates with a crowbar. Old friend and ally Jeremy, though kin to the white tormentors, helps spirit Moe to Jackson (a courageous act for which he later pays a terrible price); with Cassie and new soldier Clarence joining in the perilous journey, Stacey drives Moe to Memphis to catch a northbound train to safety.

As in the other Logan stories, the painful, authentic, vividly portrayed injustices follow one after another, each making its point: Clarence's death after a white doctor refuses to treat him; the barely averted gang-rape of a black girl found alone; the malicious vandalizing of Stacey's car. There are only occasional consoling hints of the Logans' powerful family unity; the one comfortingly safe interlude here is with Solomon Bradley, a charismatic, Harvard-educated black lawyer who runs a Memphis newspaper—his unresolved relationship with Cassie, who is on the verge of becoming a dauntless, spirited, highly intelligent woman, looks like a good subject for another book. An engrossing, capably written picture of fine young people endeavoring to find the right way in a world that persistently wrongs them.

Robert Strang

SOURCE: A review of *The Road to Memphis,* in *Bulletin of the Center for Children's Books,* Vol. 43, No. 10, June, 1990, p. 255.

Cassie Logan, now seventeen, and her older brother Stacey are now living in Jackson, which offers job and educational opportunities not available in their small farming community in Mississippi. While visiting their parents, the two young people and their friends encounter racist hostility from Statler Aames and his family, and even, it seems, from Jeremy, the Aames' cousin and childhood friend of the Logans. In a side-plot that never quite meshes, Cassie's friend Sissy becomes pregnant and coyly refuses to name the father. Comprising scenes that individually resonate with taut power, the first third of this new novel about the Logan family nevertheless seems unsure of its narrative direction. The conflicts are tellingly shown but diffusely structured, until the breaking moment when friend Moe, tired of his humiliating

abuse at the hands of the Aames boys ("Nigger, I said pick up that hat!") attacks them with a tire iron and is forced to run, involving the Logans as well as Jeremy in his suspenseful escape. That Taylor can be a skilled storyteller becomes evident once the narrative begins to incorporate dramatic as well as moral urgency. The road to Memphis is hard, as when Cassie uncovers the hatred that lies just beneath the smiling surface of a white service station owner, and complicated, as when she experiences a powerful romantic attraction for a brilliant Memphis lawyer. Readers new to the Logan saga should probably begin with *Roll of Thunder, Hear My Cry;* faithful (and persistent) fans will appreciate seeing Cassie's entry into the wider world.

Susan Schuller

SOURCE: A review of *The Road to Memphis,* in *School Library Journal,* Vol. 36, No. 6, June, 1990, p. 138.

Taylor continues the saga of the Logan family. The setting is Mississippi in 1941, and although the impending war has created some new job opportunities for blacks, discrimination and blatant racism still abound. The focus is on Cassie, now 17, her brother Stacey, and their friends, who are confronted and often humiliated by the white people they encounter. In one pivotal scene, a young man who defends himself after merciless taunting realizes he must leave Mississippi rather than face an unfair "justice" system. During that escape to Memphis, the friends face even more racist situations. Indeed, instances of white oppression and prejudice permeate the book, making it more stark than the earlier titles that emphasized family strength and unity in addition to exposing racism. Side plots involving the pregnancy of one friend, as well as the illness and death of another, add another element to the story but do not flow smoothly into the narrative. Taylor conveys the harsh realities of the time, as well as strong-willed Cassie's realization that as an adult she will have to make her own decisions and fight her own battles. Cassie's dream of becoming a lawyer and the looming war raise related questions regarding the white-controlled legal system and the injustice of fighting a war that sustains the status-quo, questions that have no easy answers. This is a dramatic, painful book, but it's more of a string of events than a narrative with strong characterizations.

Virginia B. Moore

SOURCE: A review of *The Road to Memphis,* in *Voice of Youth Advocates,* Vol. 13, No. 3, August, 1990, p. 164.

For those who have followed Cassie Logan's story in *Roll of Thunder, Hear My Cry* and *Let the Circle Be Unbroken* and for those meeting her for the first time— a black teenager living in deep Mississippi during the early 1940s—she continues to narrate her family saga with details of her poignant emotions and keen observations in this powerful, readable, and fast-moving sequel.

With her brother Stacey, she spends three harrowing nights traveling between segregated Mississippi towns and Memphis, Tennessee, in an effort to help a friend. During this time, she experiences fear, harassment, sorrow, and the exhilaration of her first romance, as rumblings of World War II begin.

In this novel, Cassie is a high school senior in Jackson, Mississippi. Her dreams of college and law school are being overshadowed by events in her rural hometown: school friends have a lover's quarrel, a black friend rages against his white tormentors, and a white youth shows regret for his role in tragic violence against a black. Remaining true to her character, she is an eavesdropping observer who is struggling toward personal maturity while at the same time being curious, unpredictable, humorous, and compassionate. She and Stacey are forced to meet the challenges of an adult world in which only black family love, community traditions, strength of heritage, and passive resistance prove heroic against white power, racism, and unjust cruelty. At the same time, they must realize that there are caring whites who are also powerless in a discriminatory society.

Reading the previous books of the series is not necessary in order to understand and enjoy this volume. Taylor's continued smooth, easy language provides readability for all ages, with a focus on universal human pride, worthy values, and individual responsibility. This action-packed drama is highly recommended.

Nancy Vasilakis

SOURCE: A review of *The Road to Memphis,* in *The Horn Book Magazine,* Vol. LXVI, No. 5, September, 1990, pp. 609-10.

Continuing the story of the Logan family begun in **Roll of Thunder, Hear My Cry** and **Let the Circle Be Unbroken,** the author now brings her protagonists to young adulthood. Cassie, spunky as ever, is concluding her last year of high school in the city of Jackson and is considering possibilities for the future. She has notions of becoming a lawyer—her interest sparked by an attraction for a handsome attorney from Memphis. Her brother Stacey, who has a job in a box factory, has recently become the proud owner of an almost-new 1938 Ford. As she did in **The Gold Cadillac,** Taylor employs the automobile as a metaphor for a journey into the dark heart of Southern racism in mid-twentieth-century America. Stacey, accompanied by Cassie and longtime chums Clarence and Willie, undertakes to help their friend Moe escape to Memphis after he is provoked into attacking and almost killing some white bullies. The trip is filled with tension; chance meetings with whites churn with potential danger. Clarence suffers what is probably a cerebral hemorrhage and dies en route. The others eventually reach their destination and safety, but, the reader senses, the respite is temporary. In spite of several compelling scenes, the novel is not a tightly constructed whole. Much of the dialogue seems repetitive, and minor

pieces of business overlong. It is our long familiarity with and affection for the Logans, one suspects, that bring the characters in this novel to life.

MISSISSIPPI BRIDGE (1990)

Kirkus Reviews

SOURCE: A review of *Mississippi Bridge,* in *Kirkus Reviews,* Vol. LVIII, No. 16, August 15, 1990, pp. 1174-75.

Readers familiar with the several other stories in which the Logans appear know that a visit to the Wallace general store will lead to painful incidents of racial injustice. This time, it's back to 1931, with Stacey Logan's contemporary and sometime friend Jeremy Simms, who is white, narrating. The once-a-week bus is coming; as the would-be riders wait at the store, Taylor contrasts their treatment (only a white may try on a hat before buying it; a black man who allows that he has a new job is cruelly forced to lie and contradict himself). The bus is full; the blacks (including the Logans' Grandmama, going to care for a sick relative) are put off to make room for whites on less urgent errands. Then the decrepit local bridge chooses this day to give way, under the bus—not exactly divine retribution, since the characters who drown are the more innocent white people, but a satisfying irony nonetheless.

Taylor, a powerful storyteller, again combines authentic incidents to create a taut plot. Jeremy's narrative, in dialect, is believable, though he gives no hint why only he, in his otherwise abusive, unredeemed family, has compassion for the blacks' situation. Taylor's cry for justice always rings true; but it would be even more potent if the other side were shown in fuller dimension.

Mary Harris Veeder

SOURCE: A review of *Mississippi Bridge,* in *Chicago Tribune—Books,* September 9, 1990, p. 6.

Taylor's tales of Depression-era Mississippi already have won prizes. The Logans, a land-owning black family whom some white neighbors consider too proud, figure again in this short piece, as seen through the eyes of Jeremy Simms, a 10-year-old white boy. Although the plot turns on a rather unusual event, the painful, petty, daily effects of racial prejudice hit hardest of all. Taylor expressively conveys the black characters' blend of anger and a self-protective surface. The book is short enough for family reading and discussion.

Betsy Hearne

SOURCE: A review of *Mississippi Bridge,* in *Bulletin of the Center for Children's Books,* Vol. 44, No. 2, October, 1990, p. 48.

Told by the white boy whose attempts at friendship with his black neighbors were recounted in *Roll of Thunder, Hear My Cry* and other books in the series about the Logan family, this is Jeremy's description of a tragedy on the Rosa Lee River. He watches as a store owner insults two black customers and as a bus driver unseats all the black travelers to accommodate a last-minute crowd of whites. His affection for two of the white passengers, a little girl and her grandmother who don't participate in the racism except by being part of a society favoring them, is equaled by his pain over the treatment of the blacks. It is the little girl and her grandmother who die when the bus hurtles over a bridge with rotten planks, and it is this irony that lends more subtle dimension to the story than has characterized some of Taylor's other indictments of racism. The conflict between an unjust father and his ethical son also add power to the scenes, which are smoothly developed in rural Southern dialect.

Anna DeWind

SOURCE: A review of *Mississippi Bridge,* in *School Library Journal,* Vol. 36, No. 11, November, 1990, pp. 119-20.

Drawing once again upon her father's stories, Taylor has created a harsh, disturbing tale of racism in Mississippi during the 1930s. Told from the viewpoint of Jeremy Simms, a ten-year-old white boy who aspires to be friends with the black children of the Logan family, this is the story of a rainy day, an overloaded bus, and the destiny of its passengers after the driver has ordered the black travelers off to make room for latecoming whites. Telescoping the injustices faced by blacks on a daily basis into one afternoon drives home the omnipresent effects of racism with a relentless force. This is an angry book, replete with examples of the insults and injuries to which the African-American characters are subjected. Jeremy, the only white character to acknowledge this unfairness, is brought to task by his father for "snivelin'" after the Logans. The book's climax is a catastrophic accident in which the bus crashes off a bridge, killing the passengers. When Jeremy asks a black rescuer how such a thing could happen, he is told, "the Lord works in mysterious ways." This is a disturbing explanation, not for its implication that the white passengers are being punished for the sins of their race so much as for the logical extension that the black characters were saved because they were kept off the bus in the first place. Well written and thought provoking, this book will haunt readers and generate much discussion.

Mary M. Burns

SOURCE: A review of *Mississippi Bridge,* in *The Horn Book Magazine,* Vol. LXVI, No. 6, November-December, 1990, pp. 747-48.

Although Mildred Taylor's novels have been deservedly acclaimed, her shorter pieces seem equally, if not more, powerful in the intensity of their focus. *Mississippi Bridge* is no exception. The story is told in the first person by Jeremy Sims, a ten-year-old white boy. Unlike most of the white community, and in particular his father, Jeremy admires the members of the black Logan family for their independence and sense of pride—exactly the qualities that antagonize the white men. This background information, developed in earlier stories, is skillfully woven into the text so that the book can be read as part of a continuing saga or as a well-crafted entity in itself. As the story opens, Jeremy watches the weekly bus emerge from the mists of a driving rainstorm into the center of his small community. Like actors in a play, various townsfolk assemble for departure, including Jeremy's former teacher, Miz Hattie, and her four-year-old granddaughter, Grace-Anne, both white; Josias Williams and the Logan children's grandmother, both black. Before the passengers board the bus, a number of incidents occur that not only indicate the social attitudes prevalent in Depression-era Mississippi but also foreshadow the climactic moment when the black passengers are forced to leave the vehicle to make room for additional white passengers. Regardless of protestations, regardless of the relative importance of the reasons for travel, there is only one principle underlying the driver's decision: whites are superior. Jeremy, more sensitive than the others, reacts with dismay, earning his father's anger. But then he becomes witness to an ironic tragedy as the bus spins out of control into the flood-swollen river. As did Thornton Wilder in *The Bridge of San Luis Rey,* Taylor has created an observer of an event who muses upon both its immediate effects and its philosophical implications: "I was crying 'cause I couldn't understand nothing about the day, about how come Miz Hattie and Grace-Anne was on that bus, and Josias, and Stacey's and them's grandmama and Rudine and her mama wasn't. . . . If the Lord was punishing, how come Grace-Anne and Miz Hattie? They ain't hurt nobody." And that is a question that haunts the reader as it haunts Jeremy, for it is not easily answered. Once again the author has successfully underscored moral dilemmas without ever losing her sure grasp of narrative development and character delineation; as always, the result is memorable.

Publishers Weekly

SOURCE: A review of *Mississippi Bridge,* in *Publishers Weekly,* Vol. 237, No. 30, July 27, 1996, p. 234.

Containing the same characters found in Taylor's series about the Logans, a black family from Mississippi, this potent short novel is told from the perspective of a 10-year-old white boy, Jeremy Simms. The year is 1931, and segregation is very much a reality in the South. Jeremy, who has been spending a rainy day at the Wallace store, is shocked when a bus driver forces Grandma Logan and the rest of his black passengers off the bus in order to make room for a group of white latecomers. The incident turns out to be a stroke of good fortune for some and a tragedy for others: minutes after its departure, the bus careens off a bridge and plunges into a creek. Using very little commentary, Taylor reveals the daily humiliations suffered by black members of a small community and explores the emotional impact of the fatal accident. The ironies and injustices presented in her story will be strongly felt and long remembered.

THE WELL (1995)

Hazel Rochman

SOURCE: A review of *The Well,* in *Booklist,* Vol. 91, No. 8, December 15, 1994, p. 754.

"Charlie Simms was always mean, and that's the truth of it." From the first line, this short, intense novel of racist violence is told with the immediacy of a family narrative. David Logan (the father in Taylor's 1977 Newbery Award winner, *Roll of Thunder, Hear My Cry*) tells a story of his boyhood in rural Mississippi at a time when "uppity niggers" can be hanged for thinking themselves equal to whites and the horror of slavery still haunts his mother's memory. The Logans are among the few black families to own land, and during a prolonged drought, they have a well of sweet water, which they share with their neighbors, black and white. Most people are grateful, but the white Simms family hates being beholden to blacks. The tense confrontation erupts in beatings and terror. The cast is large for so short a novel—it's hard sometimes to keep track of all the people in the community—but the Logan family is beautifully individualized. David is able to heed his father's warning, "Use your head, not your fists," but David's hotheaded older brother can't bear the constant humiliation. The well of the title is also a metaphor for the history of the place: both the bigotry that lies beneath the surface and the sweet strength of family ties.

Publishers Weekly

SOURCE: A review of *The Well,* in *Publishers Weekly,* Vol. 242, No. 1, January 2, 1995, p. 77.

Taylor's compact novella revisits the long-suffering Logan family, this time focusing on the boyhood of David (father of Cassie Logan from *Roll of Thunder, Hear My Cry*). In the early 1900s, all the wells in their part of Mississippi have run dry—all except for the Logans'. White neighbors come from miles around to collect water, but despite the Logans' generosity, they treat David and his family with enormous disrespect. When young Charlie Simms's taunting of the Logan boys turns physical, David's older brother Hammer chooses to retaliate—a move that causes him and his family pain from all sides. Taylor, obviously in tune with these fully-developed characters, creates for them an intense and compelling situation and skillfully delivers powerful messages about racism and moral fortitude. This insightful read stands on its own, but will have a special resonance for fans of the series.

Marie Orlando

SOURCE: A review of *The Well,* in *School Library Journal,* Vol. 41, No. 2, February, 1995, p. 100.

Another contribution to the Logan family saga, this is Father's account of an incident from his boyhood. During a drought in 1910, 10-year-old David Logan's family has the only working well in their part of Mississippi. They share their water willingly with both black and white neighbors, but white teenager Charlie Simms tests their generosity, goading David's older brother Hammer into a fight requiring restitution in the form of labor on the Simms's farm. Charlie and his brother get even for the disgrace of Hammer's beating by secretly contaminating the Logans' well with dead animals, only to be exposed and punished when a neighbor reveals their act. While David narrates, this is really Hammer's story; his pride and steely determination not to be put down are the source of the novel's action and power. Readers will feel the Logans' fear and righteous anger at the injustice and humiliation they suffer because they are black. As in *The Friendship,* Taylor has used her gift for storytelling and skillful characterization to craft a brief but compelling novel about prejudice and the saving power of human dignity.

Linda Perkins

SOURCE: A review of *The Well,* in *Wilson Library Bulletin,* Vol. 69, No. 9, May, 1995, p. 100.

Younger brother David is the storyteller in Mildred D. Taylor's *The Well.* In a preface, Taylor explains the origin of the story in her family's history. David, she notes, later becomes the father in the Logan family chronicles beginning with *Roll of Thunder, Hear My Cry.* Set in the South during the early 1900s, *The Well* revolves around the only working well in a community suffering severe drought. This well belongs to the Logans, an African American family, who generously offer water to all in need, "colored folks, and white folks, too."

Trouble begins when Charlie Simms, a mean-spirited white boy, slugs David in the jaw as he reaches for his crutch. David's older brother Hammer retaliates by shoving Charlie to the ground. In those days, blacks were lynched for merely "mouthin' off" to whites, so David fears the worst for his brother. The punishment is severe and humiliating, but the Logans manage to maintain their dignity, self-respect, and hospitality despite the bitter injustice. As David's father advises, "You gotta weigh what kind of trouble you gonna take on."

Charlie Simms is basically a villainous bully, but other "decent" folks demonstrate less obvious forms of racism as well. These ethical issues add irony and should provoke good group discussion. Once again, Taylor has taken a true incident that demonstrates the raw edge of racism and told a tense, engrossing story. Fans of the Logan family will not be disappointed.

Mary M. Burns

SOURCE: A review of *The Well,* in *The Horn Book Magazine,* Vol. LXXI, No. 4, July-August, 1995, pp. 461-62.

In a prefatory note, the author reprises her acknowledgment of the part her family's history plays in her books about the Logan family. In *The Well,* the narrative reaches back into the early days of the twentieth century, when the narrator, David Logan, the father of Cassie, Stacey, Christopher-John, and Little Man, is a boy. This story, a novella like *Song of the Trees* and *The Friendship,* delivers an emotional wallop in a concentrated span of time and action. Focused and honed, it moves rapidly from initial confrontation to denouement. It is summer, and a severe drought threatens the Mississippi community where the Logans are substantial landholders. That they are black and proud sets them apart; that they control a seemingly inexhaustible supply of water—which they share with all—makes them a target for repercussions. When David's older brother Hammer justifiably tangles with teenager Charlie Simms, the Mississippi code demands that both Logan boys will be punished. Despite this outcome, Hammer, in defiance of the times, continues to defy the malicious Charlie, who finds the ultimate retaliation in fouling the precious well. Although emphasis is on the central conflict between the Logan boys and Charlie Simms, Taylor has enriched her story by introducing characters such as Grandma Rachel, whose memories of slavery when she was denied the use of her own name suggests the long history of injustice which underlies the present moment. And the advice given David and Hammer by their father explains how the family survived adversity: "You boys better start learning how to use your heads, not your fists, when it comes to white folks. You learn to outsmart them, 'cause in the end you can't outfight them, not with your fists. They got the power, but we got our heads." Like all of Taylor's work, this story reverberates in the heart long after the final paragraph is read.

Mary Jo Peltier

SOURCE: A review of *The Well,* in *Voice of Youth Advocates,* Vol. 18, No. 3, August, 1995, p. 166.

Narrated by ten-year-old David Logan, this story of an earlier generation of the Logan clan from *Roll of Thunder, Hear My Cry* is brief and intense—a page-turner that readers are not likely to put down until finished. When all the wells in the Logan family's part of Mississippi go dry, their well still holds good, sweet water and they share it freely with black and white neighbors alike. This is not always easy for David's fiercely proud older brother Hammer, especially when the neighbors who come calling for water are the Simms, white tenant farmers who begrudge the Logan family owning 100 acres of land. Words are exchanged and tension builds until one day fourteen-year-old Charlie Simms knocks David down after demanding that David help him with his wagon. This sends Hammer into a rage and he lays Charlie out flat, breaking the law of the south—a Negro never hits a white person. David and Hammer are sentenced to work for the Simmses for the summer and are advised by their father to learn the lesson he learned at about the same age: to survive in the white man's world, you have to use your head instead of your fists. At summer's end Charlie and his younger brother Ed-Rose are not done with David and Hammer Logan, but their plans for further revenge backfire on them in an exciting climax and satisfying conclusion to the book. This is a powerful, fast-paced story and like Taylor's past novels, communicates the importance of inner strength and respect for all.

Additional coverage of Taylor's life and career is contained in the following sources published by The Gale Group: *Authors and Artists for Young Adults,* Vol. 10; *Black Writers,* Vol. 1; *Contemporary Literary Criticism,* Vol. 21; *Dictionary of Literary Biography,* Vol. 52; *Junior DISCovering Authors; Major Authors and Illustrators for Children and Young Adults; Something about the Author Autobiography Series,* Vol. 5; and *Something about the Author,* Vols. 15, 70.

Phyllis A(yame) Whitney

1903-

American author of fiction and nonfiction.

Major works include *Willow Hill* (1947), *Secret of the Samurai Sword* (1958), *Mystery of the Haunted Pool* (1960), *Mystery of the Scowling Boy* (1973), *Secret of Haunted Mesa* (1975).

INTRODUCTION

Called "America's queen of romantic suspense" and the "Grandmaster" by reviewers, Whitney, with over forty novels for young adults to her credit, is a master crafter of mysteries, romances, and intrigues about young women whose attempts to unlock secrets and solve puzzles often put them on the threshold of danger. A popular writer and commercial success—at one time she had over forty million copies of her books in print—Whitney also has garnered critical recognition for her artistry in the genre. She has received the prestigious Edgar Allen Poe Award for two of her young-adult mysteries, and award-nominations for three others. Whitney's incredible plot twists, foreign settings, complex family dynamics, sinister villains, and spooky overtones echo the eighteenth-century Gothic motif, to which Whitney adds twentieth-century themes, issues, and characters. Critics esteem her works for their realistic, likable, and spunky protagonists, who, unlike many traditional heroines of romantic and Gothic fiction, are not idealized nor sentimentalized, but rather are burdened with shortcomings that they must attempt to work out for themselves. Althea K. Helbig and Agnes Regan Perkins wrote in the *Dictionary of American Children's Fiction:* "Typically, [Whitney's YA suspense novels] are from the point of view of a young adolescent girl who feels unloved or inferior because of a lack of talent and who, with a boy her age or slightly older, unravels a series of mysterious events, often involving crime but not murder, and in so doing comes to self-understanding."

Another distinguishing feature of Whitney's work is the incorporation of a variety of exotic locales and cultures culled from her own international travels. In *Secret of the Samurai Sword*, for instance, Whitney infuses the text with hints of the Japanese traditions and customs she experienced as an American child growing up in Japan. Her stories also have been set in the Virgin Islands, the Isle of Skye in Scotland, China, and South Africa. While her mysteries and romances have been occasionally criticized for formulaic and artificial plots, reviewers applaud their swift action and vivid settings and atmospheres. Thematically, Whitney has touched upon such issues as apartheid, race relations, and the plight of Native Americans; in addition, she is concerned with the social and emotional problems of adolescents. Above all, Whit-

ney has a knack for telling suspenseful stories and for luring readers into the fantastic secrets and chilling situations of her fiction.

Biographical Information

Whitney was born in Yokohama, Japan, in 1903 to American parents. She lived in Japan, China, and the Philippines until her father's death when she was fifteen. She returned to the United States with her mother, who died two years later. After settling in Chicago with an aunt, Whitney finished high school and married a year after graduating. By that time, she was already writing stories, and managed to sell a few to magazines. In 1941, she published her first book, *A Place for Ann*, a young-adult novel that brought her a measure of success and self-sufficiency. Shortly after divorcing her husband in 1945, Whitney approached her editor about writing a book involving racial issues. Despite her editor's reservations, Whitney wrote *Willow Hill*, a story about a white girl and her high school friends confronting the integration of a housing project into their community. The book was published in 1947. Soon after, Whitney turned to writing mysteries for young adults, attracted to the challenge of plotting the complex structure of a mystery novel. Whitney once commented, "I have always written because I couldn't help it. From the age of twelve on I loved to make up stories, and I've been doing it ever since. I believe in entertaining my readers, and I also hope to make them think and feel."

Major Works

Though not her first novel for young adults, *Willow Hill* was one of Whitney's most popular and best received works, and was the work which first drew attention to her writing. The story centers on the reactions of white townspeople to the construction of a racially integrated housing project. Its main protagonist is Val Coleman, whose parents take opposing viewpoints of the issue. Harriet Ford Griswold, writing in *The Christian Science Monitor*, explained that Whitney "won the Youth Today Contest for this book . . . because her presentation of all sides of this controversial subject is so convincing." *Booklist*'s review was similarly positive: "The racial angle is very well handled and there are enough of other young people's activities to interest any teenager wishing to read about those his own age." Alice M. Jordan wrote, "The story with its grave social involvement moves swiftly, bringing in enough open-minded young people to take the lead in an effort to create a spirit of friendliness and good will."

Whitney combines history and culture with a gripping mystery in *Secret of the Samurai Sword*. Celia Bronson and her brother Stephen, fourteen and fifteen years old respectively, travel to Kyoto to visit their grandmother, who is writing a book about Japan. They soon find themselves absorbed in Japan's exotic scenery and classic customs, as well as embroiled in a mystery involving the uneasy ghost of a Samurai warrior. Critics praised the intriguing plot, the ornamental setting, and the information on ancient Japanese culture and ways of life. A *Kirkus Reviews* critic commented, "If the teen-age reader, ignorant of the structure of classical Japan, can absorb even half of the details of Japanese life offered here, this pleasant mystery will have been well worth the reading." Ruth Hill Viguers deemed *Samurai Sword* "an exceptionally good story," while Silence Buck Bellows, writing in the *Christian Science Monitor*, opined, "This book is quite a package, being a top notch mystery, a source of authentic information about Japan, and a wise and warm commentary on human relations."

While Celia and Stephen visit thier grandmother, twelve-year-old Susan Price travels ahead of her family to stay with her aunt in New York in *Mystery of the Haunted Pool*. Shortly after she arrives, Susan becomes intrigued by a family secret attached to the large old house her parents are about to rent from a retired riverboat captain. Susan helps solve the mystery, and in the process makes friends with the captain's embittered grandson, who is having difficulty adjusting to a disability. Zena Sutherland deemed the book, "A good mystery story,

with logical explanations but romantic atmosphere." She added, "The writing has pace and suspense; characterization and conversation are realistic." A reviewer for *The Booklist and Subscription Books Bulletin* noted of the book, "A plausible mystery with a well-developed plot and characterization that is above average for a mystery story."

For *Mystery of the Scowling Boy*, Whitney moved the action to the Pocono Mountains of eastern Pennsylvania, where Jan Sutton and her older brother Mike are spending the Christmas holidays with their grandparents while their parents are away. The mystery of this novel revolves around familial relationships rather than ghosts or sinister prowlers. When Jan discovers that her favorite movie star, Alanna Graham, is staying in a nearby estate, she is determined to meet her. As Jan gets to know the Graham family, she discovers that all is not well and that Alanna is being blackmailed. A *Publishers Weekly* reviewer commented, "The author is at the top of her professional form in this improbable but appealing new mystery," while Raymond J. Morafino wrote that *Scowling Boy* "is another of [Whitney's] competently plotted but routine mysteries." Morafino concluded, "The complex plot and glamorous characters will keep young readers entertained until all the mysteries are predictably resolved in time for a happy Christmas." Althea K. Helbig and Agnes Regan Perkins, writing in the *Dictionary of American Children's Fiction*, observed, "Though the story depends partly on the Gothic atmosphere of the old house and the grotesque sculptures, it is all plausible, and the ski-country setting is well evoked."

Secret of Haunted Mesa takes place in New Mexico. Jenny and her family visit Haunted Mesa Ranch, where her father is lecturing at a conference. At the ranch, Jenny meets up with Greg, one of the few young people she knows who is not smitten with her famous older sister Carol, a singer. A mystery unfolds as Jenny and Greg investigate strange-looking lights and the disappearance of Charlie, a Zuni Indian boy who steals food and kachina dolls. Although a reviewer for *The Children's Book Review Service* remarked that Whitney's "portrayal of Zuni Indians and their problems lacks accuracy, sensitivity, and depth," the reviewer concluded that the work was "a competently written mystery story." *Kirkus Reviews* was less kind. "A perfunctory mystery . . . is sandwiched in between clumsy lectures on Zuni culture and 'understanding' Anglos and a stock psychological problem—young Jenny's fear of being upstaged by her famous, folksinging sister." Sarah Law Kennerly, however, was more complimentary, concluding that the mystery will be "popular with Whitney's many fans."

Awards

Whitney was a Youth Today contest winner, and won *Book World*'s Spring Book Festival Award, both in 1947 for *Willow Hill*. She also was bestowed the Edgar Allen Poe Award from the Mystery Writers of America for the best juvenile mystery for *Mystery of the Haunted Pool* in 1961 and for *Mystery of the Hidden Hand* in 1964. The following works received Edgar Allen Poe Award nominations: *Secret of the Tiger's Eye* in 1962, *Secret of the Missing Footprint* in 1971, and *Mystery of the Scowling Boy* in 1974. Whitney won the Sequoyah Children's Book Award in 1963 for *Mystery of the Haunted Pool.* She was honored with the Grandmaster Award from the Mystery Writers of America in 1988 for lifetime achievement and with the Malice Domestic Award in 1989 for lifetime achievement.

AUTHOR'S COMMENTARY

Phyllis A. Whitney

SOURCE: "Writing the Romantic Suspense Novel," in *The Writer,* Vol. 98, No. 6, June, 1985, pp. 9-12.

The type of novel I have been writing for many years has come under assorted headings. Gothic was a favorite label for a long time, though that word has a limiting connotation, and I wrote myself away from it. Recently I have been called a romance writer, though that's a name I reject because it doesn't include mystery—an important part of my writing. If I must have a label, I prefer romantic suspense, since this term comes closest to describing mystery-romance. Whatever they are called, readers like these books and there should always be a market for them.

When I start work on a romantic suspense novel, I like to think in terms of five preliminary headings. By "preliminary" I mean that period when I am searching for a direction, and before I get into serious plotting. These are the headings I use to keep myself on the track:

1. Setting

2. Heroine's vocation (or avocation)

3. Heroine's problem

4. Other characters

5. Mystery and romance

"Setting" is less obvious than you may think. It can be some exotic place you visit, or do extensive research about, or it can mean an easily accessible spot in which *you* can create the right atmosphere. It's possible to imagine a fascinating house and the immediate area around it set down in an ordinary and familiar background. I've done it both ways, and I know the important thing for me will be my own feeling about any setting. A good deal of the emotion in a story can grow from its background, so it must be one my own imagination can respond to.

When I first choose a place to write about, I have no idea what my story will be. The setting itself will help to trigger my creative juices, and the research is sure to be filled with story ideas, as a new world opens up for me. Even when I'm making up the background out of my imagination, research is important in stimulating fresh ideas. We need to put a lot of information in before anything comes out.

Some of this research may grow from the second heading: "Heroine's work or avocation." When I started writing adult novels, I wrote only period stories. Then I began to get bored with the travails of my Victorian heroines, and for many years I've written about the present. I'm much more interested when my characters belong to the world I live in, with all its complex and exciting problems. This means that for each novel I must find out what my main character does for a living. Today's women have an independence I admire, and I want the women in my novels to fight their own battles. If you follow this course, make sure that your heroine's interests are ones you can sympathize with and understand.

I've stretched myself by writing about a woman who was a noted dress designer (when I can't thread a needle!). I got by with interesting research and by giving her a number of other matters to deal with.

When I started work on **Dream of Orchids,** there were no orchids, and of course no title. I tried to give my heroine an interest in gardening, and quickly got tired of that, since I'm no gardener. However, in reading about flowers, I became intrigued by orchids, and the following extensive research led me to the heart of my story. I find that if I just begin *somewhere,* the road will open up.

The next matter I must decide about early is a *personal* problem for my heroine. In the beginning, there can be a division between her problem and the main problems that develop for her in the course of the story. In the end, both must come together and be resolved.

In **Dream of Orchids,** my heroine leaves her successful bookstore in Long Island to go south to Key West to meet a father she hasn't seen since she was a child. There are two half-sisters there as well (who raise orchids). The personal relationships become important, and everything begins to connect. A profession of any sort, whether that of the main character, or of others in the story, can lend color and fresh interest. To say nothing of opening new plotting possibilities.

The heroine's main problem should never stand still or become repetitive and tiresome. Other elements must be brought in to affect it and develop future action. A search, for instance, can quickly become boring if it doesn't grow and change. So other problems on the main road must emerge to keep the story moving.

My fourth heading, "Other characters," now becomes

important. Working on the first three headings will suggest other people who will populate your story.

The colorful half-sisters in *Dream of Orchids* began to emerge, and when I named them Iris and Fern, their personalities developed in ways I'd never foreseen. Of course, I made notes along the way about every chance idea that came to mind, so that nothing would be lost. The story always begins to grow long before I put any of it on paper.

Time must be given to my hero and the role he needs to play. With an independent heroine, it is all too easy to leave the hero out of the action! Beware of the offstage hero who steps in only now and then. He needn't be in every scene, but he must play an active role in the story. Don't forget about him and leave him standing around for chapters at a time because you don't need him. It's necessary to figure out something important for him to do. This may not be as easy or obvious as it seems. There are a great many elements to juggle in any novel, and even heroes can be forgotten.

The emergence of the players in my drama brings me to the fifth listing, "Mystery and romance," both difficult ingredients to handle well.

Every romantic suspense novel must have the element of mystery, since this is one of the best ways to build suspense. Reader curiosity should be a strong element from the start, and it's a fine tool to use to pull the reader along. We want our readers to ask, "What is happening here? What will happen next? Where are we heading?" However, though curiosity is a useful tool, particularly in the beginning, it's never enough. Until our main character aims for a goal she can reach only after overcoming tough obstacles, we haven't really begun our story. Yet a goal and its obstacles can't be established until a great deal has been made clear to the reader. That's one reason openings are hard to write. It helps to rely first on reader curiosity. Through dialogue, action, and the main character's thoughts, we clarify what is going on, tantalizing and promising as we move ahead. When the real goal becomes evident, we're through the opening and on our way. How we get to the solution is what the story is all about. Mystery, of course, will continue right to the final scene.

The mystery and its solution seldom come to me in a single revealing flash. As the people in my story begin to flesh out and tell me about themselves, hints of mystery come to light a bit at a time. In the beginning, I may have no idea of who the villain is, or even exactly what crime has been committed. I may try out several characters in this role before I can be sure, or decide what he or she is up to. Once that matter is settled, the mystery develops on firmer ground. Now we need to watch for surprise action—action that will not only astonish our readers, but will surprise the writer as well. For this reason I don't like to outline in great detail. I plan the direction each chapter will take, and then I let

my characters play out their roles on their own, so that they sometimes do things I never expected, and thus enrich my story. This concept may seem puzzling to the reader, but the people the writer has created *should* take on a life of their own, though not entirely without control. The writer must always keep the main course of the story in mind.

Suspense is often a matter of pacing in the actual course of writing—and *rewriting*. Too much detail can kill a scene and slow down the pace, while not enough will make it lose excitement and interest. One develops a sixth sense about this rather elusive quality. In *Rainsong,* I devised what was meant to be a suspenseful scene in which my heroine finally cornered someone who had been tormenting her with frightening tricks. In my first draft, I had tossed the scene away because revelations came too quickly and spoiled the pacing. My heroine discovered that her intruder was "only a boy of sixteen," and she was no longer frightened. Suspense went out the window. When I rewrote the scene, I had a tall figure rush toward her, nearly knocking her down. She doesn't realize how young he is, and the scene is therefore much more frightening, the pacing is better (that is, stretching out suspense); when she meets him a few pages later and recognizes his youth, she is still frightened: The young can be violent, and she knows he means her harm. We don't discover right away what he is up to, since it's necessary to build *more* mystery.

Of course once any puzzle is solved, we need to move toward the next surprise and a new rising of suspense. Pacing is important here as well. Too many exciting scenes coming too close together can weary a reader. So we relax the suspense for a little while, and build it up gradually again; always that rising and falling, but with a general mounting toward the heights of a dramatic climax.

Eventually, the mystery will be solved in that final dramatic scene that is a prerequisite for a suspense novel. By the time I come to writing the big scene, my imagination is sure to take over and give me answers that I may not have imagined ahead of time—perhaps better suspense than I could figure out with my "conscious" mind. That happened with *Emerald.* While I knew what my big surprise was going to be, I still didn't know exactly how I was to get rid of the heroine's brutal, child-snatching husband. Yet everything was there in the scene for me to use, and when the time came, my creativity took charge and provided an original "weapon" for my heroine to wield.

As for the romance itself, while the hero is always important, there may be some guesswork as to who really is the hero. Unpredictable romances can be more interesting than those that are obvious from the first. If everything is in place in the first scene, you have no developing story. The scenes of emotion must, of course, be genuine, so that the reader can feel with the heroine and care about the outcome.

I have never written the torrid love scenes that editors were demanding for a while. Now that particular trend appears to be fading out to some extent. Explicit sex has lost its shock value in print and can even grow boring from all the repetition. Real emotion is much harder to achieve. It is easy to make your characters pant, but *you* have to feel something deeper for the people in your story if the reader is to be moved by your love scenes.

TITLE COMMENTARY

📖 *A PLACE FOR ANN* (1941)

Maude Adams

SOURCE: A review of *A Place for Ann*, in *The Library Journal*, Vol. 66, No. 9, May 1, 1941, p. 404.

"The House of Tomorrow" is a personal service organization started by unemployed young people on a co-operative basis. It involves arts and crafts, the restoration of an old house, and opening a day nursery. The members strengthen a wavering faith in themselves, discover their potentialities, find interesting jobs, and establish the enterprise definitely as a young people's project. While the venture is overwhelmingly successful, the difficulties encountered are quite realistic. Except for one stereotyped middle-aged man, most of the characters are well drawn. An interesting vocational novel in which imagination, courage, and personality adjustment are frankly suggested. Directed in part at the older generation for their imposed "guidance." More convincing and better motivated than *Let Polly Do It* by Amy W. Stone. I recommend it for its honesty in treating a modern problem. Illustrations by Helen Blair (some on terra cotta inserts) are distinctive.

Alice M. Jordan

SOURCE: A review of *A Place for Ann*, in *The Horn Book Magazine*, Vol. XVII, No. 4, July, 1941, p. 292.

The all too familiar plight of young people for whom no job is waiting, is the theme of this present-day story. Through Ann's enterprise and ingenuity this particular set of boys and girls pooled their ideas and discovered for themselves and others some unexpected talents for marketable work. Although there is a slight haziness about some of their services, the young people are natural, the conversations lively and convincing, while the older man who backs their venture is especially well drawn. The publishers have given the book a fine format and the illustrations [by Helen Blair] are arresting.

📖 *A STAR FOR GINNY* (1942)

Booklist

SOURCE: A review of *A Star for Ginny*, in *Booklist*, Vol. 39, No. 2, October 1, 1942, p. 37.

Determined to become an illustrator of children's books, Ginny Somerset, one of the young people in *A Place for Ann*, takes a job in the book department of a Chicago store as a step toward her goal. An up-to-date vocational story which shows something of the workings of a large department store and suggests characteristics and tempo of Chicago life.

Florence Bethune Sloane

SOURCE: A review of *A Star for Ginny*, in *The Christian Science Monitor*, December 10, 1942, p. 24.

A Star for Ginny, is a story in which a young illustrator leaves a small town to work in the book department of a large Chicago store, hoping to gain experience and information about the various types of illustration used in children's books. Ginny had to learn her lesson—"to hitch her wagon to a star" and still do good work in the job at hand. The working out of a well sustained plot and a romance provides plenty of suspense and interest for older girl readers.

📖 *WILLOW HILL* (1947)

Booklist

SOURCE: A review of *Willow Hill*, in *Booklist*, Vol. 43, No. 13, March 15, 1947, p. 227.

A story of high school people and their classes, parties, friendships, athletic games, and good times. Threatening to spoil the senior year of the principal characters is the problem of a new Negro settlement in the town. The students themselves find the solution to their difficulty. The racial angle is very well handled and there are enough of other young people's activities to interest any teenager wishing to read about those his own age. Well written.

May Lamberton Becker

SOURCE: A review of *Willow Hill*, in *New York Herald Tribune Weekly Book Review*, Vol. 23, No. 31, March 23, 1947, p. 8.

Stories for young folks about race prejudice, now rapidly increasing, are rounding out their presentation and, while preserving crusading spirit, bearing in mind that a crusade to be successful needs not only emotion but documentation. Phyllis Whitney's new story—which has won the Youth Today prize for "the most sensitive, realistic treatment of some aspect of contemporary American life and youth problems," has fire all the way through, but it has also light.

Willow Hill is a prosperous, compact community just large enough for one drug store, a civic-minded woman's club, several churches and a coeducational high school. The town is on high ground; the townspeople can look out from the gold bar of economic security and regard with growing disquiet the construction of certain buildings sprawled upon the plain below. Willow Hill feels from the first that these are likely to disrupt its ordered, suitable pattern of social mores, real estate values and preconceived ideas. This it does and more: within a year it is to unsettle their definition of democracy and drive a wedge between the articles of the pledge to the flag. For this is a government housing problem. The Hubbard Plant, a big industrial proposition, had to have workers, and some of the workers were Negroes.

Val Coleman, the senior through whose troubled mind and warm heart pass those new impressions and experiences, finds the first disruption—however slight—in her own family life. Her father, the high school gym coach, thinks "if a kid plays good basketball I want him on the team . . . and I guess I don't give a bang what anybody else thinks of his color." Her kind-hearted little mother had long ago taken all the definitions she would ever have into a mind wax to receive and marble to retain. Mutual affection held the family together—but not their opinions. There was a new line-up at school where the most popular boy was convinced you couldn't just watch your own town being ruined because the government wanted to dump something like this in its lap. Val couldn't side with him, nor with the shopkeeper, who thought her "too young to understand that angle." There was a meeting of protest, orderly, even courteous—but it meant business, and against what it meant something in Val, deeper than personal considerations, solidly set itself.

Even more trying, though, was the difficulty of starting friendly relations with colored girls in school, whose side she was on and whose suspicion, however amply she knew it to be justified, was hard to bear. Mary Evans, editor of the school paper, a post Val had herself expected, had manners as perfect as the poise of a tight rope walker and just as far from contact—for this young Negro girl had trained herself to keep her balance in precarious situations. The story moves through all-too-familiar high school situations to its climax at a basketball game that brings to an unusual test a basic American belief. But this had been tested all the way along. "Most of us," says one of the students in addressing the school, "could say the pledge in our sleep. Maybe we do say it in our sleep most of the time." Nothing in the story reaches a really violent stage— this is a book for young girls—but it will move thoughtful girls because it makes them wake up to the meaning of "those trick words—'liberty and justice for all.'"

Alice M. Jordan

SOURCE: A review of *Willow Hill*, in *The Horn Book Magazine*, Vol. XXIII, No. 3, May, 1947, pp. 218-19.

The theme of this high school story is tolerance. Its scene is a suburban town in the Middle West where a housing project for Negro families has intruded upon the complacency of the community. Beginning among the school population, the conflict over race relations spreads throughout the section, causing wide-reaching bitterness and strain. The principal participants are high school girls and boys absorbed with dates, school activities and athletics, but their elders are drawn into the situation as they are in the books by John Tunis. The story with its grave social involvement moves swiftly, bringing in enough open-minded young people to take the lead in an effort to create a spirit of friendliness and good will. Older girls will find food for thought in it.

Harriet Ford Griswold

SOURCE: A review of *Willow Hill*, in *The Christian Science Monitor*, June 12, 1947, p. 12.

Phyllis A. Whitney creates a community in her book *Willow Hill*, in which some of the white inhabitants are thrown into a furor because colored families are moving from across the tracks into the United States Government housing development at the foot of the hill and are sending their children to the high school. Vivacious Val Coleman and her mother and father are the central figures in this local turmoil, since her father is the high school basketball coach, and her mother is easily swayed by the town's social dictators who would push minorities around because of their own selfishness. The question of whether these young people shall have their opinions dictated to them by their parents, or shall make up their own minds about associating with the colored students, is fought out in the high school classrooms, cafeteria and basketball court, and even at a citizen meeting at the town hall. Phyllis A. Whitney won the Youth Today Contest for this book *Willow Hill* because her presentation of all sides of this controversial subject is so convincing.

EVER AFTER (1948)

Margaret C. Scoggin

SOURCE: A review of *Ever After*, in *New York Herald Tribune Weekly Book Review*, Vol. 25, No. 8, October 10, 1948, p. 10.

Career stories to date have followed a pattern. The heroine takes herself and her talent to a city where sooner or later she gets into her chosen work, meets most of the expected difficulties and disappointments, reaches a fairly high niche in her field, and almost always near the last page marries. The reader is led to suppose that the mingling of marriage and career is simple and the couple live happily "ever after."

Miss Whitney has challenged that happy generality and broken the pattern. Her artist heroine does indeed come to New York City where she finally achieves some success. However, she meets writer Chris Mallory and by the middle of the book the two are married, each certain that the careers of both can be worked out without any trouble at all. How they manage and whether Chris and Marcel succeed is Miss Whitney's story and she tells it seriously though with a light touch which keeps it well within the range of career story readers while it gives them food for thought. A real problem handled realistically. It will be interesting to hear what the girls say.

Booklist

SOURCE: A review of *Ever After,* in *Booklist,* Vol. 45, No. 7, December 1, 1948, p. 122.

Despite conflicting advice from friends and acquaintances on the question of career vs. marriage, Marcel Gordon felt that she and Chris Mallory could foresee difficulties and plan carefully enough for her to combine the two. Their marriage neared collapse, however, before Marcel decided to let her career take second place. The author offers no real solution but the pros and cons are reasonably presented.

THE MYSTERY OF THE GULLS (1949)

Elizabeth Johnson

SOURCE: A review of *The Mystery of the Gulls,* in *The Library Journal,* Vol. 74, No. 10, May 15, 1949, p. 827.

Mystery for younger girls than the usual Whitney audience. Twelve-year-old Taffy helps her mother run an inn on Mackinac Island where strange happenings discourage guests from coming. Will fill the need for those girls who want some mystery but not too much. Pleasant book that will be popular, but disappointing to followers of Miss Whitney who expect a little more meat. Recommended for fifth and sixth grades.

Louise S. Bechtel

SOURCE: A review of *The Mystery of the Gulls,* in *New York Herald Tribune Weekly Book Review,* Vol. 25, No. 43, June 12, 1949, p. 8.

The difference between a "teen-age" mystery and one for a "junior girl" is cleverly observed by this writer. Her twelve-year-old "Taffy" is a very real youngster, a mixture of responsibility, ambition, longing for affection, and active curiosity. She decides to solve the mystery of the hotel her mother has perhaps inherited, depending on her ability to manage it for one summer.

There are hostile gulls, a locked door, a gong that booms in the night—weird incidents that are driving the guests away. Taffy and her friend David help to straighten things out in a way satisfactory to all the adults involved. All along, they learn bits of the history and legend of the island, Mackinac, in Lake Huron. The tale is good summer reading, with nice character drawing, and Taffy is an amusing, appealing personality.

LINDA'S HOMECOMING (1950)

Virginia Kirkus' Bookshop Service

SOURCE: A review of *Linda's Homecoming,* in *Virginia Kirkus' Bookshop Service,* Vol. XVIII, No. 4, February 15, 1950, p. 104.

The author of **Willow Hill** with her penetrating understanding of the problems of young people and her gift for projecting real characters, is concerned here with the problem of adjustment facing a young person on the remarriage of one parent after the death of the other. Linda Hollis remembered her father with adoration and love. As native New Yorkers, together they had explored and loved the big city in spite of the preference of Linda's mother for the life of a small town. Two years after her father's death Linda's mother marries a man in a small town who has two children—a girl Linda's age and a ten-year-old boy. When Linda is forced to come to Centerdale, she is bitter, angry and is conscious of the resentment of her step-brother and sister, her "superiority" in being a New Yorker in a small town, and the obvious comparison with the gay happy-hearted man her father was with the solemn, quiet step-father. However, Linda begins to realize that no one can live as a self-sufficient entity, that there are responsibilities in human relationships which one cannot ignore—demands from those who love you as well as those who are unhappy and trying to make adjustments too. The adapting of Linda and her new family is slow, involving amusing and almost tragic incidents, but Linda's adjustment is natural and real to the reader. An intelligent, absorbing novel.

Bulletin of the Children's Book Center

SOURCE: A review of *Linda's Homecoming,* in *Bulletin of the Children's Book Center,* Vol. III, No. 8, July, 1950, p. 51.

When Linda Hollis's mother remarried, Linda was faced with the problem of adjusting to a new father, a new brother and sister, and a small town, after living her life in New York City, all within a short period of time. The problems were made more acute by the resentment she met with in her step-brother and sister. School activities, work in the stepfather's museum, two congenial young men, and understanding parents help all three of the children work out their problems. Characters and situations are well developed and solutions are plausible. This is a book that should be read just as a good story and for its help in adjusting to difficult situations.

Alice M. Jordan

SOURCE: A review of *Linda's Homecoming,* in *The Horn Book Magazine,* Vol. XXVI, No. 4, July, 1950, p. 289.

An unknown and bitterly resented stepfather, an unwelcome move from New York to a small town in the Midwest, and a hostile stepsister combine to make Linda unhappy and as disagreeable as possible. Her gradual adjustment provides the incidents that will hold the interest of girls in this young novel. Photography and the stepfather's direction of a museum introduce unfamiliar subjects to Linda's notice. Story and characters are entirely probable though neither girl is very attractive.

Louise S. Bechtel

SOURCE: A review of *Linda's Homecoming,* in *New York Herald Tribune Book Review,* Vol. 26, No. 48, July 16, 1950, p. 8.

Girls in junior high who like to suffer with their heroines—and many do—will enjoy Linda. At the beginning of her senior year, she was faced with a new stepfather, and with moving away from New York to a small town. She met a stepsister and brother who seemed more than she could bear. The story works out her slow adjustment to the situation, offering two contrasted beaux, and interesting sidelights on running a small museum, of which her stepfather is director, also on a high school photography club.

Linda's mother is patient and tactful, but two more true-to-life disagreeable girls than Linda and Babs have seldom been put on paper. Both hate the town of Cedarville; they are won over at the end, after much suffering on both sides. The most likable person in the book is the small boy Roddy, but the clever beau Peter also adds humor to the pages. Linda learns much about human relations that girls will like to think out with her. On the jacket, the book is labeled a "novel," which does not seem fair, for at nineteen, Linda's experiences and reactions are still adolescent, and the love story could well be read by any girl of around twelve.

THE ISLAND OF DARK WOODS (1951; also as *Mystery of the Strange Traveler,* 1967)

Bulletin of the Children's Book Center

SOURCE: A review of *The Island of Dark Woods,* in *Bulletin of the Children's Book Center,* Vol. IV, No. 6, May, 1951, p. 47.

A mediocre mystery story in which two sisters, spending a summer with their aunt on Staten Island, solve the family mystery involving their great-grandmother, a phantom stagecoach, and Santa Ana. Not only is the plot thin and too dependent on coincidence, there are definitely negative values in the manner in which the girls force their way into the house of their next door neighbor in the face of his repeated statements that he wishes to have nothing to do with them. Not recommended.

Sarah Chokla Gross

SOURCE: A review of *The Island of Dark Woods,* in *The New York Times Book Review,* June 24, 1951, p. 20.

Tomboyish Laurie Kane and her pretty sister, Ceha, knew before they reached Staten Island for a summer's visit with their aunt that she could unfold a strange story about the house next door. Aunt Serena could, and "at the right time" (a stormy afternoon) she did. But first there were Aunt Serena's home bookshop to be launched, an author to meet, and two quite different boys to know. What will particularly gratify young readers is that Laurie and Celia, with only a little help from their elders, really untangle the mystery themselves, recognizing significance in an old coin, a plush-covered book, and Mexico's Santa Ana's long-ago stay on Staten Island. The unstrained, natural humor and suspense of this second mystery by Miss Whitney make it a winner.

Louise S. Bechtel

SOURCE: A review of *The Island of Dark Woods,* in *New York Herald Tribune Book Review,* Vol. 27, No. 46, July 1, 1951, p. 6.

Those fast readers, usually female, who dash through junior mysteries, will find an unusually human and possible one in this story of Staten Island. Two amusingly contrasted sisters come to spend a summer with an aunt, an ex-school teacher now starting a bookshop. Books, a local author (we must suppose this is a self-portrait), two boys, a play, are woven into the search for a family ancestor, born in the mysterious house next door. With no horrors, a pleasant minimum of history, the appeal here is not so much the mystery as the amusing, real character of Laurie, her longing to be an author, and her belief in the mystery boy Norman. The style is not outstanding, but it is all highly preferable, for young Americans, to the doings in the [Enid] books, for girls of eleven and twelve.

LOVE ME, LOVE ME NOT (1952)

Virginia Kirkus' Bookshop Service

SOURCE: A review of *Love Me, Love Me Not,* in *Virginia Kirkus' Bookshop Service,* Vol. XX, No. 4, February 15, 1952, p. 129.

An author with keen and sympathetic discernment and a

real understanding of the problems of young people handles here the different approach of three girls to romance. The central figure is a girl from a small town, living with two others in Chicago, and getting (too easily perhaps) a job in the book department of what is probably supposed to be Marshall Field's. One of the trio is a society girl with a beau in every port—a heart-breaker, who can't be satisfied with her conquests and goes on to greener fields. The third girl is over-efficient, absorbed in her job and predestined to wear the trousers when it comes to marriage. There's plenty of incident; the characterizations are sound; the situations more or less typical. But the build up of the central theme is rather halting and carries less conviction, has less impact than many of Miss Whitney's earlier books.

Louise S. Bechtel

SOURCE: A review of *Love Me, Love Me Not,* in *New York Herald Tribune Book Review,* Vol. 28, No. 35, April 13, 1952, p. 8.

The new Phyllis Whitney is called **Love Me, Love Me Not**. The heroine is a type many will adore: a girl trying for her first job, but mostly concerned with finding a husband. First she works in a big department store book section in Chicago, then by an interesting bit of luck as food demonstrator for a big factory. The contrast between Susan and the two girls she lives with is interesting and well handled. Her "men" are a bit less valid: there are only two, which seems a smallish slice of life nowadays, and that Susan should get one of her roommate's admirers, "on the rebound," seems a bit dreary. However, he is a rare bird, a reporter who gives her some sage advice before the happy ending. It is rather a "suffering" book, but that will appeal all the more to the girls who also have been suffering with Tippy, of the [Janet] Lambert book [*Don't Cry, Little Girl*]. They "learn" a bit more about reality with Susan, for her jobs are interesting.

Bulletin of the Children's Book Center

SOURCE: A review of *Love Me, Love Me Not,* in *Bulletin of the Children's Book Center,* Vol. V, No. 9, May, 1952, p. 69.

The story of three girls who share a Chicago apartment. Susan Morris is the naive, small-town girl who is forced to work for a living but is primarily interested in finding a husband and a home. Nan Arnold is the serious young teacher with social worker inclinations. Carol Ellington is the beautiful but spoiled daughter of wealthy parents in whose apartment the three girls are living. The two young men in the story are Michael, handsome, shallow, and self-centered and Andy, earnest young newspaper reporter who sacrifices a higher salary for his integrity and wins the girl (Susan) in the end. The plot is manufactured. The characters are mere types used to forward the plot and are entirely lacking in reality. Some of the concepts are good but their value is lost in the formula writing. Not recommended.

Elizabeth Hodges

SOURCE: A review of *Love Me, Love Me Not,* in *The New York Times Book Review,* June 22, 1952, p. 16.

Susan Morris, just out of a small-town high school, comes to Chicago to job-hunt although her real goal is marriage. Work in a bookstore and later in the testing laboratory of a famous biscuit-mix factory brings her into contact with charming Michael Chase and forthright Andy Hortland, each of whom seems for a time to be the right man. Sharing an apartment with intellectual but bossy Nan and with Carol, a selfish glamour girl, gives Susan a lesson in human relations and helps her develop mature values. A lively story, told in smooth style with easy dialogue, this is sure to be popular with older girls.

STEP TO THE MUSIC (1953)

Virginia Kirkus' Bookshop Service

SOURCE: A review of *Step to the Music,* in *Virginia Kirkus' Bookshop Service,* Vol. XXI, No. 20, October 15, 1953, p. 699.

Phyllis Whitney is a puzzle to me. When she can do as extraordinarily good books for girls as **Willow Hill, Linda's Homecoming** and **Ever After** it is harder to accept the inadequacy of **Step to the Music**. One expects more than more competence from Phyllis Whitney. The emotional values here are derivative, and yet the situation posed involves depths of disturbance. The setting is Staten Island during the Civil War. There are two households chiefly involved, and in each there is internal strife, confused loyalties, or outright partisanship for North, for South. Added to that, a Southern cousin deliberately steals her Northern hostess beau right out from under, and furthermore steers his doubts into the channel of identity with the Confederacy. And yet—out of all this—the reader feels never a quiver of emotional identity with any of the disturbed characters. It is easy reading, and skillfully tailored to fit, but it just doesn't scratch the surface.

Manon R. Brown

SOURCE: A review of *Step to the Music,* in *Saturday Review,* Vol. 36, No. 46, November 14, 1953, p. 70.

Although Abigail Garrett lived a hundred years ago, young readers will accept her as one of themselves. Abbie loves people and good times; she dislikes politics, hoop skirts, and war. When her father marches away to the Civil War Abbie realizes the despair of her Southern-born mother. Though she follows the war news with interest, this is primarily the story of a young girl as she matures and falls in love.

Because she is stable and dependable people turn to Abbie with their troubles. She finds her life filled with problems and duties as well as exciting adventures and real satisfactions. Although she fancies herself in love with Douglas McIntyre, her real affection shifts to the rebellious Stuart. The history of Staten Island and the background of the Civil War add interest and authenticity to this fine story.

Lavinia R. Davis

SOURCE: A review of *Step to the Music,* in *The New York Times Book Review,* December 27, 1953, p. 14.

The scene is Staten Island in the early years of the Civil War. The characters, especially Abbie Garrett, the heroine, and her friends, Douglas and Stuart McIntyre (who have just returned to the island as the story opens), are well drawn. The episodes skillfully illustrate the theme: Abbie's development from a heedless, hero-worshiping adolescence to emotional maturity.

Miss Whitney writes with feeling and compassion. She never becomes partisan, nor does she oversimplify problems and decisions of the past. To 16-year-old Abbie, with a gentle Charleston mother and an adored father in the Union Army, the war was no conflict between absolute good and absolute evil. Nor was the choice of sides easy for the McIntyres, born in the North, who had spent happy years in the South. Since Miss Whitney has the skill to make her readers share divided allegiances, her book is a lively novel of character with a historical setting rather than just another costume story.

Jennie D. Lindquist

SOURCE: A review of *Step to the Music,* in *The Horn Book Magazine,* Vol. XXX, No. 2, April, 1954, p. 106.

The time is the Civil War and the setting Staten Island. The theme of the story centers around the problems that arose when people who loved each other differed in their sympathies. Abbie Garrett's father was a Northerner; her mother, born in Charleston, loved the South passionately. Abbie herself, her spoiled cousin, the boy with whom they both fell in love, and his less glamorous brother all felt the strain of divided loyalties. This is a good picture of the period, swift-moving and short enough to appeal to teen-age girls even if they do not ordinarily care for historical novels.

📖 *A LONG TIME COMING* (1954)

Virginia Kirkus' Bookshop Service

SOURCE: A review of *A Long Time Coming,* in *Virginia Kirkus' Bookshop Service,* Vol. XXII, No. 3, February 1, 1954, p. 65.

The author of *Love Me, Love Me Not,* and *Ever After,* and other young adult fiction tackling social and emotional problems with varying success, writes now about a homecoming to a small town and a young girl's need to live up to her family name. The results, if occasionally long winded and agonizing, have their rewards. Motherless 18 year old Christie Allard, estranged from her father since early childhood, comes to live with her Aunt Amelia in Leola which gets its economic being from the large Allard food packing plant. Among Aunt Amelia's boarders are Alan and Marge, a young minister and missionary. Among the townsfolk are the many Mexican factory workers they are trying to help, John, a foreman who wants to help too, Tidings, a manager who does not, and cheeky Tony Webb, a local newsman with whom Christie eventually falls in love. With good hard-won at last, Alan and Marge see a church and school established and Christie is reconciled with a father she had long thought unfaithful. But it's a "long time coming."

Alberta Eiseman

SOURCE: A review of *A Long Time Coming,* in *The New York Times Book Review,* March 28, 1954, p. 24.

In an engrossing, fast-paced novel Miss Whitney explores the problems of migrant labor in a Midwestern town. In Leola there is only one important industry: the Allard Company, vegetable growers and canners. The laborers who work the company's crops are bitterly resented by the local citizens and tension has permeated the whole town.

This is the unhappy picture which greets 18-year-old Christie Allard, daughter of the company's absentee owner, when she comes to Leola. Uninterested in the town's problems, anxious only to unravel her own personal conflicts, Christie nevertheless finds it impossible to stay on the sidelines. With her newly found friends— a reporter, a girl from the migrants' camp, a young minister and a social worker—she contributes actively to the improvement of local conditions. Romance comes her way, too, and a greater understanding of her own problems.

Social unrest is seldom resolved so neatly and rapidly, it seems to this reviewer, but this is a minor criticism of a very worth-while book.

The Booklist

SOURCE: A review of *A Long Time Coming,* in The *Booklist,* Vol. 50, No. 18, May 15, 1954, p. 362.

The problems of adjustment of migrant workers of Mexican descent to a small Midwest community are presented in another of this author's novels with a social purpose. The young heroine steps into the situation when her mother dies and she returns to the care of an aunt in the town dominated by the family's canning plant. The poverty of living facilities for the workers, lack of educational and recreational opportunities, charges of vandalism, and attempts by a minister, a missionary, and a few other townspeople for better community understanding all figure in the narrative with representation of the varied opinions and arguments on each aspect of the question. Incidents and characters are skillfully but obviously designed to make their point; a slight element of romance is rather lost, however.

MYSTERY ON THE ISLE OF SKYE (1955)

Anne Izard

SOURCE: A review of *Mystery on the Isle of Skye,* in *Junior Libraries*, Vol. 1, No. 8, April, 1955, p. 114.

Cathy MacLeod takes mystery to the Isle of Skye in a special box of surprises packed by her grandmother for her to open during her trip at certain stated times. Each one has its own secret and Cathy's new cousins, with whom she is traveling, and her new friends in Scotland are all drawn with her into the unraveling of the clues. This is something more than a good mystery story, for somehow the very look and feel of the country are caught up in its telling. Excellent.

The Booklist

SOURCE: A review of *Mystery on the Isle of Skye,* in *The Booklist,* Vol. 51, No. 20, June 15, 1955, p. 437.

An orphaned American girl makes a trip with unknown relatives to the Isle of Skye, the home of her ancestors, taking with her a box of tissue-wrapped "mysteries" or clues prepared by her grandmother to be worked out as Cathy goes along. Just as her grandmother had intended and hoped, the puzzling quests lead Cathy closer to the heart of Skye, to friendships, and to a permanent home with her uncle's family. Though the element of mystery is minor and the ingenious device artificial, the story is credible and holding, and the Scotch scene and history skillfully interwoven.

Virginia Haviland

SOURCE: A review of *Mystery on the Isle of Skye,* in *The Horn Book Magazine,* Vol. XXXI, No. 4, August, 1955, pp. 263, 66.

This story of a trip to Skye is saved from being a forced travel storybook by the realistic, changing relationships between Cathy and two boy cousins with whom she visits the island and by the capturing of atmosphere from legendary and historic past and unique setting. Events during Skye Week are exciting experiences to Cathy, as she makes new friends and learns to love the mountains and legendary magic of her grandmother's island. An

additional measure of happiness is provided for her by the mysteries wrapped in her grandmother's bon voyage gifts. The author bases her story of events and scenes on her own recent visit to the Misty Isle.

Bulletin of the Children's Book Center

SOURCE: A review of *Mystery on the Isle of Skye,* in *Bulletin of the Children's Book Center,* Vol. IX, No. 1, September, 1955, pp. 14-15.

A somewhat misleading title and a wholly misleading dust jacket picture. The "mystery" involves a series of packages that Cathy MacLeod's grandmother gave her just before the twelve-year-old girl set off with her aunt, uncle and two cousins on a visit to the Isle of Skye. Each package contained an object, or objects, designed to help Cathy understand Skye and learn something of her family's background there, and also to help her make friends with her relatives. This latter was especially important since Cathy's grandmother could no longer take care of her, and they both hoped that the aunt and uncle would be willing to add Cathy to their family. The packages were successful in all ways—Cathy came to know Skye and her relatives came to love her. A pleasing story despite its misleading title.

THE FIRE AND THE GOLD (1956)

Virginia Kirkus' Service

SOURCE: A review of *The Fire and the Gold,* in *Virginia Kirkus' Service,* Vol. XXIV, No. 1, January 1, 1956, p. 5.

A story of San Francisco in 1906 covers the rubble of earthquake and disrupted homes with a veneer of new understanding that emerges from the necessity to rebuild life. Melora Cranby, nineteen and doubtful that marriage with rich Quentin Seymour will bring true happiness, returns from a trip east to find her home a shambles. No longer do the problems created by a social climbing mother or her own sequestered life have any real meaning, for now Melora must get out and work to help repair the damage. So, for that matter, must Quentin. Money and position have been lost for him too, and in the year that follows the young people see each other in a new light that also illumines a hard working, satisfying future. Dependable Phyllis Whitney, this cultivates the flowers in the ashes with some facility but nevertheless emphasizes important values.

The Booklist

SOURCE: A review of *The Fire and the Gold,* in *The Booklist,* Vol. 52, No. 16, April 15, 1956, p. 344.

When Melora Cranby returns home from a visit to Chicago on April 18, 1906, to find San Francisco in flames, her determination to break her engagement to unromantic Quentin Seymour is suddenly lost in more important problems and responsibilities. As she and Quent move outside their accustomed spheres to help with the work of relief and rebuilding, both attain greater maturity. Despite Melora's temporary interest in dramatic Tony Ellis, she and Quent begin to see each other in a new light and are ready to plan their future together. Good characterization and authentic details of the 1906 San Francisco earthquake and fire compensate for the rather ordinary main theme.

Silence Buck Bellows

SOURCE: A review of *The Fire and the Gold,* in *The Christian Science Monitor,* May 10, 1956, p. 16.

The year 1956 marks the 50th anniversary of the great fire that swept San Francisco after the earthquake shock of April 18, 1906. It is in this anniversary year that Phyllis Whitney presents a youthful love story outlined against a background of ravaged San Francisco.

Nineteen-year-old Melora Cranby, returning to San Francisco from a trip to Chicago, arrives on the very morning of the disaster. Her home is deserted, except for the faithful Chinese servant Quong Sam. Following his directions, Melora finds her mother, her younger sister Cora, her younger brother Alec, and her grandmother, at Gran's house. Her father, captain of a merchant vessel, is on a voyage.

Melora is wearing Quent Seymour's diamond ring, but somehow Tony Ellis, of mixed Italian and old San Francisco family background, gets into the area of romance and persists in staying there.

The story proceeds through the days when San Francisco was rising on phoenix wings, and ends on New Year's Eve, 1906. A new year of promise is opening before the city and before Melora, too, as a person who has also come through a test by fire and has found her own mind and her own place.

The author is an able writer, has an intense interest in the history of San Francisco, and has done intensive research. All three facts show in *The Fire and the Gold.* It is definitely among those books which are more than "just another juvenile."

Ruth Hill Viguers

SOURCE: A review of *The Fire and the Gold,* in *Saturday Review,* Vol. 39, No. 25, June 23, 1956, p. 33.

Nineteen-year-old Melora returned to her San Francisco home from an Eastern visit determined to confess that her engagement to a most eligible young man was only a scheme they had evolved to stop their families' eternal matchmaking. But at home she found a state of emergency existing, much of the city in flames, and her own family "camping" in a crowded park. Suddenly her personal problems seemed too small to mention.

This is an absorbing story of San Francisco after the earthquake. Melora and her family and friends are very much alive, her growth as a person convincing, and the legendary courage and humor of the people who rebuilt San Francisco are very real.

📖 *MYSTERY OF THE GREEN CAT* (1957)

Virginia Kirkus' Service

SOURCE: A review of *Mystery of the Green Cat,* in *Virginia Kirkus' Service,* Vol. XXV, No. 14, July 15, 1957, p. 488.

What significance did the Chinese ceramic figure of a green cat hold in the mind of old Mrs. Wallenstein, their neighbor, wondered Andy, Adrian, Jill and Carol, the four children of Roger Dallas and Emily, his new wife. As the boys and girls solve the mystery they find unity as a family. San Francisco sets the stage for a good family mystery story with a credible plot which takes the reader into the past to China.

The Booklist and Subscription Books Bulletin

SOURCE: A review of *Mystery of the Green Cat,* in *The Booklist and Subscription Books Bulletin,* Vol. 54, No. 7, December 1, 1957, p. 208.

When Jill who loves mysteries comes with her younger sister to San Francisco to join their mother and a new stepfather and his two sons, she finds not only strained relationships at home but a mystery next door. As the four children become involved in ferreting out the secret of the forbidding Victorian mansion next door, its carefully guarded elderly recluse, and a missing Oriental art object, their resentments and antagonisms are resolved and family unity is achieved. A better than average mystery and credible adjustment to new family relationships.

📖 *SECRET OF THE SAMURAI SWORD* (1958)

Virginia Kirkus' Service

SOURCE: A review of *Secret of the Samurai Sword,* in *Virginia Kirkus' Service,* Vol. XXVII, No. 15, August 1, 1958, p. 551.

Celia and Stephen Bronson anticipate a lively and interesting vacation when they are invited by their grandmother to visit with her in Kyoto, where she is writing a book on Japan. The Shinto shrines, the formal gardens, the Buddhist ornaments which adorn the refreshing simplicity of their new home, more than fulfill their anticipation. But it is the uneasy ghost of a Samurai warrior, the desolate grief of an ancient Tokugawa patriarch, and the bitter conflict of a little Nisei girl, who wants desperately to lose her Japanese identity that really awaken the two American teen-agers to the root quality of traditional Japan. In solving the secret of the Samurai sword, Celia not only puts to rest the tormented spirit of the warrior, but finds a more valid basis for her own intellectual and artistic expression. If the teen-age reader, ignorant of the structure of classical Japan, can absorb even half of the details of Japanese life offered here, this pleasant mystery will have been well worth the reading.

Silence Buck Bellows

SOURCE: A review of *Secret of the Samurai Sword*, in *The Christian Science Monitor,* November 6, 1958, p. 17.

In this story, slanted to the 12-15s, Phyllis Whitney has not only produced a gripping mystery; she has also written a story that deals with the growth of international sympathy and understanding, at both adult and adolescent levels. Celia and Stephen Bronson, 14 and 15 years old respectively, have come to Japan to visit their grandmother, a writer, who is working on a book about that country. Immediately upon their arrival they make contacts with the Sato family next door. They also run into a ghost story, and actually see the "ghost." The development of the plot is thrilling, involving mysterious clues, ancient Japanese customs, and a missing Samurai sword. This book is quite a package, being a top notch mystery, a source of authentic information about Japan, and a wise and warm commentary on human relationships.

The Booklist and Subscription Books Bulletin

SOURCE: A review of *Secret of the Samurai Sword*, in *The Booklist and Subscription Books Bulletin*, Vol. 55, No. 10, January 15, 1959, p. 266.

Two Americans visiting their writer grandmother in Japan become acquainted with their neighbors, Japanese Hiro and his nisei cousin Sumiko, and with their help solve the mystery of the ghost that haunts Gran's garden. Not only a well-plotted mystery but a good story of the friendship of the four young people of different races and customs and of the nisei girl's bitter conflict between her American background and the Japanese ways to which she is expected to conform.

Ruth Hill Viguers

SOURCE: A review of *Secret of the Samurai Sword*, in *The Horn Book Magazine,* Vol. XXXV, No. 1, February, 1959, p. 47.

A summer vacation in Kyoto brings adventure and mys-

tery to an American brother and sister, and to Celia an extraordinary friendship with a Japanese artist. A vivid sense of place, understanding of Japanese customs and viewpoints, interesting contrasts in characterizations, and Miss Whitney's usual excellent storytelling make this an exceptionally good story. An eeriness in the mystery should delight ghost-story fans.

CREOLE HOLIDAY (1959)

Virginia Kirkus' Service

SOURCE: A review of *Creole Holiday,* in *Virginia Kirkus' Service,* Vol. XXVII, No. 13, July 1, 1959, p. 453.

Within the cloister of her sheltered Victorian home, eighteen-year-old Laure Beaudine dreams of the day when she will enter into her Creole father's exciting world of the theater. When she joins her father on a trip to New Orleans and is confronted with the precise and extravagant elegance of Creole life, the imaginative girl at last feels that she has claimed her birthright. Her whirlwind courtship by a dashing young Southerner settles a family feud and insures her new-found happiness. By the author of *Secret of the Samurai Sword,* this book again manifests Phyllis Whitney's talent for evoking an exotic atmosphere and portraying the excitement a young person feels at the threshold of romance. An excellent depiction of Victorian New Orleans and of the exacting standards which prevailed there within the aristocratic Creole society.

Bulletin of the Center for Children's Books

SOURCE: A review of *Creole Holiday,* in *Bulletin of the Center for Children's Books,* Vol. XIII, No. 2, October, 1959, p. 40.

When Laure Beaudine was eighteen, she went for the first time away from the cold, strict aunt who had brought her up; for the first time she met some of her Creole relatives and knew the charm of life in New Orleans. Laure's father was one of the great actors of the 1890s, but his proud mother had never forgiven his choice of profession. Laure could not convince her father that she had a talent for acting also; by the time she did impress this upon him, the girl had found that she wanted the man she loved rather than the goal of a stage career which she had so long held dear. Good writing style. The characters are consistently motivated, although some of the older members of the Beaudine family are rather stereotyped, like the two fluttery maiden aunts, dressed all in black, with high laced shoes and ancient bonnets.

Ruth Hill Viguers

SOURCE: A review of *Creole Holiday,* in *The Horn Book Magazine,* Vol. XXXV, No. 5, October, 1959, p. 390.

Creole New Orleans in the 1890s was beginning to be touched by changes, old families were gradually leaving their lovely homes in the Latin Quarter, but carnival time was as gay as ever. Such was the completely different world to which Lauré Beaudine, brought up in a strict New England home, was transported by her Creole father. All the ingredients of a romantic novel are here and they are handled well: colorful setting, a spirited heroine, variety and interesting contrasts in personalities as well as customs, and a charming romance.

MYSTERY OF THE HAUNTED POOL (1960)

Virginia Kirkus' Service

SOURCE: A review of *Mystery of the Haunted Pool,* in *Virginia Kirkus' Service,* Vol. XXVIII, No. 14, July 15, 1960, pp. 560-61.

A warm and winning story that turns into a mystery, made to order for the pre-teens. Susan Price has been sent ahead of her family to an aunt who has an antique shop in Highlands Landing, way up the Hudson. Susan and her aunt tuck themselves into Aunt Edith's crowded quarters while a search for a house for the family is on. And in the process the 12-year old girl stumbles on to a mystery, does a great deal to bring a crippled boy out of a morbid sense of guilt, helps restore a neurotic spinster to a saner outlook on life, and unearths a treasure that seems not too unlikely a find. In today's setting, history, melodrama and a wholesome sense of normal life combine to make this an above average mystery for this age group.

The Booklist and Subscription Books Bulletin

SOURCE: A review of *Mystery of the Haunted Pool,* in *The Booklist and Subscription Books Bulletin,* Vol. 57, No. 12, February 15, 1961, p. 368.

Coming to Highland Crossing on the Hudson River as an emissary to help persuade a retire driver-boat captain to rent his big old house to her family Susan Price encounters strong opposition from Captain Dan's embittered crippled grandson and stumbles on a mystery involving some old books, a face in the garden pool, a long-hidden treasure, and a snooping antique hunter. A plausible mystery with a well-developed plot and characterization that is above average for a mystery story.

Zena Sutherland

SOURCE: A review of *Mystery of the Haunted Pool,* in *Bulletin of the Center for Children's Books,* Vol. XV, No. 2, October, 1961, p. 34.

A good mystery story, with logical explanations but romantic atmosphere. The writing has pace and suspense; characterization and conversation are realistic. Susan,

visiting her aunt, becomes interested in the rumor of a family secret attached to the Teague home that her parents are about to rent. In the course of the summer she helps to solve the mystery, but—unlike many juvenile detectives—all of her involvement is believable. She also makes friends with the Teague grandson who is having trouble adjusting to a handicap, and she learns a bit about local Hudson River history. Introduced smoothly into the story are interesting descriptions of a volunteer library and a volunteer fire company of a small New York town.

SECRET OF THE TIGER'S EYE (1961)

Jane B. Jackson

SOURCE: A review of *Secret of the Tiger's Eye,* in *Kliatt Young Adult Paperback Book Guide,* Vol. XIII, No. 1, January, 1979, p. 17.

This reprint of Whitney's 1961 YA mystery has an exotic setting. Benita and Lanny Dustin are taken to South Africa by their writer-father to stay with his Aunt Persis in Cape Town while he travels around doing research. Unfortunately, Mr. Dustin also invites Joel Monroe, whom Benita hates and things get worse when, later in the story, Benita learns her father plans to marry Joel's mother. The two kids eventually overcome their mutual animosity to solve a mystery in Aunt Persis's old mansion involving a secret cave, stolen jewels, a long-ago death of Persis' adopted son, a sinister sailor with a blue thumb, and a message hidden behind the eye of a tiger-skin rug.

Whitney also takes advantage of her setting to make a very mild comment on the system of apartheid: it is too bad that people can't understand and respect each other's differences (as Joel and Benita learn to do). The book is a bit dated but could still be enjoyed by a good junior high reader.

Brenda Randolph Robinson

SOURCE: A review of *Secret of the Tiger's Eye,* in *Interracial Books for Children Bulletin,* Vol. 15, Nos. 7 & 8, 1984, p. 20.

Capetown provides the backdrop for this novel by a well-known mystery writer. Apartheid is not ignored by the author; it is woven into the fabric of the story and opposition to its practice is frequently voiced by the central characters. Unfortunately, one learns very little about events in South Africa, the people of the land or the true nature of apartheid in this novel. At the time this book was written, South Africa was experiencing one of the most explosive chapters in its history. Mass demonstrations against the implementation of apartheid, treason trials and violent police actions were daily fare. Yet, virtually none of this upheaval is reflected in the book. Capetown is described as "a clean, cheerful orderly

town." The threat of forced removal of Blacks from
urban areas is mentioned but the theme is never developed. All the major characters are liberal whites from
the U.S. The only South African featured in the novel is
a young "colored" girl who, in appearance, is indistinguishable from the whites. The author follows the regime's practice of characterizing "coloreds" as a distinct
racial group and focuses her attention on them. "Coloreds," we are informed, contain only a "trace" of
African ancestry and "are not black people just off the
reservations" but "a gentle people educated, intelligent
and long civilized." Other Africans are not given a role
in the story; they are described as "natives" who "still
lack education" and wear "bright blankets." No white
South Africans are featured. The myth about English
liberalism is repeated as is the notion that whites "have
built nearly everything." Johannesburg, the stronghold
of Afrikaners, is described as more rigidly segregated
than Capetown but we are informed that "lots of Afrikaners" are opposed to apartheid. The author takes an
admirable stand against injustice and racism in South
Africa and the U.S. She fails, however, to help her
young readers discover the root causes of discrimination
or learn more about the plight of the oppressed people of
South Africa.

THE MYSTERY OF THE GOLDEN HORN (1962)

Joyce Yen

SOURCE: A review of *The Mystery of the Golden Horn,*
in *Voice of Youth Advocates,* Vol. 13, No. 3, August,
1990, pp. 164-65.

Victoria Stewart is a problem child, at least that is what
all of her aunts think. She is failing in school, her mother
is in the hospital, and her father is teaching in Turkey.
Vicky's aunts decide to send Vicky to be with her father
in Istanbul. Vicky protests but to no avail.

In Turkey, Vicky stays with her father in an old house
of a Turkish pasha. Mrs. Byrne, an American who currently runs the house; her son Ken; and Adria March,
her cousin, are all living there, too. Adria's parents
were recently killed in a mountaineering accident in
Switzerland and Adria, who is only a high school girl,
is having some difficulties of her own. Vicky, who befriends her, becomes entangled in Adria's mess which
starts when Adria borrows Mrs. Byrne's prized Golden
Horn pin to show to her Gypsy friend Leyla. Leyla tells
Adria's fortune and discovers that both Vicky and Adria's
fortunes are intertwined. Suddenly the pin is missing and
Adria leads Vicky on a wild goose chase in hopes of
understanding and solving their fortunes.

Originally published in 1962, this is a mystery but only
in the most subtle sense of the word; there is much more
to the story. Whitney does an excellent job of describing
the various "tourist" attractions as well as the common
Turkish scenes. These bits and pieces of facts about

Turkey make the book even more interesting. Whitney
has visited Turkey and puts her feelings about and experiences with Turkey into the mystery. This is enjoyable
reading that will appeal to all readers, whether they are
mystery buffs or not.

SECRET OF THE EMERALD STAR (1964)

Lenore Glen Offord

SOURCE: A review of *Secret of the Emerald Star,* in
The New York Times Book Review, November 1, 1964,
p. 55.

Set on Staten Island, this new Whitney novel has more
plus values than ever. The mystery concerns a sinister
visitor, a stern, misguided old lady, and a jewel owned
by one of the young heroines. The story's great charm,
however, is its thesis: the worst things one can offer the
blind are pity and over-protection. A sighted girl learns
to help her blind friend in a sensible, healthy fashion,
and both find an outlet in sculpture. Fine, warm feeling
throughout.

Ruth Hill Viguers

SOURCE: A review of *Secret of the Emerald Star,* in
The Horn Book Magazine, Vol. XLI, No. 1, February,
1965, p. 54.

When thirteen-year-old Robin moved with her family to
Catalpa Court, a community of interesting old houses on
Staten Island, she was attracted by a neighbor girl of her
own age. Stella was half Cuban and had come to live
with her American grandmother, a strange, bigoted
woman. Robin was baffled at Stella's unresponsiveness
to overtures of friendliness until she realized that Stella
was blind. Then her interest in entering a class in sculpture and her wish to do a portrait head of Stella were the
beginning of a friendship that helped both girls to grow
in understanding of people of all kinds. Their success in
solving the mystery of an unpleasant stranger relieved
Stella's grandmother of a worry, made her a much more
sympathetic person and her household far happier. In
retrospect, situations and characters may seem strained;
but Miss Whitney inevitably gives mystery fans a story
that holds them—and something extra.

MYSTERY OF THE ANGRY IDOL (1965)

Nora E. Taylor

SOURCE: A review of *Mystery of the Angry Idol,* in *The
Christian Science Monitor,* November 4, 1965, p. B8.

Miss Whitney's latest book is about Jan Pendleton's
summer in historic Mystic, Conn. Once again the author
builds her story around antiques, this time an ugly figurine from China. Jan finds awakening appreciation of

Oriental beauty in her great-grandmother Althea's room full of Chinese treasures. The figurine, however, is covered with a cloth, and there is something strange and a little scary about it. Soon Jan, her new friends, and the seaport itself are tangled in a mystery. Miss Whitney's clear prose has poetic overtones that lovingly depicts the old New England seaport, its people and their ways. There is excitement, suspense, and a most satisfactory ending. Delightful pencil sketches by Al Florentine.

Ruth Hill Viguers

SOURCE: A review of *Mystery of the Angry Idol,* in *The Horn Book Magazine,* Vol. XLI, No. 6, December, 1965, p. 634.

The focus of the plot on such a device as a demonic porcelain image is typical of contrived mysteries for children. The setting, however, adds dimension to the story. Jan, visiting in Mystic, Connecticut, enjoys the fascination of history in the restored seaport. Through the stories her great-grandmother tells of her childhood in China before the Boxer Rebellion and in the old sea captain's house where her grandmother and great-grandmother now live, Jan feels a personal tie with the past. Typical of Miss Whitney's stories, the characters are real, from Jan's elderly relatives to the feuding neighbor boys. The book has variety as well as suspense.

SECRET OF THE SPOTTED SHELL (1967)

Kirkus Service

SOURCE: A review of *Secret of the Spotted Shell,* in *Kirkus Service,* Vol. XXXV, No. 1, January 1, 1967, p. 9.

The spotted shell contains a code which can be read only after the shell has been heated, and then only with the aid of the scrap of Chinese newspaper in which holes are punched—and this scrap of newspaper has gone out in the trash. From the moment Wendy Williams arrives on St. Thomas, V.I. to live with her cousins Marion and Gordon, everything is wrong; the determination of this twelve-year-old New York girl who has been shunted around from home to home while her widowed father is off building bridges to be accepted in her new and permanent home helps to set some things right again. Her reactions to her family-to-be reveal all sides of her complex character: she learns to love Cousin Marion who is bedridden with grief over the drowning of her son and the recent loss of her husband missing and presumed dead in Vietnam, Aunt Elinor, whose concern for Marion forestalls any immediate compassion for the homeless Wendy, and gentle, kindly Uncle Paul. A desperate struggle on the edge of a cliff and the joy of an old Chinese gardener in the letters of his own tongue solve the mystery of the shell. Cousin Gordon, presumed dead, is not, and Wendy has found a real home at last. No extraneous characters, no dei ex machinae, no pat solutions mar this intriguing, involving mystery plus.

Zena Sutherland

SOURCE: A review of *Secret of the Spotted Shell,* in *Bulletin of the Center for Children's Books,* Vol. 20, No. 8, April, 1967, p. 131.

One of Miss Whitney's best mystery stories. Wendy goes to the Virgin Islands to visit her cousins, the Coles, and finds on her arrival that cousin Gordon, a flyer, has disappeared; his wife, whose only child has recently died, is prostrate with shock. Marion's torpor makes it difficult for Wendy to decide what to do when she realizes that several people want a shell that clearly bears a clue to some mystery. Wendy also learns not to make hasty or intolerant judgments about people as she begins to feel less a stranger. The ending is a bit contrived: the mystery is solved, Gordon returns, Marion recovers, even Pop shows up. One of the most pleasant facets of the book is in the acceptance as natural of the fact that many Island residents are of mixed backgrounds.

The Booklist and Subscription Books Bulletin

SOURCE: A review of *Secret of the Spotted Shell,* in *The Booklist and Subscription Books Bulletin,* Vol. 63, No. 17, May 1, 1967, p. 951.

Twelve-year-old, motherless Wendy Williams, whose bridge-building father is away most of the time, eagerly looks forward to having a real home with her newly discovered cousins on St. Thomas Island. On arrival, however, she learns that her cousin Gordon Cole has disappeared under rather strange circumstances in the jungles of Vietnam and she is faced with adjusting to an unhappy, frustrating family situation. The realistic portrayal of Wendy's determined but often misguided efforts to solve her personal problems and to help clear up the mystery surrounding her cousin's disappearance are skillfully blended in a suspenseful story set against the colorful background of Virgin Island life.

Ruth Hill Viguers

SOURCE: A review of *Secret of the Spotted Shell,* in *The Horn Book Magazine,* Vol. XLIII, No. 3, June, 1967, p. 350.

Wendy, sent to live with distant relatives in the Virgin Islands, could not have arrived at a less fortunate time. The son of the family had recently been drowned; Cousin Gordon, the father, had been lost when flying his plane over the jungles of Vietnam; Cousin Marion, the mother, had given up all interest in life and seldom left her bed. Wendy felt quite unwanted. Her angry preoccupation with her own troubles surprised Cousin Marion into showing some slight interest in the girl and asking her to do a strange favor—to bring her a certain shell from Gordon's shell collection and to tell no one. The author has again caught the reader in a mesh of mysterious incidents and suspicious characters. It matters little that the intrigue seems complicated and farfetched or that unpleasant attitudes are seldom reversed so quickly; she has performed her typical magic and the mystery must be solved. Wendy is real, and girls will enjoy identifying with her; and the other characters are varied and alive. As usual, too, the setting is interesting; it is St. Thomas, vivid and very beautiful.

📖 THE MYSTERY OF THE CRIMSON GHOST (1969)

Kirkus Reviews

SOURCE: A review of *The Mystery of the Crimson Ghost,* in *Kirkus Reviews,* Vol. XXXVII, No. 5, March 1, 1969, p. 240.

Et tu Roger? Janey is crazy about Mrs. Burley's racehorse Star, Janey's friend Coral is crazy about young Roger Burley, Mrs. Burley is considered crazy for thinking that her hound dog Brutus, thirty years dead, has come back to haunt her. Roger we eventually find is the one who is really "crazy"—not that it really matters by the end of the story, except that it does clear the air around Lake Kimi in Sussex County, New Jersey. Twelve-year-old Janey, staying at the lake for the summer, falls in love with Star of Sussex, a racehorse that Mrs. Burley keeps in seclusion with her two orphaned grandsons, polite Roger and unsociable Denis. Paradoxically it was Roger who used a red light and a dog resembling Brutus to make people think his grandma is nuts; he wants to leave the ghost of a hotel half burned down decades before. Although horse lovers may disagree, the atmosphere is not very healthy and Roger comes across as the most sympathetic of the lot, not Mrs. Whitney's intention. Only for girls who, like Janey (the narrator) will forgive anything for a horse.

Patience M. Canham

SOURCE: A review of *The Mystery of the Crimson Ghost,* in *The Christian Science Monitor,* May 1, 1969, p. B6.

[T]he cover of Phyllis A. Whitney's *The Mystery of the Crimson Ghost* shows a girl on horseback and, as background, flames rising from an old house with an enormous hound baying in the flames. A tale for horse lovers with a haunted house thrown in for extra excitement? That's exactly what it is—handled with Miss Whitney's customary expertise. Girls who like a folksy first-person approach: "My name is Janey Oakes, and I might as well tell you straight off that I have a very serious and painful disease. I call it 'horse fever . . .'" will undoubtedly suck in their breath, read on avidly, and enjoy every horsey detail. Adult reviewers, predicting the outcome, read on less avidly, and give themselves a high accuracy rating at the end—but that's their loss.

Zena Sutherland

SOURCE: A review of *The Mystery of the Crimson Ghost,* in *Bulletin of the Center for Children's Books,* Vol. 22, No. 10, June, 1969, p. 166.

A mystery in which the explanation of the hideous apparition of a dog in flames, a sight that terrifies several of the characters, is explained by the fact that a large dog is seen in the red beam of a spotlight. The perpetrator is a boy who is anxious to move away from the country and knows that the neighbors are hostile to the grandmother with whom he lives, and he fosters that hostility. The protagonist is a horse-crazy girl who has been riding an animal belonging to the grandmother, and who is instrumental in solving the mystery. Despite a competent style and some suspense, this is not up to the standard of some of Whitney's books; the characters are not convincing, and the plot laboriously artificial.

📖 SECRET OF THE MISSING FOOTPRINT (1970)

Publishers Weekly

SOURCE: A review of *Secret of the Missing Footprint,* in *Publishers Weekly,* Vol. 197, No. 20, May 18, 1970, p. 39.

Phyllis Whitney, the well-known writer of mysteries for young people, has included a contemporary theme in her latest story. The mystery itself takes second place to the story of two rebellious children with a generation gap problem and the drastic steps they take in retaliation. It is mainly a story of growing up, not told in a lecturing way, but realistically, with the added dash of a mystery to keep the ball rolling.

📖 MYSTERY OF THE SCOWLING BOY (1973)

Publishers Weekly

SOURCE: A review of *Mystery of the Scowling Boy,* in *Publishers Weekly,* Vol. 203, No. 16, April 16, 1973, p. 55.

The author is at the top of her professional form in this improbable but appealing new mystery. Arriving at the Pocono Mountain home of her grandparents for the Christmas holidays, Jan is ecstatic when she finds that one of their neighbors is Alanna Graham, the famous movie star. Jan is determined to meet her idol and goes to call on her but is put off by the actress's son, Steven, an oddly unfriendly boy. Later, she does meet Alanna and is invited to her home, where it is apparent that all is not well. Miss Graham is being blackmailed and Jan's life becomes entangled in some inexplicable events, as she tries to find the guilty party or parties—among characters that include a devious housekeeper, Miss Graham's business manager, and Joe Reed, a furtive handyman.

Raymond J. Morafino

SOURCE: A review of *Mystery of the Scowling Boy,* in *School Library Journal,* Vol. 19, No. 9, May, 1973, p. 92.

Mystery of the Scowling Boy is another of [Phyllis A. Whitney's] competently plotted but routine mysteries. Spending the Christmas holidays at her grandparents' chalet in the Pocono Mountains, Jan discovers that her favorite movie star, Alanna Graham, is visiting her grandfather in a nearby mansion. Alanna turns out to be as gracious as Jan imagined, but her son, Steven, who's Jan's age, is unfriendly and seems resentful of everybody, especially his beautiful mother. As Jan gets to know the family, she perceives an undercurrent of fear and distrust in the old house and realizes that Alanna's cousin, her grandfather's nurse-housekeeper, is trying to drive Alanna away. What in Alanna's past makes her afraid of her cousin? What is the connection between handsome Jim Reed, the new handyman at Jan's grandfather's, and Alanna's family? Above all, what makes Steven so hateful? The complex plot and glamorous characters will keep young readers entertained until all the mysteries are predictably resolved in time for a happy Christmas.

SECRET OF HAUNTED MESA (1975)

Sarah Law Kennerly

SOURCE: A review of *Secret of Haunted Mesa,* in *School Library Journal,* Vol. 21, No. 9, May, 1975, p. 71.

Secret of Haunted Mesa is a better-than-average story of a teenage girl's struggle to become a person in her own right. Jenny Hanford, younger sister of Carol Hanford, who at 17 is already a famous singing star with a face and voice known to millions, has always been overshadowed by her sister. When her family visits Haunted Mesa Ranch in New Mexico Jenny is cheered that Greg, one of the few young people attending the ecology conference there, obviously prefers her to Carol. She and Greg investigate strange lights, what appears to be a blue-headed giant seen on top of Haunted Mesa, and the disappearance of a strange Indian boy. Solving the mystery plays a relatively minor part in this story which is also concerned with learning to be an independent, tolerant person capable of understanding and appreciating another culture—the American Indian—and it will undoubtedly be popular with Whitney's many fans.

Kirkus Reviews

SOURCE: A review of *Secret of Haunted Mesa,* in *Kirkus Reviews,* Vol. XLIII, No. 16, August 15, 1975, p. 920.

A perfunctory mystery—strange doings on the mesa, an Indian boy who steals kachina dolls and food from the folks below—is sandwiched in between clumsy lectures on Zuni culture and "understanding" Anglos and a stock psychological problem—young Jenny's fear of being upstaged by her famous, folksinging sister. Incidentally, we couldn't help sympathizing with sister Carol whose parents want her to give up a successful stage career to attend college and become a "person" . . . or noticing that the Indians, young Charlie and his grandfather, end up looking silly for holding a secret ceremony to get brother Harry out of jail when all it takes is a rational Anglo lawyer and simpatica Senora Consuelo to straighten everything out. . . . Others may not pay this any mind, since Consuelo's motherly chic and layers of local color overpower all else. "Who was to know what misty memories stirred on the mesa? Who was to hear the faint, far sound of a ghostly drum?" You know who.

Patricia Haber

SOURCE: A review of *Secret of Haunted Mesa,* in *Children's Book Review Service,* Vol. 4, No. 7, February, 1976, p. 65.

Although a competently written mystery story which conveys an accurate picture of the feeling of New Mexico, Ms. Whitney's portrayal of Zuni Indians and their problems lacks accuracy, sensitivity, and depth. In order to take advantage of the Shalako figure she has moved the culture hundreds of miles from its location. The generation gap that she mentions is not particular to native Americans. Characterization, in general, is slight. And it is also important that inclusion of a culture not be for the mere sake of contemporariness but that understanding of that culture be expanded.

Zena Sutherland

SOURCE: A review of *Secret of Haunted Mesa,* in *Bulletin of the Center for Children's Books,* Vol. 29, No. 9, May, 1976, pp. 151-52.

Jenny, whose family has come to Haunted Mesa Ranch because her father is lecturing at a conference there, is puzzled by Charlie, the Zuni boy who is stealing small objects and also by the moving figure she has seen on top of the mesa. She makes friends with a local resident who agrees to take her and another camp visitor to the top of the mesa, and there they find Charlie, who admits he has taken things but states firmly that he has stolen nothing, that all will be returned. The explanation, it seems, lies in the reactions of Charlie to some of the problems of today's native Americans and in the confusion of the boy's grandfather, convinced that he is raiding Spaniards when he takes things from the ranch. The author is sympathetic to the difficulties of the Indians, but the revealing of their motives and problems is not tantamount to a solution to a genuine mystery, since the denouement is fairly obvious. The book has a second plot, Jenny's resentment of the fact that her beautiful older sister, a nationally known entertainer, gets more attention. Jenny is pleased that she's involved in the "mystery," but the two aspects hardly mesh, and the book seems cluttered by this, and other, minor plot threads and characters.

📖 *DREAM OF ORCHIDS* (1985)

Kirkus Reviews

SOURCE: A review of *Dream of Orchids,* in *Kirkus Reviews,* Vol. LII, No. 21, November 1, 1984, pp. 1019-20.

As always, Whitney, headmistress of handsomely-schooled suspense, takes her heroine from "odd disquiet" to a beautifully spaced trail of deadly secrets amid lush, well-researched scenery: this time orchid culture and sunken-treasure excavation fill out the contempo-gothic mystery. Laurel York's first disquiet stirs when Marcus O'Neill, a tanned stranger, drops into her Long Island bookstore—urging her to come to the Florida Keys to visit her long-estranged father, famous novelist Clifton. (Like fathers in many a Whitney tale, Cliff left Laurel's late mother for another woman.) Now, it seems, Cliff's second wife Poppy has died, leaving their two daughters, Iris and Fern. And a tiny orchid, sent by half-sister Fern, gives Laurel her first "presentiment." But despite the old anger at her father, and her mother's posthumous warning ("Something is terribly wrong in that house"), Laurel leaves for Florida. After a history-rich drive through the Keys, she arrives to find a withdrawn Cliff, a coolly hostile Iris, and a wispy, fey Fern. Cliff's secretary, Alida Burch, seems preoccupied and upset. Then there's that sinister photograph on the wall of Laurel's room: *eyes* peering through a huge *orchid*! And what about Poppy's bizarre death in the orchid greenhouse? Or Poppy's death-threats against wealthy, middle-aged Derek—who hunts for treasure on the ocean bottom and wants to marry Iris? Well, Laurel does a bit of diving above Derek's new find—a Spanish galleon—only to meet watery danger. Next: Alida tries suicide, while rumors about Derek proliferate. And finally, after a yacht party featuring real-life pirates, murder runs rampant . . . with Laurel nearly falling victim amongst Poppy's orchids. Reliable entertainment: Whitney in full bloom.

Stephanie Zvirin

SOURCE: A review of *Dream of Orchids,* in *Booklist,* Vol. 81, No. 7, December 1, 1984, pp. 458-59.

A short course in orchid propagation and some sightseer's tips on Key West, Florida, make up the backdrop for Whitney's latest foray into the modern suspense genre. When Marcus O'Neill approaches Laurel York and tries to convince her that her long-estranged father needs her help, Laurel's first response is an angry, bristly "no." Why should she turn her life upside down for the man who deserted her and her mother? Why pretend interest in two half-sisters whom she didn't know existed? Why,

indeed. Of course, it isn't long before Laurel's anger gives way to curiosity, but her reward is a less than friendly welcome and involvement in a mystery surrounding the death of her father's second wife—an event that seems to be tearing her newfound family apart. Bound to please as a ready combination of romance and suspense, delivered in the typical Whitney idiom.

Diana Hirsch

SOURCE: A review of *Dream of Orchids,* in *School Library Journal,* Vol. 31, No. 8, May, 1985, p. 115.

Whitney has her special following for romance/suspense readers and this latest attempt will not disappoint. Laurel York runs a book store on Long Island; her father, famous novelist Cliff York, left her mother when Laurel was a child; and, although Laurel has followed his career, he is a stranger. When handsome Marcus O'Neill asks Laurel to come to the Florida Keys to meet Cliff, she accepts. York's second wife, Poppy, has died in a bizarre accident, and her two daughters, Fern and Iris, are feuding over the will and over Derek Phillips, engaged to Iris but loved by Fern. Laurel finds herself in the midst of mystery—Poppy's death may not have been an accident—she cut herself and bled to death in the orchid house because the door had been wedged shut. Aside from the cutesy flower names, Whitney paints a vivid picture of the Florida landscape while blending enough romantic and sinister overtones to keep the pages turning.

📖 *THE SINGING STONES* (1990)

Denise Perry Donavin

SOURCE: A review of *The Singing Stones,* in *Booklist,* Vol. 86, No. 8, December 15, 1989, p. 770.

Whitney's newest heroine, Lynn McLeod, is an ombudsman for terminally ill children who is suddenly summoned to assist the daughter of her first husband. But the child is not physically ill. She is haunted by the near-fatal accident that crippled her father and the threatening presence of her wicked stepmother (whom everyone believes to be the epitome of quiet kindness). Lynn enters the complicated family situation with great reluctance, bewitched by the spiritualist philosophies of one character yet driven by her own sympathy for a child in distress. A terrific work of romantic suspense in a contemporary setting.

Kirkus Reviews

SOURCE: A review of *The Singing Stones,* in *Kirkus Reviews,* Vol. LVII, No. 24, December 15, 1989, p. 1782.

Again, the setting is the Blue Ridge Mountains of Virginia, and there's a smidgen of psychic/paranormal shudders and speculation as in *Rainbow in the Mist*—along with, as always, Whitney's cast of bothered characters, most shaded by a pall of suspicion as dark deeds ensue, and a brisk surprise when evil is unmasked.

Lynn McLeod, child psychiatrist dealing with ill children, married architect Stephen Asche when she was 19, but Stephen became bewitched by Oriana, an exotic dancer, and Lynn divorced him and left Virginia. Now comes a letter from Julian, related vaguely to Stephen, begging Lynn to heal ten-year-old Jill, daughter of Stephen and the ever-absent Oriana: Jill is cowering in a shell of fear. Will Lynn come to her old home where crippled Stephen is grimly holed up, his career and spirit gone? Sure, she will. Among those awaiting are: Julian's wife Vivian, who, like him, is a New Age buff; nasty Carla, Jill's dance tutor, gloweringly ever-present; Stephen's brother Everett and wife, who seem to have enveloped Stephen's former enterprises; and Stephen's nasty nurse. There will be murders (past and present) uncovered and attempted, as well as sinister vandalism, before the mystery of Stephen's injury at what was a cliff side murder site can be solved—and before Jill's secret can be unlocked. As for the Singing Stones (a strange rock formation), well, "There's some sort of . . . of *power* there." There's also an express "regression" into Lynn's past life by Julian for New Age titillation.

More rock-solid, reliable Whitney, so just sing along.

Shirley A. Bathgate

SOURCE: A review of *The Singing Stones,* in *Voice of Youth Advocates,* Vol. 13, No. 2, June, 1990, p. 112.

A brief prologue introduces Lynn McLeod, clinical psychologist; describes the beautiful but lonely house in Virginia's Blue Ridge Mountains where most of the story is set; and suggests the suspense which soon engrosses the reader. The secluded house is home to Stephen Asche, once Lynn's husband; his troubled daughter; and a host of other relatives and caretakers. An accident has left Stephen in a wheelchair and young Jilly emotionally crippled. Although 12 years have not healed all the hurt, Lynn, despite misgivings, accepts an invitation from Stephen's stepmother to come and try to help the seriously withdrawn ten year old. Lynn is slowly, subtly drawn into the lives of everyone in the strange household as deadly old secrets, accidents, murders, and new mysteries are encountered. Old passions are revived as Jilly is helped.

The mystery and suspense are everything Whitney fans have come to expect. However, unusual views of destiny, karma, reincarnation, and forgiveness cloud the romantic elements of the story and make for unrealistic characters and situations. Severe emotional problems are cured almost overnight with virtually no treatment; characters change too abruptly to be believed. Despite these flaws, Whitney fans will enjoy the book.

Lindsey Wilson

SOURCE: A review of *The Singing Stones,* in *School Library Journal,* Vol. 36, No. 8, August, 1990, p. 177.

Lynn McLeod, a child psychologist, is awaiting the start of a much-needed vacation when a letter arrives altering her plans. She is invited to the home of her ex-husband, Stephen Asche, to help his troubled daughter, Jilly. Upon her arrival, Lynn finds herself drawn into a series of unexplicable events. Jilly is being secretive to protect her father; her mother and father have withdrawn from Jilly's life into worlds of their own. The plot thickens, of course, and mystery fans will applaud this addition to any collection.

WOMAN WITHOUT A PAST (1991)

Martin Brady

SOURCE: A review of *Woman without a Past,* in *Booklist,* Vol. 87, No. 16, April 15, 1991, p. 1603.

Whitney may be in her eighties now, but her burning desire to craft popular, readable psychological suspense hasn't waned a bit. *Woman without a Past,* her thirty-fifth novel, combines the typical expectations of the genre with the author's unfailing devotion to accurate research into time and place. Our heroine, Molly Hunt, is a budding young star in the world of suspense fiction, yet her psyche is still wounded from the sudden, violent death of her husband. A chance meeting in her publisher's office is the incident that sweeps Molly physically into the Old South ambience of Charleston, South Carolina, and emotionally onto a trail that leads to the discovery of the truth about her parentage and her place within the Mountfort family. The ax-swinging climax is certainly in tune with haunting events, and Molly does make connections with a mysterious but attractive gentleman. Stock up for the author's rabid following.

Claudia Moore

SOURCE: A review of *Woman without a Past,* in *School Library Journal,* Vol. 37, No. 12, December, 1991, p. 150.

Startled to learn that she may have been stolen as a baby prior to her adoption by the parents who raised her, author Molly Hunt flies to Charleston, SC, to meet her twin sister. Once there she seeks to unravel the mystery about her theft, learns that she will inherit the family estate, and struggles to cope with strange pranks and the death of a cousin. Whitney continues to use channeling to heighten interest, but it is not as strong here as in *Rainbow in the Mist.* The characters of Molly and her twin, Amelia, are particularly well drawn as one can contrast their similarities and their differences. Whitney's background research is obvious in this aspect of the story and in the flavor of old Charleston and its tradition-oriented families. This is a good, modern gothic novel sure to please those hooked on the genre.

📖 STAR FLIGHT (1993)

Kirkus Reviews

SOURCE: A review of *Star Flight*, in *Kirkus Reviews*, Vol. LXI, No. 13, July 1, 1993, p. 817.

In this (for Whitney) overly talky and cluttered mystery/suspense novel, set in a scenic area of western North Carolina, a young widow from California sets out to discover the true story of two deaths decades apart.

Lauren Castle's late husband, filmmaker Jim, has been accidentally killed while working on a documentary concerning the career of fabled actor Roger Brandt, who still lives on beautiful Lake Lure. In 1938, the movie idol had made a film—as well as a child—with his lover, the lovely Victoria Fraser. The child was raised elsewhere, and Victoria, presumably distraught that Roger would stay forever with his wife, Camilla, committed suicide. Or did she? Lauren, meanwhile, has told no one except former boyfriend Gordon (now a forest ranger) that she is the granddaughter of Victoria and Roger. Now in North Carolina to sleuth, Lauren pinballs here and there, picking up bits of info and chatting with: blunt but chummy Gretchen Fraser, Victoria's sister; Gordon's mother Finella, who's heavily into making products from the kudzu vine; Natalie Brandt, Roger's daughter, an artist who has painted a spooky picture of a UFO-like object landing on the local mountain peak; Camilla, who introduces Lauren to Victoria's old dresser, Betty; and hirsute Ty, Gretchen's brother, who is mighty strange and beats drums in the wild. At the close, when all's made plain, there's a climb to what might be a sky-high grave.

This time the story seems crowded, and Whitney has not allowed her mob of suspects space and time; readers may feel overwhelmed by the plethora of chat and surfeit of chatterers. But even the best of the pros can lob one into the underbrush—not that Whitney's following will care.

Denise Perry Donavin

SOURCE: A review of *Star Flight*, in *Booklist*, Vol. 90, No. 1, September 1, 1993, p. 38.

This tangled contemporary tale of murder and romance is haunted by an adulterous affair between two Hollywood stars of the 1930s. Lauren Castle, granddaughter of this liaison, visits the North Carolina site of her mother's supposed suicide after Lauren's husband dies in a mysterious accident while filming at this haunted location. As Whitney weaves stories from the past with Lauren's present-day search, the novelist sets up an assembly line of possible villains: is it the dead woman's brother? sister? ex-lover? the ex-lover's wife? the ex-lover's granddaughter? The villainess is not terribly surprising, but the suspense is well plotted in this swift-moving novel by a pro.

📖 DAUGHTER OF THE STARS (1994)

Denise Perry Donavin

SOURCE: A review of *Daughter of the Stars*, in *Booklist*, Vol. 91, No. 2, September 15, 1994, p. 115.

Whitney's new novel takes place in Harper's Ferry, where a young woman discovers a family her mother has kept secret throughout her life. Lacey Elliot reads a letter addressed to her mother in order to protect her during convalescence, only to discover a family she has never known. The letter is a plea for help, and Lacey responds by showing up in Harper's Ferry in her mother's stead. She falls in love with a writer whom she meets on the ferry and is introduced to an aunt, her great-grandmother, and cousins, while learning of her fathers unsolved murder. The tension from that long-ago incident is revived by the reappearance of the major suspect, her grandfather. Whitney lives up to her reputation with this contemporary romance steeped in American history.

Claudia Moore

SOURCE: A review of *Daughter of the Stars*, in *School Library Journal*, Vol. 41, No. 3, March, 1995, p. 236.

A light, fast-paced mystery. Lacey returns to the town of her birth, Harper's Ferry, WV, and becomes involved in trying to learn who killed her father 30 years ago. The multifaceted plot is further enriched (and complicated) by flashbacks to the Civil War, as ancestors motivate contemporary characters' actions. (It's unfortunate that there's no family tree to help keep characters in their proper time period.) Only Lacey's personality is fully developed. Although keeping the time periods straight may challenge some readers, this quick read provides a look at Harper's Ferry's key role in the preliminary days of the Civil War.

Additional coverage of Whitney's life and career is contained in the following sources published by The Gale Group: *Contemporary Authors New Revision Series*, Vol. 60; *Junior DISCovering Authors*; and *Major Authors and Illustrators for Children and Young Adults*, Vols. 1, 30.

CUMULATIVE INDEXES

How to Use This Index

The main reference

Baum, L(yman) Frank 1856–
1919 .... **15**

list all author entries in this and previous volumes of *Children's Literature Review:*

The cross-references

See also CA 103; 108; DLB 22; JRDA
MAICYA; MTCW; SATA 18; TCLC 7

list all author entries in the following Gale biographical and literary sources:

AAYA = Authors & Artists for Young Adults
AITN = Authors in the News
BLC = Black Literature Criticism
BLCS = Black Literature Criticism Supplement
BW = Black Writers
CA = Contemporary Authors
CAAS = Contemporary Authors Autobiography Series
CABS = Contemporary Authors Bibliographical Series
CANR = Contemporary Authors New Revision Series
CAP = Contemporary Authors Permanent Series
CDALB = Concise Dictionary of American Literary Biography
CDBLB = Concise Dictionary of British Literary Biography
CLC = Contemporary Literary Criticism
CMLC = Classical and Medieval Literature Criticism
DAB = DISCovering Authors: British
DAC = DISCovering Authors: Canadian
DAM = DISCovering Authors: Modules
    DRAM: Dramatists Module; MST: Most-Studied Authors Module;
    MULT: Multicultural Authors Module; NOV: Novelists Module;
    POET: Poets Module; POP: Popular Fiction and Genre Authors Module
DC = Drama Criticism
DLB = Dictionary of Literary Biography
DLBD = Dictionary of Literary Biography Documentary Series
DLBY = Dictionary of Literary Biography Yearbook
HLC = Hispanic Literature Criticism
HW = Hispanic Writers
JRDA = Junior DISCovering Authors
LC = Literature Criticism from 1400 to 1800
MAICYA = Major Authors and Illustrators for Children and Young Adults
MTCW = Major 20th-Century Writers
NCLC = Nineteenth-Century Literature Criticism
NNAL = Native North American Literature
PC = Poetry Criticism
SAAS = Something about the Author Autobiography Series
SATA = Something about the Author
SSC = Short Story Criticism
TCLC = Twentieth-Century Literary Criticism
WLC = World Literature Criticism, 1500 to the Present
WLCS = World Literature Criticism Supplement
YABC = Yesterday's Authors of Books for Children

Author Index

CUMULATIVE INDEX TO NATIONALITIES

Nationality Index

CUMULATIVE INDEX TO TITLES

Title Index

Title Index

Title Index

Title Index

Title Index

Title Index

Title Index

Title Index

Title Index

ISBN 0-7876-3224-4